THE FOUNDING
OF
MASSACHUSETTS

Historians and the Sources

THE FOUNDING
OF
MASSACHUSETTS

Historians and the Sources

EDITED BY

EDMUND S. MORGAN

YALE UNIVERSITY

THE BOBBS-MERRILL COMPANY, INC.

A Subsidiary of Howard W. Sams & Co., Inc.

PUBLISHERS · INDIANAPOLIS · NEW YORK · KANSAS CITY

Introduction

Out of the records and documents that have escaped destruction, out of what he calls "original sources," the historian reconstructs the past. He tells us not only what happened but also why it happened, and he often tells the story so convincingly that we fail to detect how partial, how artful, indeed how flimsy it may be: We assume that the sources, if we took the pains to read them ourselves, would tell us the same story. This book is a reminder that what happened, what the sources say happened, and what historians say happened are not necessarily the same thing.

A work of history is always more orderly than the sources on which it depends. The historian, after studying the sources, arrives at a way of arranging the facts and ideas derived from them. The record of events, patchy, contradictory, and disconnected, passes through his mind and emerges in a pattern or sequence that makes sense, an interpretation. The writing of history, whatever else it may be, is a creative ordering of past events.

To a degree, everyone who tries to put experience into words must undertake a similar ordering. A man describing a traffic accident, a baseball game, or a love affair does not attempt to tell everything. Whether he is talking or writing to one listener or to many or simply to himself, he omits some things and stresses others. What he had expected to happen or wanted to happen or thought ought to happen is likely to give form to his account of what did happen. But the historian's ordering of events is more deliberate. He usually deals with records made by several people; and he views the events they describe from a more distant perspective. The pattern he discerns or imposes is the product of more care and thought and is compounded from a greater variety of information than is usually available to a person who is simply writing a letter or making a note about something he has seen or heard or done.

Because the historian has a larger perspective and exercises more care, he is frequently able to relate and explain events more objectively than an eyewitness or participant. He tries to be impartial, which is not always the case with participants. Nevertheless, consciously or unconsciously, he is subject to a similar tendency to see events as he wants to see them, to see things happening as he thinks they ought to have happened. The order he imposes on the past may consist of ignoring information that his experience in a different time and place has led him to consider unimportant. The motives he attributes to the actors are likely to be those which he thinks he or his contemporaries would feel in the same situation. He may even attempt to justify a particular view of human nature or society by selecting events from the past and attributing to the participants motives that seem to exemplify that view.

It is never easy for a historian to recognize the pressures that lead him to a particular interpretation. The very act of creation itself may impose a certain pressure. Once a pattern begins to appear to a reader of the sources, it gradually acquires an attractiveness that distracts his attention from discordant facts. Ultimately, it may appear as inevitable, as the *only* way of ordering the events; and when he writes his account, his interpretative pattern will itself assume the guise of fact. Recognizing this danger, serious historians and teachers of history always insist on the need for continual recurrence to the sources. If one wishes to discover the past as it was, it is necessary to return to the sources.

Of what use, then, is it to read or write history? Why not simply publish and read the sources? One reason is that a historian who has studied the sources for a given period or episode can usually offer guidance of some kind to anyone else engaged in the same task. Whether he wrote two and a half centuries ago, like Cotton Mather, or only forty years ago, like James Truslow Adams, a man who has studied the sources is likely to have something to say to another doing the same thing. Another reason is that few people have time to read all the sources relevant even to a brief historical period. The surviving records and documents are so voluminous that everyone derives his picture of the past in large measure from the abbreviated, orderly narratives of historians. Even historians gain most of their knowledge, outside their particular specialties, from other historians.

Usually, people rely on histories written in their own generation, because historians of earlier times appear to be less objective than those whose experiences and assumptions parallel our own. Unless, however, we have compared one historian's account of some specific episode with another's and with the sources on which both are based, we are likely to attribute to historians of all periods an omniscience that none possesses, and by consequence we are likely to see the past as more orderly than it was. The purpose of this book is to make available under one cover the basic sources for a historical episode, together with the accounts that four different historians have created out of those sources. The episode chosen is the founding of the Massachusetts Bay colony in the years from 1628 to 1634.

Massachusetts Bay was not the first permanent settlement in New England; the Pilgrim Fathers had founded Plymouth in 1620, and a few straggling settlers had lived in the Bay area before 1628. But with the formation of the Massachusetts Bay Company and with the arrival on the scene of Governor John Winthrop in 1630, Massachusetts became the spearhead of Puritan emigration to the New World. During the next four years, under Winthrop's leadership, the colony gained a firm foothold, and by the time he was temporarily removed from the governorship in 1634 it was possible to discern the main outlines of the political, social, and religious institutions that were to prevail throughout New England during the colonial period and that still exert their influence on American civilization.

The story of the founding is told in every history of the United States. The sources for it are abundant but encompassable. It seems therefore an appropriate point at which to examine the relationship between the historian and his sources. Here are most of the surviving documents written in Massachusetts Bay before 1634, as well as a number of pertinent ones written in England before 1630. Here also are accounts by four historians who had access to these sources and who can each offer assistance to anyone else trying to make sense out of them. The documents are given in their entirety, with no attempt to eliminate passages that seem unimportant or irrelevant. In two cases, those of John Winthrop's journal and the Records of the Massachusetts Bay Company, entries falling after the terminal date of May 1634 are omitted, but there are no omissions within the period covered. It is my hope that the sources in their full complexity and disorder will enable the reader to attempt for himself the creative ordering of a small, sample segment of the past and thus experience some of the problems and some of the excitement of practicing the historian's art. At the same time, I hope that a study of the similar efforts of four distinguished historians will lead the reader to a new appreciation not only of the historian's limitations, but also of his creative achievement and literary skill, in presenting his generation with an orderly, usable past.

I have placed the historians first and the sources second, because the historians all furnish a certain amount of background information that may prove helpful in understanding the sources. But some readers may prefer to go to the sources first. In whatever order one proceeds, one of the pleasures of studying the sources is to find in them things that one had not quite expected. Out of sensitivity to the unexpected comes new understanding.

As a point of departure for his own discoveries, the reader may wish to bear in mind some of the questions to which historians have sought answers in these sources:

What did the members of Massachusetts Bay Company hope to achieve by their colony? Were the aims of the actual settlers different from those of the company? Were religious and economic motives in conflict? Did the colony in the initial years fulfill the expectations of the founders and settlers?

What became of the Massachusetts Bay Company after the transfer of the charter to the New World? Was the company now the colony? Did the company charter become the only basis of the colony's government? Is there any evidence of a social compact or covenant among the settlers? What relationship did the colony bear to the government of England? What legal limitations existed on the authority of the colony's government? Did the Massachusetts government violate those limitations, and, if so, how? What political rights did the charter allow to settlers? Why were new "freemen" admitted? Why was John Winthrop not reelected governor in 1634?

Is the colonial government of Massachusetts properly described as an oligarchy? a theocracy? a democracy? What relationship existed between church and state? Did clergymen hold political office? How did the government regulate economic activity? How were the settlers supplied? How did they earn their livings?

Why is Massachusetts considered a Puritan colony? If Massachusetts was founded and settled by Puritans, is it possible from
the sources to arrive at a definition of Puritanism? Is there evidence of hostility to Puritanism among the settlers? How did the
code of morals established in Massachusetts differ from that established by law in the present United States?

Historians have offered different answers to these questions. The
reader should note the disagreements and variations among their
answers and should compare these answers with the evidence of the
sources on which they are based.

Edmund S. Morgan

New Haven, Connecticut
July 1964

Contents

PART ONE

The Historians

1
Cotton Mather

The New England Puritans were highly self-conscious about their achievements and began interpreting themselves for posterity as soon as they arrived in the New World. Their children and grandchildren continued the process. Cotton Mather (1663–1728), son of Increase Mather, grandson of Richard Mather and of John Cotton, was extremely proud of his forebears but even more proud of his erudition. In writing about the founding of Massachusetts he could draw upon family traditions and on the memories of participants who were still living; but he also took pains to study the sources, and in addition to those printed in this book he probably had access to some that have since disappeared.

Mather published his magnum opus, the *Magnalia Christi Americana,* in 1702, at a time when, with the original Massachusetts charter revoked, the colony was governed under a new charter, obtained from King William in 1691 by Increase Mather. Though the Mathers defended this new charter as the best obtainable, neither they nor other New Englanders were happy about the fact that it provided for a governor appointed by the King of England. Cotton Mather was therefore concerned to defend ancestral values against possible royal interference. At the same time, however, he and his father were engaged in theological and ecclesiastical disputes with some of their fellow New Englanders (notably Solomon Stoddard of Northampton) who wished to extend membership in the New England churches to persons whose piety would not have satisfied the founders. This appeared to the Mathers as a more serious threat to their religious inheritance than that posed by royal governors. The *Magnalia,* besides being a serious work of history, was an attempt to recall New Englanders to ancestral standards by recounting the exploits and defining the beliefs of their fathers. The modern reader, however, will perceive how far Cotton Mather had himself come from the founders, in taste and temperament at least, by comparing his florid style with the lean words of the sources. The passage that follows comprises Chapters IV and V of Book I.

3

CHAP. IV.

Paulo Majora! *Or, The* Essays *and* Causes *which
produced the Second, but largest Colony of*
NEW-ENGLAND; *and the manner
wherein the First Church of this* New-Colony *was gathered.*

1. WORDS full of *Emphasis,* are those which my Reader may find Written by a Learned and Pious Minister of the Church of *England;* and I hope I may without offence tender to the Reader the Words of *such* an Author.

Some among us (*writes he*) are angry with *Calvin* for calling Humane Rites, *Tolerabiles Ineptias;* they will not at the great Day be *such* unto the rigorous Imposers, who made them *the Terms of Communion.* How will you at that Day lift up your Faces before your Master and your Judge, when he shall demand of you, *what is become of those his Lambs which you drove into the Wilderness by needless Impositions?*

The Story of the Flocks thus *driven into the Wilderness* has begun to be related: And we would relate it without all Intemperate Expressions of our anger against our *Drivers,* before whom the People must *needs go,* as they did: It becomes not an *Historian,* and it less becomes a *Christian,* to be *Passionate.* Nevertheless, *Poetry* may *dare* to do something at the Description of that which *drove* those *Drivers;* and with a few Lines fetch'd from the most famous *Epic Poem* of Dr. *Blackmore,* we will describe the Fury.

—*A* Fury *crawl'd from out her Cell,*
The Bloodiest Minister of Death *and* Hell.
A monstrous Shape, a foul and hideous Sight,
Which did all Hell *with her dire Looks affright.*
Huge full-gorg'd Snakes *on her lean Shoulders hung,*
And Death's *dark Courts with their loud hissing rung.*
Her Teeth *and* Claws *were* Iron, *and her* Breath
Like Subterranean Damps, *gave present* Death.
Flames *worse than* Hell's, *shot from her Bloody* Eyes,

And Fire! *and* Sword! *Eternally she cries.*
No certain Shape, no Feature regular,
No Limbs distinct in th'odious Fiend *appear.*
Her Squalid, Bloated Belly *did arise,*
Swoll'n with black Gore *to a prodigious Size:*
Distended vastly by a mighty Flood
Of slaughter'd Saints, *and constant* Martyr's *Blood.*
A Monster *so deform'd, so fierce as this,*
It self a Hell, *ne're saw the* dark Abyss!
Horrow *till now, the uggliest Shape esteem'd,*
So much out-done, an harmless Figure *seem'd.*
Envy, *and* Hate, *and* Malice *blush'd to see*
Themselves Eclips'd *by such Deformity.*
Her Feav'rish Heat *drinks down a Sea of* Blood,
Not of the Impious, *but the* Just *and* Good:
'Gainst whom she burns with unextinguish'd Rage,
Nor can th'Exhausted World *her Wrath asswage.*

It was PERSECUTION; a *Fury* which we consider not as pos-
sessing *the Church of* England, but as inspiring a *Party* which
have unjustly Challenged the Name of *the Church of* England,
and which, whenever *the Church of* England shall any more encourage her *Fall,* will become like that of the *House* which our
Saviour saw Built upon the *Sand.*

2. There were more than a few attempts of the *English,* to
People and Improve the Parts of *New-England,* which were to the
Northward of *New-Plymouth;* but the Designs of those Attempts
being aim'd no higher than the Advancement of some *Worldly
Interests,* a constant Series of Disasters has confounded them, until
there was a Plantation erected upon the nobler Designs of *Christianity;* and that Plantation, tho' it has had more Adversaries than
perhaps any one upon Earth; yet, *having obtained help from God,
it continues to this Day.* There have been very fine Settlements in
the *North-East* Regions; but what is become of them? I have
heard that one of our Ministers once Preaching to a Congregation
there, urged them to approve themselves a *Religious People* from
this Consideration, *That otherwise they would contradict the main
end of Planting this Wilderness;* whereupon a well-known Person,
then in the Assembly, cry'd out, *Sir, You are mistaken, you think*

you are Preaching to the People at the Bay; *our main End was to catch Fish.* Truly 'twere to have been wished, that something more excellent had been the *main End* of the *Settlements* in that brave Country, which we have, even long since the arrival of that more Pious Colony at the *Bay,* now seen dreadfully *unsettled,* no less than *twice* at least, by the Sword of the Heathen, after they had been replenished with many *Hundreds* of People, who had thriven to many *Thousands* of Pounds; and had all the force of the *Bay* too, to assist them in the maintaining of their Settlements. But the same or the like inauspicious things attended many other Endeavours, to make Plantations upon such a *Main End* in several other Parts of our Country, before the Arrival of those by whom the *Massachuset* Colony was at last formed upon more glorious *Aims:* All proving like the Habitations of the *foolish, cursed before they had taken root.* Of all which *Catastrophe's,* I suppose none was more sudden than that of Monsieur *Finch,* whom in a Ship from *France,* trucking with the *Massachuset-Natives;* those Bloody Salvages, coming on Board without any other *Arms,* but *Knives* concealed under *Flaps,* immediately Butchered with all his Men, and set the Ship on Fire. Yea, so many Fatalities attended the *Adventurers* in their Essays, that they began to suspect that the *Indian* Sorcerers had laid the place under some *Fascination;* and that the *English* could not prosper upon such *Enchanted Ground,* so that they were almost afraid of *Adventuring* any more.

3. Several Persons in the West of *England,* having by Fishing-Voyages to Cape *Ann,* the Northern Promontory of the *Massachuset-Bay,* obtained some Acquaintance with those Parts; the News of the good Progress made in the New Plantation of *Plymouth,* inspired the renowned Mr. *White,* Minister of *Dorchester,* to prosecute the Settlement of such another Plantation here for the Propagation of *Religion.* This good Man engaged several Gentlemen about the Year 1624. in this Noble Design; and they employ'd a most Religious, Prudent, Worthy Gentleman, one Mr. *Roger Conant,* in the Government of the Place, and of their Affairs upon the Place; but thro' many Discouragements, the Design for a while almost fell unto the Ground. That great Man greatly grieved hereat, wrote over to this Mr. *Roger Conant,* that if he and three Honest Men more would yet stay upon the Spot, he would procure a *Patent* for them, and send them over *Friends, Goods,*

Provisions, and what was necessary to assist their Undertakings. Mr. *Conant,* then looking out a Scituation more Commodious for a *Town,* gave his Three disheartned Companions to understand, that he did believe God would make this Land a Receptacle for his People, and that if *they* should leave him, yet *he* would not stir; for he was confident he should not long want Company; which Confidence of his caused them to abandon the thoughts of leaving him. Well, it was not long before the Council of *Plymouth* in *England,* had by a Deed bearing Date, *March* 19. 1627. Sold unto some Knights and Gentlemen about *Dorchester,* viz. Sir *Henry Roswel,* Sir *John Young, Thomas Southcott, John Humphrey, John Endicot,* and *Simon Whetcomb,* and their Heirs and Assigns, and their Associates for ever, that Part of *New-England* which lyes between a great River call'd *Merimack,* and a certain other River there call'd *Charles River,* in the bottom of the *Massachuset-Bay.* But shortly after this, Mr. *White* brought the aforesaid Honourable Persons into an Acquaintance with several other Persons of Quality about *London;* as, namely, Sir *Richard Saltonstall, Isaac Johnson, Samuel Adderly, John Ven, Matthew Cradock, George Harwood, Increase Nowel, Richard Perry, Richard Bellingham, Nathanael Wright, Samuel Vassal, Theophilus Eaton, Thomas Goff, Thomas Adams, John Brown, Samuel Brown, Thomas Hutchings, William Vassal, William Pinchon,* and *George Foxcraft.* These Persons being associated unto the former, and having bought of them all their Interest in *New-England* aforesaid, now consulted about settling a *Plantation* in that Country, whither such as were then called *Non-Conformists,* might with the Grace and Leave of the King make a peaceable *Secession,* and enjoy the Liberty and the Exercise of their own Perswasions, about the Worship of the Lord Jesus Christ. Whereupon Petitioning the King to confirm what they had thus purchased with a New *Patent,* he granted them one, bearing Date from the Year 1628. which gave them a Right unto the Soil, holding their Titles of Lands, as of the Manor of *East Greenwich* in *Kent,* and in common *Soccage.* By this *Charter* they were empowered yearly to *Elect* their own Governour, Deputy-Governour and Magistrates; as also to make such *Laws* they should think suitable for the Plantation: But as an acknowledgment of their dependance upon *England,* they might not make any Laws Repugnant unto those of the Kingdom; and the Fifth part of all the *Oar* of *Gold* or *Silver* found in the Territory, belong'd unto the Crown. So, soon after Mr. *Cradock* being by the Company chosen Governour, they sent over Mr. *Endicott* in the Year 1628. to carry on the Plantation, which the *Dorchester*-Agents had lookt out for them, which was at a Place called Nahumkeick. Of which place I have somewhere met with an odd Observation, that the Name of it was rather *Hebrew* than *Indian;* for בְהוּם *Nahum,* signifies Comfort, and חֵיק *Keik,* signifies an *Haven;* and our *English* not only found it an *Haven of Comfort,* but happened also to put an *Hebrew Name* upon it; for they call'd it *Salem,* for the *Peace* which they had and hoped in it; and *so it is called unto this Day.*

4. An Entrance being thus made upon the Design of Planting a Country of *English* and *Reformed* Churches; they that were concerned for the Plantation, made their Application to Two Non-Conformists Ministers, that they would go over to serve the *Cause of God and of Religion* in the beginning of those *Churches.* The one of these was Mr. *Higginson,* a Minister in *Leicestershire,* silenced for his Non-Conformity; the other was Mr. *Skelton,* a Minister of *Lincolnshire,* suffering also for his Non-Conformity: Both of which were Men eminent for Learning and Virtue, and who thus driven out of their Native Country, sought their Graves on the *American-Strand,* whereon the Epitaph might be inscribed that was on *Scipio's, Ingrata Patria, ne Mortui quidem Habebis Ossa.* These Ministers came over to *Salem,* in the Summer of the Year 1629. and with these there came over a considerable number of Excellent Christians, who no sooner arrived, but they set themselves about the Church-Work, which was their *Errand* hither.

'Tis true, there were two other *Clergy-Men,* who came over about the same time; nevertheless, there has been very little Account given of their Circumstances; except what a certain little *Narrative-Writer* has offered us, by saying, *There were Two that began to hew Stones in the Mountains, for the Building of the Temple here; but when they saw all sorts of Stones would not fit in the Building, the one betook himself to the Seas again, and the other to Till the Land;* for which cause, burying all further mention of them among the Rubbish, in the *Foundation* of the Colony, we will proceed with our Story; which is now to tell us, That the Passage of these our *Pilgrims* was attended with many Smiles of

Heaven upon them. They were blessed with a Company of honest *Seamen;* with whom the Ministers and Passengers constantly served God, Morning and Evening; *Reading, Expounding* and *Applying* the Word of God, *singing* of His Praise, and *seeking* of His Peace; to which Exercises they added on the *Lord's Day* two Sermons, and a *Catechising:* And sometimes they set apart an whole Day for *Fasting* and *Prayer,* to obtain from Heaven a good success in their Voyage, especially when the Weather was much against them, whereto they had very Remarkable Answers; but the *Seamen* said, *That they believed these were the First* Sea-*Fasts that ever were kept in the World.* At length, *Per varios Casus, per Tot Discrimina Rerum,* they Landed at *the Haven of Rest* provided for them.

5. The persecuted Servants of God, under the *English* Hierarchy, had been in *a Sea of Ice mingled with Fire;* tho' the *Fire* scalded them, yet such Cakes of *Ice* were over their Heads, that there was no getting out: But the *Ice* was now broken, by the *American* Offers of a Retreat for the pure Worshippers of the Lord into a *Wilderness.*

The Report of the CHARTER granted unto the Governour and Company of the *Massachuset-Bay,* and the Entertainment and Encouragement, which Planters began to find in that *Bay,* came with a, —*Patrias, age, desere Sedes,* and caused many very deserving Persons to transplant themselves and their Families into *New-England. Gentlemen* of Ancient and Worshipful Families, and *Ministers* of the Gospel, then of great Fame at Home, and *Merchants, Husbandmen, Artificers,* to the Number of some Thousands, did for Twelve Years together carry on this Transplantation. It was indeed a *Banishment,* rather than a *Removal,* which was undergone by this glorious Generation, and you may be sure sufficiently *Afflictive* to Men of Estate, Breeding and Conversation. As the *Hazard* which they ran in this Undertaking was of such *Extraordinariness,* that nothing less than a strange and strong Impression from *Heaven* could have thereunto moved the Hearts of such as were in it; so the *Expence* with which they carried on the Undertaking was truly *Extraordinary.* By Computation, the *Passage* of the *Persons* that peopled *New-England,* cost at least Ninety Five Thousand Pound: The Transportation of their first small Stock of *Cattel* great and small, cost no less than Twelve Thousand

Pound, besides the Price of the *Cattel* themselves: The *Provisions* laid in for Subsistence, till *Tillage* might produce more, cost Forty Five Thousand Pounds; the *Materials* for their first Cottages cost Eighteen Thousand Pounds; their Arms, Ammunition and Great Artillery, cost Twenty Two Thousand Pounds; besides which Hundred and Ninety Two Thousand Pounds, the *Adventurers* laid out in *England,* what was not Inconsiderable. About an *Hundred and Ninety Eight Ships* were employed in passing the *Perils of the Seas,* in the Accomplishment of this Renowned Settlement; whereof, by the way, but *one* miscarried in those *Perils.*

Briefly, The God of Heaven served as it were, a *Summons* upon the *Spirits* of His People in the English Nation; stirring up the Spirits of Thousands which never saw the *Faces* of each other, with a most Unanimous Inclination to leave all the Pleasant Accommodations of their Native Country, and go over a Terrible *Ocean,* into a more Terrible *Desart,* for the *pure Enjoyment of all his Ordinances.* It is now Reasonable that before we pass any further, the *Reasons* of this Undertaking should be more exactly made known unto *Posterity,* especially unto the *Posterity* of those that were the *Undertakers,* lest they come at length to Forget and Neglect *the true Interest of* New-England. Wherefore I shall now Transcribe some of *them* from a Manuscript, wherein they were then tendred unto Consideration.

General Considerations for the Plantation of New-England.

First, It will be a Service unto the *Church* of great Consequence, to carry the *Gospel* into *those* Parts of the World, and Raise a *Bulwark* against the Kingdom of *Antichrist,* which the *Jesuites* labour to Rear up in *all* Parts of the World.

Secondly, All other Churches of *Europe* have been brought under *Desolations;* and it may be feared that the like Judgments are coming upon *Us;* and who knows but God hath provided this place to be a *Refuge* for many, whom he means to save out of the *General Destruction.*

Thirdly, The Land grows weary of her *Inhabitants,* insomuch that *Man,* which is the most precious of all Creatures, is here more vile and base than the Earth he treads upon: *Children, Neighbours* and *Friends,* especially the *Poor,* are counted the greatest *Burdens,* which if things were right, would be the chiefest Earthly *Blessings.*

Fourthly, We are grown to that Intemperance in all *Excess of Riot,* as no mean Estate almost will suffice a Man to keep Sail with his *Equals,* and he that fails in it, must live in Scorn and Contempt: Hence it comes to pass, that all *Arts* and *Trades* are carried in that Deceitful Manner, and Unrighteous Course, as it is almost Impossible for a good upright Man to maintain his constant Charge, and live comfortably in them.

Fifthly, The *Schools* of Learning and Religion are so corrupted, as (besides the unsupportable Charge of Education) most Children, even the Best, Wittiest, and of the Fairest Hopes, are perverted, corrupted, and utterly overthrown, by the multitude of evil Examples and Licentious Behaviours in these *Seminaries.*

Sixthly, The *whole Earth* is the *Lord's Garden,* and he hath given it to the Sons of *Adam,* to be Tilled and Improved by them: Why then should we stand Starving here for Places of Habitation, and in the mean time suffer whole Countries, as profitable for the use of Man, to lye waste without any Improvement?

Seventhly, What can be a better or nobler Work, and more worthy of a *Christian,* than to erect and support a *reformed particular Church* in its Infancy, and unite our Forces with such a Company of Faithful People, as by a timely Assistance may grow Stronger and Prosper; but for want of it, may be put to great Hazards, if not be wholly Ruined.

Eighthly, If any such as are known to be Godly, and live in Wealth and Prosperity here, shall forsake all this to join with this *Reformed Church,* and with it run the Hazard of an hard and mean Condition, it will be an Example of great Use, both for the removing of *Scandal,* and to give more *Life* unto the *Faith* of God's People in their Prayers for the Plantation, and also to encourage others to join the more willingly in it.

6. Mr. *Higginson,* and Mr. *Skelton,* and other good People that arrived at *Salem,* in the Year 1629. resolved, like their Father *Abraham,* to begin their Plantation with *calling on the Name of the Lord.* The great Mr. *Hildersham* had advised our first Planters

to agree fully upon their Form of *Church Government,* before their coming into *New-England;* but they had indeed agreed little further than in this general Principle, *That the Reformation of the Church was to be endeavoured according to the written Word of God.* Accordingly ours, now arrived at *Salem,* consulted with their Brethren at *Plymouth,* what Steps to take for the more exact Acquainting of themselves *with,* and Conforming themselves *to,* that *written Word:* And the *Plymotheans,* to their great Satisfaction, laid before them what *Warrant,* they judged, that they had in the *Laws* of our Lord Jesus Christ, for every Particular in their *Church Order.*

Whereupon having the Concurrence and Countenance of their Deputy Governour, the Worshipful *John Endicot,* Esq; and the approving Presence of Messengers from the Church of *Plymouth,* they set apart the Sixth Day of *August,* after their Arrival, for *Fasting* and *Prayer,* for the settling of a *Church-State* among them, and for their making a *Confession of their Faith,* and entering into an Holy *Covenant,* whereby that *Church-State* was formed.

Mr. *Higginson* then became the Teacher, and Mr. *Skelton* the Pastor, of the Church thus constituted at *Salem;* and they lived very *peaceably* in *Salem* together, till the Death of Mr. *Higginson,* which was about a Twelvemonth after, and then of Mr. *Skelton,* who did not long survive him. Now the *Covenant* whereto these *Christians* engaged themselves, which was about Seven Years after solemnly *renewed* among them, I shall here lay before all the *Churches* of God, as it was then expressed and inforced.

We Covenant with our Lord, and one with another; and we do Bind our selves in the presence of God, to walk together in all his Ways, according as he is pleased to reveal himself unto us in his blessed Word of Truth; and do explicitely, in the Name and Fear of God, profess and protest to walk as followeth, thro' the Power and Grace of our Lord Jesus Christ.

We Avouch the Lord to be our God, and our selves to be his People, in the truth and simplicity of our Spirits.

We Give our selves to the Lord Jesus Christ, and the Word of his Grace for the Teaching, Ruling and Sanctifying of us in Matters of Worship and Conversation, resolving to cleave unto him alone for Life and Glory, and to reject all contrary Ways, Canons, and Constitutions of Men in his Worship.

We Promise to walk with our Brethren, with all Watchfulness and Tenderness, avoiding Jelousies and Suspicions, BackBitings, Censurings, Provokings, secret Risings of Spirit against them; but in all Offences to follow the Rule of our Lord Jesus, and to bear and forbear, give and forgive, as he hath taught us.

In Publick or Private, we will willingly Do nothing to the Offence of the Church; but will be willing to take Advice for our selves and ours, as occasion shall be presented.

We will not in the Congregation be forward either to show our own Gifts and Parts in Speaking or Scrupling, or there discover the Weakness or Failings of our Brethren; but attend an orderly Call thereunto, knowing how much the Lord may be dishonoured, and his Gospel, and the Profession of it, slighted by our Distempers and Weaknesses in Publick.

We Bind our selves to study the Advancement of the Gospel in all Truth and Peace; both in Regard of those that are within or without; no way slighting our Sister Churches, but using their Counsel, as need shall be; not laying a stumbling-block before any, no, not the Indians, whose good we desire to promote; and so to converse, as we may avoid the very appearance of Evil.

We do hereby promise to carry our selves in all lawful Obedience to those that are over us, in Church or Commonwealth, knowing how well-pleasing it will be to the Lord, that they should have Encouragement in their Places, by our not grieving their Spirits thro' our Irregularities.

We Resolve to approve our selves to the Lord in our particular Callings; shunning Idleness, as the Bane of any State; nor will we deal hardly or oppressingly with any, wherein we are the Lord's Stewards.

Promising also unto our best Ability to Teach our Children and Servants the Knowledge of God, and of His Will, that they may serve Him also; and all this not by any strength of our own, but by the Lord Christ; whose Blood we desire may sprinkle this our Covenant made in His Name.

By this *Instrument* was the *Covenant of Grace* Explained, Received, and Recognized, by the *First Church* in this Colony, and *applied* unto the Evangelical Designs of a *Church-Estate* before the Lord: This *Instrument* they afterwards often read over, and renewed the *Consent* of their Souls unto every Article in it; espe-

cially when their Days of *Humiliation* invited them to lay hold
on particular Opportunities for doing so.

So you have seen the *Nativity* of the *First Church* in the *Massachuset*-Colony.

7. As for the Circumstances of *Admission* into this Church,
they left it very much unto the Discretion and Faithfulness of
their Elders, together with the Condition of the Persons to be
admitted. Some were admitted by expressing their Consent unto
their *Confession* and *Covenant;* some were admitted after their
first Answering to *Questions* about *Religion,* propounded unto
them; some were admitted, when they had presented in *Writing*
such things, as might give *Satisfaction* unto the People of God
concerning them; and some that were admitted, *Orally* addressed
the People of God in such Terms, as they thought proper to ask
their *Communion* with; which *Diversity* was perhaps more *Beautiful,* than would have been a more *Punctilious Uniformity:* But
none were admitted without regard unto a Blameless and Holy
Conversation. They did all agree with their Brethren of *Plymouth*
in this Point, *That the Children of the Faithful were Church-
Members, with their Parents; and that their Baptism was a Seal of
their being so;* only before their admission to Fellowship in a
Particular Church, it was judged Necessary, that being free from
Scandal, they should be examined by the *Elders* of the Church,
upon whose Approbation of their *Fitness,* they should Publickly
and Personally own the *Covenant;* so they were to be received
unto the Table of the Lord: And accordingly the Eldest Son of
Mr. *Higginson,* being about Fifteen Years of Age, and laudably
Answering all the Characters expected in a *Communicant,* was
then so Received.

8. It is to be Remembred, that some of the Passengers, who
came over with those of our first *Salemites,* observing that the
Ministers did not use the *Book of Common-Prayer* in their Administrations; that they Administred the *Baptism* and the *Supper* of
the Lord, without any unscriptural *Ceremonies;* that they resolved
upon using *Discipline* in the Congregation against Scandalous
Offenders, according to the Word of God; and that some *Scandalous* Persons had been denied *Admission* into the Communion of
the Church; they began (*Frankford*-Fashion) to raise a deal of
Trouble hereupon. *Herodiana Malitia, nascentem persequi Reli-
gionem!* Of these there were especially *Two* Brothers; the one

a Lawyer, the other a Merchant, *both* Men of Parts, Estate and Figure in the Place. These gather'd a Company together, *separate* from the publick Assembly; and *there* the *Common-Prayer-Worship* was after a sort upheld among such as would resort unto them. The Governour perceiving a Disturbance to arise among the People on this Occasion, sent for the *Brothers;* who accused the Ministers, as *departing from the Orders of the Church of* England; adding, *That they were Separatists, and would be shortly Anabaptists;* but for themselves, *They would hold unto the Orders of the Church of* England. The Answer of the Ministers to these Accusations, was, *That they were neither* Separatists *nor* Anabaptists; *that they did not separate from the Church of* England, *nor from the Ordinances of God there, but only from the Corruptions and Disorders of that Church: That they came away from the* Common-Prayer *and* Ceremonies, *and had suffered much for their Non-conformity in their Native Land; and therefore being in a place where they might have their Liberty, they neither could nor would use them; inasmuch as they judged the Imposition of these things to be a sinful Violation of the Worship of God.* The Governour, the Council, the People, generally approved of the Answer thus given by the Ministers; but these Persons returned into *England* with very furious *Threatnings* against the Church thus Established; however the *threatned Folks* have *lived so long,* that the *Church* has *out-lived* the grand *Climacterical* Year of Humane Age; it now Flourishing more than *Sixty-three* Years after its first Gathering under the Pastoral Care of a most Reverend and Ancient Person, even Mr. *John Higginson,* the *Son* of that excellent Man who laid the Foundations of that Society.

CHAP. V.

Peregrini Deo Curæ: *Or, The Progress of the* New-Colony;

with some *Account of the* Persons, *the* Methods,

and the Troubles, *by which it came to* Something.

1. The *Governour* and *Company* of the *Massachuset-Bay* then in *London,* did in the Year 1629. after exact and mature Debates, Conclude, that it was most Convenient for the *Government,* with the Charter of the Plantation, to be transferred into the Plantation it self; and an *Order of Court* being drawn up for that End, there

was then Chosen a New *Governour,* and a New *Deputy-Governour,* that were willing to remove themselves with their Families thither on the first Occasion. The Governour was *John Winthrop,* Esq; a Gentleman of that Wisdom and Virtue, and those manifold Accomplishments, that After-Generations must reckon him no less a *Glory,* than he was a *Patriot* of the Country. The Deputy-Governour was *Thomas Dudley,* Esq; a Gentleman, whose *Natural* and *Acquired* Abilities, joined with his excellent *Moral* Qualities, Entitled him to all the great Respects with which his Country on all Opportunities treated him. Several most Worthy *Assistants* were at the same time chosen to be in this *Transportation;* moreover, several other *Gentlemen* of prime Note, and several famous *Ministers* of the Gospel, now likewise embarked themselves with these Honourable *Adventurers:* Who Equipped a *Fleet,* consisting of Ten or Eleven Ships, whereof the Admiral was, *The Arabella* (so called in Honour of the Right Honourable the Lady *Arabella Johnson,* at this time on Board) a Ship of Three Hundred and Fifty Tuns; and in some of the said Ships there were Two Hundred Passengers; all of which Arrived before the middle of *July,* in the Year 1630. safe in the Harbours of *New-England.* There was a time when the *British Sea* was by *Clements,* and the other Ancients, called Ὠκεανοσ ἀχέραντοσ, *The unpassable Ocean.* What then was to be thought of the vast *Atlantick Sea,* on the Westward of *Britain?* But this *Ocean* must now be *passed!* An Heart of Stone must have dissolved into *Tears* at the Affectionate *Farewel,* which the Governour and other Eminent Persons took of their Friends, at a *Feast* which the Governour made for them, a little before their going off; however they were acted by Principles that could carry them thro' *Tears* and *Oceans;* yea, thro' *Oceans* of *Tears:* Principles that enabled them to leave, *Dulcia Limina, atq; amabilem Larem, quem & parentum memoria, atq; ipsius* (to use *Stupius* words) *Infamiae Rudimenta Confirmant.* Some very late *Geographers* do assure us, that the Breadth of the *Atlantick Sea* is commonly over-reckoned by *Six,* by *Eight,* by *Ten* Degrees. But let that Sea be as narrow as they please, I can assure the Reader the passing of it was no little *Trial* unto those worthy People that were now to pass it.

2. But the most notable Circumstance in their *Farewel,* was their Composing and Publishing of what they called, *The humble*

request of His Majesties Loyal Subjects, the Governour and Company lately gone for New-England, *to the rest of their Brethren in and of the Church of* England; *for the obtaining of their Prayers, and the removal of Suspicions and Misconstructions of their Intentions.* In this Address of theirs, notwithstanding the trouble they had undergone for desiring to see the Church of *England Reformed* of several things, which they thought its *Deformities,* yet they now called the Church of *England* their *Dear Mother;* acknowledging that such *Hope* and *Part* as they had obtained in the *Common Salvation* they had *sucked from her Breasts;* therewithal entreating their many *Reverend Fathers and Brethren* to recommend them unto the Mercies of God, in their constant Prayers, as a *Church* now springing out of their own Bowels. *You are not Ignorant* (said they) *that the Spirit of God stirred up the Apostle* Paul, *to make a continual mention of the Church at* Philippi, *which was a Colony from* Rome; *let the same Spirit, we beseech you, put you in Mind, that are the Lord's Remembrancers, to pray for us without ceasing, who are the weak* Colony *from your selves.* And after such Prayers, they Concluded, *What Goodness you shall extend unto us, in this or any other Christian Kindness, we your Brethren in Christ shall Labour to Repay, in what Duty we are or shall be able to perform; promising so far as God shall enable us, to give him no rest on your Behalfs; wishing our Heads and Hearts may be Fountains of Tears for your everlasting Welfare, when we shall be in our Poor Cottages in the Wilderness, overshadowed with the Spirit of Supplication, thro' the manifold Necessities and Tribulations, which may not altogether unexpectedly, nor we hope unprofitably, befal us.*

3. *Reader,* If ever the *Charity* of a Right Christian, and Enlarged Soul, were exemplarily seen in its proper *Expansions,* 'twas in the Address which thou hast now been Reading: But if it now puzzel the Reader to Reconcile these Passages with the *Principles* declared, the *Practices* followed, and the *Persecutions* undergone, by these *American Reformers,* let him know, that there was more than one *Distinction,* whereof these excellent Persons were not Ignorant. First, They were able to Distinguish between the *Church of England,* as it *contained* the whole *Body of the Faithful,* scattered throughout the Kingdoms, tho' of different Perswasions about some *Rites* and *Modes* in Religion; many Thousands of

whom our *Nor-Angles* knew could comply with many things, to
which *our Consciences* otherwise enlightned and perswaded could
not yeild such a Compliance: And the *Church of England,* as it
was *confined* unto a certain Constitution by *Canons,* which pronounced *Ipso Facto,* Excommunicate all those who should affirm
that the *Worship* contained in the Book of *Common-Prayer,* and
Administrations of Sacraments, is unlawful, or that any of the
Thirty Nine Articles are Erroneous, or that any of the *Ceremonies*
commanded by the Authority of the Church might not be Approved, Used and Subscribed; and which will have to be *Accursed*
all those, who maintain that there are in the Realm any other
Meetings, Assemblies or Congregations of the King's Born Subjects, than such as by the Laws of the Land are allowed, which
may rightly Challenge to themselves the Name of *True* and *Lawful*
Churches: And by which, all those that refuse to *Kneel* at the
Reception of the Sacrament, and to be present at Publick *Prayers,*
according to the *Orders* of the Church, about which there are
prescribed many Formalities of *Responses,* with Bowing at the
Name of JESUS, are to be denied the *Communion;* and all who
dare not submit their Children to be *Baptized* by the Undertaking
of *God-Fathers,* and receive the *Cross* as a dedicating Badge of
Christianity, must not have *Baptism* for their Children: Besides
an *Et-Caetera* of how many more *Impositions!* Again, they were
able to distinguish between the *Church of England,* as it kept the
true *Doctrine* of the *Protestant Religion,* with a Disposition to
pursue the *Reformation* begun in the former Century, among
whom we may Reckon such Men, as the famous *Assembly of*
Divines at *Westminster,* who all but *Eight* or *Nine,* and the *Scots,*
had before then lived in *Conformity;* and *the Church of England,*
as limiting that Name unto a certain *Faction,* who together with
a *Discipline* very much *Unscriptural,* vigorously prosecuted the
Tripartite Plot of *Arminianism* and Conciliation with *Rome,* in
the *Church,* and unbounded *Prerogative* in the *State;* who set themselves to Cripple as fast as they could the more Learned, Godly,
Painful *Ministers* of the Land, and Silence and Ruin such as could
not Read a *Book for Sports on the Lord's Days;* or did but use
a *Prayer* of their own Conceiving, before or after Sermon; or did
but Preach in an *Afternoon,* as well as in a Morning, or on a
Lecture, or on a *Market,* or in aniwise discountenance *Old* Super-

stitions, or *New* Extravagancies; and who at last threw the Nation into the lamentable Confusions of a *Civil War*. By the Light of this *Distinction,* we may easily perceive what *Church of England* it was, that our *New-England* Exiles called, *Their Mother;* though their *Mother* had been so harsh to them, as to turn them out of Doors, yet they highly honoured Her; believing that it was not so much their *Mother,* but some of their angry *Brethren;* abusing the Name of their *Mother,* who so harshly treated them; and all the harm they wished her, was to see her put off those *Ill Trimmings,* which at her first coming out of the Popish *Babylon,* she had not so fully laid aside. If any of those *envious Brethren* do now call these *Dissenters,* as not very long since a great Prelate in a Sermon did, *The Bastards of the Church of England,* I will not make the Return which was made upon it by a Person of Quality then present; but instead thereof humbly Demand, who are the *Truer Sons* to the Church of *England;* they that hold all the *Fundamentals of Christianity* embraced by that Church, only Questioning and Forbearing a few *Disciplinary Points,* which are confessed *Indifferent* by the greatest Zealots for them; or they that have made *Britain* more unhabitable than the *Torrid Zone?* For the poor *Non-Conformists,* by their *hot* pressing of those *Indifferencies,* as if they had been the only *Necessaries,* in the mean time utterly subverting the *Faith* in the important Points of *Predestination, Free-will, Justification, Perseverance,* and some other things, which that Church requires all her Children to give their *Assent* and *Consent* unto? If the *Former; then,* say I, the First Planters of *New England* were *Truer Sons* to the Church of *England,* than that part of the *Church,* which, then by their misemploying their heavy *Church-keys,* banished them into this Plantation. And indeed, the more Genuine among the most Conformable *Sons of the Church,* did then accordingly wish all Prosperity to their *New-English* Brethren; in the Number of whom I would particularly Reckon that faithful Man, Mr. *Edward Symons,* Minister of *Rayn* in *Essex;* who in a Discourse printed *Anno* 1637, does thus Express himself, *Many now promise to themselves nothing but successive Happiness at* New-England; *which for a time, thro' God's Mercy, they may enjoy; and I pray God, they may a long time, but in this World there is no Happiness perpetual.* Nor would I on this Occasion leave unquoted some notable Words of

the Learned, Witty, and Famous Dr. *Fuller*, in his Comment on
Ruth, Page 16. *Concerning our Brethren which of late left this
Kingdom, to advance a Plantation in* New-England, *I think the
Counsel best, that King* Joash *prescribed unto* Amaziah, Tarry at
Home: *Yet as for those that are already gone, far be it from us
to conceive them to be such, to whom we may not say,* God speed:
But let us Pity them, and Pray for them. I conclude of the two
Englands, *what our Saviour saith of the two Wines,* No Man
having tasted of the Old, presently desireth the New; for he saith,
The Old is better.

4. Being happily arrived at *New-England,* our new Planters
found the difficulties of a rough and hard *Wilderness* presently
assaulting them: Of which the worst was the *Sickliness* which
many of them had contracted by their other difficulties. Of those
who soon dy'd after their first Arrival, not the least considerable
was the Lady *Arabella,* who left an Earthly *Paradice* in the Family
of an *Earldom,* to Encounter the Sorrows of a *Wilderness,* for the
Entertainments of a *pure Worship* in the *House of God;* and
then immediately left that *Wilderness* for the Heavenly *Paradise,*
whereto the Compassionate *Jesus,* of whom she was a *Follower,*
called her. We have Read concerning a Noble Woman of *Bohemia,*
who forsook her Friends, her Plate, her House and All; and
because the Gates of the City were Guarded, crept through the
Common-Sewer, that she might enjoy the *Institutions* of our Lord
at another Place where they might be had. The Spirit which acted
that Noble Woman, we may suppose carried this Blessed Lady
thus to and thro' the Hardships of an *American* Desart. But as
for her Virtuous Husband, *Isaac Johnson,* Esq;

———— *He try'd*

To Live without her, lik'd it not, and Dy'd.

His *Mourning* for the Death of His Honourable Consort was too
bitter to be extended a *Year;* about a Month after *her* Death, *his*
ensued, unto the extream loss of the whole Plantation. But at
the *End* of this *perfect and upright Man;* there was not only *Peace,*
but *Joy;* and his *Joy* particularly expressed it self, *That God had
kept his Eyes open so long as to see* One Church *of the Lord Jesus
Christ gathered in these Ends of the Earth, before his own going
away to Heaven.* The *Mortality* thus threatning of this New
Plantation, so *enlivened* the Devotions of this good People, that

they set themselves by *Fasting* and *Prayer* to obtain from God the removal of it; and their Brethren at *Plymouth* also attended the like Duties on their Behalf: The Issue whereof was, that in a little time they not only had *Health* restored, but they likewise enjoyed the special Direction and Assistance of God in the further Prosecution of their Undertakings.

5. But there were Two terrible Distresses more, besides that of *Sickness,* whereto this People were exposed in the beginning of their Settlement: Tho' a most seasonable and almost unexpected *Mercy from Heaven* still rescued them out of those Distresses. One thing that sometimes extreamly exercised them, was a *Scarcity of Provisions;* in which 'twas wonderful to see their *Dependance* upon God, and God's *Mindfulness* of them. When the parching Droughts of the *Summer* divers times threatned them with an utter and a total Consumption to the Fruits of the Earth, it was their manner, with *Heart-melting,* and I may say, *Heaven-melting* Devotions, to *Fast* and *Pray* before God; and on the very Days, when they *poured out the Water* of their *Tears* before him, he would *shower down the Water* of his *Rain* upon their Fields; *while they were yet speaking, he would hear them;* insomuch that the Salvages themselves would on that Occasion admire *the English-man's God!* But the *Englishmen* themselves would Celebrate their Days of *Thanksgiving* to him. When their *Stock* was likewise wasted so far, which divers times it was, that they were come *to the last Meal in the Barrel,* just then, unlook'd for, arrived several Ships from other Parts of the World loaden with Supplies, among which, One was by the *Lord Deputy of Ireland* sent hither, altho' he did not know the *Necessities* of the Country, to which he sent her; and if he had *known* them, would have been thought as unlikely as any Man living to have helpt them: In these Extremities, 'twas marvellous to see how *Helpful* these good People were to one another, following the Example of their most liberal Governour *Winthrop,* who made an *equal Distribution* of what he had in his own Stores among the Poor, *taking no thought for to Mor-row!* And how *Content* they were; when an Honest Man, as I have heard, inviting his Friends to a Dish of *Clams,* at the Table gave Thanks to Heaven, who *had given them to suck the abundance of the Seas, and of the Treasures hid in the Sands!*

Another thing that gave them no little Exercise, was *the Fear of the Indians,* by whom they were sometimes *Alarm'd.* But this Fear was wonderfully prevented, not only by *Intestine Wars* happening then to fall out among those *Barbarians,* but chiefly by the *Small-Pox,* which prov'd a *great Plague* unto them, and particularly to one of the *Princes* in the *Massachuset-Bay,* who yet seemed hopefully to be *Christianiz'd* before he Dy'd. This Distemper getting in, I know not how, among them, swept them away with a most prodigious Desolation, insomuch that altho' the *English* gave them all the assistances of *Humanity* in their Calamities, yet there was, it may be, not *One* in *Ten* among them left alive, of those *few* that liv'd; many also *fled* from the Infection, leaving the Country a meer *Golgotha* of unburied Carcases; and as for the *rest,* the *English* treated them with all the Civility imaginable; among the Instances of which Civility, let this be reckoned for *One,* that notwithstanding the *Patent* which they had for the Country, they fairly *purchased* of the Natives the several *Tracts* of Land which they afterwards *possessed.*

6. The People in the Fleet that arriv'd at *New-England,* in the Year 1630, left the Fleet almost, as the *Family* of *Noah* did the *Ark,* having a whole World before them to be peopled. *Salem* was already supplied with a competent Number of Inhabitants; and therefore the Governour, with most of the Gentlemen that Accompanied him in his Voyage, took their first Opportunity to prosecute further Settlements about the bottom of the *Massachuset-Bay:* But where-ever they sat down, they were so mindful of their *Errand into the Wilderness,* that still one of their *First Works* was to gather a *Church* into the *Covenant* and *Order* of the Gospel. First, There was a Church thus gathered at *Charles-Town,* on the North side of *Charles's* River; where keeping a Solemn *Fast* on *August* 27. 1630, to Implore the Conduct and Blessing of Heaven on their Ecclesiastical Proceedings, they chose Mr. *Wilson,* a most Holy and Zealous Man, formerly a Minister of *Sudbury,* in the County of *Suffolk,* to be their Teacher; and altho' he now submitted unto an *Ordination,* with an *Imposition of such Hands* as were by the Church invited so to pronounce the Benediction of Heaven upon him; yet it was done with a *Protestation* by all, that it should be only as a sign of his *Election* to the Charge of his *New Flock,* without any Intention that he should thereby Renounce the Ministry he had received in *England.* After the gathering of the Church

at *Charles-Town*, there quickly followed another at the Town of *Dorchester*.

And after *Dorchester* there followed another at the Town of *Boston*, which Issued out of *Charles-Town;* one Mr. *James* took the Care of the Church at *Charles-Town*, and Mr. *Wilson* went over to *Boston*, where they that formerly belonged unto *Charles-Town*, with Universal Approbation became a *distinct Church* of themselves. To *Boston* soon succeeded a Church at *Roxbury;* to *Roxbury*, one at *Lyn;* to *Lyn*, one at *Watertown;* so that in one or two Years time there were to be seen *Seven Churches* in this Neighbourhood, all of them attending to what the *Spirit* in the *Scripture said unto them;* all of them *Golden Candelsticks*, illustrated with a very sensible *Presence* of our Lord Jesus Christ amoug them.

7. It was for a matter of *Twelve Years* together, that Persons of all Ranks, well affected unto *Church-Reformation*, kept sometimes *Dropping*, and sometimes *Flocking* into *New-England*, tho' some that were coming into *New-England* were not suffered so to do. The Persecutors of those *Puritans*, as they were called, who were now *Retiring* into that *Cold Country* from the *Heat* of their Persecution, did all that was possible to hinder as many as was possible from enjoying of that *Retirement*. There were many *Countermands* given to the Passage of People that were now steering of this *Western Course;* and there was a sort of *Uproar* made among no small part of the Nation, that this People should not be *let go*. Among those bound for *New-England*, that were so stopt, there were especially Three Famous Persons, whom I suppose their Adversaries would not have so studiously detained at Home, if they had *foreseen* Events; those were *Oliver Cromwel*, and Mr. *Hambden*, and Sir *Arthur Haselrig:* Nevertheless, this is not the only Instance *of Persecuting Church-mens* not having the *Spirit of Prophecy*. But many others were diverted from an intended Voyage hither by the pure *Providence* of God, which had *provided* other Improvements for them; and of this take one Instance instead of many. Before the woful Wars which broke forth in the *Three Kingdoms*, there were divers Gentlemen in *Scotland*, who being uneasie under the *Ecclesiastical Burdens* of the Times, wrote unto *New-England* their Enquiries, Whether they might be there suffered freely to Excercise their *Presbyterian Church-Government?* And it was freely answered, *That they might*. Hereupon they sent

over an Agent, who pitched upon a Tract of Land near the Mouth of *Merimack River,* whither they intended then to Transplant themselves: But altho' they had so far proceeded in their Voyage, as to be *Half-Seas* thorough; the manifold Crosses they met withal, made them give over their Intentions; and the Providence of God so ordered it, that some of those very Gentlemen were afterwards the *Revivers* of that well-known *Solemn League and Covenant,* which had so great an Influence upon the following Circumstances of the Nations. However, the number of those who did actually arrive at *New England* before the Year 1640. have been computed about *Four Thousand;* since which time far more have gone out of the Country than have come to it; and yet the God of Heaven so smiled upon the *Plantation,* while under an *easie* and *equal* Government, the Designs of Christianity in well-formed *Churches* have been carried on, that no History can *parallel* it. That saying of *Eutropius* about *Rome,* which hath been sometimes applied unto the Church, is capable of some Application to this little part of the Church: *Nec Minor ab Exordio, nec major Incrementis ulla.* Never was any Plantation brought unto such a Considerableness, in a space of time so Inconsiderable! An *Howling Wilderness* in a few Years became a *Pleasant Land,* accommodated with the *Necessaries,* yea, and the *Conveniencies* of *Humane Life;* the *Gospel* has carried with it a *fulness of all other Blessings;* and (albeit, that Mankind generally, as far as we have any Means of enquiry, have increased, in one and the same given Proportion, and so no more than *doubled* themselves in about Three-Hundred and Sixty Years, in all the past Ages of the World, since the fixing of the present Period of Humane Life) the Four-Thousand *First Planters,* in less than Fifty Years, notwithstanding all *Transportations* and *Mortalities,* increased into, they say, more than an *Hundred Thousand.*

2
George Bancroft

By the time George Bancroft (1800–1891) began his monumental *History of the United States* (10 volumes; Boston, 1834–1874), statesmen, orators, and journalists had begun to look upon the pioneers of seventeenth-century New England as the "founding fathers" of the American nation. Bancroft, sharing this view along with an enthusiasm for Jacksonian democracy, was disposed to see the settlement of Massachusetts as an episode in the history of popular liberty. Like Cotton Mather, he thought that God had taken an active part in the settlement, and, like Mather, he wished to enlist God and the founding fathers on his side; but as his side was that of democracy, his notion concerning what had been founded differed from Mather's, and he chose different events for emphasis. The selection beginning on page 29 is from Volume I, pages 371–394 of the first edition, published in 1834.

Bancroft began revising the early volumes of his history before completing the later ones; and subsequent editions, of which there were many, revealed changes both in his literary style and in his understanding of events. For example, compare the following four paragraphs from the last edition, published in 1883 ("the author's last revision") with the corresponding passage from our selection (i.e., the first five paragraphs, beginning "The charter . . ." and ending ". . . original patentees.") :

The charter, which was cherished for more than half a century as the most precious boon, constituted a body politic by the name of the Governor and Company of the Massachusetts Bay in New England. The administration of its affairs was intrusted to a governor, deputy, and eighteen assistants, who were annually, on the last Wednesday of Easter term, to be elected by the freemen or members of the corporation, and to meet once a month or oftener "for despatching such businesses as concerned the company or plantation." Four times a year the governor, assistants, and all the freemen were to be summoned to "one great, general, and solemn assembly;" and these "great and general courts" were invested with full powers to choose and admit into the company so many as they should think fit, to elect and constitute all requisite subordinate officers, and to make laws and ordinances for the welfare of the company and for the government of the lands and the inhabitants of the plantation, "so as such laws and ordinances be not contrary and repugnant to the laws and statutes of the realm of England."

"The principle and foundation of the charter of Massachusetts," wrote Charles II. at a later day, when he had Clarendon for his adviser, "was the freedom of liberty of conscience." The governor, or his deputy, or two of the assistants, was empowered, but not required, to administer the oaths of supremacy and allegiance to every person who should go to inhabit the granted lands; and, as the statutes establishing the common prayer and spiritual courts did not reach beyond the realm, the silence of the charter respecting them released the colony from their power. The English government did not foresee how wide a departure from English usages would grow out of the emigration of Puritans to America; but, as conformity was not required of the new commonwealth, the persecutions in England were a guarantee that the immense majority of emigrants would be fugitives who scrupled compliance with the common prayer. Freedom of Puritan worship was the purpose and the result of the colony. The proceedings of the company, moreover, did not fall under the immediate supervision of the king, and did not need his assent; so that self-direction, in ecclesiastical as well as civil affairs, passed to the patentees, subject only to conflicts with the undefined prerogative of the king, and the unsettled claim to superior authority by parliament.

The company was authorized to transport to its territory any persons, whether English or foreigners, who would go willingly, would become lieges of the English king, and were not restrained "by especial name;" and they were encouraged to do so by a promise of favor to the commerce of the colony with foreign parts, and a total or partial exemption from duties for seven and for twenty-one years. The emigrants and their posterity were ever to be considered as natural-born subjects, entitled to all English liberties and immunities.

The corporate body alone was to decide what liberties the

colonists should enjoy. All ordinances published under its seal were to be implicitly obeyed. Full legislative and executive authority was conferred on the company, but the place where it should hold its courts was not named.

Most, though not all, of Bancroft's revisions were of this kind, reducing the dramatic contrasts of his first narrative and in some cases reversing his interpretation.

In later editions Bancroft eliminated footnotes. Since those in the first edition were abbreviated, the reader who wishes to trace Bancroft's sources beyond the limits of this volume may find the following expansions convenient:

Bentley or Bentley's Salem. William Bentley, "A Description and History of Salem," Massachusetts Historical Society, *Collections,* first series, VI (1799), 212–288.

Chalmers. George Chalmers, *Political Annals of the Present United Colonies, from their Settlement to the Peace of 1763* (London, 1780).

Colony Laws. *The Charters and General Laws of the Colony and Province of Massachusetts Bay* (Boston, 1814).

Col. Records. The manuscript volumes later edited by Nathaniel B. Shurtleff as *The Records of the Governor and Company of the Massachusetts Bay* (5 vols. in 6; Boston, 1853–1854).

Douglass. William Douglass, *A Summary, Historical and Political, of the First Planting, Progressive Improvements, and Present State of the British Settlements in North-America* (2 vols.; Boston, 1749–1751, 1755; London, 1760).

Dudley. Thomas Dudley's letter to the Countess of Lincoln, which had been printed in *Massachusetts, or the First Planters of New England* (Boston, 1696) and reprinted in Massachusetts Historical Society, *Collections,* first series, VIII (1802). The later publication by the New Hampshire Historical Society, from the original manuscript, did not appear until 1834, the year when Bancroft's own work was published. See pages 157–173.

Ebeling. Christoph Daniel Ebeling, *Erdbeschreibung und Geschichte von Amerika* (7 vols.; Hamburg, 1793–1816).

Felt's Annals of Salem. Joseph Barlow Felt, *The Annals of Salem, from its first Settlement* (Salem, 1827).

Grahame. James Grahame, *The History of the Rise and Progress of the United States of North America, till the British Revolution in 1688* (2 vols.; London, 1827).

Hazard. Ebenezer Hazard (ed.), *Historical Collections; Consisting of State Papers and other Authentic Documents; Intended as Materials for an History of the United States of America* (2 vols.; Philadelphia, 1792–1794). The passages cited from this work are selections from Records of the Massachusetts Bay Company and letters from the Company to Endecott and to Skelton and Higginson in 1629. See pages 302–479.

Hubbard. William Hubbard, *A General History of New England, from the Discovery to MDCLXXX* (Cambridge, Mass., 1815). Hubbard (1621–1704) came to New England in 1635. The early part of his work depends heavily on Winthrop's journal.

Hutchinson. Thomas Hutchinson, *The History of Massachusets-Bay* (3 vols., Boston, 1764–1828).

Hutchinson's Coll. Thomas Hutchinson (ed.), *A Collection of Original Papers Relative to the History of the Colony of Massachusets-Bay* (Boston, 1769).

Mass. Hist. Coll. Massachusetts Historical Society, *Collections*. Beginning publication in 1792, this serial contained mostly original documents of the seventeenth and eighteenth centuries. It had reached twenty-four volumes by 1834.

Mather. Cotton Mather, *Magnalia Christi Americana* (London, 1702).

Montesquieu. Charles de Secondat, Baron de la Brède et de Montesquieu, *De l'Esprit des Loix* (Geneva, 1748); *The Spirit of Laws,* translated from the French (London, 1750).

Neal's N. E. Daniel Neal, *The History of New England* (2 vols.; London, 1720, 1747, 1754).

Oldmixon. John Oldmixon, *The British Empire in America, Containing the History of the Discovery, Settlement, Progress and present State of all the British Colonies, on the Continent and Islands of America* (2 vols.; London, 1708).

Prince. Thomas Prince, *A Chronological History of New-England* (Boston, 1736–1755, 1826).

Records. See Col. Records.

Robertson. William Robertson, *The History of America, Books IX and X, containing the History of Virginia to the Year 1688; and of New England to the Year 1652* (London, 1796; Philadelphia, 1799).

Winthrop. John Winthrop, *The History of New England from 1630 to 1649,* James Savage (ed.), (2 vols.; Boston, 1825–1826). Winthrop's journal. Savage brought out a new edition, with corrections, in 1853, from which the selection on pages 204–282 has been reprinted.

Most of the above volumes are either secondary works (written long after the events described, without firsthand knowledge) or early printings of documents included in the present volume. In the selection below, the dates included in brackets were printed by Bancroft in the margins of the text.

From

A History of the United States

The charter, which bears the signature of Charles I., and which was cherished for more than half a century as the most precious boon, established a corporation, like other corporations within the realm. The associates were constituted a body politic by the name of the Governor and Company of the Massachusetts Bay in New England. The administration of its affairs was entrusted to a Governor, Deputy, and eighteen assistants, who were to be annually elected by the stockholders, or members of the corporation. Four times a year, or oftener if desired, a general assembly of the freemen was to be held; and to these assemblies, which were invested with the necessary powers of legislation, inquest, and superintendence, the most important affairs were referred. No provision required the assent of the king to render the acts of the body valid; in his eye it was but a trading corporation, not a civil government; its doings were esteemed as indifferent as those of any guild or company in England; and if powers of jurisdiction in America were conceded, it was only from the nature of the business, in which the stockholders were to engage.

For the charter designedly granted great facilities for colonization. It allowed the company to transport to its American territory any persons, whether English or foreigners, who would go willingly, would become lieges of the English king, and were not restrained "by especial name." It empowered, but it did not require,[1] the governor to administer the oaths of supremacy and allegiance; yet it was far from conceding to the patentees the privilege of freedom of worship. Not a single line alludes to such a purpose; nor can it be implied by a reasonable construction from any clause in the charter. The omission of an express guarantee left religious liberty unprovided for and unprotected. The instrument confers on the colonists the rights of English subjects; it does not confer on them new and greater rights. On the contrary, they are strictly forbidden to make laws or ordinances, repugnant to the laws and statutes of the realm of England. The express concession of power to administer the oath of supremacy, demonstrates that universal religious toleration was not designed; and the freemen of the corporation, it should be remembered, were not at that time Separatists. Even Higginson, and Hooker, and Cotton were still ministers of the church of England; nor could the patentees foresee, nor the English government anticipate, how wide a departure from English usages, would grow out of the emigration of puritans to America.[2]

The political condition of the colonists was not deemed by king Charles a subject worthy of his consideration. Full legislative and executive authority was conferred not on the emigrants but on the company, of which the emigrants could not be active members, so long as the charter of the corporation remained in England. The associates in London were to establish ordinances, to settle forms of government, to name all necessary officers, to prescribe their duties, and to establish a criminal code. Massachusetts was not erected into a province, to be governed by laws of its own enact-

---

[1] Grahame, v. I, p. 244, 245, is right as to that fact and no further. On the contested question he follows Neal, while Chalmers and Robertson have sustained an opposite view. I have written with confidence, because I have been favored with an ample, and to my mind, a conclusive opinion on the subject from the author of the Commentaries on the Constitution of the U. S.; whose opinions derive their weight less from his eminent station than from his profound learning and genius. The European who would understand our form of government, must study the Commentaries of Story.

[2] The editor of Winthrop did me the kindness to read to me unpublished letters, which are in his possession, and which prove that the Puritans in England were amazed as well as alarmed at the boldness of their brethren in Massachusetts.

ment; it was reserved for the corporation to decide, what degree of civil rights its colonists should enjoy. The charter on which the freemen of Massachusetts succeeded in erecting a system of independent representative liberty, did not secure to them a single privilege of self-government; but left them, as the Virginians had been left, without one valuable franchise, at the mercy of a corporation within the realm. This was so evident, that some of those, who had already emigrated, clamored that they were become slaves.[3]

It was equally the right of the corporation, to establish the terms on which new members should be admitted to its freedom. Its numbers could be enlarged or changed only by its own consent.

It was perhaps implied, though it was not expressly required, that the affairs of the company should be administered in England; yet the place for holding the courts was not specially appointed. What if the corporation should vote the emigrants to be freemen, and call a meeting beyond the Atlantic? What if the governor, deputy, assistants, and freemen should themselves emigrate, and thus break down the distinction between the colony and the corporation? The history of Massachusetts is the counterpart to that of Virginia; the latter obtained its greatest liberty by the abrogation of the charter of its company; the former by a transfer of its charter and a daring construction of its powers by the successors of the original patentees.

The charter had been granted in March; in April preparations were hastening for the embarkation of new emigrants. The government which was now established for Massachusetts, merits commemoration, though it was never duly organized. It was to consist of a governor and counsellors; of whom eight out of the thirteen were appointed by the corporation in England; three were to be named by these eight; and, as it was said, to remove all grounds of discontent, the choice of the remaining two counsellors was granted to the colonists as a liberal boon. The board, when thus constituted, was invested with all the powers of legislation, justice, and administration. Such was the inauspicious dawn of civil and religious liberty on the Bay of Massachusetts.[4]

[3] Hazard, v. i. p. 257.
[4] Col. Records. Hazard, v. i. p. 256–268, and 268–271. Bentley in i. Mass. Hist. Coll. v. vi. 235, 236.

Benevolent instructions to Endicot were at the same time issued. "If any of the salvages," such were the orders long and uniformly followed in all changes of government, and placed on record more than half a century before William Penn proclaimed the principles of peace on the borders of the Delaware, "pretend right of inheritance to all or any part of the lands granted in our patent, we pray you endeavor to purchase their tytle, that we may avoid the least scruple of intrusion." "Particularly publish, that no wrong or injury be offered to the natives."[5]

The departure of the fleet for America was now anxiously desired. The colonists were to be cheered by the presence of religious teachers; and the excellent and truly catholic John Higginson, an eminent non-conforming minister, receiving an invitation to conduct the emigrants, esteemed it as a call from heaven.[6] The propagation of the gospel among the heathen was earnestly desired; in pious sincerity they resolved if possible to redeem these wrecks of human nature; the colony seal was an Indian, erect, with an arrow in his right hand, and the motto, "Come over and help us;"[7]—a device of which the appropriateness has been lost by the modern substitution of the favorite line of Algernon Sidney;—and three additional ministers attended the expedition. The company of emigrants was winnowed before sailing; and servants of ill life were discharged. "No idle drone may live amongst us;"[8] was the spirit as well as the law of the dauntless community, which was to turn the sterility of New-England into a cluster of wealthy states.

As the ships were bearing Higginson and his followers out of sight of their native land, they remembered it, not as the scene of their sufferings from intolerance, but as the home of their fathers and the dwelling place of their friends. They did not say "Farewell Babylon! farewell Rome! but, FAREWELL DEAR ENGLAND."[9]

It was in the last days of June [1629] that the little band of two hundred arrived at Salem; where the "corruptions of the English church" were never to be planted, and where a new "reformation" was to be reduced to practice. They found neither church nor

[5] Hazard, v. i. p. 263, 277.
[6] Hutchinson's Coll. p. 24, 25. Hubbard, p. 112.
[7] Douglass, v. i. p. 409. Douglass is almost as rash as Oldmixon.
[8] Hazard, v. i. p. 284, 283, 256.
[9] Mather, b. iii. c. i. S. 12.

town; eight or ten pitiful hovels, one more stately tenement for the Governor, and a few cornfields were the only proofs, that they had been preceded by their countrymen. The whole body of old and new planters now amounted to three hundred; of whom one third joined the infant settlement at Charlestown.[10]

To the great European world the few tenants of the mud-hovels and log-cabins at Salem might appear too insignificant to merit notice; to themselves they were as the chosen emissaries of God; outcasts from England yet favorites with heaven; destitute of security, of convenient food and shelter, and yet blessed beyond all mankind, for they were the depositories of the purest truth, and the selected instruments to kindle in the wildnerness the beacon of pure religion, of which the undying light should not only penetrate the wigwams of the heathen, but spread its benignant beams across the darkness of the whole civilized world. The emigrants were not so much a body politic, as a church in the wilderness; with no benefactor around them but nature, no present sovereign but God. An entire separation was made between state and church; religious worship was established on the basis of the independence of each separate religious community; all officers of the church were elected by its members; and these rigid Calvinists, of whose rude intolerance the world has been filled with malignant calumnies, established a covenant, cherishing, it is true, the severest virtues, but without one tinge of fanaticism. It was an act of piety not of study; it favored virtue not superstition; inquiry and not submission. The people were enthusiasts but not bigots.[11] The church was self-constituted.[12] It did not ask the assent of the king; or recognize him as its head; its officers were set apart and ordained among themselves;[13] it used no liturgy; it rejected unnecessary ceremonies; and reduced the simplicity of Calvin to a still plainer standard. The motives, which controlled their decisions, were so deeply seated in

10 Higginson's whole account is, of course, the highest authority. See Hutchinson's Collection, p. 32–50, and i. Mass. Hist. Coll. v. i. p. 117–124. Charlestown Records in Prince, p. 261.

11 See the covenant in Neal's N. E. v. i. 141–143, and in Bentley's Salem, App. No. iv.

12 Hubbard, p. 116–120. Prince, p. 263, 264. Neal's N. E., v. i. p. 144.

13 Felt's Annals of Salem, p. 573. An accurate and useful work, the fruit of much original research.

the very character of their party, that the doctrine and discipline, then established at Salem, remained the rule of puritans in New England.

There existed even in this little company a few individuals, to whom the new system was unexpected; and in John and Samuel Browne, they found able leaders. Both were members of the colonial council, they had been favorites of the corporation in England; and one of them an experienced and meritorious lawyer, had been a member of the board of Assistants in London.[14] They declared their dissent from the church of Higginson; and at every risk of union and tranquillity, they insisted upon the use of the English liturgy. But should the emigrants give up the very purpose for which they had crossed the Atlantic? Should not even the forests of Massachusetts be safe against the intrusion of the hierarchy, before which they had fled? They were, in one sense, a garrison, set for the defence of the territory against insincere friends not less than open foes. They deemed the coëxistence of their liberty and of prelacy impossible; anticipating invasions of their rights, they feared to find in the adherents of the establishment, persons, who would act as spies in the camp and betray them to their persecuting adversaries; the form of religion, from which they had suffered, was therefore attacked, not as a sect but as a tyranny.[15] The charter had conferred on the company the right of expelling from its colonial domains every person, whose presence seemed a detriment to its welfare;[16] and the instructions from the company required the enforcement of the provision.[17] Finding it to be a vain attempt to persuade the Brownes to relinquish their resolute opposition, and believing that their speeches tended to produce disorder and dangerous feuds, Endicot sent them to England in the returning ships; and faction, deprived of its leaders, died away.[18]

Winter [1629–30] brought disease and the sufferings incident

[14] Hazard, v. i. p. 267, 269.

[15] Montesquieu, L. xxv. c. ix. Hutchinson, quoting the remark, omits the best part of it.

[16] Colony Laws, p. 15, 16.

[17] "If any prove incorrigible, ship such persons home by the Lyon's Whelp." Hazard, v. i. p. 263.

[18] Prince, p. 264. Bentley, p. 241, 242. Mather, b. i. c. 4. S. 3. Eliot, in i. Mass. Hist. Coll. v. ix. p. 3–6. Chalmers, 144–146. Neal's N. E. v. i. p. 144, 145. The liberal Ebeling, v. i. p. 869, defends the measure.

to early settlements. Above eighty, almost half of the emigrants, died before spring;[19] lamenting only, that they were removed from the world before beholding the perfect establishment of their religion. Higginson himself fell a victim to a hectic fever; the future prosperity of New England, and the glories of the many churches, which were to adorn and gladden the wilderness, were the cheering visions, that in the hour of death floated before his eyes.[20]

The Brownes returned to England, breathing ineffectual menaces.[21] The ships also carried with them a description of New England by Higginson; a tract, of which three editions were published within a few months, so intense an interest in the new colony had been diffused throughout the realm.

For the concession of the Massachusetts Charter seemed to the puritans like a summons from Heaven, inviting them to America. There the gospel might be taught in its purity; and the works of nature would alone be the safe witnesses of their devotions. England by her persecutions proved herself weary of her inhabitants, who were now esteemed more vile, than the earth on which they trod. Habits of expense degraded men of moderate fortune; and even the schools, which should be the fountains of living waters, had become corrupt. The new world shared in the Providence of God; it had claims, therefore, to the benevolence and exertions of man. What nobler work, than to abandon the comforts of England, and plant the church in the remote citadel, which the advocates of a false religion should never scale?

But was it right, a scrupulous conscience demanded, to fly from persecutions? Yes, they answered, for persecutions might lead their posterity to abjure the truth. The certain misery of their wives and children was the most gloomy of their forebodings; and it must have been a stern sense of duty, which could command the powerful emotions of nature to be silent, and set aside all considerations of physical evils as the fears of too carnal minds. The rights of the natives offered an impediment more easily removed; much land had been desolated by the plague; and the good leave of the Indians might be purchased. The ill success of other plantations could not

[19] Dudley, p. 38. Prince, p. 271.
[20] Mather, b. iii. c. i. S. 14.
[21] Hazard, v. i. p. 287, 289.

chill the rising enthusiasm; former enterprize had aimed at profit; the present object was purity of religion; the earlier settlements had been filled with a lawless multitude; it was now proposed to form "a peculiar government," and to colonize "the best." Such were the "Conclusions,"[22] which were privately circulated among the puritans of England.

On the suggestion of the generous Matthew Cradock, the governor of the company,[23] it was proposed [July 28, 1629] that the charter should be transferred to those of the freemen, who should themselves inhabit the colony; and the question immediately became the most important, that could be debated. An agreement was at once formed at Cambridge in England [Aug. 24] between men of fortune and education, that they would themselves embark for America, if, before the last of September, the whole government should be legally transferred to them and the other freemen of the company, who should inhabit the plantation.[24] The plan was sufficient to excite in the family of John Winthrop and in many of the purest men in England, the desire to emigrate. "I shall call that my country," said the younger Winthrop to his father, "where I may most glorify God, and enjoy the presence of my dearest friends. Therefore herein I submit myself to God's will and yours, and dedicate myself to God and the company, with the whole endeavors, both of body and mind. The Conclusions, which you sent down, are unanswerable; and it cannot but be a prosperous action, which is so well allowed by the judgments of God's prophets, undertaken by so religious and wise worthies in Israel, and indented to God's glory in so special a service."[25] Two days after the contract had been executed, the subject was again brought before the court. A serious debate ensued, and continued the next day, when it was fully and with general consent declared, that the

[22] Hutchinson's Coll. p. 27–31. Mather, b. i. c. iv. S. 5.

[23] Prince, p. 262. Savage on Winthrop, v. i. p. 2. I have carefully consulted the Colony Records, which are in general in a good state of preservation, and which are diffuse on the subject of the transfer of the charter.

[24] Hutchinson's Coll. p. 25, 26.

[25] Winthrop, v. i. p. 359, 360. The publicity of the admirable letter is due to Savage.

government and the patent should be transferred beyond the Atlantic and settled in New England.[26]

This vote was simply a decision of the question, where the future meetings of the company should be held; and yet it effectually changed a commercial corporation into an independent provincial government. The measure was believed to be consistent with the principles of the charter. The corporation did not sell itself; the corporation emigrated. They could not assign the patent; but they could call a legal meeting at London or on board ship in an English harbor; and why not in the port of Salem as well as at the Isle of Wight? In a cabin or under a tree at Charlestown, as well as at the house of Goffe in London? The propriety of the measure in a juridical point of view, cannot be sustained;[27] but whatever may be thought of the legality of the decision, it certainly conferred no new franchises or power on the emigrants, unless they were already members of the company; it admitted no new freemen; it gave to Massachusetts a present government; but the corporation, though it was to meet in New England, retained in its full integrity the right conferred by the charter, of admitting freemen according to its pleasure. The manner in which that power was to be exercised, would control the early political character of Massachusetts.

At the court, convened for the purpose of appointing officers who would emigrate [Oct. 20, 1629], John Winthrop, a man approved for piety, liberality and wisdom, was chosen governor, and the whole board of assistants selected for America. Yet as the hour of departure drew near, the consciousness of danger spread such terrors, that even the hearts of the strong began to fail. One and another of the magistrates declined. It became necessary to hold a court at Southampton [Mar. 18, 1630] for the election of three substitutes among the assistants; and of these three one never went. Even after they had embarked, a court was held on board the Arbella, and Thomas Dudley was chosen Deputy Governor in the place of Humphrey, who staid behind.[28] Dudley emigrated,

26 Records, v. i. p. 31.; "soe far as it may be done legally." Yet Sept. 29, 1629, a committee was raised "to take advice of Learned Counsell, whether the same may be legally done or no." Records, v. i. p. 33.

27 Story's MS. opinion.

28 Records, v. i. p. 54. Prince, p. 264. 266, 267. 270. 272. 274, 275. Hutchinson, v. i. p. 23, 24.

and had hardly reached America, before he repented that he had come; the country had been described in too favorable colors.[29] It was principally the calm decision of Winthrop which sustained the courage of his companions.[30]

The whole number of ships employed during the season was seventeen; and they carried over not far from fifteen hundred souls. About eight hundred, all of them puritans, inclined to the party of the independents, many of them men of high endowments, large fortune, and the best education, scholars, well versed in all the learning of the times, clergymen, who ranked among the most eloquent and pious in the realm, embarked with Winthrop for their asylum, bearing with them the charter, which was to be the basis of their liberties.[31] Religion did not expel the feelings of nature; before leaving Yarmouth they published to the world the grounds of their removal, and bade an affectionate farewell to the church of England and to the land of their nativity. "Our hearts," say they, "shall be fountains of tears for your everlasting welfare, when we shall be in our poor cottages in the wilderness."

The emigrants were a body of sincere believers, desiring purity of religion, and not a colony of philosophers, bent upon universal toleration; reverence for the peculiarities of their faith led them to a land, which was either sterile or overgrown with an unprofitable

[29] Dudley's Letter as before.

[30] Ibid. i. Mass. H. Coll. v. viii. 38.

[31] For the history of Massachusetts in the remainder of this chapter, the Records of the Colony were a principle source. The History of Winthrop in the incomparably accurate edition and with the Commentary of Savage is of still greater historical value and of equal authenticity. Hubbard, Mather, Prince, Neal, Oldmixon, and Chalmers, are of little service in comparison. The Mass. Hist. Coll. are rich in authentic materials, none of which I have neglected. The excellent Letter of Dudley, Winthrop's Correspondence, Johnson's Wonderworking Providence, have been carefully consulted, and shorter tracts and letters almost without number. Hutchinson's Collection is full of important documents for the history of N. E. His history is an excellent guide; but I have followed the contemporaries of the events which I describe. Snow, Felt, and Francis, have treated their respective subjects with ability and research. Besides the recent edition of the Colony Laws, I have before me the folio of 1660. Many documents are in Hazard. Many more are on file in the State House; and I have examined hundreds of them; gleaning but little new information, where men like Prince and Savage had been gathering before me. The original materials for the early history of New England are exceedingly copious; the circumstances, attending every considerable event may be traced with minuteness.

vegetation. They emigrated to a new hemisphere, where distance might protect them from inquisition; to a soil of which they had purchased the exclusive possession, with a charter of which they had acquired the entire control, for the sake of reducing to practice the doctrines of religion and the forms of civil liberty, which they cherished more than life itself. They constituted a corporation to which they themselves might establish at their pleasure the terms of admission. They held in their own hands the key to their asylum, and maintained their right of closing its doors against the enemies of its harmony and its safety.

In June and July the ships which bore Winthrop and his immediate companions, arrived to a scene of gloom; such of the earlier emigrants as had survived the previous winter, were poor and weak from sickness; their corn and bread were hardly enough for a fortnight's supply. Instead of offering a welcome, they thronged to the new comers to be fed. Nearly two hundred servants, who had been sent over at a great expense, received their liberty, free from all engagements; their labor, such was the excessive scarcity, was worth less than the cost of their maintenance.

The selection of places for the new plantations became the immediate care. The bay and the adjoining rivers were examined; if Charlestown was the place of the first sojourning, it was not long before the fires of civilization, never more to be quenched, were kindled in Boston and the adjacent villages. The dispersion of the company was esteemed a grievance; but no time was left for long deliberation; and those who had health began to build. Yet sickness delayed the progress of the work; and death often withdrew the laborer from the fruit of his exertions. Every hardship was encountered. The emigrants lodged at best in tents of cloth and in miserable hovels; they beheld their friends "weekly, yea almost daily, drop away before their eyes;" in a country abounding in secret fountains, they perished for the want of good water. Many of them had been accustomed to plenty and ease, the refinements of cultivated life and the conveniences of luxury. Woman was there to struggle against unforeseen hardships, unwonted sorrows; the men who defied trials for themselves, were miserable at beholding those whom they cherished, dismayed by the horrors which encompassed them. The virtues of Arbella Johnson, a daughter of the house of Lincoln, could not break through the gloomy shadows that surrounded her; and as she had been ill before her arrival, grief soon hurried her to the grave. Her husband, one of the first men in the colony, zealous for pure religion, in life "the greatest furtherer of the plantation," and by his bequests a benefactor of the infant state, was subdued by the force of disease and afflictions; but "he died willingly and in sweet peace," making a "most godly end." Winthrop lost a son, though not by disease. A hundred or more, some of them of the board of assistants, men who had enjoyed high consideration, and had been revered with confidence as the inseparable companions of the common misery or the common success, disheartened by the scenes of woe, and dreading famine and death, deserted Massachusetts and sailed for England. Before December two hundred at the least had died. Yet as the brightest lightnings are kindled in the darkest clouds, the general distress did but augment the piety and confirm the fortitude of the colonists. Their enthusiasm was softened by the mildest sympathy with suffering humanity; while a sincere religious faith kept guard against despondency and weakness. Not a hurried line, not a trace of repining, appears in their records; the congregations always assembled at the stated times, whether in the open fields or under the shade of an ancient tree; in the midst of want they abounded in hope; in the solitudes of the wilderness, they believed themselves in company with the Greatest, the most Benevolent of Beings. Honor is due not less to those who perished than to those who survived; to the martyrs the hour of death was an hour of triumph; such as is never witnessed in more tranquil seasons; just as there can be no gorgeous sunset, but when the vapors of evening gather in heavy masses round the west, to reflect the glories of declining day. For that placid resignation, which diffuses grace round the bed of sickness, and makes death too serene for sorrow and too beautiful for fear, no one was more remarkable than the daughter of Thomas Sharp, whose youth and sex, and as it seemed unequalled virtues, won the warmest eulogies of the austere Dudley. Even children caught the spirit of the place; and in their last hours awoke to the awful mystery of the impending change, awaited its approach in the tranquil confidence of faith, and went to the grave full of immortality. The survivors bore all things meekly, "remembering the end of their coming hither." "We here enjoy God and Jesus Christ," wrote Winthrop to his wife, whom pregnancy had detained in England, "and is not this enough? I thank God I like so well to be here, as I do not repent my coming. I would not have altered my course, though I had foreseen all these afflictions. I never had more content of mind."

Such were the scenes in the infant settlements of Massachusetts. In the two following years the colony had not even the comfort of receiving large accessions. In 1631 ninety only came over; a smaller number than had returned the preceding year. In 1632 no more than two hundred and fifty arrived. Men dreaded the hazards of the voyage and the wilderness; and waited to learn the success of the first adventurers. Those who had deserted, excused their cowardice by defaming the country. Dudley wrote plainly of the hardships to be encountered; and, moreover, the apprehension was soon raised and never quieted, that the liberties of the colonists would be subverted by the government in England.

Purity of religion and civil liberty were the objects nearest the wishes of the emigrants. The first court of assistants [Aug. 23, 1630] took measures for the support of the ministers. As others followed, the form of the administration was considered; that the liberties of the people might be secured against the encroachments of the rulers; "for," say they, "the waves of the sea do not more certainly waste the shore, than the minds of ambitious men are led to invade the liberties of their brethren." By the charter, fundamental laws were to be enacted in the assembly of all the freemen of the colony; and a general court was accordingly convened at Boston [Oct. 19, 1630] to settle the government. More than one hundred persons, many of them old planters and members of no church, were admitted to the franchises of the corporation; the inconvenience of gathering the whole body for purposes of legislation became but the greater and the more apparent; and the people did but reserve to themselves the right of filling such vacancies as might occur in the board of assistants. Thus the government became for a season an elective aristocracy; the magistrates holding their offices for no limited period, were to choose the governor and deputy from among themselves; and were entrusted with every branch of political power.

This arrangement was temporary. At the next general court [May 18, 1631] the freemen began to revoke a part of the authority, of which they had been too lavish. The former ordinance was now modified by a declaratory act, which did not, it is true, limit the duration of office to a year, but reserved to the commons a right of annually making in the board such changes as a majority should desire. If the right thus asserted should not be exercised, the former magistrates remained in power without the formality of a new election. And a law of still greater moment, pregnant with evil and with good, was at the same time established. "To the end the body of the commons may be preserved of honest and good men, it was ordered and agreed, that for the time to come, no man shall be admitted to the freedom of this body politic but such as are members of some of the churches within the limits of the same." The principle of universal suffrage was the usage of Virginia; Massachusetts, resting for its defence on its unity and its enthusiasm, gave all power to the select band of religious votaries, into which the avenues could be opened only by the elders. The elective franchise was thus confined to a small proportion of the whole population, and the government rested on an essentially aristocratic foundation. But it was not an aristocracy of wealth; the polity was a sort of theocracy; the servant or the bondman, if he were a member of a church, might be a freeman of the company. Other states have limited the possession of political rights to the opulent; to free-holders; to the first-born; the colonists of Massachusetts had emigrated for the enjoyment of purity of religion; and, while they scrupulously refused to the clergy even the least shadow of political power, they deliberately entrusted the whole government to those of the laity, over whose minds the ministers would probably exercise an unvarying influence. It was the reign of the church; it was a commonwealth of the chosen people in covenant with God.

The motive of this limitation of the elective franchise lay in the dangers, which were apprehended from England; and which seemed to require a devoted union, confirmed by the strongest ties and consecrated by the holiest rites of religion. The public mind of the colony was in other respects ripening for the practice of democratic liberty. It could not rest satisfied with leaving the assistants in possession of all authority and of an almost independent existence; and the magistrates, with the exception of the passionate Ludlow, were willing to yield. It was, therefore, agreed, at the next general court [May 8, 1632], that the governor and assistants should be annually chosen. The people, satisfied with the recognition of their right, re-elected their former magistrates, and carried themselves with silence and modesty. The germ of a representative government was already visible; each town was ordered to choose two men, to appear at the next court of assistants, and concert a plan for the establishment of a public treasury. The measure had become necessary; for the levy, made by the assistants alone, had already awakened alarm and opposition.

A transition to a more perfect form of government soon ensued. Two years had not elapsed, before the people had become yet more jealous of their liberties, and previous to the general court [1634] the freemen in each town, of themselves, as it were by a general impulse, chose deputies to consider in advance, what subjects should be brought before the general court. The charter also was carefully examined; the opinion of the governor was required in explanation of its provisions and the best mode for carrying them into effect. It was plain, that the legislative authority was reserved to the whole body of freemen; "the patent," thought Winthrop, "allows no deputies at all, but only by inference;" yet the welfare of the colony would not permit the assembling of the whole people. The governor, therefore, proposed a select committee to be chosen by the respective towns, with power to amend the legislation of the assistants, to sanction assessments, and to dispose of lands. The advice was discreet; the conduct of the people was still better.

The day for the assembling of the general court arrived. The magistrates and the clergy were aware of the democratic tendencies of the freemen; and John Cotton, who had newly joined the colony, attempting by the exercise of professional influence to raise a barrier against the swelling tide, preached an election sermon against rotation in office. To eject an honest magistrate from his post was compared to the injustice of turning a private man out of his freehold. The question, having thus been decided in the pulpit, remained to be settled by the electors at the polls; and they reversed the opinion by choosing a new governor and deputy. The mode of taking the votes was at the same time reformed; and instead of the erection of hands, the ballot-box was now introduced. Thus "the people established a reformation of such things as they judged to be amiss in the government."

It was then decreed, that the whole body of the freemen should be convened only for the election of the magistrates; to whom in conjunction with the deputies to be chosen by the several towns, the powers of legislation and appointment were henceforward entrusted. Thus did the epidemic of America break out in Massachusetts just fifteen years after its first appearance in Virginia. The trading corporation had become a representative democracy.

The pride of newly acquired power proceeded to investigate the conduct of the first administration; and to censure the usurpations of authority by the assistants. But the laws which were dictated by a spirit of jealous liberty, are of far deeper interest. The people of Virginia in March, 1624, and perhaps at an earlier session, had asserted for its popular branch the exclusive right of laying taxes. It was now made the rule in Massachusetts, that the immediate representatives of the freemen alone might raise money or dispose of lands. Arbitrary taxation was strangled in the American colonies in their infancy. Thus early did they establish the principles, which at a greater hazard and for a greater object, were again and triumphantly declared after the lapse of nearly a century and a half. Thus early did the freemen of Massachusetts unconsciously echo back the voice of the people of Virginia; like the solitary mountain, replying to the thunder, or like deep, calling unto deep. The state was filled with the hum of village politicians; "the freemen of every town in the Bay were busy in inquring into their liberties and privileges." With the exception of the principle of universal suffrage, now so happily established, the annual representative democracy was as perfect two centuries ago as it is to-day. The dangers which the enemies of popular liberty now feign to apprehend, were then considered imminent. "Elections cannot be safe there long," said the lawyer Lechford. The same prediction has been made these two hundred years; and all the while the civil government has remained secure. The public mind has been in perpetual agitation; like the vast rocking-stone, it is still easily shaken, even by slight and transient impulses; but after all its vibrations it follows the laws of the moral world and safely and steadily recovers its balance, as surely as that the power of gravity continues unchanged.

3
James Truslow Adams

Nearly a century after George Bancroft, James Truslow Adams (1878–1949) told the story of the founding of Massachusetts for a generation that was less disposed than either Bancroft's or Cotton Mather's to see the hand of God in human affairs. By 1921 the "muckrakers" had exposed greed, corruption, and hypocrisy behind many revered American institutions; and Charles Beard had pushed the exposure into the past in his influential *Economic Interpretation of the Constitution,* which tried to demonstrate that the architects of the American republic were moved by a desire to protect their investments. Other historians looked for economic motives elsewhere in the American past; and James Truslow Adams, after a thorough study of the sources, found economic considerations to be more important than religion in *The Founding of New England* (1921). The passage that follows is from pages 118–163 and is incorporated here by the kind permission of the Adams estate and of Little, Brown and Company.

CHAPTER VI
New England and the Great Migration

During the years that the Pilgrims had thus been struggling to found a tiny commonwealth on an inhospitable bit of the long American coast-line, events had been moving rapidly on the more crowded stage of the Old World. In France, the power of the Huguenots had been hopelessly crushed by the fall of Rochelle in 1628; while in England, affairs were evidently approaching a crisis, due to the incompetence of the government of Charles, with its disgraceful military failures abroad, and its illegal financial exactions at home. No one was safe from the ruin of his fortune or the loss of his freedom. The nobility and gentry, subject to the imposition of forced loans, faced imprisonment if they refused to pay; and those below the rank of gentleman were the unwilling hosts of a horde of ruffians, the unpaid and frequently criminal soldiery returned from unsuccessful foreign ventures, and billeted upon them by the government. The laws against Catholics were largely suspended to please the Queen, who was of that faith, and the prospects were daily growing darker for the Puritan and patriot elements, both within and without the Church. Religious toleration as an avowed governmental policy was not, as yet, seriously considered by any considerable body of men outside of Holland, the notable example of which country had failed to influence England, where the control of the church was evidently passing into the hands of Laud and his party. The time had thus come when the King must face a united opposition of the soundest men in the country—of those who feared alike for their property, their liberty, and their religion.

The formation of the Puritan party, drawing into its fold men animated by any or all of these motives, in varying proportions, coincided with the beginning of the great increase in emigration to Massachusetts, which was to carry twenty thousand persons to the shores of New England between 1630 and 1640. But if attention is concentrated too exclusively upon the history of the continental colonies in North America, and, more particularly, of those in New England, the impression is apt to be gained that this swarming out of the English to plant in new lands was largely confined to Massachusetts and its neighbors, and to the decade named. The conclusion drawn from these false premises has naturally been that Puritanism, in the New England sense, was the only successful colonizing force. We do not wish to minimize the value of any deeply felt religious emotion in firmly planting a group of people in a new home. Such value was justly recognized by one of the wisest practical colonizers of the last century,[1] who was not himself of a religious temperament, but who, to secure the firm establishment of his colony, would "have transplanted the Grand Lama of Tibet with all his prayer wheels, and did actually nibble at the Chief Rabbi."[2] The Puritan colonies, nevertheless, not only were far from being the only permanent ones, but them-

[1] Gibbon Wakefield. Cf. pp. 156–163 of his *View of the Art of Colonization;* Oxford, ed. 1914.

[2] Dr. Garnett, cited by H. E. Egerton, *Origin and Growth of Greater Britain* (Oxford, 1903), p. 107.

selves were not always equally successful; and it is well to point out that many elements, besides peculiarity of religious belief, entered into the success of the New England colonies, as contrasted with the conspicuous failure of the Puritan efforts in the Caribbean.

At the beginning of the increased emigration to Massachusetts, colonizing, indeed, had ceased to be a new and untried business. To say nothing of the numerous large and small French, Dutch, and Spanish settlements firmly established in the New World, and the English already planted on the mainland, the latter nation had successfully colonized the islands of Bermuda in 1612, St. Kitts in 1623, Barbadoes and St. Croix in 1625, and Nevis and Barbuda three years later. By the time John Winthrop led his band to the shores of Massachusetts Bay, besides the five hundred Dutch in New Amsterdam, ten thousand Englishmen were present, for six months of each year, in Newfoundland, engaged in the fisheries there; nine hundred had settled permanently in Maine and New Hampshire; three hundred within the present limits of Massachusetts; three thousand in Virginia; between two and three thousand in Bermuda; and sixteen hundred in Barbadoes; while the numbers in the other colonies are unknown.[3] The figures are striking also for the year 1640, or slightly later, at which date the tide is too often considered as having flowed almost wholly toward the Puritan colonies of New England for the preceding ten years. The number in Massachusetts at that time had risen to fourteen thousand, in Connecticut to two thousand, and in Rhode Island to three hundred. Maine and New Hampshire however, contained about fifteen hundred, Maryland the same number, Virginia nearly eight thousand, Nevis about four thousand, St. Kitts twelve to thirteen thousand, and Barbadoes eighteen thousand six hundred. There are no contemporary figures for Barbuda, St. Croix, Antigua, Montserrat, and other settlements.[4] At the end, therefore, of what

[3] *Cal. State Pap., Col., 1574–1660*, p. 26; *A Century of Population Growth* (Census Bureau, 1909), p. 9; C. P. Lucas, *Historical Geography of the British Colonies* (Oxford, 1905), vol. II, pp. 13, 179.

[4] *Century of Population*, p. 9; F. B. Dexter, "Estimates of Population in American Colonies," *American Antiquarian Society Proceedings*, 1889, vol. V, pp. 25, 32; Lucas, *Historical Geography*, pp. 142 f. 181. In 1645, there were 18,300 effective men in Barbadoes, which would indicate a much larger population. The population is given as 30,000 whites in 1650. F. W. Pitman, *Development of the British West Indies* (Yale Univ. Press, 1917), p. 370.

has often been considered a period of distinctly Puritan emigration, we find that approximately only sixteen thousand Englishmen had taken their way to the Puritan colonies, as against forty-six thousand to the others; which latter figure, moreover, is undoubtedly too low, owing to the lack of statistics just noted. Nor does the above statement take into account the thousands of Englishmen who emigrated to Ireland during the same period, and whose motives were probably similar to those animating the emigrants to the New World, however different their destinations may have been. There had, indeed, been a "great migration," resulting in an English population in America and the West Indies, by 1640 or thereabout, of over sixty-five thousand persons; but it is somewhat misleading to apply the term solely to the stream of emigrants bound for the Puritan colonies, who were outnumbered three to one by those who went to settlements where religion did not partake of the "New England way." Although young John Winthrop might write of his brother that it "would be the ruine of his soule to live among such company" as formed the colony of Barbadoes in 1629,[5] nevertheless, the population of that island had risen to nearly nineteen thousand in another decade, whereas that of Massachusetts had reached only fourteen thousand.

If, in addition, we recall the fact that, approximately, not more than one in five of the adult males who went even to Massachusetts was sufficiently in sympathy with the religious ideas there prevalent to become a church member, though disfranchised for not doing so, we find that in the "great migration" the Puritan element, in the sense of New England church-membership, amounted to only about four thousand persons out of about sixty-five thousand. In the wider sense, indeed, Puritanism, in its effect on legal codes and social usages, is found present, in greater or less degree, in almost all the colonies, island and mainland, but the influence of the form that it took in New England was to be wholly disproportionate upon the nation which evolved from the scattered continental settlements.

If, however, we shift from our usual point of view and, instead of studying the English emigration of the time in the light of the leaders who reached New England, consider the great body

[5] Winthrop Papers, *Mass. Hist. Soc. Coll.*, Series V, vol. VIII, p. 22.

of those who left the shores of England, we shall have to account for those fourteen emigrants out of every fifteen, who, although willing to leave their homes and all they had held dear, yet shunned active participation in the Bible Commonwealths. It is evident that other causes, besides the quarrels in the Church and the tyranny of Laud, must have been operative on a large scale, to explain the full extent of the movement. It seems probable that the principal cause that induced such an extraordinary number of people, from the ranks of the lesser gentry and those below them, to make so complete a break in their lives as was implied by leaving all they had ever known for the uncertainties of far-off lands, was economic. They came for the simple reason that they wanted to better their condition. They wanted to be rid of the growing and incalulable exactions of government. They wanted to own land; and it was this last motive, perhaps, which mainly had attracted those twelve thousand persons out of sixteen thousand who swelled the population of Massachusetts in 1640, but were not church members; for the Puritan colonies were the only ones in which land could be owned in fee simple, without quit-rent or lord, and in which it was freely given to settlers.[6]

The local sources in England of the great migration, and the relations of that movement to local economic conditions, have not received adequate treatment as yet, and the subject is somewhat obscure; but apparently it was the eastern and southeastern counties that furnished the main supply of immigrants for the New World. It was in these counties that the artisans from Flanders had sought refuge, when driven abroad by Alva, as well as the Huguenots from France. In these counties, also, the enclosures, which were of such far-reaching economic influence, had taken place earlier than elsewhere, while wages there showed a lower ratio to subsistence than in the north.[7] The special area in which the inhabitants were most

[6] B. W. Bond, Jr., *The Quit-rent System in the American Colonies* (Yale Univ. Press, 1919), pp. 15, 35.

[7] Cunningham, *English Industry,* vol. II, pp. 36, 38; W. A. S. Hewins, *English Trade and Finance, chiefly in the 17th Century* (London, 1892), p. 108; R. H. Tawney, *The Agrarian Problem, in the 16th Century* (New York, 1912), p. 405; W. J. Ashley, *Introduction to English Economic History and Theory* (London, 1893), vol. II, pp. 286–88; G. Slater, "The Inclosure of Common Fields considered geographically," *Geographical Journal* (London), vol. XXIX, pp. 39 f.; M. Aurosseau, "The Arrangement of Rural Populations," *Geographical Review,* vol. X, pp. 321 f.

disposed to seek new homes was that around the low country drain-
ing into the Wash; and throughout the early seventeenth century
economic and agrarian agitation was notably constant in that particular region,[8] the period of heaviest emigration—that between
1630 and 1640—marking, perhaps, its years of greatest economic
readjustment and strain. The rise in rents and land-values had,
indeed, been enormous during the preceding half-century.[9] But
this agricultural prosperity had been so closely bound up with the
great expansion of the cloth industry, that in this section it may
be said to have been wholly dependent upon it.[10] From 1625 to
1630, however, the business of the clothiers suffered a very severe
decline, which continued for some years, and the effects of which
were very marked in the agricultural industries as well.[11] In Norwich, for example, the Mayor and Aldermen complained that,
owing to the dearth of food, and to the great increase of unemploy-
ment due to bad trade conditions, the amount necessary for poor
relief had to be doubled.[12] Moreover, as is always the case in
periods of great economic alteration, the change had not affected
all classes in the community alike. The yeomanry, who were less
influenced by the rapidly rising scale of living, and so could save
a much larger proportion of their increased gains from the high
agricultural prices, were improving their position at the expense
of the gentry.[13] Enterprising traders, in the cloth and other indus-

[8] Newton, *Puritan Colonisation,* p. 79.

[9] *Victoria History of County of Lincoln* (London, 1906), vol. II, p. 334.

[10] *Victoria History of County of Suffolk* (London, 1911), vols. I, pp. 661,
676, and II, p. 268.

[11] *Ibid.,* vol. II, p. 266.

[12] *Cal. State Pap., Domestic, 1629-31,* p. 419. Cf. also, *Ibid.* pp. 8, 403, 419.
A few years earlier, Sir Wm. Pelham, writing to his brother-in-law, said: "Our
country was never in that wante that now itt is, and more of munnie than Corne,
for theare are many thousands in thease parts whoo have soulde all thay have
even to theyr bedd straw, and cann not get worke to earne any munny. Dogg's
flesh is a dainty dish," etc. *Lincolnshire Notes and Queries,* vol. I, p. 16.

[13] "Our yeomanry, whose continuall under living, saving, and the immunities
from the costly charge of these unfaithfull times, do make them so as to grow
with the wealth of this world, that whilest many of the better sort, as having past
their uttermost period, do suffer an utter declination, these onely doe arise, and
doe lay such strong, sure, and deep foundations that from thence in time are
derived many noble and worthy families." Robt. Reyce, *Suffolk Breviary,* 1618
(ed. London, 1902), p. 58.

tries, who had acquired fortunes, but who naturally were not of the old families, were pushing in and buying country estates, and, like all *nouveaux riches,* were asserting their new and unaccustomed position by raising the scale of living.[14] Many of the gentry, on the other hand, unable to adjust themselves to the new economic conditions or to take advantage of them, and yet unwilling to give up their comparative position in the county, found themselves "overtaken," as a contemporary writer says, "with too well meaning and good nature," and so were "inforced sometimes to suffer a revolution" in their domestic affairs.[15] About the years of the emigration, however, there seem to have been financial difficulties and economic unrest among all the classes, due to the immediate crisis in the cloth trade, as well as to the more general conditions of the time.

The district in which these economic changes were at work was also the one in which Puritanism had taken its strongest hold, and the leaders both of the Puritan movement at home and of colonization abroad "formed a veritable clan, intimately bound together by ties of blood, marriage, and neighborhood, acting together in all that concerned colonization on the one hand and autocratic rule on the other."[16] We have already seen, in an earlier chapter, how the trading companies had brought into working contact the great nobles, city merchants, and country gentlemen, and accustomed them to act together as, perhaps, nothing else could have done, thus paving the way for the formation of the Puritan party.

In addition to this foundation, the leaders were united by ties based upon social and blood-relationship, many of which were of great importance in the affairs of both Old and New England. Among many such, we may note that John Endicott was a parishioner of the Reverend John White, who was interested in the Cape Ann fishing company with John Humphrey. Humphrey, in turn, was a brother-in-law of the Earl of Lincoln, one of the

[14] *History of Suffolk,* vol. I, p. 673.

[15] Reyce, *Breviary,* p. 60.

[16] C. M. Andrews, Introduction to Newton, *Puritan Colonisation,* p. viii. Robert Reyce, writing of the gentry, in 1618, says: "So againe what with the enterlacing of houses in marriage (a practise at this day much used for the strengthening of families therby) such is the religious unity wherewith in all good actions they doe concur, that whatsoever offendeth one displeaseth all, and whosever satisfieth one contenteth all." *Breviary,* p. 60.

most earnest of the Puritan peers, and son-in-law of Viscount Say
and Sele. Lincoln's other brothers-in-law were Isaac Johnson and
John Gorges, the latter a son of Sir Ferdinando. Lincoln's steward,
Thomas Dudley, was a parishioner of John Cotton. The Earl of
Holland was a brother of the Earl of Warwick, who was the leader
of the Puritans. The latter's interests in Parliament were attended
to by Lord Brooke, while his man of business was Sir Nathaniel
Rich. The Riches and the Barringtons were neighbors and close
friends. Lady Joan Barrington, who was a correspondent of many
of the New England emigrants, was an aunt of John Hampden and
Oliver Cromwell, and Roger Williams at one time applied for the
hand of her niece. Many of these were deeply interested in the
attempt to found a Puritan colony in the Caribbean, as were also
Gregory Gawsell, John Gurdon, and Sir Edward Moundeford, who
were all three country neighbors and intimate friends of John
Winthrop and his family circle.[17]

At the time that our story has now reached, there were two
projects for Puritan settlement in which members of this clan were
particularly interested, that of the island of Old Providence in the
Caribbean Sea, and that of the remnants of the Cape Ann fishing
attempt, which was mentioned in the preceding chapter. The latter
somewhat ill-judged effort, in 1623, to combine as a single enterprise an agricultural colony on land and a fishing business at sea,
had been abandoned two years later, with a loss of £3000.[18] Most
of the men had been withdrawn, but Roger Conant, with a few
others, decided to remain in America, transferring their homes to
the location of what was in a few years to be known as Salem.
Thinking that something might still be saved from the wreck, a
few of the Adventurers in England plucked up courage, and having
interested fresh capitalists, including Thomas Dudley, secured the
services of John Endicott as local governor, and, in 1628, were
granted a patent from the Council for New England.[19] The Puritan

[17] Newton, *Puritan Colonisation*, pp. 61 ff.; E. J. Carpenter, *Roger Williams*
(New York, 1909), pp. 16–21.

[18] J. White, *The Planter's Plea* (Force Tracts), p. 39.

[19] White, *Planter's Plea*, p. 43; T. Dudley, "Letter to the Countess of Lincoln,"
in Young's *Chronicles of the first Planters of Massachusetts* (Boston, 1846), p.
310; cf. Osgood, *American Colonies*, vol. I, p. 130.

character of the new undertaking would be sufficiently evidenced by the names of White and his parishioner Endicott, Humphrey, and Dudley, did we not know also that the Earl of Warwick, who seven years before had secured the patent for the Pilgrims, now acted in obtaining that for the New England Company.[20] Sir Ferdinando Gorges, to whom Warwick applied, gave his consent, provided that the new patent should not be prejudicial to the interests of his son Robert, and distinctly stated that the new colony was to found a place of refuge for Puritans.[21] The grant, which extended from three miles north of the River Merrimac to three miles south of the Charles, conflicted with that bestowed on Gorges and Mason in 1622, as well as with that of Robert Gorges of similar date. As the same limits were confirmed in the royal charter to the Company of Massachusetts Bay in 1629, the seeds of future discord were sown in these conflicting titles.[22]

Endicott was at once dispatched, with a few followers, to take possession, and to prepare the way for a larger body to be sent in the succeeding year. The little band, with which he arrived in September, 1628, together with the old settlers already on the spot, made up a company of only fifty or sixty people, most of whom seem to have done little but "rub out the winter's cold by the Fire-side," "turning down many a drop of the Bottell, and burning Tobacco with all the ease they could," while they discussed the progress they would make in the summer.[23] There was, however, much sickness among them, which may have accounted in part for their close hearth-keeping. From what we know of Endicott's harsh manners and lack of wisdom in dealing with delicate situations, it may be assumed that his superseding of Conant in the office of local governor was not made more palatable by any grace in his announcement of the fact; and, in any case, ill-feeling developed between the old and new planters. This, however, was

[20] There was no uniform designation until the issue of the charter of 1629, the company being variously styled "the New England Company," "the Company of Adventurers for New England in America," etc. Thornton, *Landing at Cape Anne*, p. 57 *n*.

[21] Gorges, *Briefe Narration*, p. 80 (written many years later).

[22] Haven, *Lowell Lectures*, pp. 153 f.

[23] White, *Planter's Plea*, p. 43; E. Johnson, *Wonder-working Providence of Sions Saviour in New-England* (ed. New York, 1910), p. 45.

smoothed over by Conant's own tact, and affairs were adjusted "so meum and tuum that divide the world, should not disturb the peace of good christians."[24] Morton, owing to his unsympathetic neighbors, the Pilgrims, was temporarily in England, and so absent from his crew at Merry Mount; but Endicott promptly visited that very un-Puritan and somewhat dangerous settlement, and having hewn down the offending May-pole, "admonished them to look ther should be better walking."[25] It is possible that, before winter set in, preparations may have been made for a second settlement at Charlestown to forestall the claims of Oldham in that locality.[26]

Endicott's whole mission at this time, indeed, seems to have been merely to prepare the way for others; and in the following year, six ships were dispatched, carrying over four hundred people, with cattle and additional supplies.[27] Four clergymen, including Skelton and Higginson, were also sent, for the spiritual welfare of the colony, and the conversion of the Indians, which latter object, at this stage of the enterprise, was officially declared to be the main end of the plantation.

Meanwhile, the number of those in England interested in the venture continued to grow, and a royal charter, under the broad seal, was granted March 4, 1629, in the names of Sir Henry Rose-well, Sir John Younge, Thomas Southcott, John Humphrey, John Endicott, and their associates, the total membership of the company being about one hundred and ten.[28] The grant followed somewhat closely that received by the Virginia Company in 1609, the patentees being joint proprietors of the plantation, with rights of ownership and government similar to those enjoyed by the earlier

[24] W. Hubbard, *History of New England* (1815), p. 110.

[25] Bradford, *Plymouth,* p. 238.

[26] The Robert Gorges claim had been sold in two parts, one to Sir Wm. Brereton and one to John Dorrell and John Oldham. J. G. Palfrey, *History of New England* (Boston, 1859), vol. I, p. 294; cf. T. Prince, *Chronological History of New England* (Arber reprint, London, 1897), p. 483; and Cradock's instructions in Young, *Chron. Mass.,* pp. 147 ff., 171.

[27] Prince, *New England,* p. 489; Young, *Chron. Mass.,* pp. 132, 216. The number included 35 of the Leyden congregation bound for Plymouth.

[28] *Records of the Governor and Company of the Massachusetts Bay in New England* (ed. N. B. Shurtleff, Boston, 1853), vol. I, p. 5 (hereafter cited as *Massachusetts Records*). The charter is given on pp. 1–20. S. F. Haven, prefatory chapter to the Company's Records, in *Archeologia Americana,* 1857, vol. III, pp. cxxxiv-cxxxvi.

London Company. A General Court, to meet quarterly, was provided for, and annually, at the Easter session, this court was to elect a governor, deputy governor and a board of assistants, consisting of eighteen members. By an important clause, six of the latter, together with the governor or his deputy, constituted a quorum, and were therefore required to be present at the sittings of the court. The General Court, consisting of the members of the Company, known as freemen, was also given the power to add to its number, and to make such necessary laws and ordinances as should not be repugnant to the laws of England. The first governor was Mathew Cradock, with Thomas Goffe as deputy, the Assistants including Sir Richard Saltonstall, Isaac Johnson, John Humphrey, John Endicott, Increase Nowell, Theophilus Eaton, and John Browne. It was this charter of a proprietary company, skillfully interpreted to fit the needs of the case, and constantly violated as to its terms, which formed the basis of the commonwealth government of Massachusetts for over half a century.

The company, so organized, proceeded to arrange for a local government in Massachusetts, confirming Endicott as governor, and associating with him a council of thirteen. This was to include the three clergymen then there, the two Brownes, and two of the old planters, if the latter group should desire such representation. Efforts were made to conserve as equitably as possible the rights of those former settlers, and other instructions for the conduct of the company's affairs were forwarded to Endicott a few weeks after the grant of the charter.[29] Writing home, at the end of the first summer, Higginson stated that, on their arrival, they had found "aboute a half score houses, and a fair house newly built for the Governor," and that, including the newcomers and old settlers, about three hundred people were planted in the colony, of whom two thirds were at Salem and the remainder at Charlestown.[30] "But that which is our greatest comfort and means of defence above all others," he continued, "is that we have here the true religion and holy ordinances of Almighty God taught amongst us. Thanks be to God, we have here plenty of preaching, and diligent catechising, with strict and careful exercise."

29 Young, *Chron. Mass.*, pp. 141–71.
30 F. Higginson, *New England's Plantation;* Young, *Chron. Mass.*, pp. 258 f.

As we noted in an earlier chapter, many writers have insisted greatly upon the rigid distinction between the Pilgrims, as Separatists, and the Puritans, as mere Noncomformists. Not only, however, were the members of the several communities by no means agreed as to what constituted Separatism and Nonconformity, but in the American wilderness, such distinctions rapidly ceased to have any but a disputatious value, with, at intervals, political reverberations in England. The Pilgrims, at the time of their emigration from Holland, may have been strict Separatists or on the way to becoming mere non-Separatist Independent Puritans;[31] and the leaders of the churches of Massachusetts for many years denied any Separatism on their own part or that of the Pilgrims. John Cotton wrote categorically, in 1647, that "for New England there is no such church of the Separation at al that I know of."[32] On the other hand, many, of all shades of religious belief, refused to acknowledge this view of the matter. They found it impossible to answer Roger Williams's query as to "what is that which Mr. Cotton and so many hundreths fearing God in New England walk in, but a way of separation?"[33] Indeed, in view of the open and patent facts, the only possible answer was the casuistical one of Cotton and the other leaders, that they had separated, "not from the Churches in Old England, as no Churches, but from some corruptions found in them."[34] As these corruptions were held to include the polity and ritual of the English Church, and as members of the New England churches, though they might listen to its preaching, were not allowed to be in communion with it, and as no Church of England services were permitted on New England soil, the point as to whether or not the New England Puritans were Separatists is a mere matter of terms. It depends upon the question how far a minority of any organization, social, political, or religious, can go in denying the validity of its ideas, in refusing to

[31] C. Burrage, *English Dissenters*, vol. I, p. 357.

[32] *Master John Cotton's Answer to Master Roger Williams* (*Narraganset Club Publications*, Providence, 1867, vol. II, p. 203).

[33] R. Williams, *Mr. Cotton's Letter examined and answered* (*Narraganset Club Publications*, vol. I, p. 109).

[34] *Narraganset Club Publications*, vol. II, p. 234.

conform to its practices, and in not allowing them to be used, and still consider themselves as being in the organization. Opinions will always differ, and it is as impossible to decide to-day whether the Puritans became Separatists as it was for themselves and their critics to decide at the time.

The question of terms is not especially important, but the question of polity, as it was developed in the little church at Salem, is immensely so, for it undoubtedly gave a very great impetus to the growth of Congregationalism in Massachusetts, and, indeed, has been called "the chief point of departure in the ecclesiastical history of New England," which was so inextricably interwoven with its political history. In no other part of the country has a more distinct and persistent type of thought and character been developed than in that section; and in this regard we have already noted the important influences of the geographic environment. But the impress of its institutional life was no less effective upon the minds of its people. It was not Puritanism alone that developed the type; for, we repeat, the Puritan strain may be traced in the legislation and social life of many of the English settlements, and the Puritanism of any individual to-day may derive quite as directly from an ancestral Bermudian, Georgian, Jamaican Commonwealth man, Carolinian Scotch Covenanter, or Pennsylvanian Ulsterite, as from a settler in Salem or Plymouth. But wherever we find Congregationalism, town government, and the village school, we may trace the triple influence straight to New England.

It is impossible to say what may have been the precise ideas as to church government held by the groups which emigrated with Endicott and in the following year, but the evidence seems clear that, at least as far as Endicott was concerned, they were identical with those of the Pilgrims, or were unconsciously derived from them after arrival. Dr. Fuller, who visited Salem during the sickness of the first winter, was not only a physician but a deacon of the Plymouth church. With him Endicott discussed the question of church polity, and, as a result, wrote to Governor Bradford that "I am by him satisfied touching your judgments of the outward forme of Gods worshipe. It is, as farr as I can gather, no other than is warranted by the evidence of truth, and the same which I have proffessed and maintained ever since the Lord in mercie

revealed him selfe unto me."[35] A few weeks later, after the arrival
of Skelton and Higginson, the Salem church was organized, with
the former as pastor, and the latter as teacher, the members being
united by a church covenant, which became one of the essential
features of the New England church system.[36] In that system,
every local church was independent, choosing and ordaining its
own pastor, teachers, and ruling elders, and was composed of such
Christians only as could satisfy the other church members of their
converted state.[37] "The stones that were to be laid in Solomon's
temple," wrote Cotton, with characteristic far-fetched use of Old
Testament texts, "were squared and made ready before they were
laid in the building . . . and, wherefore so, if not to hold forth
that no members were to be received into the Church of Christ,
but such as were rough-hewn, and squared, and fitted to lie close
and levell to Christ and to his members?"[38]

Although the church government was democratic in form, and
thus of influence in fostering democratic beliefs as to government
in general, it must be remembered that at probably no period
during the life of the charter, did the number of church members
include more than a very distinct minority of the population.
Lechford's statement, that three quarters of the people were outside the pale of the church in 1640, seems borne out by other
testimony, and this proportion appears not to have been greatly
changed till near the end of the century.[39] The influence of this
democratic form of church organization, however, was clearly foreseen by King James in his dictum, "No bishop, no king"; and of
even greater effect in its logical political consequence was the

[35] Bradford, *Plymouth,* p. 265; Burrage thinks the Pilgrim influence slight,
differing from most authorities. *English Dissenters,* vol. I, pp. 360 ff. Cf. W.
Walker, *History of Congregational Churches in U. S.* (New York, 1894), pp.
101 ff.

[36] Bradford, *Plymouth,* pp. 265 f. The covenant of 1629 and the enlarged one
of 1636 are in W. Walker, *Creeds and Platforms of Congregationalism* (New
York, 1893), pp. 116 ff. Cf. C. Burrage, *The Church Covenant Idea* (Philadelphia, 1904), pp. 88 ff.

[37] Cf. T. Lechford, "Plain dealing or Newes from New England"; *Mass. Hist.
Soc. Coll.,* Series III, vol. III, pp. 63–75.

[38] John Cotton, *The Way of the Churches of Christ in New England* (London,
1645), p. 54.

[39] Lechford, *Plain Dealing,* p. 143; A. E. McKinley, *Suffrage Franchise in the
Thirteen English Colonies* (University of Pennsylvania Publications, 1905), p. 313.

employment of the covenant. In defending its use in the church, Cotton, in the volume already quoted, was forced onto broader ground. "It is evident," he wrote, "by the light of nature, that all civill Relations are founded in Covenant. For, to passe by naturall Relations between Parents and Children, and violent Relations between Conquerors and Captives; there is no other way given wherby a people (sui Juris) free from naturall and compulsory engagements, can be united or combined together into one visible body."[40]

It is difficult to overestimate the influence which, in time, these two ideas, of a democratic church polity and a voluntary covenant as the only basis for a civil government, would come to exert upon those holding them; but for the moment, the result was the forcible expulsion from the community of two members who did not hold them. John and Samuel Browne, both men of good estate, the one a merchant and the other a lawyer, and both original patentees of the Company, had left England for Salem in the spring of 1629, with high recommendation to Endicott from the Company at home, as men much trusted and respected.[41] When the Salem church was organized, the two brothers, who were both on the council, objected, accusing the ministers of having become Separatists, which they denied. As the Brownes refused to give up the use of the prayer-book, and held private services with their followers, Endicott, either from personal feeling or from a real fear that the trouble would disrupt the colony, took a strong stand, and shipped them back to England.[42] There is no contemporary account of the details, and it is therefore as unwise, perhaps, to condemn Endicott, as it is unjustifiable to speak of the Brownes as "anarchical," or, with an odd lack of humor, as "Schismatical."[43] Endicott was mildly censured by the Company in England, who wrote that they conceived that "it is possible some undigested councells have too sudainely bin put in execution, wch may have ill construccion with the state heere;" while the ministers were asked to clear themselves

[40] Cotton, *The Way of the Churches,* p. 4.

[41] T. Hutchinson, *History of Massachusetts* (Salem, 1795), vol. I, p. 19; Young, *Chron. Mass.,* p. 168.

[42] Hutchinson, *History,* vol. I, p. 19; Morton, *New England's Memorial,* pp. 100 f.

[43] Young's epithets, in *Chron. Mass.,* p. 160 n.

if innocent, or else to look back upon their "miscarriage with repentance." In time the Brownes seem to have been settled with satisfactorily on a cash basis.[44]

While progress was thus being made in the establishment of the Massachusetts Bay colony, another project for a Puritan settlement was rapidly taking form. After the dissolution of the Virginia Company, the quarrel between the Sandys and Warwick factions was continued in the courts of the Somers Islands, or Bermuda Company, and its affairs were going from bad to worse, largely owing to the frequent changes in the person of the governor as the two factions succeeded each other in power at home. In April, 1629, Sir Nathaniel Rich received a long letter from Governor Bell, in regard to various matters, in the course of which he described two islands lying in the Caribbean, in either of which he thought one year would "be more profitable than seven years here," and placed the disposition of both islands in Warwick's hands.[45]

It was a momentous time. Hardly more than a few days before, Parliament had been angrily dissolved by the King, not to meet again for eleven years. Eliot, Selden, and seven other of the popular leaders had been committed to the Tower. In every direction, Puritans of distinction, and even such lesser men as John Humphrey and John Winthrop, were made to feel the hostility of the court. The recent successful colonization of St. Kitts and Barbadoes by the Earls of Carlisle and Marlborough, both members of the court party, and hostile to the Warwicks and Riches, combined with the flattering report of the new-found islands by Bell, induced Warwick, whose affairs had not been going well, to make an immediate counter-move. With Rich, Gawsell, and others, he provided £2000, and dispatched two ships for the Caribbean under letters of marque. They arrived at Providence about Christmas, the company beginning to make ready for the larger body which was to arrive in the spring, precisely as Endicott had done at Salem. "The aim and desire above all things," wrote the promoters of the enterprise, "is to plant the true and sincere Religion and worship of God, which in the Christian world is now very much opposed." At first, the utmost secrecy was maintained as to the

[44] *Massachusetts Records,* vol. I, pp. 409, 407, 52, 54, 61, 69.
[45] Newton, *Puritan Colonisation,* pp. 32 f.

real aims of Warwick and his associates; and it was only in December of the following year, after the main body of the colonists had already been planted, that letters-patent for the islands were procured from the King.[46]

There can be no doubt, however, that the matter was well known to Winthrop and others of those who were contemplating emigratior in the summer of 1629. Not only was Gawsell a neighbor and friend of Winthrop, but all steps taken by the Massachusetts group seem to have been talked over with Warwick and Rich.[47] John Winthrop, now in his forty-third year, who was living the life of a country squire at Groton, in Suffolk, and was a small office-holder under government, had been anxiously watching the course of affairs. Of a sensitive and deeply religious nature, strongly attached to the Puritan cause, he could not but regard the future with the greatest anxiety. "The Lord hath admonished, threatened, corrected and astonished us," he wrote to his wife in May, 1629, "yet we growe worse and worse, so as his spirit will not allwayes strive with us, he must needs give waye to his fury at last. . . . We sawe this, and humbled not ourselves, to turne from our evill wayes, but have provoked him more than all the nations rounde about us: therefore he is turninge the cuppe toward us also, and because we are the last, our portion must be, to drinke the verye dreggs which remaine. My dear wife, I am veryly persuaded, God will bringe some heavye Affliction upon this lande, and that speedylye."[48] In addition to his fear that all hope of civil, as well as of even a moderate degree of religious, liberty was rapidly fading, Winthrop was also much troubled by the prospects for his personal social and financial position. A few months earlier, he had written to his son Henry, at that time a settler in Barbadoes, that he then owed more than he was able to pay without selling his land; and throughout all his letters and papers of the period runs the same strain of anxiety over money matters.[49] Although possessed of a modest estate, which, when subsequently sold,

[46] *Ibid.*, pp. 48, 50. 53, 95, 86. This island had been confused, until recently, with New Providence in the Bahamas.

[47] *Ibid.*, p. 47.

[48] R. C. Winthrop, *Life and Letters of John Winthrop* (Boston, 1869), vol 1, p. 296.

[49] *Ibid.*, vol. 1, 286.

realized £4200,[50] the demands of a large family, and the increased
cost of living, were more than he could meet. In June, he was,
in addition, deprived of his office under the Master of the Wards,
and wrote to his wife that "where we shall spende the rest of or
short tyme I knowe not: the Lorde, I trust, will direct us in
mercye."[51]

With the discussion then going on in Puritan circles as to Endicott's settlement at Salem, and with his neighbors actively interested
in the colony at Providence, it was natural that Winthrop should
seriously consider the thought of emigrating. Just at this time,
a paper consisting of arguments for and against settling a plantation in New England was being circulated among the group of
Puritans mentioned earlier in this chapter. The reasons given in
favor of it were mainly religious and economic. The first dwelt
upon the glory of opposing Anti-Christ, in the form of the French
Jesuits in Canada, and of raising "a particular church" in New
England, while the second referred to the supposed surplus population at home, and to the standard and cost of living which had
"growne to that height of intemperance in all excesse of Riott,
as noe mans estate allmost will suffice to keepe saile with his
aequalls."[52]

The document, which has come down to us in at least four different forms, was possibly drafted by Winthrop himself, though
the evidence is only inferential, and it has also been attributed to
the Reverend John White and others.[53] It is interesting to note
that John Hampden wrote to Sir John Eliot, then in prison, for
a copy of it.[54] Whether or not Winthrop was the author, several
copies, one of them indorsed "May, 1629," contain memoranda
of "Particular considerations in the case of J. W.," in which he

[50] Letter from J. Winthrop, Jr.; *Mass. Hist. Soc. Coll.,* Series V, vol. VIII,
p. 28. Winthrop had appraised it at £5760. R. C. Winthrop, *J. Winthrop,* vol.
II, p. 78.

[51] *Ibid.,* vol. I, pp. 214 ff, 301 f.

[52] R. C. Winthrop, *J. Winthrop,* vol. I, pp. 308, 328.

[53] The editor of this life of Winthrop (vol. I, pp. 308, 318) naturally claims
it for his ancestor. Channing thinks it probable (*History,* vol. I, p. 327); but
Doyle does not (*Puritan Colonies,* vol. I, p. 85). Cf. *Mass. Hist. Soc. Proceedings,* Series I, vols. VIII, pp. 413–30, and XII, pp. 237 ff.

[54] Letter of Dec. 8, 1629; *Ibid.,* vol. VIII, p. 427.

wrote that the success of the plan had come to depend upon him, for "the chiefe supporters (uppon whom the rest depends) will not stirr wthout him," and that his wife and children are in favor of it. "His meanes," moreover, he wrote, "heer are so shortened (now 3 of his sonnes being com to age have drawen awaie the one half of his estate) as he shall not be able to continue in that place and imployment where he now iss, his ordinary charg being still as great almost as when his meanes was double"; and that "if he lett pass this opportunitie, That talent wch God hath bestowed uppon him for publicke service is like to be buried."[55] "With what comfort can I live," he added in one version, "wth 7 or 8 servts in that place and condition where for many years I have spent 3: or 400 li yearly and maintained a greater chardge?"[56] The prospects in England, for his wife and children, lay heavily on his mind. "For my care of thee and thine," he wrote to the former, after the die was cast, "I will say nothing. The Lord knows my heart, that it was one great motive to draw me into this course."[57]

His judgment regarding the ending of the opportunity for a public career for such as himself in England was obviously wrong, as events developed there. The England which retained a Pym, a Hampden, an Eliot, and a Cromwell, may well have offered scope for the talents of a Winthrop. As our eyes are usually fastened on this side of the water, we are apt to think of the Pilgrims, Puritans, and other immigrants as starting their careers by coming here. We rarely consider them in the light of leaving behind them other possible careers in England. It is no disparagement of the courage with which they faced the wilderness, to think of them, for a moment, as Englishmen, abandoning their place in the struggle at home, and to consider the type of mind which thus preferred to exchange the simplifications of unpeopled America for the complexities of the situation in England. Is it, perhaps, altogether fanciful, to attribute, in slight part, that deeply ingrained feeling of Americans, that they wish to have nothing to do with the problems of the world at large, to this choice of the

55 *Mass. Hist. Soc. Proceedings,* Series I, vol. VIII, p. 420. The wording is slightly different in the version in R. C. Winthrop, *J. Winthrop,* vol. I, p. 327.

56 *Mass. Hist. Soc. Proceedings,* Series I, vol. XII, p. 238.

57 Letter of Jan. 15, 1630; R. C. Winthrop, *J. Winthrop,* vol. I, p. 366.

founders in abandoning their place in the struggles of Europe for a more untrammeled career on a small provincial stage?

Winthrop's reasons have been thus dwelt upon, because, in the motives given by him who was the purest, gentlest, and broadest-minded of all who were to guide the destinies of the Bay Colony, we presumably find the highest of those which animated any of the men who sought its shores. As we descend the scale of character, the religious incentives narrow and disappear, as does also the desire for honorable public service, and the economic factor alone remains.

In July, a few weeks after Winthrop lost his office, Isaac Johnson, a brother-in-law of the Earl of Lincoln, wrote to Emanuel Downing, a brother-in-law of Winthrop, asking them to meet at Sempringham, the Earl's seat in Lincolnshire, whither they both went on the 28th.[58] There they undoubtedly met Dudley, Johnson, Humphrey, and others of that family and social group. All those gathered there, so far as we know, were keenly interested in the project for Massachusetts. As they were also in close touch with Warwick, Rich, and others of those who were just at the moment planning to send out the colony to Providence in September, it is probable that both places were considered, and Warwick continued for years to urge Winthrop and his group to move to the southern colony. The decision, however, was in favor of Massachusetts; and, a few weeks later, on August 26, Saltonstall, Dudley, Johnson, Humphrey, Winthrop, and seven others, signed an agreement by which they bound themselves to be ready, with their families and goods, by the first of the following March, to embark for New England, and to settle there permanently.[59]

There was one clause in the agreement, of incalculable importance. "Provided always," so it read, "that before the last of September next, the whole Government, together with the patent for the said plantation, be first, by an order of court, legally transferred and established to remain with us and others which shall

[58] *Mass. Hist. Soc. Coll.*, Series IV, vol. VI, pp. 29 f. Sempringham is a tiny hamlet, and of the beautiful house of the Earls of Lincoln, only the garden wall remains. W. F. Rawnsley, *Highways and Byways in Lincolnshire* (London, 1914), p. 38. The house is mentioned in Camden's *Brittania* (ed. London, 1806), vol. II, p. 334.

[59] R. C. Winthrop, *J. Winthrop*, vol. I, pp. 344 f.

inhabit upon the said Plantation."[60] Possibly as a result of consultation with the Cambridge signers, Governor Cradock, at a meeting of the court of the Company a month earlier, had read certain propositions, "conceived by himself," which anticipated this condition. They seem to have struck those present as serious and novel, and of such importance in their possible consequences as to call for deferred consideration in great secrecy. The matter was brought up at a number of successive meetings, and it was only after much debate, objections on the part of many, and the taking of legal advice, that the court finally voted that the charter and government might be removed to America.[61] By such transfer, and the use made of the charter in New England, what was intended to be a mere trading company, similar to those which had preceded it, became transformed into a self-governing commonwealth, whose rulers treated the charter as if it were the constitution of an independent state. Such an interpretation could not legally be carried beyond a certain point, and the attempt was bound to break down under the strain.

The step, in its far-reaching consequences, was one of the most important events in the development of the British colonies, but its story remains a mystery. It was a completely new departure, but may have been suggested to the leaders by the act of the Pilgrims in buying out their English partners and thus in effect, though without any legal authority, constituting themselves a self-governing community. There has been much discussion as to whether the absence in the original charter of any words indicating that the corporation was to remain in England was due to accident or design. It is impossible to prove the point either way, for Winthrop's statement, of somewhat uncertain application and written many years later, does not seem conclusive against the other facts and probabilities.[62] The proceedings at the meetings of the court show clearly, at least, that many of the most active patentees had had no inkling of any such conscious alteration of the docu-

---

[60] *Ibid.*, p. 345.

[61] *Massachusetts Records,* vol. I, pp. 49–52, 55.

[62] R. C. Winthrop, *J. Winthrop,* vol. II, p. 443; C. Deane, in *Mass. Hist. Soc. Proceedings,* Series I, vol. XI, pp. 166 ff.; Mellen Chamberlain, *Ibid.,* Series II, vol. VIII, p. 110; J. Parker in *Lowell Lectures,* pp. 365 ff.; and Osgood, *American Colonies,* vol. I, pp. 145 ff., 183.

ment at the time of issue, nor does it seem likely that Charles I would have knowingly consented. If the charter were intentionally so worded as to create "the Adventurers a Corporation upon the Place,"[63] for the purpose the wording was later made to serve, then such of the leaders as arranged the matter consciously hoodwinked both the government and many of their own associates.

At length, however, the consent of the patentees was obtained, after their counsel had approved the legality of the step; and in October, in contemplation of the removal of the government to America, Winthrop was elected Governor, and Humphrey, Deputy, in place of those who were to remain behind.[64] Eight months later, in the early summer of 1630, Winthrop and a band of between nine hundred and a thousand immigrants landed in America, and settled what were later known as the towns of Charlestown, Boston, Medford, Watertown, Roxbury, Lynn, and Dorchester.[65] Eighty of the inhabitants already planted at Salem under Endicott had died during the winter, and of those who formed the present settlements, about two hundred succumbed between the time of leaving England and the end of December, including Johnson, his wife the Lady Arbella, the Reverend Mr. Higginson, and other important members of the colony.[66]

The settlers, apparently, did not have time to house themselves properly before winter came on, and many, particularly of the poor, had to face the icy winds of a New England January with no better shelter than a canvas tent.[67] Provisions, even in England, were exceedingly scarce and dear that year, partly, some claimed, because of the large quantities taken out by emigrants to New England and the other plantations.[68] Massachusetts had evidently not received her share, if such had been the case, and famine soon

[63] Decision of the English Chief Justices in 1677; *Acts Privy Council, Colonial,* vol. I, p. 724. Cf. *Ibid.,* p. 841.

[64] *Massachusetts Records,* vol. I, pp. 59 f. At the last moment, as Humphrey's sailing was delayed, Dudley was elected in his place. *Ibid.,* p. 70.

[65] The ships did not all arrive together. Some were delayed until the first week in July. John Winthrop, *History of New England* (ed. Boston, 1853), vol. I, p. 34. Cf. Young, *Chron. Mass.,* pp. 310 ff.

[66] Dudley's Letter, in Young, *Chron. Mass.,* pp. 311, 319.

[67] J. Winthrop, *History,* vol. I, p. 52.

[68] *Cal. St. Pap., Dom., 1628-9,* p. 266; *Acts Privy Council, Colonial,* vol. I, p. 154.

faced the settlers, who were forced to live partly on mussels and acorns.[69] Even upon their arrival in the summer, food had been so scarce that they had been forced to give their liberty to a hundred and eighty servants, entailing a loss of between three and four hundred pounds.[70] The cold, which had held off until December 24, suddenly came on in extreme severity, and "such a Christmas eve they had never seen before." The contrast with the Christmas Day which the Warwick settlers were passing at Providence, in the Caribbean, was complete; and Humphrey and Downing, who were in frequent conference with the earl and with Rich, kept writing to advise Winthrop to move the colony farther south, if only to the Hudson River.[71] At a critical moment, the ship Lion, which Winthrop had had the foresight to send at once to England for provisions, arrived with a new supply; but so deep was the discouragement, that many returned in her to the old home, never to come back. Others, however, were of sterner stuff, and took passage in the same boat to fetch their families.[72]

At last the winter passed, and with the summer came renewed hope. The public business had been temporarily managed by the Assistants only, and the first General Court was not held until October. At that session the charter was violated in an important point, in that the freemen relinquished their right to elect the governor and the deputy. Thereafter, it was ruled, these were to be elected by the Assistants only, with whom they were to have the power of making laws and appointing officers.[73] The extent of this limitation of the right of election, which was revoked, however, at the next General Court, is evident from the fact that in March, in contemplation of the probability of there being less than nine Assistants left in the colony, it was agreed that seven should constitute a court. In fact, the charter was continually violated in that regard, as the number of Assistants, for over fifty years,

[69] R. Clap, Memoirs, in Young, *Chron. Mass.*, p. 352.

[70] Dudley's Letter, *Ibid.*, p. 312.

[71] Letters in *Mass. Hist. Soc. Coll.*, Series IV, vol. VI, pp. 3, 8, 38.

[72] Hutchinson, *History*, vol. I, p. 29. For details of the first winter, as noted by one of the poorer emigrants, cf., Letter to Wm. Pond from his son, *Mass. Hist. Soc. Proceedings*, Series II, vol. VIII, pp. 471 ff.

[73] *Massachusetts Records*, vol. I, pp. 73, 78, 79.

was never more than about one half of the required eighteen.[74]

The Assistants, into whose hands the control of the government now passed, were probably a majority of the entire voting population of the colony. According to the terms of the charter only members of the Company, or the so-called freemen, had the right to vote at its meetings. After the "sea-change" which was presumed to have altered that document into "something rich and strange" in the way of political constitutions, those meetings became the political assemblies of the colony, and the freemen of the Company became the only enfranchised voters of the state. While two thousand persons were settled in Massachusetts about the time of that October meeting, it is probable that not more than sixteen to twenty members of the Company had crossed the ocean, of whom a number had returned or died.[75] If the charter were indeed the written constitution of a state, it was unique among such instruments in that it thus limited all political rights, in a community of two thousand persons, to a tiny self-perpetuating oligarchical group of not more than a dozen citizens. Ninety-nine and one half per cent of the population was thus unenfranchised and unrepresented, and even denied the right of appeal to the higher authorities in England.

Such was the situation, brought about with full knowledge and intention, and as long as possible persisted in, by the Puritan leaders. Those leaders, as we have such clear proof in the case of the noblest of them, John Winthrop, seem to have come to Massachusetts with three distinct and clearly understood objects. They wished, first, to found and develop a peculiar type of community, best expressed by the term Bible-Commonwealth, in which the political and religious elements, in themselves and in their relations to one another, should be but two aspects of the same method of so regulating the lives of individuals as to bring them into harmony with the expressed will of God, as interpreted by the self-appointed rulers. Secondly, both as religious zealots, who felt that they had come into possession of ultimate truth, and as active-minded Englishmen, desirous of an outlet for their admin-

---

[74] *Massachusetts Records*, vol. I, p. 84; Hutchinson, History, vol. I, p. 293*n*. Cf. *Acts Privy Council, Colonial*, vol. I, p. 842.

[75] Palfrey, *History*, vol. I, pp. 313, 323.

istrative energies, they considered themselves as the best qualified rulers and the appointed guardians for the community which they had founded. Lastly, having been largely determined by economic considerations in venturing their fortunes in the enterprise, they looked with fear, as well as jealousy, upon any possibility of allowing control of policy, of law and order, and of legislation concerning person and property, to pass to others.

In such a church-state, no civil question could be considered aside from its possible religious bearings; no religious opinion could be discussed apart from its political implications. It was a system which could be maintained permanently only by the most rigid denial of political free speech and religious toleration. Fortunately, however, it contained within itself the seeds of its own dissolution. Apart from other factors, the church-covenant idea, brought by the Pilgrims, accepted by Endicott, and indorsed by the three churches formed by the Winthrop colonists, in 1630, at Dorchester, Charlestown, and Watertown, was the seed of a democratic conception of the state, which grew so persistently as to defy all efforts of its own planters to destroy it. The attitude of the two most influential Massachusetts leaders, lay and ecclesiastical, is not a matter of inference. "Democracy," wrote Winthrop, after stating that there "was no such government in Israel," is "amongst civil nations, accounted the meanest and worst of all forms of government." To allow it in Massachusetts would be "a manifest breach of the 5th. Commandment."[76] "Democracy," wrote John Cotton to Lord Say and Sele, "I do not conceive that ever God did ordeyne as a fit government eyther for church or commonwealth. If the people be governors who shall be governed?"[77] We have already quoted Gooch's statement that "democracy is the child of the Reformation, not of the Reformers." The democracy of Massachusetts, slow in developing, was the child of the church-covenant and of the frontier, not of the Puritan leaders.

While the latter were thus attempting to found and maintain an aristocracy or oligarchy to guard a church polity which was unconsciously but implicitly democratic,[78] their position was ren-

---

[76] R. C. Winthrop, *J. Winthrop*, vol. II, p. 430. I have modernized the spelling.

[77] Hutchinson, *History*, Appendix, vol. I, p. 437.

[78] Cf. H. L. Osgood, "Political Ideas of the Puritans"; *Political Science Quarterly*, vol. VI, p. 21.

dered precarious at the very outset, and increasingly so as time went on, by the necessary presence in the colony of that large unenfranchised class which was not in sympathy with them. As we have seen, even under strong social and political temptation, three quarters of the population, though probably largely Puritan in sentiment and belief, persistently refused to ally themselves with the New England type of Puritan church. Their presence in the colony was undoubtedly due to economic motives, more especially, perhaps, the desire to own their lands in fee. It must also have been due to economic considerations on the part of the Puritan rulers. The planting of a Bible-Commonwealth might have been possible without these non-church members, but the creation of a prosperous and populous state was not, as was evidenced by statistics throughout its life. Even of the first thousand who came with Winthrop, it is probable that many were without strong religious motives; that few realized the plans of the leaders; and it is practically certain that the great bulk of them had never seen the charter.

Many of the more active soon wished to have some voice in the management of their own affairs; and at the October meeting of the General Court, one hundred and eight, including Conant, Maverick, and Blackstone among the old planters, requested that they be made freemen.[79] It became evident to the dozen or so men who alone possessed the governing power, that some extension of the franchise would be necessary if the leading spirits among their two thousand subjects were not to emigrate again to other colonies, or to foment trouble at home. On the other hand, the extension of the franchise was, in their minds, fraught with the perils already indicated. The decision to extend the franchise, but to limit its powers, and to violate the terms of the charter by placing the election of the governor and deputy in the hands of the Assistants instead of the freemen, was probably the result of an effort to solve this problem. Before the next meeting of the General Court in the following May, at which the new freemen were to be admitted, further thought had evidently been devoted to the question, and another solution arrived at. Winthrop was chosen Governor, not by the Assistants, as voted at the pre-

[79] *Massachusetts Records,* vol. I, pp. 79, 80.

ceding meeting, but by "the general consent of the Court, according to the meaning of the patent"; and the momentous resolution was adopted that "noe man shall be admitted to the freedome of this body polliticke, but such as are members of some of the churches within the lymitts of the same."[80] The first attempt on the part of its unenfranchised subjects to secure a larger share of political liberty had resulted merely in establishing, more firmly than before, the theocratical and oligarchical nature of the government.

Chapter VII

An English Opposition Becomes a New England Oligarchy

In an earlier chapter, in discussing the problems which confronted Elizabeth, we spoke of an established church as a necessity in her day from all three standpoints—of religion, morals, and politics. We also touched upon the simplicity of problems as they appear to those in opposition, as contrasted with their aspect to those who bear the responsibility of power. In England, in the earlier part of the seventeenth century, in spite of the example of Holland, the doctrine of the necessity of a state church, to which all men must conform, in their capacity of citizens as well as of Christians, was still held, although the influence of the "dissidence of dissent," as the logical outcome of individual interpretation of the Bible, was beginning to be felt. Voices were being raised in many quarters denouncing the intolerance of the various sects, both Anglican and Puritan; and, although the Protestants might consider that the religious glacier which held all men in its embrace was as rigidly frozen as ever, the ice was, in truth, rapidly melting beneath the surface. To Englishmen in tolerant Leyden, John Robinson was preaching that "magistrates are kings and lords over men properly and directly, as they are their subjects, and not as they are Christ's," and that by "compulsion many become atheists, hypocrites, and Familists, and being at first constrained to practise against conscience, lose all conscience afterwards."[1] In England, Chilling-

---

80 *Massachusetts Records,* vol. I, p. 87.
1 Robinson, *Works,* vol. II, p. 41.

worth, through the doctrine of the innocence of error, was elevating toleration into a principle of justice and a practicable rule of government.[2] In the New World, Roger Williams was soon to begin his life-long struggle against what he vehemently denounced as "that body-killing, soule-killing, and State-killing doctrine" of religious persecution by the arm of the civil power.[3]

We cannot, perhaps, blame men for not being in advance of their age, or even for being behind it. The founders of the Bay Colony were but little qualified, by reason of the narrowness of their views and the intensity with which they were held, to lead men to any higher ground than that which they had been accustomed to tread. Moreover, having changed their place from members of an opposition to members of a government, their new responsibilities would tend to foster even more strongly that fear of innovation which is nearly always characteristic of the middle-class man in power. The exercise of authority is apt to prove an intoxicating draught, even to the best-intentioned men who have been unaccustomed to it; and, of the tiny group who now claimed absolute sway over two thousand subjects, rapidly increasing to sixteen thousand, none had held any position of administrative importance in the old country. Some of them had, indeed, occupied offices, but they were rather of a nature to encourage that intolerance of contradiction, and tendency to arbitrary action upon a small stage, which are apt, in time, to become characteristic of the petty judge, the schoolmaster and the clergyman. Of Endicott's whole career in England, for example, we know only that his rector spoke of him as "a man well knowne to divers persons of good note,"[4] which, in reference to a parishioner in a small country town, more probably referred to his moral character than to any administrative experience. Winthrop had held an unimportant position in a law court. Dudley had managed the estate of a nobleman. Cotton was the rector of a large provincial parish. The work which they and the other leaders did was done honestly; and although the course they pursued, in regard both to the religious qualification for the franchise, and to

---

[2] Cited by A. A. Seaton, *The Theory of Toleration under the later Stuarts* (Cambridge Univ. Press, 1911), p. 56.

[3] *Mr. Cotton's Letter examined; Narr. Club Pub.*, vol. I, p. 44.

[4] White, *Planter's Plea*, p. 43.

the later persecutions for religious beliefs, was, in the long run, to hamper the growth of the colony and to be partly responsible for the eventual loss of the charter, they should not be too severely condemned, perhaps, for the illegal and unjust, as well as politically unwise, course, upon which they now entered. It must be said, however, that, when the great opportunity was offered them of advancing the cause of religious liberty, they turned aside. To the new voices being raised on behalf of justice and humanity, the Massachusetts leaders were as deaf as Laud and the Anglican hierarchy. Equally, and for the same reason, each party solidly and consciously blocked the path to toleration in so far as lay in its power.

The problems of government in the new country soon came thick upon the little group from the opposition in the old. The notorious Morton, for example, was once more singing and trading in "his old nest in the Massachusetts," in the autumn of the year in which Winthrop landed. There were valid reasons, notably his selling fire-arms to the Indians, which might have served adequately as warrant for his arrest by the authorities; but when that action was decided upon, the alleged grounds bore a curiously trumped-up appearance. In the official order for his apprehension, no crime was mentioned; and in his sentence the only matters cited were the "many wrongs he hath done" the Indians, and the theft of a canoe from them.[5] Whatever the moral nature of his intercourse with the natives, it was not likely that, from their standpoint, there had been any very serious crime committed against them by a man living almost isolated in their midst, and whose sole business was trading with them. The convenient, but apparently unfounded, suspicions of a murder committed by him in England, and a warrant procured from the Chief Justice for his shipment thither, could not have served as a basis for any sentence inflicted in Massachusetts.[6] The probable truth is that the Puritans either wanted to teach the discontented "old planters" a lesson, for which purpose Morton offered himself as an easy victim, or they suspected, what was indeed the fact, that he was in communication with

[5] *Massachusetts Records,* vol. I, pp. 74 f.
[6] Bradford, *Plymouth,* p. 253.

Gorges.[7] Obviously, neither of these could be openly alleged as a cause for the punishment they inflicted, which was extraordinarily severe. He was put in the stocks and deported to England; his entire property was confiscated, and his house burned to the ground. Set at liberty in England with little delay, he got into communication with Gorges, and was soon joined by two other victims of colonial methods.

Gorges, though a stanch supporter of the Church of England, was in close relations with the Puritan peers. He and Warwick were having constant dealings, as both were active in the Council for New England, and his son John was a brother-in-law of the Earl of Lincoln, in whose house, as we have seen, the Massachusetts project took shape. There is nothing to indicate any hostility upon his part to the Massachusetts colony until 1632; and the several emissaries whom he secretly sent there were probably dispatched for the sole purpose of seeing whether or not the settlers were encroaching upon the lands claimed by himself and his son Robert, whose rights, it will be recalled, he specifically reserved when he consented to the granting of the Massachusetts charter. The grantees of that instrument, however, denied that the Gorges rights had any legal validity, and claimed and occupied the disputed land as their own. A quarrel was, therefore, inevitable, and as the Puritans, it must be confessed, had little respect for legality themselves, they could, when need required, be counted upon to take such steps as they might see fit to oppose any action of Gorges.

Winthrop had been scarcely a month on the shores of the Bay, when another newcomer arrived in the shape of one of the most picturesque and mysterious characters who were ever to stroll on Boston Common. Sir Christopher Gardiner, Knight of the Sepulchre (somewhat whited), suddenly appeared, with no ostensible business, but with that unexpected phenomenon in the Puritan colony, a pretty young mistress. To be sure, he called her cousin, but it was soon suspected, as Bradford somewhat quaintly wrote, that "she (after the Italian manner) was his concubine."[8] In spite

<hr>

[7] C. F. Adams, *New English Canaan of Thomas Morton* (Prince Soc., Boston, 1883), p. 41. For a fair and full account, cf. the same author's *Three Episodes* vol. I, pp. 240–50. Morton's own account is in his *New English Canaan,* pp 108 ff.

[8] Bradford, *Plymouth,* p. 294.

of the fact that a late defender has claimed that "he was unfitted for the quiet pleasures of domestic life,"[9] he seems to have made some efforts in that direction; for the authorities soon received word from London to the effect that he had two wives there, who were then in conference, and of whom one was calling loudly for his conversion, and the other for his destruction.[10] On the first of March, 1631, it was ordered by the Massachusetts court that he and seven others should be sent prisoners to England by the good ship Lyon;[11] but the knight, getting word of what was proposed, fled to the Indians.[12] Some weeks later he was taken into custody by the Plymouth people, who asserted that they had found on his person evidence that he was a Roman Catholic.[13] While he was lodged in jail in Boston, letters addressed to him by Gorges, as well as one to the absent Morton, came into the hands of Winthrop, who opened them, and decided that they indicated a design on the part of Gorges to regain possession of his land—an ambition not wholly unnatural.[14] Whether or not the authorities decided that it was wiser that Gardiner should not appear in England to add his testimony to that of Morton, nothing further seems to have been done to carry into effect the order for his deportation, and he was soon set at liberty.

Meanwhile a lonely settler from Maine had appeared in Boston, and had looked with favor upon Gardiner's fair companion. He decided to marry the lady and to take her back to the Eveless Eden of the Androscoggin. Gardiner himself accompanied them, and the curiously assorted trio spent the winter together at Brunswick, from which season there was an odd echo in the Maine law courts nine years later, when Gardiner's host, and not himself, was properly sued for a warming-pan stolen by the knight during his chilly stay. In the summer of 1632, Gardiner landed in England just in time to add his witness to that of Morton and Ratcliffe in Gorges's attack upon the Massachusetts charter.[15]

9 P. Oliver, *The Puritan Commonwealth* (Boston, 1856), p. 35.
10 Dudley's Letter, in Young, *Chron. Mass.*, p. 333.
11 *Massachusetts Records*, vol. I, p. 83.
12 J. Winthrop, *History*, vol. I, p. 65.
13 Bradford, *Plymouth*, p. 295.
14 J. Winthrop, *History*, vol. I, p. 68.
15 C. F. Adams, *Mass. Hist. Soc. Proceedings*, Series I, vol. xx, p. 80.

Ratcliffe, who was a mentally unbalanced servant of Cradock, had apparently talked loosely about the government and the Salem church. For these "mallitious and scandulous speeches," as the crime was designated in his sentence by the court, he was whipped, had both his ears cut off, was fined the impossible sum of £40, and banished from the colony.[16] He was not long in joining Morton and Gardiner in England, and becoming one more arrow in Gorges's quiver.

These cases, moreover, though they proved more important individually, in their reaction upon the colony, by no means stood alone. A certain Thomas Gray, for an unspecified crime, was banished, his house was pulled down, and all Englishmen were enjoined from giving him shelter, "under such penalty as the Court shall thinke meete to inflicte." Thomas Dexter, for saying, "This captious government will bring all to naught," adding that "the best of them was but an atturney, &c.," was put in the stocks, fined £40, and disfranchised. Henry Lynn, "for writeing into England falsely and mallitiously against the government and execuccion of justice here," was ordered whipped and banished; while Thomas Knower was put in the stocks for saying that, if punished, he would have the legality of his sentence tried in England.[17]

The course of justice, if no worse than in contemporary England, was evidently but little improved by its passage overseas, or by being administered by those who had been so loud in their denunciations of the summary methods of Laud and the High Commission. It seemed to many, as to the "old planter" Blackstone, that the tyranny of the "Lord-Bishops" had merely been exchanged for that of the "Lord-Brethren"; and it was evident also that the fixed policy of the leaders was to allow no appeals from their decisions to the home courts of England. All the colonists, therefore, who would not, on the one hand, wholly refrain from criticizing the policy and acts of the leaders, and, on the other, prove themselves acceptable to the clergy, and so secure the franchise by being elected freemen, were wholly without representation, without voice in the making of their laws, and without recourse to the courts and king at home.

---

[16] *Massachusetts Records*, vol. I, p. 88; J. Winthrop, *History*, vol. I, p. 67.
[17] *Massachusetts Records*, vol. I, pp. 77, 101, 103, 104, 102.

As the charter was that of a trading corporation, the levying of taxes was a mere development of the right to assess shareholders, and, therefore, extended only to freemen. But no such legal restriction was observed, and from the beginning, the authorities taxed the non-freemen equally with themselves, though denying them the political rights which they themselves possessed.[18] Indeed, not only their property was thus subject to enactments in which they had no voice, but their time and the work of their hands as well; for the General Court passed a law that all except members of the court, and officers of the church and commonwealth, were liable to be impressed for manual labor on all public works.[19] The town meeting, indeed, seems to have been the only place in which the great majority of the colonists could legally make their voice heard at all, and there only upon questions concerning the most trivial local matters.

The New England town, already noted as one of the three typical institutions in the development and influence of that section, may be considered in its origin as "the politically active congregation," bound together, in addition to its church ties, by a peculiar agrarian policy.[20] Originating at Plymouth, it became universal throughout the Puritan colonies on the mainland, and was reproduced with extraordinary fidelity of detail wherever New Englanders migrated. The New England colonies, for the most part, neither sold nor rented their land, but granted it freely in fee to actual settlers, in rough proportion to their present ability to use it.[21] In general most of it was granted primarily to towns, which owned it in their corporate capacity; and by them it was allotted to individuals in the form of home-lots or arable land and meadow. The remainder formed the "common," for the use of all, under certain restrictions.

---

[18] H. L. Osgood, "New England Colonial Finance in the 17th Century"; *Political Science Quarterly*, vol. XIX, p. 82.

[19] *Massachusetts Records*, vol. I, p. 124.

[20] M. Eggleston, *The Land System of the New England Colonies*, Johns Hopkins Univ. Studies, Baltimore, 1886. Cf. also C. M. Andrews, *The River Towns of Conn.*, J. H. U. S., 1889; W. E. Foster, *Town Government in Rhode Island*, J. H. U. S., 1886; A. B. Maclear, *Early New England Towns*, Columbia Univ. Studies, 1908; H. L. Osgood, *American Colonies*, vol. I, pp. 424 ff.; and for English towns on Long Island, J. T. Adams, *History of the Town of Southampton* (Bridgehampton, 1918), pp. 94–103.

[21] The occasional few and unimportant exceptions do not affect the general statement.

The whole land-system, as well as the methods of cultivation, exhibited many striking resemblances to those of our early Teutonic ancestors; and, some years ago, these coincidences were largely insisted upon as cases of genuine survival.[22] It is more probable that a return to favorable wilderness conditions merely strengthened those primitive elements still remaining in the manorial system, with which the settlers were familiar in England. As we have already pointed out, the geographical environment in New England, as contrasted with that of the other colonies, tended strongly to develop the type of compact settlement. This was further reinforced by the form of emigration, which was distinctly of neighborhood groups, and by the type of church government.

The exigencies of the situation, when the settlers first landed, had necessitated their dispersal in various communities, whose members at once found it needful to manage their local affairs to some extent by meeting together among themselves. The charter made no provision for any but a general government; nor, under it, did the company have any legal right to incorporate other bodies. These more or less informal local governments were, therefore, extra-legal both before and after the passage of a township act by which it was attempted specifically to give them certain rights of local administration. At the town meetings, which at first were spontaneous, and afterward regulated, all the inhabitants had the right to be present and to take part in the discussion of public affairs, although only the freemen were entitled to vote, except upon a few questions of minor importance. The distinction was somewhat similar to that in the churches, which all could attend, but in the management of which only church members had a voice. The town meeting, therefore, was a completely democratic institution in only one of its aspects, although it came to have great influence upon both political theory and practice.

A further development brought these local communities into working relations with the General Court. Owing to the distance

---

[22] Cf. H. B. Adams, *The Germanic Origin of New England Towns,* J. H. U. S., 1882; Id., *Village Communities of Cape Anne and Salem,* J. H. U. S., 1883; G. E. Howard, *Local Constitutional History of the U. S.,* J. H. U. S., 1889. Too enthusiastic believers should read "The Survival of Archaic Communities," in F. W. Maitland, *Collected Papers* (Cambridge Univ. Press, 1911), vol. II, pp. 313 ff.

of the scattered settlements from Boston, and the danger of all the freemen being absent at once from their homes, it was enacted, in 1634, that every town should elect two or three deputies, who should have the power of the whole, and who should act as their representatives in the General Court.[23] As the charter provided that seven of the eighteen Assistants must be present in the Court in order to constitute a quorum, that body was now composed of a small number of Assistants and a steadily growing number of Deputies. As the Virginia House of Burgesses had been established in 1619, and the Bermuda Assembly in 1620, the representative government provided for in Massachusetts was the third in the colonies.[24]

Owing to the close alliance maintained between the clergy and the Magistrates, as the Assistants soon came to be called, the body of deputies grew to be considered the more popular element in the Court. It was clear that real grievances and the democratic influences at work in the town meeting were likely to develop into attacks upon the arbitrary power of the very limited body of freemen. The form that the struggle assumed was that of a contest, lasting twenty years, between the deputies and the magistrates, with the influence of the clergy constantly on the side of the latter. The freemen themselves were, indeed, not all in favor of the arbitrary exercise of power by the small oligarchical group which for so long remained in control. As early as 1631, the people of Watertown, when taxed for fortifying Newtown, declared that "it was not safe to pay moneys after that sort, for fear of bringing themselves and posterity into bondage."[25] Although legally in the right, they accepted Winthrop's interpretation of the charter, which is interesting as showing how completely the unjustified transformation from a company into a commonwealth had already been effected in the minds of the leaders.

Although the people, until well into the eighteenth century, probably had little thought of becoming independent of England, it seems clear from all the acts of the leaders, especially the transfer

[23] *Massachusetts Records,* vol. I, p. 118.

[24] Cf. J. H. Lefroy, *On the Constitutional History of the Bermudas* (Westminster, 1881), p. 6.

[25] J. Winthrop, *History,* vol. I, p. 84.

of the charter itself, that it was their intention, even before leaving England, to govern in as complete independence of that country as future circumstances might permit. They wished, it is true, to found a state for the glory of God and the establishment of true religion, but in which, nevertheless, they themselves should constitute the supreme power. Every encroachment upon it, from any direction, was grudgingly yielded to; and it is not unlikely that, even then, some of them dreamed of an actual political independence. "We are not a free state," wrote Pyncheon to Winthrop, in 1646, evidently with this in mind; "neither do I think it our wisdom to be a free state; though we had our liberty, we cannot *as yet* subsist without England."[26]

The political history of Massachusetts under the charter was thus made up of two separate elements. The first was the resistance of the governing group to any effort of England, legal or illegal, to assert her rights, even justly, over her colony; and the second was the struggle of a part of the colonists themselves, for toleration and liberty, against the governing class. Even had the colony never separated from England, we should, in all probability, have come to possess the same measure of civil liberty and religious toleration that the English have to-day; but that separation having taken place, had the Puritan oligarchy retained and extended their power, we should have but little of either. It is, therefore, the second conflict which, although less dramatic, is the more vital in the history of human freedom. We must now turn to consider the earliest important attacks from both of the quarters indicated.

Of those from across the water, the first was launched, as could well have been foreseen, by Sir Ferdinando Gorges, and was brought upon the colony directly through the policy pursued by its leaders. The untiring interest of Gorges in the affairs of New England, and his hope of yet creating a profitable settlement there for himself, were both well known to the Puritans. The old knight had spent vastly greater sums in the effort to plant the wilderness than had been contributed by any individual among themselves. He had attempted the colonization of Maine at a time when the men who were now engaged in banishing his agents were hardly more than children.[27] He had made no effort to disturb the Pil-

---

[26] *Mass. Hist. Soc. Coll.,* Series IV, vol. VI. p. 383. The italics are mine.
[27] Winthrop was a lad of 19 in 1607, and Endicott but 16.

grims during their ten-years' stay at Plymouth, and would probably have left the Massachusetts settlers also in peace, had it not been for their denial of the rights he claimed in a part of the soil they had preëmpted, and for their treatment of his emissaries. The Massachusetts authorities, by throwing down the gauntlet, had created a powerful enemy who was not slow in picking it up.

In 1632, Gorges and Mason, with the assistance of Gardiner, Morton, and Ratcliffe, prepared a petition, which was presented to the Privy Council in December.[28] Winthrop stated that among many false accusations and "some truths misrepeated," it accused the colony of separating from the Church of England, and of threatening to cast off its political allegiance.[29] Supporters of the company in England hastily put into motion those unseen agencies that were most efficacious in doing business at the court of Charles; and, in spite of what seemed overwhelming odds against them, in courtly influence, won an unexpected victory, even gaining a word of commendation from the King.[30] Their success is involved in a mystery, which, however, we suspect might be unlocked by that same "golden key" which the Pilgrims were using contemporaneously at another of the royal doors. Meanwhile, the Council for New England had requested that the Company's charter be presented for examination, and Humphrey had been forced to confess that it was in New England, stating that, though he had often written for it, he had been unable to obtain it.[31]

The demand, however, was repeated from a more powerful source two years later. In 1633, Laud had become Archbishop of Canterbury, and had declared war upon the Puritans. Colonial affairs, which had heretofore been considered, when considered at all, by the Privy Council, were now put into the hands of a body styled "the Lords Commissioners for Plantations in General," which was headed by the Archbishop, and given almost royal powers in both civil and ecclesiastical matters, including that of revoking all charters and patents unduly obtained.[32] Gorges uti-

---

[28] *Acts Privy Council, Colonial,* vol. I, p. 183.

[29] J. Winthrop, *History,* vol. I, p. 122.

[30] J. Winthrop, *History,* vol. I, p. 123n.

[31] Records Council for New England; *American Antiquarian Society Proceedings,* 1866, p. 107.

[32] C. M. Andrews, *British Committees, Commissions, and Councils of Trade and Plantations, 1622–1675,* J. H. U. S., 1908, pp. 16 f.

lized this new opportunity, and at once began to work upon the Archbishop's hatred of Puritanism, in order to recover his own legal claims. On February 21, 1634, the Board, having taken into consideration the great numbers of persons "known to be ill-affected and discontented, as well with the Civil as Ecclesiastical government," who were daily resorting to New England, ordered that Cradock produce the Massachusetts charter.[33] Upon receipt of Cradock's first letter requesting its return, the authorities at Boston decided to return an evasive answer, ignoring the Council's demand. After the first communication had been followed by an official copy of the order itself, word was returned by Winslow, who was acting as agent for both Plymouth and Massachusetts, that the charter could not be sent except by a vote of the General Court, which body would not meet until September.[34]

Meanwhile, Gorges was plying the English authorities with letters advising that a governor, "neither papistically nor scizmatically affected," be appointed for New England, modestly suggesting that he himself was an eminently proper person for the office, and urging that the Massachusetts charter be repealed.[35] His wish was gratified as to the first two points, and it looked as if he was at last to see the shores of that land which had been the chief object of his thoughts for thirty years. Winslow, whose suit, at first, had seemingly prospered, was suddenly and dramatically confronted, in the presence of Laud, with his old enemy Morton of Merry Mount, and, as a result of the latter's accusations, was temporarily committed to prison.[36]

The grandiose scheme that Gorges had conceived contemplated the division of all New England among certain members of the old Council, and the validating of the individual assignments by legal sanctions. It was also arranged that the charter should then be resigned by that body, which had only too truly become, as the declaration read, "a Carcass in a manner breathless."[37] This was done in April, and in the following month a writ of *Quo War-*

[33] *Acts Privy Council, Colonial,* vol. I, p. 199. The order is given in Hubbard, *History,* p. 153.

[34] J. Winthrop, *History,* vol. I, pp. 161, 163.

[35] Baxter, *Gorges,* vol. III, pp. 261–75.

[36] Bradford, *Plymouth,* p. 330.

[37] Hazard, *Hist. Coll.,* vol. I, p. 391.

ranto was entered, to deprive the Massachusetts company of its own charter, as the final step in the transformation of New England. Aside from the play of conflicting influences involved, the leaders, by their handling of affairs, had, without question, violated the terms of that instrument, and so had given their adversaries a reputable cause to plead. The verdict was adverse to the Company, judgment was entered against such of the patentees as appeared, and the remainder were outlawed. The patentees, however, refused to acknowledge the action of the courts, and the charter was not returned, though again demanded two years later.[38] Meanwhile, Gorges's new-risen hopes had been wholly dashed. Though he had been appointed governor, the King had provided him with no funds from the empty treasury, and Gorges's own resources were always inadequate for his undertakings. Mason, who was aiding him, suddenly died. The ship which was to have carried the knight to his new province broke as it was being launched, and delay followed delay, while the aspect of public affairs was rapidly changing.

This favorable turn, however, was not foreseen in the colony, and immediately upon receipt of the news of the appointment of the new Commission for Plantations, the Massachusetts government prepared for armed resistance. A sentry was posted on a hill near Boston, to give notice of the arrival of any hostile ships; £600 was raised for the completion of the fortifications on Castle Island; a military committee was appointed; and, a few weeks later, the clergy were consulted as to what should be done if a general governor were sent out from England. Their unanimous answer was that "We ought not to accept him, but defend our lawful possessions (if we are able), otherwise to avoid or protract."[39] It must be recalled that the Massachusetts settlers were as yet Englishmen, and not independent Americans; and the home government, whose subjects they were, could hardly regard these acts and utterances otherwise than as rank rebellion, however different an aspect they

---

[38] Hutchinson, *History,* vol. I, p. 85; Hutchinson, *Papers* (Prince Soc., Albany, 1865), vol. I, p. 119.

[39] *Massachusetts Records,* vol. I, pp. 136–39; J. Winthrop, *History,* vol. I, pp. 170, 183. They were also asked whether it was lawful to retain the cross in the royal ensign, Endicott having chosen this inopportune moment to give an example of his blundering fanaticism, by cutting it out. *Massachusetts Records,* vol. I, pp. 136, 147; J. Winthrop, *History,* vol. I, pp. 175, 183, 199.

might come to wear in the eyes of ourselves as heirs of a subsequent and successful revolution. Political events in England soon developed in such a way as to prevent any very serious consideration of colonial affairs for another quarter of a century, and the policy of "avoid or protract," seemed temporarily to serve all purposes.

The colonial government, which had thus assumed what was practically a position of avowed independence of the king and courts of England, next decided to take up a stronger line in regard to its own subjects in the colony itself, for the spirit of the Watertown freemen against taxation had evidently spread. Just prior to the meeting of the General Court in the spring of 1634, every town deputed two men to consider such matters as might come up; and after consultation, a demand was made upon the governor to allow them to inspect the charter. Having found upon examination that the General Court was the only legal body entitled to legislate, they apparently inquired why that power had been usurped by the magistrates. Winthrop replied that it was because the General Court had become unwieldy in size; and he made the suggestion that, for the present, "they might, at the general court, make an order, that, once in the year, a certain number should be appointed (upon summons from the governor) to revise all laws, etc., and to reform what they found amiss therein; but not to make any new laws, but prefer their grievances to the court of assistants; and that no assessments should be laid upon the country without the consent of such a committee, nor any lands disposed of."[40] It is difficult to conceive of a more complete abrogation of the rights of even the very limited body of freemen; and, though Winthrop does not tell us how this astonishing offer was received, the records leave us in no doubt. At the meeting of the General Court, it was immediately voted that there should be no trial for life or banishment except by a jury summoned by themselves; that there should be four such courts a year, not to be dissolved without their own consent; that none but the General Court had power to make laws or to elect and remove officials; and that none but the General Court had power to dispose of lands or to raise money by taxation.[41]

[40] J. Winthrop, *History*, vol. I, p. 153.
[41] *Massachusetts Records*, vol. I, pp. 117 ff.

Another incident, of less importance, but interesting as showing the feeling abroad and the means by which it might, for a time, be suppressed, occurred at a meeting of the inhabitants of Boston later in the year, to choose some men to divide additional townland. The voting was by secret ballot, for the first time, and Winthrop, Coddington, and the other leaders failed of election. The first stated in his account of the affair, that the electors chose mostly men of "the inferior sort," fearing that the richer men would give the poor an unfairly small proportion of land, the policy, he added, having been to leave a large amount undivided for newcomers and commons.[42] The argument, which was sound, might perhaps have been considered sounder by the discontented, had the governor himself, for example, not acquired by that time above eighteen hundred acres, Saltonstall sixteen hundred, and Dudley seventeen hundred.[43] After Winthrop had made a speech, and the Reverend Mr. Cotton had "showed them that it was the Lord's order among the Israelites to have all such businesses committed to the elders," a new vote was ordered and the magistrates were elected.[44]

It was evident that, if the little group of leaders, lay and ecclesiastic, were to retain power permanently, in view of the spirit evinced by the people, and the extremely rapid growth of the population, it could be only by securing a firmer hold upon the body of magistrates and the election of freemen. A few months previously, Cotton had preached a sermon arguing that the magistrates, who were annually elected under the charter, were entitled to be perpetually reëlected, except for "just cause"; and he compared their rights to office with those of a man in his freehold estate.[45] This suggestion seems to have borne fruit something more than a year afterward, when, it having been shown "from the word of God, etc., that the principal magistrates ought to be for life," it was voted that a council should be created, to have such powers as the General Court should grant them, and not to be subject to removal except for crimes or "other weighty cause." This, of

[42] J. Winthrop, *History*, vol. I, p. 181.
[43] Adams, *Three Episodes*, vol. I, p. 365.
[44] J. Winthrop, *History*, vol. I, p. 181.
[45] *Ibid.*, vol. I, p. 157.

course, was again a violation of the charter, and, like so much of the reactionary legislation, was due to the direct influence of the clergy.[46] Though Winthrop, Dudley, and Endicott were elected to the new offices, the council was never granted any powers, and the plan failed.[47]

Of somewhat more practical service, in view of the fact that church membership was an indispensable qualification for the franchise, was the law, passed at the same court, that no new churches could be organized without the approbation of the magistrates and a majority of the elders of the preëxisting churches, and that no man could become a freeman who was not a member of a church so approved of. By this means a degree of control, at least, could be maintained over the great numbers of newcomers now arriving.

We do not wish to convey the impression that the leaders of the colony were animated by mere love of power or a vulgar ambition, strong though the former was in most of them. But the danger to the liberties of their subjects was no less great because Winthrop and Cotton were wholly convinced of the divine nature of their mission. It is too frequently assumed that despotic acts are necessarily those of a self-conscious despot; whereas, in most cases, they are merely the readiest means employed for reaching ends which authority may think itself rightly privileged, or morally bound, to attain. Charles and Laud were no less certain than the rulers of Church and State in Massachusetts, that their mandate was a heavenly one. Liberty cannot mean one thing in old England and another in New, nor can intolerance be condoned in the one and condemned in the other. The King and the Archbishop were no more closely allied, nor more bent upon forcing their own will upon that of the people, than were the civil and ecclesiastical powers of the little American commonwealth, however worthy or unworthy the motives of each may have been. Pride in the valiant work that the Massachusetts leaders did in subduing the wilderness, and in the sacrifices that they made for their religious beliefs, has tended to make their descendants, in the words of the old

46 R. C. Winthrop, *J. Winthrop,* vol. II, p. 271.
47 J. Winthrop, *History,* vol. I, p. 220; *Massachusetts Records,* vol. I, pp. 167, 174, 195, 264.

English saw, "to their faults a little blind, and to their virtues very kind"; but if the nations of the world are to grow in mutual understanding and brotherly feeling, their histories must be written from the standpoint of justice to all, and not from that of a mistaken national piety.

4
Samuel Eliot Morison

During the past twenty-five years, the economic interpretation of history that seemed so plausible in the twenties and thirties has gradually begun to appear too one-sided. Historians today are wary of attributing events in any period to a single cause. This development came very early to the study of the founding of New England. In 1927 Kenneth Murdock's biography of Increase Mather suggested how much might be learned by taking the Puritans' ideas seriously. Since then, Perry Miller's studies of *The New England Mind,* together with Samuel Eliot Morison's *Builders of the Bay Colony* and his histories of Harvard College, have transformed and deepened the study of New England Puritanism. No other area of American history has received more intensive or more imaginative treatment by modern scholars. Professor Morison's *Builders of the Bay Colony,* which appeared on the three-hundredth anniversary of John Winthrop's arrival in Massachusetts, is a good example of this new approach to the Puritans.

John Winthrop, Esquire
1. THE PURITAN SQUIRE

In the early part of the reign of Henry VIII, a bright country lad named Adam Winthrop told his father that he was through with farming, and went up to London to seek his fortune. There, in a ten years' apprenticeship to a member of the Clothworkers' gild, he learned the secrets of that ancient trade and mystery of working up wool into cloth. After his indenture was up he became journeyman, then master clothier, and full-fledged member of the gild. At the age of forty-six, having acquired a fortune, and in a fair way to become Master of the Worshipful Company of Clothworkers,

Adam did what Englishmen in his position have done time out of mind: purchased a country estate and joined the landed gentry. Such estates were easily come by in that day, for Henry VIII had laid violent hands on the vast possessions of the monasteries, and was finding new owners for them, with the double purpose of increasing his revenue, and enlarging his following. So Adam purchased, for £408 18s. 3d., the manor of Groton in Suffolk, formerly belonging to the Abbey of Bury St. Edmunds, with the manor house and all the singular its buildings, tenements, messuages, and hereditaments; with all rights of pasturage, fishing, and wood-cutting; with its wardships, heriots, mercates, mills, and tolls; with the right and duty to hold court baron for the free tenants and court leet for the customary tenants, and the presentation of Groton Church. All thus, with much additional land, was inherited by his son, the second Adam Winthrop, who practiced law in London for a time, but during the greater part of his life found sufficient occupation in farming and governing Groton Manor. He acquired a coat of arms, and a settled position among the country gentry of Suffolk, where his son John was born in January of the Armada year, 1588.

Groton to-day is a tiny village on a hillside, overlooking the market town of Boxford. An ancient mulberry tree marks the site of Groton Hall, but the old parish church is still there, with the tombs of the early Winthrops. Suffolk is the most homely part of Old England, to a New Englander: a gently rolling country of quiet horizons, less wooded than most parts of New England to-day, but with the regular irregularity and even unevenness which Westerners find so charming (or exasperating) in Massachusetts. Stone walls enclosing meadow and tillage, mowing and pasture; narrow roads winding and dipping in unexpected ways; and always a smooth-crested hill to vary the skyline. The old houses, too, are of the style and proportion of our seventeenth-century New England dwellings, though covered with plaster and thatch instead of clapboard and cedar shingle; the same great central chimney, overhanging second story, high-pitched roof, and small casements with leaded diamond panes. Out in the country they stand, surrounded by farm buildings (barn doors opening on the side, in the old New England pattern), or generously spaced about a village green, like a New England town common.

Here is our very homeland. In an afternoon's drive of seventy or eighty miles, we may visit Framlingham, Ipswich, Dedham, Braintree, Boxford, Groton, Sudbury, and Haverhill, and spend the night at Cambridge. Suffolk is the heart of East Anglia, the section of England, which, according to Havelock Ellis' 'Study of British Genius,' has produced the greatest statesmen, scientists, ecclesiastics, scholars, and artists in English history, and which has always been distinguished for a profound love of liberty and independence. In East Anglia, the puritan movement bit deepest. From East Anglia came the heaviest contingent for the planting of Massachusetts Bay; and Massachusetts as colony and commonwealth, by every known test of eminence, has produced more distinguished men and women in proportion to her population, than any other state of the Union.

The lordship of the Manor of Groton involved many duties and obligations. Adam Winthrop, like many a country gentleman of to-day, was a self-made business man; but we must not carry the analogy further by supposing that he had nothing to do but make over the mansion, join the local smart set, and pretend that his farm paid its expenses. To be a country gentleman in Elizabethan England meant to be an active member of the governing class: a justice of the peace, holding petty sessions and sitting on the bench with fellow magistrates at the quarter-sessions and grand assizes. The early magistrates of Massachusetts Bay were of this class. They had been local leaders and rulers over the same sort of people who came with them, a fact which explains both the deference that they obtained, and the ability that they displayed. Yet the founders of New England made no attempt to transplant the manorial system or hereditary government to our soil. They were through with feudalism, as they were through with ritualism.

John Winthrop was Justice of the Peace at eighteen, and in a few years' time began to hold court leet for his father, and act as steward of the manor: excellent training in administration. In addition he had to direct the ordinary farming work of the demesne, and of outlying estates that he owned or leased. Adam the second's diary is full of entries that carry us back almost to his namesake, and forward to the other day in New England: sowing, reaping, and threshing wheat, rye, pease, and barley; calvings and foalings; dogs biting sheep and cows in the corn; riving logs and thatching

roofs; drowning the meadow and casting the pond; clowns a-woo-
ing maids, and getting them with child; together with a few items
typical of the period, such as highway robberies, forced loans to
the Queen's Majesty, news of King James' progress from the
North.

So John Winthrop grew up an English squire, governing and
directing the common English rustic, and mingling socially with
his peers. Besides, his family maintained contacts with the City
and the University. Both Adam and John practised law in London,
and kept up with the solid members of the city livery companies;
Adam also served as auditor of Trinity College, Cambridge.
Groton was about the same distance from that university town as
Groton, Massachusetts, is from ours; so it was a pleasant recreation
for Adam to ride up to Cambridge four times a year to go through
the college books, to play bowls with the dons, eat the great audit
dinner, and drink the heavy audit ale. He entered John at Trinity
at the age of fourteen, only a little younger than the average freshman. The boy remained there less than two years. Few sons of
the country gentry took university degrees in those days unless they
were destined for the Church. We may infer from John's severe
remarks on the dissoluteness of Cambridge undergraduates, and
from sending his eldest son to Trinity College, Dublin, that further
residence in college was regarded as a waste of time. For the
Winthrops were puritans, and of all puritanic tenets, perhaps the
most lasting in New England is the prohibition to waste your
'precious time.'

The time has come, the Walrus said, to talk of puritanism and
the puritans. I had hoped to get through this book without that
disagreeable task of definition; but it cannot be done. What then
is meant by puritanism, and who were the puritans?

Puritanism was a way of life based on the belief that the Bible
was the word of God, and the whole word of God. Puritans were
the Englishmen who endeavored to live according to that light.
Having been so round, I must shade off, for puritanism has had
various meanings at different times. Originally a nickname (οἱ
καθαροί, *puritani*) flung about on the theological controversies of
the late Roman Empire, it was revived in Queen Elizabeth's reign
to describe that party of English Protestants who wished to carry

out the Reformation to its logical conclusion, and purge the Anglican Church of forms and ceremonies for which there was no warrant in the Bible; or, to use a phrase of Cartwright which became a watchword for one party and a jest for their opponents, to restore the Christian Church 'pure and unspotted.' At first it was applied only to persons within the Church of England; but by 1630, the term puritan had been stretched to include separatists like the Pilgrims who obtained purity outside the Anglican communion, and even the Scots Presbyterians, who had a different organization. Further, the Church of England puritans were divided into nonconformists, who disobeyed the law rather than compromise with conscience, and the conformable puritans like John White and John Winthrop who performed or attended the prescribed services according to the Book of Common Prayer, while hoping for better things.

Beside this purely religious meaning of puritanism, there was a moral aspect. Persons who read the Bible and sincerely believed in it, adopted or attempted a very exacting code of morals; and as they believed that this code was gospel ordinance, they endeavored to enforce it on others. Such persons were originally called precisians, and were not necessarily puritans in a religious sense. The most thoroughly puritanic diary I have ever read, full of moans and groans over the mildest peccadilloes of himself and others, is that of Samuel Ward, master of Sidney Sussex College, a stout Royalist and Anglican who was expelled by Cromwell. We mean this moral preciseness when we use the term puritanism to-day; yet moral puritanism is by no means confined to the Protestant or English-speaking churches. The Catholic counter-reformation of the sixteenth century was quite as puritanic in a moral sense as the Protestant reformation. Jansenism was a puritanical movement within the Gallican church in France; and no sect within the last century has been more puritanical in a moral sense than the Catholic Church in Ireland. In England there was what we might call high church puritanism, of which the 'divine Herbert' was the highest example. King Charles and Bishop Laud were both persons of high moral standards. Laud's ecclesiastical courts were as zealous to punish immorality as to enforce conformity; and the reforms that he began in the University of Oxford were continued by its later puritan rulers. If Bishop and King had not attempted religious innovations in the direction of Rome, if they had respected the ritual and doctrine of the Church as Elizabeth or even Archbishop Bancroft had left them, the puritans might never have become associated with radicalism and democracy.

And what of the political side of puritanism? Charles Borgeaud, and other political scientists, have traced democracy to puritanism. I do not think that this theory will hold water, although there is something in it. The Englishman of 1630 was politically mature, compared with other Europeans. He was beginning to feel his way toward popular government, and during the Interregnum he went far on that road. As we have seen in the case of the Salem Church, the congregational polity which one branch of the puritans favored, made laymen the governing body of the church. But the connection between puritanism and political liberalism was fortuitous. English puritans in 1630 rallied to representative government and traditional English liberty because that was their only refuge against innovating Bishops and a high church King; but in New England where they had things their own way, their political spirit was conservative and their temper autocratic. If American democracy came out of puritan New England (and it may equally well be traced to Virginia), it came from the English and not the puritan in our ancestors, and from the newness not the puritanism of New England.

We would do well then to remember that puritanism in the seventeenth century had a purely religious connotation. I will not detain my readers here with a summary of their beliefs and practices; these will appear as the lives of those commonwealth builders, puritans all, unfold. Yet pardon me if I caution you against certain current delusions about the early puritans upon which historians have placed the stamp of authority. The one is that they were mainly preoccupied with hell and damnation. On the contrary, fire-and-brimstone sermons, and poems such as Wigglesworth's 'Day of Doom,' belong to a later generation or to the eighteenth century, when puritan pastors tried to frighten their backsliding congregations into good behavior. The second delusion is that puritanism is synonymous with Calvinism. Broadly speaking the English puritan theologians were Calvinist in their theology rather than Lutheran or Arminian; but being learned in the ancient tongues they derived their ideas mainly from the Bible and the

Fathers. Calvin's 'Institutes' was never to them a sacred book, and I have found Calvin less frequently quoted in their writings than English theologians like Ames, Perkins, and Whitaker. A third delusion is that puritans were prohibitionists, or indirectly responsible for prohibition. Their faith put more stress on the joys of the inner life than on those of the senses, but they made no attempt to proscribe one of God's good creatures, whose temperate use was sanctioned by the Bible, and by our Lord's example. Finally, readers of New England history must be cautioned against ascribing to puritanism alone a coarseness that was common to the age, and a bigotry that was common to all Christian sects, and still is far too common. We will not often find breadth of mind among the English puritans; but we will find a spiritual depth that belongs only to the great ages of religious experience.

John Winthrop was happy to have lived in the golden age of English puritanism, when some of its early fanaticism had been sloughed off, without losing the bloom of youth. It had not altogether broken with the stately and cadenced ritual of the Book of Common Prayer; it had grasped firm hold of the evangelistic principle, the 'tidings of great joy' that our Saviour brought to men. Whatever puritanism may have come to mean in later ages—and I will freely admit that its more recent manifestations have been negative, narrow, and altogether unlovely—it meant three hundred years ago, a high sincerity of purpose, an integrity of life, and an eager searching for the voice of God. The intellectual strength of the puritan was his knowledge of the Bible; the moral strength of the puritan was his direct approach to God. No puritan ever said, as did the children of Israel when they heard the thunder and the trumpet blasts on Mount Sinai, 'Let not God speak to us, lest we die.' His home, his study, his meeting-house, were filled with the reverberations of the awful and gracious voice for which he listened. If he rejected the intercession of the saints, it was because he would meet God face to face. If he despised the ancient pageantry of worship, it was because he would have no false and sensual symbols between him and his Redeemer. Often, like the ancient Hebrews, he misunderstood the voice of God. Often he mistook for it the echo of his own wants and passions. But the desire to hear it, the sense that life consisted in hearing and obeying it, never left him.

The Winthrops were puritans of that sort, as we may infer from the books they read, the friends they valued, and the preachers they liked to hear. One of John's uncles was a friend to John Fox, compiler of the Book of Martyrs. They were conforming puritans, for the presentation of the living at Groton was in their hands, so they would not choose a 'dumb minister' who could do nothing but read out of the Prayer-Book, but a 'godly, learned and painefull (painstaking)' vicar who would neither bend the knee nor wear the surplice, and would hurry through morning prayer to preach a meaty sermon on Christian duty and doctrine. Their delight in sermons helps to make puritans incomprehensible to the present age, which values sermons inversely to their length. 'She hath in her time taken inttollerable paines to hear sermons,' wrote one of that day of his mother; although when a girl she could not imagine what ailed people 'to keep such a strirre in praying, reading, and running to sermons.' Among persons whose minds were filled with thoughts of God, and the desire to learn and do his will, a sermon by a learned and pious man was of absorbing interest and assistance. One of the 'common grevances groaninge for reformation' of which John Winthrop complains, is the punishment of laymen 'for goeing to another parrish to heare a sermon when there is none in there owne.'

We have a fairly full record of John Winthrop's religious experiences in a diary that he kept of his inner life. The family portraits show him, his father, and his son, to have been of the dark, sanguine, and passionate type of Englishman; so we may believe John when he tells us that he was 'wild and dissolute' as a lad, and at all times tempted by the lusts of the flesh. He first drew near to God when lying ill at Trinity College. Backsliding followed, but shortly after his first marriage, at the age of seventeen, he came 'to some peace and comfort in God and in his wayes.' It was long, however, before he reached that serene conviction of divine favor which the puritans called conversion. Numerous *experienciae* of his riper years record constant wrestling with animal desires, long periods of prayer, stern self-abasement, and joy at recovering the pathway of life. His ideal was to devote every waking moment to God, when not engaged in his calling, or in reasonable recreation. It was a matter of self-congratulation that his horseback journeys to London could be employed in praying, singing, and meditation, instead of 'eyes runninge upon every object,' and 'thoughts varieing with everye occasion.' These soul-searching records were common among sincere puritans of that time. They gave rise to what is known as the New England conscience, which was nothing more nor less than the English puritan conscience, transplanted. They could easily be carried to a morbid excess, and often were. John Winthrop's *experiencia* is often tiresome, and even ludicrous in one instance, where he gives his reasons for giving up shooting birds out of season: (1) it is illegal; (2) it offends his neighbors; (3) 'it wastes great store of tyme'; (4) 'it toyles a man's bodye overmuche'; (5) it endangers his life; (6) it brings no profit; (7) the penalty, if caught, would be heavy; (8) 'it brings a man of worth and godliness into some contempt'; (9) after he has gone shooting with 'woundes of conscience,' he has missed most of the 'fowle' that came his way, and often returned with an empty bag! One may suspect that the last reason, which would suffice for most men, was really the first; and one may trace to this sort of thing that tendency toward self-deception, still strong to-day in those of puritanic antecedents, and apt to slop over into hypocrisy.

John Winthrop was a more pronounced puritan than his father. Adam's diaries deal with material things; John's only with religion, until he sets sail for America. Adam could be merry; John regarded mirth and jollity out of place in an earnest life. Adam was at ease among his fellows; John felt lonely among the jovial magistrates at quarter-sessions. 'O Lord, keepe me that I be not discouraged!' he confides to his diary. 'Thou tellest me, and all experience tells me, that in this way there is the least companie, and that those which doe walke openly in this way shalbe despised, pointed at, hated of the world, . . . called puritans, nice fooles, hipocrites.' This entry in his diary reminds us that the term puritan was still one of opprobrium. If you had cried 'Puritan! Puritan!' at a stout fellow embarking for New England, he would have knocked you down. Doubtless he would have prayed God to be forgiven, but he would have knocked you down first. The puritans called themselves the People of God, or simply Christians, for they believed that their faith was what Christ and his apostles preached. It was not until the end of the century that they came to accept the term puritan for themselves, and to glory in it.

For all these soul-strivings one gathers from the Winthrop family papers the impression of a busy, wholesome, happy family life. There was plenty of quiet recreation, even after John decided it did not pay to go shooting: falconry, badger hunting with hounds, shooting with bows and arrows at a mark, good cheer at family gatherings. To his four successive wives, John was a tender husband. No woman could want more affectionate letters than those of John Winthrop to his 'sweet wife' Margaret, mingling gossip with kind messages and talk of God, ending 'many kisses of love I sende thee. Farewell. Thy faithful loving husband, John Winthrop.'

Yet there is much uneasiness in that quiet household at Groton, and grave forebodings for the future of the family, of the Church, and of England. As early as 1624 there is a hint that John Winthrop might follow his brother's example and emigrate to Ireland, could he find opportunity. Manners and conditions were fast changing, much as they are now, and to the same dismay of quiet gentlemen with limited incomes. The rich were getting richer and the poor becoming poorer. It was becoming difficult to bring up children properly. The universities were full of riot and frivolity. Luxury was so rife among the landed gentry, that people like the Winthrops could not keep up with them. Saddle horses and rustic serving men no longer suffice for a gentleman; you must have liveried servants, and the latest model coach. Manners are corrupted. 'He that hath not for every word an oath . . . they say hee is a puritan, a precise fool, not fit to hold a gentleman company.' Wild parties become good form. It was Chief Justice Popham, says John Aubrey, who 'was the greatest howse-keeper in England; would have at Littlecote 4 or 5 more lords at a time. His wife (Harvey) was worth to him, I thinke, £60,000, and she was as vaine as he, . . . and in her husband's absence would have all the woemen of the countrey thither, and feast them, and make them drunke, as she would be herselfe.'

These changes are brought home to us by a contemporary ballad, a satire on the times:

> You talke of Newe England; I truly beleeve
> Oulde England's growne newe and doth us deceave.
> I'le aske you a question or two, by your leave:
> And is not ould England growne new?

Wher are your ould souldiers with slashes and skarrs
That never used drinkeinge in noe time of warrs,
Nor sheddinge of blood in madd drunken Jarrs?
    And is not ould England growne new!

And what is become of your Bills and your Bowes,
Your Bucklers and Targetts that never feard blowes?
They'r turnd to stillatoes and other vaine showes.
    And is not ould England growne new?

New Captaines are come that never did Fight
But with Potts in the daie and Puncks in the night—
And all ther chieff caire is to keepe ther swords bright!
    And is not ould England growne new?

Wher are your ould Courttiers that used to ryde
With forty blewe coates and footmen beside?
They'r turn'd to six horses, a coach with a guyde!
    And is not ould England growne new?

And what is become of your ould fashiond clothes,
Your longsided Dublett and your trunck hose?
They'r turn'd to new fashions—but what the Lord knowes!
    And is not ould England growne new?

Now your gallaint and his tayllor some halfe yeare together
To fitt a new sute to a new hatt and fether,
Of gould or of silver, silke, cloth stuff, or lether.
    And is not ould England growne new?

You have new fashon'd Beards and new fashon'd locks
And new fashon's hatts for new pated blocks,
And moor new diseases besides the French Pox!
    And is not ould England growne new?

New Fashons in houses, new Fashons at table,
The ould servants discharged, the new are moor able;
And every ould custome is but an ould fable!
    And is not ould England growne new?

New trickings, new goeings, new measurs, new paces,
New hedds for your men, for women new faces;
And twenty new tricks to mend ther bad cases!
    And is not ould England growne new?

New houses are built and the ould ones pull'd downe,
Untill the new houses sell all the ould ground,
And then the house stands like a horse in a pounde!
    And is not ould England growne new?

New tricks in the Law, new leases, new houlds,
New bodies they have—they look for new soules
When the mony is payde all for buildinge ould Powles!
    And is not ould England growne new?

Then talke you noe more of New England!
New England is wher ould England did stand,
Newe furnnishd, newe fashond, new woman'd, new man'd
    And is not ould England growne newe![1]

Political conditions were even worse than the social. The horizon was darkly overcast with clouds of the counter-reformation. Bishop Laud is the King's right-hand man. Conformity is the order of the day. Preachers and lecturers are silenced, sermons forbidden, and all ministers who will not wear a surplice, genuflect, and make an altar of the communion table, are under suspicion. The Queen is a Catholic. Discreet Papal emissaries and sleek Catholic chaplains swarm at court. The King refuses to lift a finger to help his Protestant brother-in-law the Elector Palatine. Spanish infantry under Wallenstein overrun the Palatinate, Cardinal Richelieu destroys the power of the French Huguenots; yet the English government has not a word to say. Putting these things together, how could an English puritan doubt that his country had been caught in the backwash of the Catholic reaction, that the days of Queen Mary would return, and once more the flesh of Protestant martyrs would roast at Smithfield?

A crisis came in the spring of 1629: Parliament is always puritan; so King Charles shall govern without Parliament. March 2.

---

[1] Bodleian Library, Ashmole MSS., XXXVI, 37.

The day of the three resolutions declaring every supporter of High Church and royal prerogative a capital enemy to this Kingdom and Commonwealth, resolutions passed with a tumult of ayes, and the usher of the Black Rod thundering at the door, and speaker Finch held down in his chair, so he will not end the session. The Royal Guard breaks in, carries off the puritan leaders to the tower, and for eleven years King Charles governs without a parliament.

John Winthrop, as a known puritan, loses his attorneyship at the Court of Wards and Liveries, but that is the least of his troubles. 'My dear Wife,' he writes on May 15, 1629, 'I am verily persuaded, God will bringe some heavye Affliction upon this lande, and that speedylye; but be of good comfort . . . If the Lord seeth it wilbe good for us, he will provide a shelter & a hidinge place for us and others, as a Zoar for Lott, Sarephtah for his prophet; if not, yet he will not forsake us.'

2. THE TRANSFER OF THE CHARTER

For some time, several prominent puritans of Lincolnshire have been talking of emigrating to New England. The social center of this group is Tattershall, the seat of the Earl of Lincoln, near Sempringham and Boston. John Humfry, treasurer of the old Dorchester adventurers, is the person who, with Master John White of Dorchester, has aroused the interest of this nucleus, and in the course of his negotiations Humfry marries Lady Sarah Fiennes, the Earl's daughter. Other members of the group are Isaac Johnson, a wealthy landowner of Rutland, and husband to Lady Arbella Fiennes; Thomas Dudley of Northampton, former captain of English volunteers under Henry of Navarre, lately a devoted parishioner of John Cotton at Boston, and sometime steward to the Earl of Lincoln; his successor in that office, a young Cambridge graduate named Simon Bradstreet, who is about to marry Dudley's daughter Anne. Thomas Leverett, alderman of Boston, and Richard Bellingham, recorder of the borough, are probably also of their circle of friends. Several are members of the Governor and Company of the Massachusetts Bay. Why not transfer the charter and government of the Company to the soil of New England, and make it the framework of a puritan commonwealth?

Such a thing had never been done before, but why not now? The

Massachusetts Bay Company was a joint-stock corporation, organized very much as business corporations are to-day. The stockholders or freemen chose the president and board of directors—there called Governor and Assistants—to manage the company's affairs. Freemen and officers met quarterly in a Great and General Court, to choose officers and keep track of the Company's business. The Company's offices are in London; the colony at Salem is subordinate to them, just as British India, for almost two hundred years, was subordinate to the General Court of the East India Company in London. In the Massachusetts Bay charter, no mention was made of the place where the company must hold its meetings. Whether by accident, or by greasing the palm of some government clerk who drafted the document, this important proviso was left out. The puritan leaders must have read, in Captain John Smith's works if not elsewhere, how annoying it was for colonists to be subject to meddlesome orders and instructions from English business men who knew nothing about American conditions. And every one remembered that the Virginia charter had been confiscated in 1624, because it was in London where the Crown could lay hands on it.

Whoever conceived this idea of transferring the charter, it was not Winthrop. Either the London group of stockholders—Saltonstall, Eaton, and their friends—or the Lincolnshire group, was responsible. When they came to discuss the transfer, it appeared that Matthew Cradock, the Governor of the Company, could not or would not emigrate, although he would and did provide money generously. Nor would any Assistant take the governorship. The principal persons who wished to emigrate with the charter agreed that the one man for that position was John Winthrop, and that without him they would not go.

However justified this decision was, it is still a mystery why Winthrop should have been selected as the leader. He was not a member of the Massachusetts Bay Company, nor related to any member. In the affairs of his county he does not appear to have been more prominent than any other squire or magistrate. But as attorney at the Court of Wards and Liveries, with an extensive clientage among county families, his acquaintance was wide; and we may therefore infer that the 'chief Undertakers' of the transfer had been impressed by his character and ability.

It took Winthrop some time to make up his mind. Fortunately we can follow the arguments, pro and con as they presented themselves to him, and to others. One or more papers, with arguments for and against emigration, were circulated among leading puritans. John White had a copy, Winthrop a second, and Sir John Eliot a third, which John Hampden asked to borrow. Whether White or Winthrop had the larger share in drafting these papers is uncertain; but the most detailed copy, containing 'Particular Considerations in the case of J: W:'[2] is found among Winthrop's papers, together with a letter from his friend and neighbor Robert Ryece, combating the idea of emigration. The gist of Ryece's arguments was that English puritans should stick together, and that Winthrop was too elderly (forty-one!) and gentle for the task. 'The Church and Common welthe heere . . . hathe more neede of your beste abyllytie in these dangerous tymes then any remote plantation.' 'Plantations ar for yonge men, that can enduer all paynes and hunger.' 'How harde wyll it bee for one browghte up amonge boockes and learned men to lyve in a barbarous place, where there is no learnynge and less cyvillytie.' And finally, he quoted John Smith's History of Virginia, to prove that good order was hard to maintain in a new settlement, and gospel order impossible.

Winthrop, like men in every age who felt the urge to pioneer, was not to be turned aside by timorous and prudent considerations. He felt an inward call to New England, which he was candid enough to admit came in part from personal ambition. For some years, one infers, Winthrop had felt a longing for some greater public service than his attorneyship and the local magistracy. He had drafted petitions to Parliament, and very likely had looked forward to becoming a member at the next election; but the King had decided to summon no more parliaments. 'If he should refuse this opportunitye' for New England, writes Winthrop of himself, 'that talent which God hath bestowed upon him for publike service, were like to be buried.' His means were straitened by losing his attorneyship, by half the family estate going to his boys; and keeping up with the Joneses of that day was repugnant to him, as we have seen. Mistress Winthrop and their three grown sons were keen to go. But beyond these personal considerations, Winthrop was deeply apprehensive of the future, in view of the recent fate

---

[2] Not John White, as the arguments used could not have been applied to his circumstances.

of Protestant churches in Europe, and disgusted with social conditions at home. He longed to get away from the 'Ould England grown newe' of the ballad, from corruption in almost every phase of English life; to found a New England that would preserve the waning virtues of the old. This opportunity to lead a colony and shape it according to the word of God, was not one to be lost. He accepted the governorship.

The Massachusetts Bay Company, in the meantime, was holding its meetings in London, at the house of Governor Cradock or Deputy-Governor Goffe. At a General Court on July 28, 1629, 'Mr. Governour reade certain proposicions conceived by himselfe, that for the advancement of the plantacion, the inducing and encouraging persons of worth and qualitie to transplant themselves and famylyes thether, and for other weighty reasons therein contained,—to transferr the government of the plantacion to those that shall inhabite there, and not to continue the same in subordination to the Company heer, as now it is. This business occasioned some debate,' and the decision was postponed to the next General Court.

On the same day that this discussion was going on in London, John Winthrop and his brother-in-law Emmanuel Downing were riding north from Groton to visit the Lincoln family seat. His horse got into a soft spot in the fen country, and gave the future Governor a bad ducking; but fortunately he did not construe this accident as an omen of disaster. At Tattershall the whole question was threshed out with Johnson, Humfry, and Dudley. These three accompanied Winthrop on his return journey. At Cambridge they met Increase Nowell and William Pynchon, stockholders who had been at the Company meeting, together with Saltonstall and William Vassall, who also were officers of the Company. I like to imagine that they met in some room of Emmanuel College, where Isaac Johnson had graduated and one of his brothers was still a student, together with Sir Richard Saltonstall's son and two sons of Thomas Dudley; and where John Harvard was just finishing his freshman year. On August 26, 1629, they signed and dated at Cambridge a compact, which with the Charter is the basis of the Commonwealth of Massachusetts.

It is fully and faithfully agreed amongst us, . . . that . . . we will be ready in our persons . . . to embarke for the said plantation by the first of March next, . . . to the end to passe the seas (under God's protection) to inhabite and continue in New England. *Provided always,* that before the last of September next the whole government together with the patent for the said plantation be first by an order of court legally transferred and established to remain with us and others which shall inhabite upon the said plantation.

Six signers of this Cambridge Agreement reached London in time for the meeting of the General Court on August 29, summoned to decide upon the question of removal. After a long debate, say the records, Deputy-Governor Goffe put it to the question, as followeth: 'As many of you as desire to have the pattent and the government of the plantacion to be transferred to New England, soe as it may bee done legally, hold up your hands. So many as will not, hold upp *your* hands.' The ayes had it.

After this momentous decision events moved rapidly toward the founding of the Massachusetts colony. At a General Court on October 20, 1629, 'having received of extraordinary great commendacions of Mr. John Wynthrop, both for his integritie and sufficiencie, as being one every [way] well fitted and accomplished for the place of Governour,' he was so elected for the ensuing year.

Under Winthrop's lead in East Anglia, Saltonstall's in London, and White's in the West Country, preparations for the voyage moved so rapidly that the first ship sailed in February, 1630, and fourteen vessels of the fleet had cleared from England by June. In view of the long time it takes nowadays to prepare even a naval conference or a tercentennial, it seems almost incredible that in the slow-moving days of horse and sail, when even good roads were wanting, when the beef for a long voyage had to be bought on the hoof, and the corn on the stalk, only nine months were required to assemble sixteen vessels all found and sound, and a thousand colonists prepared in mind, body and estate for a fresh start in the New World. One would think that nine months would have been little enough, in that newspaperless age, even to make known the transfer proposition. It was, wrote one of these pioneers in his old age, 'as if a Royal Herald, through our Nation from Berwick to Cornwall had made Proclamation to summon and muster up volunteers to appear in New England for His Sacred Majesties Service, there to attend further orders.' Surely the proposed emigration had long been discussed in every puritan center; and, owing to the bad turn of events in church and state, thousands of puritans were 'r'aring to go.'

Almost the entire financial burden was shouldered by the actual colonists, so that the future planters would not suffer as the Pilgrim Fathers had, from servitude to English merchants. Members of the Company who did not wish to emigrate resigned whatever office in the Company they might hold; and Winthrop persuaded them not to withdraw their subscriptions from the joint stock, which was used for ships, supplies, and free passage for poor but desirable emigrants.

At this point I cannot refrain from quoting the English historian, Arthur Percival Newton, who has made English colonization his lifelong study:

> The Massachusetts migration was an event entirely without precedent in the modern world; Virginia, Newfoundland, and Guiana had attracted merely the adventurers and the needy; the Mayflower pilgrims, though later ages have glorified them, were too few in number, too humble in station, and too far removed from the main currents of English life to be of importance; but now sober, well-to-do men of middle age, to whom the spirit of adventure was entirely foreign, were contemplating a transfer of themselves, their families, and their goods to new homes across the seas, there to found not a colony, but a commonwealth. . . . Winthrop and White, guided as they felt by a Higher Power, were resolved upon a course that was new. The men of the future had their way and the great human stream was directed to the New England shore.

If the leaders of the Bay Colony were idealists, their handling of the practical details shows that they were no strangers to big business. The West Country emigrants embarked from Bristol and Plymouth; those from East Anglia, London, the Home Counties and the Midlands, from Southampton. Thus it was hoped to avoid the usual detention at the Downs, consuming stores and breeding sickness, while waiting for an easterly breeze. Master John Cotton, Vicar of St. Botolph's church at Boston, who accompanied the Lincolnshire group to Southampton, there preached the farewell

sermon on the text of 2 Samuel VII, 10: 'Moreover I will appoint
a place for my people Israel, and will plant them, that they may
dwell in a place of their own, and move no more; neither shall
the children of wickedness afflict them any more, as beforetime.'

A most interesting and significant sermon it was, striking the
notes of faith, learning, conversion, public spirit, and righteous-
ness, which make the puritan scale. Master Cotton must have made
the hearts of his hearers swell with that radiant joy that comes to
the devout of every faith, when they feel that God is with them.
He rehearsed all the arguments for the New England colony, which
we have already heard. He begged the emigrants to take root in
the ordinances of God, when the Lord would make them a fruitful
vineyard. 'Goe forth, every man that goeth, with a publick spirit,'
with that 'care of universall helpfulnesse' which was so strong in
the primitive church. 'Have a tender care . . . to your children,
that they doe not degenerate as the Israelites did.' 'Offend not the
poore Natives, but as you partake in their land, so make them
partakers of your precious faith.' And forget not Old England:—
'Oh pray for the peace of Jerusalem, they shall prosper that love
her. . . . Forget not the wombe that bore you and the breasts that
gave you sucke. Even ducklings hatched under an henne, though
they take the water, yet will still have recourse to the wing that
hatched them: how much more should chickens of the same feather,
and yolke?'

It is pleasant to record that the point pressed home with this
farmyard simile, has penetrated so deeply that this year Bostonians
of New England are helping to restore the stately church of St.
Botolph, where John Cotton served before he emigrated.

Cotton's sermon was of a nature to inspire these new children
of Israel with the belief that they were the Lord's chosen people;
destined, if they kept the covenant with him, to people and fructify
this new Canaan in the western wilderness.

What hee hath planted he will maintaine. Every plantation
his right hand hath not planted shalbe rooted up, but his owne
plantation shall prosper and flourish. When he promiseth peace
and safety, what enemies shall be able to make the promise of
God of none effect? Neglect not walls and bulwarkes, and fortifications for your owne defence; but ever let the Name of the

Lord be your strong Tower; and the word of his Promise, the Rocke of your Refuge. His word that made heaven and earth will not faile, till heaven and earth be no more.

In the course of the voyage, Governor Winthrop delivered a sermon entitled A Model of Christian Charity, in which he struck with even greater emphasis the note of public spirit already sounded by John Cotton; and called it by the deeper and better name of Love. 'We are a company,' he said, 'professing ourselves fellow members of Christ,' for which reason though we come from many regions and divers classes, 'we ought to account ourselves knitt together by this bond of love.' Our immediate object is to seek out a new home 'under a due forme of Government both civill and ecclesiasticall.' Hence 'the care of the publique must oversway all private respects. . . . The end is to improve our lives to do more service to the Lord . . . that ourselves and posterity may be the better preserved from the common corruptions of this evil world.'

How may this be effected? First and foremost by love. 'Wee must love brotherly without dissimulation; wee must love one another with a pure hearte fervently. We must bear one another's burdens.' For 'we are entered into a covenant' with God 'for this worke. We have taken out a Commission; the Lord hath given us leave to draw our own Articles . . . If the Lord shall please to heare us, and bring us in peace to the place wee desire, then hath hee ratified this Covenant and sealed our Commissions, [and] will expect a strict performance of the Articles contained in it.' But if we fail him, 'the Lord will surely breake out in wrathe against us.'

Now the onely way to avoyde this shipwracke, and to provide for our posterity, is to followe the counsell of Micah, to doe justly, to love mercy, to walke humbly with our God. For this end, wee must be knitt together in this work as one man . . . Soe shall wee keepe the unitie of the spirit in the bond of peace . . . Wee shall finde that the God of Israell is among us, when tenn of us shall be able to resist a thousand of our enemies; when hee shall make us a prayse and glory that men shall say of succeeding plantations, 'the lord make it like that of NEW ENG-LAND.' For wee must Consider that wee shall be as a Citty upon a hill. The eies of all people are uppon Us, soe that if wee shall deale falsely with our god in this worke wee have undertaken, and soe cause him to withdrawe his present help from us, wee shall be made a story and a by-word through the world . . . Therefore lett us choose life, that wee and our seede may live by obeyeing his voyce and cleaveing to him, for hee is our life and our prosperity.

Herein is the clearest statement we have of the principles that guided the leaders of the Bay Colony, and their conception of the sort of commonwealth they were to found. It explains much that followed, both good and bad, in the early history of Massachusetts. We need not expect men who believe that they have a commission directly from God, to be eager to share their responsibility or power with others. We should not look to them to be tolerant of other points of view, to suffer the foxes to spoil the vines which they have tenderly planted. The rights of the individual they will hold as nothing in the scales against the public interest, as they conceive it. King Charles I, too, believed in his divine commission. John Winthrop will serve his people according to his lights, and serve them well; but he will make some of the same mistakes as those of his sovereign.

From the high seriousness of this sermon, we may turn to the tender affection in John Winthrop's farewell letter to his wife, who remained behind to care for Groton Manor until it could be sold.

My faithful and dear wife,—It pleaseth God, that thou shouldst once againe heare from me before our departure, and I hope this shall come safe to thy hands, I know it wilbe a great refreshinge to thee. And blessed be his mercye, that I can write thee so gud newes, that we are all in verye gud health, and, havinge tryed our shipps entertainment now more then a weeke, we finde it agree very well with us, our boyes are well and cheerfull, and have no minde of home. They lye both with me, and sleepe as soundly in a rugge (for we use no sheets heer) as ever they did at Groton; and soe I doe my selfe, (I prayse God). the winde hath been against us this weeke and more; but this day it is come faire to the North, so as we are preparinge (by Gods assistance) to sett sayle in the morninge . . . And now (my sweet soule) I must once againe take my last farewell of thee in old England, It goeth verye neere to my heart to leave thee;

but I know to whom I have committed thee, even to him who loves the much better that any husband can . . . and (if it be for his glorye) will bringe us togither againe with peace and comfort. oh, how it refreseheth my heart, to thinke, that I shall yet againe see thy sweet face in the lande of the livinge— that lovely countenance, that I have so much delighted in, and beheld with so great contente! . . . I hope, the course we have agreed upon wilbe some ease to us both. mundayes and frydayes, at 5: of the clocke at night, we shall meet in spiritt till we meet in person. yet, if all these hopes should faile, blessed be our God, that we are assured we shall meet one day, if not as husband and wife, yet in a better condition, let that staye and comfort thy heart. neither can the sea drowne thy husband, nor enemyes destroye, nor any adversity deprive thee of thy husband or children. therefore I will onley take thee now and my sweet children in mine armes, and kisse and embrace you all, and so leave you with my God. Farewell, farewell . . .

Thine wheresoever   JO: WINTHROP.

from Aboard the Arbella,
  rydinge at the Cowes march 28, 1630.

Winthrop's journal, the most precious chronicle of the Bay Colony, begins the next day with this entry: 'Easter Monday. Riding at the Cowes, near the Isle of Wight, in the *Arbella,* a ship of three hundred and fifty tons, whereof Capt. Peter Milbourne was master, being manned with fifty-two seamen, and twenty-eight pieces of ordnance.' She was a stout, well-found ship, larger than the average emigrant vessel, and as the *Eagle* had seen hard service as a privateer of Sir Kenelm Digby. She was the admiral or flagship of a fleet of four (the *Talbot, Ambrose,* and *Jewel*) which decided to set forth together, leaving the other seven to follow as soon as might be. The last Court of Assistants of the Company to be held in England, had a few days before assembled in the *Arbella's* cabin. Winds came westerly, and it was ten days more before they got clear of the Isle of Wight; as late as April 6 ex-Governor Cradock came aboard at Yarmouth for a farewell visit, and was given a parting salute from the ship's battery. The next day, presumably, Master John White arrived to get his 'Humble Request' signed 'on the dotted line'; since that charming if somewhat deceptive farewell to the Reverend Brethren of the Church of England is dated 'from Yarmouth aboord the *Arbella,* April 7, 1630.' The Lady Arbella Johnson herself was on board, with the Squire her husband; as well as Master George Phillips, who became the first minister of Watertown, the Saltonstall, Dudley, and Bradstreet families, William Pynchon, with some score of humbler folk, and numerous horses and cattle. Even the family dogs were not forgotten, for we hear of a settler the next winter, swapping his pup with an Indian for a peck of corn. It is not likely that they brought much furniture other than a favorite chair or two; for there would have been no room for massive court cupboards or four-posters, and no economy in bringing tables and settles which could easily be made from New England pine. But there must have been many household utensils in pottery, pewter, iron, brass, and silver, irreplaceable in a new country.

We may suppose that the voyage was a 'pious and Christian-like passage' such as Higginson had enjoyed the year before on the *Talbot,* with morning and evening prayer, two sermons every Sabbath, and the watches changed 'with singing a psalm, and prayer that was *not* read out of a book.'

There was plenty of excitement as well, since war was still on with France. Many other vessels were sighted, and some were spoken. The *Arbella* was cleared for action when eight sail, supposed to be corsairs of Dunkirk, hove in sight. Cannon were well charged, women and children placed amidships, while each man ground his cutlass to a razor edge and prepared for rough work. On the return voyage three of the Winthrop fleet 'were set upon by Dunkirkers' in the English Channel, and badly mauled; but on this occasion the ships proved to be peaceable merchantmen. Later a small Frenchman scuttled off before the wind when the *Arbella* put forth her 'ancient' (ensign), and the *Jewel* and *Ambrose* almost picked a quarrel with a friendly Dutchman, thinking him French. Two ships were spoken bound for Quebec, which the English had taken the previous summer; and Captain Milbourne went aboard for a conference.

Transatlantic voyages were unpleasant at best, in the short-ended high-pooped vessels of that day: six to twelve weeks tossing at sea amid the effluvia of men and cattle in crowded quarters; but the voyage of the *Arbella,* by Winthrop's account, was better than the average. Three of the four ships were usually within sight and hail, so that boats passed back and forth in calm weather, dinners were exchanged, and on one important occasion the *Arbella* borrowed a midwife from the *Jewel*. There was plenty of fun aboard. After the first gale a line was stretched from the steerage to the mainmast, and the seasick who 'lay groaning in the cabins' were fetched out on deck and required to 'sway it up and down till they were warm, and by this means they soon grew well and merry.' Games and horse-play with the seamen kept the young people's minds off their stomachs, and they 'gave themselves to drink hot waters very immoderately.' A maid-servant took so much of this seasick cure that she passed out, and all but away. After passing Cape Sable they were becalmed in thirty fathoms, so the *Arbella* was hove to 'and took, in less than two hours, with a few hooks, sixty-seven codfish, most of them very great fish, some a yard and a half long, and a yard in compass.' Did the Governor consult his conscience as well as his yardstick before he handed down that yarn to posterity?

On June 8, just two months out, the *Arbella,* now alone, raised the bald summits of Mount Desert. It was one of those heaven-sent June days in the Gulf of Maine, with clear sunshine, light fleecy clouds, and an off-shore wind: 'so pleasant a sweet air as did much refresh us, and there came a smell off the shore like the smell of a garden.' The *Arbella* proceeded cautiously, picking up landmarks like the Camden Hills. On June 10, Cape Porpoise and Agamenticus were sighted, and Boon Island weathered. The next day she stood off and on between Cape Ann and the Isles of Shoals, waiting for a southwest gale to moderate. In the night Cape Ann was weathered, and at daybreak on June 12 Marblehead loomed up on the western horizon. The *Arbella* fired two guns, sent her fast rowing skiff ahead, and received a visit from Isaac Allerton, on his way down east in a fishing shallop. Then with colors streaming and sails bellying to a light easterly breeze, she fanned through the main ship channel between Baker's Island and Little Misery, a stately and beautiful sight. Having reached good shelter and holding ground off Mingo Beach or Plum Cove, she came to an anchor for the first time since leaving soundings in the channel of old England.

Governor Endecott came aboard in the early afternoon, to learn that he was no longer governor; and while the gentry were rowed three miles to Salem, to sup on 'a good Venison pasty and good beer' the rest of the passengers landed on the near-by Beverly shore to feast on delicious wild strawberries, a heaven-sent refreshment after eight weeks of ship diet. The next day Masconomo, sagamore of Agawam, came aboard to pay his respects and see what he could pick up; and on June 14 the *Arbella* was warped up Beverly Harbor to a final anchorage in the North River, then Salem's front door.

The *Lion* was already there, the *Mary and John* had dumped her passengers at Nantasket; and one by one the rest of the fleet straggled in—the *Talbot* taking three months, and losing fourteen passengers. By the end of the summer almost a thousand people and two hundred head of cattle had been landed. The Bay Colony was already thrice as populous as New Plymouth, founded ten years earlier.

A preliminary exploration convinced Winthrop and the Assistants of the Company that Boston Bay should be the center of population and government rather than Salem. Charlestown, where a settlement had been started under Endecott's order the year before, was selected as the temporary capital. In the old minute book of the Massachusetts Bay Company, following the record of the last Court of Assistants held in England on March 23, 1630, there comes, in Simon Bradstreet's hand, that of the first Court of Assistants held on the soil of Massachusetts, at Charlestown on August 23. Governor Winthrop, Deputy-Governor Dudley, Sir Richard Saltonstall, Roger Ludlow, Edward Rossiter, Increase Nowell, Thomas Sharpe, William Pynchon, and Simon Bradstreet, made up this first political assembly; and their first item of business was to provide house and maintenance for two ministers, George Phillips and John Wilson.

The transfer of the charter was completed; the trading company of the Massachusetts Bay was dead; the Commonwealth of Massachusetts was born.

3. GOVERNOR OF THE MASSACHUSETTS

To tell the story of the rest of John Winthrop's life would be to relate the history of the Bay Colony until his death in 1649. During nine of those nineteen years he was properly addressed as 'The Right Worshipful John Winthrop, Esquire, Governour of the Massachusetts'; and during the other ten years he served as

Deputy-Governor or Assistant. At all times he was a most devoted public servant, neglecting his private affairs to the ruin of his estate, and during the critical first winter his faith, energy, and steadfastness kept the colony together.

Governor Winthrop intended to form a compact settlement protected by a fort, at Newtowne (Cambridge); but the multitude proved too great for him to shepherd into one fold. There were many pleasant places on the harbor, and along the winding valleys of the Charles and Mystic. Medford, Watertown, Roxbury, Dorchester, and Lynn were founded before the winter set in. Owing to lack of fresh water at Charlestown, several of the magnates accepted an invitation of William Blaxton of Beacon Hill, a solitary survivor of the Gorges colony, to move over to Shawmut or Trimountain; and the Court of Assistants 'ordered that Trimountaine shalbe called Boston' on September 7. The first General Court summoned since the transfer of the charter was held there the following month in order to reëlect the officers, whose terms had expired.

During the first winter there was much sickness and suffering. The people arrived too late to plant a crop, and the months that followed were critical indeed. Busy months for Winthrop, but sad, for his son Henry was drowned shortly after the arrival, and some of his nearest and dearest friends fell victims to disease and hardship. Endecott's plantation at Salem had been weakened from sickness, and had little provision to spare. The Indians' supplies were inadequate; and though Samuel Maverick, the Episcopalian proprietor of Winnesimmet, 'a man of very loving and curteous behaviour, very ready to entertaine strangers,' did what he could, there was a limit to the hospitality that he and the old planters could offer. So the people lived largely on the salt junk and hardtack left over from the voyage. One hundred and eighty indented servants had to be turned loose to fend for themselves.

'It was not accounted a strange thing in those days to drink water, and to eat samp or hominy without butter or milk,' remembered Roger Clap. Smelt, clams, and mussels kept many from actual starvation; but the Englishman of that period considered himself starving without beef, bread and beer; and even to-day, if you will try a steady diet of shellfish and spring water for a week, you may feel some sympathy for these puritan colonists bereft of

their stout British fare. Scurvy set in, and a contagious fever, probably typhus. Young Lady Arbella died, and her husband Isaac
Johnson, not yet thirty: 'a holy man and wise, and died in sweet
peace, leaving some part of his substance to the colony.' He was
buried in what is now the King's Chapel burying ground in Boston;
and such love had he inspired among the people in the short
months he had been with them, that for years after Bostonians
would direct that their bodies might be laid as near his as might
be. Biting cold set in Christmas Eve; and many of the people were
yet inadequately housed, living and dying in bark wigwams or
sailcloth tents, 'soe that almost in every family, lamentation, mourning and woe was heard, and no fresh food to be had to cherish
them.'

We are fortunate to have the 'low-down' on the situation, in a
letter from a Suffolk yeoman to his father.

> Her is good stor of feishe ife we had botes to goo 8 or 10
> leges to sea to feishein. her are good stor of weield foule but
> they ar hard to come bye. It is hardur to get a shoot then it is
> in ould eignland . . . The cuntrey is not so as we ded expecte
> it tharefor lovinge father I wolld intret you that you woolld
> send me a ferckeine of buttr & a hogseit of mault onground for
> we dreinck notheinge but walltre . . . we do not know how longe
> we may subseiste for we can not live her witheought provis-
> seyenes from ould eignland . . . beseides God hath tacken away
> the chefeiste stud in the land, Mr Johnson & the ladye arabella
> his wife wiche wase the cheiffeste man of estate in the land &
> on that woold a don moste good.

There was much discontent among the common sort, who found
it more difficult to adjust themselves than the gentry, and were
probably less moved by religious motives. The hired servants made
trouble, as they always do in a new country. One such named
Ratcliffe, for 'foul, scandalous invectives against our church and
government,' was whipped, cropped, and was banished, *pour en-
courager les autres*. Similar punishment, together with branding
and life imprisonment, was at the time being inflicted by Star
Chamber for like utterances against Laud.

The month of February, 1631, just before this discouraging

letter was written, was the worst time. According to the writer there was some bad profiteering: £5 for a pig and £3 for a goat, but there was charity as well. The Governor gave freely of what he had. His last batch of bread was in the oven, and his last handful of meal given away to a poor man, when a relief ship appeared. This was the *Lion,* which the Governor had prudently sent back to Bristol for provisions; and which had been well stocked by the devoted efforts of John White and other friends of the colony. Her arrival was the occasion for a February thanksgiving day. She brought a quantity of lemon juice which cured the scurvy, and her cargo of grain, peas and barrelled beef was distributed among the several towns, at the Company's charge. Another ship with corn from Virginia, and one or two from Ireland, with all kind of provision, ended the shortage by planting time, and a good crop was put in that spring. Many discouraged settlers returned in these ships, and of them 'many died by the way and after they were landed.'

Only a few hundred persons came to Massachusetts Bay in 1631 and 1632, but the following year the full tide of the Great Emigration set in; Boston harbor frequently contained ten or a dozen ships at a time bearing recruits for the puritan Canaan. For in 1633 William Laud, from a position of great influence, was promoted to one of great power as well—the Archbishopric of Canterbury. Ritualism was now forced on every parish, puritan tracts were suppressed, more puritan lecturers silenced, and the gentry forbidden to keep chaplains. Archbishop Laud was even more efficient than the Massachusetts authorities proved to be, in enforcing a superficial uniformity. He succeeded in stopping up every hole, save emigration, through which puritan feeling could find vent; so many puritans emigrated and others bided their time. By 1643 there were a score of towns and churches in the jurisdiction of Massachusetts Bay, with over sixteen thousand people, more than all the rest of English America put together.

Edward Johnson in his 'Wonder Working Providence of Sions Saviour in New England' computes the total cost of this Great Emigration as £192,000—in purchasing power equivalent to something between ten and twenty million dollars to-day. The original stockholders of the Company contributed a small part of this sum, charitable persons gave much; but the most was paid out by the settlers themselves. 'Gentle Reader,' asks Johnson, 'where had this poore people this great sum of money? the mighty Princes of the Earth never opened their Coffers for them, and the generality of these men were meane and poore in the things of this life, but sure it is the work is done, let God have the glory, who hath now given them food to the full, and some to spare for other Churches.'

The transfer of the charter did not give the Bay Colony a completely workable government; only a bare framework, and practical independence. Fourteen years were required for the complete evolution of the government from that of trading corporation to commonwealth. The government thus established was not a democracy, and was not intended to be; but the puritan builders left out of their foundations two principles of government, the feudal and the hereditary, upon which democracy had always found it difficult to raise a house. They made no attempt to establish manors, as did the proprietors of Carolina, Maryland, and New York. Nor did they admit the least hereditary element into their government. In 1635 Lord Say and Sele, Lord Brook, and other persons of quality in the puritan party proposed, as the conditions of their removal, that the commonwealth of Massachusetts should consist of two ranks of men, gentlemen and freeholders, the former constituting an hereditary colonial House of Lords, and the latter electing a House of Commons. The Massachusetts magistrates wanted badly such men as these. Like other Englishmen they dearly loved a lord, especially when he combined social eminence with puritan orthodoxy. They instructed John Cotton to reply in the name of the government, that although it was the custom of the country—a country barely six years old!—to regard such men as the gentry, as well as 'others of meaner estate' who showed their worth; and although the Colony would be glad to elect to office any member of a 'noble or generous family with a spirit and gifts fit for government,' yet 'if God should not delight to furnish some of their posterity with gifts fit for magistracy' it would not be proper 'if we should call them forth, when God hath not, to public authority.' Their lordships took the hint, and did not emigrate.

However, the point of departure for this rejection of the heredity principle was not democracy, but godliness. As we have seen from Winthrop's shipboard sermon, the leaders of the emigration, already invested with authority as Assistants of the Company, conceived that they had a divine commission to govern the Colony according to gospel ordinance. They did not propose to share this authority any further than circumstances required. The charter, to be sure, established a definite form of government and definite days of election: the Governor, Deputy-Governor and eighteen Assistants must be annually elected by the General Court, consisting of all freemen or stockholders of the Corporation; and the freemen, in General Court, had the supreme legislative power. But what is a charter between friends? It so happened that no freeman of the Company who was not also an Assistant, crossed in the Winthrop fleet. Hence the first government assembly on the American side of the Atlantic was a Court of Assistants at Charlestown. This court took a very important step to enhance its power individually and collectively. It appointed six of its nine members to be magistrates or judges, 'in all things to have the like power that justices of the peace hath in England for reformacion of abuses and punishing of offenders,' and it soon became the practice to consider every Assistant, when elected, a magistrate *ex officio*.[3] At the next meeting of the Court of Assistants it assumed supreme judicial power, in sentencing Thomas Morton to deportation. At the first meeting of the General Court, consisting of exactly six Assistants beside the two chief magistrates, it was decided, in direct violation of charter terms, that the Governor and Deputy-Governor be elected out of the Assistants, by the Assistants. In other words, the first Board of Assistants, not one half of the legal number, arrogated to themselves complete legislative, executive, and judicial power. And for the first four years of the settlement they exercised it.

This governing oligarchy, with Winthrop at its head, showed a keen political sense in knowing when and how far to yield its power; and every concession had to be purchased at a heavy price. The first was in the matter of extending the body of freemen, who annually elected the Assistants. At the meeting of the General Court in October, 1630, over one hundred settlers, both old planters and new, demanded the franchise. Winthrop saw perfectly well

---

[3] For this reason I shall follow the seventeenth-century practice of using the terms Assistant and Magistrate interchangeably.

that they could not be denied. Accordingly these and a few others
were enfranchised the following May. But at the same time the
Court declared that no one in future could be a freeman or voter,
unless a church member. And a church member, as understood
by the polity already established in Salem, meant not merely a
church goer, or member of a parish, but a communicant, admitted
only after he had satisfied the brethren that he was one of the
'visible saints.' Thus the electors were limited to God's elect: a
logical restriction for the Bible Commonwealth that Winthrop
intended to found. 'Do ye not know that the Saints shall judge
the world? (I. Cor. VI, 2),' as John Cotton observed to Lord Say
and Sele, 'and Solomon maketh it the joy of a commonwealth,
when the righteous are in authority.'

This ghostly qualification for the franchise lasted until 1664,
though it did not apply to local government after 1647, or to the
portions of Maine and New Hampshire annexed to Massachusetts
Bay between 1639 and 1658. Church-member suffrage was the
rock on which the Bible Commonwealth was built; and the only
movement to widen the franchise, the remonstrance of Robert
Child, was promptly suppressed. In a sense, however, this sort
of franchise was democratic, for it made no account of social standing or estate. Many poor men, who needed charity to live, became
freemen because they fulfilled the religious qualification; while
rich men who could not get a church to take them in, were left
without the vote. Narrow as the franchise was, it cut through the
community vertically, not horizontally.

The first body of Visible Saints thus honored with the vote were
not content merely to elect the Assistants. At the annual election
in 1632, the latter were forced to allow them to elect the Governor
and Deputy-Governor as well; and in 1635 they extorted the right
to use secret paper ballots. Grains of Indian corn for the *ayes* and
beans for the *noes* were substituted in 1644 for paper ballots, and
the freemen were encouraged to vote at home in their respective
towns; but they much preferred to vote in person at Boston on the
'last Wednesday in Easter terme' (the day before Ascension) as
the charter prescribed; and Election Day became a sort of spring
holiday for the Colony. The freemen assembled at the town house
(on the site of the Old State House), listened to an election sermon,

dropped their corn or beans or papers in the ballot box, and delivered the sealed-up ballots from the towns to be counted. As the maximum vote cast by this very select electorate was never more than a few hundred, the result was soon announced. The Governor, Deputy-Governor and Assistants for the ensuing year were sworn in, and the Great and General Court opened its session. Spring became so firmly associated with elections in the New England mind, that the date was not essentially changed in Massachusetts until 1831. Even now there is a survival of the old spring election in the anniversary week of the Congregational clergy, and in the annual drumhead election of a commander for the Ancient and Honorable Artillery Company, at Boston Common.

It must not be supposed that this annual election was agreeable to John Winthrop and the Magistrates. It was simply a necessity which the plain terms of the charter, and the wishes of the freemen imposed upon them. John Cotton, who came over in 1633, strongly supported their idea of government as a sacred stewardship, and preached an election sermon to the effect that magistrates once elected should never be defeated save for just cause. The freemen promptly repudiated this doctrine by electing Thomas Dudley governor for the ensuing year. Winthrop put a good face on it, and invited the new governor and assistants to the banquet which had been prepared at his house[4] for a different administration. Magnanimity toward opponents was one of Winthrop's most attractive traits. Roger Williams he attempted to shield, and his friendship retained. In his Journal much evil is recorded in sadness, but nothing in malice. Sir Harry Vane, the figurehead of the Antinomian controversy, 'showed himself a true friend to New England, and a man of noble and generous mind.' Thomas Dudley was 'a very wise and just man, and one that would not be trodden under foot by any man.'

Dudley had the privilege of presiding over the first Massachusetts legislature that contained elected representatives of the freemen, and not merely assistants. This was a serious breach in

---

[4] A few doors down State Street from the Old State House, on the site of the Exchange Building. Later he built a house on the site of the Old South meetinghouse, Washington Street.

the exclusive power of the magistracy. Watertown, which seems
to have contained more upstanding lovers of liberty than any other
of the first settlements, objected to a tax levy made by assistants
alone. Master George Phillips, the minister, and elder Richard
Browne assembled the people and declared 'that it was not safe
to pay moneys after that sort, for fear of bringing themselves and
posterity into bondage.' So soon had the echoes of Runnymede
reached the New England forest. In consequence they were haled
before Winthrop, admonished and silenced, but not convinced.
The Governor and his colleagues, as a gracious concession, then
invited each town to appoint members of an advisory committee
on taxation. The freemen, not to be put off with such chaff, chose
deputies just before the spring election of 1634, and respectfully
requested the Governor to give them a look at the Charter, which
hitherto had been carried about on state occasions in its large
leather-covered case, to impress the populace. (It did not impress
Morton of Merrymount, who declared that the vulgar sort of
people took it for a musical instrument, and guessed that the
Governor had been a fiddler in his youth!) Winthrop yielded.
One can imagine the deputies poring over the parchment, wading
heavily through its redundant phraseology, and finally with a shout
of triumph finding just what they expected to find:

> . . . Greate and Generall Courts of the saide Company: In
> all and every, or any of which saide Greate and Generall Courts
> soe assembled, Wee doe for Us, our heires and successors, give
> and graunte to the said Governor and Company and their suc-
> cessors . . . to make lawes and ordinances for the good and
> welfare of the saide Company, and for the government and
> ordering of the saide landes and plantation, and the people
> inhabiting and to inhabite the same, as to them from tyme to
> tyme shalbe thought meete. soe as such lawes and ordinances
> be not contrarie or repugnant to the lawes and statutes of this
> our realme of England.

That little visit to the Governor's house punctured the legislative
power of the oligarchy. The deputies of the freemen took their
seats in the General Court, sitting as one house with the Assistants,
and pushed through three important resolutions, which may be

said to have founded representative government in Massachusetts Bay:

> That none but the Generall Court hath power to chuse and admitt Freemen.
>
> That none but the Generall Court hath power to make and establishe lawes, nor to elect and appoynct officers . . .
>
> That none but the Generall Court hath power to rayse moneyes and taxes and to dispose of lands. . . .

In the meantime, trouble had begun within the Board of Assistants. It was due to a practice which the puritans believed to be enjoined by the Epistles of St. Paul, of calling each other to account for their faults, and speaking their minds without the tact and reticence usual in personal intercourse among gentlemen. Deputy-Governor Dudley, an energetic old soldier some ten years Winthrop's senior, early became obsessed with the idea that the Governor was too soft, evasive, and lenient. Early in 1632 he offered to resign his position, 'because he must needs discharge his conscience in speaking freely; and he saw that bred disturbance.' The Assistants denied his right to resign, and Winthrop, with amazing tactlessness, proceeded to call his colleague to account for selling seven and a half bushels of corn to poor men, in return for ten to be paid at the next harvest; and for building at Newtowne what he regarded as a luxurious house. 'There arose hot words about it.' Dudley justified himself and called the Governor weak, speeches which (says Winthrop) he bore 'with more patience than . . . upon a like occasion, at another time.'

The storm subsided at dinner, but arose again when Winthrop announced that the time had come to let the freemen choose Governor and Deputy-Governor and not merely the Assistants. At that Roger Ludlow, one of the West Countrymen of Dorchester 'grew into passion, and said that then we should have no government,'—he would return to England if they allowed such a thing. Then another squabble, about the men of Watertown being compelled to watch and ward at Newtowne. 'Thus the day was spent and no good done, which was the more uncomfortable to most of them, because they had commended this meeting to God in more earnest manner than ordinarily at other meetings.' What a New

England small-town flavor the whole session has, even as Winthrop tells it!

Seven days later Dudley consented to withdraw his resignation, 'and the governor and he being reconciled the day before, all things were carried very lovingly amongst all.' But the love did not last long. A little meeting was arranged between the three chief officers, the secretary of the Colony (Increase Nowell), and four ministers. First, the matter of the Governor's removing the frame of his house from Newtowne to Boston, was threshed out. Then Dudley brought in a series of charges to the effect that Winthrop had of his own authority, without vote of the Court of Assistants, lent twenty-eight pounds of powder to Plymouth, had allowed Watertown to erect a fish weir, had allowed the crop-eared and banished Ratcliffe to stay until spring (when a winter departure would have probably lost him his life); and a few similar acts of tyranny. Hot words passed again, counter-charges, and the ministers apparently had some difficulty to restrain these pillars of the state from coming to blows. The best that could be done for the present was to agree to disagree. In the end, however, the two became reconciled over the marriage of their children, and sealed it in a manner that reveals the vein of tenderness in the Puritan heart:

> The governor and deputy went to Concord to view some land for farm, and, going down the river about four miles, they made choice of a place for one thousand acres for each of them . . . The governor yielded him the choice. So, at the place where the Deputy's land was to begin, there were two great stones, which they called the Two Brothers, in remembrance that they were brothers by their children's marriage, and did so brotherly agree, and for that a little creek near those stones was to part their lands.

Canoeists on the placid Concord may still see, on the Bedford side, the two boulders which mark the reconciliation of these founders of the Commonwealth.

If the Assistants' assumed duty to be their brothers' keepers produced unedifying scenes in their worshipful Court, they were as a unit when their collective power was called into question. A very tender point was their assumption of magisterial powers. An incident which Winthrop does not mention in his journal, no doubt because he realized it did him small credit, is in a letter of Israel Stoughton, deputy from Dorchester. When the first deputies were admitted to the General Court, in 1634, the Assistants, by a rather doubtful construction of the Charter, claimed a 'negative voice' or veto on the deputies' decisions, as if an upper house; while the deputies naturally wished to make their superior numbers felt in a unicameral assembly—like the *tiers état* at the opening of the French Revolution. A pro-magisterial sermon by John Cotton bore them down for a time, and the matter rested. Israel Stoughton then drew up a brief against the 'negative voice.' It was passed around among the ministers, and by Cotton sent to Winthrop, then Deputy-Governor. At the next General Court Winthrop, to Stoughton's astonishment, denounced him as a 'worme,' a 'troubler of Israel,' 'an underminder of the state'; and accused him of having declared that the Assistants were ministers with no discretional authority, not magistrates.

Stoughton demanded that his brief be read to disprove the charge. He observed that the meaning had been perverted for want of a comma. Stoughton then read it aloud himself, and brought out what he really had said, that the Assistants' authority was both ministerial and magisterial, but not arbitrary. Nothing would satisfy the Assistants, however, but to have the brief burned. 'Let the booke be burnt if that pleases them,' said Stoughton, and burnt it was. Still the Assistants were not satisfied, Ludlow and Winthrop returning to the charge, and insisted that Stoughton, for sedition, be disqualified for office for three years. The deputies, still somewhat surprised at their own audacity in getting into the General Court, weakly submitted, and Stoughton was disqualified. But general feeling was that both Ludlow and Winthrop had 'too much forgott and over shott' themselves; and in the election of 1636 John Haynes was chosen governor, Ludlow defeated as assistant, and Winthrop chosen to the board by a much reduced vote. 'He is indeed a man of men,' concludes Stoughton. 'But he is but a man; and some say they have idolized him, and do now confesse their error. My opinion is . . . that he is a godly man, and a worthy Magistrate notwithstanding some few passages at which some have stumbled.'

The matter of the negative voice came to a head a few years

later, over the *cause célèbre* of Goody Sherman and her stray sow. This poor widow accused Robert Keayne, a wealthy and grasping merchant, of having impounded her errant swine, and sued him for recovery of lost property. Acquitted in the Court of Assistants, she appealed to the General Court (the supreme judicial as well as the supreme legislative assembly), which voted to reverse the judgment. The Assistants then claimed a negative on the appeal against themselves. The reverend clergy were called into consultation, the whole colony was in an uproar, and a forcible denial of negative voice was only prevented by the eloquence of Winthrop, on the ground that a unicameral legislature would be democratic. 'If we should change from a mixt aristocratie to a mere Democratie, first we should have no warrant in scripture for it: there was no such government in Israel . . . a Democratie is, amongst most civil nations, accounted the meanest and worst of all forms of government.' That Massachusetts was not yet ripe for democracy may be conceded; but it must have been a sad outlook for the average Englishman in the Bay Colony to learn that no forms of government which were unknown to the ancient Hebrews would be permitted. However, Winthrop's speech had its effect; the negative voice was admitted; and the General Court separated into a House of Deputies and a House of Assistants. If, as is claimed, this was the first full-fledged bicameral legislature in the English colonies, a monument on Beacon Hill to Goody Sherman's sow, as the mother of Senates, would seem to be in order.

Throughout this controversy, two of the magistrates, Richard Saltonstall and Richard Bellingham, stood with the deputies against their own class. This occasioned much grief to Winthrop, and doubtless inflicted on them sundry repetitions of his shipboard sermon. Yet he took pains to record in his journal his belief that 'these gentlemen were such as feared God, and endeavoured to walk by the rule of his word' and 'in all those differences and agitations they continued in brotherly love' with their fellow magistrates, 'and in the exercise of all friendly offices to each other.'

By 1644, then, the transition of the Massachusetts Bay government from trading company to commonwealth was complete. The officers, originally intended to serve as president and board of directors of a joint-stock corporation, were now governor and executive council and upper house and superior court of justice of a colony. They were elected annually by the freemen, who were originally the stockholders of the company, and now the holders of a franchise determined by sanctity. A new representative body, the House of Deputies, had been created in order to obviate the necessity of personal attendance by the freemen to exercise their legislative rights. It was a typically English political compromise, satisfying nobody, expressing no logical system or consistent theory, yet working because it was composed of politically minded Englishmen, ready to compromise their dearest convictions if only government might go on. This government proved powerful enough to preserve Massachusetts independent of all outside control, to defend it from domestic and foreign enemies, to regulate the economic life of the community, and to maintain law and order on the edge of the wilderness.

In the development of American institutions, this revamped trading company of the Massachusetts Bay was momentous. For the transferred and transformed charter proved so workable a constitution that other colonies, even beyond New England, used it as a model; and in the American revolution most of the thirteen colonies adopted state constitutions on the same principle. The particular features of this government which proved successful and enduring were the election of all officials at stated intervals, and the use of the ballot. It did not much matter that the Massachusetts electorate was confined to members of the puritan churches; that could be and was remedied later. The important thing was that representatives, assistants, and the governor himself, had to go before the voters on a fixed day every year. In contrast to the English or parliamentary system, this corporate mode of election put an almost continuous check on the government. It became an essential principle of every state constitution and of the federal constitution; and the ballot enabled the freemen to exercise their rights without undue publicity.

Despite these concessions in a democratic direction, the Assistants, with their combined power as upper chamber, court of appeals, and executive council, remained the most powerful part of the Massachusetts government; and the civil list of Assistants reads like the chronicle of Israel before the flood. Although ten to fifteen were annually elected, only thirty-five new names appear in forty-eight years. John Winthrop was governor or assistant for nineteen years, when he died. John Endecott was assistant or governor for twenty-three years, and governor for ten years more, when he died. Simon Bradstreet earned a promotion to the governorship by fifty years' faithful service on the Board of Assistants. He was nine times reëlected governor, but forced into premature retirement at the age of eighty-nine by the arrival of a new charter. It has often been wondered why the freemen, whose deputies often quarrelled with the Assistants, did not elect a new board. The probable answer lies in a complaint of the General Court in 1652, of the scarcity of persons 'fit for magistracie.' Men with the qualities, the education and the training for so many-sided an office were rare in a colony; and if the freemen of the Bay had set their faces toward democracy, they still wished to be governed by their best, not their average men.

Winthrop, who thought much on political science, submitted to popular participation in legislation, but always protested against 'referring matter of counsel or judicature to the body of the people, *quia* the best part is always the least, and of that best part the wiser part is always the lesser. The old law was, Choose ye out judges, etc., and thou shalt bring the matter to the judge, etc.' In the more democratic Connecticut, where men of little learning or judgment were elected to high office, Winthrop observed that the state business was actually done by the parsons, 'who, though they were men of singular wisdom and godliness, yet stepping out of their course, their actions wanted that blessing which otherwise might have been expected.' In his own 'Government of the Massachusetts' he was satisfied that there was a proper balance between the rights of the freemen and the authority of the magistrates; 'a mixt Aristocratie, and no wayes Arbitrary.'

Governor Winthrop was an intense patriot, and his country was New England. Massachusetts, a word uncouth to English ears, was not a word to conjure with in the seventeenth century. The people called themselves New Englanders, and their jurisdiction, the Bay. It was doubtless Winthrop's intention that the Bay take in all New England. He was bitterly disappointed that Haynes and Hooker set up a separate government for their river towns, when they emigrated to the Connecticut in 1635; but Hooker and Haynes found the polity of Massachusetts too oligarchical for their taste. When the Eaton and Davenport company came to Boston, the

Court offered them practically any township or tract they might choose, in order to keep them in the Bay Colony; but Eaton and Davenport thought the government of Massachusetts too lax, and its trade too crowded; so they founded a theocracy and commercial center at New Haven.

Relations between 'the River' and 'the Bay' were not very pleasant for a number of years, William Pynchon's colony at Springfield being one of several bones of contention. Governor Winthrop received an angry epistle from Hooker accusing the Bay authorities of malice and hatred toward them in cramping the River Colony; of instructing innkeepers to 'entertain their guests with invectives against Connecticut,' of even sending out boats to immigrant ships in Boston harbor to tell the passengers what a terrible place Connecticut was. Winthrop replied in the most humorous letter we have from his pen. The picture of himself peddling anti-River propaganda through barroom and waterside gossip, evidently tickled his fancy. 'Your large and lovinge lettre . . . makes me a little merrye,' says he; but our Hartford friends, having opened the back door on the frontier, and invited all and sundry to that 'most fatt and pleasant country' must not take it amiss if the head of the Bay house endeavor to keep his family together, and prevent the lad who took the coat from getting the cloak too. 'We are brethren,' he continues in a more serious vein. 'One in consotiation, in the same worke of God, in the same community of perill'; then for God's sake, let us 'labor in peace and love.'

A solution of these ill-boding disputes was provided by the New England Confederation, the league of Bible commonwealths of which Winthrop was an architect. It is pleasant to record that after the first meeting at Boston to organize the Confederation, Thomas Hooker wrote 'to his much Honoured freind John Wyntropp[5] Esquier, Governor of the plantations on the Matcheshusets Bay,' a glowing expression of gratitude for his 'candid and cordiall cariage in a matter of so great consequence,' and his 'speciall prudence to settle a foundation of safety and prosperity in succeeding ages.' Herein we may discern the gift of prophecy descending on the doubting Thomas, for, if the New England

---

[5] This appears to have been the contemporary pronunciation of Winthrop. My late friend Henry H. Edes, a great stickler for traditional Boston pronunciation, always said Governor Wint'rup, John Hahv'd, John Eli't, and Funnel Hall.

Confederation did not survive the century, the federal principle did; and it is not the least of Winthrop's glories that he helped to bring into practice a principle of immeasurable benefit to these States, and of wide promise to the world.

In relations with the mother country, Winthrop would not brook the slightest interference with the charter, or the self-government of the Bay. As we shall see when we come to the remonstrance of Robert Child, Massachusetts Bay acted as a free state. When King Charles sent for the charter in 1634, and gave Gorges and Mason a commission to govern New England, Governor Winthrop mounted ordnance at the Castle, put the militia in a state of preparedness, and had the beacon constructed on Beacon Hill to arouse the country in case of invasion. During the English Civil War he maintained the neutrality of the Bay, and promptly punished the captain of a parliamentary privateer which fired on a royalist vessel in Boston Harbor. When certain members of Parliament offered to confer favors on Massachusetts, Winthrop persuaded the General Court to decline, lest by admitting Parliamentary jurisdiction over the colony an inconvenient precedent be established.

He was particularly disturbed by the persistent efforts of the Earl of Warwick and his associates to attract settlers from the Bay to the Caribbean; and John Humfry, who lent himself to these schemes, was one toward whom Winthrop found it most difficult to exercise Christian charity. Humfry was a curious character. Though an original Dorchester Adventurer, active in promoting the emigration of 1630 and in sending relief ships, he soon began talking of removing the Massachusetts Bay colony further South. He was elected an Assistant even before emigrating, and received a good land grant at Lynn, and belonged to the church; but was unsuccessful and discontented, finally accepting the governorship of Warwick's island in the West Indies. Winthrop records in his journal, that when the ship in which Humfry was returning neared the English coast, several passengers spoke reproachfully of New England. Gales and tempests promptly arose, and tossed them about, until, in imminent peril, they prayed the Lord to pardon them for speaking ill of New England. The prayers of Master George Phillips, who had wisely refrained from these revilings, saved them from being dashed on the rocks, and brought them to the haven where they would be. 'Yet the Lord followed them on shore,' says Winthrop. Some were forsaken by friends, one lost two children by the plague, one of Humfry's daughters went mad, and two others, both under ten years of age, were found to have been 'often abused by divers lewd persons, and filthiness in his family.'

That is the kind of statement which flies up in your face when you are beginning to think that the puritans were pretty good fellows. It shows us what a chasm separates the thoughts of even the best men of that time and persuasion, from ourselves. Shall we laugh, or should we weep at the God of John Winthrop, whose interest in New England prosperity is such that he raises a gale to drown the 'knockers,' decides to save them because a good 'booster' is on board, and then visits his wrath on their innocent children with the most revolting of crimes?

The puritans, taking literally some of the ill-tempered outbursts of the Hebrew prophets, and the parables and oriental imagery that Our Lord employed in his teaching, believed that every occurrence, however trivial or loathsome, was God's will. At the same time they conceived God as infinitely just. They craved to know God's will toward them and their commonwealth, and his opinion of the manner in which they were keeping the covenant. This case of the Humfry children caused the colony great scandal and shame. There were long conferences with the elders as to whether or not the criminals should suffer death by Mosaic law. Among others, Charles Chauncy, first scholar of his time at Cambridge, and a former fellow of Trinity, applied his mind to the problem. God must have permitted the crime; yet God was just. What could be the explanation? *For I the Lord, thy God, am a jealous God, visiting the sins of the fathers upon the children unto the third and fourth generation of them that hate me. . . .*

Yet that conclusion was not inevitable for a sincere puritan. Governor Bradford of the Plymouth Colony, musing over this and other sexual outbreaks in New England, deduced three reasons for them: (1) the Devil was working hard to shame them; (2) '—as it is with waters when their streames are stopped or dammed up, when they gett passage they flow with more violence . . . then when they are suffered to rune quietly in their owne chanels'; (3) '— hear (as I am verily perswaded) is not more evills in this kind, nor nothing nere so many by proportion as in other places; but they are more discovered and seen and made publick by due serch, inquisition, and due punishment.' These common-sense conclusions, one must admit, stamp the self-educated Pilgrim as a man of greater breadth than the eminent Governor of the Bay. One feels the force in the remark of Thomas Hutchinson, a century later, that Winthrop 'was of a more catholic spirit than some of his brethren before he left England, but afterwards he grew more contracted.'

Undoubtedly Bradford's second reason was the correct one. The puritan standard of sexual morality was too high for the meaner sort of people. Early marriage and frequent childbearing was a healthy outlet for the independent yeomen and gentry; but the indented servants, who caused almost all the trouble, were recruited from the brutish elements of a coarse age. Forbidden marriage while serving their time, and forced to heavy labor in the fields, they found an outlet where they could. Precisely the same sort of trouble occurred with the indented servants in Virginia, and for the same reason.

At this point I wish to take issue with Mr. James Truslow Adams' pronouncement that the puritans took a 'morbid interest in the most indecent sexual matters.'[6] If Winthrop and Bradford had passed over these events, leaving them to be discovered in the court records, our modern puritan-baiters would have enjoyed accusing them of concealment, hypocrisy, and 'ignoring the facts of life.' It seems hard that their frank human interest in such facts should be considered morbid. There was something more to it, however, than curiosity. The puritan chroniclers classed sexual outbreaks, monstrous births, and the like, with earthquakes and cyclones: regrettable phenomena to be reported along with the contrary evidence of God's favor. Puritan housewives do not sweep the dirt under the bed. Winthrop is not morbid and obscene, but simply natural and coarse like Shakespere, when he writes of a certain man: 'He was ripped out of his mother's belly, and never sucked, nor saw father nor mother, nor they him.'

Winthrop's superstition has also attracted the scorn of superior

[6] *Founding of New England.* p. 265, note. This was *à propos* stripping suspects for examination for marks of witchcraft, a part of the regular procedure against witches in all countries in the seventeenth century.

minds in later times. His stories of the snake which crept into the elder's seat at the Cambridge synod, and of the mice eating his son's Prayer-Book but respecting the Psalms and Greek Testament, have often been quoted to show what a petty and barbarous community Massachusetts must have been, when the mind of its chief magistrate worked that way. Superstition, like persecution and coarse language, was part and parcel of the age in which Winthrop lived, and he was no better nor worse than the average educated Englishman of the time. The University of Cambridge was all stirred up in 1626 by the discovery of a small book called 'A Preparation to the Cross' in the maw of a codfish. Samuel Ward, master of Sidney Sussex, thought 'it may be a special admonition to us at Cambridge,' and even Archbishop Ussher wrote, 'The incident is not lightly to be passed over.'

In his private affairs Governor Winthrop was not what New Englanders would call a good manager. He consistently neglected them for the public business. For many years he refused a salary, spending the proceeds of the sale of Groton Manor in public concerns, when there was no money in the colony treasury. He gave generous hospitality as befitted the station of chief magistrate, although so temperate in his own habits that his friends called his attention to Paul's precept to Timothy: 'drink no longer water, but use a little wine for thy stomach's sake.'

He was almost recklessly charitable, and died 'land poor.'

> What goods he had he did not spare;
>   The Church and Commonwealth
> Had of his Goods the greatest share,
>   Kept nothing for himself

declares Perciful Lowle with truth, in his 'Funeral Elegie on the Death of the Memorable and Truly Honourable John Winthrope Esq.'

A dishonest agent in England embezzled the Governor's property there; and a rascally steward of his Ten Hills estate on the Mystic, diverted to his own use the profits of the Governor's crops and cattle. Winthrop did not mind these losses at Ten Hills so much as the discovery, after the steward was sacked, that the neighbors had taken advantage of the man's unfaithfulness to make some very questionable bargains, which some of them insisted on carrying out to the letter. To Ezekiel Rogers, the minister of Rowley, he wrote on this subject, 'I suppose you intended me a Courtesye in offeringe to accept a heifer for your 2 Calves and 4 *l.*, and accordingly I desired Mr. Carlton to choose one for you; and I think if you value your Calves . . . of a weeke old at 5 *l.* or 6 *l.* (which is the most they can be worth) and my heifer (as I sould her fellowes before winter) at 13 *l.* you will find yourselfe mystaken, but that is a small matter between yourselfe and me.' One could hardly tell a parson more tactfully that he was a close bargainer.

Winthrop never appeared to better advantage than in one of those tempests in the colonial teapot, the Hingham militia affair. The town of Hingham, under the lead of the minister Peter Hobart and his three stout brothers, mutinied against an unpopular militia officer imposed on them by the Court. Winthrop was accused of exceeding his powers in dealing with the mutineers. Hingham petitioned the General Court against him, and a process equivalent to impeachment took place. As in the famous impeachments of history, the motives were political. Saltonstall, Bellingham, and a bare majority of the deputies, conceiving 'that the magistrates exercised two much power, and that the people's liberty was thereby in danger,' baffled by their defeat in the matter of the negative voice and in their efforts to get a definite law code adopted, were resolved to make an example of Winthrop. The rest, feeling that authority was too much slighted, that the existence of the colony was at stake, defended him. Winthrop left the bench, placed himself in the position of one on trial, and insisted that the whole thing be thrashed out, and a clean-cut decision be reached. He got it, because the Magistrates threatened to appeal to a clerical board of arbitration, and the deputies knew from past experience that the clergy would always uphold the magistrates, right or wrong.

So Winthrop was acquitted, and the chief petitioners and rioters fined. It must have been an impressive scene when Governor Dudley read the sentence in the crowded Boston meetinghouse, and Winthrop resumed his seat among his colleagues, and delivered himself of this 'little speech' on liberty:

I entreat you to consider, that when you choose magistrates, you take them from among yourselves, men subject to like passions as you are. Therefore when you see infirmities in us, you should reflect upon your own, and that would make you bear the more with us, and not be severe censurers of the failings of your magistrates, when you have continual experience of the like infirmities in yourselves and others . . . When you agree with a workman to build you a ship or house, he undertakes as well for his skill as for his faithfulness, for it is his profession, and you pay him for both. But when you call one to be a magistrate, he doth not profess nor undertake to have sufficient skill for that office, nor can you furnish him with gifts, therefore you must run the hazard of his skill and ability . . .

Concerning liberty, I observe a great mistake in the country about that. There is a twofold liberty, natural (I mean as our nature is now corrupt) and civil or federal. The first is common to man with beasts and other creatures. By this, man, as he stands in relation to man simply, hath liberty to do what he lists; it is a liberty to evil as well as to good. This liberty is incompatible and inconsistent with authority, and cannot endure the least restraint of the most just authority. The exercise and maintaining of this liberty makes men grow more evil, and in time to be worse than brute beasts: . . . The other kind of liberty I call civil or federal . . . This liberty is the proper end and object of authority, and cannot subsist without it; and it is a liberty to that only which is good, just and honest. This liberty you are to stand for, with the hazard (not only of your goods, but) of your lives, if need be. Whatsoever crosseth this, is not authority, but a distemper thereof. This liberty is maintained and exercised in a way of subjection to authority; it is of the same kind of liberty wherewith Christ hath made us free . . .

Other events and controversies in which Winthrop took a leading part might be related, and some have been postponed to later chapters; but I have told enough for you to judge what manner of man he was. Keeping in mind the basis and principle by which he governed, that he and his fellow magistrates were God's vicegerents divinely commissioned to maintain gospel ordinance in a new

colony, Winthrop justified those 'extraordinary great commendacions' of him. Without that basis, he would not have been Winthrop. From his fellows of the ruling class, strong and able men,
he stands out as a superior man of noble character, with a single
eye to the common weal. One may regret that he did not more
often insist on that comparative mildness and mercy in administration which was natural to him. One welcomes the tradition that
upon his deathbed, when Dudley pressed him to sign an order for
banishing a dissenter, he refused, saying 'he had done too much
of that work already.' Yet Winthrop's capacity to take advice and
yield to the majority, was part of his equipment for leadership.

There is no better summary of the Governor's life than that of
William Hubbard, the earliest historian of Massachusetts: 'A
worthy gentleman, who had done good in Israel, having spent not
only his whole estate . . . but his bodily strength and life, in the
service of the country; not sparing, but always as the burning
torch, spending . . .'

PART TWO
The Sources

The Sources

To understand fully any historical event would be to know every-thing that happened before it, everything that has happened since, and everything that was happening at the same time. To study any part of the past by itself is to do violence to the seamless continuity of history. But it is only by such an act of violence that we can study the past at all. The four historians from whose writings the previous extracts are taken were all writing about a larger segment of time than the five or six years that have been isolated for study here; but none of them attempted to encompass the whole human past. Although they used earlier and later materials to assist them in understanding the founding of Massachusetts, they had to derive most of their information, so far as the years 1628–1634 are con-cerned, from the documents that follow. These are not the only Massachusetts documents that survive from the period. There are numerous other letters and papers, including some written in Eng-land, that reflect information coming from the colony. There are also papers written later by people who had been in Massachusetts at this time or who had talked with people who had been there. Nevertheless, any understanding of what happened in Massa-chusetts from 1628 to 1634 has always depended and will always depend primarily on the documents that follow.

In reprinting them here, I have indicated the authorship of each but have not furnished footnotes to identify persons and places or to explain obscure allusions and archaic words. The documents are not, in this sense, edited. The object has been to present the reader with as close an approximation of the raw materials as typography will allow.

1

Francis Higginson on the Commodities and Discommodities of New England

Francis Higginson (1587–1630) was sent by the Massachusetts Bay Company in 1629 to minister to the spiritual needs of the settlers at Salem. Educated at Emmanuel College, Cambridge, he had won esteem among Puritans as minister of a church at Leicester. At Salem he and another Puritan minister, Samuel Skelton, gathered a church on congregational principles in July 1629, and they were chosen its first ministers. Higginson died in August of the following year. His account of New England, printed in London in 1630, went through three editions in that year. The text that follows is that of the third edition, entitled *"New-Englands Plantation or, A Short and True Description of the Commodities and Discommodities of that Country. Written by Mr. Higgeson, a reverend Divine now there resident. Whereunto is added a Letter, sent by Mr. Graves an Enginere, out of New England. The third Edition, enlarged."* Mr. Graves was probably Thomas Graves, an engineer sent by the Company and frequently mentioned in the Records.

TO THE READER.

Reader, doe not disdaine to reade this Relation: and looke not here to have a large Gate and no building within: a full-stuffed Tittle with no matter in the Booke: But here reade the truth, and that thou shalt find without any frothy bumbasting words, or any quaint new-devised additions, onely as it was written (not intended for the Presse) by a reverend Divine now there living, who onely sent it to some Friends here, which were desirous of his Relations; which is an Epitomy of their proceedings in the Plantation. And for thy part if thou meanest to be no Planter nor Venturer doe but lend thy good Prayers for the furtherance of it. And so I rest a Well-Wisher to all the good designes both of them which are gone, and of them that are to goe.

M. S.

New-Englands
Plantation.

Letting passe our Voyage by Sea, we will now begin our discourse on the shore of *New-England.* And because the life and wel-fare of every Creature heere below, and the commodiousnesse of the Countrey whereas such Creatures live, doth by the most wise ordering of Gods providence, depend next unto himselfe, upon the temperature and disposition of the foure Elements, Earth, Water, Aire, and Fire (For as of the mixture of all these, all sublunary things are composed; so by the more or lesse injoyment of the wholesome temper and convenient use of these, consisteth the onely well-being both of Man and Beast in a more or lesse comfortable measure in all Countreys under the Heavens) Therefore I will indeavour to shew you what *New-England* is by the consideration of each of these apart, and truly indeavour by Gods helpe to report nothing but the naked truth, and that both to tell you of the discommodities as well as of the commodities, though as the idle Proverbe is, *Travellers may lye by autoritie,* and so may take too much sinfull libertie that way. Yet I may say of my selfe as once *Nehemiah* did in another case: *Shall such a Man as I lye?* No verily: It becommeth not a Preacher of Truth to be a Writer of Falshod in any degree: and therefore I have beene carefull to report nothing of *new* England but what I have partly seene with mine owne Eyes, and partly heard and inquired from the mouths of verie honest and religious persons, who by living in the Countrey a good space of time have had experience and knowledge of the state thereof, & whose testimonies I doe beleeve as my selfe.

First therefore of the Earth of *New-England* and all the appertenances thereof: It is a Land of divers and sundry sorts all about *Masathulets* Bay, and at *Charles* River is as fat blacke Earth as can be seene any where: and in other places you have a clay soyle, in other gravell, in other sandy, as it is all about our Plantation at *Salem,* for so our Towne is now named, *Psal.* 76. 2.

The forme of the Earth here in the superficies of it is neither too flat in the plainnesse, nor too high in Hils, but partakes of both in a mediocritie, and fit for Pasture, or for Plow or meddow ground, as Men please to employ it: though all the Countrey bee as it were a thicke Wood for the generall, yet in divers places there is much ground cleared by the *Indians,* and especially about the Plantation: and I am told that about three miles from us a Man may stand on a little hilly place and see divers thousands of acres of ground as good as need to be, and not a Tree in the same. It is thought here is good Clay to make Bricke and Tyles and Earthen-Pot as need to be. At this instant we are setting a Bricke-Kill on worke to make Brickes and Tyles for the building of our Houses. For Stone, here is plentie of Slates at the Ile of Slate in *Masathulets* Bay, and Lime-stone, Free-stone, and Smooth-stone, and Iron-stone, and Marble-stone also in such store, that we have great Rocks of it, and a Harbour hard by. Our Plantation is from thence called Marble-harbour.

Of Minerals there hath yet beene but little triall made, yet we are not without great hope of being furnished in that Soyle.

The fertilitie of the Soyle is to be admired at, as appeareth in the aboundance of Grasse that groweth everie where both verie thicke, verie long, and verie high in divers places: but it groweth verie wildly with a great stalke and a broad and ranker blade, because it never had been eaten with Cattle, nor mowed with a Sythe, and seldome trampled on by foot. It is scarce to be beleeved how our Kine and Goats, Horses and Hogges doe thrive and prosper here and like well of this Countrey.

In our Plantation we have already a quart of Milke for a penny: but the aboundant encrease of Corne proves this Countrey to bee a wonderment. Thirtie, fortie, fiftie, sixtie are ordinarie here: yea *Joseph's* encrease in *Ægyt* is out-stript here with us. Our planters hope to have more then a hundred fould this yere: and all this while I am within compasse; what will you say of two hundred fould and upwards? It is almost incredible what great gaine some of our English Planters have had by our Indian Corne. Credible persons have assured me, and the partie himselfe avouched the truth of it to me, that of the setting of 13 gallons of Corne hee hath had encrease of it 52 Hogsheads, every Hogshead holding seven Bushels of *London* measure, and every Bushell was by him sold and trusted to the *Indians* for so much Beaver as was worth 18 shillings; and so of this 13 Gallons of Corne which was worth 6 shillings 8 pence, he made about 327 pounds of it in the yeere following, as by reckoning will appeare: where you may see how God blessed husbandry in this Land. There is not such greate and plentifull eares of Corne I suppose any where else to bee found but in this Country: because also of varietie of colours, as red, blew, and yellow, &c. and of one Corne there springeth foure or five hundred. I have sent you many Eares of divers colours that you might see the truth of it.

Little Children here by setting of Corne may earne much more then their owne maintenance.

They have tryed our *English* Corne at new *Plimmouth* Plantation, so that all our severall Graines will grow here verie well, and have a fitting Soyle for their nature.

Our Governor hath store of greene pease growing in his garden as good as ever I eat in *England*.

This Countrey aboundeth naturally with store of rootes of great varietie and good to eat. Our Turnips, Parsnips and Carrots are here both bigger and sweeter then is ordinarily to bee found in *England*. Here are store of Pumpions, Cowcombers, and other things of that nature which I know not. Also divers excellent Pot-herbs grow abundantly among the Grasse, as Strawberrie leaves in all places of the Countrey, and plentie of strawberries in their time, and Penyroyall, Wintersaverie, Sorrell, Brookelime, Liverwort, Caruell and Watercresses, also Leekes and Onions are ordinarie, and divers Physicall Herbs. Here are also aboundance of other sweet Hearbs delightfull to the smell, whose names we know not, &c. and plentie of single Damaske Roses verie sweete; and two kinds of Herbes that beare two kinds of Flowers very sweet, which they say, are as good to make Cordage or Cloath as any Hempe or Flaxe we have.

Excellent Vines are here up and downe in the Woodes. Our Governour hath already planted a Vineyard with great hope of encrease.

Also, Mulberries, Plums, Raspberries, Corrance, Chesnuts, Filberds, Walnuts, Smalnuts, Hurtleberies, & Hawes of Whitethorne neere as good as our Cherries in *England,* they grow in plentie here.

For Wood there is no better in the World I thinke, here being foure sorts of Oke differing both in the Leafe, Timber, and Colour, all excellent good. There is also good Ash, Elme, Willow, Birch, Beech, Saxafras, Juniper, Cipres, Cedar, Spruce, Pines, & Firre that will yeeld abundance of Turpentine, Pitch, Tarre, Masts and other materials for building both of Ships and Houses. Also here are store of Sumacke Trees, they are good for dying and tanning of Leather, likewise such trees yeeld a precious Gem called Wine Benjamen, that they say is excellent for perfumes. Also here be divers Roots and Berries wherewith the *Indians* dye excellent holding colours that no raine nor washing can alter. Also, wee have materials to make Sope-Ashes and Salt-Peter in aboundance.

For Beasts there are some Beares, and they say some Lyons also; for they have been seen at Cape *Anne.* Also here are severall sorts of Deere, some whereof bring three or foure young ones at once, which is not ordinarie in *England.* Also Wolves, Foxes, Beavers, Otters, Martins, great wild Cats, & a great Beast called a Molke as bigge as an Oxe. I have seen the Skins of all these Beasts since I came to this Plantation excepting Lyons. Also here are great store of squerrels, some greater, and some smaller and lesser: there are some of the lesser sort, they tell me, that by a certaine Skill will fly from Tree to Tree though they stand farre distant.

Of the Waters of New-England, *with the things belonging to the same.*

New-England hath Water enough both salt and fresh, the greatest Sea in the World, the *Atlanticke* Sea runs all along the Coast thereof. There are abundance of Ilands along the Shore, some full of Wood and Mast to feed Swine; and others cleere of Wood, and fruitfull to beare Corne. Also wee have store of excellent harbours for Ships, as at Cape *Anne,* and at *Masathulets* Bay, and at *Salem,* and at many other places: and they are the better because for Strangers there is a verie difficult and dangerous passage into them, but unto such as are well acquainted with them, they are easie and safe enough. The aboundance of Sea-Fish are almost beyond beleeving, and sure I should scarce have beleeved it, except I had seene it with mine owne Eyes. I saw great store of Whales, and Crampusse, and such aboundance of Mackerils that it would astonish one to behold, likewise Cod-Fish in aboundance on the Coast, and in their season are plentifully taken. There is a Fish called a Basse, a most sweet & wholesome Fish as ever I did eate, it is altogether as good as our fresh Sammon, and the season of their comming was begun when wee came first to *New-England* in *June,* and so continued about three months space. Of this Fish our Fishers take many hundreds together, which I have seene lying on the shore to my admiration; yea their Nets ordinarily take more then they are able to hale to Land, and for want of Boats and Men they are constrained to let a many goe after they have taken them, and yet sometimes they fill two Boates at a time with them. And besides Basse wee take plentie of Scate and Thornbacks, and abundance of Lobsters, and the least Boy in the Plantation may both catch and eat what he will of them. For my owne part I was soone cloyed with them, they were so great, and fat, and lussious. I have seene some my selfe that have weighed 16 pound, but others have had divers times so great Lobsters as have weighed 25 pound, as they assure mee. Also heere is abundance of Herring, Turbut, Sturgion, Cuskes, Hadocks, Mullets, Eeles, Crabbes, Muskles and Oysters. Besides there is probability that the Countrey is of an excellent temper for the making of Salt: for since our comming our Fishermen have brought home very good Salt which they found candied by the standing of the Sea water and the heat of the Sunne, upon a Rocke by the Sea shore: and in divers salt Marishes that some have gone through, they have found some Salt in some places crushing under their Feete and cleaving to their Shooes.

And as for fresh Water the Countrey is full of dainty Springs, and some great Rivers, and some lesser Brookes; and at *Masa-thulets* Bay they digged Wels and found Water at three Foot deepe in most places: and neere *Salem* they have as fine cleare Water as we can desire, and we may digge Wels and find Water where we list.

Thus wee see both Land and Sea abound with store of blessings for the comfortable sustenance of Man's life in *New-England*.

Of the Aire of New-England *with the temper and Creatures in it.*

The Temper of the Aire of *New-England* is one speciall thing that commends this place. Experience doth manifest that there is hardly a more healthfull place to be found in the World that agreeth better with our English bodyes. Many that have beene weake and sickly in old *England,* by comming hither have beene thoroughly healed and growne healthfull strong. For here is an extraordinarie cleere and dry Aire that is of a most healing nature to all such as are of a Cold, Melancholy, Flegmatick, Rheumatick temper of Body. None can more truly speake hereof by their owne experience then my selfe. My Friends that knew me can well tell how verie sickly I have bin and continually in Physick, being much troubled with a tormenting paine through an extraordinarie weaknesse of my Stomacke, and aboundance of Melancholicke humors; but since I came hither on this Voyage, I thanke God, I have had perfect health, and freed from paine and vomiting, having a Stomacke to digest the hardest and coursest fare, who before could not eat finest meat; and whereas my Stomacke could onely digest and did require such drinke as was both strong and stale, now I can and doe often times drink *New-England* water verie well; and I that have not gone without a Cap for many yeeres together, neither durst leave off the same, have now cast away my Cap, and doe weare none at all in the day time: and whereas before-time I cloathed my selfe with double cloathes and thicke Wast-coates to keepe me warme, even in the Summer time, I doe now goe as thin clad as any, onely wearing a light Stuffe Cassocke upon my Shirt, and Stuffe Breeches of one thicknesse without Linings. Besides I have one of my Children that was formerly most lamentably handled with sore breaking out of both his hands and feet of the King's-evill, but since he came hither hee is very well over he was, and there is hope of perfect recoverie shortly even by the very wholesomnesse of the Aire, altering, digesting and drying up the cold and crude humours of the Body: and therefore I thinke it is a wise course for al cold complections to come to take Physick in *New England:* for a sup of *New-England's* Aire is better then a whole draught of old *England's* Ale. In the Summer time in the midst of *July* and *August,* it is a good deale hotter then in old *England:* and in Winter *January* and *February* are much colder as they say: but the Spring and Autumne are of a middle temper.

Fowles of the Aire are plentifull here, and of all sorts as we have in *England* as farre as I can learne, and a great many of strange Fowles which wee know not. Whilst I was writing these things, one of our Men brought home an Eagle which hee had killed in the Wood: they say they are good meate. Also here are many kinds of excellent Hawkes, both Sea Hawkes & Land Hawkes: and my selfe walking in the Woods with another in company, sprung a Partridge so bigge that through the heavinesse of his Body could fly but a little way: they that have killed them, say they are as bigge as our Hens. Here are likewise aboundance of Turkies often killed in the Woods, farre greater then our English Turkies, and exceeding fat, sweet and fleshy, for here they have aboundance of feeding all the yeere long, as Straw-berries, in Summer all places are full of them, and all manner of Berries and Fruits. In the Winter time I have seene Flockes of Pidgeons, and have eaten of them: they doe fly from Tree to Tree as other Birds doe, which our Pidgeons will not doe in *England:* they are of all colours as ours are, but their wings and tayles are far longer, and therefore it is likely they fly swifter to escape the terrible Hawkes in this Country. In Winter time this Country doth abound with wild Geese, wild Duckes, and other Sea Fowle, that a great part of winter the Planters have eaten nothing but roast meate of divers Fowles which they have killed.

Thus you have heard of the Earth, Water and Aire of *New-England,* now it may bee you expect something to bee said of the Fire proportionable to the rest of the Elements. Indeede I thinke *New-England,* may boast of this Element more then of all the rest: for though it bee here somewhat cold in the winter, yet here we have plenty of Fire to warme us, and that a great deale cheaper then they sel Billets and Faggots in *London:* nay, all *Europe* is not able to afford to make so great Fires as *New-England.* A poore servant here that is to possesse but 50 Acres of Land, may afford to give more wood for Timber & Fire as good as the world yeelds, then many Noble men in *England* can afford to do. Here is good living for those that love good Fires. And although *New-England* have no Tallow to make Candles of, yet by the aboundance of the Fish thereof, it can afford Oyle for Lampes. Yea our Pine-Trees that are the most plentifull of all wood, doth allow us plenty of Candles which are very usefull in a House: and they are such Candles as the *Indians* commonly use, having no other, and they are nothing else but the wood of the Pine Tree cloven in two little slices something thin, which are so full of the moysture of Turpentine and Pitch, that they burne as cleere as a Torch. I have sent you some of them that you may see the experience of them.

Thus of *New-England's* commodities, now I will tell you of some discommodities that are here to be found.

First, in the Summer season for these three months, *June, July,* and *August,* we are troubled much with little Flyes called Musketoes, being the same they are troubled with in Lincolneshiere and the Fens: and they are nothing but Gnats, which except they bee smoked out of their houses are troublesome in the night season.

Secondly, in the Winter season for two months space, the earth is commonly covered with Snow, which is accompanied with sharp biting Frosts, something more sharpe then is in old *England,* and therefore are forced to make great Fires.

Thirdly, the countrey being very full of Woods, and Wildernesses, doth also much abound with Snakes and Serpents of strange colours, and huge greatnesse: yea there are some Serpents called Rattlesnakes that have Rattles in their Tailes, that will not fly from a man as others will, but will flye upon him and sting him so mortally, that hee will dye within a quarter of an houre after, except the partie stinged have about him some of the root of an Hearbe called Snake-weed to bite on, and then hee shall receive no harme: but yet seldome falles it out that any hurt is done by these. About three yeares since, an *Indian* was stung to death by one of them, but wee heard of none since that time.

Fourthly and lastly, Here wants as it were good company of honest Christians to bring with them Horses, Kine and Sheepe to make use of this fruitfull Land: great pitty it is to see so much good ground for Corne & for Grasse as any is under the Heavens, to ly altogether unoccupied, when so many honest Men and their

Families in old *England* through the populousnesse thereof, do make very hard shift to live one by the other.

Now, thus you know what *New-England* is, as also with the commodities and discommodities thereof: now I will shew you a little of the Inhabitants thereof, and their government.

For their Governors they have Kings, which they call *Sagga-mores,* some greater, and some lesser, according to the number of their Subjects.

The greatest *Saggamores* about us can not make above three hundred Men, and other lesse *Saggamores* have not above fifteene Subjects, and others neere about us but two.

Their Subjects above twelve yeares since were swept away by a great & grievous Plague that was amongst them, so that there are verie few left to inhabite the Country.

The *Indians* are not able to make use of the one fourth part of the Land, neither have they any setled places, as Townes to dwell in, nor any ground as they challenge for their owne posses-sion, but change their habitation from place to place.

For their Statures, they are a tall and strong limmed People, their colours are tawny, they goe naked, save onely they are in part covered with Beasts Skins on one of their shoulders, and weare something before their privities: their Haire is generally blacke, and cut before like our Gentelewomen, and one locke longer then the rest, much like to our Gentelmen, which fashion I thinke came from hence into *England*.

For their weapons, they have Bows and Arrowes, some of them headed with Bone, and some with Brasse: I have sent you some of them for an example.

The Men for the most part live idely, they doe nothing but hunt and fish: their wives set their Corne and doe all their other worke. They have little Houshold stuffe, as a kettle, and some other Vessels like Trayes, Spoones, Dishes and Baskets.

Their Houses are verie little and homely, being made with small Poles pricked into the ground, and so bended and fastned at the tops, and on the sides they are matted with Boughes and covered on the Roofe with Sedge and old Mats, and for their beds that they take their rest on, they have a Mat.

They doe generally professe to like well of our comming and planting here; partly because there is abundance of ground that they cannot possesse nor make use of, and partly because our being heere will bee a meanes both of reliefe to them when they want, and also a defence from their Enemies, wherewith (I say) before this Plantation began, they were often indangered.

For their religion, they doe worship two Gods, a good God and an evill God: the good God they call *Tantum,* and their evill God whom they feare will doe them hurt, they call *Squantum.*

For their dealing with us, we neither feare them nor trust them, for fourtie of our Musketeeres will drive five hundred of them out of the Field. We use them kindly, they will come into our Houses sometimes by halfe a douzen or halfe a score at a time when we are at victuals, but will aske or take nothing but what we give them.

We purpose to learne their language as soone as we can, which will be a meanes to do them good.

Of the present condition of the Plantation,

and what it is.

When we came first to *Nehumkek,* we found about halfe a score Houses, and a faire House newly built for the Governor, we found also aboundance of Corne planted by them, very good and well liking. And we brought with us about two hundred Passengers and Planters more, which by common consent of the old Planters were all combined together into one Body Politicke, under the same Governor.

There are in all of us both old and new Planters about three hundred, whereof two hundred of them are setled at *Nehumkek,* now called *Salem:* And the rest have planted themselves at *Masathulets* Bay, beginning to build a Towne there which wee doe call *Cherton,* or *Charles* Towne.

We that are setled at *Salem* make what haste we can to build Houses, so that within a short time we shall have a faire Towne.

We have great Ordnance, wherewith wee doubt not but wee shall fortifie our selves in a short time to keepe out a potent Adversary. But that which is our greatest comfort, and meanes of defence above all other, is, that we have here the true Religion and holy Ordinances of Almightie God taught amongst us: Thankes be to God, wee have here plenty of Preaching, and diligent Catechizing, with strickt and carefull exercise, and good and commendable orders to bring our People into a Christian conversation with whom wee have to doe withall. And thus wee doubt not but God will be with us, and *if God be with us, who can be against us?*

Here ends Master Higgeson's Relation of
New-England.

A Letter sent from New-England,
by Master Graves, *Engynere*
now there resident.

Thus much I can affirme in generall, that I never came in a more goodly Country in all my life, all things considered: if it hath not at any time beene manured and husbanded, yet it is very beautifull in open Lands, mixed with goodly woods, and againe open plaines, in some places five hundred Acres, some places more, some lesse, not much troublesome for to cleere for the Plough to goe in, no place barren, but on the tops of the Hils; the grasse & weedes grow up to a man's face, in the Lowlands & by fresh Rivers aboundance of grasse and large Meddowes without any Tree or shrubbe to hinder the Sith. I never saw except in Hungaria, unto which I alwayes paralell this countrie, in all our most respects, for every thing that is heere eyther sowne or planted prospereth far better then in old England: the increase of Corne is here farre beyond expectation, as I have seene here by experience in Barly, the which because it is so much above your conception I will not mention. And Cattle doe prosper very well, and those that are bredd here farr greater then those with you in England. Vines doe grow here plentifully laden with the biggest Grapes that ever I saw, some I have seene foure inches about, so that I am bold to say of this countrie, as it is commonly said in *Germany* of *Hungaria,* that for Cattel, Corne, and Wine it excelleth. We have many more hopefull commodities here in this countrie, the which time will teach to make good use of: In the meane time wee abound with such things which next under God doe make us subsist, as Fish, Foule, Deere, and sundrie sorts of fruits, as musk-millions water-millions, India-Pompions, Indian-Pease Beanes, & many other odde fruits that I cannot name; all which are made good and pleasant through this maine blessing of God, the health-fulnesse of the countrie which far exceedeth all parts that ever I have beene in: It is observed that few or none doe here fal sicke, unless of the Scurvy that they bring from aboard the Ship with

them, whereof I have cured some of my companie onely by labour.
[Thus making an end of an imperfect Description, and committing
you to God, &c.

A Catalogue of such needefull things as every Planter doth or ought to provide to go to *New-England*

as namely for one man, which being doubled, may serve for as
many as you please, *viz.*
Victuals for a whole yeere for a man, and so after the rate for more.

8 *Bushels of meale.*	1 *Gallon of Oyle.*
2 *Bushels of pease.*	2 *Gallons of Vinegar.*
2 *Bushels of Otemeale.*	1 *Firkin of Butter.*
1 *Gallon of Aquavitæ.*	

Apparell.

1 *Monmoth Cap.*	3 *Paire of Stockings.*
3 *Falling bands.*	4 *Paire of Shooes.*
3 *Shirts.*	2 *Paire of Sheets.*
1 *Wast-coat.*	7 *Ells of Canvas to make a bed*
1 *Suit of Canvase.*	*and boulster.*
1 *Suit of Frize.*	1 *Paire of Blankets.*
1 *Suit of Cloth.*	1 *Course Rug.*

Armes.

1 *Armor compleat.*	1 *Bandilier.*
1 *Long peece.*	20 *Pound of Powder.*
1 *Sword.*	60 *Pound of Lead.*
1 *Belt.*	1 *Pistoll and Goose shot.*

Tooles.

1 *Broad Howe.*	1 *Broad Axe.*
1 *Narrow Howe.*	1 *Felling Axe.*
1 *Steele Handsawe.*	1 *Gimblet.*
1 *Whipsawe.*	1 *Hatchet.*
1 *Hammer.*	2 *Frowes.*
1 *Shovell.*	1 *Hand-Bill.*

1 *Spade.*	1 *Grindstone.*
2 *Augres.*	1 *Pickaxe.*
4 *Chissels.*	*Nayles of all sorts.*
2 *Percers stocked.*	

Houshold implements.

1 *Iron pot.*	1 *Spit.*
1 *Kettel.*	*Wooden Platters.*
1 *Frying pan.*	*Dishes.*
1 *Gridiron.*	*Spoons.*
2 *Skellets.*	*Trenchers.*

Spices.

Sugar.	*Cinnamon.*
Pepper.	*Nutmegs.*
Cloves.	*Fruit.*
Mace.	

Also there are divers other things necessary to bee taken over to this Plantation, as Bookes, Nets, Hookes and Lines, Cheese, Bacon, Kine, Goats, &c.

The names of the most remarkable places in *New-England.*

The old names.	The new names.
Cape *Cod.*	Cape *James.*
The Harbor of Cape *Cod.*	*Milford* Haven.
Chawum.	*Barwick.*
Accomack.	*Plimouth.*
Sagoquas.	*Oxford.*
Massachusets Mount.	*Cheuit* Hils.
Massachusets River.	*Charles* River.
Totan.	*Famouth.*
A great Bay by Cape *Anne.*	*Bristow.*
Cape *Tragabig sanda.*	Cape *Anne.*
Naembeck.	*Bastable,* so named by King *Charles:* But by the new Planters now called *Salem.*
Aggawom.	*Southampton.*
Smiths Iles.	*Smiths* Iles.

Passasaquack.
Accominticus.
Sassanows Mount.
Sowocatuck.
Bahanna.
A good Harbor within
  that Bay.
Ancociscos Mount.
Ancocisco.
Anmoughcawgen.
Kenebecka.
Sagadahock.
Pemmayquid.
Segocket.
Mecadacut.
Pennobscot.
Nusket.
Monahigan.
Matinack.
Metinacus.

Hull.
Boston.
Snowdon hill.
Ipswich.
Dartmouth.
Sandwich.

Shuters hill.
The *Base.*
Cambridge.
Edenborow.
Leth.
S. Johns towne.
Norwich.
Dunbarton.
Aberden.
Low mounds.
Barties Iles.
Willowbies Iles.
Haughtons Iles.

But whosoever desireth to know as much as yet can be discovered, I advise them to buy Captaine *John Smiths* booke of the description of *New-England* in Folio; and reade from Fol. 203. to the end; and there let the Reader expect to have full content.

2

Some brief collections out of a letter that Mr. Higginson *sent to his friends at* Leicester

Thomas Hutchinson (1711–1780), lieutenant governor and later governor of Massachusetts, made the history of the colony his avocation. He wrote three volumes on the subject and collected papers and documents relating to it. Some of his papers were destroyed when a mob attacked his house in 1765. (They suspected, wrongly, that he had advocated passage of the Stamp Act.) Hutchinson published many of the papers that survived the mob in *A Collection of Original Papers Relative to the History of Massachusetts-Bay* (Boston, 1769). Among these (pages 47–50), under the above title, was the following copy of a part of a letter written by Francis Higginson from Salem in 1629 or 1630.

There are certainly expected here the next spring the coming of 60 familyes out of Dorcettershire, who have by letters signified so much to the Governour to desyre him to appoint them places of habitations; they bringing their ministers with them. Also many families are expected out of Lincolnshire and a minister with them, and a great company of godly christians out of London. Such of you as come from Leister, I would counsell you to come quickly, and that for two reasons. 1st, if you linger too long, the passages of Jordan through the malice of Sathan, may be stopped; that you can not come if you would. 2dly, Those that come first speed best here, and have the priviledge of choosing choise places of habitations. Little children of 5 years ould may by setting corne one month be able to get their owne maintenance abundantly. Oh what a good worke might you that are rich do for your poore brethren, to helpe them with your purses onely to convey them hither with their children and families, where they may live as well both for soule and body as any where in the world. Besides they will recompense the cost by helping to build houses and plant your ground for a tyme; which shall be difficult worke at the first, except you have the helpe of many hands. Mr. Johnson out of Lincolnshire and many others have helped our godly christians hither, to be employed in their worke, for a while, and then to live of themselves. We have here about 40 goats that give milke, and as many milch kyne; we have 6 or 7 mares and an horse, and do every day expect the coming of half a score mares more, and 30 kyne by two shipps that are to follow us. They that come let them bring mares, kyne, and sheepe as many as they can: Ireland is the best place to provide sheepe, and lyes in the way. Bring none that are in lambe, nor mares in foale; for they are in more danger to perish at sea. Of all trades carpenters are most needful, therefore bring as many as you can. It were a wise course for those that are of abilityes to joyne together and buy a shipp for the voyage and other merchandize. For the governor would that any man may employ his stocke in what merchandises he please, excepting only beaver skins, which the company of merchants reserve to themselves, and the managing of the publique stocke. If any be of the mynde to buy a shipp, my cousin Nowel's counsell would be good. Also one Mr. [Beecher] a very godly man and the master of the ship we went in, and likewise one Mr. Graves the master's maite, dwelling in Wapping may herein staund you in sted. The payment of the transportation of things is wondrous deare, as 5*l* a man and 10*l* a horse and commonly 3*l* for every tunne of goodes: So that a little more then will pay for the passage will purchase the possession of a ship for all together.

No man hath or can have a house built for him here unlesse he comes himselfe, or else sends servants before to do it for him. It was an errour that I now perceive both in myselfe, and others did conceive by not rightly understanding the merchaunts meaning. For we thought that all that put in their money into the common stocke should have a house built for them, besides such a portion of land; but it was not so. They shall indeed have so much land allotted to them when they come to take possession of it and make use of it, but if they will have houses they must build them. Indeed we that are ministers, and all the rest that were entertained and sent over and maintained by the rest of the company, as their servants, for such a tyme in such employments, all such are to have houses built them of the companies charge and no others nor otherwise. They that put money into the stocke, as they do a good worke to helpe forwards so worthy a plantation, so all the gayne they are like to have, is according to the increase of the stocke at 3 yeares end, by the trade of beaver, besides the lands which they shall enjoy when they will.

All that come must have victualls with them for a twelve month, I meane they must have meale, oatmeale and such like sustenaunce of food, till they can gett increase of corne by their owne labour. For, otherwise, so many may come without provision at the first, as that our small beginnings may not be sufficient to maintayne them.

Before you come be carefull to be strongly instructed what things are fittest to bring with you for your more comfortable passage at sea, as also for your husbandrey occasions when you come to the land. For when you are once parted with England you shall meete neither with taverns nor alehouse, nor butchers, nor grosers, nor apothecaries shops to help what things you need, in the midst of the great ocean, nor when you are come to land, here are yet neither markets nor fayres to buy what you want. Therefore be sure to furnish yourselves with things fitting to be had before you come; as meale for bread, malt for drinke, woolen and linnen cloath, and leather for shoes, and all manner of car-penters tooles, and a good deale of iron and steele to make nails, and lockes, for houses and furniture for ploughs and carts, and glasse for windowes, and many other things which were better for you to think of them there than to want them here.

Whilst I was writing this letter my wiffe brought me word that the fishers had caught 1600 basse at one draught, which if they were in England were worth many a pound.

3
Thomas Dudley

Thomas Dudley (1574–1653), who came to Massachusetts as deputy governor in 1630, had been steward to the Earl of Lincoln, a nobleman sympathetic to Puritanism. Dudley's early career in Massachusetts, including his altercations with John Winthrop, figures in other pages of this volume. He served as governor in 1634, 1640, 1645, and 1650. His letter to the Countess of Lincoln was first published from a manuscript copy by the New Hampshire Historical Society, in its *Collections*, Volume IV (1834), pages 224–249, from which it is reprinted here.

The reader should note that in the seventeenth century Englishmen followed the Julian calendar, in which dates were ten days behind those of the Gregorian calendar, and the new year began on March 25. Dudley dated his letter March 12, 1630. By the Gregorian calendar this was actually March 22, 1631.

To the Right Honourable, my very good Lady,
the Lady BRIDGET, *Countess of Lincoln.*

MADAM,

Your letters (which are not common nor cheap) following me hither into *New England,* and bringing with them renewed testimonies of the accustomed favours you honoured me with in the *old,* have drawn from me this narative retribution, which (in respect of your proper interest in some persons of great note amongst us) was the thankfullest present I had to send over the seas. Therefore I humbly intreat your Honour this be accepted as payment from him, who neither hath, nor is any more, than

> Your Honour's
> Old
> Thankful Servant,
> THOMAS DUDLEY.

Boston in *New England,*
  March 12th 1630.

For the satisfaction of your Honour, and some friends, and for the use of such as shall hereafter intend to increase our plantation in *New England,* I have in the throng of domestick, and not altogether free from publick business, thought fit to commit to memory our present condition, and what hath befallen us since our arrival here; which I will do shortly, after my usual manner, and must do rudely, having yet no table, nor other room to write in, than by the fire-side upon my knee, in this sharp winter; to which my family must have leave to resort, though they break good manners, and make me sometimes forget what I would say, and say what I would not.

[*At this point a part of the manuscript is missing. It apparently contained an account of the Bays and Rivers, and then a brief notice of the Indian tribes living on them.*]

. . . Sachim in New England whom I saw the last somer. Upon the river of Naponset neere to the Mattachusetts feilds dwelleth *Chicka Talbott,* who hath betweene 50 and 60 subjects. This man least favoureth the English of any Sagamore (for soe are the kinges with us called, as they are Sachims Southwards) wee are acquainted with, by reason of the old quarrell betweene him and those of Plymouth, wherein hee lost 7 of his best men, yet hee lodged one night the last winter at my house in freindly manner. About 70 or 80 miles westward from theis, are seated the Nipnett men, whose Sagamore wee know not, but wee heare their numbers exceed any but the Pecoates and the Narragansets, and they are the only people wee yet heare of in the inland Country. Uppon the river of Mistick is seated Saggamore *John,* and uppon the river Sawgus, Sagamore *James* his brother, both soe named by the English.—The elder brother *John* is a handsome young [*one line missing*] conversant with us, affecting English Apparell and howses and speaking well of our God. His brother *James* is of a farr worse disposition, yet repaireth often to us. Both theis brothers command not above 30 or 40 men for aught I can learne. Neer to Salem dwelleth 2 or 3 families, subject to the Saggamore of Agawam, whose name he tould mee, but I have forgotten it. This Sagamore hath but few subjects and them and himself tributary to Sagamore *James,* havinge beene before the last yeare (in James

his minority) tributary to *Chicka Talbott*. Uppon the river Merimack is seated Sagamore *Passaconaway,* having under his command
4 or 500 men, being esteemed by his countrymen a false fellow,
and by us a wich. For any more northerly I know not, but leave
it to after relacons. Haveing thus breifly and disorderly, especially
in my description of the Bays and Rivers set downe what is come
to hand touching the [*one line missing*]

Now concerninge the English that are planted here, I find that
about the year 1620, certaine English sett out from Leyden, in
Holland, intending their course for Hudson's river; the mouth
whereof lyeth south of the river of the Pecoates, but ariseth as
I am informed, northwards in about 43 degrees, and soe a good
part of it within the compass of our Patent. Theis being much
weather beaten and wearied with seeking the river after a most
tedious voyage, arrived at length in a small Bay, lyeing north east
from Cape Cod, where, landing about the moenth of December,
by the favour of a calm winter, such as was never seene here since,
beganne to build their dwellinges in that place, which now is
called New Plymouth, where, after much sicknes, famine, povertie
and great mortality, (through all which God by an unwonted
Providence caryed them) they are now groune upp to a people,
healthfull, wealthy, politique and religious: such thinges doth the
Lord for those that waite for his mercies. Theis of Plymouth came
with Patents from King *James,* and have since obtained others
from our Sovereigne King *Charles,* haveing a Governour and
Counsaile of their owne. There was about the same time one
Mr. *Wesen,* an English merchant, who sent diverse men to plant
and trade who sate downe by the river Wesaguscus, but theis not
comeing for soe good ends as those of Plymouth, spedd not soe
well, for the most of them dyinge and languishing away, they
who survived were rescued by those of Plymouth out of the hands
of *Chicka Talbott,* and his Indians, who oppressed these weake
English, and intended to have distroyed them, and the Plymotheans
also, as is set downe in a tract written by Mr. Winslow of Plymouth. Also since, one Capt. *Wollastone* wth. some 30 with him,
came neer to the same place, and built on a hill, which he named
Mount Wollaston; but being not supplied with renewed provisions,
they vanished away as the former did. Also, diverse merchants
of Bristow and some other places have yearly for theis 8 years

or thereabouts sent ships hether at the fishing times to trade for Beaver where there factors dishonestly for their gaines, have furnished the Indians with guns, swords, powder and shott.

Touching the plantacon which wee here have begun, it fell out thus:—About the yeare 1627, some friends beeing togeather in Lincolnshire, fell into some discourse about New England, and the plantinge of the gospell there; and after some deliberation wee imparted our reasons by lres. and messages to some in London and the west country, where it was likewise deliberately thought uppon, and at length with often negotiation soe ripened that in the year 1628, wee procured a patent from his Matie for our planting betweene the Matachusets Bay and Charles River on the south and the River of Merimack on the North; and 3 miles on eyther side of those Rivers and Bay; as allso for the goverment of those who did or should inhabit wth. in that compass: and the same yeare, we sent Mr. *John Endicott* and some wth. him to beginne a plantacon; and to strengthen such as hee should find there, which wee sent hether from Dorchester and some places adjoyning; from whom the same year receiveinge hopeful newes, the next yeare, 1629, wee sent diverse shipps over wth. about 300 people, and some cowes, goates and horses, many of which arrived safely. Theis by their too large commendacons of the Country, and the commodities thereof, invited us soe strongly to goe on that Mr. Wenthropp of Suffolke (who was well knowne in his owne country and well approved heere for his pyety, liberality, wisedom and gravity) cominge in to us, wee came to such resolution that in April, 1630, wee sett saile from old England with 4 good shipps. And in May following, 8 more followed; 2 haveing gone before in February and March, and 2 more following in June and August, besides another set out by a private merchant. Theis 17 shipps arrived all safe in New England for the increase of the plantacon here this yeare 1630—but made a long, a troublesome and costly voyage, beeing all windbound long in England, and hindred with contrary winds, after they sett saile and soe scattered wth. mists and tempests that few of them arrived together. Our 4 shipps which sett out in Aprill arrived here in June and July, where wee found the Colony in a sadd and unexpected condition, above 80 of them beeing dead the winter before, and many of those alive, weake and sicke; all the corne

and bread amongst them all, hardly sufficient to feed upon a fortnight, insomuch that the remainder of 180 servents wee had the
two yeares before sent over, cominge to us for victualls to sustaine
them, wee found ourselves wholly unable to feed them by reason
that the provisions shipped for them were taken out of the shipp
they were put in, and they who were trusted to shipp them in
another, failed us, and left them behind; whereupon necessity
enforced us to our extreme loss to give them all libertie, who had
cost us about 16 or 20 £. a person furnishing and sending over.
But bearing theis things as wee might, wee beganne to consult
of the place of our sitting downe; for Salem, where wee landed,
pleased us not.—And to that purpose, some were sent to the Bay
to search upp the rivers for a convenient place; who uppon their
returne, reported to have found a good place uppon Mistick; but
some other of us seconding theis to approve or dislike of their
judgment, wee found a place [*that*] liked us better, 3 leagues up
Charles river; and thereuppon unshipped our goods into other
vessells and with much cost and labour, brought them in July to
Charlestowne: but there receiveing advertisements by some of the
late arrived shipps from London and Amsterdam, of some French
preparations against us (many of our people brought with us
beeing sick of feavers and the scurvy, and wee thereby unable to
carry up our ordinance and baggage soe farr) wee were forced
to change counsaile and for our present shelter to plant dispersedly,
some at Charles Towne which standeth on the North side of the
mouth of Charles river; some on the south side thereof, which
place wee named Boston; (as wee intended to have done the place
wee first resolved on) some of us upon Mistick, which wee named
Meadford; some of us westwards on Charles river, 4 miles from
Charles Towne, which place wee named Watertowne; others of
us 2 miles from Boston, in a place wee named Rocksbury; others
uppon the river of Sawgus betweene Salem and Charles Towne;
and the western men 4 miles South from Boston, at a place wee
named Dorchester. This dispersion troubled some of us, but helpe
it wee could not; wanting ability to remoove to any place fitt to
build a Towne uppon, and the time too short to deliberate any
longer, least the winter should surprize us before wee had builded
our houses. The best counsel wee could find out was, to build a
fort to retire to, in some convenient place, if an enemy pressed

thereunto, after wee should have fortified ourselves against the
injuries of wett and cold. So ceasing to consult further for that
time, they who had health to labour fell to building, wherein many
were interrupted with sicknes and many dyed weekely, yea almost
dayley. Amongst whom were Mrs. *Pinchon,* Mrs. *Coddington,*
Mrs. *Philips,* and Mrs. *Alcock,* a sister of Mr. *Hookers.* Insomuch
that the shipps beeing now uppon their returne, some for England,
some for Ireland, there was, as I take it not much less than an
hundred (some think many more) partly out of dislike of our
government which restrained and punished their excesses, and
partly through fear of famine, not seeing other meanes than by
their labour to feed themselves, which returned back againe. And
glad were wee so to bee ridd of them. Others also afterwards
heareing of men of their owne disposition, which were planted
at Pascataway, went from us to them, whereby though our numbers
were lessened, yet wee accounted ourselves nothing weakened by
their removeall. Before the departure of the shipps, we contracted
with Mr. *Peirce* Mr. of the Lyon of Bristow, to returne to us with
all speed with fresh supplies of victualls, and gave him directions
accordingly. With this shipp returned Mr. *Revil,* one of the 5
undertakers here for the joint stock of the company; and Mr. *Vassall.* one of the assistants, and his family; and also Mr. *Bright,*
a minister, sent hither the yeare before. The shipps beeinge gone,
victualls wastinge, and mortality increasinge, wee held diverse
fasts in our severall congregations, but the Lord would not yet
bee depricated; for about the beginning of September, dyed Mr.
Gager, a right godly man, a skilful chirurgeon, and one of the
deacons of our congregation; and Mr. *Higginson,* one of the ministers of Salem, a zealous and a profitable preacher;—this of a
consumption, that of a feaver, and on the 30th of September, dyed
Mr. *Johnson* another of the 5 undertakers (the Lady *Arrabella,*
his wife, being dead a month before.) This gentleman was a
prime man amongst us, haveing the best estate of any, zealous
for religion and greatest furtherer of this plantation. He made
a most godly end, dying willingly, professing his life better spent
in promoting this plantacon than it would have beene any other
way. He left to us a loss greater than the most conceived.—
Within a month after, dyed Mr. *Rossiter,* another of our assistants,
a godly man, and of a good estate, which still weakened us more;

so that there now were left of the 5 undertakers but the Governour, Sir *Richard Saltonstall* and myselfe, and 7 other of the Assistants. And of the people who came over with us, from the time of their setting saile from England in Aprill, 1630, untill December followinge, there dyed by estimacon about 200 at the least—Soe lowe hath the Lord brought us! Well, yet they who survived were not discouraged, but bearing God's corrections with humilitye and trusting in his mercies, and considering how after a greater ebb hee had raised upp our neighbours at Plymouth, wee beganne againe in December to consult about a fitt place to build a towne uppon, leaveinge all thoughts of a Fort, because uppon any invasion wee were necesarily to loose our howses when wee should retire thereunto; soe after diverse meetings at Boston, Roxbury and Waterton on the 28th day of December, wee grew to this resolucon to bind all the Assistants (Mr. *Endicott* and Mr. *Sharpe* excepted, which last purposeth to return by the next shipps into England) to build howses at a place, a mile East from Waterton, neere Charles river, the next spring, and to winter there the next year, that soe by our examples and by removeing the ordinance and munition thether, all who were able, might be drawne thether, and such as shall come to us hereafter to their advantage bee compelled soe to doe, and soe if God would, a fortified Towne might there grow upp, the place fitting reasonably well thereto. I should before have mentioned how both the English and Indian corne beeinge at tenne shillings a strike, and beaver beeinge valued a. 6 shilling a pound, wee made laws to restraine the selling of corne to the Indians, and to leave the price of beaver at libertie, which was presently sold for tenne and 20 shillings a pound. I should alsoe have remembred how the halfe of our cowes and almost all our mares and goats, sent us out of England dyed at sea in their passage hither, and that those intended to be sent us out of Ireland were not sent at all; all which togeather with the loss of our six months building, occasioned by our intended removeall to a Towne to bee fortified weakened our estates, especially the estates of the undertakers, who were 3 or 4000£. engaged in the joynt stock, which was now not above soe many hundreds; yet many of us laboured to beare it as comfortably as wee could, remembringe the end of our comeinge hether and knowinge the power of God who canne support and raise us againe, and useth to bring his servants lowe that the meeke may bee made glorious by deliverance. Psal. 112.

In the end of this December, departed from us the shipp Handmaid of London, by which wee sent away one *Thomas Morton,* a proud insolent man who has lived here diverse years, and had beene an Attorney in the West Countryes while he lived in England. Multitude of complaintes were received against him for injuries doone by him both to the English and Indians, and amongst others for shootinge hail shott at a troope of Indians, for not bringing a Cannowe unto him to cross a river withall, whereby hee hurt one, and shott through the garments of another; for the satisfacon of the Indians wherein, and that it might appear to them and to the English that wee meant to doe justice impartially, wee caused his hands to be bound behind him and sett his feete in the bill bowes, and burned his howse to the ground, all in the sight of the Indians, and soe kept him prisoner till wee sent him for England, whether wee sent him, for that my Lord Cheife Justice there soe required that he might punish him cappitally for fowler misdemeaners there perpetrated as wee were informed.

I have no leasure to review and insert things forgotton, but out of due time and order must sett them downe as they come to memory.—About the end of October this year, 1630, I joyned with the Governour and Mr. *Maverecke* in sendinge out our pinnace to the Narragansetts to trade for corne to supply our wants, but after the pynace had doubled Cape Cod, shee putt into the next harbour shee found, and there meetinge with Indians, who shewed their willingness to truck, shee made her voyage their, and brought us 100 bushells of corne, at about 4s. a bushell, which helped us somewhat. From the coast where they traded, they saw a very large island, 4 leagues to the east, which the Indians commended as a fruitefull place, full of good vines, and free from sharpe frosts, haveing one only entrance into it, by a navigable river, inhabitted by a few Indians, which for a trifle would leave the island, if the English would sett them uppon the maine; but the pynace haveinge noe direction for discovery, returned without sayling to it, which in 2 houers they might have done. Uppon this coast, they found store of vines full of grapes dead ripe, the season beeing past—whether wee purpose to send the next yeare sooner, to make some small quantitie of wine, if God enable us, the vines growinge thinne with us and wee not haveinge yett any leasure to plant vineyards. But now haveing some leasure to discourse of the motives for other men's comeinge to this place, or their abstaininge from it, after my breif manner I say this;—That if any come hether to plant for worldly ends that canne live well at home, he committs an errour, of which he will soone repent him. But if for spirituall, and that noe particular obstacle hinder his removeall, hee may find here what may well content him vizt: materialls to build, fewell to burne, ground to plant, seas and rivers to fish in, a pure ayer to breathe in, good water to drinke, till wine or beare canne be made; which, togeather with the cowes, hoggs and goates brought hether allready, may suffice for food; for as for foule and venison, they are dainties here as well as in England. For cloaths and bedding, they must bringe them wth. them, till time and industry produce them here. In a word, wee yett enjoy little to be envyed, but endure much to be pittyed in the sicknes and mortallitye of our people. And I do the more willingly use this open and plaine dealinge, least other men should fall short of their expectacons when they come hether, as wee to our great prejudice did, by meanes of letters sent us from hence into England, wherein honest men out of a desire to draw over others to them, wrote somewhat hyperbolically of many things here. If any godly men, out of religious ends, will come over to helpe us in the good worke wee are about, I think they cannot dispose of themselves nor of their estates more to God's glory, and the furtherance of their owne reckoninge; but they must not bee of the poorer sort yett, for diverse years; for wee have found by experience that they have hindred, not furthered the worke—And for profaine and deboshed persons, their oversight in comeinge hether is wondered at, where they shall find nothing to content them. If there bee any endued with grace and furnished with meanes to feed themselves and theirs for 18 months, and to build and plant, lett them come over into our Macedonia and helpe us, and not spend themselves and their estates in a less profittable employment; for others I conceive they are not yet fitted for this busines.

Touching the discouragements which the sicknes and mortality which every first year hath seized upon us, and those of Plymouth as appeareth before, may give to such who have cast any thoughts this way (of which mortality it may bee said of us allmost as of the Egiptians, that there is not an howse where there is not one dead, and in some howses many) the naturall causes seem to bee in the want of warm lodginge, and good dyet, to which Englishmen are habittuated at home; and in the suddain increase of heate which they endure that are landed here in somer, the salt meates at sea haveinge prepared their bodyes thereto, for those onely 2 last yeares dyed of feavers who landed in June and July; as those of Plymouth who landed in the winter dyed of the scirvy, as did our poorer sort, whose howses and bedding kept them not sufficiently warm, nor their dyet sufficiently in heart. Other causes God may have, as our faithfull minister Mr. *Wilsoune* (lately handlinge that poynt) shewed unto us, which I forbeare to mention, leaving this matter to the farther dispute of phisitions and divines—Wherefore to returne, upon the third of January dyed the daughter of Mr. *Sharpe,* a godly virginne, making a comfortable end, after a long sicknes. The plantacon here received not the like loss of any woman since wee came hether, and therefore shee well deserves to be remembred in this place; and to add to our sorrowes, uppon the 5th day, came letters to us from Plymouth, advertiseinge us of this sadd accident followinge.—About a fortnight before, there went from us in a shallop to Plymouth 6 men and a girle, who in an hour or two before night, on the same day they went forth, came near to the mouth of Plymouth Bay, but the wind then comeing strongly from the shore, kept them from entering and drove them to sea wards, and they haveing no better means to helpe themselves, lett down their killick, that soe they might drive the more slowly, and bee nearer land when the storm should cease. But the stone slipping out of the killick, and thereby they driving faster than they thought all the night, in the morninge, when they looked out, they found themselves out of sight of land, which soe astonished them, the frost being extreme and their hands soe benummed with cold, that they could not handle their oares, neyther had any compass to steare by, that they gave themselves for lost, and lay downe to dye quietly, onely one man who had more naturall heate and courage remaining then the rest, continued soe long lookinge for land, that the morning waxing clearer, hee discovered land, and with difficulty hoysted the saile, and soe the winde a little turninge, 2 days after they were driven from

Plymouth Bay, they arrived at a shore unknowne unto them. The stronger helped the weaker out of the boate and takeing their saile on shore, made a shelter thereof, and made a fire; but the frost had soe peirced their bodyes that one of them dyed about 3 days after their landinge, and most of the others grew worse, both in bodye and courage;—noe hope of releife beeinge within their veiw. Well, yett the Lord pittyinge them and two of them who onely could use their leggs goeing abroad, rather to seeke then to hope to find helpe, they mett first with 2 Indian women, who sent unto them an Indian man, who informed them that Plymouth was within 50 miles, and offered togeather to procure releife for them, which they gladly accepting, hee perfourmed, and brought them 3 men from Plymouth (the governour and counsell of Plymouth liberally rewardinge the Indian and tooke care for the safety of our people) who brought them all alive in their boate thether, save one man, who with a guide chose rather to goe over land, but quickly fell lame by the way, and getting harbour at a trucking house the Plymotheans had in those partes: there he yet abides. At the others landing at Plymouth, one of them dyed as hee was taken out of the boate; another (and he the worst in the company) rotted from the feete upwards where the frost had gotten most hold, and soe dyed within *in* a few days. The other 3, after God had blessed the Chirurgeon's skill used towards them, returned safe to us. I sett downe this the more largely, partly because the first man that dyed was a godly man of our congregation; one *Richard Garrad,* who, at the time of his death, more feared hee should dishonour God than cared for his own life;—As allso because diverse boates have been in manifest perill this year, yett the Lord preserved them all, this one excepted. Amongst those who dyed about the end of this Jannuary, there was a girle of 11 years old, the daughter of one *John Ruggles* of whose family and kindred dyed so many, that for some reason it was matter of observacon amongst us; who in the time of her sicknes expressed to the minister and to those about her, soe much faith and assurance of salvation, as is rarely found in any of that age, which I thought not unworthy here to committ to memory; and if any taxe mee for wastinge paper with recordinge theis small matters, such may consider that little mothers bring fourth little children, small common wealths;—matters of small moment, the reading whereof yett is not to be despised by the judicious, because small things in the beginning of naturall or politique bodyes are as remarkable as greater in bodyes full growne.

Upon the 5 of February, arrived here Mr. *Peirce* with the ship Lyon of Bristow with supplyes of victuals from England, who had sett fourth from Bristow the first of December before. He had a stormy passage hether, and lost one of his saylors not far from our shore, who in a tempest having helped to take in the spritt saile, lost his hold as he was comeinge downe and fell into the sea; where after long swimminge hee was drouned, to the great dolour of those in the shipp, who beheld so lamentable a spectacle, without beeing able to minister help to him; the sea swa soe high and the shipp drove soe fast before the wind, though her sailes were taken downe. By this shipp wee understood of the fight of 3 of our shipps and 2 English men of war comeing out of the straites with 14 Dunkirkes, upon the coast of England as they returned from us in the end of the last summer, who through God's goodness with the loss of some 13 or 14 men out of our 3 shipps; and I know not how many out of the 2 men of war gott at length clear of them. The Charles, one of our 3, a stout shipp of 300 tunne, beeing soe torne, that shee had not much of her left whole above water.—

By this shipp wee also understood the death of many of those who went from us the last year to Old England, as likewise of the mortallity there, whereby wee see are graves in other places as well as with us.

Allso to increase the heape of our sorrows, wee received advertisement by lers. from our friends in England, and by the reports of those who came hether in this shipp to abide with us, (who were about 26) that they who went discontentedly from us the last year, out of their evill affections towards us, have raised many false and scandalous reports against us, affirminge us to be BROWNISTS in religion, and ill affected to our state at home and that theis vile reports have wonne credit with some who formerly wished us well. But wee doe desire, and cannot but hope, that wise and impartial men will at length consider that such malecontents have ever pressed this manner of casting dirt to make others seeme as fowle as themselves, and that our godly freinds, to whome wee have beene known, will not easily believe that wee are not soe

soon turned from the profession wee soe long have made in our
native country: And for our further cleareinge, I truely affirm,
that I know noe one person who came over with us the last yeare
to bee altered in judgment and affection, eyther in eccliasticall or
civill respects since our comeing hither; but wee doe continue to
pray dayly for our Soveraigne lord the King, the Queene, the
Prince, the royal blood, the counsaile and whole state, as duty
bindes us to doe, and reason perswades others to believe, for
how ungodly and unthankfull should wee bee if wee should not
thus doe, who came hether by vertue of his Maj.ties letters patent,
and under his gracious protection, under which shelter wee hope
to live safely, and from whome [whose?] kingdom and subjects,
wee now have received and hereafter expect reliefe. Lett our
friends therefore give noe credit to such malicious aspersions, but
be more ready to answer for us, then we hear they have been: we
are not like those which have dispensations to lye; but as wee were
free enough in Old England, to turne our in sides outwards, som-
times to our disadvantage, very unlike is it that now (beeinge
procul a fulmine) wee should be so unlike ourselves: lett therefore
this bee sufficient for us to say, and others to heare in this matter.

Amongst others who dyed about this time was Mr. *Robert
Welden,* whom in the time of his sickness, wee had chosen to bee
Captaine of 100 foote, but before hee tooke possession of his
place, he dyed the 16 of this February, and was buried as a soldier
with 3 volleys of shott. Upon the 22 day of February, wee held a
general day of Thanksgiveinge throughout the whole Colony for
the safe arrivall of the shipp which came last with our provisions.

About this time, wee apprehended one *Robert Wright,* who had
been sometimes a lynnen draper in Newgate market, and after that
a brewer on the Banke side and on Thames streete. This man wee
lately understood had made an escape in London from those who
came to his howse to apprehend him for clipping the kinges coyne
[*one or two words wanting*] had stolen after us.—Uppon his
examinacon, hee confessed the fact and his escape, but affirmed hee
had the kinges pardon for it, under the broade seale, which hee
yett not being able to proove, and one to whome he was known
chargeing him with untruth in some of his answers, wee therefore
committed him to prison, to be sent by the next shipp into England.

Likewise, wee were lately informed that one Mr. *Gardiner,* who arrived here a month before us (and who had passed here for a knight by the name of Sr. *Christopher Gardiner* all this while) was noe knight, but instead thereof, had two wives now liveinge in an house at London, one of which came about September last from Paris in France (where her husband had left her years before) to London, where she had heard her husband had marryed a second wife, and whom by enquiryg she found out, and they both condoling each others estate, wrote both their lres. to the governour (by Mr. *Pierce* who had conference with both the women in the presence of Mr. *Allerton* of Plymouth;) his first wife desiring his returne and conversion; his second, his destruccon for his foule abuse, and for robbing her of her estate, of a part whereof she sent an Inventory hether, compriseinge therein many rich jewels, much plate and costly lynnen. This man had in his family (and yet hath) a gentlewoman whom he called his kinswoman, and whom one of his wives in her letter, names *Mary Grove,* affirming her to be a knowne harlot, whose sending back into Old England shee allso desired, togeather with her husband. Shortly after this intelligence, wee sent to the house of the said *Gardiner* (which was 7 miles from us) to apprehend him and his woman, with a purpose to send them both to London to his wives there; but the man, who haveing heard some rumour from some who came in the shipp, that lres. were come to the Governor, requireing justice against him, was readily prepared for flight, soe soone as he should see any crossinge the river, or likely to apprehend him, which hee accordingly perfourmed; for hee dwelling aloone, easily discerned such who were sent to take him, halfe a mile before they approached his house, and with his peece on his neck, went his way, as most men think northwards, hopeing to find some English there like to himselfe; but likely enough it is, which way so ever hee went, hee will loose himselfe in the woods and be stopped with some rivers in his passing, notwithstanding his compass in his pockett, and soe with hunger and cold, will perish before hee find the place hee seekes. His woman was brought unto us and confessed her name, and that her mother dwells 8 miles from Beirdly in Salopshire, and that *Gardiner's* father dwells in or neare Gloucester, and was (as shee said) brother to *Stephen Gardiner,* Bishop of Winchester, and did disinherit his sonne for his 26 years absence in his travailes in France, Italy, Germany and Turkey; that he had (as he told her) marryed a wife in his travailes, from whom hee was devorced, and the woman long since dead; that both herselfe and *Gardiner* were both Catholiques till of late, but were now Protestants; that shee takes him to be a knight, but never heard when he was knighted. The woman was impenitent and close, confessing noe more then was wrested from her by her owne contradictions, soe wee have taken order to send her to the two wives in Old England to search her further.

Upon the 8 of March, from after it was faire day light untill about 8 of the clock in the forenoon, there flew over all the towns in our plantacons soe many flocks of doves, each flock conteyning many thousands, and some soe many that they obscured the light, that passeth credit, if but the truth should bee written; and the thing was the more strange, because I scarce remember to have seene tenne doves since I came into this country. They were all turtles, as appeared by diverse of them we killed flying, somewhat bigger than those of Europe, and they flew from the north east to the south west; but what it portends I know not.

The shipp now waits but for wind, which when it blows, there are ready to go aboard therein for England Sr. *Richard Saltonstall,* Mr. *Sharpe,* Mr. *Coddington,* and many others, the most whereof purpose to returne to us again, if God will. In the meane time, wee are left a people poor and contemptible, yet such as trust in God and are contented with our condition, beeing well assured that he will not faile us nor forsake us.

I had almost forgotten to add this, that the wheate we received by this last shipp stands us in 13 or 14 shillinges a strike, and the pease about 11s. a strike, besides the adventure, which is worth 3 or 4 shillinges a strike, which is an higher price than I ever tasted bread of before.

Thus, MADAM, I have as I canne, told your Hon. all ourmatters, knowinge your wisedome canne make good use thereof. If I live not to perfourme the like office of my dutie hereafter, likely it is some other will doe it better.

Before the depparture of the Shipp (wch. yet was wind bound) there came unto us Sagamore *John* and one of his subjects requireinge sattisfaction for the burning of two wigwams by some of the English, which wiggwams were not inhabitted, but stod in a place convenient for their shelter, when uppon occasion they should travaile that wayes. By examination, wee found that some English fowlers haveing retired into that which belonged to the subject and leaveinge a fire therein carelessly which they had kindled to warm them, were the cause of burninge thereof; for that which was the Sagamores, wee could find no certaine proofe how it was fired, yet least hee should thinke us not scedulous enough to find it out, and soe should depart discontentedly from us, wee gave both him and his subject satisfaction for them both.

The like accident of fire allso befell Mr. *Sharpe* and Mr. *Colborne* upon the 17 of this March, both whose howses, which were as good, and as well furnished as the most in the plantacon, were in 2 houres space burned to the ground, togeather with much of their househould stuff, apparell and other thinges, as allsoe some goods of others who sojourned wth. them in their howses; God soe pleaseing to exercise us with corrections of this kind, as hee hath done with others: for the prevention whereof in our new towne, intended this somer to bee builded, wee have ordered that noe man there shall build his chimney with wood, nor cover his house with thatch, which was readily assented unto, for that diverse other howses have beene burned since our arrivall (the fire allwaies beginninge in the woodden chimneys) and some English wigwams, which have taken fire in the roofes covered with thatch or boughs.

And that this shipp might returne into Old England with heavy newes, uppon the 18 day of March, came one from Salem and told us, that uppon the 15 thereof, there dyed Mrs. *Skelton,* the wife of the other minister there, who, about 18 or 20 dayes before, handling cold thinges in a sharpe morninge, put herselfe into a most violent fitt of the wind colleck and vomitting, which continuinge, shee at length fell into a feaver and soe dyed as before. She was a godly and an helpfull woman, and indeed the maine pillar of her family, haveinge left behind her an husband and 4 children, weake and helpeles, who canne scarce tell how to live without her—She lived desired and dyed lamented, and well deserves to bee honourably remembred.

Uppon the 25 of this March, one of Waterton haveing lost a calfe, and about 10 of the clock at night, hearinge the howlinge of some wolves not farr off, raysed many of his neighbours out of their bedds, that by dischargeinge their muskeets neere about the place where hee heard the wolves, hee might so putt the wolves to flight, and save his calfe—The wind serveing fitt to cary the report of the musketts to Rocksbury, 3 miles off at such a time; the inhabitants there tooke an alarme beate upp their drume, armed themselves, and sent in post to us in Boston to raise us allsoe. Soe in the morninge the calfe beeinge found safe, the wolves affrighted, and our danger past, wee went merrily to breakefast.

I thought to have ended before, but the stay of the shipp and my desire to informe your honr. of all I canne, hath caused this addition, and every one haveinge warninge to prepare for the shipps departure tomorrow, I am now this 28th of March, 1631, sealing my lres.

4
John Winthrop

John Winthrop, as the preceding pages have made clear, was the key figure in the founding of Massachusetts. Even if none of his papers had survived, his preeminence would still be apparent from other sources. But Winthrop was himself the most assiduous recorder of the events in which he participated. From the time he set foot on the *Arbella* until his death in 1649, he kept a journal, the historical purpose of which is suggested by the fact that after the first few days he refrained from using the first person singular and wrote of himself as "the governor." Apart from the Records of the Massachusetts Bay Company, this journal is the richest single source of information about early Massachusetts, but it is not the only one that Winthrop left us. He and the other members of his family saved many of the letters they received both from one another and from outsiders. These, together with the journal and other papers, were preserved in the family from generation to generation until they were deposited in the library of the Massachusetts Historical Society.

The letters and papers, with other surviving Winthrop documents from other libraries, have been published by the Society, first in various volumes of its *Collections* and now in a magnificent edition-in-progress of *Winthrop Papers* (Boston, 1929–   ) arranged chronologically and extending over several generations of the family from 1498 onward. By permission of the Society, selections from this edition are here reprinted, along with Winthrop's journal from March 29, 1630, the date on which he began it, up to the time of his retirement from the governorship in May 1634. The text of the journal has been taken from James Savage's edition (Boston, 1853), pages 1–158, the last to be made by transcription from the original manuscript.

The selections are arranged as follows: numbers 1–6 are letters and papers antedating the time of Winthrop's arrival in New England (*Winthrop Papers*, II, 138–145, 151–152, 218–219, 224–226, 231–233, 282–295); number 7 is Winthrop's journal to May 14, 1634; numbers 8–18 are letters and papers dating from July 16, 1630, to May 22, 1634 (*Winthrop Papers*, II, 301–302, 303–304, 312–313, 314, 319–320; III, 17–19, 19–20, 20–21, 24–26, 139–140, 166–168). Note that Winthrop followed the same system of dating as Thomas Dudley.

1. Reasons to be Considered, and Objections with Answers[1]

Reasons to be considered for justifieinge the undertakeres of the intended Plantation in New England, and for incouraginge such whose hartes God shall move to joyne with them in it.

(1 It will be a service to the Church of great consequence to carry the Gospell into those parts of the world, to helpe on the comminge of the fullnesse of the Gentiles, and to raise a Bulworke against the kingdome of Ante-Christ which the Jesuites labour to reare up in those parts.

(2) All other Churches of Europe are brought to desolation, and our sinnes, for which the Lord beginnes allreaddy to frowne upon us, and to cutte us short doe threatne evill times to be com-minge upon us, and whoe knowes, but that God hath provided this place to be a refuge for many whome he meanes to save out of the generall callamity, and seeinge the Church hath noe place lefte to flie into but the wildernesse, what better worke can there be, then to goe and provide tabernacles and foode for her against she comes thether:

(3 This Land growes weary of her Inhabitantes, soe as man whoe is the most praetious of all creatures, is here more vile and base then the earth we treade upon, and of lesse prise among us then an horse or a sheepe, masters are forced by authority to entertaine servants, parents to mainetaine there owne children, all

---

[1] This manuscript, the first draft of which was probably composed by Winthrop in the spring or early summer of 1629, is one of several surviving versions.

townes complaine of the burthen of theire poore, though we have taken up many unnessicarie yea unlawfull trades to mainetaine them, and we use the authoritie of the Law to hinder the increase of our people, as by urginge the Statute against Cottages, and inmates, and thus it is come to passe, that children servantes and Neighboures especially if they be poore are compted the greatest burthens, which if thinges weare right would be the cheifest earthly blessinges.

(4) The whole earth is the Lords garden and he hath given it to the sonnes of men with a gen[eral] Commission: Gen: 1: 28: increace and multiplie, and replenish the earth and subdue it, which was againe renewed to Noah, the end is double and naturall, that man might enjoy the fruits of the earth, and God might have his due glory from the creature: why then should we stand striving here for places of habitation etc. (many men spending as much labour and coste to recover or keepe sometimes an acre or twoe of Land, as would procure them many C[hundred] as good or better in another Countrie) and in the meane time suffer a whole Continent as fruitfull and convenient for the use of man to lie waste without any improvement?

(5) We are growne to that height of Intemperance in all excesse of Riott, as noe mans estate allmost will suffice to keepe saile with his aequalls: and he, whoe failes herein, must live in scorne and contempt. Hence it comes that all artes and Trades are carried in that deceiptfull and unrighteous course, as it is allmost impossible for a good and upright man to mainetayne his charge and live comfortablie in any of them.

(6) The Fountaines of Learning and Religion are soe corrupted as (besides the unsupportable charge of there education) most children (even the best witts and of faierest hopes) are perverted, corrupted, and utterlie overthrowne by the multitude of evill examples and the licentious government of those Seminaries, where men straine at knatts, and swallowe camells, use all severity for mainetaynance of cappes, and other accomplymentes, but suffer all ruffianlike fashions, and disorder in manners to passe uncontrolled.

(7) What can be a better worke, and more honorable and worthy a Christian then to helpe raise and supporte, a particular Church while it is in the Infancy, and to joyne his forces with

such a company of faithfull people, as by a timely assistance may growe stronge and prosper, and for wante of it may be put to great hazard, if not wholy ruined:

(8 If any such are knowne to be Godly, and live in wealth and prosperity here shall forsake all this, to joyne themselves with this Church and to runne an Hazard with them of an hard and meane condition, it will be an example of great use both for removinge the scandall of worldly and sinister respects which is cast upon the Adventurers: to give more life to the faith of Gods people, in theire praiers for the Plantation, and to incorrage others to joyne the more willingly in it:

(9) It appeares to be a worke of God for the good of his Church in that he hath disposed the hartes of soe many of his wise and faithfull servantes both ministers, and others not onely to approve of the enterprise but to interest themselves in it, some in theire persons, and estates, other by there serious advise and helpe otherwise, and all by there praiers for the wealfare of it Amos 3: the Lord revealeth his secreat to his servantes the profits, it is likely he hath some great worke in hand which he hath revealed to his prophetts among us whom he hath stirred up to encourage his servantes to this Plantation, for he doeth not use to seduce his people by his owne prophetts, but committe that office to the ministrie of false prophetts and lieing sperittes.

Diverse objections which have beene made against this Plantation, with theire answears and Resolutions:

Ob: 1: We have noe warrant to enter upon that Land which hath beene soe longe possessed by others: *ans:* That which lies common, and hath never beene replenished or subdued is free to any that possesse and improve it: For God hath given to the sonnes of men a double right to the earth; theire is a naturall right, and a Civill Right. The first right was naturall when men held the earth in common every man sowing and feeding where he pleased: then as men and theire Cattell encreased they appropriated certaine parcells of Grownde by inclosinge and peculiar manuerance, and this in time gatte them a Civill right: such was the right which Ephron the Hittite had in the feild of Mackpelah wherein Abraham could not bury a dead Corpes without leave though for the out partes of the Countrie which lay common he dwelt upon then, and tooke the frute of them at his pleasure: the like did Jacob, whoe fedde his Cattell as bouldly in Hamors Land, (for he is said to be Lord of the Countrie) and in other places where he came, as the native Inhabitantes themselves: and that in those times and places men accompted noething theire owne, but that which they had appropriated by theire owne industry, appeares plainely by this, that Abimileckes servantes in there owne Countrie, when they ofte contended with Isaackes servantes about welles which they had digged, yet never strove for the Land wherein they weare: Soe likewise betweene Jacob and Laban, he would not take a kidde of Labans without speaciall contracte; but he makes noe bargaine with them for the Land where they fedde, and it is very probable that if the Countrie had not beene as free for Jacob as for Laban, that covetous wretch would have made his advantage of it, and have upbraided Jacob with it as he did with his Cattell: As for the Natives in New England, they inclose noe Land, neither have any setled habytation, nor any tame Cattle to improve the Land by, and soe have noe other but a Naturall Right to those Countries. soe as if we leave them sufficient for their use, we may lawfully take the rest, there being more then enough for them and us:

2 We shall come in with the good leave of the natives who finde benifight allreaddy by our Neighbourhood, and learne from us to improve a parte to more use then before they could doe the whole: and by this meanes we come in by valuable purchase, for they have of us that, which will yeeld them more benifight, then all that Land which we have from them.

3 God hath consumed the Natives with a great Plauge in those partes, soe as there be few Inhabitantes lefte.

Ob: 2: It will be a great wrong to our Church and Countrie to take awaye the good people, and we shall lay it the more open to the Judgment feared:

Ans: 1 The departinge of good people from a Countrie doe not cause a Judgment but forshew it, which may occasion such as remaine to turne from there evill waies, that they may praevent it, or to take some other course that they may escape it:

2 Such as goe awaye are of noe observation in respect of those

whoe remaine and they are likely to doe more good there then here, and since Christes time the Church is to be considered as universall without distinction of Countries, soe as he that doeth good in one place serves the Church in all places in regard of the unity.

3 It is the revealed will of God that the Gospell should be preached to all nations, and though we know not whether those Barbarians will receive it at first or noe, yet it is a good worke to serve Gods providence in offering it to them (and this is fittest to be doone by Godes owne servantes) for God shall have glory by it though they refuse it, and there is good hope that the Posterity shall by this meanes be gathered into Christes sheepefould.

Ob: 3 We have feared a Judgment a great while, but yet we are safe, it weare better therefore to stay till it come, and either we may flie then, or if we bee overtaken in it we may well content ourselves to suffer with such a Church as ours is:

Ans: It is likely that this consideration made the Churches beyound the Seas as the Pallatinate, Rochell etc. to sitt still at home, and not looke out for shelter, while they might have founde it; but the woefull spectacle of theire ruine may teach us more wisdome to avoide the Plauge when it is foreseene, and not to tarry as they did till it overtake us. If they weare now at theire former liberty we may be sure they would take other Courses for theire safty and though halfe of them had miscarried in theire escape, yet had it not beene soe miserable to them selves nor scandalous to Religion, as this desperate backsliding and abjuering the trewth, which many of the ancient Professours among them, and the whole Posteritie which remaine are now plundged into:

Ob: 4: The ill successe of other Plantations may tell us what will become of this:

Ans: 1 None of the former sustained any great damage but Virginia which happned through there owne slouth and security.

2 The argument is not good for thus it standes: some Plantations have miscarried therefore we should not make any, it consistes of particulars and soe concludes noethinge we might as well reason thus, many houses have beene burnt by killes; therefore we should use none, many shippes have beene cast awaye therefore we should content ourselves with our home commodities and not adventure

mens lives at Sea for those thinges which we might live without: Some men have beene undoone by being advanced to great places, therefore we should refuse all praeferment: etc:

3 The fruite of any publike designe is not to be discerned by the immediate successe it may appeare in time that the former Plantations weare all to good use.

4 There weare great and fundamentall errors in the former which are like to be avoided in this: For: 1: their mayne end was Carnall and not Religious: 2. They used unfitt instrumentes, a multitude of rude and misgovernd persons the very scumme of the Land: 3: They did not establish a right forme of goverment.

(Ob: 5.) It is attended with many and great difficulties:

Ans: Soe is every good action, the Heathen could say Ardua virtutis via, and the way of Gods kingdome which is the best waye in the world is accompanied with most difficulties streight is the gate, and narrow is the waye that leadeth to life: againe the difficulties are noe other then such as many dayly meete with, and such as God hath brought others well through them:

(Ob: 6. It is a worke above the power of the undertakers:

Ans: 1 The wealfare of any body consists not soe much in quantitie as in a due proportion and disposition of partes, and we see other Plantations have subsisted diverse yeares and prospered from weaker meanes:

2 It is noe wonder for great things to arise from smale and contemptible beginnings it hath beene often seene in kingdomes and states, and may as well hould in townes and plantations. The Waldenses weare scattred into the Alpes, and mountaines of Peidmont by small companies but they became famous Churches whereof some remaine to this day, and it is certaine that the Turckes, Venetians, and other States weare very weake in their beginninges:

Ob: 7 The Countrie affordes noe naturall fortifications:

Ans: Noe more did Holland and many other places which had greater enimies and neerer at hand and God doth use to place his people in the middest of perilles, that they may trust in him and not in outward meanes of safety; soe when he would chouse a place to plante his onely beloved people in, he seated them not in an Iland or other place fortified by nature, but in a plaine Countrie, besette with potent and bitter enimies rounde about, yet soe longe as they served him and trusted in his helpe they weare safe, soe the Apostle Saint Paull saith of himselfe and his fellow labourours that they weare coumpassed with dangers on every side and weare dayly under the sentence of death, that they might learne to trust in the livinge God:

Ob: 8: The place affordeth not comfortable meanes to the first planters and our breedinge here at home hath made us unfitte for the hardshippe we are like to endure there

Ans: 1 Noe place of it selfe hath afforded sufficient to the first Inhabitantes, such thinges as we stand in neede of are usually supplied by Gods blessing upon the wisdome and industry of man, and whatsoever we stand in neede of is treasured up in the earth by the Creator, and to be feched thense by the sweate of our browes:

2 We must learne with Paull to want as well as to abounde; if we have foode and rayment (which are there to be had) we ought to be contented, the difference in the quality may a little displease us but it cannot hurt us.

3 It may be God will by this meanes bringe us to repent of our former Intemperance and soe cure us of that desease which sends many amongst us untimely to our graves and others to Hell. Soe he carried the Isralites into the wildernesse and made them forgette the fleshpotts of Egipt which was some pinch to them at first but he disposed it to their good in the end, Deu: 8: 3: 16:

Ob: 9 We must looke to be praeserved by miracle if we subsiste and soe we shall tempt God

Ans: 1 They who walke under ordinary meanes of safety and supply doe not tempt God but such will our condition be in this Plantation, therefore etc. the proposition can not be denied, the assumption we prove thus, that place is as much secured from ordinary dangers as many C[hundred] in the civill partes of the world and we shall have as much provision beforehand as such townes doe use to provide against a seige or dearth and sufficient meanes for raising sufficient store to succeed against that be spent If it be denied that we shall be as secure as other places, we answeare that many of our Sea townes, and such as are upon the confines of enimies countries in the continent lie more open and neerer to danger then we shall and though such townes have some-time beene burnt or spoiled yet men tempt not God to dwell still in them, and though many houses in the Countrie amongst us lie open to Robbers and theeves (as many have found by sad experience) yet noe man will say that those that dwell in such places must be praeserved by miracle:

2 Though miracles be now ceased yet men may expecte a more then ordinarie blessing from God upon all lawfull meanes where the worke is the Lords and he is sought in it according to his will, for it is usuall with him to encrease or weaken the strenth of the meanes as he is pleased or displeased with the Instrumentes and the action; else we must conclude that God hath lefte the goverment of the world and committed all power to the Creature that the successe of all thinges should wholely depend upon second causes

3 We appeale to the judgment of Soldieres if 500 men may not in one mounth raise a fortification which with sufficient munition and victuall they may not make good against 3000 for many mounths and yet without miracle:

4 We demand an instance of any Prince or state that hath raised 3000 soldieres and hath victuald them for vi or viii mounths with shippinge and munition answerable to invade a place soe far distant as this is from any forraine enimie and where they must runne an hazard of Repulse and noe bootie or just title of soveranitie to allure them:

Ob: 10 If it succeed ill it will raise a scandall upon our profession:

Ans: It is noe rule in Philosophie much lesse in divinity to judge the action by the successe the enterprize of the Israelites against Benjamin succeeded ill twice yet the action was good and prospered in the end. The Erle of Beziers in France and Tholosuye [*sic*] miscarried in the defence of a just cause of Religion and theire hereditarie right against the unjust violence of the Earle Montford and the Popes Legatt. The Duke of Saxony and the Landgrave had ill successe in the defence of the Gospell against Charles the 5th wherein the Duke and his Children lost their whole Inheritance to this day: The Kinge of Denmarck and other Princes of the union had ill successe in the defence of the Palatinate and the Liberty of Germanie yet their profession suffered not with their persons except it weare with the adversaries of Religion and soe it was noe scandall given.

2. *The Agreement at Cambridge*

The true coppie of the Agreement of Cambridge, August. 26. 1629.

Upon due consideracion of the state of the plantacion now in hand for new England, wherein wee (whose names are herunto subscribed) have ingaged ourselves: and having weighed the greatnes of the worke in regard of the consequence, Gods glory and the churches good: As also in regard of the difficultyes and discouragements which in all probabilityes must be forcast upon the prosecucion of this businesse: Considering withall that this whole adventure growes upon the joynt confidence we have in each others fidelity and resolucion herein, so as no man of us would have adventured it without assurance of the rest: Now for the better encourragement of ourselves and others that shall joyne with us in this action, and to the end that every man may without scruple dispose of his estate and afayres as may best fitt his preparacion for this voyage, It is fully and faithfully agreed amongst us, and every of us doth hereby freely and sincerely promise and bynd himselfe in the word of a Christian and in the presence of God who is the searcher of all hearts, that we will so really endevour the prosecucion of this worke, as by Gods assistaunce we will be ready in our persons, and with such of our severall familyes as are to go with us and such provisions as we are able conveniently to furnish ourselves withall, to embarke for the said plantacion by the first of march next, at such port or ports of this land as shall be agreed upon by the Company, to the end to passe the Seas (under Gods protection) to inhabite and continue in new England. Provided always that before the last of September next the whole governement together with the Patent for the said plantacion bee first by an order of Court legally transferred and established to remayne with us and others which shall inhabite upon the said plantacion. And provided also that if any shall be hindered by such just and inevitable Lett or other cause to be allowed by 3 parts of foure of these whose names are hereunto subscribed, then such persons for such tymes and during such letts to be dischardged of this bond. And we do further promise every one for himselfe that shall fayle to be ready through his owne default by the day appointed, to pay for every dayes default the summe of 3 *li.* to the

use of the rest of the Company who shall be ready by the same
day and tyme.

This was done by order of Court the 29th of August. 1629.

RICH: SALTONSTALL.   ISAACK JOHNSON
THO: DUDLEY   JOHN HUMFREY
WILLIAM VASSALL   THO: SHARP
NICHO: WEST.   INCREASE NOWELL

              JOHN WINTHROP
              WILL: PINCHON
              KELLAM BROWNE
              WILLIAM COLBRON.

3.   *John Winthrop to his Wife*

*To my verye loving wife Mrs. Winthrop the elder
at Groton Suffolk dd.*

LONDON March 10: 1629 [–30].
MINE OWNE, MINE ONELY, MY BEST BELOVED, Me thinkes it
is verye longe since I sawe or heard from my beloved, and I misse
allreadye the sweet comfort of thy most desired presence: but the
rich mercye and goodnesse of my God makes supplye of all wants:
Blessed be his great and holy name. Ah my good wife, we now
finde what blessinge is stored up in the favour of the Lorde, he
onely sweetens all conditions to us, he takes of our cares and feares
from us, he supports us in our dangers, he disposeth all our affaires
for us, he will guide us by his counsell in our pilgrimage, and
after will bringe us to glorye.

John is returned from S: Hampton, where he lefte our boyes
well and merrye: and this morninge we are ridinge thither, and
from thence I shall take my last farewell of thee till we meet in
new E: or till midsomer that it please God our shipps returne.
my deare wife be of good courage, it shall goe well with thee
and us, the haires of thy head are numbred, he who gave his onely
beloved to dye for thee, will give his Angells charge over thee:
therefore rayse up thy thoughts, and be merrye in the Lorde, labour

to live by thy Faith; if thou meet with troubles or difficultyes, be not dismayed, God doth use to bringe his children into the streights of the redd sea etc: that he may shew his power and mercye in makinge a waye for them: All his courses towardes us, are but to make us knowe him and love him, the more thy heart drawes towards him in this, the freer shall thy condition be from the evill of Affliction.

Our freinds heer are all in health (blessed be God) and desire to be heartyly commended to thee. I am exceedingly beholdinge to my good brother and sister D[owning], I can fasten no recompénce upon them for all the chardge my selfe and my company have putt them to. I have received much kindnesse also from my Lady Mildmay and from others, whereof some have been meer strangers to me, the Lord reward them: It doth much incourage us to see, how the eyes and hearts of all good people are upon us, breathinge many sweet prayers and blessinges after us. Commende my hearty love to all our freindes, I cannot now name them, but thou knowest whom I meane.

Nowe I beseech the Lord and father of mercye to blesse thee and all thy companye, my daughter W: Ma: Mat: Sam: Deane, and the litle one unknowne, Tho: Am: and the rest: tell Am: I am very much beholdinge to her brother, desire her to give him thankes for me: tell my n[eighbor] Culpacke I am beholdinge to his sonne in lawe for oysters he sent me, but could not see him to give him thankes. my deare wife farewell, once againe let us kisse and imbrace, so in teares of sweet Affection I rest Thine ever
JO: WINTHROP.

4. *John Winthrop to his Wife*

To M. W. the Elder at groton.

MY FAITHFULL AND DEARE WIFE, It pleaseth God that thou shouldest once againe heare from me before our departure, and I hope this shall come safe to thy hands, I knowe it wilbe a great refreshinge to thee: And blessed be his mercye, that I can write thee so good newes, that we are all in verye good health, and

havinge tryed our shipps entertainment now more then a weeke,
we finde it agree very well with us, our boyes are well and cheerfull, and have no minde of home, they lye both with me, and
sleepe as soundly in a rugge (for we use no sheets heer) as ever
they did at Groton, and so I doe my selfe (I prayse God). the
winde hath been against us this weeke and more, but this day it
is come faire to the North, so as we are preparinge (by Godes
assistance) to sett sayle in the morninge: we have onely 4: shippes
ready, and some 2: or 3: hollandes goe alonge with us: the rest
of our fleet (beinge 7: shippes) will not be ready this senight.
we have spent now 2: sabbaths on shipp board, very comfortably
(God be praysed) and are daylye more and more incouraged to
looke for the Lords presence to goe alonge with us: Hen: Kinges-
burye hath a childe or 2: in the Talbott sicke of the measells, but
like to doe well: one of my men had them at Hampton, but he
was soone well againe. we are in all our 11: shippes, about 700:
persons passengers; and 240 Cowes, and about 60: horses. the
shippe which went from Plimouth carried about 140: persons,
and the shippe which goes from Bristowe, carrieth about 80:
persons. And now (my sweet soule) I must once againe take
my last farewell of thee in old England, it goeth verye neere to
my heart to leave thee, but I know to whom I have committed
thee, even to him, who loves the[e] much better than any husband
can, who hath taken account of the haires of thy head, and putts
all thy teares in his bottle, who can, and (if it be for his glorye)
will bringe us togither againe with peace and comfort. oh how
it refresheth my heart to thinke that I shall yet againe see thy sweet
face in the lande of the livinge: that lovely countenance, that I
have so much delighted in, and beheld with so great contente! I
have hetherto been so taken up with businesse, as I could seldome
looke backe to my former happinesse, but now when I shalbe at
some leysure, I shall not avoid the remembrance of thee, nor the
greife for thy absence: thou hast thy share with me, but I hope,
the course we have agreed upon wilbe some ease to us both,
mundayes and frydayes at 5: of the clocke at night, we shall meet
in spiritt till we meet in person. yet if all these hopes should faile,
blessed be our God, that we are assured, we shall meet one day,
if not as husband and wife, yet in a better condition, let that staye
and comfort thy heart, neither can the sea drowne thy husband,
nor enemyes destroye, nor any adversity deprive thee of thy hus-

band or children. therefore I will onely take thee now and my sweet children in mine armes, and kisse and embrace you all, and so leave you with my God. farewell farewell. I blesse you all in the name of the Lord Jesus; I salute my daughter Winth: Matt, Nan and the rest, and all my good neighbors and freindes pray all for us. farewell.

Comende my blessinge to my sonne John. I cannot now write to him, but tell him I have committed thee and thine to him, labour to drawe him yet nearer to God, and he wilbe the surer staffe of comfort to thee. I cannot name the rest of my good freinds, but thou canst supply it. I wrote a weeke since to thee and mr. Leigh and diverse others. Thine wheresoever

JO: WINTHROP.

From Aboard the ARBELLA rydinge at the COWES march 28. 1630.

I would have written to my brother and sister Gostlinge, but it is neer midnight, let this excuse and commende my love to them and all theirs.

5. *The Humble Request*

THE HUMBLE
REQUEST OF HIS
Majesties loyall Subjects, the
Governour and the Company late
gone for *New England;* to the rest
of their Brethren in and of the
Church of ENGLAND.[1]

Reverend FATHERS *and* BRETHREN:

The generall rumour of this solemne Enterprise, wherin our selves with others, through the providence of the Almightie, are ingaged, as it may spare us the labour of imparting our occasion unto you, so it gives us the more incouragement to strengthen our selves by the procurement of the prayers & blessings of the Lords faithfull Servants: For which end wee are bold to have recourse unto you, as those whom *God* hath placed nearest his throne of Mercy; which as it affords you the more opportunitie, so it im-

[1] London, printed for John Bellamie, 1630. For a discussion of the authorship, see Frances Rose-Troup, *John White* (New York, 1930), 204–212, 433; Henry Wilder Foote, in Mass. Historical Society, *Proceedings,* LXIII. 196–201.

poseth the greater bond upon you to intercede for his people in all their straights, we beseech you therefore by the mercies of the LORD JESUS to consider us as your Brethren, standing in very great need of your helpe, and earnestly imploring it. And howsoever your charitie may have met with some occasion of discouragement through the misreport of our intentions, or through the disaffection, or indiscretion, of some of us, or rather, amongst us: for wee are not of those that dreame of perfection in this world; yet we desire you would be pleased to take notice of the principals, and body of our company, as those who esteeme it our honour, to call the *Church* of *England,* from whence wee rise, our deare Mother, and cannot part from our native Country, where she specially resideth, without much sadnes of heart, and many teares in our eyes, ever acknowledging that such hope and part as wee have obtained in the common salvation, we have received in her bosome, and suckt it from her breasts: wee leave it not therfore, as loathing that milk wherewith we were nourished there, but blessing God for the parentage and education, as members of the same body shall alwayes rejoyce in her good, and unfainedly grieve for any sorrow that shall ever betide her, and while we have breath, syncerely desire and indeavour the continuance & abundance of her welfare, with the inlargement of her bounds in the kingdome of CHRIST JESUS.

Be pleased therefore *Reverend* FATHERS & BRETHREN to helpe forward this worke now in hand; which if it prosper, you shall bee the more glorious, howsoever your judgment is with the LORD, and your reward with your GOD. It is an usuall and laudable exercise of your charity to commend to the prayers of your Congregations the necessities and straights of your private neighbours; Doe the like for a Church springing out of your owne bowels. We conceive much hope that this remembrance of us, if it be frequent and fervent, will bee a most prosperous gale in our sailes, and provide such a passage and welcome for us, from the GOD of the whole earth, as both we which shall finde it, and your selves, with the rest of our friends, who shal heare of it, shall be much inlarged to bring in such daily returnes of Thanks-givings, as the specialties of his Providence and Goodnes may justly challenge at all our hands. You are not ignorant, that the Spirit of GOD stirred up the Apostle *Paul* to make continuall mention of the Church of *Philippi* (which was a Colonie from *Rome)* let the same Spirit, we beseech you, put you in mind, that are the Lords remembrancers, to pray for us without ceasing (who are a weake Colony from your selves) making continuall request for us to GOD in all your prayers.

What we intreat of you that are the Ministers of GOD, that we also crave at the hands of all the rest of our Brethren, that they would at no time forget us in their private solicitations at the throne of Grace.

If any there be, who through want of cleare intelligence of our course, or tendernesse of affection towards us, cannot conceive so well of our way as we could desire, we would intreat such not to despise us, nor to desert us in their prayers & affections, but to consider rather, that they are so much the more bound to expresse the bowels of their compassion towards us, remembring alwaies that both Nature and Grace, doth ever binde us to relieve and rescue with our utmost & speediest power, such as are deare unto us, when wee conceive them to be running uncomfortable hazards.

What goodnes you shall extend to us in this or any other Christian kindnesse, wee your Brethren in CHRIST JESUS shall labour to repay in what dutie wee are or shall be able to performe, promising so farre as God shall enable us to give him no rest on your behalfes, wishing our heads and hearts may be as fountaines of teares for your everlasting welfare, when wee shall be in our poore Cottages in the wildernesse, over-shadowed with the spirit of supplication, through the manifold necessities and tribulations which may not altogether unexpectedly, nor, we hope, unprofitably befall us. And so commending you to the grace of GOD in CHRIST, wee shall ever rest

Your assured Friends
and Brethren,

From *Yarmouth*
aboord the *Arbella*
April 7, 1630.

Jo: Winthrope GOV.	*Rich: Saltonstall.*
Charles Fines.	*Isaac Johnson.*
	Tho: Dudley.
George Philipps.	*William Coddington*
&c.	&c.

6.   *A Modell of Christian Charity.*

Written
On Boarde the Arrabella,
On the Attlantick Ocean.
By the Honorable JOHN WINTHROP Esquire.
In His passage, (with the great Company of Religious people,
of which Christian Tribes he was the Brave Leader and famous
Governor;) from the Island of Great Brittaine, to New-England
in the North America. Anno 1630.

Christian Charitie.
A MODELL HEREOF.

God Almightie in his most holy and wise providence hath soe
disposed of the Condicion of mankinde, as in all times some must
be rich some poore, some highe and eminent in power and dignitie;
others meane and in subjeccion.

THE REASON HEREOF.

1. REAS: *First,* to hold conformity with the rest of his workes,
being delighted to shewe forthe the glory of his wisdome in the
variety and differance of the Creatures and the glory of his power,
in ordering all these differences for the preservacion and good of
the whole, and the glory of his greatnes that as it is the glory of
princes to have many officers, soe this great King will have many
Stewards counting himselfe more honoured in dispenceing his
guifts to man by man, then if hee did it by his owne immediate
hand.

2. REAS: *Secondly,* That he might have the more occasion to
manifest the worke of his Spirit: first, upon the wicked in mod-
erateing and restraineing them: soe that the riche and mighty
should not eate upp the poore, nor the poore, and dispised rise
upp against theire superiours, and shake off theire yoake; 2ly in
the regenerate in exerciseing his graces in them, as in the greate
ones, theire love mercy, gentlenes, temperance etc., in the poore
and inferiour sorte, theire faithe patience, obedience etc:

3. REAS: Thirdly, That every man might have need of other,

and from hence they might be all knitt more nearly together in the Bond of brotherly affeccion: from hence it appeares plainely that noe man is made more honourable then another or more wealthy etc., out of any perticuler and singuler respect to himselfe but for the glory of his Creator and the Common good of the Creature, Man; Therefore God still reserves the propperty of these guifts to himselfe as Ezek: 16. 17. he there calls wealthe his gold and his silver etc. Prov: 3. 9. he claimes theire service as his due honour the Lord with thy riches etc. All men being thus (by divine providence) rancked into two sortes, riche and poore; under the first, are comprehended all such as are able to live comfortably by theire owne meanes duely improved; and all others are poore according to the former distribution. There are two rules whereby wee are to walke one towards another: JUSTICE and MERCY. These are allwayes distinguished in theire Act and in theire object, yet may they both concurre in the same Subject in eache respect; as sometimes there may be an occasion of shewing mercy to a rich man, in some sudden danger of distresse, and allsoe doeing of meere Justice to a poor man in regard of some perticuler contract etc. There is likewise a double Lawe by which wee are regulated in our conversacion one towardes another: in both the former respects, the lawe of nature and the lawe of grace, or the morrall lawe or the lawe of the gospell, to omitt the rule of Justice as not propperly belonging to this purpose otherwise then it may fall into consideracion in some perticuler Cases: By the first of these lawes man as he was enabled soe withall [is] commaunded to love his neighbour as himselfe upon this ground stands all the precepts of the morrall lawe, which concernes our dealings with men. To apply this to the works of mercy this lawe requires two things first that every man afford his help to another in every want or distresse Secondly, That hee performe this out of the same affeccion, which makes him carefull of his owne good according to that of our Saviour Math: [7.12] Whatsoever ye would that men should doe to you. This was practised by Abraham and Lott in entertaineing the Angells and the old man of Gibea.

The Lawe of Grace or the Gospell hath some differance from the former as in these respectes first the lawe of nature was given to man in the estate of innocency; this of the gospell in the estate of regeneracy: 2ly, the former propounds one man to another, as the same fleshe and Image of god, this as a brother in Christ allsoe, and in the Communion of the same spirit and soe teacheth us to put a difference betweene Christians and others. Doe good to all especially to the household of faith; upon this ground the Israelites were to putt a difference betweene the brethren of such as were strangers though not of the Canaanites. 3ly. The Lawe of nature could give noe rules for dealeing with enemies for all are to be considered as freinds in the estate of innocency, but the Gospell commaunds love to an enemy. proofe. If thine Enemie hunger feede him; Love your Enemies doe good to them that hate you Math: 5. 44.

This Lawe of the Gospell propoundes likewise a difference of seasons and occasions there is a time when a christian must sell all and give to the poore as they did in the Apostles times. There is a tyme allsoe when a christian (though they give not all yet) must give beyond theire abillity, as they of Macedonia. Cor: 2. 6. likewise community of perills calls for extraordinary liberallity and soe doth Community in some speciall service for the Churche. Lastly, when there is noe other meanes whereby our Christian brother may be releeved in this distresse, wee must help him beyond our ability, rather then tempt God, in putting him upon help by miraculous or extraordinary meanes.

This duty of mercy is exercised in the kindes, Giveing, lending, and forgiveing.

Quest. What rule shall a man observe in giveing in respect of the measure?

Ans. If the time and occasion be ordinary he is to give out of his aboundance—let him lay aside, as god hath blessed him. If the time and occasion be extraordinary he must be ruled by them; takeing this withall, that then a man cannot likely doe too much especially, if he may leave himselfe and his family under probable meanes of comfortable subsistance.

Objection. A man must lay upp for posterity, the fathers lay upp for posterity and children and he is worse than an Infidell that provideth not for his owne.

Ans: For the first, it is plaine, that it being spoken by way of Comparison it must be meant of the ordinary and usuall course of fathers and cannot extend to times and occasions extraordinary; for the other place the Apostle speakes against such as walked inordinately, and it is without question, that he is worse then an Infidell whoe throughe his owne Sloathe and voluptuousnes shall neglect to provide for his family.

OBJECTION. The wise mans Eies are in his head (saith Salomon) and foreseeth the plague, therefore wee must forecast and lay upp against evill times when hee or his may stand in need of all he can gather.

ANS: This very Argument Salomon useth to perswade to liberallity. Eccle: [11.1.] cast thy bread upon the waters etc.: for thou knowest not what evill may come upon the land Luke 16. make you freinds of the riches of Iniquity; you will aske how this shall be? very well. for first he that gives to the poore lends to the lord, and he will repay him even in this life an hundred fold to him or his. The righteous is ever mercifull and lendeth and his seed enjoyeth the blessing; and besides wee know what advantage it will be to us in the day of account, when many such Witnesses shall stand forthe for us to witnesse the improvement of our Tallent. And I would knowe of those whoe pleade soe much for layeing up for time to come, whether they hold that to be Gospell Math: 16. 19. Lay not upp for yourselves Treasures upon Earth etc. if they acknowledge it what extent will they allowe it; if onely to those primitive times lett them consider the reason whereupon our Saviour groundes it, the first is that they are subject to the moathe, the rust the Theife. Secondly, They will steale away the hearte, where the treasure is there will the heart be allsoe. The reasons are of like force at all times therefore the exhortacion must be generall and perpetuall which [applies] allwayes in respect of the love and affeccion to riches and in regard of the things themselves when any speciall service for the churche or perticuler distresse of our brother doe call for the use of them; otherwise it is not onely lawfull but necessary to lay upp as Joseph did to have ready uppon such occasions, as the Lord (whose stewards wee are of them) shall call for them from us: Christ gives us an Instance of the first, when hee sent his disciples for the Asse, and bidds them answer the owner thus, the Lord hath need of him; soe when the Tabernacle was to be builte his [servant] sends to his people to call for their silver and gold etc.; and yeildes them noe other reason but that it was for his worke, when Elisha comes to the widowe of Sareptah and findes her prepareing to make ready her pittance for herselfe and family, he bids her first provide for him, he challengeth first gods parte which shee must first give before shee must serve her owne family, all these teache us that the lord lookes that when hee is pleased to call for his right in any thing wee have, our owne Interest wee have must stand aside, till his turne be served, for the other wee need looke noe further then to that of John 1. he whoe hath this worlds goodes and seeth his brother to neede, and shutts upp his Compassion from him, how dwelleth the love of god in him, which comes punctually to this Conclusion: if thy brother be in want and thou canst help him, thou needst not make doubt, what thou shouldst doe, if thou lovest god thou must help him.

QUEST: What rule must wee observe in lending?

ANS: Thou must observe whether thy brother hath present or probable, or possible meanes of repayeing thee, if ther be none of these, thou must give him according to his necessity, rather than lend him as hee requires; if he hath present meanes of repayeing thee, thou art to looke at him, not as an Act of mercy, but by way of Commerce, wherein thou arte to walke by the rule of Justice, but, if his meanes of repayeing thee be onely probable or possible then is hee an object of thy mercy thou must lend him, though there be danger of looseing it Deut: 15. 7. If any of thy brethren be poore etc. thou shalt lend him sufficient that men might not shift off this duty by the apparant hazzard, he tells them that though the Yeare of Jubile were at hand (when he must remitt it, if hee were not able to repay it before) yet he must lend him and that chearefully: it may not greive thee to give him (saith hee) and because some might object, why soe I should soone impoverishe my selfe and my family, he adds with all thy Worke etc. for our Saviour Math: 5. 42. From him that would borrow of thee turne not away.

QUEST: What rule must wee observe in forgiveing?

ANS: Whether thou didst lend by way of Commerce or in mercy, if he have noething to pay thee [thou] must forgive him (except in cause where thou hast a surety or a lawfull pleadge) Deut. 15. 2. Every seaventh yeare the Creditor was to quitt that which hee lent to his brother if hee were poore as appeares ver: 8[4]: save when there shall be noe poore with thee. In all these and like Cases Christ was a generall rule Math: 7. 22. Whatsoever

ye would that men should doe to you doe yee the same to them
allsoe.

QUEST: What rule must wee observe and walke by in cause
of Community of perill?

ANS: The same as before, but with more enlargement towardes
others and lesse respect towards our selves, and our owne right
hence it was that in the primitive Churche they sold all had all
things in Common, neither did any man say that that which he
possessed was his owne likewise in theire returne out of the Cap-
tivity, because the worke was greate for the restoreing of the
church and the danger of enemies was Common to all Nehemiah
exhortes the Jewes to liberallity and readines in remitting theire
debtes to theire brethren, and disposeth liberally of his owne to
such as wanted and stands not upon his owne due, which hee
might have demaunded of them, thus did some of our forefathers
in times of persecucion here in England, and soe did many of the
faithfull in other Churches whereof wee keepe an honourable
remembrance of them, and it is to be observed that both in Scriptures and latter stories of the Churches that such as have beene
most bountifull to the poore Saintes especially in these extraordinary times and occasions god hath left them highly Commended
to posterity, as Zacheus, Cornelius, Dorcas, Bishop Hooper, the
Cuttler of Brussells and divers others observe againe that the
scripture gives noe causion to restraine any from being over liberall
this way; but all men to the liberall and cherefull practise hereof
by the sweetest promises as to instance one for many, Isaiah 58. 6:
Is not this the fast that I have chosen to loose the bonds of wick-
ednes, to take off the heavy burdens to lett the oppressed goe free
and to breake every Yoake, to deale thy bread to the hungry and
to bring the poore that wander into thy house, when thou seest
the naked to cover them etc. then shall thy light breake forthe as
the morneing, and thy healthe shall growe speedily, thy righteous-
nes shall goe before thee, and the glory of the lord shall embrace
thee, then thou shalt call and the lord shall Answer thee etc.
2. 10: If thou power out thy soule to the hungry, then shall thy
light spring out in darknes, and the lord shall guide thee continually, and satisfie thy Soule in draught, and make fatt thy bones,
thou shalt be like a watered Garden, and they shall be of thee
that shall build the old wast places etc. on the contrary most heavy

cursses are layd upon such as are straightened towards the Lord and his people Judg: 5. [23] Cursse ye Meroshe because the[y] came not to help the Lord etc. Pro: [21. 13] Hee whoe shutteth his eares from hearing the cry of the poore, he shall cry and shall not be heard: Math: 25. [41] Goe ye curssed into everlasting fire etc. [42.] I was hungry and ye fedd mee not. Cor: 2. 9. 16. [6.] He that soweth spareingly shall reape spareingly.

Haveing allready sett forth the practise of mercy according to the rule of gods lawe, it will be usefull to lay open the groundes of it allsoe being the other parte of the Commaundement and that is the affeccion from which this exercise of mercy must arise, the Apostle tells us that this love is the fullfilling of the lawe, not that it is enough to love our brother and soe noe further but in regard of the excellency of his partes gieveing any motion to the other as the Soule to the body and the power it hath to sett all the faculties on worke in the outward exercise of this duty as when wee bid one make the clocke strike he doth not lay hand on the hammer which is the immediate instrument of the sound but setts on worke the first mover or maine wheele, knoweing that will certainely produce the sound which hee intends; soe the way to drawe men to the workes of mercy is not by force of Argument from the goodnes or necessity of the worke, for though this course may enforce a rationall minde to some present Act of mercy as is frequent in experience, yet it cannot worke such a habit in a Soule as shall make it prompt upon all occasions to produce the same effect but by frameing these affeccions of love in the hearte which will as natively bring forthe the other, as any cause doth produce the effect.

The diffinition which the Scripture gives us of love is this Love is the bond of perfection. First, it is a bond, or ligament. 2ly, it makes the worke perfect. There is noe body but consistes of partes and that which knitts these partes together gives the body its perfeccion, because it makes eache parte soe contiguous to other as thereby they doe mutually participate with eache other, both in strengthe and infirmity in pleasure and paine, to instance in the most perfect of all bodies, Christ and his church make one body: the severall partes of this body considered aparte before they were united were as disproportionate and as much disordering as soe many contrary quallities or elements but when christ comes and by his spirit and love knitts all these partes to himselfe and each to other, it is become the most perfect and best proportioned body in the world Eph: 4. 16. "Christ by whome all the body being knitt together by every joynt for the furniture thereof according to the effectuall power which is in the measure of every perfeccion of partes a glorious body without spott or wrinckle the ligaments hereof being Christ or his love for Christ is love 1 John: 4. 8. Soe this definition is right Love is the bond of perfeccion.

From hence wee may frame these Conclusions.

1 first all true Christians are of one body in Christ 1. Cor. 12. 12. 13. 17. [27.] Ye are the body of Christ and members of [your?] parte.

2ly. The ligamentes of this body which knitt together are love.

3ly. Noe body can be perfect which wants its propper ligamentes.

4ly. All the partes of this body being thus united are made soe contiguous in a speciall relacion as they must needes partake of each others strength and infirmity, joy, and sorrowe, weale and woe. 1 Cor: 12. 26. If one member suffers all suffer with it, if one be in honour, all rejoyce with it.

5ly. This sensiblenes and Sympathy of each others Condicions will necessarily infuse into each parte a native desire and endeavour, to strengthen defend preserve and comfort the other.

To insist a little on this Conclusion being the product of all the former the truthe hereof will appeare both by precept and patterne i. John. 3. 10. yee ought to lay downe your lives for the brethren Gal: 6. 2. beare ye one anothers burthens and soe fulfill the lawe of Christ.

For patterns wee have that first of our Saviour whoe out of his good will in obedience to his father, becomeing a parte of this body, and being knitt with it in the bond of love, found such a native sensiblenes of our infirmities and sorrowes as hee willingly yeilded himselfe to deathe to ease the infirmities of the rest of his body and soe heale theire sorrowes: from the like Sympathy of partes did the Apostles and many thousands of the Saintes lay downe theire lives for Christ againe, the like wee may see in the members of this body among themselves. 1. Rom. 9. Paule could have beene contented to have beene seperated from Christ that the Jewes might not be cutt off from the body: It is very observable which hee professeth of his affectionate part[ak]eing with every

member: whoe is weake (saith hee) and I am not weake? whoe
is offended and I burne not; and againe. 2 Cor: 7. 13. therefore
wee are comforted because yee were comforted. of Epaphroditus
he speaketh Phil: 2. 30. that he regarded not his owne life to
[do] him service soe Phebe. and others are called the servantes of
the Churche, now it is apparant that they served not for wages or
by Constrainte but out of love, the like wee shall finde in the histories of the churche in all ages the sweete Sympathie of affeccions
which was in the members of this body one towardes another,
theire chearfullnes in serveing and suffering together how liberall
they were without repineing harbourers without grudgeing and
helpfull without reproacheing and all from hence they had fervent
love amongst them which onely make[s] the practise of mercy
constant and easie.

The next consideracion is how this love comes to be wrought;
Adam in his first estate was a perfect modell of mankinde in all
theire generacions, and in him this love was perfected in regard of
the habit, but Adam Rent in himselfe from his Creator, rent all
his posterity allsoe one from another, whence it comes that every
man is borne with this principle in him, to love and seeke himselfe
onely and thus a man continueth till Christ comes and takes possession of the soule, and infuseth another principle love to God
and our brother. And this latter haveing continuall supply from
Christ, as the head and roote by which hee is united get the pre-
dominency in the soule, soe by little and little expells the former
1 John 4. 7. love cometh of god and every one that loveth is borne
of god, soe that this love is the fruite of the new birthe, and none
can have it but the new Creature, now when this quallity is thus
formed in the soules of men it workes like the Spirit upon the drie
bones Ezek. 37. [7] bone came to bone, it gathers together the
scattered bones or perfect old man Adam and knitts them into one
body againe in Christ whereby a man is become againe a liveing
soule.

The third Consideracion is concerning the exercise of this love,
which is twofold, inward or outward, the outward hath beene
handled in the former preface of this discourse, for unfolding the
other wee must take in our way that maxime of philosophy, Simile
simili gaudet or like will to like; for as it is things which are
carved with disafeccion to eache other, the ground of it is from a

dissimilitude or [*blank*] ariseing from the contrary or different nature of the things themselves, soe the ground of love is an apprehension of some resemblance in the things loved to that which affectes it, this is the cause why the Lord loves the Creature, soe farre as it hath any of his Image in it, he loves his elect because they are like himselfe, he beholds them in his beloved sonne: soe a mother loves her childe, because shee throughly conceives a resemblance of herselfe in it. Thus it is betweene the members of Christ, each discernes by the worke of the spirit his owne Image and resemblance in another, and therefore cannot but love him as he loves himselfe: Now when the soule which is of a sociable nature findes any thing like to it selfe, it is like Adam when Eve was brought to him, shee must have it one with herselfe this is fleshe of my fleshe (saith shee) and bone of my bone shee conceives a great delighte in it, therefore shee desires nearenes and familiarity with it: shee hath a greate propensity to doe it good and receives such content in it, as feareing the miscarriage of her beloved shee bestowes it in the inmost closett of her heart, shee will not endure that it shall want any good which shee can give it, if by occasion shee be withdrawne from the Company of it, shee is still lookeing towardes the place where shee left her beloved, if shee heare it groane shee is with it presently, if shee finde it sadd and disconsolate shee sighes and mournes with it, shee hath noe such joy, as to see her beloved merry and thriveing, if shee see it wronged, shee cannot beare it without passion, shee setts noe boundes of her affeccions, nor hath any thought of reward, shee findes recompence enoughe in the exercise of her love towardes it, wee may see this Acted to life in Jonathan and David. Jonathan a valiant man endued with the spirit of Christ, soe soone as hee Discovers the same spirit in David had presently his hearte knitt to him by this linement of love, soe that it is said he loved him as his owne soule, he takes soe great pleasure in him that hee stripps himselfe to adorne his beloved, his fathers kingdome was not soe precious to him as his beloved David, David shall have it with all his hearte, himselfe desires noe more but that hee may be neare to him to rejoyce in his good hee chooseth to converse with him in the wildernesse even to the hazzard of his owne life, rather then with the greate Courtiers in his fathers Pallace; when hee sees danger towards him, hee spares neither care paines, nor perill to divert it, when Injury was offered his beloved David, hee could not beare it, though from his owne father, and when they must parte for a Season onely, they thought theire heartes would have broake for sorrowe, had not theire affeccions found vent by aboundance of Teares: other instances might be brought to shewe the nature of this affeccion as of Ruthe and Naomi and many others, but this truthe is cleared enough. If any shall object that it is not possible that love should be bred or upheld without hope of requitall, it is graunted but that is not our cause, for this love is allwayes under reward it never gives, but it allwayes receives with advantage: first, in regard that among the members of the same body, love and affection are reciprocall in a most equall and sweete kinde of Commerce. 2ly [3ly], in regard of the pleasure and content that the exercise of love carries with it as wee may see in the naturall body the mouth is at all the paines to receive, and mince the foode which serves for the nourishment of all the other partes of the body, yet it hath noe cause to complaine; for first, the other partes send backe by secret passages a due proporcion of the same nourishment in a better forme for the strengthening and comforteing the mouthe. 2ly the labour of the mouthe is accompanied with such pleasure and content as farre exceedes the paines it takes: soe is it in all the labour of love, among christians, the partie loveing, reapes love againe as was shewed before, which the soule covetts more then all the wealthe in the world. 2ly [4ly]. noething yeildes more pleasure and content to the soule then when it findes that which it may love fervently, for to love and live beloved is the soules paradice, both heare and in heaven: In the State of Wedlock there be many comfortes to beare out the troubles of that Condicion; but let such as have tryed the most, say if there be any sweetnes in that Condicion comparable to the exercise of mutuall love.

From the former Consideracions ariseth these Conclusions.

1 First, This love among Christians is a reall thing not Imaginarie.

2ly. This love is as absolutely necessary to the being of the body of Christ, as the sinewes and other ligaments of a naturall body are to the being of that body.

3ly. This love is a divine spirituall nature free, active strong

Couragious permanent under valueing all things beneathe its propper object, and of all the graces this makes us nearer to resemble the virtues of our heavenly father.

4ly, It restes in the love and wellfare of its beloved, for the full and certaine knowledge of these truthes concerning the nature use, [and] excellency of this grace, that which the holy ghost hath left recorded 1. Cor. 13. may give full satisfaccion which is needfull for every true member of this lovely body of the Lord Jesus, to worke upon theire heartes, by prayer meditacion continuall exercise at least of the speciall [power] of this grace till Christ be formed in them and they in him all in eache other knitt together by this bond of love.

It rests now to make some applicacion of this discourse by the present designe which gave the occasion of writeing of it. Herein are 4 things to be propounded: first the persons, 2ly, the worke, 3ly, the end, 4ly the meanes.

1. For the persons, wee are a Company professing our selves fellow members of Christ, In which respect onely though wee were absent from eache other many miles, and had our imploymentes as farre distant, yet wee ought to account our selves knitt together by this bond of love, and live in the excercise of it, if wee would have comforte of our being in Christ, this was notorious in the practise of the Christians in former times, as is testified of the Waldenses from the mouth of one of the adversaries Aeneas Sylvius, mutuo [solent amare] penè antequam norint, they use to love any of theire owne religion even before they were acquainted with them.

2ly. for the worke wee have in hand, it is by a mutuall consent through a speciall overruleing providence, and a more then an ordinary approbation of the Churches of Christ to seeke out a place of Cohabitation and Consorteshipp under a due forme of Government both civill and ecclesiasticall. In such cases as this the care of the publique must oversway all private respects, by which not onely conscience, but meare Civill pollicy doth binde us; for it is a true rule that perticuler estates cannott subsist in the ruine of the publique.

3ly. The end is to improve our lives to doe more service to the Lord the comforte and encrease of the body of christe whereof wee are members that our selves and posterity may be the better preserved from the Common corrupcions of this evill world to serve the Lord and worke out our Salvacion under the power and purity of his holy Ordinances.

4ly for the meanes whereby this must bee effected, they are 2fold, a Conformity with the worke and end wee aime at, these wee see are extraordinary, therefore wee must not content our selves with usuall ordinary meanes whatsoever wee did or ought to have done when wee lived in England, the same must wee doe and more allsoe where wee goe: That which the most in theire Churches maineteine as a truthe in profession onely, wee must bring into familiar and constant practise, as in this duty of love wee must love brotherly without dissimulation, wee must love one another with a pure hearte fervently wee must beare one anothers burthens, wee must not looke onely on our owne things, but allsoe on the things of our brethren, neither must wee think that the lord will beare with such faileings at our hands as hee dothe from those among whome we have lived, and that for 3 Reasons.

1. In regard of the more neare bond of mariage, betweene him and us, wherein he hath taken us to be his after a most strickt and peculiar manner which will make him the more Jealous of our love and obedience soe he tells the people of Israell, you onely have I knowne of all the families of the Earthe therefore will I punishe you for your Transgressions.

2ly, because the lord will be sanctified in them that come neare him. Wee know that there were many that corrupted the service of the Lord some setting upp Alters before his owne, others offering both strange fire and strange Sacrifices allsoe; yet there came noe fire from heaven, or other sudden Judgement upon them as did upon Nadab and Abihu whoe yet wee may thinke did not sinne presumptuously.

3ly When God gives a speciall Commission he lookes to have it stricktly observed in every Article, when hee gave Saule a Commission to destroy Amaleck hee indented with him upon certaine Articles and because hee failed in one of the least, and that upon a faire pretence, it lost him the kingdome, which should have beene his reward, if hee had observed his Commission: Thus stands the cause betweene God and us, wee are entered into Covenant with him for this worke, wee have taken out a Commission, the Lord hath given us leave to drawe our owne Articles wee have professed to enterprise these Accions upon these and these ends, wee have hereupon besought him of favour and blessing: Now if the Lord shall please to heare us, and bring us in peace to the place wee desire, then hath hee ratified this Covenant and sealed our Commission, [and] will expect a strickt performance of the Articles contained in it, but if wee shall neglect the observacion of these Articles which are the ends wee have propounded, and dissembling with our God, shall fall to embrace this present world and prosecute our carnall intencions, seekeing great things for our selves and our posterity, the Lord will surely breake out in wrathe against us be revenged of such a perjured people and make us knowe the price of the breache of such a Covenant.

Now the onely way to avoyde this shipwracke and to provide for our posterity is to followe the Counsell of Micah, to doe Justly, to love mercy, to walke humbly with our God, for this end, wee must be knitt together in this worke as one man, wee must entertaine each other in brotherly Affeccion, wee must be willing to abridge our selves of our superfluities, for the supply of others necessities, wee must uphold a familiar Commerce together in all meekenes, gentlenes, patience and liberallity, wee must delight in eache other, make others Condicions our owne rejoyce together, mourne together, labour, and suffer together, allwayes haveing before our eyes our Commission and Community in the worke, our Community as members of the same body, soe shall wee keepe the unitie of the spirit in the bond of peace, the Lord will be our God and delight to dwell among us, as his owne people and will commaund a blessing upon us in all our wayes, soe that wee shall see much more of his wisdome power goodnes and truthe then formerly wee have beene acquainted with, wee shall finde that the God of Israell is among us, when tenn of us shall be able to resist a thousand of our enemies, when hee shall make us a prayse and glory, that men shall say of succeeding plantacions: the lord make it like that of New England: for wee must Consider that wee shall be as a Citty upon a Hill, the eies of all people are uppon us; soe that if wee shall deale falsely with our god in this worke wee have undertaken and soe cause him to withdrawe his present help from us, wee shall be made a story and a by-word through the world, wee shall open the mouthes of enemies to speake evill of the wayes of god and all professours for Gods sake; wee shall shame the faces of many of gods worthy servants, and cause theire prayers to be turned into Cursses upon us till wee be consumed out of the good land whether wee are goeing: And to shutt upp this discourse with that exhortacion of Moses that faithfull servant of the Lord in his last farewell to Israell Deut. 30. Beloved there is now sett before us life, and good, deathe and evill in that wee are Commaunded this day to love the Lord our God, and to love one another to walke in his wayes and to keepe his Commaunde-ments and his Ordinance, and his lawes, and the Articles of our Covenant with him that wee may live and be multiplyed, and that the Lord our God may blesse us in the land whether wee goe to possesse it: But if our heartes shall turne away soe that wee will not obey, but shall be seduced and worshipp [serve *cancelled*] other Gods our pleasures, and proffitts, and serve them; it is pro-pounded unto us this day, wee shall surely perishe out of the good Land whether wee passe over this vast Sea to possesse it;

> Therefore lett us choose life,
> that wee, and our Seede,
> may live; by obeyeing his
> voyce, and cleaveing to him,
> for hee is our life, and
> our prosperity.

7. *The Journal of John Winthrop*
March 29, 1630–May 14, 1634

THE HISTORY OF NEW ENGLAND.

ANNO DOMINI, 1630, MARCH 29, MONDAY.

Easter Monday.]   Riding at the Cowes, near the Isle of Wight, in the Arbella, a ship of three hundred and fifty tons, whereof Capt. Peter Milborne was master, being manned with fifty-two seamen, and twenty-eight pieces of ordnance, (the wind coming to the N. by W. the evening before,) in the morning there came aboard us Mr. Cradock, the late governour, and the masters of his two ships, Capt. John Lowe, master of the Ambrose, and Mr. Nicholas Hurlston, master of the Jewel, and Mr. Thomas Beecher, master of the Talbot, (which three ships rode then by us,—the Charles, the Mayflower, the William and Francis, the Hopewell, the Whale, the Success and the Trial being still at Hampton and not ready,) when, upon conference, it was agreed, that (in regard it was uncertain when the rest of the fleet would be ready) these four ships should consort together; the Arbella to be admiral, the Talbot vice-admiral, the Ambrose rear-admiral, and the Jewel a captain; and accordingly articles of consortship were drawn between the said captains and masters; whereupon Mr. Cradock took leave of us, and our captain gave him a farewell with four or five shot.

About ten of the clock we weighed anchor and set sail, with the wind at N., and came to an anchor again over against Yarmouth, and the Talbot weighed likewise, and came and anchored by us. Here we met with a ship of Hampton, called the Plantation, newly come from Virginia. Our captain saluted her, and she us again; and the master, one Mr. [*blank*] *Graves,* came on board our ship, and stayed with us about two or three hours, and in the meantime his ship came to an anchor by us.

Tuesday, 30.] In the morning, about ten of the clock, the wind being come to the W. with fair weather, we weighed and rode nearer Yarmouth. When we came before the town, the castle put forth a flag; our captain saluted them, and they answered us again. The Talbot, which rode farther off, saluted the castle also.

Here we saw, close by the shore of the Isle of Wight, a Dutch ship of one thousand tons, which, being bound to the East Indies, about two years since, in passing through the Needles, struck upon a rock, and being forced to run ashore to save her men, could never be weighed since, although she lies a great height above the water, and yet she hath some men aboard her.

Wednesday, 31.] The wind continued W. and S. W. with rain. Our captain and some of our company went to Yarmouth for supply of wood and other provisions; (our captain was still careful to fill our empty casks with water).

Thursday, April 1.] The wind continued very strong at W. and by S. with much rain.

Friday, 2.] We kept a fast aboard our ship and the Talbot. The wind continued still very high at W. and S. and rainy. In the time of our fast, two of our landmen pierced a rundlet of strong water, and stole some of it, for which we laid them in bolts all the night, and the next morning the principal was openly whipped, and both kept with bread and water that day.

Saturday, 3.]   The wind continued still at W. and with continual storms and rain.

Sunday, 4.]   Fair, clear weather. In the morning the wind W. and by N., but in the afternoon S. S. W. This evening the Talbot weighed and went back to the Cowes, because her anchor would not hold here, the tide set with so strong a race.

Monday, 5.]   The wind still W. and S. with fair weather. A maid of Sir Richard Saltonstall fell down at the grating by the cook-room, but the carpenter's man, who occasioned her fall unwittingly, caught hold of her with incredible nimbleness, and saved her; otherwise she had fallen into the hold.

Tuesday, 6.]   Capt. Burleigh, captain of Yarmouth castle, a grave, comely gentleman, and of great age, came aboard us and stayed breakfast, and, offering us much courtesy, he departed, our captain giving him four shot out of the forecastle for his farewell. He was an old sea captain in Queen Elizabeth's time, and, being taken prisoner at sea, was kept prisoner in Spain three years. Himself and three of his sons were captains in Roe's voyage.

The wind was now come about to N. E. with very fair weather.

In the afternoon Mr. Cradock came aboard us, and told us, that the Talbot, Jewel, and Ambrose were fallen down into Stoke's Bay, intending to take their way by St. Helen's Point, and that they desired we could come back to them. Hereupon we came to council, and wrote unto them to take the first opportunity of the wind to fall down to us, and Mr. Cradock presently went back to them, our captain giving him three shot out of the steerage for a farewell.

Our captain called over our landmen, and tried them at their muskets, and such as were good shot among them were enrolled to serve in the ship, if occasion should be.

The lady Arbella and the gentlewomen, and Mr. Johnson and some others went on shore to refresh themselves.

Wednesday, 7.]   Fair weather, the wind easterly, in the morning a small gale, but in the afternoon it came about to the south. This afternoon our other consorts came up to us, and about ten or twelve Flemings, and all anchored by us, and the masters of the Jewel and of the Ambrose came aboard us, and our captain and they went on shore.

Towards night there came from the W. a Fleming, a small man-of-war, with a Brazil man which he had taken prize, and came to anchor by us.

Thursday, 8.] About six in the morning (the wind being E. and N. and fair weather) we weighed anchor and set sail, and before ten we gat through the Needles, having so little wind as we had much to do to stem the tide, so as the rest of our fleet (we being nine in all, whereof some were small ships, which were bound for Newfoundland) could not get out all then till the ebb. In the afternoon the wind came S. and W. and we were becalmed, so as being not able to get above three or four leagues from the Needles, our captain tacked about, and putting his fore-sheets aback stays, he stayed for the rest of the fleet, and as they came by us we spake to them, and about eight in the evening we let fall an anchor, intending to stop till the ebb. But before ten at night the wind came about to the N. a good gale; so we put up a light in the poop, and weighed and set sail, and by daylight, Friday 9, we were come to Portland; but the other ships being not able to hold up with us, we were forced to spare our mainsail, and went on with a merry gale. In the morning we descried from the top eight sail astern of us, (whom Capt. Lowe told us he had seen at Dunnose in the evening.) We supposing they might be Dunkirkers, our captain caused the gunroom and gundeck to be cleared; all the hammocks were taken down, our ordnance loaded, and our powder-chests and fireworks made ready, and our landmen quartered among the seamen, and twenty-five of them appointed for muskets, and every man written down for his quarter.

The wind continued N. [*blank*] with fair weather, and after noon it calmed, and we still saw those eight ships to stand towards us; having more wind than we, they came up apace, so as our captain and the masters of our consorts were more occasioned to think they might be Dunkirkers, (for we were told at Yarmouth, that there were ten sail of them waiting for us;) whereupon we all prepared to fight with them, and took down some cabins which were in the way of our ordnance, and out of every ship were thrown such bed matters as were subject to take fire, and we heaved out our long boats, and put up our waste cloths, and drew forth our men, and armed them with muskets and other weapons, and instruments for fireworks; and for an experiment our captain shot a ball of wild-fire fastened to an arrow out of a cross-bow, which burnt in the water a good time. The lady Arbella and the other women and children were removed into the lower deck, that they might be out of danger. All things being thus fitted, we went to prayer upon the upper deck. It was much to see how cheerful and comfortable all the company appeared; not a woman or child that showed fear, though all did apprehend the danger to have been great, if things had proved as might well be expected, for there had been eight against four, and the least of the enemy's ships were reported to carry thirty brass pieces; but our trust was in the Lord of Hosts; and the courage of our captain, and his care and diligence, did much encourage us. It was now about one of the clock, and the fleet seemed to be within a league of us; therefore our captain, because he would show he was not afraid of them, and that he might see the issue before night should overtake us, tacked about and stood to meet them, and when we came near we perceived them to be our friends,—the Little Neptune, a ship of some twenty pieces of ordnance, and her two consorts, bound for the Straits; a ship of Flushing, and a Frenchman, and three other English ships bound for Canada and Newfoundland. So when we drew near, every ship (as they met) saluted each other, and the musketeers discharged their small shot; and so (God be praised) our fear and danger was turned into mirth and friendly entertainment. Our danger being thus over, we espied two boats on fishing in the channel; so every of our four ships manned out a skiff, and we bought of them great store of excellent fresh fish of divers sorts.

Saturday, 10.]   The wind at E. and by N. a handsome gale with fair weather. By seven in the morning we were come over against Plimouth.

About noon the wind slacked, and we were come within sight of the Lizard, and towards night it grew very calm and a great fog, so as our ships made no way.

This afternoon Mr. Hurlston, the master of the Jewel, came aboard our ship, and our captain went in his skiff aboard the Ambrose and the Neptune, of which one Mr. Andrew Cole was master. There he was told, that the bark Warwick was taken by the Dunkirkers, for she came single out of the Downs about fourteen days since, intending to come to us to the Wight, but was never heard of since. She was a pretty ship of about eighty tons and ten pieces of ordnance, and was set out by Sir Ferdinando

Gorges, Capt. Mason, and others, for discovery of the great lake in New England, so to have intercepted the trade of beaver. The master of her was one Mr. Weatherell, whose father was master of one of the cattle ships, which we left at Hampton.

This day two young men, falling at odds and fighting, contrary to the orders which we had published and set up in the ship, were adjudged to walk upon the deck till night with their hands bound behind them, which accordingly was executed; and another man, for using contemptuous speeches in our presence, was laid in bolts till he submitted himself, and promised open confession of his offence.

I should have noted before, that the day we set sail from the Cowes, my son Henry Winthrop went on shore with one of my servants to fetch an ox and ten wethers, which he had provided for our ship, and there went on shore with him, Mr. Pelham and one of his servants. They sent the cattle aboard, but returned not themselves. About three days after, my servant and a servant of Mr. Pelham's came to us to Yarmouth, and told us they were all coming to us in a boat the day before, but the wind was so strong against them, as they were forced on shore in the night, and the two servants came to Yarmouth by land, and so came on ship-board, but my son and Mr. Pelham (we heard) went back to the Cowes and so to Hampton. We expected them three or four days after, but they came not to us, so we have left them behind, and suppose they will come after in Mr. Goffe's ships. We were very sorry they had put themselves upon such inconvenience, when they were so well accommodated in our ship. This was not noted before, because we expected daily their return; and upon this occasion I must add here one observation, that we have many young gentlemen in our ship, who behave themselves well, and are conformable to all good orders.

About ten at night it cleared up with a fresh gale at N. and by W., so we stood on our course merrily.

Sunday, 11.]   The wind at N. and by W. a very stiff gale.

About eight in the morning, being gotten past Scilly, and standing to the W. S. W. we met two small ships, which falling in among us, and the Admiral coming under our lee, we let him pass, but the Jewel and Ambrose, perceiving the other to be a Brazil man, and to take the wind of us, shot at them and made them stop and fall after us, and sent a skiff aboard them to know what they were. Our captain, fearing lest some mistake might arise, and lest they should take them for enemies which were friends, and so, through the unruliness of the mariners some wrong might be done them, caused his skiff to be heaved out, and sent Mr. *Graves,* one of his mates and our pilot, (a discreet man,) to see how things were, who returned soon after, and brought with him the master of one of the ships and Mr. Lowe and Mr. Hurlston. When they were come aboard us, they agreed to send for the captain, who came and showed his commission from the Prince of Orange. In conclusion he proved to be a Dutchman, and his a man-of-war of Flushing, and the other ship was a prize he had taken laden with sugar and tobacco; so we sent them aboard their ships again, and held on our course. In this time (which hindered us five or six leagues) the Jewel and the Ambrose came foul of each other, so as we much feared the issue, but, through God's mercy, they came well off again, only the Jewel had her foresail torn, and one of her anchors broken. This occasion, and the sickness of our minister and people, put us all out of order this day, so as we could have no sermons.

Monday, 12.]   The wind more large to the N. a stiff gale, with fair weather. In the afternoon less wind, and our people began to grow well again. Our children and others, that were sick, and lay groaning in the cabins, we fetched out, and having stretched a rope from the steerage to the mainmast, we made them stand, some of one side and some of the other, and sway it up and down till they were warm, and by this means they soon grew well and merry.

Tuesday, 13.]   The night before it was calm, and the next day calm and close weather, so as we made little way, the wind with us being W.

Wednesday, 14.]   The wind S. W. rainy weather, in the morning.

About nine in the forenoon the wind came about to N. N. W. a stiff gale; so we tacked about and steered our course W. S. W.

This day the ship heaved and set more than before, yet we had but few sick, and of these such as came up upon the deck, and stirred themselves, were presently well again; therefore our captain set our children and young men to some harmless exercises, which the seamen were very active in, and did our people much good, though they would sometimes play the wags with them. Towards night we were forced to take in some sail to stay for the vice-admiral, which was near a league astern of us.

[*Large blank.*]

Thursday, 15.] The wind still at N. N. W. fair weather, but less wind than the day and night before, so as our ship made but little way.

At noon our captain made observation by the cross-staff, and found we were in forty-seven degrees thirty-seven minutes north latitude.

All this forenoon our vice-admiral was much to leeward of us; so after dinner we bare up towards her, and having fetched her up and spoken with her, the wind being come to S. W. we tacked about and steered our course N. N. W. lying as near the wind as we could, and about four of the clock, with a stiff gale, we steered W. and by N. and at night the wind grew very strong, which put us on to the W. amain.

About ten at night the wind grew so high, and rain withal, that we were forced to take in our topsail, and having lowered our mainsail and foresail, the storm was so great as it split our foresail and tore it in pieces, and a knot of the sea washed our tub overboard, wherein our fish was a-watering. The storm still grew, and it was dark with clouds, (though otherwise moonlight,) so as (though it was the Jewel's turn to carry the light this night, yet) lest we should lose or go foul one of another, we hanged out a light upon our mizzen shrouds, and before midnight we lost sight of our vice-admiral.

Our captain, so soon as he had set the watch, at eight in the evening called his men, and told them he feared we should have a storm, and therefore commanded them to be ready upon the deck, if occasion should be; and himself was up and down the decks all times of the night.

Friday, 16.] About four in the morning the wind slacked a little, yet it continued a great storm still, and though in the afternoon it blew not much wind, yet the sea was so high as it tossed us more than before, and we carried no more but our mainsail, yet our ship steered well with it, which few such ships could have done.

About four in the afternoon, the wind still W. and by S. and rainy, we put on a new foresail and hoisted it up, and stood N. W. All this day our rear-admiral and the Jewel held up with us.

This night was very stormy.

All the time of the storm few of our people were sick, (except the women, who kept under hatches,) and there appeared no fear or dismayedness among them.

[*Large blank.*]

Saturday, 17.]   The wind S. W. very stormy and boisterous. All this time we bore no more sail but our mainsail and foresail, and we steered our course W. and by N.

This day our captain told me, that our landmen were very nasty and slovenly, and that the gundeck, where they lodged, was so beastly and noisome with their victuals and beastliness, as would much endanger the health of the ship. Hereupon, after prayer, we took order, and appointed four men to see to it, and to keep that room clean for three days, and then four others should succeed them, and so forth on.

The wind continued all this day at S .W. a stiff gale. In the afternoon it cleared up, but very hazy. Our captain, about four of the clock, sent one to the top to look for our vice-admiral, but he could not descry him, yet we saw a sail about two leagues to the leeward, which stood toward the N. E.

We were this evening (by our account) about ninety leagues from Scilly, W. and by S. At this place there came a swallow and lighted upon our ship.

Sunday, 18.]   About two in the morning the wind N. W.; so we tacked about and steered our course S. W. We had still much wind, and the sea went very high, which tossed our ship continually.

After our evening sermon, about five of the clock, the wind came about to S. E. a good gale, but rainy; so we steered our course W. S. W. and the ship's way was about nine leagues a watch; (a watch is four hours).

This day the captain sent to top again to discover our vice-admiral. We descried from thence to the eastward a sail, but we knew not what she was.

About seven of the clock the Jewel bare up so near as we could speak each to other, and after we bated some sail; so she went ahead of us, and soon after eight put forth her light.

Monday, 19.]   In the morning the wind was come about to the N. W. a good gale and fair weather; so we held our course, but the ship made not so good way as when the wind was large.

This day, by observation and account, we found ourselves to be in forty-eight degrees north latitude, and two hundred and twenty leagues W. from the meridian of London.

Here I think good to note, that all this time since we came from the Wight, we had cold weather, so as we could well endure our warmest clothes. I wish, therefore, that all such as shall pass this way in the spring have care to provide warm clothing; for nothing breeds more trouble and danger of sickness, in this season, than cold.

In the afternoon the wind came to S. W. a stiff gale, with rain; so we steered westerly, till night; then the wind came about to N. W. and we tacked again and stood S. W.

Our rear-admiral being to leeward of us, we bare up to him. He told us all their people were in health, but one of their cows was dead.

Tuesday, 20.]   The wind southerly, fair weather, and little wind. In the morning we stood S. and by E., in the afternoon W. and by N.

Wednesday, 21.]   Thick, rainy weather; much wind at S. W.

Our captain, over night, had invited his consorts to have dined with him this day, but it was such foul weather as they could not come aboard us.

Thursday, 22.]   The wind still W. and by S. fair weather; then W. N. W.

This day at noon we found ourselves in forty-seven degrees and forty-eight minutes, and having a stiff gale, we steered S. W. about four leagues a watch, all this day and all the night following.

Friday, 23.]   The wind still W. N. W. a small gale, with fair weather. Our captain put forth his ancient in the poop, and heaved out his skiff, and lowered his topsails, to give sign to his consorts that they should come aboard us to dinner, for they were both a good way astern of us, and our vice-admiral was not yet seen of us since the storm, though we sent to the top every day to descry her.

About eleven of the clock, our captain sent his skiff and fetched aboard us the masters of the other two ships, and Mr. Pynchon, and they dined with us in the round-house, for the lady and gentlewomen dined in the great cabin.

This day and the night following we had little wind, so as the sea was very smooth, and the ship made little way.

Saturday, 24.] The wind still W. and by N., fair weather and calm all that day and night. Here we made observation again, and found we were in forty-five degrees twenty minutes, north latitude.

Sunday, 25.] The wind northerly, fair weather, but still calm. We stood W. and by S. and saw two ships ahead of us as far as we could descry.

In the afternoon the wind came W. and by S. but calm still. About five of the clock, the rear-admiral and the Jewel had fetched up the two ships, and by their saluting each other we perceived they were friends, (for they were so far to windward of us as we could only see the smoke of their pieces, but could not hear them). About nine of the clock, they both fell back towards us again, and we steered N. N. W. Now the weather begins to be warm.

Monday, 26.] The wind still W. and by S. close weather, and scarce any wind.

The two ships, which we saw yesterday, were bound for Canada. Capt. Kirk was aboard the admiral. They bare up with us, and falling close under our lee, we saluted each other, and conferred together so long till his vice-admiral was becalmed by our sails, and we were foul one of another; but there being little wind and the sea calm, we kept them asunder with oars, etc., till they heaved out their boat, and so towed their ship away.

They told us for certain, that the king of France had set out six of his own ships to recover the fort from them.

About one of the clock Capt. Lowe sent his skiff aboard us, (with a friendly token of his love to the governour,) to desire our captain to come aboard his ship, which he did, and there met the masters of the other ships and Capt. Kirk, and before night they all returned to their ships again, Capt. Lowe bestowing some shot upon them for their welcome.

The wind now blew a pretty gale, so as our ship made some way again, though it were out of our right course N. W. by N.

Tuesday, 27.]   The wind still westerly, a stiff gale, with close weather. We steered W. N. W. About noon some rain, and all the day very cold. We appointed Tuesdays and Wednesdays to catechize our people, and this day Mr. Phillips began it.

Wednesday, 28.]   All the night, and this day till noon, the wind very high at S. W., close weather, and some rain. Between eleven and twelve, in a shower, the wind came W. N. W., so we tacked about and stood S. W.

Thursday, 29.]   Much wind all this night at W. and by N. and the sea went very high, so as the ship rolled very much, because we sailed but with one course; therefore, about twelve, our captain arose and caused the foretopsail to be hoisted, and then the ship went more steady. He caused the quartermaster to look down into the hold to see if the cask lay fast and the . . . .*

In the morning the wind continued with a stiff gale; rainy and cold all the day.

We had been now three weeks at sea, and were not come above three hundred leagues, being about one third part of our way, viz., about forty-six north latitude, and near the meridian of the Terceras.

This night Capt. Kirk carried the light as one of our consorts.

Friday, 30.]   The wind at W. N. W., a strong gale all the night and day, with showers now and then.

We made observation, and found we were in forty-four north latitude. At night the wind scanted towards the S. with rain; so we tacked about and stood N. W. and by N.

Saturday, May 1.]   All the night much wind at S. S. W. and rain. In the morning the wind still strong, so as we could bear little sail, and so it continued a growing storm all the day, and towards night so much wind as we bore no more sail but so much as should keep the ship stiff. Then it grew a very great tempest all the night, with fierce showers of rain intermixed, and very cold.

Lord's day, 2.]   The tempest continued all the day, with the wind W. and by N., and the sea raged and tossed us exceedingly; yet, through God's mercy, we were very comfortable, and few or none sick, but had opportunity to keep the Sabbath, and Mr. Phil-

* [Several words illegible.]

lips preached twice that day. The Ambrose and Jewel were separated far from us the first night, but this day we saw them again, but Capt. Kirk's ships we saw not since.

Monday, 3.]   In the night the wind abated, and by morning the sea was well assuaged, so as we bare our foresail again, and stood W. S. W.; but all the time of the tempest we could make no way, but were driven to the leeward, and the Ambrose struck all her sails but her mizzen, and lay a hull. She brake her main yard. This day we made observation, and found we were in forty-three and a half north latitude. We set two fighters in the bolts till night, with their hands bound behind them. A maid-servant in the ship, being stomach-sick, drank so much strong water, that she was senseless, and had near killed herself. We observed it a common fault in our young people, that they gave themselves to drink hot waters very immoderately.

Tuesday, 4.]   Much wind at S. W., close weather. In the morning we tacked about and stood N. W. and about ten in the morning W. N. W., but made little way in regard of the head sea.

Wednesday, 5.]   The wind W. and by S. thick, foggy weather, and rainy; so we stood N. W. by W. At night the Lord remembered us, and enlarged the wind to the N.; so we tacked about and stood our course W. and by S. with a merry gale in all our sails.

Thursday, 6.]   The wind at N. a good gale, and fair weather. We made observation and found we were forty-three and a half north latitude; so we stood full west, and ran, in twenty-four hours, about thirty leagues.

Four things I observed here. 1. That the declination of the pole star was much, even to the view, beneath that it is in England. 2. That the new moon, when it first appeared, was much smaller than at any time I had seen it in England. 3. That all the way we came, we saw fowls flying and swimming, when we had no land near by two hundred leagues. 4. That wheresoever the wind blew, we had still cold weather, and the sun did not give so much heat as in England.

Friday, 7.]   The wind N. and by E. a small gale, very fair weather, and towards night a still calm. This day our captain and Mr. Lowe dined aboard the Jewel.

Saturday, 8.]   All the night calm. In the morning the wind

S. W. a handsome gale; so we tacked and stood N. W. and soon after, the wind growing more large, we stood W. N. W. with a good gale. About four of the clock we saw a whale, who lay just in our ship's way, (the bunch of his back about a yard above water). He would not shun us; so we passed within a stone's cast of him, as he lay spouting up water.

Lord's day, 9.]   The wind still S. W. a good gale, but close weather and some rain; we held on our course W. N. W. About nine it cleared up, and towards night a great fog for an hour or two.

We were now in forty-four and a half north latitude, and a little west of Corvos.

Monday, 10.]   The wind S. S. W. a good gale and fair weather; so we stood W. and by N. four or five leagues a watch, all this day. The wind increased, and was a great storm all the night. About midnight our rear-admiral put forth two lights, whereby we knew that some mischance had befallen her. We answered her with two lights again, and bare up to her, so near as we durst, (for the sea went very high, and she lay by the lee) and having hailed her, we thought she had sprung aleak; but she had broken some of her shrouds; so we went a little ahead of her, and, bringing our fore-sail aback stays, we stayed for her, and, about two hours after, she filled her sails, and we stood our course together, but our captain went not to rest till four of the clock, and some others of us slept but little that night.

Tuesday, 11.]   The storm continued all this day, till three in the afternoon, and the sea went very high, so as our ship could make no way, being able to bear no more but our mainsail about midmast high. At three there fell a great storm of rain, which laid the wind, and the wind shifting into the W. we tacked and stood into the head sea, to avoid the rolling of our ship, and by that means we made no way, the sea beating us back as much as the wind put us forward.

We had still cold weather, and our people were so acquainted with storms as they were not sick, nor troubled, though we were much tossed forty-eight hours together, viz., twenty-four during the storm, and as long the next night and day following, Wednesday, 12, when as we lay as it were a hull, for want of wind, and rolling continually in a high grown sea. This day was close and rainy.

Complaint was made to our captain of some injury that one of the under officers of the ship had done to one of our landmen. He called him and examined the cause, and commanded him to be tied up by the hands, and a weight to be hanged about his neck; but, at the intercession of the governour, (with some difficulty,) he remitted his punishment.

At night the wind blew at S. E. a handsome gale, with rain; so we put forth our sails and stood W. and by S.

Thursday, 13.] Toward morning the wind came to the south-westerly, with close weather and a strong gale, so as before noon we took in our topsails, (the rear-admiral having split her fore-topsail) and we stood west-southerly.

Friday, 14.] The wind W. S. W., thick, foggy weather, and in the afternoon rainy. We stood W. and by S. and after W. and by N. about five leagues a watch. We were in forty-four and a half. The sun set N. W. and by N. one third northerly. And towards night we stood W.

Saturday, 15.] The wind westerly all this day; fair weather. We tacked twice to small purpose.

Lord's day, 16.] As the 15 was.

Monday, 17.] The wind at S. a fine gale and fair weather. We stood W. and by S. We saw a great drift; so we heaved out our skiff, and it proved a fir log, which seemed to have been many years in the water, for it was all overgrown with barnacles and other trash. We sounded here and found no ground at one hundred fathom and more. We saw two whales. About nine at night the wind grew very strong at S. W. and continued so, with much rain, till one of the clock; then it ceased raining, but the wind came to the W. with more violence. In this storm we were forced to take in all our sails, save our mainsail, and to lower that so much as we could.

Tuesday, 18.] In the morning the wind slacked, but we could stand no nearer our course than N. and we had much wind all this day. In the afternoon we tacked and stood S. by E. Towards night (our rear-admiral being near two leagues to leeward of us) we bare up, and drawing near her, we descried, some two leagues more to leeward, two ships, which we conceived were those two of Capt. Kirk's, which parted from us in the storm, May 2. We had still cold weather.

Wednesday, 19.]   The wind S. S. W.; close and rainy; little wind. We tacked again and stood W.; but about noon the wind came full W. a very strong gale; so we tacked again and stood N. by E. and at night we took off our main bonnet, and took in all our sails, save our main-course and mizzen. We were now in forty-four degrees twelve minutes north, and by our account in the midway between the false bank and the main bank. All this night a great storm at W. by N.

Thursday, 20.]   The storm continued all this day, the wind as it was, and rainy. In the forenoon we carried our forecourse and stood W. S. W., but in the afternoon we took it in, the wind increasing, and the sea grown very high; and lying with the helm a-weather, we made no way but as the ship drove. We had still cold weather.

[1] In the great cabin, at nine at night, etc., and the next day again, etc. The storm continued all this night.

Friday, 21.]   The wind still N. W.; little wind, and close weather. We stood S. W. with all our sails, but made little way, and at night it was a still calm.

A servant of one of our company had bargained with a child to sell him a box worth 3*d*. for three biscuits a day all the voyage, and had received about forty, and had sold them and many more to some other servants. We caused his hands to be tied up to a bar, and hanged a basket with stones about his neck, and so he stood two hours.

Saturday, 22.]   The wind S. S. W. much wind and rain. Our spritsail laid so deep in as it was split in pieces with a head sea at the instant as our captain was going forth of his cabin very early in the morning to give order to take it in. It was a great mercy of God, that it did split, for otherwise it had endangered the breaking of our bowsprit and topmasts at least, and then we had no other way but to have returned for England, except the wind had come east. About ten in the morning, in a very great fret of wind, it chopt suddenly into the W. as it had done divers times before, and so continued with a small gale and [we] stood N. and by W. About four in the afternoon there arose a sudden storm of

[1] In the margin of the MS. the word "fast" is written by the governour, and a later reader has put in a 🖙 pointing at the paragraph.

wind and rain, so violent as we had not a greater. It continued thick and boisterous all the night.

About seven we descried a sail ahead of us, towards the N. and by E. which stood towards us. Our captain, supposing it might be our vice-admiral, hoisted up his mainsail, which before was struck down aboard, and came up to meet her. When we drew near her we put forth our ancient, and she luffed up to get the wind of us; but when she saw she could not, she bare up, and hoisting up her foresail, stood away before the wind; yet we made all the signs we could, that we meant her no harm, but she would not trust us. She was within shot of us, so as we perceived she was a small Frenchman, which we did suppose had been driven off the bank. When she was clear of us, she stood her course again, and we ours.

This day at twelve we made observation, and were about forty-three, but the storm put us far to the N. again. Still cold weather.

Lord's day, 23.]   Much wind, still westerly, and very cold weather.

Monday, 24.]   The wind N. W. by N. a handsome gale, and close weather and very cold. We stood S. W. About noon we had occasion to lie by the lee to straighten our mizzen shrouds, and the rear-admiral and Jewel, being both to windward of us, bare up and came under our lee, to inquire if anything were amiss with us; so we heard the company was in health in the Jewel, but that two passengers were dead in the Ambrose, and one other cow.

Tuesday, 25.]   The wind still N. W.; fair weather, but cold. We went on with a handsome gale, and at noon were in forty-three and a half; and the variation of the compass was a point and one-sixth. All this day we stood W. S. W. about five or six leagues a watch, and towards night the wind enlarged, with a cold dash of snowy rain, and then we ran in a smooth sea about eight or nine leagues a watch, and stood due W.

Wednesday, 26.]   The wind still N. W. a good gale and fair weather, but very cold still; yet we were about forty-three. At night we sounded, but found no ground.

Thursday, 27.]   The wind N. W. a handsome gale; fair weather. About noon it came about to the S. W. and at night rain, with a stiff gale, and it continued to rain very hard till it was near midnight.

This day our skiff went aboard the Jewel for a hogshead of meal, which we borrowed, because we could not come by our own, and there came back in the skiff the master of the Jewel and Mr. Revell; so our captain stayed them dinner, and sent for Capt. Lowe; and about two hours after dinner, they went aboard their own ships, our captain giving Mr. Revell three shot, because he was one of the owners of our ship.

We understood now, that the two which died in the Ambrose were Mr. Cradock's servants, who were sick when they came to sea; and one of them should have been left at Cowes, if any house would have received him.

In the Jewel, also, one of the seamen died—a most profane fellow, and one who was very injurious to the passengers, though much against the will of the master.

At noon we tacked about and stood W. and by N. and so continued most part of that day and night following, and had much rain till midnight.

Friday, 28.] In the morning the wind veered to the W. yet we had a stiff gale, and steered N. W. and by N. It was so great a fog all this day, as we had lost sight of one of our ships, and saw the other sometimes much to leeward. We had many fierce showers of rain throughout this day.

At night the wind cleared up, and we saw both our consorts fair by us; so that wind being very scant, we tacked and stood W. and by S. A child was born in the Jewel about this time.

Saturday, 29.] The wind N. W. a stiff gale, and fair weather, but very cold; in the afternoon full N. and towards night N. and by E.; so we stood W.

Lord's day, 30.] The wind N. by E. a handsome gale, but close, misty weather, and very cold; so our ship made good way in a smooth sea, and our three ships kept close together. By our account we were in the same meridian with Isle Sable, and forty-two and a half.

Monday, 31.] Wind N. W. a small gale, close and cold weather. We sounded, but had no ground. About noon the wind came N. by E. a stiff, constant gale and fair weather, so as our ship's way was seven, eight, and sometimes twelve leagues a watch. This day, about five at night, we expected the eclipse, but there was not any, the sun being fair and clear from three till it set.

June 1, Tuesday.] The wind N. E. a small gale, with fair, clear weather; in the afternoon full S., and towards night a good gale. We stood W. and by N. A woman in our ship fell in travail, and we sent and had a midwife out of the Jewel. She was so far ahead of us at this time, (though usually we could spare her some sail,) as we shot off a piece and lowered our topsails, and then she brailed her sails and stayed for us.

This evening we saw the new moon more than half an hour after sunset, being much smaller than it is at any time in England.

Wednesday, 2.] The wind S. S. W., a handsome gale; very fair weather, but still cold; in the evening a great fog. We stood W. and by N. and W. N. W.

Our captain, supposing us now to be near the N. coast, and knowing that to the S. there were dangerous shoals, fitted on a new mainsail, that was very strong, and double, and would not adventure with his old sails, as before, when he had sea-room enough.

Thursday, 3.] The wind S. by W. a good steady gale, and we stood W. and by N. The fog continued very thick, and some rain withal. We sounded in the morning, and again at noon, and had no ground. We sounded again about two, afternoon, and had ground about eighty fathom, a fine gray sand; so we presently tacked and stood S. S. E., and shot off a piece of ordnance to give notice to our consorts, whom we saw not since last evening.

The fog continued all this night, and a steady gale at S. W.

Friday, 4.] About four in the morning we tacked again (the wind S. W.) and stood W. N. W. The fog continued all this day, so as we could not see a stone's cast from us; yet the sun shone very bright all the day. We sounded every two hours, but had no ground. At night we tacked again and stood S. In the great cabin, fast.

Saturday, 5.] In the morning the wind came to N. E. a handsome gale, and the fog was dispersed; so we stood before the wind W. and by N., all the afternoon being rainy. At night we sounded, but had no ground. In the great cabin, thanksgiving.

It rained most part of this night, yet our captain kept abroad, and was forced to come in in the night to shift his clothes.

We sounded every half watch, but had no ground.

Lord's day, 6.] The wind N. E. and after N., a good gale,

but still foggy at times, and cold. We stood W. N. W., both to make Cape Sable, if we might, and also because of the current, which, near the west shore sets to the S., that we might be the more clear from the southern shoals, viz., of Cape Cod.

About two in the afternoon we sounded and had ground at about eighty fathom, and the mist then breaking up, we saw the shore to the N. about five or six leagues off, and were (as we supposed) to the S. W. of Cape Sable, and in forty-three and a quarter. Towards night it calmed and was foggy again, and the wind came S. and by E. We tacked and stood W. and by N., intending to make land at Aquamenticus, being to the N. of the Isles of Shoals.

Monday, 7.] The wind S. About four in the morning we sounded and had ground at thirty fathom, and was somewhat calm; so we put our ship a-stays, and took, in less than two hours, with a few hooks, sixty-seven codfish, most of them very great fish, some a yard and a half long, and a yard in compass. This came very seasonably, for our salt fish was now spent, and we were taking care for victuals this day (being a fish day).

After this we filled our sails, and stood W. N. W. with a small gale. We hoisted out a great boat to keep our sounding the better.* The weather was now very cold. We sounded at eight, and had fifty fathom, and, being calm, we heaved out our hooks again, and took twenty-six cods; so we all feasted with fish this day. A woman was delivered of a child in our ship, stillborn. The woman had divers children before, but none lived, and she had some mischance now, which caused her to come near a month before her time, but she did very well. At one of the clock we had a fresh gale at N. W. and very fair weather all that afternoon, and warm, but the wind failed soon.

All the night the wind was W. and by S. a stiff gale, which made us stand to and again, with small advantage.

Tuesday, 8.] The wind still W. and by S., fair weather, but close and cold. We stood N. N. W. with a stiff gale, and, about three in the afternoon, we had sight of land to the N. W. about ten leagues, which we supposed was the Isles of Monhegan, but it proved Mount Mansell. Then we tacked and stood W. S. W. We had now fair sunshine weather, and so pleasant a sweet air

* [This sentence has a line drawn through it.]

as did much refresh us, and there came a smell off the shore like the smell of a garden.

There came a wild pigeon into our ship, and another small land bird.

Wednesday, 9.] In the morning the wind easterly, but grew presently calm. Now we had very fair weather, and warm. About noon the wind came to S. W.; so we stood W. N. W. with a handsome gale, and had the main land upon our starboard all that day, about eight or ten leagues off. It is very high land, lying in many hills very unequal. At night we saw many small islands, being low land, between us and the main, about five or six leagues off us; and about three leagues from us, towards the main, a small rock a little above water. At night we sounded and had soft oozy ground at sixty fathom; so, the wind being now scant at W. we tacked again and stood S. S. W. We were now in forty-three and a half. This high land, which we saw, we judged to be at the W. cape of the great bay, which goeth towards Port Royal, called Mount Desert, or Mount Mansell, and no island, but part of the main. In the night the wind shifted oft.

Thursday, 10.] In the morning the wind S. and by W. till five. In the morning a thick fog; then it cleared up with fair weather, but somewhat close. After we had run some ten leagues W. and by S. we lost sight of the former land, but made other high land on our starboard, as far off as we could descry, but we lost it again.

The wind continued all this day at S. a stiff, steady gale, yet we bare all our sails, and stood W. S. W. About four in the afternoon we made land on our starboard bow, called the Three Turks' Heads, being a ridge of three hills upon the main, whereof the southmost is the greatest. It lies near Aquamenticus. We descried, also, another hill, more northward, which lies by Cape Porpus. We saw, also, ahead of us, some four leagues from shore, a small rock, not above a flight shot over, which hath a dangerous shoal to the E. and by S. of it, some two leagues in length. We kept our luff and weathered it, and left it on our starboard about two miles off. Towards night we might see the trees in all places very plainly, and a small hill to the southward of the Turks' Heads. All the rest of the land to the S. was plain, low land. Here we had a fine fresh smell from shore. Then, lest we should not get clear of the ledge of rocks, which lie under water from within a flight shot of the said rock, (called Boone Isle,) which we had now brought N. E. from us, towards Pascataquac, we tacked and stood S. E. with a stiff gale at S. by W.

Friday, 11.] The wind still S. W., close weather. We stood to and again all this day within sight of Cape Ann. The Isles of Shoals were now within two leagues of us, and we saw a ship lie there at anchor, and five or six shallops under sail up and down.

We took many mackerels, and met a shallop, which stood from Cape Ann towards the Isles of Shoals, which belonged to some English fishermen.

Saturday, 12.] About four in the morning we were near our port. We shot off two pieces of ordnance, and sent our skiff to Mr. Peirce his ship (which lay in the harbour, and had been there [blank] days before). About an hour after, Mr. Allerton came aboard us in a shallop as he was sailing to Pemaquid. As we stood towards the harbour, we saw another shallop coming to us; so we stood in to meet her, and passed through the narrow strait between Baker's Isle and Little Isle, and came to an anchor a little within the islands.

After Mr. Peirce came aboard us, and returned to fetch Mr. Endecott, who came to us about two of the clock, and with him Mr. Skelton and Capt. Levett. We that were of the assistants, and some other gentlemen, and some of the women, and our captain, returned with them to Nahumkeck, where we supped with a good venison pasty and good beer, and at night we returned to our ship, but some of the women stayed behind.

In the mean time most of our people went on shore upon the land of Cape Ann, which lay very near us, and gathered store of fine strawberries.

An Indian came aboard us and lay there all night.

Lord's day, 13.] In the morning, the sagamore of Agawam and one of his men came aboard our ship and stayed with us all day.

About two in the afternoon we descried the Jewel; so we manned out our skiff and wafted them in, and they went as near the harbour as the tide and wind would suffer.

Monday, 14.] In the morning early we weighed anchor, and

the wind being against us, and the channel so narrow as we could not well turn in, we warped in our ship and came to an anchor in the inward harbour.

In the afternoon we went with most of our company on shore, and our captain gave us five pieces.

[*Large blank.*]

Thursday, 17.]   We went to Mattachusetts, to find out a place for our sitting down. We went up Mistick River about six miles.

We lay at Mr. Maverick's, and returned home on Saturday. As we came home, we came by Nataskott, and sent for Capt. Squib ashore—(he had brought the west-country people, viz., Mr. Ludlow, Mr. Rossiter, Mr. Maverick, etc., to the bay, who were set down at Mattapan,)—and ended a difference between him and the passengers; whereupon he sent his boat to his ship, (the Mary and John,) and at our parting gave us five pieces. At our return we found the Ambrose in the harbour at Salem.

Thursday, July 1.]   The Mayflower and the Whale arrived safe in Charlton harbour. Their passengers were all in health, but most of their cattle dead, (whereof a mare and horse of mine). Some stone horses came over in good plight.

Friday, 2.]   The Talbot arrived there. She had lost fourteen passengers.

My son, Henry Winthrop, was drowned at Salem.

Saturday, 3.]   The Hopewell, and William and Francis arrived.

Monday, 5.]   The Trial arrived at Charlton, and the Charles at Salem.

Tuesday, 6.]   The Success arrived. She had [*blank*] goats and lost [*blank*] of them, and many of her passengers were near starved, etc.

Wednesday, 7.]   The Lion went back to Salem.

Thursday, 8.]   We kept a day of thanksgiving in all the plantations.

[*Large blank.*]

Thursday, August 18.]   Capt. Endecott and —— Gibson were married by the governour and Mr. Wilson.

Saturday, 20.]   The French ship called the Gift, came into the harbour at Charlton. She had been twelve weeks at sea, and lost one passenger and twelve goats; she delivered six.

Monday we kept a court.

Friday, 27.]   We, of the congregation, kept a fast, and chose Mr. Wilson our teacher, and Mr. Nowell an elder, and Mr. Gager and Mr. Aspinwall, deacons. We used imposition of hands, but with this protestation by all, that it was only as a sign of election and confirmation, not of any intent that Mr. Wilson should renounce his ministry he received in England.

September 20.]   Mr. Gager died.

30.]   About two in the morning, Mr. Isaac Johnson died; his wife, the lady Arbella, of the house of Lincoln, being dead about one month before. He was a holy man, and wise, and died in sweet peace, leaving some part of his substance to the colony.

The wolves killed six calves at Salem, and they killed one wolf.

Thomas Morton adjudged to be imprisoned, till he were sent into England, and his house burnt down, for his many injuries offered to the Indians, and other misdemeanours. Capt. Brook, master of the Gift, refused to carry him.

[Large blank.]

Finch, of Watertown, had his wigwam burnt and all his goods.

Billington executed at Plimouth for murdering one.

Mr. Phillips, the minister of Watertown, and others, had their hay burnt.

The wolves killed some swine at Saugus.

A cow died at Plimouth, and a goat at Boston, with eating Indian corn.

October 23.]   Mr. Rossiter, one of the assistants, died.

25.]   Mr. Colburn (who was chosen deacon by the congregation a week before) was invested by imposition of hands of the minister and elder.

The governour, upon consideration of the inconveniences which had grown in England by drinking one to another, restrained it at his own table, and wished others to do the like, so as it grew, by little and little, to disuse.

29.]   The Handmaid arrived at Plimouth, having been twelve

weeks at sea, and spent all her masts, and of twenty-eight cows she lost ten. She had about sixty passengers, who came all well; John Grant, master.

Mr. Goffe wrote to me, that his shipping this year had utterly undone him.

She brought out twenty-eight heifers, but brought but seventeen alive.*

November 11.] The master came to Boston with Capt. Standish and two gentlemen passengers, who came to plant here, but having no testimony, we would not receive them.

10.] [*blank*] Firmin, of Watertown, had his wigwam burnt. Divers had their hay-stacks burnt by burning the grass.

27.] Three of the governour's servants were from this day to the 1 of December abroad in his skiff among the islands, in bitter frost and snow, being kept from home by the N. W. wind, and without victuals. At length they gat to Mount Wollaston, and left their boat there, and came home by land. Laus Deo.

December 6.] The governour and most of the assistants, and others, met at Roxbury, and there agreed to build a town fortified upon the neck between that and Boston, and a committee was appointed to consider of all things requisite, etc.

14.] The committee met at Roxbury, and upon further consideration, for reasons, it was concluded, that we could not have a town in the place aforesaid: 1. Because men would be forced to keep two families. 2. There was no running water; and if there were any springs, they would not suffice the town. 3. The most part of the people had built already, and would not be able to build again. So we agreed to meet at Watertown that day sen'night, and in the meantime other places should be viewed.

Capt. Neal and three other gentlemen came hither to us. He came in the bark Warwick, this summer, to Pascataqua, sent as governour there for Sir Ferdinando Gorges and others.

21.] We met again at Watertown, and there, upon view of a place a mile beneath the town, all agreed it a fit place for a fortified town, and we took time to consider further about it.

24.] Till this time there was (for the most part) fair, open weather, with gentle frosts in the night; but this day the wind

---

* [This sentence has a line drawn through it in the manuscript.]

came N. W., very strong, and some snow withal, but so cold as some had their fingers frozen, and in danger to be lost. Three of the governour's servants, coming in a shallop from Mistick, were driven by the wind upon Noddle's Island, and forced to stay there all that night, without fire or food; yet, through God's mercy, they came safe to Boston next day, but the fingers of two of them were blistered with cold, and one swooned when he came to the fire.

26.] The rivers were frozen up, and they of Charlton could not come to the sermon at Boston till the afternoon at high water.

Many of our cows and goats were forced to be still abroad for want of houses.

28.] Richard Garrett, a shoemaker of Boston, and one of the congregation there, with one of his daughters, a young maid, and four others, went towards Plimouth in a shallop, against the advice of his friends; and about the Gurnett's Nose the wind overblew so much at N. W. as they were forced to come to a killock at twenty fathom, but their boat drave and shaked out the stone, and they were put to sea, and the boat took in much water, which did freeze so hard as they could not free her; so they gave themselves for lost, and, commending themselves to God, they disposed themselves to die; but one of their company espying land near Cape Cod, they made shift to hoist up part of their sail, and, by God's special providence, were carried through the rocks to the shore, where some gat on land, but some had their legs frozen into the ice, so as they were forced to be cut out. Being come on shore they kindled a fire, but, having no hatchet, they could get little wood, and were forced to lie in the open air all night, being extremely cold. In the morning two of their company went towards Plimouth, (supposing it had been within seven or eight miles, whereas it was near fifty miles from them). By the way they met with two Indian squaws, who, coming home, told their husbands that they had met two Englishmen. They thinking (as it was) that they had been shipwrecked, made after them, and brought them back to their wigwam, and entertained them kindly; and one of them went with them the next day to Plimouth, and the other went to find out their boat and the rest of their company, which were seven miles off, and having found them, he holp them what he could, and returned to his wigwam, and fetched a hatchet, and built them a wigwam and covered it, and gat them wood (for they were so weak and frozen, as they could not stir;) and Garrett died about two days after his landing; and the ground being so frozen as they could not dig his grave, the Indian hewed a hole about half a yard deep, with his hatchet, and having laid the corpse in it, he laid over it a great heap of wood to keep it from the wolves. By this time the governour of Plimouth had sent three men to them with provisions, who being come, and not able to launch their boat, (which with the strong N. W. wind was driven up to the high water mark,) the Indian returned to Plimouth and fetched three more; but before they came, they had launched their boat, and with a fair southerly wind were gotten to Plimouth, where another of their company died, his flesh being mortified with the frost; and the two who went towards Plimouth died also, one of them being not able to get thither, and the other had his feet so frozen as he died of it after. The girl escaped best, and one Harwood, a godly man of the congregation of Boston, lay long under the surgeon's hands; and it was above six weeks before they could get the boat from Plimouth; and in their return they were much distressed; yet their boat was very well manned, the want whereof before was the cause of their loss.

January.] A house at Dorchester was burnt down.

February 11.] Mr. Freeman's house at Watertown was burned down, but, being in the daytime, his goods were saved.

5.] The ship Lyon, Mr. William Peirce, master, arrived at Nantasket. She brought Mr. Williams, (a godly minister,) with his wife, Mr. Throgmorton, [blank] Perkins, [blank] Ong, and others, with their wives and children, about twenty passengers, and about two hundred tons of goods. She set sail from Bristol, December 1. She had a very tempestuous passage, yet, through God's mercy, all her people came safe, except Way his son, who fell from the spritsail yard in a tempest, and could not be recovered, though he kept in sight near a quarter of an hour. Her goods also came all in good condition.

8.] The governour went aboard the Lyon, riding by Long Island.

9.] The Lyon came to an anchor before Boston, where she rode very well, notwithstanding the great drift of ice.

10.] The frost brake up; and after that, though we had many

snows and sharp frost, yet they continued not, neither were the
waters frozen up as before. It hath been observed, ever since this
bay was planted by Englishmen, viz., seven years, that at this day
the frost hath broken up every year.

The poorer sort of people (who lay long in tents, etc.) were
much afflicted with the scurvy, and many died, especially at Boston
and Charlestown; but when this ship came and brought store of
juice of lemons, many recovered speedily. It hath been always
observed here, that such as fell into discontent, and lingered after
their former conditions in England, fell into the scurvy and died.

18.] Capt. Welden, a hopeful young gentleman, and an experienced soldier, died at Charlestown of a consumption, and was
buried at Boston with a military funeral.

Of the old planters, and such as came the year before, there
were but two, (and those servants,) which had the scurvy in all
the country. At Plimouth not any had it, no not of those, who
came this year, whereof there were above sixty. Whereas, at their
first planting there, near the half of their people died of it.

A shallop of Mr. Glover's was cast away upon the rocks about
Nahant, but the men were saved.

Of those which went back in the ships this summer, for fear
of death or famine, etc., many died by the way and after they were
landed, and others fell very sick and low, etc.

The Ambrose, whereof Capt. Lowe was master, being new
masted at Charlton, spent all her masts near Newfoundland, and
had perished, if Mr. Peirce, in the Lyon, who was her consort,
had not towed her home to Bristol. Of the other ships which
returned, three, viz., the Charles, the Success, and the Whale, were
set upon by Dunkirkers, near Plimouth in England, and after long
fight, having lost many men, and being much torn, (especially the
Charles,) they gat into Plimouth.

The provision, which came to us this year, came at excessive
rates, in regard of the dearness of corn in England, so as every
bushel of wheat-meal stood us in fourteen shillings, peas eleven
shillings, etc. Tonnage was at £6.11.

22.] We held a day of thanksgiving for this ship's arrival,
by order from the governour and council, directed to all the
plantations.

[March 16.] About noon the chimney of Mr. Sharp's house

in Boston took fire, (the splinters being not clayed at the top,) and taking the thatch burnt it down, and the wind being N. W., drove the fire to Mr. Colburn's house, being [*blank*] rods off, and burnt that down also, yet they saved most of their goods.

23.]   Chickatabot came with his sannops and squaws, and presented the governour with a hogshead of Indian corn.

After they had all dined, and had each a small cup of sack and beer, and the men tobacco, he sent away all his men and women, (though the governour would have stayed them, in regard of the rain and thunder). Himself and one squaw and one sannop stayed all night, and, being in English clothes, the governour set him at his own table, where he behaved himself as soberly, etc., as an Englishman. The next day after dinner he returned home, the governour giving him cheese and peas and a mug and some other small things.

26.]   John Sagamore and James his brother, with divers sannops, came to the governour to desire his letter for recovery of twenty beaver skins, which one Watts in England had forced him of. The governor entertained them kindly, and gave him his letter with directions to Mr. Downing in England, etc.

The night before, alarm was given in divers of the plantations. It arose through the shooting off some pieces at Watertown, by occasion of a calf, which Sir Richard Saltonstall had lost; and the soldiers were sent out with their pieces to try the wilderness from thence till they might find it.

29.]   Sir Richard Saltonstall and his two daughters, and one of his younger sons, (his two eldest sons remained still in the country,) came down to Boston, and stayed that night at the governour's, and the next morning, by seven of the clock, accompanied with Mr. Peirce and others in two shallops, they departed to go to the ship riding at Salem. The governour gave them three drakes at their setting sail, the wind being N. W. a stiff gale and full sea. Mr. Sharp went away at the same time in another shallop.

About ten of the clock, Mr. Coddington and Mr. Wilson, and divers of the congregation, met at the governour's, and there Mr. Wilson, praying and exhorting the congregation to love, etc., commended to them the exercise of prophecy in his absence, and designed those whom he thought most fit for it, viz., the governour, Mr. Dudley, and Mr. Nowell the elder. Then he desired the governour to commend himself and the rest to God by prayer;

which being done, they accompanied him to the boat, and so they went over to Charlestown to go by land to the ship. This ship set sail from Salem, April 1, and arrived at London (all safe) April 29.

April.] The beginning of this month we had very much rain and warm weather. It is a general rule, that when the wind blows twelve hours in any part of the east, it brings rain or snow in great abundance.

4.] Wahginnacut, a sagamore upon the River Quonehtacut which lies west of Naragancet, came to the governour at Boston, with John Sagamore, and Jack Straw, (an Indian, who had lived in England and had served Sir Walter Raleigh, and was now turned Indian again,) and divers of their sannops, and brought a letter to the governour from Mr. Endecott to this effect: That the said Wahginnacut was very desirous to have some Englishmen to come plant in his country, and offered to find them corn, and give them yearly eighty skins of beaver, and that the country was very fruitful, etc., and wished that there might be two men sent with him to see the country. The governour entertained them at dinner, but would send none with him. He discovered after, that the said sagamore is a very treacherous man, and at war with the Pekoath (a far greater sagamore). His country is not above five days' journey from us by land.

12.] At a court holden at Boston, (upon information to the governour, that they of Salem had called Mr. Williams to the office of a teacher,) a letter was written from the court to Mr. Endecott to this effect: That whereas Mr. Williams had refused to join with the congregation at Boston, because they would not make a public declaration of their repentance for having communion with the churches of England, while they lived there; and, besides, had declared his opinion, that the magistrate might not punish the breach of the Sabbath, nor any other offence, as it was a breach of the first table; therefore, they marvelled they would choose him without advising with the council; and withal desiring him, that they would forbear to proceed till they had conferred about it.

13.] Chickatabot came to the governour, and desired to buy some English clothes for himself. The governour told him, that English sagamores did not use to truck; but he called his tailor and gave him order to make him a suit of clothes; whereupon he gave the governour two large skins of coat beaver, and, after he and his men had dined, they departed, and said he would come again three days after for his suit.

14.]   We began a court of guard upon the neck between Roxbury and Boston, whereupon should be always resident an officer and six men.*

An order was made last court, that no man should discharge a piece after sunset, except by occasion of alarm.

15.]   Chickatabot came to the governour again, and he put him into a very good new suit from head to foot, and after he set meat before them; but he would not eat till the governour had given thanks, and after meat he desired him to do the like, and so departed.

21.]   The house of John Page of Watertown was burnt by carrying a few coals from one house to another: a coal fell by the way and kindled in the leaves.

One Mr. Gardiner, (calling himself** Sir Christopher Gardiner, knight of the golden melice,) being accused to have two wives in England, was sent for; but he had intelligence, and escaped, and travelled up and down among the Indians about a month; but, by means of the governour of Plimouth, he was taken by the Indians about Namasket, and brought to Plimouth, and from thence he was brought, by Capt. Underhill and his Lieut. Dudley, May 4, to Boston.

16.]   There was an alarm given to all our towns in the night, by occasion of a piece which was shot off, (but where could not be known,) and the Indians having sent us word the day before, that the Mohawks were coming down against them and us.

17.]   A general court at Boston. The former governour was chosen again, and all the freemen of the commons were sworn to this government. At noon, Cheeseborough's house was burnt down, all the people being present.

27].   There came from Virginia into Salem a pinnace of eighteen tons, laden with corn and tobacco. She was bound to the north, and put in there by foul weather. She sold her corn at ten shillings the bushel.

---

* [This sentence has a line drawn through it in the manuscript.]
** [The preceding four words have a line drawn through them in the manuscript.]

June 14.]   At a court, John Sagamore and Chickatabot being told at last court of some injuries that their men did to our cattle, and giving consent to make satisfaction, etc., now one of their men was complained of for shooting a pig, etc., for which Chickatabot was ordered to pay a small skin of beaver, which he presently paid.

At this court one Philip Ratcliff, a servant of Mr. Cradock, being convict, ore tenus, of most foul, scandalous invectives against our churches and government, was censured to be whipped, lose his ears, and be banished the plantation, which was presently executed.

25.]   There came a shallop from Pascataqua, which brought news of a small English ship come thither with provisions and some Frenchmen to make salt. By this boat, Capt. Neal, governour of Pascataqua, sent a packet of letters to the governour, directed to Sir Christopher Gardiner, which, when the governour had opened, he found it came from Sir Ferdinando Gorges, (who claims a great part of the Bay of Massachusetts). In the packet was one letter to Thomas Morton, (sent prisoner before into England upon the lord chief justice's warrant:) by both which letters it appeared, that he had some secret design to recover his pretended right, and that he reposed much trust in Sir Christopher Gardiner.

These letters we opened, because they were directed to one, who was our prisoner, and had declared himself an ill willer to our government.

27.]   There came to the governour Capt. Southcot of Dorchester, and brought letters out of the White Angel, (which was lately arrived at Sauco). She brought [*blank*] cows, goats, and hogs, and many provisions, for the bay and for Plimouth. Mr. Allerton returned in this ship, and by him we heard, that the Friendship, which put out from Barnstable [*blank*] weeks before the Angel, was forced home again by extremity of foul weather, and so had given over her voyage. This ship, the Angel, set sail from [*blank*].

July 4.]   The governor built a bark at Mistick, which was launched this day, and called the Blessing of the Bay.

6.]   A small ship of sixty tons arrived at Natascott, Mr. Graves master. She brought ten passengers from London. They came with a patent to Sagadahock, but, not liking the place, they came hither. Their ship drew ten feet, and went up to Watertown, but she ran on ground twice by the way. These were the company called the Husbandmen, and their ship called the Plough. Most of them proved familists and vanished away.

13.] Canonicus' son, the great sachem of Naraganset, came to the governour's house with John Sagamore. After they had dined, he gave the governour a skin, and the governour requited him with a fair pewter pot, which he took very thankfully, and stayed all night.

14.] The ship called the Friendship, of Barnstable, arrived at Boston, after she had been at sea eleven weeks, and beaten back again by foul weather. She set sail from Barnstable again about the midst of May. She landed here eight heifers, and one calf, and five sheep.

21.] The governour, and deputy, and Mr. Nowell, the elder of the congregation at Boston, went to Watertown to confer with Mr. Phillips, the pastor, and Mr. Brown, the elder of the congregation there, about an opinion, which they had published, that the churches of Rome were true churches. The matter was debated before many of both congregations, and, by the approbation of all the assembly, except three, was concluded an error.

22.] The White Angel came into the bay. She landed here twenty-one heifers.

26.] A small bark of Salem, of about twelve tons, coming towards the bay, John Elston and two of Mr. Cradock's fishermen being in her, and two tons of stone, and three hogsheads of train oil, was overset in a gust, and, being buoyed up by the oil, she floated up and down forty-eight hours, and the three men sitting upon her, till Henry Way his boat, coming by, espied them and saved them.

29.] The Friendship set sail for the Christopher Islands, and ran on ground behind Conant's Island.

30.] The White Angel fell down for Plimouth, but, the wind not serving, she came to an anchor by Long Island, and ran on ground a week after, near Gurnett's Nose.

Mr. Ludlow, in digging the foundation of his house at Dorchester, found two pieces of French money: one was coined in 1596. They were in several places, and above a foot within the firm ground.

August 8.]   The Tarentines, to the number of one hundred, came in three canoes, and in the night assaulted the wigwam of the sagamore of Agawam, by Merimack, and slew seven men, and wounded John Sagamore, and James, and some others, (whereof some died after,) and rifled a wigwam where Mr. Cradock's men kept to catch sturgeon, took away their nets and biscuit, etc.

[*Large blank.*]

19.]   The Plough returned to Charlestown, after she had been on her way to the Christopher Islands about three weeks, and was so broke she could not return home.

31.]   The governour's bark, called the Blessing of the Bay, being of thirty tons, went to sea.

September 6.]   The White Angel set sail from Marble Harbour.

About this time last year the company here set forth a pinnace to the parts about Cape Cod, to trade for corn, and it brought here above eighty bushels. This year again the Salem pinnace, being bound thither for corn, was, by contrary winds, put into Plimouth, where the governour, etc., fell out with them, not only forbidding them to trade, but also telling them they would oppose them by force, even to the spending of their lives, etc.; whereupon they returned, and acquainting the governour of Massachusetts with it, he wrote to the governour of Plimouth this letter, here inserted, with their answer, which came about a month after.

The wolves did much hurt to calves and swine between Charles River and Mistick.

At the last court, a young fellow was whipped for soliciting an Indian squaw to incontinency. Her husband and she complained of the wrong, and were present at the execution, and very well satisfied.

At the same court, one Henry Linne was whipped and banished, for writing letters into England full of slander against our government and orders of our churches.

17.]   Mr. Shurd of Pemaquid, sent home James Sagamore's wife, who had been taken away at the surprise at Agawam, and writ that the Indians demanded [*blank*] fathom of wampampeague and [*blank*] skins for her ransom.

27.]   At a court, one Josias Plaistowe and two of his servants were censured for stealing corn from Chickatabot and his men, (who were present,) the master to restore two fold, and to be degraded from the title of a gentleman, and fined five pounds, and his men to be whipped.

[*Blank.*]

October 4.]   The Blessing went on a voyage to the eastward.

11.]   The governour, being at his farm house at Mistick, walked out after supper, and took a piece in his hand, supposing he might see a wolf, (for they came daily about the house, and killed swine and calves, etc.;) and, being about half a mile off, it grew suddenly dark, so as, in coming home, he mistook his path, and went till he came to a little house of Sagamore John, which stood empty. There he stayed, and having a piece of match in his pocket, (for he always carried about him match and a compass, and in summer time snake-weed,) he made a good fire near the house, and lay down upon some old mats, which he found there, and so spent the night, sometimes walking by the fire, sometimes singing psalms, and sometimes getting wood, but could not sleep. It was (through God's mercy) a warm night; but a little before day it began to rain, and, having no cloak, he made shift by a long pole to climb up into the house. In the morning, there came thither an Indian squaw, but perceiving her before she had opened the door, he barred her out; yet she stayed there a great while essaying to get in, and at last she went away, and he returned safe home, his servants having been much perplexed for him, and having walked about, and shot off pieces, and hallooed in the night, but he heard them not.

22.]   The governour received a letter from Capt. Wiggin of Pascataquack, informing him of a murder committed the third of this month at Richman's Isle, by an Indian sagamore, called Squidrayset, and his company, upon one Walter Bagnall, called Great Watt, and one John P——, who kept with him. They, having killed them, burnt the house over them, and carried away their guns and what else they liked. He persuaded the governour to send twenty men presently to take revenge; but the governour, advising with some of the council, thought best to sit still awhile, partly because he heard that Capt. Neal, etc., were gone after them, and partly because of the season, (it being then frost and snow,) and want of boats fit for that expedition. This Bagnall was sometimes servant to one in the bay, and these three years had dwelt alone in the said isle, and had gotten about £400 most in goods. He was a wicked fellow, and had much wronged the Indians.

25.] The governour, with Capt. Underhill and others of the officers, went on foot to Sagus, and next day to Salem, where they were bountifully entertained by Capt. Endecott, etc., and, the 28th, they returned to Boston by the ford at Sagus River, and so over at Mistick.

A plentiful crop.

30.] The governour, having erected a building of stone at Mistick, there came so violent a storm of rain, for twenty-four hours, from the N. E. and S. E. as (it being not finished, and laid with clay for want of lime) two sides of it were washed down to the ground; and much harm was done to other houses by that storm.

Mr. Pynchon's boat, coming from Sagadahock, was cast away at Cape Ann, but the men and chief goods saved, and the boat recovered.

November 2.] The ship Lyon, William Peirce master, arrived at Natascot. There came in her the governour's wife, his eldest son, and his wife, and others of his children, and Mr. Eliot, a minister, and other families, being in all about sixty persons, who all arrived in good health, having been ten weeks at sea, and lost none of their company but two children, whereof one was the governour's daughter Ann, about one year and a half old, who died about a week after they came to sea.

3.] The wind being contrary, the ship stayed at Long Island, but the governour's son came on shore, and that night the governour went to the ship, and lay aboard all night; and the next morning, the wind coming fair, she came to an anchor before Boston.

4.] The governour, his wife and children, went on shore, with Mr. Peirce, in his ship's boat. The ship gave them six or seven pieces. At their landing, the captains, with their companies in arms, entertained them with a guard, and divers vollies of shot, and three drakes; and divers of the assistants and most of the people, of the near plantations, came to welcome them, and brought and sent, for divers days, great store of provisions, as fat hogs, kids, venison, poultry, geese, partridges, etc., so as the like joy and manifestation of love had never been seen in New England. It was a great marvel, that so much people and such store of provisions could be gathered together at so few hours' warning.

11.]   We kept a day of thanksgiving at Boston.

17.]   The governour of Plimouth came to Boston, and lodged in the ship.

23.]   Mr. Peirce went down to his ship, which lay at Nantascot. Divers went home with him into England by Virginia, as Sir Richard Saltonstall his eldest son and others; and they were six weeks in going to Virginia.

The congregation at Watertown (whereof Mr. George Phillips was pastor) had chosen one Richard Brown for their elder, before named, who, persisting in his opinion of the truth of the Romish church, and maintaining other errors withal, and being a man of a very violent spirit, the court wrote a letter to the congregation, directed to the pastor and brethren, to advise them to take into consideration, whether Mr. Brown were fit to be continued their elder or not; to which, after some weeks, they returned answer to this effect: That if we would take the pains to prove such things as were objected against him, they would endeavour to redress them.

December 8.]   The said congregation being much divided about their elder, both parties repaired to the governour for assistance, etc.; whereupon he went to Watertown, with the deputy governour and Mr. Nowell, and the congregation being assembled, the governour told them, that being come to settle peace, etc., they might proceed in three distinct respects: 1. As the magistrates, (their assistance being desired). 2. As members of a neighbouring congregation. 3. Upon the answer which we received of our letter, which did no way satisfy us. But the pastor, Mr. Phillips, desired us to sit with them as members of a neighbouring congregation only, whereto the governour, etc., consented.

Then the one side, which had first complained, were moved to open their grievances; which they did to this effect: That they could not communicate with their elder, being guilty of errors, both in judgment and conversation. After much debate of these things, at length they were reconciled, and agreed to seek God in a day of humiliation, and so to have a solemn uniting; each party promising to reform what hath been amiss, etc.; and the pastor gave thanks to God, and the assembly brake up.

January 27.] The governour, and some company with him, went up by Charles River about eight miles above Watertown, and named the first brook, on the north side of the river, (being a fair stream, and coming from a pond a mile from the river,) Beaver Brook, because the beavers had shorn down divers great trees there, and made divers dams across the brook. Thence they went to a great rock, upon which stood a high stone, cleft in sunder, that four men might go through, which they called Adam's Chair, because the youngest of their company was Adam Winthrop. Thence they came to another brook, greater than the former, which they called Masters' Brook, because the eldest of their company was one John Masters. Thence they came to another pointed rock, having a fair ascent on the west side, which they called Mount Feake, from one Robert Feake, who had married the governour's daughter-in-law. On the west side of Mount Feake, they went up a very high rock, from whence they might see all over Neipnett, and a very high hill due west, about forty miles off, and to the N. W. the high hills by Merrimack, above sixty miles off.

February 7.] The governour, Mr. Nowell, Mr. Eliot, and others, went over Mistick River at Medford, and going N. and by E. among the rocks about two or three miles, they came to a very great pond, having in the midst an island of about one acre, and very thick with trees of pine and beech; and the pond had divers small rocks, standing up here and there in it, which they therefore called Spot Pond. They went all about it upon the ice. From thence (towards the N. W. about half a mile,) they came to the top of a very high rock, beneath which, (towards the N.) lies a goodly plain, part open land, and part woody, from whence there is a fair prospect, but it being then close and rainy, they could see but a small distance. This place they called Cheese Rock, because, when they went to eat somewhat, they had only cheese, (the governour's man forgetting, for haste, to put up some bread).

14.] The governour and some other company went to view the country as far as Neponsett, and returned that night.

[*Large blank.*]

17.]   The governour and assistants called before them, at Boston, divers of Watertown; the pastor and elder by letter, and the others by warrant. The occasion was, for that a warrant being sent to Watertown for levying of £8, part of a rate of £60, ordered for the fortifying of the new town, the pastor and elder, etc., assembled the people and delivered their opinions, that it was not safe to pay moneys after that sort, for fear of bringing themselves and posterity into bondage. Being come before the governour and council, after much debate, they acknowledged their fault, confessing freely, that they were in an error, and made a retractation and submission under their hands, and were enjoined to read it in the assembly the next Lord's day. The ground of their error was, for that they took this government to be no other but as of a mayor and aldermen, who have not power to make laws or raise taxations without the people; but understanding that this government was rather in the nature of a parliament, and that no assistant could be chosen but by the freemen, who had power likewise to remove the assistants and put in others, and therefore at every general court (which was to be held once every year) they had free liberty to consider and propound anything concerning the same, and to declare their grievances, without being subject to question, or, etc., they were fully satisfied; and so their submission was accepted, and their offence pardoned.

March 5.]   The first court after winter. It was ordered, that the courts (which before were every three weeks) should now be held the first Tuesday in every month.

Commissioners appointed to set out the bounds of the towns.

14.]   The bark Warwick arrived at Natascott, having been at Pascataquack and at Salem to sell corn, which she brought from Virginia. At her coming into Natascott, with a S. E. wind, she was in great danger, by a sudden gust, to be cast away upon the rocks.

19.]   She came to Winysemett.

Mr. Maverick, one of the ministers of Dorchester, in drying a little powder, (which took fire by the heat of the fire pan,) fired a small barrel of two or three pounds, yet did no other harm but singed his clothes. It was in the new meeting-house, which was thatched, and the thatch only blacked a little.

April 3.]   At a court at Boston, the deputy, Mr. Dudley, went away before the court was ended, and then the secretary delivered the governour a letter from him, directed to the governour and assistants, wherein he declared a resignation of his deputyship and place of assistant; but it was not allowed.

At this court an act was made expressing the governour's power, etc., and the office of the secretary and treasurer, etc.

9.]   The bark Warwick, and Mr. Maverick's pinnace, went out towards Virginia.

12.]   The governour received letters from Plimouth, signifying, that there had been a broil between their men at Sowamset and the Naraganset Indians, who set upon the English house there to have taken Owsamequin, the sagamore of Packanocott, who was fled thither with all his people for refuge; and that Capt. Standish, being gone thither to relieve the three English, which were in the house, had sent home in all haste for more men and other provisions, upon intelligence that Canonicus, with a great army, was coming against them. Withal they writ to our governour for some powder to be sent with all possible speed, (for it seemed they were unfurnished). Upon this the governour presently despatched away the messenger with so much powder as he could carry, viz., twenty-seven pounds.

16.]   The messenger returned, and brought a letter from the governour, signifying, that the Indians were retired from Sowams to fight with the Pequins, which was probable, because John Sagamore and Chickatabott were gone with all their men, viz., John Sagamore with thirty, and Chickatabott with [*blank*] to Canonicus, who had sent for them.

A wear was erected by Watertown men upon Charles River, three miles above the town, where they took great store of shads.

A Dutch ship brought from Virginia two thousand bushels of corn, which was sold at four shillings sixpence the bushel.

May 1.]   The governour and assistants met at Boston to consider of the deputy his deserting his place. The points discussed were two. The 1st, upon what grounds he did it: 2d, whether it were good or void. For the 1st, his main reason was for public peace; because he must needs discharge his conscience in speaking freely; and he saw that bred disturbance, etc. For the 2d, it was maintained by all, that he could not leave his place, except by the same power which put him in; yet he would not be put from his contrary opinion, nor would be persuaded to continue till the general court, which was to be the 9th of this month.

Another question fell out with him, about some bargains he had made with some poor men, members of the same congregation, to whom he had sold seven bushels and an half of corn to receive ten for it after harvest, which the governour and some others held to be oppressing usury, and within compass of the statute; but he persisted to maintain it to be lawful, and there arose hot words about it, he telling the governour, that, if he had thought he had sent for him to his house to give him such usage, he would not have come there; and that he never knew any man of understanding of other opinion; and that the governour thought otherwise of it, it was his weakness. The governour took notice of these speeches, and bare them with more patience than he had done, upon a like occasion, at another time. Upon this there arose another question, about his house. The governour having formerly told him, that he did not well to bestow such cost about wainscotting and adorning his house, in the beginning of a plantation, both in regard of the necessity of public charges, and for example, etc., his answer now was, that it was for the warmth of his house, and the charge was little, being but clapboards nailed to the wall in the form of wainscot. These and other speeches passed before dinner. After dinner, the governour told them, that he had heard, that the people intended, at the next general court, to desire, that the assistants might be chosen anew every year, and that the governour might be chosen by the whole court, and not by the assistants only. Upon this, Mr. Ludlow grew into passion, and said, that then we should have no government, but there would be an interim, wherein every man might do what he pleased, etc. This was answered and cleared in the judgment of the rest of the assistants, but he continued stiff in his opinion, and protested he would then return back into England.

Another business fell out, which was this. Mr. Clark of Watertown had complained to the governour, that Capt. Patrick, being removed out of their town to Newtown, did compel them to watch near Newtown, and desired the governour, that they might have the ordering within their own town. The governour answered him, that the ordering of the watch did properly belong to the constable; but in those towns where the captains dwelt, they had thought fit to leave it to them, and since Capt. Patrick was removed, the constable might take care of it; but advised him withal to acquaint the deputy with it, and at the court it should be ordered. Clark went right home and told the captain, that the governour had ordered, that the constable should set the watch, (which was false;) but the captain answered somewhat rashly, and like a soldier, which being certified to the governour by three witnesses, he sent a warrant to the constable to this effect, that whereas some difficulty was fallen out, etc., about the watch, etc., he should, according to his office, see due watch should be kept till the court had taken order in it. This much displeased the captain, who came to this meeting to have it redressed. The governour told the rest what he had done, and upon what ground; whereupon they refused to do anything in it till the court.

While they were thus sitting together, an Indian brings a letter from Capt. Standish, then at Sowams, to this effect, that the Dutchmen (which lay for trading at Anygansett or Naragansett) had lately informed him, that many Pequins (who were professed enemies to the Anagansetts) had been there divers days, and advised us to be watchful, etc., giving other reasons, etc.

Thus the day was spent and no good done, which was the more uncomfortable to most of them, because they had commended this meeting to God in more earnest manner than ordinary at other meetings.

May 8.]   A general court at Boston. Whereas it was (at our first coming) agreed, that the freemen should choose the assistants, and they the governour, the whole court agreed now, that the governour and assistants should all be new chosen every year by the general court, (the governour to be always chosen out of the assistants;) and accordingly the old governour, John Winthrop, was chosen; accordingly all the rest as before, and Mr. Humfrey and Mr. Coddington also, because they were daily expected.

The deputy governour, Thomas Dudley, Esq., having submitted the validity of his resignation to the vote of the court, it was adjudged a nullity, and he accepted of his place again, and the governour and he being reconciled the day before, all things were carried very lovingly amongst all, etc., and the people carried themselves with much silence and modesty.

John Winthrop, the governour's son, was chosen an assistant.

A proposition was made by the people, that every company of trained men might choose their own captain and officers; but the governour giving them reasons to the contrary, they were satisfied without it.

Every town chose two men to be at the next court, to advise with the governour and assistants about the raising of a public stock, so as what they should agree upon should bind all, etc.

This court was begun and ended with speeches for the, etc., as formerly.*

The governour, among other things, used this speech to the people, after he had taken his oath: That he received gratuities from divers towns, which he received with much comfort and content; he had also received many kindnesses from particular persons, which he would not refuse, lest he should be accounted uncourteous, etc.; but he professed, that he received them with a trembling heart, in regard of God's rule, and the consciousness of his own infirmity; and therefore desired them, that hereafter they would not take it ill, if he did refuse presents from particular persons, except they were from the assistants, or from some special friends; to which no answer was made; but he was told after, that many good people were much grieved at it, for that he never had any allowance towards the charge of his place.

24.]   The fortification upon the Corn Hill at Boston was begun.

25.]   Charlestown men came and wrought upon the fortification.

Roxbury the next, and Dorchester the next.

26.]   The Whale arrived with Mr. Wilson, Mr. Dummer, and about thirty passengers, all in health; and of seventy cows lost but two. She came from Hampton, April 8th. Mr. Graves was master.

June 5.]   The William and Francis, Mr. Thomas master, with about sixty passengers, whereof Mr. Welde and old Mr. Batchelor (being aged 71) were, with their families, and many other honest men; also, the Charles of Barnstable, with near eighty cows and six mares, Mr. Hatherly, the merchant, and about twenty passengers, all safe, and in health. They set sail, viz., the William and Francis from London, March the 9th, and the Charles from Barnstable, April 10th, and met near Cape Ann. Mr. Winslow of Plimouth came in the William and Francis.

* [This sentence has a line drawn through it in the manuscript.]

12.]   The James, Mr. Grant master, arrived. Her passage was eight weeks from London. She brought sixty-one heifers and lost forty, and brought twelve passengers.

13.]   A day of thanksgiving in all the plantations, by public authority, for the good success of the king of Sweden, and Protestants in Germany, against the emperour, etc., and for the safe arrival of all the ships, they having not lost one person, nor one sick among them.

14.]   The governour was invited to dinner aboard the Whale. The master fetched him in his boat, and gave him three pieces at his going off.

The French came in a pinnace to Penobscot, and rifled a trucking house belonging to Plimouth, carrying thence three hundred weight of beaver and other goods. They took also one Dixy Bull and his shallop and goods.*

One Abraham Shurd of Pemaquid, and one Capt. Wright, and others, coming to Pascataquack, being bound for this bay in a shallop with £200 worth of commodities, one of the seamen, going to light a pipe of tobacco, set fire on a barrel of powder, which tare the boat in pieces. That man was never seen: the rest were all saved, but the goods lost.

The man, that was blown away with the powder in the boat at Pascataquack, was after found with his hands and feet torn off. This fellow, being wished by another to forbear to take any tobacco, till they came to the shore, which was hard by, answered, that if the devil should carry him away quick, he would take one pipe. Some in the boat were so drunk and fast asleep, as they did not awake with the noise.

A shallop of one Henry Way of Dorchester, having been missing all the winter, it was found that the men in her, being five, were all killed treacherously by the eastern Indians.

Another shallop of his being sent out to seek out the other, was cast away at Aquamenticus, and two of the men drowned. A fishing shallop at Isle of Shoals was overset. One Noddle, an honest man of Salem, carrying wood in a canoe, in the South River, was overturned and drowned.

July.]   At a training at Watertown, a man of John Oldham's, having a musket, which had been long charged with pistol bullets,

* [This sentence has a line drawn through it in the manuscript.]

not knowing of it, gave fire, and shot three men, two into their bodies, and one into his hands; but it was so far off, as the shot entered the skin and stayed there, and they all recovered.

The congregation at Boston wrote to the elders and brethren of the churches of Plimouth, Salem, etc., for their advice in three questions: 1. Whether one person might be a civil magistrate and a ruling elder at the same time? 2. If not, then which should be laid down? 3. Whether there might be divers pastors in the same church?—The 1st was agreed by all negatively; the 2d doubtfully; the 3d doubtful also.

[*Large blank.*]

The strife in Watertown congregation continued still; but at length they gave the separatists a day to come in, or else to be proceeded against.

5.]   At the day, all came in and submitted, except John Masters, who, though he were advised by divers ministers and others, that he had offended in turning his back upon the sacrament, and departing out of the assembly, etc., because they had then admitted a member whom he judged unfit, etc.; yet he persisted. So the congregation (being loath to proceed against him) gave him a further day; 8, at which time, he continuing obstinate, they excommunicated him; but, about a fortnight after, he submitted himself, and was received in again.

[*Blank.*]

At Watertown there was (in the view of divers witnesses) a great combat between a mouse and a snake; and, after a long fight, the mouse prevailed and killed the snake. The pastor of Boston, Mr. Wilson, a very sincere, holy man, hearing of it, gave this intepretation: That the snake was the devil; the mouse was a poor contemptible people, which God had brought hither, which should overcome Satan here, and dispossess him of his kingdom. Upon the same occasion, he told the governour, that, before he was resolved to come into this country, he dreamed he was here, and that he saw a church arise out of the earth, which grew up and became a marvellous goodly church.

After many imparlances and days of humiliation, by those of

Boston and Roxbury, to seek the Lord for Mr. Welde his disposing, and the advice of those of Plimouth being taken, etc., at
length he resolved to sit down with them of Roxbury.

[*Large blank.*]

August 3.]   The deputy, Mr. Thomas Dudley, being still discontented with the governour, partly for that the governour had
removed the frame of his house, which he had set up at Newtown,
and partly for that he took too much authority upon him, (as he
conceived,) renewed his complaints to Mr. Wilson and Mr. Welde,
who acquainting the governour therewith, a meeting was agreed
upon at Charlestown, where were present the governour and
deputy, Mr. Nowell, Mr. Wilson, Mr. Welde, Mr. Maverick, and
Mr. Warham.   The conference being begun with calling upon
the Lord, the deputy began,—that howsoever he had some particular grievances, etc.; yet, seeing he was advised by those present,
and divers of the assistants, to be silent in them, he would let
them pass, and so come first to complain of the breach of promise,
both in the governour and others, in not building at Newtown.
The governour answered, that he had performed the words of the
promise; for he had a house up, and seven or eight servants abiding
in it, by the day appointed: and for the removing of his house, he
alleged, that, seeing that the rest of the assistants went not about
to build, and that his neighbours of Boston had been discouraged
from removing thither by Mr. Deputy himself, and thereupon had
(under all their hands) petitioned him, that (according to the promise he made to them when they first sate down with him at Boston,
viz., that he would not remove, except they went with him) he
would not leave them;—this was the occasion that he removed his
house.   Upon these and other speeches to this purpose, the ministers went apart for one hour; then returning, they delivered their
opinions, that the governour was in fault for removing of his
house so suddenly, without conferring with the deputy and the
rest of the assistants; but if the deputy were the occasion of discouraging Boston men from removing, it would excuse the governour *a
tanto*, but not *a toto*.   The governour, professing himself willing
to submit his own opinion to the judgment of so many wise and
godly friends, acknowledged himself faulty.

After dinner, the deputy proceeded in his complaint, yet with this protestation, that what he should charge the governour with, was in love, and out of his care of the public, and that the things which he should produce were but for his own satisfaction, and not by way of accusation. Then demanded he of him the ground and limits of his authority, whether by the patent or otherwise. The governour answered, that he was willing to stand to that which he propounded, and would challenge no greater authority than he might by the patent. The deputy replied, that then he had no more authority than every assistant, (except power to call courts, and precedency, for honor and order). The governour answered, he had more; for the patent, making him a governour, gave him whatsoever power belonged to a governour by common law or the statutes, and desired him to show wherein he had exceeded, etc.; and speaking this somewhat apprehensively, the deputy began to be in passion, and told the governour, that if he were so round, he would be round too. The governour bad him be round, if he would. So the deputy rose up in great fury and passion, and the governour grew very hot also, so as they both fell into bitterness; but, by mediation of the mediators, they were soon pacified. Then the deputy proceeded to particulars, as followeth:

1st. By what authority the governour removed the ordnance and erected a fort at Boston.—The governour answered, that the ordnance lying upon the beach in danger of spoiling, and having often complained of it in the court, and nothing done, with the help of divers of the assistants, they were mounted upon their carriages, and removed where they might be of some use: and for the fort, it had been agreed, above a year before, that it should be erected there: and all this was done without any penny charge to the public.

2d. By what authority he lent twenty-eight pounds of powder to those of Plimouth.—Governour answered, it was of his own powder, and upon their urgent distress, their own powder proving naught, when they were to send to the rescue of their men at Sowamsett.

3d. By what authority he had licensed Edward Johnson to sit down at Merrimack.—Governour answered, that he had licensed him only to go forth on trading, (as he had done divers others,) as belonging to his place.

4th. By what authority he had given them of Watertown leave

to erect a wear upon Charles River, and had disposed of lands to
divers, etc.—Governour answered, the people of Watertown, falling very short of corn the last year, for want of fish, did complain,
etc., and desired leave to erect a wear; and upon this the governour
told them, that he could not give them leave, but they must seek it
of the court; but because it would be long before the courts began
again, and, if they deferred till then, the season would be lost, he
wished them to do it, and there was no doubt but, being for so
general a good, the court would allow of it; and, for his part, he
would employ all his power in the court, so as he should sink
under it, if it were not allowed; and besides, those of Roxbury
had erected a wear without any license from the court. And for
lands, he had disposed of none, otherwise than the deputy and
other of the assistants had done,—he had only given his consent,
but referred them to the court, etc. But the deputy had taken more
upon him, in that, without order of court, he had empaled, at
Newtown, above one thousand acres, and had assigned lands to
some there.

5th. By what authority he had given license to Ratcliff and
Grey (being banished men) to stay within our limits.—Governour
answered, he did it by that authority, which was granted him in
court, viz., that, upon any sentence in criminal causes, the governor
might, upon cause, stay the execution till the next court. Now
the cause was, that, being in the winter, they must otherwise have
perished.

6th. Why the fines were not levied.—Governour answered, it
belonged to the secretary and not to him: he never refused to sign
any that were brought to him; nay, he had called upon the secretary
for it; yet he confessed, that it was his judgment, that it were not
fit, in the infancy of a commonwealth, to be too strict in levying
fines, though severe in other punishments.

7th. That when a cause had been voted by the rest of the court,
the governour would bring new reasons, and move them to alter the
sentence:—which the governour justified, and all approved.

The deputy having made an end, the governour desired the
mediators to consider, whether he had exceeded his authority or
not, and how little cause the deputy had to charge him with it; for
if he had made some slips, in two or three years' government, he
ought rather to have covered them, seeing he could not be charged

that he had taken advantage of his authority to oppress or wrong
any man, or to benefit himself; but, for want of a public stock, had
disbursed all common charges out of his own estate; whereas the
deputy would never lay out one penny, etc.; and, besides, he could
shew that under his hand, that would convince him of a greater
exceeding his authority, than all that the deputy could charge him
with, viz., that whereas Binks and Johnson were bound in open
court to appear at next court to account to, etc., he had, out of
court, discharged them of their appearance. The deputy answered,
that the party, to whom they were to account, came to him and confessed that he was satisfied, and that the parties were to go to Virginia; so he thought he might discharge them.

Though the governour might justly have refused to answer these
seven articles, wherewith the deputy had charged him, both for
that he had no knowledge of them before, (the meeting being only
for the deputy his personal grievances,) and also for that the governour was not to give account of his actions to any but to the
court; yet, out of his desire of the public peace, and to clear his
reputation with those to whom the deputy had accused him, he was
willing to give him satisfaction, to the end, that he might free him
of such jealousy as he had conceived, that the governour intended
to make himself popular, that he might gain absolute power, and
bring all the assistants under his subjection; which was very im-
probable, seeing the governour had propounded in court to have
an order established for limiting the governour's authority, and had
himself drawn articles for that end, which had been approved and
established by the whole court; neither could he justly be charged
to have transgressed any of them. So the meeting breaking up,
without any other conclusion but the commending the success of it
by prayer to the Lord, the governour brought the deputy onward
of his way, and every man went to his own home. See two pages
after.

5.] The sachem, who was joined with Canonicus, the great
sachem of Naragansett, called Mecumeh, after Miantonomoh, being at Boston, where [he] had lodged two nights with his squaw,
and about twelve sanapps, being present at the sermon, three of
his sanapps went, in the meantime, and brake into a neighbour's
house, etc. Complaint being made thereof to the governour, after

evening exercise, he told the sachem of it, and with some difficulty caused him to make one of his sanapps to beat them, and then sent them out of the town; but brought the sachem and the rest of [the] company to his house, and made much of them, (as he had done before,) which he seemed to be well pleased with; but that evening he departed.

At a court not long before, two of Chickatabott's men were convented and convicted for assaulting some English of Dorchester in their houses, etc. They were put in the bilboes, and Chickatabot required to beat them, which he did.

[*Large blank.*]

The congregation of Boston and Charlestown began the meeting-house at Boston, for which, and Mr. Wilson's house, they had made a voluntary contribution of about one hundred and twenty pounds.

[*Blank.*]

14.] Fair weather and small wind, and N. E. at Boston, and, at the same time, such a tempest of wind N. E. a little without the bay, as no boat could bear sail, and one had her mast borne by the board. So again, when there hath [been] a very tempest at N. W. or W. in the bay, there hath been a stark calm one league or two off shore.

This summer was very wet and cold, (except now and then a hot day or two,) which caused great store of musketoes and rattle-snakes. The corn, in the dry, sandy grounds, was much better than other years, but in the fatter grounds much worse, and in Boston, etc., much shorn down close by the ground with worms.

The windmill was brought down to Boston, because, where it stood near Newtown, it would not grind but with a westerly wind.

Mr. Oldham had a small house near the wear at Watertown, made all of clapboards, burnt down by making a fire in it when it had no chimney.

This week they had in barley and oats, at Sagus, above twenty acres good corn, and sown with the plough.

Great store of eels and lobsters in the bay. Two or three boys have brought in a bushel of great eels at a time, and sixty great lobsters.

The Braintree company, (which had begun to sit down at Mount Wollaston,) by order of court, removed to Newtown. These were Mr. Hooker's company.

The governour's wife was delivered of a son, who was baptized by the name of William. The governour himself held the child to baptism, as others in the congregation did use. William signifies a common man, etc.

30.] Notice being given of ten sagamores and many Indians assembled at Muddy River, the governour sent Capt. Underhill, with twenty musketeers, to discover, etc.; but at Roxbury they heard they were broke up.

September 4.] One Hopkins, of Watertown, was convict for selling a piece and pistol, with powder and shot, to James Saga-more, for which he had sentence to be whipped and branded in the cheek. It was discovered by an Indian, one of James's men, upon promise of concealing him, (for otherwise he was sure to be killed).

[Large blank.]

The ministers afterward, for an end of the difference between the governour and deputy, ordered, that the governour should procure them a minister at Newtown, and contribute somewhat towards his maintenance for a time; or, if he could not, by the spring, effect that, then to give the deputy, toward his charges in building there, twenty pounds. The governour accepted this order, and promised to perform it in one of the kinds. But the deputy, having received one part of the order, returned the same to the governour, with this reason to Mr. Wilson, that he was so well persuaded of the governour's love to him, and did prize it so much, as if they had given him one hundred pounds instead of twenty pounds, he would not have taken it.

Notwithstanding the heat of contention, which had been be-tween the governour and deputy, yet they usually met about their affairs, and that without any appearance of any breach or discontent; and ever after kept peace and good correspondency together, in love and friendship.

One Jenkins, late an inhabitant of Dorchester, and now removed to Cape Porpus, went with an Indian up into [the] country with store of goods to truck, and, being asleep in a wigwam of one of Passaconamy's men, was killed in the night by an Indian, dwelling near the Mohawks' country, who fled away with his goods, but was fetched back by Passaconamy. There was much suspicion, that the Indians had some plot against the English, both for that many Naragansett men, etc., gathered together, who, with those of these parts, pretended to make war upon the Neipnett men, and divers insolent speeches were used by some of them, and they did not frequent our houses as they were wont, and one of their pawawes told us, that there was a conspiracy to cut us off to get our victuals and other substance. Upon this there was a camp pitched at Boston in the night, to exercise the soldiers against need might be; and Capt. Underhill (to try how they would behave themselves) caused an alarm to be given upon the quarters, which discovered the weakness of our people, who, like men amazed, knew not how to behave themselves, so as the officers could not draw them into any order. All the rest of the plantations took the alarm and answered it; but it caused much fear and distraction among the common sort, so as some, which knew of it before, yet through fear had forgotten, and believed the Indians had been upon us. We doubled our guards, and kept watch each day and night.

14.] The rumour still increasing, the three next sagamores were sent for, who came presently to the governour.

16, being the Lord's day.] In the evening Mr. Peirce, in the ship Lyon, arrived, and came to an anchor before Boston. He brought one hundred and twenty-three passengers, whereof fifty children, all in health; and lost not one person by the way, save his carpenter, who fell overboard as he was caulking a port. They had been twelve weeks aboard, and eight weeks from the Land's End. He had five days east wind and thick fog, so as he was forced to come, all that time, by the lead; and the first land he made was Cape Ann.

22.] The Barnstable ship went out at Pullen Point to Marble Harbour.

27.]   A day of thanksgiving at Boston for the good news of the prosperous success of the king of Sweden, etc., and for the safe arrival of the last ship and all the passengers, etc.

October 18.]   Capt. Camock, and one Mr. Godfry, a merchant, came from Pascataquack in Captain Neal his pinnace, and brought sixteen hogsheads of corn to the mill. They went away November [*blank*].

25.]   The governour, with Mr. Wilson, pastor of Boston, and the two captains, etc., went aboard the Lyon, and from thence Mr. Peirce carried them in his shallop to Wessaguscus. The next morning Mr. Peirce returned to his ship, and the governour and his company went on foot to Plimouth, and came thither within the evening. The governour of Plimouth, Mr. William Bradford, (a very discreet and grave man,) with Mr. Brewster, the elder, and some others, came forth and met them without the town, and conducted them to the governour's house, where they were very kindly entertained, and feasted every day at several houses. On the Lord's day there was a sacrament, which they did partake in; and, in the afternoon, Mr. Roger Williams (according to their custom) propounded a question, to which the pastor, Mr. Smith, spake briefly; then Mr. Williams prophesied; and after the governour of Plimouth spake to the question; after him the elder; then some two or three more of the congregation. Then the elder desired the governour of Massachusetts and Mr. Wilson to speak to it, which they did. When this was ended, the deacon, Mr. Fuller, put the congregation in mind of their duty of contribution; whereupon the governour and all the rest went down to the deacon's seat, and put into the box, and then returned.

27.]   The wind N. W., Mr. Peirce set sail for Virginia.

31, being Wednesday.]   About five in the morning the governour and his company came out of Plimouth; the governour of Plimouth, with the pastor and elder, etc., accompanying them near half a mile out of town in the dark. The Lieut. Holmes, with two others, and the governour's mare, came along with them to the great swamp, about ten miles. When they came to the great river, they were carried over by one Luddam, their guide, (as they had been when they came, the stream being very strong, and up to the crotch;) so the governour called that passage Luddam's Ford. Thence they came to a place called Hue's Cross. The governour, being displeased at the name, in respect that such things might hereafter give the Papists occasion to say, that their religion was first planted in these parts, changed the name, and called it Hue's Folly. So they came, that evening, to Wessaguscus, where they were bountifully entertained, as before, with store of turkeys, geese, ducks, etc., and the next day came safe to Boston.

About this time Mr. Dudley, his house, at Newtown, was preserved from burning down, and all his family from being destroyed by gunpowder, by a marvellous deliverance;—the hearth of the hall chimney burning all night upon a principal beam, and store of powder being near, and not discovered till they arose in the morning, and then it began to flame out.

Mr. John Eliot, a member of Boston congregation, and one whom the congregation intended presently to call to the office of teacher, was called to be a teacher to the church at Roxbury; and though Boston laboured all they could, both with the congregation of Roxbury and with Mr. Eliot himself, alleging their want of him, and the covenant between them, etc., yet he could not be diverted from accepting the call of Roxbury, November 5. So he was dismissed.

About a fortnight before this, those of Charlestown, who had formerly been joined to Boston congregation, now, in regard of the difficulty of passage in the winter, and having opportunity of a pastor, one Mr. James, who came over at this time, were dismissed from the congregation of Boston.

The congregation of Watertown discharged their elder, Richard Brown, of his office, for his unfitness in regard of his passion and distemper in speech, having been oft admonished and declared his repentance for it.

21.] The governour received a letter from Capt. Neal, that Dixy Bull and fifteen more of the English, who kept about the east, were turned pirates, and had taken divers boats, and rifled Pemaquid, etc.,—23. Hereupon the governour called a council, and it was agreed to send his bark with twenty men, to join with those of Pascataquack, for the taking of the said pirates.

22.] A fast was held by the congregation of Boston, and Mr. Wilson (formerly their teacher) was chosen pastor, and [*blank*] Oliver a ruling elder, and both were ordained by imposition of hands, first by the teacher, and the two deacons, (in the name of the congregation,) upon the elder, and then by the elder and the deacons upon the pastor.

December 4.]   At a meeting of all the assistants, it was agreed, in regard that the extremity of the snow and frost had hindered the making ready of the bark, and that they had certain intelligence, that those of Pascataquack had sent out two pinnaces and two shallops, above a fortnight before, to defer any further expedition against the pirates till they heard what was done by those; and for that end it was agreed, to send presently a shallop to Pascataquack to learn more, etc.

5.]   Accordingly, the governour despatched away John Gallopp with his shallop. The wind being very great at S. W., he could reach no farther than Cape Ann harbour that night; and the winds blowing northerly, he was kept there so long, that it was January the 2d before he returned.

By letters from Capt. Neal and Mr. Hilton, etc., it was certified, that they had sent out all the forces they could make against the pirates, viz., four pinnaces and shallops, and about forty men, who, coming to Pemaquid, were there windbound about three weeks.

It was further advertised, by some who came from Penobscott, that the pirates had lost one of their chief men by a musket shot from Pemaquid; and that there remained but fifteen, whereof four or five were detained against their wills; and that they had been at some English plantations, and taken nothing from them but what they paid for; and that they had given another pinnace in exchange for that of Mr. Maverick, and as much beaver and otter as it was worth more, etc.; and that they had made a law against excessive drinking; and that their order was, at such times as other ships use to have prayer, they would assemble upon the deck, and one sing a song, or speak a few senseless sentences, etc. They also sent a writing, directed to all the governours, signifying their intent not to do harm to any more of their countrymen, but to go to the southward, and to advise them not to send against them; for they were resolved to sink themselves rather than be taken: Signed underneath, Fortune le garde, and no name to it.

January 1.]   Mr. Edward Winslow chosen governour of Plimouth, Mr. Bradford having been governour about ten years, and now by importunity gat off.

9.]   Mr. Oliver, a right godly man, and elder of the church of

Boston, having three or four of his sons, all very young, cutting down wood upon the neck, one of them, being about fifteen years old, had his brains beaten out with the fall of a tree, which he had felled. The good old father (having the news of it in as fearful a manner as might be, by another boy, his brother) called his wife (being also a very godly woman) and went to prayer, and bare it with much patience and honor.

17.] The governour, having intelligence from the east, that the French had bought the Scottish plantation near Cape Sable, and that the fort and all the ammunition were delivered to them, and that the cardinal, having the managing thereof, had sent some companies already, and preparation was made to send many more the next year, and divers priests and Jesuits among them,—called the assistants to Boston, and the ministers and captains, and some other chief men, to advise what was fit to be done for our safety, in regard the French were like to prove ill neighbours (being Papists;) at which meeting it was agreed, that a plantation and a fort should forthwith be begun at Natascott, partly to be some block in an enemy's way, (though it could not bar his entrance,) and especially to prevent an enemy from taking that passage from us; and also, that the fort begun at Boston should be finished;—also, that a plantation should be begun at Agawam, (being the best place in the land for tillage and cattle,) least an enemy, finding it void, should possess and take it from us. The governour's son (being one of the assistants) was to undertake this, and to take no more out of the bay than twelve men; the rest to be supplied at the coming of the next ships.

A maid servant of Mr. Skelton of Salem, going towards Sagus, was lost seven days, and at length came home to Salem. All that time she was in the woods, having no kind of food, the snow being very deep, and as cold as at any time that winter. She was so frozen into the snow some mornings, as she was one hour before she could get up; yet she soon recovered and did well, through the Lord's wonderful providence.

[*Large blank.*]

About the beginning of this month of January the pinnaces, which went after the pirates, returned, the cold being so great as they could not pursue them; but, in their return, they hanged up at Richman's Isle an Indian, one Black Will, one of those who had there murdered Walter Bagnall. Three of the pirates' company ran from them and came home.

[*Large blank.*]

February 21.]   The governour and four of the assistants, with three of the ministers, and others, about twenty-six in all, went, in three boats, to view Natascott, the wind W., fair weather; but the wind arose at N. W. so strong, and extreme cold, that they were kept there two nights, being forced to lodge upon the ground, in an open cottage, upon a little old straw, which they pulled from the thatch. Their victuals also grew short, so as they were forced to eat muscles,—yet they were very mean,—and came all safe home the third day after, through the Lord's special providence. Upon view of the place, it was agreed by all, that to build a fort there would be of too great charge, and of little use; whereupon the planting of that place was deferred.

22, or thereabouts.]   The ship William, Mr. Trevore master, arrived at Plimouth with some passengers and goods for the Massachusetts Bay; but she came to set up a fishing at Scituate, and so to go to trade at Hudson's River.

By this ship we had intelligence from our friends in England, that Sir Ferdinando Gorges and Capt. Mason (upon the instigation of Sir Christopher Gardiner, Morton, and Ratcliff) had preferred a petition to the lords of the privy council against us, charging us with many false accusations; but, through the Lord's good providence, and the care of our friends in England, (especially Mr. Emanuel Downing, who had married the governour's sister, and the good testimony given on our behalf by one Capt. Wiggin, who dwelt at Pascataquack, and had been divers times among us,) their malicious practice took not effect. The principal matter they had against us was, the letters of some indiscreet persons among us, who had written against the church government in England, etc., which had been intercepted by occasion of the death of Capt. Levett, who carried them, and died at sea.

26.]   Two little girls of the governour's family were sitting

under a great heap of logs, plucking of birds, and the wind driving
the feathers into the house, the governour's wife caused them to
remove away. They were no sooner gone, but the whole heap of
logs fell down in the place, and had crushed them to death, if
the Lord, in his special providence, had not delivered them.

March.] The governour's son, John Winthrop, went, with
twelve more, to begin a plantation at Agawam, after called
Ipswich.

[Large blank.]

One John Edye, a godly man of Watertown congregation, fell
distracted, and, getting out one evening, could not be found; but,
eight days after, he came again of himself. He had kept his
strength and colour, yet had eaten nothing (as must needs be
conceived) all that time. He recovered his understanding again
in good measure, and lived very orderly, but would, now and then,
be a little distempered.

[Blank.]

April 10.] Here arrived Mr. Hodges, one of Mr. Peirce his
mates. He came from Virginia in a shallop, and brought news
that Mr. Peirce's ship was cast away upon a shoal four miles from
Feake Isle, ten leagues to the N. of the mouth of Virginia Bay,
November 2d, about five in the morning, the wind S. W., through
the negligence of one of his mates, who had the watch, and kept
not his lead as he was exhorted. They had a shallop and their
ship's boat aboard. All that went into the shallop came safe on
shore, but the ship's boat was sunk by the ship's side, and *[blank]*
men drowned in her, and ten of them were taken up alive into
the shallop. There were in the ship twenty-eight seamen and ten
passengers. Of these were drowned seven seamen and five passengers, and all the goods were lost, except one hogshead of
beaver; and most of the letters were saved, and some other small
things, which were driven on shore the next day, when the ship
was broken in pieces. They were nine days in much distress,
before they found any English. Plimouth men lost four hogsheads,

900 pounds of beaver, and 200 otter skins. The governour of Massachusetts lost, in beaver and fish, which he sent to Virginia, etc., near £100. Many others lost beaver, and Mr. Humfrey, fish.

[*Large blank.*]

May.]   The William and Jane, Mr. Burdock master, arrived with thirty passengers and ten cows or more. She came in six weeks from London.

[*Blank.*]

The Mary and Jane arrived, Mr. Rose master. She came from London in seven weeks, and brought one hundred and ninety-six passengers, (only two children died). Mr. Coddington, one of the assistants, and his wife, came in her. In her return she was cast away upon Isle Sable, but [*blank*] men were saved.

By these ships we understood, that Sir Christopher Gardiner, and Thomas Morton, and Philip Ratcliff, (who had been punished here for their misdemeanours,) had petitioned to the king and council against us, (being set on by Sir Ferdinando Gorges and Capt. Mason, who had begun a plantation at Pascataquack, and aimed at the general government of New England for their agent there, Capt. Neal). The petition was of many sheets of paper, and contained many false accusations, (and among some truths misrepeated,) accusing us to intend rebellion, to have cast off our allegiance, and to be wholly separate from the church and laws of England; that our ministers and people did continually rail against the state, church, and bishops there, etc. Upon which such of our company as were then in England, viz., Sir Richard Saltonstall, Mr. Humfrey, and Mr. Cradock, were called before a committee of the council, to whom they delivered in an answer in writing; upon reading whereof, it pleased the Lord, our gracious God and Protector, so to work with the lords, and after with the king's majesty, when the whole matter was reported to him by Sir Thomas Jermin, one of the council, (but not of the committee, who yet had been present at the three days of hearing, and spake much in the commendation of the governour, both to the lords and after to his majesty,) that he said, he would have them severely punished, who did abuse his governour and the plantation; that the defendants were dismissed with a favorable order for their encouragement, being assured from some of the council, that his majesty did not intend to impose the ceremonies of the church of England upon us; for that it was considered, that it was the freedom from such things that made people come over to us; and it was credibly informed to the council, that this country would, in time, be very beneficial to England for masts, cordage, etc., if the Sound should be debarred.

We sent forth a pinnace after the pirate Bull, but, after she had been forth two months, she came home, having not found him. After, we heard he was gone to the French.

A Dutch pink arrived, which had been to the southward a trading.

June 2.] Capt. Stone arrived with a small ship with cows and some salt. The governour of Plimouth sent Capt. Standish to prosecute against him for piracy. The cause was, being at the Dutch plantation, where a pinnace of Plimouth coming, and Capt. Stone and the Dutch governour having been drinking together, Capt. Stone, upon pretence that those of Plimouth had reproached them of Virginia, from whence he came, seized upon their pinnace, (with the governour's consent,) and offered to carry her away, but the Dutchmen rescued her; and the next day the governour and Capt. Stone entreated the master of the pinnace (being one of the council of Plimouth) to pass it by, which he promised by a solemn instrument under his hand; yet, upon their earnest prosecution at court, we bound over Capt. Stone (with two sureties) to appear in the admiralty court in England, etc. But, after, those of Plimouth, being persuaded that it would turn to their reproach, and that it could be no piracy, with their consent, we withdrew the recognizance.

15.] Mr. Graves, in the ship Elizabeth Bonadventure, from Yarmouth, arrived with ninety-five passengers, and thirty-four Dutch sheep, and two mares. They came from Yarmouth in six weeks; lost not one person, but above forty sheep.

19.] A day of thanksgiving was kept in all the congregations, for our delivery from the plots of our enemies, and for the safe arrival of our friends, etc.

July 2.] At a court it was agreed, that the governour, John

Winthrop, should have, towards his charges this year, £150, and the money, which he had disbursed in public business, as officers' wages, etc., being between two and three hundred pounds, should be forthwith paid.

12.]   Mr. Edward Winslow, governour of Plimouth, and Mr. Bradford, came into the bay, and went away the 18th. They came partly to confer about joining in a trade to Connecticut, for beaver and hemp. There was a motion to set up a trading house there, to prevent the Dutch, who were about to build one; but, in regard the place was not fit for plantation, there being three or four thousand warlike Indians, and the river not to be gone into but by small pinnaces, having a bar affording but six feet at high water, and for that no vessels can get in for seven months in the year, partly by reason of the ice, and then the violent stream, etc., we thought not fit to meddle with it.

24.]   A ship arrived from Weymouth, with about eighty passengers, and twelve kine, who sate down at Dorchester. They were twelve weeks coming, being forced into the Western Islands by a leak, where they stayed three weeks, and were very courteously used by the Portugals; but the extremity of the heat there, and the continual rain brought sickness upon them, so as [blank] died.

Much sickness at Plimouth, and above twenty died of pestilent fevers.

Mr. Graves returned, and carried a freight of fish from hence and Plimouth.

By him the governour and assistants sent an answer to the petition of Sir Christopher Gardiner, and withal a certificate from the old planters concerning the carriage of affairs, etc.

August 6.]   Two men servants to one Moodye, of Roxbury, returning in a boat from the windmill, struck upon the oyster bank. They went out to gather oysters, and, not making fast their boat, when the flood came, it floated away, and they were both drowned, although they might have waded out on either side; but it was an evident judgment of God upon them, for they were wicked persons. One of them, a little before, being reproved for his lewdness, and put in mind of hell, answered, that if hell were ten times hotter, he had rather be there than he would serve his master, etc. The occasion was, because he had bound himself for divers years, and saw that, if he had been at liberty, he might have had greater wages, though otherwise his master used him very well.

Mr. Graves returned. He carried between five and six thousand weight of beaver, and about thirty passengers. Capt. Walter Neal, of Pascataquack, and some eight of his company, went with him. He had been in the bay above ten days, and came not all that time to see the governour. Being persuaded by divers of his friends, his answer was, that he was not well entertained the first time he came hither, and, besides, he had some letters opened in the bay; ergo, except he were invited, he would not go see him. The 13th day he wrote to the governour, to excuse his not coming to see him, upon the same reasons. The governour returned him answer, that his entertainment was such as time and place could afford, (being at their first coming, before they were housed, etc.) and retorted the discourtesy upon him, in that he would thrust himself, with such a company, (he had five or six gentlemen with him,) upon a stranger's entertainment, at such an unseasonable time, and having no need so to do; and for his letters, he protested his innocency, (as he might well, for the letters were opened before they came into the bay;) and so concluded courteously, yet with plain demonstration of his error. And, indeed, if the governour should have invited him, standing upon those terms, he had blemished his reputation.

There is mention made before of the answer, which was returned to Sir Christopher Gardiner his accusations, to which the governour and all the assistants subscribed, only the deputy refused. He made three exceptions: 1. For that we termed the bishops reverend bishops; which was only in repeating the accuser's words. 2. For that we professed to believe all the articles of the Christian faith, according to the scriptures and the common received tenets of the churches of England. This he refused, because we differed from them in matter of discipline, and about the meaning of Christ's descension into hell; yet the faithful in England (whom we account the churches) expound it as we do, and not of a local descent, as some of the bishops do. 3. For that we gave the king the title of sacred majesty, which is the most proper title of princes, being the Lord's anointed,* and the word a mere civil word, never applied in scripture to any divine thing, but sanctus used always, (Mr. Knox called the queen of Scotland by the same title). Yet

* [The preceding four words have a line drawn through them.]

by no reasons could he be drawn to yield to these things, although they were allowed by divers of the ministers and the chief of Plimouth.

There was great scarcity of corn, by reason of the spoil our hogs had made at harvest, and the great quantity they had even in the winter, (there being no acorns;) yet people lived well with fish and the fruit of their gardens.

Sept. 4.] The Griffin, a ship of three hundred tons, arrived, (having been eight weeks from the Downs). This ship was brought in by John Gallop a new way by Lovell's Island, at low water, now called Griffin's Gap. She brought about two hundred passengers, having lost some four, whereof one was drowned two days before, as he was casting forth a line to take mackerel. In this ship came Mr. Cotton, Mr. Hooker, and Mr. Stone, ministers, and Mr. Peirce, Mr. Haynes, (a gentleman of great estate,) Mr. Hoffe, and many other men of good estates. They gat out of England with much difficulty, all places being belaid to have taken Mr. Cotton and Mr. Hooker, who had been long sought for to have been brought into the high commission; but the master being bound to touch at the Wight, the pursuivants attended there, and, in the mean time, the said ministers were taken in at the Downs. Mr. Hooker and Mr. Stone went presently to Newtown, where they were to be entertained, and Mr. Cotton stayed at Boston. On Saturday evening, the congregation met in their ordinary exercise, and Mr. Cotton, being desired to speak to the question, (which was of the church,) he showed, out of the Canticles, 6, that some churches were as queens, some as concubines, some as damsels, and some as doves, etc. He was then (with his wife) propounded to be admitted a member. The Lord's day following, he exercised in the afternoon, and being to be admitted, he signified his desire and readiness to make his confession according to order, which he said might be sufficient in declaring his faith about baptism, (which he then desired for his child, born in their passage, and therefore named Seaborn). He gave two reasons why he did not baptize it at sea, (not for want of fresh water, for he held, sea water would have served:) 1, because they had no settled congregation there; 2, because a minister hath no power to give the seals but in his own congregation. He desired his wife might also be admitted

a member, and gave a modest testimony of her, but withal requested, that she might not be put to make open confession, etc.,
which he said was against the apostle's rule, and not fit for
women's modesty; but that the elders might examine her in private.
So she was asked, if she did consent in the confession of faith
made by her husband, and if she did desire to be admitted, etc.;
whereto she answered affirmatively; and so both were admitted,
and their child baptized, the father presenting it, (the child's
baptism being, as he did then affirm, in another case, the father's
incentive for the help of his faith, etc).

The said 4th of September, came in also the ship called the
Bird, (Mr. Yates master). She brought [*blank*] passengers, having
lost [*blank;*] and [*blank*] cows, having lost [*blank;*] and four
mares. She had been twelve weeks at sea, being, at her first
coming out, driven northerly to fifty-three.

About ten days before this time, a bark was set forth to Connecticut and those parts, to trade.

John Oldham, and three with him, went over land to Connecticut, to trade. The sachem used them kindly, and gave them
some beaver. They brought of the hemp, which grows there
in great abundance, and is much better than the English. He
accounted it to be about one hundred and sixty miles. He brought
some black lead, whereof the Indians told him there was a whole
rock. He lodged at Indian towns all the way.

12.]   Capt. John Stone (of whom mention is made before)
carried himself very dissolutely in drawing company to drink,
etc., and being found upon the bed in the night with one Bar-
croft's wife, he was brought before the governour, etc., and though
it appeared he was in drink, and no act to be proved, yet it was
thought fit he should abide his trial, for which end warrant was
sent out to stay his pinnace, which was ready to set sail; whereupon
he went to Mr. Ludlow, one of the assistants, and used braving
and threatening speeches against him, for which he raised some
company and apprehended him, and brought him to the governour,
who put him in irons, and kept a guard upon him till the court,
(but his irons were taken off the same day). At the court his
indictment was framed for adultery, but found ignoramus by the
great jury; but, for his other misdemeanors, he was fined £100,

which yet was not levied of him; and ordered upon pain of death to come here no more, without license of the court; and the woman was bound to her good behaviour.

17.]   The governour and council met at Boston, and called the ministers and elders of all the churches, to consider about Mr. Cotton his sitting down. He was desired to divers places, and those who came with him desired he might sit down where they might keep store of cattle; but it was agreed, by full consent, that the fittest place for him was Boston, and in that respect those of Boston might take farms in any part of the bay not belonging to other towns; and that (keeping a lecture) he should have some maintenance out of the treasury. But divers of the council, upon their second thoughts, did after refuse this contribution.

October 2.]   The bark Blessing, which was sent to the southward, returned. She had been at an island over against Connecticut, called Long Island, because it is near fifty leagues long, the east part about ten leagues from the main, but the west end not a mile. There they had store of the best wampampeak, both white and blue. The Indians there are a very treacherous people. They have many canoes so great as one will carry eighty men. They were also in the River of Connecticut, which is barred at the entrance, so as they could not find above one fathom of water. They were also at the Dutch plantation upon Hudson's River, (called New Netherlands,) where they were very kindly entertained, and had some beaver and other things, for such commodities as they put off. They showed the governour (called Gwalter Van Twilly) their commission, which was to signify to them, that the king of England had granted the river and country of Connecticut to his own subjects; and therefore desired them to forbear to build there, etc. The Dutch governour wrote back to our governour, (his letter was very courteous and respectful, as it had been to a very honorable person,) whereby he signified, that the Lords the States had also granted the same parts to the West India Company, and therefore requested that we would forbear the same till the matter were decided between the king of England and the said lords.

The said bark did pass and repass over the shoals of Cape Cod, about three or four leagues from Nantucket Isle, where the breaches are very terrible, yet they had three fathom water all over.

[*Large blank.*]

The company of Plimouth sent a bark to Connecticut, at this time, to erect a trading house there. When they came, they found the Dutch had built there, and did forbid the Plimouth men to proceed; but they set up their house notwithstanding, about a mile above the Dutch. This river runs so far northward, that it comes within a day's journey of a part of Merrimack called [*blank,*] and so runs thence N. W. so near the Great Lake, as [allows] the Indians to pass their canoes into it over land. From this lake, and the hideous swamps about it, come most of the beaver which is traded between Virginia and Canada, which runs forth of this lake; and Patomack River in Virginia comes likewise out of it, or very near, so as from this lake there comes yearly to the Dutch about ten thousand skins, which might easily be diverted by Merrimack, if a course of trade were settled above in that river.

10.]   A fast was kept at Boston, and Mr. Leverett, an ancient, sincere professor, of Mr. Cotton's congregation in England, was chosen a ruling elder, and Mr. Firmin, a godly man, an apothecary of Sudbury in England, was chosen deacon, by imposition of hands; and Mr. Cotton was then chosen teacher of the congregation of Boston, and ordained by imposition of the hands of the presbytery, in this manner: First, he was chosen by all the congregation testifying their consent by erection of hands. Then Mr. Wilson, the pastor, demanded of him, if he did accept of that call. He paused, and then spake to this effect: that howsoever he knew himself unworthy and unsufficient for that place; yet, having observed all the passages of God's providence, (which he reckoned up in particular) in calling him to it, he could not but accept it. Then the pastor and the two elders laid their hands upon his head, and the pastor prayed, and then, taking off their hands, laid them on again, and, speaking to him by his name, they did thenceforth design him to the said office, in the name of the Holy Ghost, and did give him the charge of the congregation, and did thereby (as by a sign from God) indue him with the gifts fit for his office; and lastly did bless him. Then the neighboring ministers, which were present, did (at the pastor's motion) give him the right hands of fellowship, and the pastor made a stipulation between him and the congregation. When Mr. Cotton accepted of the office, he commended to the congregation such as were to come over, who were of his charge in England, that they might be comfortably provided for.

The same day, Mr. Grant, in the ship James, arrived at Salem, having been but eight weeks between Gravesend and Salem. He brought Capt. Wiggin and about thirty, with one Mr. Leveridge, a godly minister, to Pascataquack, (which the Lord Say and the Lord Brook had purchased of the Bristol men,) and about thirty for Virginia, and about twenty for this place, and some sixty cattle. He brought news, that the Richard, a bark of fifty tons, which came forth with the Griffin, being come above three hundred leagues, sprang such a leak, as she was forced to bear up, and was put in at Weymouth.

11.] A fast at Newtown, where Mr. Hooker was chosen pastor, and Mr. Stone teacher, in such a manner as before at Boston.

The wolves continued to do much hurt among our cattle; and this month, by Mr. Grant, there came over four Irish greyhounds, which were sent to the governour by Mr. Downing, his brother-in-law.

[*Very large blank.*]

November.] A great mortality among the Indians. Chickatabot, the sagamore of Naponsett, died, and many of his people. The disease was the small pox. Some of them were cured by such means as they had from us; many of their children escaped, and were kept by the English.

Capt. Wiggin of Pascataquack wrote to the governour, that one of his people had stabbed another, and desired he might be tried in the bay, if the party died. The governour answered, that if Pascataquack lay within their limits, (as it was supposed,) they would try him.

A small ship of about sixty tons was built at Medford, and called the Rebecca.

This year a watermill was built at Roxbury, by Mr. Dummer.

The scarcity of workmen had caused them to raise their wages to an excessive rate, so as a carpenter would have three shillings the day, a laborer two shillings and sixpence, etc.; and accordingly those who had commodities to sell advanced their prices sometime double to that they cost in England, so as it grew to a general complaint, which the court, taking knowledge of, as also of some further evils, which were springing out of the excessive rates of wages, they made an order, that carpenters, masons, etc., should take but two shillings the day, and laborers but eighteen pence, and that no commodity should be sold at above four pence in the shilling more than it cost for ready money in England; oil, wine, etc., and cheese, in regard of the hazard of bringing, etc., [excepted]. The evils which were springing, etc., were: 1. Many spent much time idly, etc., because they could get as much in four days as would keep them a week. 2. They spent much in tobacco and strong waters, etc., which was a great waste to the commonwealth, which, by reason of so many foreign commodities expended, could not have subsisted to this time, but that it was supplied by the cattle and corn, which were sold to new comers at very dear rates, viz., corn at six shillings the bushel, a cow at £20,—yea, some at £24, some £26,—a mare at £35, an ewe goat at 3 or £4; and yet many cattle were every year brought out of England, and some from Virginia. Soon after order was taken for prices of commodities, viz., not to exceed the rate of four pence in the shilling above the price in England, except cheese and liquors, etc.

The ministers in the bay and Sagus did meet, once a fortnight, at one of their houses by course, where some question of moment was debated. Mr. Skelton, the pastor of Salem, and Mr. Williams, who was removed from Plimouth thither, (but not in any office, though he exercised by way of prophecy,) took some exception against it, as fearing it might grow in time to a presbytery or superintendency, to the prejudice of the churches' liberties. But this fear was without cause; for they were all clear in that point, that no church or person can have power over another church; neither did they in their meetings exercise any such jurisdiction, etc.

[*Large blank.*]

News of the taking of Machias by the French. Mr. Allerton of Plimouth, and some others, had set up a trading wigwam there, and left in it five men and store of commodities. La Tour, governour of the French in those parts, making claim to the place, came to displant them, and, finding resistance, killed two of the men, and carried away the other three, and the goods.

[*Large blank.*]

Some differences fell out still, now and then, between the governour and the deputy, which yet were soon healed. It had been ordered in court, that all hands should help to the finishing of the fort at Boston, and all the towns in the bay had gone once over, and most the second time; but those of Newtown being warned, the deputy would not suffer them to come, neither did acquaint the governour with the cause, which was, for that Salem and Sagus had not brought in money for their parts. The governour, hearing of it, wrote friendly to him, showing him that the intent of the court was, that the work should be done by those in the bay, and that, after, the others should pay a proportionable sum for the house, etc., which must be done by money; and therefore desired him that he would send in his neighbours. Upon this, Mr. Haynes and Mr. Hooker came to the governour to treat with him about it, and brought a letter from the deputy full of bitterness and resolution not to send till Salem, etc. The governour told them it should rest till the court, and withal gave the letter to Mr. Hooker with this speech: I am not willing to keep such an occasion of provocation by me. And soon after he wrote to the deputy (who had before desired to buy a fat hog or two of him, being somewhat short of provisions) to desire him to send for one, (which he would have sent him, if he had known when his occasion had been to have made use of it,) and to accept it as a testimony of his good will; and, lest he should make any scruple of it, he made Mr. Haynes and Mr. Hooker (who both sojourned in his house) partakers with him. Upon this the deputy returned this answer: "Your overcoming yourself hath overcome me. Mr. Haynes, Mr. Hooker, and myself, do most kindly accept your good will; but we desire, without offence, to refuse your offer, and that I may only trade with you for two hogs;" and so very lovingly concluded.—The court being two days after, ordered, that Newtown should do their work as others had done, and then Salem, etc., should pay for three days at eighteen pence a man.

11.]   The congregation of Boston met to take order for Mr.

Cotton's passage and house, and his and Mr. Wilson's maintenance. Mr. Cotton had disbursed eighty pounds for his passage,
and towards his house, which he would not have again; so there
was about £60 raised (by voluntary contribution) towards the
finishing of his house, and about £100 towards their maintenance.
At this meeting there arose some difference between the governour
and Mr. Cottington, who charged the governour, that he took
away the liberty of the rest, because (at the request of the rest)
he had named some men to set out men's lands, etc., which
grew to some heat of words; but the next Lord's day they both
acknowledged openly their failing, and declared that they had
been reconciled the next day.

[*Large blank.*]

26.] Mr. Wilson (by leave of the congregation of Boston,
whereof he was pastor) went to Agawam to teach the people of
that plantation, because they had yet no minister. Whiles he was
there, December 4, there fell such a snow (knee deep) as he could
not come back for [*blank*] days, and a boat, which went thither,
was frozen up in the river.

December 5.] John Sagamore died of the small pox, and
almost all his people; (above thirty buried by Mr. Maverick of
Winesemett in one day). The towns in the bay took away many
of the children; but most of them died soon after.

James Sagamore of Sagus died also, and most of his folks. John
Sagamore desired to be brought among the English, (so he was;)
and promised (if he recovered) to live with the English and serve
their God. He left one son, which he disposed to Mr. Wilson,
the pastor of Boston, to be brought up by him. He gave to the
governour a good quantity of wampompeague, and to divers others
of the English he gave gifts, and took order for the payment of
his own debts and his men's. He died in a persuasion that he
should go to the Englishmen's God. Divers of them, in their
sickness, confessed that the Englishmen's God was a good God;
and that, if they recovered, they would serve him.

It wrought much with them, that when their own people forsook them, yet the English came daily and ministered to them;
and yet few, only two families,* took any infection by it. Among

* [The preceding three words have a line drawn through them.]

others, Mr. Maverick of Winesemett is worthy of a perpetual*
remembrance. Himself, his wife, and servants, went daily to
them, ministered to their necessities, and buried their dead, and
took home many of their children. So did other of the neighbours.

This infectious disease spread to Pascataquack, where all the
Indians (except one or two) died.

One Cowper of Pascataquack, going to an island, upon the
Lord's day, to fetch some sack to be drank at the great house, he
and a boy, coming back in a canoe, (being both drunk,) were
driven to sea and never heard of after.

At the same plantation, a company having made a fire at a tree,
one of them said, Here this tree will fall, and here will I lie; and
accordingly it fell upon him and killed him.

It pleased the Lord to give special testimony of his presence in
the church of Boston, after Mr. Cotton was called to office there.
More were converted and added to that church, than to all the
other churches in the bay, (or rather the lake, for so it were more
properly termed, the bay being that part of sea without between
the two capes, Cape Cod and Cape Ann). Divers profane and
notorious evil persons came and confessed their sins, and were
comfortably received into the bosom of the church. Yea, the Lord
gave witness to the exercise of prophecy, so as thereby some were
converted, and others much edified. Also, the Lord pleased greatly
to bless the practice of discipline, wherein he gave the pastor,
Mr. Wilson, a singular gift, to the great benefit of the church.

After much deliberation and serious advice, the Lord directed
the teacher, Mr. Cotton, to make it clear by the scripture, that the
minister's maintenance, as well as all other charges of the church,
should be defrayed out of a stock, or treasury, which was to be
raised out of the weekly contribution; which accordingly was
agreed upon.

27.]   The governour and assistants met at Boston, and took
into consideration a treatise, which Mr. Williams (then of Salem)
had sent to them, and which he had formerly written to the governour and council of Plimouth, wherein, among other things,
he disputes their right to the lands they possessed here, and concluded that, claiming by the king's grant, they could have no title,

* [The preceding two words have a line drawn through them.]

nor otherwise, except they compounded with the natives. For this, taking advice with some of the most judicious ministers, (who much condemned Mr. Williams's error and presumption,) they gave order, that he should be convented at the next court, to be censured, etc. There were three passages chiefly whereat they were much offended: 1, for that he chargeth King James to have told a solemn public lie, because in his patent he blessed God that he was the first Christian prince that had discovered this land: 2, for that he chargeth him and others with blasphemy for calling Europe Christendom, or the Christian world: 3, for that he did personally apply to our present king, Charles, these three places in the Revelations, viz., [*blank.*]

Mr. Endecott being absent, the governour wrote to him to let him know what was done, and withal added divers arguments to confute the said errors, wishing him to deal with Mr. Williams to retract the same, etc. Whereto he returned a very modest and discreet answer. Mr. Williams also wrote to the governour, and also to him and the rest of the council, very submissively, professing his intent to have been only to have written for the private satisfaction of the governour etc., of Plimouth, without any purpose to have stirred any further in it, if the governour here had not required a copy of him; withal offering his book, or any part of it, to be burnt.

At the next court he appeared penitently, and gave satisfaction of his intention and loyalty. So it was left, and nothing done in it.

January 21.]   News came from Plimouth, that Capt. Stone, who this last summer went out of the bay or lake, and so to Aquamenticus, where he took in Capt. Norton, putting in at the mouth of Connecticut, in his way to Virginia, where the Pequins inhabit, was there cut off by them, with all his company, being eight. The manner was thus: Three of his men, being gone ashore to kill fowl, were cut off. Then the sachem, with some of his men, came aboard, and staid with Capt. Stone in his cabin, till Capt. Stone (being alone with him) fell on sleep. Then he knocked him on the head, and all the rest of the English being in the cook's room, the Indians took such pieces as they found there ready charged, and bent them at the English; whereupon one took a piece, and by accident gave fire to the powder, which blew up the deck; but most of the Indians, perceiving what they went about, shifted overboard, and after they returned, and killed such as remained, and burned the pinnace. We agreed to write to the governour of Virginia, (because Stone was one of that colony,) to move him to revenge it, and upon his answer to take further counsel.*

20.] Hall and the two others, who went to Connecticut November 3, came now home, having lost themselves and endured much misery. They informed us, that the small pox was gone as far as any Indian plantation was known to the west, and much people dead of it, by reason whereof they could have no trade.

At Naragansett, by the Indians' report, there died seven hundred; but, beyond Pascataquack, none to the eastward.

24.] The governour and council met again at Boston, to consider of Mr. Williams's letter, etc., when, with the advice of Mr. Cotton and Mr. Wilson, and weighing his letter, and further considering of the aforesaid offensive passages in his book, (which, being written in very obscure and implicative phrases, might well admit of doubtful interpretation,) they found the matters not to be so evil as at first they seemed. Whereupon they agreed, that, upon his retractation, etc., or taking an oath of allegiance to the king, etc., it should be passed over.

[*Very large blank.*]

An Englishman of Sacoe, travelling into the country to trade, was killed by the Indians.

[*Very large blank.*]

30.] John Seales, who ran from his master to the Indians, came home again. He was at a place twelve miles off, where were seven Indians, whereof four died of the pox while he was there.

[*Large blank.*]

February 1.] Mr. Cradock's house at Marblehead was burnt down about midnight before, there being then in it Mr. Allerton, and many fishermen, whom he employed that season, who all were

* [A line has been drawn diagonally across the last four sentences.]

preserved by a special providence of God, with most of his goods therein, by a tailor, who sate up that night at work in the house, and, hearing a noise, looked out and saw the house on fire above the oven in the thatch.

This winter was very mild, little wind, and most S. and S. W. but oft snows, and great. One snow, the 15th of this month, was near two feet deep all over.

[Large blank.]

Such of the Indians' children as were left were taken by the English, most whereof did die of the pox soon after, three only remaining, whereof one, which the governour kept, was called Know-God, (the Indians' usual answer being, when they were put in mind of God, Me no know God).

[Large blank.]

22.]   The grampus came up towards Charlestown against the tide of ebb.

[Large blank.]

This season Mr. Allerton fished with eight boats at Marble Harbour.*

[Large blank.]

By this time seventeen fishing ships were come to Richman's Isle and the Isle of Shoals.

March 4.]   By order of court a mercate was erected at Boston, to be kept upon Thursday, the fifth day of the week, being the lecture day. Samuel Cole set up the first house for common entertainment, and John Cogan, merchant, the first shop.

Upon offer of some new comers to give liberally towards the building of a galley for defence of the bay, and upon consultation with divers experienced seamen and others, it was thought fitter for our condition to build a vessel forty feet in length, and twenty-

* [This sentence has a line drawn through it.]

one in breadth, to be minion proof, and the upper deck musket proof, to have one sail, and to carry whole culverin and other small pieces, eight in all. This was found to be so chargeable, and so long time ere it could be finished, that it was given over.

At this court all swamps, above one hundred acres, were made common, etc. Also Robert Cole, having been oft punished for drunkenness, was now ordered to wear a red D about his neck for a year.

[*Blank.*]

7.]   At the lecture at Boston a question was propounded about veils. Mr. Cotton concluded, that where (by the custom of the place) they were not a sign of the women's subjection, they were not commanded by the apostle. Mr. Endecott opposed, and did maintain it by the general arguments brought by the apostle. After some debate, the governour, perceiving it to grow to some earnestness, interposed, and so it brake off.

[*Large blank.*]

Among other testimonies of the Lord's gracious presence with his own ordinances, there was a youth of fourteen years of age (being the son of one of the magistrates) so wrought upon by the ministry of the word, as, for divers months, he was held under such affliction of mind, as he could not be brought to apprehend any comfort in God, being much humbled and broken for his sins, (though he had been a dutiful child, and not given up to the lusts of youth,) and especially for his blasphemous and wicked thoughts, whereby Satan buffeted him, so as he went mourning and languishing daily; yet, attending to the means, and not giving over prayer, and seeking counsel, etc., he came at length to be freed from his temptations, and to find comfort in God's promises, and so, being received into the congregation, upon good proof of his understanding in the things of God, he went on cheerfully in a Christian course, falling daily to labor, as a servant, and as a younger brother of his did, who was no whit short of him in the knowledge of God's will, though his youth kept him from daring to offer himself to the congregation.—Upon this occasion it is not impertinent (though no credit nor regard be to be had of dreams in these days) to report a dream, which the father of these children had at the same time, viz., that, coming into his chamber, he found his wife (she was a very gracious woman) in bed, and three or four of their children lying by her, with most sweet and smiling countenances, with crowns upon their heads, and blue ribbons about their leaves.* When he awaked, he told his wife his dream, and made this interpretation of it, that God would take of her children to make them fellow heirs with Christ in his kingdom.

[*Large blank.*]

Satan bestirred himself to hinder the progress of the gospel, as, among other practices, appeared by this: He stirred up a spirit of jealousy between Mr. James, the pastor of Charlton, and many of his people, so as Mr. Nowell, and some others, who had been dismissed from Boston, began to question their fact of breaking from Boston, and it grew to such a principle of conscience among them, as the advice of the other ministers was taken in it, who, after two meetings, could not agree about their continuance or return.

[*Large blank.*]

One Mr. Morris, ensign to Capt. Underhill, taking some distaste in his office, requested the magistrates, that he might be discharged of it, and so was, whereby he gave offence to the congregation of Boston, so as, being questioned and convinced of sin in forsaking his calling, he did acknowledge his fault, and, at the request of the people, was by the magistrates chosen lieutenant to the same company, for he was a very stout man and an experienced soldier.

April 1.] Order was taken for ministering an oath to all house keepers and sojourners, being twenty years of age and not freemen, and for making a survey of the houses and lands of all freemen.

Notice being sent out of the general court to be held the 14th

* [The preceding five words have a line drawn through them.]

day of the third month, called May, the freemen deputed two of each town to meet and consider of such matters as they were to take order in at the same general court; who, having met, desired a sight of the patent, and, conceiving thereby that all their laws should be made at the general court, repaired to the governour to advise with him about it, and about the abrogating of some orders formerly made, as for killing of swine in corn, etc. He told them, that, when the patent was granted, the number of free-men was supposed to be (as in like corporations) so few, as they might well join in making laws; but now they were grown to so great a body, as it was not possible for them to make or execute laws, but they must choose others for that purpose: and that how-soever it would be necessary hereafter to have a select company to intend that work, yet for the present they were not furnished with a sufficient number of men qualified for such a business, neither could the commonwealth bear the loss of time of so many as must intend it. Yet this they might do at present, viz., they might, at the general court, make an order, that, once in the year, a certain number should be appointed (upon summons from the governour) to revise all laws, etc., and to reform what they found amiss therein; but not to make any new laws, but prefer their grievances to the court of assistants; and that no assessment should be laid upon the country without the consent of such a committee, nor any lands disposed of.

3.]   The governour went on foot to Agawam, and because the people there wanted a minister, spent the Sabbath with them, and exercised by way of prophecy, and returned home the 10th.

20.]   John Coggeshall, gentleman, being dismissed from the church of Roxbury to Boston, though he were well known and approved of the church, yet was not received but by confession of his faith, etc.

[Very large blank.]

May 3.]   News came of the death of Hockin and the Plimouth man at Kenebeck, (and of the arrival of the ship at Pemaquid which brought thirty passengers for this place).

The occasion of the death of those men at Kenebeck was this: The Plimouth men had a grant, from the grand patentees of New England, of Kenebeck, with liberty of sole trade, etc. The said

Hockin came in a pinnace, belonging to the Lord Say and Lord Brook at Pascataquack, to trade at Kenebeck. Two of the magistrates of Plimouth, being there, forbad him; yet he went up the river; and, because he would not come down again, they sent three men in a canoe to cut his cables. Having cut one, Hockin presented a piece, and sware he would kill him that went to cut the other. They bad him do if he durst, and went on to cut it. Thereupon he killed one of them, and instantly one in the Plimouth pinnace (which rode by them, and wherein five or six men stood with their pieces ready charged) shot and killed Hockin.

15.] At the general court at Boston, upon the complaint of a kinsman of the said Hockin, John Alden, one of the said magistrates of Plimouth, who was present when Hockin was slain, being then at Boston, was called and bound with sureties not to depart out of our jurisdiction without leave had; and withal we wrote to Plimouth to certify them what we had done, and to know whether they would do justice in the cause, (as belonging to their jurisdiction,) and to have a speedy answer, etc. This we did, that notice might be taken, that we did disavow the said action, which was much condemned of all men, and which was feared would give occasion to the king to send a general governour over; and besides had brought us all and the gospel under a common reproach of cutting one another's throats for beaver.

[*Blank.*]

By this time the fort at Boston was in defence, and divers pieces of ordnance mounted in it.

[*Large blank.*]

Those of Newtown complained of straitness for want of land, especially meadow, and desired leave of the court to look out either for enlargement or removal, which was granted; whereupon they sent men to see Agawam and Merimack, and gave out they would remove, etc.

[*Large blank.*]

14.] At the general court, Mr. Cotton preached, and delivered this doctrine, that a magistrate ought not to be turned into the condition of a private man without just cause, and to be publicly convict, no more than the magistrates may not turn a private man out of his freehold, etc., without like public trial, etc. This falling in question in the court, and the opinion of the rest of the ministers being asked, it was referred to further consideration.

The court chose a new governour, viz., Thomas Dudley, Esq., the former deputy; and Mr. Ludlow was chosen deputy; and John Haines, Esq., an assistant, and all the rest of the assistants chosen again.

At this court it was ordered, that four general courts should be kept every year, and that the whole body of the freemen should be present only at the court of election of magistrates, etc., and that, at the other three, every town should send their deputies, who should assist in making laws, disposing lands, etc. Many good orders were made this court. It held three days, and all things were carried very peaceably, notwithstanding that some of the assistants were questioned by the freemen for some errors in their government, and some fines imposed, but remitted again before the court brake up. The court was kept in the meeting-house at Boston, and the new governour and the assistants were together entertained at the house of the old governour, as before.*

* [The last nineteen words have a line drawn through them.]

8. *John Winthrop to his Wife*

To my verye loving Wife mrs. Winthrop the elder, at Groton in Suffolk neere Sudburye. from N: England.

CHARLETON IN N[EW] ENGLAND July 16 1630

MY DEARE WIFE, Blessed be the Lord our good God and mercifull father, that yet hath preserved me in life and health to salute thee, and to comforte thy longe longinge heart, with the joyfull newes of my wellfare, and the wellfare of thy beloved children.

We had a longe and troublesome passage, but the Lord made it safe and easye to us: and though we have mett with many and great troubles (as this bearer can certifie thee) yet he hath pleased to uphold us, and to give us hope of a happye issue.

I am so overpressed with businesse, as I have no tyme for these or other mine owne private occasions. I onely write now, that thou mayest knowe that yet I live and am mindfull of thee, in all my affaires: the larger discourse of all thinges thou shalt receive from my brother Downinge, which I must sende by some of the last shippes. We have mett with many sadd and discomfortable thinges, as thou shalt heare after: and the Lordes hande hath been heavy upon my selfe in some verye neere to me: my sonne Henry, my sonne Henrye, ah poore childe, yet it greives me much more for my deare daughter, the Lord strengthen and comfort her heart, to beare this crosse patiently: I knowe thou wilt not be wantinge to her in this distresse: yet for all these thinges (I prayse my God) I am not discouraged, nor doe I see cause to repent, or dispaire of those good dayes heere, which will make amends for all.

I shall expect thee next sommer (if the Lord please) and by that tyme I hope to be provided for thy comfortable entertainment: my most sweet wife, be not disheartened, trust in the Lord, and thou shalt see his faithfullnesse. Comende me heartyly to all our kinde friendes at Castleins, Groton hall, mr. Leigh and his wife, my neighbour Cole and all the rest of my neighbours and their wives, both rich and poore.

Remember me to them at Assington hall, and Codenham hall, mr. Brande mr. Alston mr. Mott and their wives, goodman Ponde, Charles Newton etc: The good Lord be with thee and blesse thee and all our children and servantes commende my love to them all, I kisse and embrace thee my deare wife and all my Children, and leave thee in his arms who is able to preserve you all, and to fullfill our joye in our happye meetinge in his good tyme, Amen. Thy faithfull husband

JO: WINTHROP.

I shall write to my sonne John by London.

9. *John Winthrop to his Wife*

MY DEARE WIFE, I wrote to thee by my brother Arthur, but I durst write no more, then I need not care though it miscarried, for I found him the olde man still, yet I would have kept him to ease my brother, but that his owne desire to returne and the scarcitye of provisions heer, yeilded the stronger reason to let him goe. Now (my good wife) let us joyne in praysinge our mercifull God, that (howsoever he hath Afflicted us, both generally and perticularly mine owne family in his stroke upon my sonne Henry) yet my selfe and the rest of our children and familye are safe and in health, and that he upholds our heartes that we fainte not in all our troubles, but can yet waite for a good issue. And howsoever our fare be but coarse in respect of what we formerly had (pease, pud-dinges, and fish, beinge our ordinary diet) yet he makes it sweet and wholsome to us, that I may truely say I desire no better: Be-sides in this, that he beginnes with us thus in Affliction, it is the greater argument to us of his love, and of the goodnesse of the worke, which we are about, for Sathan bends his forces against us, and stirres up his instruments to all kinde of mischeife, so that I thinke heere are some persons who never shewed so much wick-ednesse in England as they have doone heer. Therefore be not discouraged (my deare wife) by any thinge thou shalt heere from hence, for I see no cause to repente of our comminge hether, and thou seest (by our experience) that God can bringe safe hether (even the tenderest woemen and the yongest children as he did many in diverse shippes, though the voyage were more teadious then formerly hath been knowne in this season) be sure to be warme clothed, and to have store of fresh provisions, meale, egges putt up in salt or grounde mault, butter ote meale, pease, and fruits, and a large stronge chest or 2: well locked, to keepe these provisions in, and be sure they be bestowed in the shippe where they may be readyly come by, (which the boatswaine will see to and the quarter masters, if they be rewarded before hande) but for these thinges my sonne will take care: be sure to have ready at sea 2: or 3: skillettes of severall syzes, a large fryinge panne, a small stewinge panne, and a Case to boyle a pudding in; store of linnen for use at sea, and sacke to bestowe amonge the saylers: some drinkinge vessells, and peuter and other vessells. and for phisick you shall need no other but a pound of Doctor Wrightes Electuarium lenitium, and his direction to use it a gallon of juice of scirvy grasse to drinke a litle [for?] 5: or 6: morninges togither with some saltpeter dissolved in it, and a little grated or sliced nutmege.

Thou must be sure to bringe no more companye, then so many

as shall have full Provision for a yeare and halfe for though the
earth heere be very fertile yet there must be tyme and meanes to
rayse it, if we have corne enough we may live plentifully: yet all
these are but the meanes which God hath ordayned to doe us good
by: our eyes must be towardes him, who as he can withhould
blessing from the strongest meanes, so he can give sufficient vertue to the weakest. I am so streightned with must businesse, as
can no waye satisfie my selfe in wrightinge to thee. the Lorde will
in due tyme lett us see the faces of each other againe to our great
comforte: Now the Lord in mercye blesse guide and supporte thee,
I kisse and embrace thee my deare wife, I kisse and blesse you all
my deare children, Forth, Mary, Deane, Sam and the other: the
Lorde keepe you all and worke his true feare in your heartes. the
blessing of the Lorde be upon all my servantes whom salute from
me, Jo: Sanford, Amy etc. Goldston, Pease, Chote etc.: my good
freindes at Castlins and all my good neighbours, Goodman Cole
and his good wife, and all the rest:

Remember to come well furnished, with linnen, woollen, some
more beddinge, brasse, peuter, leather bottells, drinkinge hornes
etc.: let my sonne, provide 12: axes of severall sortes of the Braintree Smithe, or some other prime workman, whatever they coste,
and some Augers great and smale, and many other necessaryes
which I cant now thinke of, as Candle, Sope, and store of beife
suett, etc.: once againe farewell my deare wife. Thy faithfull
husband

Jo: Winthrop.

CHARLTON IN N: ENGLAND JULY 23: 1630.

10. *John Winthrop to his Wife*

MY DEARE WIFE, The blessinge of God allsufficient be upon thee
and all my deare ones with thee for ever.

I prayse the Good Lord, though we see much mortalitye sicknesse
and trouble, yet (such is his mercye) my selfe and children, with
most of my family are yet livinge and in health, and enjoye prosperity enough, if the Afflictions of our bretheren did not hold
under the comfort of it. The Lady Arbella is dead, and good mr.
Higginson, my servant, old Waters of Neyland and many others:

thus the Lord is pleased still to humble us, yet he mixes so many mercyes with his corrections, as we are perswaded he will not cast us off, but in his due tyme, will doe us good, accordinge to the measure of our Afflictions, he stayes but till he hath purged our corruptions, and healed the hardnesse and error of our heartes, and stripped us of our vaine confidence in this arme of flesh, that he may have us relye wholy upon himselfe. The French shippe so longe expected, and given for lost, is now come safe to us, about a fortnight since, havinge been 12: weekes at sea, and yet her passingers (beinge but fewe) all safe and well, but one: and her goates, but 6: livinge of 18: so as now we are somewhat refreshed with suche goodes and provisions as she brought, though much thereof hath received damage by wett. I prayse God, we have many occasions of comfort heer, and doe hope, that our dayes of Affliction will soone have an ende, and that the Lord will doe us more good in the ende, then we could have expected, that will abundantly recompence for all the trouble we have endured. yet we may not looke at great thinges heer, it is enough that we shall have heaven, though we should passe through hell to it. we heer enjoye God and Jesus Christ, is not this enough? What would we have more? I thanke God, I like so well to be heer, as I doe not repent my comminge: and if I were to come againe, I would not have altered my course, though I had foreseene all these Afflictions: I never fared better in my life, never slept better, never had more content of minde, which comes meerly of the Lordes good hande, for we have not the like meanes of these comfortes heer which we had in England, but the Lord is allsufficient, blessed be his holy name, if he please, he can still uphold us in this estate, but if he shall see good to make us partakers with others in more Affliction, his will be doone, he is our God, and may dispose of us as he sees good.

I am sorrye to parte with thee so soone, seeinge we meet so seldome, and my much businesse hath made me too ofte forgett mundayes and frydayes, I longe for the tyme, when I may see thy sweet face againe, and the faces of my deare children. but I must breake off, and desire thee to commende me kindly to all my good freindes and excuse my not writinge at this tyme, if God please once to settle me I shall make amendes. I will name nowe but such as are nearest to thee, my brother and sister Gost[lin] mr. Leigh etc.

Castleins, my neigh[bor] Cole and his good wife, with the rest of
my goode neighbors tenantes and servantes. the good Lord blesse
thee, and all our children and famylye. So I kisse my sweet wife
and my deare children and rest thy faithfull husband
                                            Jo: Winthrop.
I would have written to Maplested if I had tyme. thou must
excuse me, and remember me kindly to them all
    this is the 3: lettre I have written to thee from n[ew] England

Sept. 9. 1630.

11. *John Winthrop to John Winthrop, Jr.*

My good sonne, The good Lord blesse you ever.
    I have written to your mother, and to your unckle Downinge at
large of all things heere, to which I must referre you, in regarde
of my muche businesse and little leysure heere.
    I shall expecte your mother and you and the rest of my Com-
panye heere next springe (if God will.) I praye take order (if it
be possible) to make even reconinges with all before you come
over, and gett a good shippe, and 40: hogsheads of meale at least,
well cleansed from the branne, and layd abroad 3: or 4: dayes
before it be packed, pease and otemeale well dryed, as muche as
you can, good store of drye suffolk cheese, brought loose, or
packed in verye drye mault, butter and tryed suett, sugar and
fruite, pepper and Ginger, store of Coarse rugges, bothe to use
and sell, a hoggeshead of wine vinegar and another of verjuice,
bothe in good Caske and Iron bounde. we have lost muche by
badd Caske. bestow everye thinge in even hoggeshedes if you
can, for it will save muche in the Charge of fraught: bringe some
good oyle, pitche and tarre, and a good peece of an old Cable to
make okum, for that which was sent is muche loste. some more
Cowes would be brought, espec[ially] 2: new milche, which must
be well mealed and milked by the waye, and some goates [and]
espec[ially] sheepe (if they can be had). bring some store of
garlick and onyons, and conserve of redd roses, Allum and Alloes,
oyled skins, bothe Calf and sheepe, and some worsted ribbeinge
of several sises. this is the 3: lettre I have written to you from

heere. Comende me to all our freindes, my love and blessinge
to your brother and sisters, your sister Winthrop, and cosin Matt,
my love and service to mr. Gurdon and his wife, salutations to
mr. Jacie mr. Chamber and the rest of the good ministers, mr.
Mott, and mr. Brand. I layd out 15 *li.* to mr. Goffe for a Cowe
for his sonne. Comend me to all my good neighbours, mr. Jarrold,
william Ponde and the rest. those who were to have Cowes
delivered heere and fayled must have their monye again, my cosen
[*blank*] of Rattlesden, 20 *li.* I can think of no other, but mrs.
Sandes 15 *li.* Comend me to her, and if you see them at Graces
remember me to them. the Lord blesse you. farewell. your
loving father

                                                JO: WINTHROP.
Sept: 9. 1630.

12.   *John Winthrop to his Wife*

To Mar: Win: the Elder at groton. ddd.

MY SWEET WIFE, The blessinge of the Allmighty be upon thee
and thine for ever.

There is a shipp arrived at Plimmouth, some 30: miles from us,
which came from London the 10th of August, and was twelve
weekes at sea in such tempests, as she spent all her mastes yet
of 60: passingers she lost but one: all the rest (through the Lordes
great mercy) are safe and in health: Edy of Boxted, who came
in her, tould me a fortnight since that he had many lettres in the
shippe for me, but I heer not yet of them: which makes me now
(havinge opportunity to send to Plimmouth) to write these fewe
lines to thee, least the shippe should be gone before I have received
my lettres, and can returne answeare to them. thou shalt understand by this, how it is with us since I wrote last (for this [is]
the 3: or 4th lettre I have written to thee since I came hether) that
thou maiest see the goodnesse of the Lord towardes me, that when
so many have dyed, and many yet languishe, my selfe and my
children are yet livinge and in health, yet I have lost 12: of my
family, viz. Walters and his wife and 2: of his children; mr.
Gager and his man: Smith of Buxall and his wife and 2: children:
the wife of Taylor of Haverill and their childe: my sonne H:

makes the 12. and besides many other of lesse note as Jeff: Ruggles of Sudbury and divers others of that towne (about 20:) the Lord hath stripped us of some principall persons: mr. Johnson and his Lady, mr. Rossiter, mrs. Philips and others unknowne to thee. we conceive that this disease grewe from ill diet at sea and proved infectious. I write not this to discourage thee, but to warne thee and others to provide well for the sea and by Godes helpe the passage wilbe safe and easy how longe soever. be carefull (I intreate thee) to observe the directions in my former lettres, and I trust that, that God, who hath so gratiously preserved and blessed us hetherto, will bringe us to see the faces of each other with abundance of joye. my deare wife, we are heer in a Paradice, though we have not beife and mutton etc: yet (God be praysed) we want them not; our Indian Corne answeares for all, yet heere is foule and fish in great plenty. I will heer breake off, because I hope to receive lettres from thee soone, and to have opportunity of writinge more largely. I will say nothinge of my love to thee, and of my longinge desires towardes thee, thou knowest my heart. neither can I mention salutations to my good freindes, other then in general, in my next I hope to supply all. Now the Lord our good God, be with thee and all my children, and company with thee, Grace and peace be with you all, so I kisse my sweet wife, and all my deare children, and blesse you in the Lord, farewell. Thy faithfull husband

Jo: Winthrop.

Boston in Mattachusets Nov: 29. 1630.

Thou must excuse my not writing to my sonne Jo[hn] and other of my freindes at this tyme, for I deferre it till I receive my lettres.

13. ——— Pond to William Pond*

To my Lovinge Fathere William Ponde at Etherston in Suffolcke give theis

Moste Lovinge and Kinde Father and mother, my humble deuteye remembreid unto you trusteinge in god you are in good

---

* [It is not clear how this letter came to be among the Winthrop papers.]

hellthe and I pray remembr my love unto my Brother Joseife, and thanck him for his kindnes that I found at his hand at London wich wase not the valleu of fardin   I knowe Lovinge father and do confese that I wase an undeuteyefull Cheilld unto you when I liveied withe you and by you for the wiche I am muche sorrowfull and greveid for it trusteinge in god that he will so geide me that I will never offend you so aney more and I truste in god that you will forgive me for it and my wreightein unto you is to lete you undurestand what a cuntrey theis new Eingland is whar we live   her ar but fewoe eingeines and a gret sorte of them deyeid theis winture it wase thought it wase of the plage   thay ar a craftey peple and thaye will cussen and cheat and thay ar a suttell peple and whareas we ded expect gret stor of bever her is littell or non to be had and thar Sackemor John waiethe it and maney of us truck withe them and it leyethe us maney tymes in 8*s* a pound   thay ar proper men and clen Jointeide men and maney of them go nackeid withe a skein abought thare loines but now s[o]me of them get eingellishe menes parell   and the cuntrey is verey rockey and heilley and s[o]me champine ground and the soile is verey flete and her is s[o]mee good ground and marshe ground but her is no myckellmes springe   cattell threive well here but thay give small stor of mylck   the best cattell for proffeit is sweines and a good sweine is her at 5*li* preise and a goote is worthe 3*li* a gadene gote   her is teimbur good store and ackornes good stor and her is good stor of feishe If we had botes to goo 8 or x leges to sea to fishe in   her ar good stor of weield foule but thay ar hard to c[o]me bye   it is hardur to get a shoot then it is in ould eingland   and Peple her ar subgecte to deicesesse for her have deyeid of the skurveye and of the bur[n]inge fever too hundreid and ode   beseides maney leyethe lame and all sudberey men are ded but thre and thee woomen and sume cheilldren   and provisseyones ar her at a wondurfule rat   wheat mell is xiiij*s* a bushell and pese x*s* and mault x*s* and eindey seid wheat is xv*s* and thare other wheat is x*s* buttr xii*d* a pound and chese is 8*d* a pound and all kind of speyseis verey der and allmoste non to be got and if theis ship had not cume when it ded we had bine put to a woonderfule straighte but thanckes be to god for sendinge of it in   I resayveid from the shipe a hogseite of mell and the governer tellethe me of a hundreid waight of chesse the wiche I have resayveid parte of it I humbley thancke you for it I ded expecte too coves the wiche I had non nor I do not arenestly deseyer that you shoold send me aney becauese the cuntrey is not so as we ded expecte it tharefor Lovige father I wolld intret you that you woolld send me a ferckeine of buttr and a hogseit of mault onground for we dreinck notheinge but walltre and a corse clothe of fouer pound preise so it be thicke and for the fraute if you of youer Love will send them I will paye the fraute for her is notheinge to be gote withe ought we had c[o]memodeytes to go up in to the este partes amonckest the eingeines to truck for her whare we live her is no bever and her is no clothe to be had to mack no parell and shoes ar at 5s a payer for me and that clothe that is woorthe 2s 8d a yard is woorthe her 5s so I pray father send me fouer or five yardes of clothe to mack us sume parell and Lov[i]nge fathere thoue I be far disstante from you yet I pray you remembure me as youer cheield and we do not know how longe we may subeseiste for we can not live her witheought provisseyones from ould eingland thare fore I pray do not put away youer shopestufe for I theinck that in the eind if I live it must be my leveinge for we do not know how longe theis plantacyon will stand for s[o]me of the marchantes that ded up hould it have turned of thare men and have givene it overe beseides god hath tacken away the chefeste stud in the land Mr. Johnson and the ladye arabella his wife wiche wase the cheiffeste man of estate in the land and on that woold a don moste good

her cam over xxv passeingares and thare cume backe agayn fouer skore and od parsones and as maney more wolld a cume if thay had whare withe all to bringe them hom for her ar maney that cam over the laste yere wiche wase woorthe too hundreid poundes afore they cam ought of ould eingland that betwine theis and myckellmes wille be hardly worthe xxxli so her we may live if we have suppleyes everey yere from ould eingland other weyse we can not subeseiste I maye as I will worck hard sete an ackorne of eindey wheat and if we do not set it withe fishe and that will coste xxs and if we set it witheought fishe thay shall have but a por crope so father I pray consedre of my cause for her will be but a verey por beinge and no beinge withe ought Lovinge father youer helpe withe provisseyones from ould eingland I had thought to a cam home in theis sheipe for my provisseyones ware all moste

all spente but that I humbley thanck you for youer gret love and
kindnes in sendinge me s[o]me provissyones or elles I shold and
myne a bine half famiuyshed but now I will if it plese god that
I have my hellthe I will plant what corne I can and if provisseyones
be no cheper betwein theis and myckellmes and that I do not her
from you what I wase beste to do I purpose to c[o]me hom at
myckellmes   my wife remembur hur humble deutey unto you and
to my mother and my Love to mye brother Joseife and to Sarey
myler   thus I leve you to the protectyon of Allmytey god
                                                    [*No signature*]
from WALLTUR TOUNE in new eingland
the 15 of marche 1630[/31]

we ware wondurfule seick as we cam at sea withe the small Poxe
no man thought that I and my leittell cheilld woolld a liveid and
my boye is lame and my gurell too and thar deyeid in the sheip
that I cam ine xiiij parsones.

14. *John Winthrop to Margaret Winthrop*

MY DEAR WIFE, I have small hope that this should come to thy
hands, in regard of the longe staye of the shipe heer, so as thou
maiest be well onward of thy waye hether before these can come
to England: therefore I write little to thyselfe and my sonne and
those whom I expect to see heer shortly, if it shall so please the
Lorde. And blessed be his holy and glorious name that he hath
so far magnified his mercy towards us, that when so many have
been layd in their graves since we parted, yet he hath pleased to
preserve us unto this hope of a joyfull meetinge, that we may see
the faces of each other againe, the faces of our children and sweet
babes: these thinges I durst scarce think off heertofore, but now
I embrace them ofte, and delight my heart in them, because I
trust, that the Lord our God, who hath kept me and so many of
my Company in health and safety amonge so many dead Corps,
through the heat of the summer and the Cold of winter, and hath
also preserved thee in the perill of childbirth, and upheld thy
heart in the middest of so many discouragements, with the life of

all thy companye, will of his owne goodnesse and free mercye
preserve us and ours still that we shall meet in joye and peace,
which I dayly pray for, and shall expect in the Lords good tyme:
who still continues his favour and blessinge upon thee and our
sweet babes and all thy companye. For our little daughter, doe
as thou thinkest best. the Lord direct thee in it. if thou bringest
her, she wilbe more trouble to thee in the shipp then all the rest
I knowe my sister wilbe tender of her till I may send for her.
bringe Amy and Anne Gostlin with thee if thou canst. if they
come not, they will much wronge themselves. they need feare
no want here, if they wilbe guided by Gods word: otherwise they
can looke to prosper no where. I prayse God I want nothinge but
thee and the rest of my family: Commend my Love and blessinge
to them all: and to all my neighbours and freinds, but I have
desired my brother Gostlin to performe that. remember to bringe
juice of Limons to sea with thee, for thee and thy company to
eate with your meat as sauce. but of these things my sonne hath
direction: so again I kisse thee my sweet wife and commend thee
and all ours to the Lord, and rest Thine

Jo. Winthrop

March 28, 1631

15. *John Winthrop to John Winthrop, Jr.*

*To my verye lovinge Sonne mr. John Winthrop at London deliver
if he be come away my brother Downing may open this Letter*

My good sonne, The blessinge of the Allmighty be upon thy
soule and life forever.

Amonge many the sweet mercyes of my God towards me in
this strange lande, where we have mett many troubles and adver-
sityes, this is not the least, and that which affords much Comfort
to my heart, that he hath given me a lovinge and dutyfull sonne:
God allsufficient rewarde thee abundantly for all thy Care and
paynes in my Affairs, and for all that Love and dutye thou hast
shewed to thy good mother. I doubt not but thou shalt finde it
in outward blessings, for thou art under the promise of havinge

thy dayes prolonged: but I desire especially thou mayest finde it
in the manifestation of the Goodwill of the Lord towards thee,
and in those sp[irit]uall blessings, which may fatten thy soule.

This shipp stayinge so longe here, I am allmost out of hope
that my Lettres should come to thy hands: for though I thinke
verye longe till I see you all heere, yet I would rather you stayed,
though it were 2 or 3 months, to come with mr. Peirce, partly
because of his skill and Care of his passingers, and partly that we
might be the better provided of housing etc. to entertain you:
for we are much streightned yet that waye, and we have had divers
houses burnt, and now within these two dayes, mr. Sharpe and
mr. Colburne, both of our towne, had their houses burnt to the
ground, and much goods lost: thus it pleaseth the Lord still to
humble us. I doubt not, but he will doe us the more good at
the last.

I have written to your unckle D[owning] concerninge all our
businesse fearing you should be come awaye. I have sent the
Assignment sealed. I lefte all my bonds and writings in my Cup-
bord at Groton, or els at London.

Bringe no provision with you, but meale and pease, and some
otemeale and Sugar, fruit, figges and pepper, and good store of
Saltpeeter, and Conserve of redd roses, and mithridate, good store
of pitche and ordinarye suett, or tallowe. bringe none but wine
vinegar, and not much of that, and be sure that the Caske be good,
store of oyled Calves skins of the largest, and the strongest welt
leather shoes and stockins for Children: and hats of all Syzes. if
you could bring two or three hundred sheepskins and lambs skins
with the wooll on, dyed redd, it would be a good Comodytye
heere, and the coursest woollen clothe (so it be no flockes,) and
of sadd Colours, and some redd, milstones some 2 foot and some
3 foote over, with brasses ready cast and ringes, and mill bills,
store of shoemakers thread, and hobnayles, Chalk and Chalkeline
and a paire of 2 or more of large steele Compasses, store of course
linnen: some birdlime.

When you have cleered all things in England, if you have any
moneye lefte, you may bring some with you, (not above 100*li*) and
the rest leave with your unckle D[owning] or dispose of it as
your owne occasions may require. any wise matt. must have 400*li*
and there wilbe much due to your sister Winthrop which were

best to be left in England. but you must advise with your uncle D[owning] about these things, for I am so full of businesse heere, as I cant think of mine owne affaires as I should. you must allso consider what you would have for your selfe, and how you would imploy it.

I never had lettre yet from your brother F[orth] if he intends to come hether, it were good he solde his lande and payd his sister her 100*li* which he promised when I putt over his lande to him. you shall need bringe no more Cowes for I have enough. The good Lord blesse you and bringe you and all my Company hither in safty   so I rest your lovinge father

JO. WINTHROP

MASSACHUSETTS March 28, 1631

I hope the Lorde hathe provided a good husband for your sister Winthrop. mr. Coddington is well affected to her. if he proceed I wish you to further it, for he is a godly man and of good estate.

16. *John Endecott to John Winthrop*

RIGHT WORSHIPFUL, I did expect to have beene with you in person at the court, and to that end I put to sea yesterday and was driven back againe the wind being stiffe against us. And there being no canoe or boat at Sagust I must have beene constrained to goe to Mistick and thence about to Charles town, which at this time I durst not be so bold, my bodie being at this present in an ill condition to wade or take cold, and therefore I desire you to pardon mee. Though otherwise I could have much desired it, by reason of many occasions and businesses. There are at Mr. Hewson's plantations 5 or 6 kine verie ill and in great danger, I feer they will hardlie escape it, whereof twoe are myne and all I have, which are worse than any of the rest. I left myne there this winter to doe Mr. Skelton a pleasure to keep his for him here at Salem, that he might have the benefit of their milk. And I understand by Wincoll that they have been ill tended and he saith almost starved. Beside they have fed on acornes and they cannot digest them, for that they vomitt exceedinglie and are so bound in their bodies that he is faine to rake them and to use all his skill to maintaine life in them. I have willed him to be there till he can bring them to some strength againe if it be possible. And I have given him malt to make them mashes of licoris and annis seedes, and long pepper, and such other things as I had to drench them. I could wish when Manning hath recovered his strength that you would free him; for he will never doe you or Mr. Hewson service, for when he was well he was as negligent as the worst of them. Mr. Skelton, myselfe and the rest of the congregation desire to be thankfull to God and yourselfe for your benevolence to Mr. Haughton's child. The Lord restore it you. I prevailed with much adoe with Sir Richard for an old debt heere which he thought was desperate, to contribute it, which I hope I shall make good for the child. I think Mr. Skelton hath written to you, whome he thinks stands most in neede of contribution of such provisions as you will be pleased to give amongst us of that which was sent over. The yeele-potts you sent for are made, which I had in my boate, hoping to have brought them with mee. I caused him to make but two for the present, if you like them and his prices (for he worketh for himselfe) you shall have as many as you desire. He selleth them for 4 shillings a pieece. Sir, I desired the rather to have beene at court because I heare I am much com-playned on by goodman Dexter, for striking him. I acknowledge I was too rash in strikeing him, understanding since that it is not lawfull for a justice of peace to strike. But if you had seene the manner of his carriadge, with such daring of mee with his armes on kembow etc. It would have provoked a very patient man But I will write noe more of it but leave it till we speak before you face to face. Onely thus farre further, that he hath given out if I had a purse he would make mee empty it, and if he cannot have justice here he will doe wonders in England, and if he cannot prevale there, hee will trie it out with mee heere at blowes. Sir, I desire that you will take all into consideration. If it were lawfull to trie it at blowes and hee a fitt man for mee to deale with, you should not heare mee complaine; but I hope the Lord hath brought mee off from that course. I thought good further to wryte what my judgment is for the dismissing of the court till corne be sett. It will hinder us that are farre off exceedingly, and not further you there. Mens labour are precious here in corne setting tyme, the

plantations being yet so weak. I will be with you, the Lord assisting mee, as soone as conveniently I can. In the meane while I
committ you to his protection and safeguard that never failes his
children, and rest Your unfeigned loving friend to command

JO: ENDECOTT

SALEM, the 12th of Aprill, 1631

17.   John Winthrop to Sir Simonds D'Ewes

*To the right wor[shi]p[fu]ll his muche honored friend and Cosin
Sir Simeon Dewes at Lavenham in Suff. deliver*

WORTHY SIR, Yours by younge Hamond I received, and cannot
but most thankfully accept your kind remembrance of me, and
your good Affection to this work, which the Lords owne hande hath
begunne and uphelde hetherto, and in the prosperitye whereof,
some blessinge and comforte may redounde to all the Churches
of Christ. For our estate heere both Politick and Eccl[es]ia[stica]ll,
I knowe, you are allreadye sufficiently informed: and althoughe
we cannot professe a perfection in either (which is not to be looked
for in this worlde) yet it is suche, as the Lords holy and wise
servants (suche as he hath vouchsaffed to bestowe upon us both
formerly and now of late) doe approve of, and accordingly doe
joyne with us in the same Course: I meane especially those 2
rever[en]d and faithfull min[iste]rs Mr. Cotton and Mr. Hooker,
who lately arrived heere with their familyes in as good healthe
(praysed be God) as when they came forthe, althoughe Mrs. Cotton was delivered of a sonne at sea, who was since baptised on
shore and named Seaborne.

For your advise about our Affaires, I am muche beholden to
your Care of us, and doe concurre with your opinion in the most,
as our practice dothe declare, and shalbe somewhat rectified by
your advice, at present, and more as our meanes may be enlarged:
but in the last, both our practice and Judgment differ from yours:
but I suppose we should soone be agreed if you were heere to see
the state of things, as we see them: I think not fitt to enter into
particulars because Lettres are subject to miscarrye, but you can

conceive my meaning. I cannot enlarge towards you as your Love
deserves. I hope you will consider my occasions and many Lettres
which I must write. How you should imploye any stock heere,
except you sende some faithfull man to manage it, I cannot advise
you; onely you may drive a trade with the Lord heere, in helping
forwarde the worke of the Gospell, by sending over some poore
godly familyes with a yeares provision, which I account one of the
best workes which may be performed at this season: If you will
please to rayse a Colonye heere in that manner (which would not
be difficult for your self with such godly frends as you may have
to joyn with you) I would take off any further trouble from you
about it, but I leave it to your Consideration. So with my hearty
salutation and due respect to your selfe and your Ladye, I commende you to the Lord and take my leave. I rest Yours to doe you
service in the Lord

JO: WINTHROP

MASSACHUSETTS N: ENG: Sept. 26: 1633

18.   *John Winthrop to Sir Nathaniel Rich*

To his honor[a]ble freind Sir Nath[anie]ll Riche Knight at
Warwick howse in Holburne London deliver

WORTHYE SIR, That you are pleased amonge your many and
weighty imployments to spende so many searious thoughts and
good wishes upon us, and the worke of the Lord in our hands, I
must needs acknowledge it amonge other the speciall favours of
God towards us, and an undoubted testimonye of your sincere
Love towards us: which makes me the more carefull to satisfie
your desire, of beinge truely informed of our estate (this being
the first safe meanes of Conveyance since I received yours in
October last) you may please therefore to understand that first,
for the number of our people, we never took any surveigh of them,
nor doe we intend it, except inforced through urgent occasion
(Davids example stickes somewhat with us) but I esteeme them
to be in all about 4000 soules and upwarde: in good health (for

the most parte) and well provided of all necessaryes: so as
(through the Lords speciall providence) there hath not died above
2 or 3 growne persons, and about so many Children all the last
yeare, it being verye rare to heare of any sick of agues or other
diseases, nor have I knowne of any quartan Ague amonge us since
I came into the Countrye. For Our subsistence heere, the meanes
hetherto hath beene the yearly access of new Commers, who have
supplied all our wants, for Cattle, and the fruits of our labours,
as boarde, pale, smithes work etc: if this should faile, then have
we other meanes which may supple us, as fishe, viz: Codd, basse
and herringe, for which no place in the world exceeds us, if we
can compass salt at reasonable rate: our grounds likewise are
apt for hempe and flaxe and rape seeds, and all sorts of rootes
pumpins and other fruits, which for tast and wholesomeness far
excede those in England: our grapes allso (wherewith the Countrye
abonds) afford a good harde wine. Our ploughes goe on with
good successe, we are like to have 20 at worke next yeare: our
lands are aptest for Rye and oats. Our winters are sharpe and
longe, I may reckon 4 monthes for storeing of Cattle, but we find
no difference whither they be housed or goe abroad: our summers
are somewhat more fervent in heat then in England. Our Civill
Government is mixt: the freemen choose the magistrats everye
yeare (and for the present they have chosen Tho: Dudly esqr.
Governour) and at 4 Courts in the yeare 3 out of each towne
(there being 8 in all) doe assist the magistrats in making of lawes,
imposing taxes, and disposing of lands: our Juries are chosen by
the freemen of everye towne. Our Churches are governed by
Pastors, Teachers ruling Elders and Deacons, yet the power lies
in the wholl Congregation and not in the Presbitrye further then
for order and precedencye. For the natives, they are neere all dead
of the small Poxe, so as the Lord hathe cleared our title to what
we possess. I shall now acquaint you with a sadd accident which
lately fell out between our neighbours of Plimouth and some of
the Lorde Saye his servants at Pascat[aqua] They of Pl[imouth]
having engrossed all the Cheif places of trade in N: E: viz: Kenebeck, Penobscott, Narigancet, and Conecticott, have erected trading
houses in all of them. The Lords Pinace going with 3 men and
a boye to trade at Kenebeck, were forbidden, and persisting in
their purpose 2 of the magistrats of Pl[imouth] viz: Jo: Alden

and Jo: Howlande and about 9 more, came up to them in their
pinace and sent 3 men in a Canoe to cutt the Cables of the
Pas[cataqua] pinace (her master one Hockin having given them
provoking speeches) and stood in their owne pinace with their
peeces charged and ready to shoote: after they had cutt one Cable,
Hockin came up, and asked them if they ment to caste away his
vessell etc: and sware withall that he would kill him that should
come to cutt the other: whereupon (the Canoa being driven away
with the strength of the streame) they took out him that steered
her and putt in another, and sent them againe to cutt the other
Cable, which while one was doeing, (for it was cutt) Hockin shott
one of them in the Canoa dead, upon which one of pl[imouth]
men out of their Pinace shott at Hockin and killed him upon the
place, wherupon another of Hockins company coming up upon
the decke one of Pl[imouth] men asked Howland if he should
kill him allso, but he forbade him saying he feard there had been
too many killed allready: the pinace being then driven on shoare
and in danger, the Pl[imouth] men saved her, and putt one
of their own men into her to carry her homewards toward
Pasc[ataqua] upon the reporte of this we were muche greived, that
suche an occasion should be offerd to our enemys to reproache our
profession and that suche an injurye should be offered to those
hon[our]able persons who for love of us and for furtherance of
our beginnings here, had so farre eng[aged] themselv[es] with
us, so as we wrote to them to knowe the truethe of the matter, and
whither they would advowe it: the wrote to us againe relatinge
the matter in effecte as I have expressed, with justification of the
facte etc: yet declaringe their sorrowe, that it had hapned so sadlye,
otherwise then they intended: but they did not doubt but their
Grant would beare them out: upon this, we refuse to holde communion with them, till they give better satisfaction, and havinge
the said Alden before us, at a gen[era]l Court, we took security
of him for his forthcoming and wrote to them what and wherefore we had done it: and upon their answeare, that themselves
would doe justice in the Cause, we remitted him to them, as having
no jurisdiction in it, to trye it ourselves. All that we ayme at is
that they may come to see their sinne and repente of it: which if
they shall doe, I would intreat you to intercede with the Lords for
them, that the injury and discourtesy may be passed by, upon such

satisfaction as they can make. I can think of nothing more at present to acquaint you with: so desiringe the continuance of your care and prayers for us, as we wish and rejoyce in the successe of your like undertakings to the Southward I take leave and rest Yours ever to be Commanded in the Lord

JO: WINTHROP

BOSTON MASSACHU[SE]TS N: E: May 22, 1634
heere are 6 shipps lately arived with passengers and Cattle, most of them came in 6 weekes space   we have setled a plantation 20 miles to the northward, neere Merimacke. Mr. Parker is to be minister there.

5

Records of the Massachusetts
Bay Company

The Massachusetts Bay Company traced its ancestry to a company of English merchants known as the Dorchester Adventurers, which had founded a fishing settlement on Cape Ann in 1623. The company had been authorized to make the settlement by the Council for New England, a group of merchants, gentlemen, and noblemen to whom King James I had given the whole of New England in 1620. When the fishing at Cape Ann proved unsuccessful financially, the Dorchester Adventurers sold their claims to a new group of investors, known as the New England Company, most of whose members came from London and East Anglia. This group, after obtaining a charter of its own from the Council for New England in 1628, consolidated its position still further in the following year by securing another charter directly from the king, by which it became known as the Massachusetts Bay Company. The manner in which the royal charter was obtained is not clear, but what it said and what the members of the company did with it are a matter of record.

When that record was first published (*The Records of the Governor and Company of the Massachusetts Bay in New England,* Nathaniel B. Shurtleff, ed. [5 vols., Boston, 1853–54]), special type was cast in order to reproduce the abbreviations that are found in all seventeenth-century manuscripts. Modern editors have abandoned such attempts to reproduce the appearance of a manuscript in print. In the succeeding pages are printed the text of the royal charter and the records of the company through May 14, 1634, with most of the abbreviations expanded, from Volume I, pages 3–121, 361–369, and 383–409.

The original spelling and punctuation have been retained, except that modern usage has been followed in the spelling of expanded abbreviations and in the transcription of the letters *i, j, u,* and *v.* Abbreviations in common use today have been retained, as have the abbreviations of first names in which the first few letters of the name are followed by a colon. Brackets around words or letters indicate that the reading of these in the manuscript is doubtful. Words that are bracketed *and* italicized are interlineations in the manuscript.

A blank space indicates a blank in the manuscript, and the italic letter *x* indicates a lost or illegible word. The letter *x* may also, however, be the roman numeral for ten. The context will in every case indicate which use of *x* is intended. Where Roman numerals are used to designate sums of money, the abbreviations for pound, shilling, and penny (£, *s, d*) have been expanded; but where figures are given in Arabic numerals, these abbreviations have been retained, and the pound sign has been placed in front of the numeral, rather than after it.

Additions to the manuscript made at a date subsequent to 1634, including marginal summaries of the entries, have been omitted. As in the original publication of the records, lists of persons admitted to freemanship have been placed at the end, along with the letters written in 1629 by the company to the settlers. The explanatory footnotes have been adapted from those of the original editor, Nathaniel B. Shurtleff.

The Charter
of the
Colony of the Massachusetts Bay
in New England.
1628–29.

CHARLES, BY THE GRACE OF GOD, Kinge of England, Scotland, Fraunce, and Ireland, Defendor of the Fayth, etc., To ALL to whome theis Presentes shall come, Greeting. WHEREAS our most deare and royall father Kinge James, of blessed memory, by his Highness letters patentes beareing date at Westminster the third day of November, in the eighteenth yeare of his raigne, HATH given and graunted unto the Councell established at Plymouth in the County of Devon, for the planting, ruling, ordering, and governing of Newe England in America, and to their successors and assignes for ever: All that parte of America lyeing and being in bredth from forty degrees of northerly latitude from the equi-

noctiall lyne, to forty eight degrees of the saide northerly latitude
inclusively, and in length of and within all the breadth aforesaid
throughout the maine landes from sea to sea, together, also, with
all the firme landes, soyles, groundes, havens, portes, rivers, waters,
fishing, mynes, and myneralls, aswell royall mynes of gould and
silver, as other mynes and myneralls, precious stones, quarries,
and all and singuler other commodities, jurisdictions, royalties,
priviledges, franchesies, and prehemynences, both within the said
tract of lande upon the mayne, and also within the islandes and
seas adjoining: PROVIDED alwayes, That the saide islandes or any
the premises by the said letters patentes intended and meant to be
graunted were not then actuallie possessed or inhabited by any
other Christian Prince or State, nor within the boundes, lymittes,
or territories of the Southerne Colony then before graunted by
our said deare father, to be planted by divers of his loveing subjectes in the south partes. TO HAVE and to houlde, possesse, and
enjoy all and singuler the aforesaid continent, landes, territories,
islands, hereditamentes, and precinctes, seas, waters, fishinges, with
all and all manner their commodities, royalties, liberties, prehemynences, and profittes that should from thenceforth arise from
thence, with all and singuler their appurtenances, and every parte
and parcell thereof, unto the saide Councell and their successors
and assignes for ever, To the sole and proper use, benefitt, and
behoofe of them the saide Councell and their successors and
assignes for ever: To be houlden of our saide most deare and
royall father, his heires, and successors, as of his mannor of
Eastgreenewich, in the County of Kent, in free and common
Soccage, and not in Capite nor by Knightes Service. YEILDINGE
and paying therefore to the saide late Kinge, his heires, and successors the fifte parte of the oare of gould and silver which should,
from tyme to tyme, and at all tymes then after, happen to be found,
gotten, had, and obteyned in, att, or within any of the saide landes,
lymyttes, territories, and precinctes, or in or within any parte or
parcell thereof, for or in respect of all and all manner of duties,
demaunds, and services whatsoever to be don, made, or paide to
our saide dear father, the late Kinge, his heires, and successors,
As in and by the saide letters patentes (amongest sundrie other
clauses, powers, priviledges, and grauntes therein conteyned) more
at large appeareth. AND WHEREAS the saide Councell, established

at Plymouth, in the County of Devon, for the plantinge, ruling, ordering, and governing of Newe England in America, have, by their deede, indented under their common seale, bearing date the nyneteenth day of March last past, in the third yeare of our raigne, given, graunted, bargained, soulde, enfeoffed, aliened, and confirmed to Sir Henry Rosewell, Sir John Young, knightes, Thomas Southcott, John Humphrey, John Endecott, and Symon Whetcombe, their heires and associates for ever, All that parte of Newe England in America aforesaid which lyes and extendes betweene a greate river there commonlie called Monomack, alias Merriemack, and a certen other river there called Charles river, being in the bottome of a certayne bay there commonlie called Massachusettes, alias Mattachusettes, alias Massatusettes bay, and also all and singuler those landes and hereditamentes whatsoever lyeing within the space of three English myles on the south parte of the saide Charles river, or of any or everie parte thereof: And also all and singuler the landes and hereditamentes whatsoever, lyeing and being within the space of three English myles to the southwarde of the southermost parte of the saide bay, called Massachusettes, alias Mattachusetes, alias Massatusetes bay: And also all those landes and hereditamentes whatsoever which lye and be within the space of three English myles to the northward of the saide river called Monomack, alias Merrymack, or to the northward of any and every parte thereof: And all landes and hereditamentes whatsoever, lyeing within the lymyttes aforesaide, north and south, in latitude and bredth, and in length and longitude, of and within all the bredth aforesaide, throughout the mayne landes there, from the Atlantick and westerne sea and ocean on the east parte, to the south sea on the west parte, and all landes and groundes, place and places, soyles, woodes and wood groundes, havens, portes, rivers, waters, fishinges, and hereditamentes whatsoever, lyeing within the said boundes and lymyttes, and everie parte and parcell thereof: And also all islandes lyeing in America aforesaide, in the saide seas, or either of them, on the westerne or easterne coastes or partes of the saide tractes of lande by the saide indenture mentioned to be given, graunted, bargained, sould, enfeoffed, aliened, and confirmed, or any of them: And also all mynes and myneralls, as well royall mynes of gould and silver, as other mynes and myneralls whatsoever in the saide landes and premisses, or any parte thereof: And all jurisdictions, rightes, royalties, liberties, freedomes, ymmunities, priviledges, franchises, preheminences, and commodities whatsoever, which they, the saide Councell, established at Plymouth, in the County of Devon, for the planting, ruling, ordering, and governing of Newe England in America, then had or might use, exercise, or enjoy in and within the saide landes and premisses by the saide indenture mentioned to be given, graunted, bargained, sould, enfeoffed, and confirmed, or in or within any parte or parcell thereof. TO HAVE and to hould the saide parte of Newe England in America which lyes and extendes and is abutted as aforesaide, and every parte and parcell thereof: And all the saide islandes, rivers, portes, havens, waters, fishinges, mynes and mineralls, jurisdictions, franchises, royalties, liberties, priviledges, commodities, hereditamentes, and premisses whatsoever, with the appurtenances, unto the saide Sir Henry Rosewell, Sir John Younge, Thomas Southcott, John Humfrey, John Endecott, and Simon Whetcombe, their heires and assignes, and their associattes, to the onlie proper and absolute use and behoofe of the said Sir Henry Rosewell, Sir John Younge, Thomas Southcott, John Humfrey, John Endecott, and Symon Whettcombe, their heires and assignes, and their associattes, for evermore. TO BE HOULDEN of us, our heires and successors, as of our mannor of Eastgreenewich, in the County of Kent, in free and common Socage, and not in Capite, nor by knightes service, YEILDING and payeing therefore unto us, our heires and successors, the fifte parte of the oare of goulde and silver which shall, from tyme to tyme, and all tymes hereafter, happen to be founde, gotten, had, and obteyned in any of the saide landes within the saide lymyttes, or in or within any parte thereof, for and in satisfaction of all manner duties, demaunds, and services whatsoever, to be donn, made, or paid to us, our heires or successors, as in and by the said recited indenture more at large maie appeare. NOWE knowe yee, that wee, at the humble suite and petition of the saide Sir Henry Rosewell, Sir John Younge, Thomas Southcott, John Humfrey, John Endecott, and Simon Whetcombe, and of others whome they have associated unto them, HAVE, for divers good causes and considerations us moveing, graunted and confirmed, And by theis presentes of our especiall grace, certen knowledge, and meere motion, doe graunt and confirme unto the saide Sir Henry Rosewell, Sir John

Younge, Thomas Southcott, John Humfrey, John Endecott, and Simon Whetcombe, and to their associates hereafter named, (videlicet,) Sir Richard Saltonstall, knight, Isaack Johnson, Samuel Aldersey, John Ven, Mathew Cradock, George Harwood, Increase Nowell, Richard Perry, Richard Bellingham, Nathaniell Wright, Samuell Vassall, Theophilus Eaton, Thomas Goffe, Thomas Adams, John Browne, Samuell Browne, Thomas Hutchins, William Vassall, William Pinchion, and George Foxcrofte, their heires and assignes, All the saide parte of Newe England in America, lyeing and extending betweene the boundes and lymittes in the said recited indenture expressed, and all landes and groundes, place and places, soyles, woodes and wood groundes, havens, portes, rivers, waters, mynes, mineralls, jurisdictions, rightes, royalties, liberties, freedomes, immunities, priviledges, franchises, preheminences, hereditamentes, and commodities whatsoever to them the saide Sir Henry Rosewell, Sir John Younge, Thomas Southcott, John Humfrey, John Endecott, and Simon Whetcombe, their heires and assignes, and to their associattes, by the saide recited indenture given, graunted, bargayned, solde, enfeoffed, aliened, and confirmed, or mentioned or intended thereby to be given, graunted, bargayned, sold, enfeoffed, aliened, and confirmed. TO HAVE and to hould the saide parte of Newe England in America, and other the premisses hereby mentioned to be graunted and confirmed, and every parte and parcell thereof, with the appurtenances, to the saide Sir Henry Rosewell, Sir John Yonge, Sir Richard Saltonstall, Thomas Southcott, John Humfrey, John Endecott, Simon Whetcombe, Isaack Johnson, Samuell Aldersey, John Ven, Mathewe Cradock, George Harwood, Increase Nowell, Richard Pery, Richard Bellingham, Nathaniell Wright, Samuell Vassall, Theophilus Eaton, Thomas Goffe, Thomas Adams, John Browne, Samuell Browne, Thomas Hutchins, William Vassall, William Pinchion, and George Foxcrofte, their heires and assignes for ever, to their onlie proper and absolute use and behoofe for evermore. To be holden of us, our heires and successors, as of our mannor of Eastgreenewich aforesaid, in free and common Socage, and not in Capite nor by knightes service, AND ALSO YEILDING and paying therefore to us, our heires and successors, the fifte parte onlie of all oare of gould and silver, which, from tyme to tyme, and att all tymes hereafter, shalbe there gotten, had, or obteyned, for all services, exactions, and demaunds whatsoever, according to the tenure and reservation in the said recited indenture expressed. AND FURTHER knowe yee, That, of our more especiall grace, certen knowledg, and meere motion, Wee have given and graunted, And by theis presentes doe for us, our heires and successors, give and graunt unto the said Sir Henry Rosewell, Sir John Younge, Sir Richard Saltonstall, Thomas Southcott, John Humfrey, John Endecott, Symon Whetcombe, Isaack Johnson, Samuell Aldersey, John Ven, Mathewe Cradock, George Harwood, Increase Nowell, Richard Pery, Richard Bellingham, Nathaniel Wright, Samuell Vassall, Theophilus Eaton, Thomas Goffe, Thomas Adams, John Browne, Samuell Browne, Thomas Hutchins, William Vassall, William Pinchion, and George Foxcrofte, their heires and assignes, All that parte of Newe England in America which lyes and extendes betweene a great river there commonlie called Monomack river, alias Merrimack river, and a certen other river there called Charles river, being in the bottome of a certen bay there commonlie called Massachusettes, alias Mattachusettes, alias Massatusettes bay: And also all and singuler those landes and hereditamentes whatsoever, lyeing within the space of three Englishe myles on the south parte of the saide river called Charles river, or of any or every parte thereof: And also all and singuler the landes and hereditamentes whatsoever lyeing and being within the space of three Englishe myles to the southward of the southermost parte of the said baye called Massachusettes, alias Mattachusettes, alias Massatusetes bay: And also all those landes and hereditamentes whatsoever which lye and be within the space of three English myles to the northward of the saide river called Monomack, alias Merrymack, or to the norward of any and every parte thereof, and all landes and hereditamentes whatsoever, lyeing within the lymittes aforesaide, north and south, in latitude and bredth, and in length and longitude, of and within all the bredth aforesaide, throughout the mayne landes there from the Atlantick and westerne sea and ocean on the east parte, to the south sea on the west parte: And all landes and groundes, place and places, soyles, woodes and wood groundes, havens, portes, rivers, waters, and hereditamentes whatsoever, lyeing within the said boundes and lymyttes, and every parte and parcell thereof, and also all islandes in America aforesaide, in the saide seas, or either of them, on the westerne or easterne coastes, or partes of the saide tractes of landes hereby mentioned to be given and graunted, or any of them, and all mynes and myneralls, aswell royall mynes of gould and silver as other mynes and myneralls whatsoever, in the said landes and premisses, or any parte thereof, and free libertie of fishing in or within any the rivers or waters within the boundes and lymyttes aforesaid, and the seas thereunto adjoining: And all fishes, royal fishes, whales, balan, sturgions, and other fishes, of what kinde or nature soever that shall at any tyme hereafter be taken in or within the saide seas or waters, or any of them, by the said Sir Henry Rosewell, Sir John Younge, Sir Richard Saltonstall, Thomas Southcott, John Humfrey, John Endecott, Simon Whetcombe, Isaack Johnson, Samuell Aldersey, John Ven, Mathewe Cradock, George Harwood, Increase Noell, Richard Pery, Richard Bellingham, Nathaniell Wright, Samuell Vassall, Theophilus Eaton, Thomas Goffe, Thomas Adams, John Browne, Samuell Browne, Thomas Hutchins, William Vassall, William Pinchion, and George Foxcrofte, their heires and assignes, or by any other person or persons whatsoever there inhabiting, by them, or any of them, to be appointed to fishe therein. PROVIDED, alwayes, that yf the said landes, islandes, or any other the premisses herein before mentioned, and by theis presentes intended and meant to be graunted, were, at the tyme of the graunting of the saide former letters patentes, dated the third day of November, in the eighteenth yeare of our said deare fathers raigne aforesaide, actuallie possessed or inhabited by any other Christian Prince or State, or were within the boundes, lymyttes, or territories of that Southerne Colony then before graunted by our said late father to be planted by divers of his loveing subjectes in the south partes of America, That then this present graunt shall not extend to any such partes or parcells thereof, soe formerly inhabited or lyeing within the boundes of the southerne plantation as aforesaide, but as to those partes or parcells soe possessed or inhabited by such Christian Prince or State, or being within the bounders aforesaid, shalbe utterly voyd, theis presentes or any thinge therein conteyned to the contrarie notwithstanding. TO HAVE and to hould, possesse and enjoy the saide partes of Newe England in America, which lye, extend, and are abutted as aforesaide, and every parte and parcell thereof: And all the islandes, rivers, portes, havens, waters, fishinges, fishes, mynes, myneralls, jurisdictions, franchises, royalties, liberties, priviledges, commodities, and premisses whatsoever, with the appurtenances, unto the said Sir Henry Rosewell, Sir John Younge, Sir Richard Saltonstall, Thomas Southcott, John Humfrey, John Endecott, Simon Whetcombe, Isaack Johnson, Samuell Aldersey, John Ven, Mathewe Cradock, George Harwood, Increase Nowell, Richard Perry, Richard Bellingham, Nathaniell Wright, Samuell Vassall, Theophilus Eaton, Thomas Goffe, Thomas Adams, John Browne, Samuell Browne, Thomas Hutchins, William Vassall, William Pinchion, and George Foxcroft, their heires and assignes forever, to the onlie proper and absolute use and behoufe of the said Sir Henry Rosewell, Sir John Younge, Sir Richard Saltonstall, Thomas Southcott, John Humfrey, John Endecott, Simon Whetcombe, Isaac Johnson, Samuell Aldersey, John Ven, Mathewe Cradocke, George Harwood, Increase Nowell, Richard Pery, Richard Bellingham, Nathaniell Wright, Samuell Vassall, Theophilus Eaton, Thomas Goffe, Thomas Adams, John Browne, Samuell Browne, Thomas Hutchins, William Vassall, William Pinchion, and George Foxcroft, their heires and assignes forevermore. TO BE HOLDEN of us, our heires and successors, as of our mannor of Eastgreenewich, in our Countie of Kent, within our realme of England, in free and common soccage, and not in Capite nor by knightes service, and also yeilding and paying therefore to us, our heires and successors, the fifte parte onlie of all oare of gould and silver which, from tyme to tyme, and at all tymes hereafter, shalbe there gotten, had, or obteyned for all services exactions, and demaundes whatsoever. PROVIDED alwaies, and our expresse will and meaninge is, That onlie one fifte parte of the gould and silver oare abovementioned in the whole, and noe more be reserved or payeable unto us, our heires and successors, by collour or vertue of theis presentes. The double reservations or recitalls aforesaid, or any thinge herein conteyned, notwithstanding. AND FORASMUCH as the good and prosperous successe of the plantation of the saide partes of Newe England aforesaide intended by the said Sir Henry Rosewell, Sir John Younge, Sir Richard Saltonstall, Thomas Southcott, John Humfrey, John Endecott Simon Whetcombe, Isaack Johnson, Samuell Aldersey, John Ven Mathewe Cradock, George Harwood, Increase Noell, Richard Pery Richard Bellingham, Nathaniell Wright, Samuell Vassall, Theophi

lus Eaton, Thomas Goffe, Thomas Adams, John Browne, Samuell
Browne, Thomas Hutchins, William Vassall, William Pinchion,
and George Foxcrofte, to be speedily sett upon, cannot but cheifly
depend, next under the blessing of Almightie God and the support
of our royall authoritie, upon the good government of the same,
To the ende that the affaires and busyssinesses which, from tyme
to tyme, shall happen and arise concerning the saide landes and
the plantation of the same, maie be the better mannaged and
ordered. WEE HAVE FURTHER hereby, of our especiall grace, certen
knowledge, and meere motion, given, graunted, and confirmed,
And for us, our heires and successors, doe give, graunt, and confirme unto our saide trustie and welbeloved subjectes, Sir Henry
Rosewell, Sir John Younge, Sir Richard Saltonstall, Thomas South-
cott, John Humfrey, John Endicott, Simon Whetcombe, Isaack
Johnson, Samuell Aldersey, John Ven, Mathewe Cradock, George
Harwood, Increase Nowell, Richard Pery, Richard Bellingham,
Nathaniell Wright, Samuel Vassall, Theophilus Eaton, Thomas
Goffe, Thomas Adams, John Browne, Samuell Browne, Thomas
Hutchins, William Vassall, William Pinchion, and George Fox-
crofte: AND for us, our heires and successors, wee will and ordeyne,
That the saide Sir Henry Rosewell, Sir John Yong, Sir Richard
Saltonstall, Thomas Southcott, John Humfrey, John Endicott,
Symon Whetcombe, Isaack Johnson, Samuell Aldersey, John Ven,
Mathewe Cradock, George Harwood, Increase Noell, Richard
Pery, Richard Bellingham, Nathaniell Wright, Samuell Vassall,
Theophilus Eaton, Thomas Goffe, Thomas Adams, John Browne,
Samuell Browne, Thomas Hutchins, William Vassall, William
Pinchion, and George Foxcrofte, and all such others as shall here-
after be admitted and made free of the Company and Society
hereafter mentioned, shall, from tyme to tyme, and at all tymes
for ever hereafter, be, by vertue of theis presentes, one body
corporate and politique in fact and name, by the name of the Governor and Company of the Mattachusettes Bay in Newe England:
And them by the name of the Governor and Company of the
Mattachusettes Bay in Newe England, one bodie politique and
corporate in deede, fact, and name, Wee doe for us, our heires
and successors, make, ordeyne, constitute, and confirme by theis
presentes, and that by that name they shall have perpetuall succes-
sion: And that by the same name they and their successors shall,

and maie be capeable and enabled, aswell to implead and to be impleaded, and to prosecute, demaund, and aunswere, and be aunsweared unto, in all and singuler suites, causes, quarrells, and actions of what kinde or nature soever. And also to have, take possesse, acquire, and purchase any landes, tenementes, or heredi-tamentes, or any goodes or chattells, And the same to lease, graunt. demise, alien, bargaine, sell, and dispose of as other our liege people of this our realme of England, or any other corporation or body politique of the same maie lawfullie doe: AND, FURTHER, that the said Governor and Companye and their successors maie have for ever one common seale, to be used in all causes and occasions of the said Company, and the same seale maie alter, chaunge, breake, and newe make, from tyme to tyme, at their pleasures. AND OUR will and pleasure is, And wee doe hereby for us, our heires and successors, ordeyne and graunte, That, from henceforth for ever, there shalbe one Governor, one Deputy Gov-ernor, and eighteene Assistantes of the same Company, to be from tyme to tyme constituted, elected, and chosen out of the freemen of the saide Company, for the tyme being, in such manner and forme as hereafter in theis presentes is expressed. Which said officers shall applie themselves to take care for the best disposeing and ordering of the generall buysines and affaires of, for, and concerning the saide landes and premisses hereby mentioned to be graunted, and the plantacion thereof, and the government of the people there. AND FOR the better execution of our royall pleasure and graunte in this behalf, WEE doe, by theis presentes, for us, our heires and successors, nominate, ordeyne, make, and constitute our welbeloved the saide Mathewe Cradocke to be the first and present Governor of the said Company, and the saide Thomas Goffe to be Deputy Governor of the saide Company, and the saide Sir Richard Saltonstall, Isaack Johnson, Samuell Aldersey, John Ven, John Humfrey, John Endecott, Simon Whetcombe, Increase Noell, Richard Pery, Nathaniell Wright, Samuell Vas-sall, Theophilus Eaton, Thomas Adams, Thomas Hutchins, John Browne, George Foxcrofte, William Vassall, and William Pin-chion to be the present Assistantes of the saide Company, to continue in the saide severall offices respectivelie for such tyme and in such manner as in and by theis presentes is hereafter declared and appointed. AND, FURTHER, wee will, and by theis presentes for us, our heires and successors, doe ordeyne and graunt, That the Governor of the saide Company, for the tyme being, or in his absence, by occasion of sicknes or otherwise, the Deputie Governor, for the tyme being, shall have authoritie, from tyme to tyme, upon all occasions, to give order for the assembling of the saide Company, and calling them together to consult and advise of the businesses and affaires of the saide Company. And that the said Governor, Deputie Governor, and Assistantes of the saide Company, for the tyme being, shall or maie once every moneth, or oftener at their pleasures, assemble, and houlde, and keepe a Courte or Assemblie of themselves, for the better ordering and directing of their affaires. And that any seaven or more persons of the Assistantes, togither with the Governor or Deputie Governor, soe assembled, shalbe saide, taken, held, and reputed to be, and shalbe, a full and sufficient Courte or Assemblie of the saide Company for the handling, ordering, and dispatching of all such buysinesses and occurrentes as shall, from tyme to tyme, happen touching or concerning the said Company or plantation, and that there shall or maie be held and kept by the Governor or Deputie Governor of the said Company, and seaven or more of the said Assistantes, for the tyme being, upon every last Wednesday in Hillary, Easter, Trinity, and Michas termes respectivelie for ever, one greate, generall, and solempe Assemblie, which foure Generall Assemblies shalbe stiled and called the Foure Greate and Generall Courtes of the saide Company: IN all and every or any of which saide Great and Generall Courtes soe assembled, WEE DOE, for us, our heires and successors, give and graunte to the said Governor and Company, and their successors, That the Governor, or, in his absence, the Deputie Governor, of the saide Company for the tyme being, and such of the Assistantes and freemen of the saide Company as shalbe present, or the greater nomber of them soe assembled, whereof the Governor or Deputie Governor and six of the Assistantes, at the least to be seaven, shall have full power and authoritie to choose, nominate, and appointe such and soe many others as they shall thinke fitt, and that shall be willing to accept the same, to be free of the said Company and Body, and them into the same to admitt, and to elect and constitute such officers as they shall thinke fitt and requisite for the ordering, mannaging, and dispatching of the affaires of the saide Governor

and Company and their successors, And to make lawes and ordinances for the good and welfare of the saide Company, and for
the government and ordering of the saide landes and plantation,
and the people inhabiting and to inhabite the same, as to them
from tyme to tyme shalbe thought meete. Soe as such lawes and
ordinances be not contrarie or repugnant to the lawes and statutes
of this our realme of England. AND our will and pleasure is, And
wee doe hereby for us, our heires and successors, establish and
ordeyne, That yearely once in the yeare for ever hereafter, namely,
the last Wednesday in Easter tearme yearely, the Governor, Deputy Governor, and Assistantes of the said Company, and all other
officers of the saide Company, shalbe, in the Generall Court or
Assembly to be held for that day or tyme, newly chosen for the
yeare ensueing by such greater parte of the said Company for the
tyme being, then and there present, as is aforesaide. AND YF it
shall happen the present Governor, Deputy Governor, and Assistantes by theis presentes appointed, or such as shall hereafter be
newly chosen into their roomes, or any of them, or any other of
the officers to be appointed for the said Company, to dye or to be
removed from his or their severall offices or places before the saide
generall day of election, (whome wee doe hereby declare for any
misdemeanor or defect to be removeable by the Governor, Deputie
Governor, Assistantes, and Company, or such greater parte of them
in any of the publique Courtes to be assembled as is aforesaid,)
That then, and in every such case, it shall and maie be lawfull to
and for the Governor, Deputie Governor, Assistantes, and Company aforesaide, or such greater parte of them soe to be assembled
as is aforesaide, in any of their assemblies, to proceade to a newe
election of one or more others of their Company in the roome or
place, roomes or places, of such officer or officers soe dyeing or
removed, according to their discretions. And ymmediatly upon
and after such election and elections made of such Governor,
Deputie Governor, Assistant or Assistantes, or any other officer
of the saide Company in manner and forme aforesaid, the authoritie, office, and power before given to the former Governor,
Deputie Governor, or other officer and officers soe removed, in
whose steede and place newe shalbe soe chosen, shall, as to him,
and them, and everie of them, cease and determine. PROVIDED,
also, and our will and pleasure is, That aswell such as are by theis

presentes appointed to be the present Governor, Deputie Governor, and Assistantes of the said Company as those that shall succeed them, and all other officers to be appointed and chosen as aforesaid, shall, before they undertake the execution of their saide offices and places, respectivelie take their corporall oathes for the due and faithfull performance of their duties in their severall offices and places, before such person or persons as are by theis presentes hereunder appointed to take and receive the same; That is to saie, the saide Mathewe Cradock, whoe is hereby nominated and appointed the present Governor of the saide Company, shall take the saide oathes before one or more of the Masters of our Courte of Chauncery for the tyme being, unto which Master or Masters of the Chauncery Wee doe, by theis presentes, give full power and authoritie to take and administer the said oathe to the said Governor accordinglie. And after the saide Governor shalbe soe sworne, then the said Deputy Governor and Assistantes, before by theis presentes nominated and appointed, shall take the said severall oathes to their offices and places respectivelie belonging before the said Mathew Cradock, the present Governor, soe formerlie sworne as aforesaide. And every such person as shallbe, at the tyme of the annuall election, or otherwise upon death or removeall, be appointed to be the newe Governor of the said Company, shall take the oathes to that place belonging before the Deputy Governor or two of the Assistantes of the said Company, at the least, for the tyme being. And the newe elected Deputie Governor and Assistantes, and all other officers to be hereafter chosen as aforesaide, from tyme to tyme, to take the oathes to their places respectivelie belonging before the Governor of the said Company for the tyme being. Unto which said Governor, Deputie Governor, and Assistantes, Wee doe by theis presents give full power and authoritie to give and administer the said oathes respectively, according to our true meaning hearein before declared, without any commission or further warrant to be had and obteyned of us, our heires or successors in that behalf. AND WEE DOE FURTHER, of our especiall grace, certen knowledge, and meere motion, for us, our heires and successors, give and graunte to the said Governor and Company, and their successors for ever, by theis presentes, That it shalbe lawfull and free for them and their assignes, at all and every tyme and tymes hereafter, out of any our realmes or domynions whatsoever, to take, leade, carry, and transport for and into their voyages, and for and towardes the said plantation in Newe England, all such and soe many of our loving subjectes, or any other strangers that will become our loving subjectes, and live under our allegiance, as shall willinglie accompany them in the same voyages and plantation, and also shipping, armour, weapons, ordinance, munition, powder, shott, corne, victualls, and all manner of clothing, implementes, furniture, beastes, cattle, horses, mares, marchandizes, and all other thinges necessarie for the saide plantation, and for their use and defence, and for trade with the people there, and in passing and returning to and fro, any lawe or statute to the contrarie hereof in any wise notwithstanding, and without payeing or yeilding any custome or subsedie either inward or outward to us, our heires or successors, for the same, by the space of seaven yeares from the day of the date of theis presentes. PROVIDED, that none of the saide persons be such as shalbe hereafter by especiall name restrayned by us, our heires or successors. AND for their further encouragement, Of our especiall grace and favor, wee doe by theis presentes for us, our heires and successors, yeild and graunt to the saide Governor and Company, and their successors, and every of them, their factors and assignes, That they and every of them shalbe free and quitt from all taxes, subsidies, and customes in Newe England for the like space of seaven yeares, and from all taxes and impositions for the space of twenty and one yeares upon all goodes and merchandises at any tyme or tymes hereafter, either upon importation thither, or exportation from thence into our realme of England, or into any other our domynions, by the said Governor and Company, and their successors, their deputies, factors, and assignes, or any of them, EXCEPT onlie the five poundes per centum due for custome upon all such goodes and merchandizes, as after the saide seaven yeares shalbe expired shalbe brought or imported into our realme of England, or any other of our dominions, according to the auncient trade of merchantes, which five poundes per centum onlie being paide, it shall be thenceforth lawfull and free for the said adventurers the same goodes and merchandizes to export and carry out of our said domynions into forraine partes, without any custome, tax, or other dutie to be paid to us, our heires or successors, or to any other officers or ministers of us, our heires and successors. PROVIDED, that the said goodes and merchandizes be shipped out within thirteene monethes after their first landing within any parte of the saide domynions. AND WEE DOE for us, our heires and successors, give and graunte unto the saide Governor and Company and their successors, That whensoever, or soe often as any custome or subsedie shall growe due or payeable unto us, our heires or successors, according to the lymittation and appointment aforesaide, by reason of any goodes, wares, or merchandizes to be shipped out, or any retorne to be made of any goodes, wares, or merchandize, unto or from the said partes of Newe England hereby mentioned to be graunted as afore-saide, or any the landes or territories aforesaide, That then and soe often and in such case the farmors, customers, and officers of our customes of England and Ireland, and everie of them for the tyme being, upon request made to them by the saide Governor and Company, or their successors, factors, or assignes, and upon convenient security to be given in that behalf, shall give and allowe unto the said Governor and Company, and their successors, and to all and everie person and persons free of that company as afore-saide, six monethes tyme for the payement of the one halfe of all such custome and subsidy as shalbe due and payeable unto us, our heires and successors, for the same, For which theis our letters patentes, or the duplicate or the inrollement thereof, shalbe unto our saide officers a sufficient warrant and discharge. NEVERTHE-LES, our will and pleasure is, That yf any of the saide goodes, wares, and merchandize which be or shalbe at any tyme hereafter landed or exported out of any of our realmes aforesaide, and shalbe shipped with a purpose not to be carried to the partes of Newe England aforesaide, but to some other place, That then such payment, dutie, custome, imposition, or forfeyture shalbe paid or belonge to us, our heires and successors, for the said goodes, wares, and merchandize soe fraudulently sought to be transported, as yf this our graunte had not benn made nor graunted. AND WEE DOE further will, And by theis presentes for us, our heires and successors, firmely enjoin and commaunde as well the Treasorer, Chauncellor, and Barons of the Exchequer of us, our heires and successors, as also all and singuler the customers, farmors, and collectors of the customes, subsidies, and impostes, and other the officers and ministers of us, our heires and successors, whatsoever, for the tyme being, That they and every of them, upon the shewing forth unto them of theis letters patentes, or the duplicate or exemplification of the same, without any other writt or warrant whatsoever from us, our heires or successors, to be obteyned or sued forth, doe and shall make full, whole, entire, and due allowance and cleare discharge unto the saide Governor and Company, and their successors, of all customes, subsidies, impositions, taxes, and duties whatsoever that shall or maie be claymed by us, our heires and successors, of or from the said Governor and Company and their successors, for or by reason of the said goodes, chattels, wares, merchandizes, and premises to be exported out of our saide domynions, or any of them, into any parte of the saide landes or premises hereby mentioned to be given, graunted, and confirmed, or for or by reason of any of the saide goodes, chattells, wares, or merchandizes to be imported from the said landes and premises hereby mentioned to be given, graunted, and confirmed, into any of our saide dominions or any parte thereof, as aforesaide, excepting onlie the saide five poundes per centum hereby reserved and payeable after the expiration of the saide terme of seaven yeares, as aforesaid, and not before. And theis our letters patentes, or the inrollment, duplicate, or exemplification of the same shalbe for ever hereafter from time to tyme, as well to the Treasorer, Chauncellor, and Barons of the Exchequer of us, our heires and successors, as to all and singuler the customers, farmors, and collectors of the customes, subsidies, and impostes of us, our heires and successors, and all searchers and other the officers and ministers whatsoever of us, our heires and successors for the time being, a sufficient warrant and discharge in this behalf. AND FURTHER, our will and pleasure is, And wee doe hereby, for us, our heires and successors, ordeyne, declare, and graunte to the saide Governor and Company, and their successors, That all and every the subjectes of us, our heires or successors, which shall goe to and inhabite within the saide landes and premisses hereby mentioned to be graunted, and every of their children which shall happen to be borne there, or on the seas in goeing thither or retorning from thence, shall have and enjoy all liberties and immunities of free and naturall subjectes within any of the domynions of us, our heires or successors, to all intentes, constructions, and purposes whatsoever, as yf they and everie of them were borne within the realme of England. And that the Governor and Deputie Governor of the said Company for the tyme being, or either of them, and any two or more of such of the saide Assistantes as shalbe thereunto appointed by the saide Governor and Company, at any of their courtes or assemblies to be held as aforesaide, shall and maie att all tymes, and from tyme to tyme hereafter, have full power and authoritie to minister and give the oathe and oathes of supremacie and allegiance, or either of them, to all and everie person and persons which shall at any tyme or tymes hereafter goe or passe to the landes and premisses hereby mentioned to be graunted to inhabite in the same. AND wee doe, of our further grace, certen knowledg and meere motion, give and graunt to the saide Governor and Company, and their successors, That it shall and maie be lawfull to and for the Governor or Deputie Governor and such of the Assistantes and Freemen of the said Company for the tyme being as shalbe assembled in any of their Generall Courtes aforesaide, or in any other Courtes to be specially summoned and assembled for that purpose, or the greater parte of them, (whereof the Governor or Deputie Governor and six of the Assistantes, to be alwaies seaven,) from tyme to tyme to make, ordeine, and establishe all manner of wholesome and reasonable orders, lawes, statutes, and ordinances, directions, and instructions not contrarie to the lawes of this our realme of England, aswell for setling of the formes and ceremonies of government and magistracy fitt and necessary for the said plantation and the inhabitantes there, and for nameing and stiling of all sortes of officers, both superior and inferior, which they shall finde needefull for that governement and plantation, and the distinguishing and setting forth of the severall duties, powers, and lymyttes of every such office and place, and the formes of such oathes warrantable by the lawes and statutes of this our realme of England as shalbe respectivelie ministred unto them, for the execution of the said severall offices and places, as also for the disposing and ordering of the elections of such of the said officers as shalbe annuall, and of such others as shalbe to succeede in case of death or removeall, and ministring the said oathes to the newe elected officers, and for impositions of lawfull fynes, mulctes, imprisonment, or other lawfull correction, according to the course of other corporations in this our realme of England,

and for the directing, ruling, and disposeing of all other matters and thinges whereby our said people, inhabitantes there, maie be soe religiously, peaceablie, and civilly governed, as their good life and orderlie conversation maie wynn and incite the natives of country to the knowledg and obedience of the onlie true God and Savior of mankinde, and the Christian fayth, which, in our royall intention and the adventurers free profession, is the principall ende of this plantation. WILLING, commaunding, and requiring, and by theis presentes for us, our heires and successors, ordeyning and appointing, That all such orders, lawes, statutes, and ordinances, instructions, and directions, as shalbe soe made by the Governor or Deputie Governor of the said Company, and such of the Assistantes and Freemen as aforesaide, and published in writing under their common seale, shalbe carefullie and dulie observed, kept, performed, and putt in execution, according to the true intent and meaning of the same. And theis our letters patentes, or the duplicate or exemplification thereof, shalbe to all and everie such officers, superior and inferior, from tyme to tyme, for the putting of the same orders, lawes, statutes, and ordinances, instructions, and directions in due execution against us, our heires and successors, insufficient warrant and discharge. AND WEE doe further, for us, our heires and successors, give and graunt to the said Governor and Company, and their successors, by theis presentes, That all and everie such cheife commaunders, captaines, governors, and other officers and ministers, as by the said orders, lawes, statutes, ordinances, instructions, or directions of the said Governor and Company for the tyme being, shalbe from tyme to tyme hereafter ymploied either in the government of the saide inhabitantes and plantation, or in the waye by sea thither or from thence, according to the natures and lymyttes of their offices and places respectively, shall from tyme to tyme hereafter for ever within the precinctes and partes of Newe England hereby mentioned to be graunted and confirmed, or in the waie by sea thither, or from thence, have full and absolute power and authoritie to correct, punishe, pardon, governe, and rule all such the subjectes of us, our heires and successors, as shall from tyme to tyme adventure themselves in any voyadge thither or from thence, or that shall at any tyme hereafter inhabite within the precinctes and partes of Newe England aforesaid, according to the orders, lawes, ordinances, instructions, and directions aforesaid, not being repugnant to the lawes and statutes of our realme of England, as aforesaid. AND WEE DOE further, for us, our heires and successors, give and graunte to the said Governor and Company and their successors, by theis presentes, That it shall and maie be lawfull to and for the cheife commaunders, governors, and officers of the said company for the time being, who shalbe resident in the said parte of Newe England in America, by theis presentes graunted, and others there inhabiting, by their appointment and direction from tyme to tyme, and at all tymes hereafter, for their speciall defence and safety, to incounter, expulse, repell, and resist by force of armes, aswell by sea as by lande, and by all fitting waies and meanes whatsoever, all such person and persons as shall at any tyme hereafter attempt or enterprise the destruction, invasion, detriment, or annoyance to the said plantation or inhabitantes: And to take and surprise, by all waies and meanes whatsoever, all and every such person and persons, with their shippes, armour, munition, and other goodes, as shall in hostile manner invade or attempt the defeating of the said plantation, or the hurt of the said Company and inhabitantes. NEVERTHELES, our will and pleasure is, And wee doe hereby declare to all Christian Kinges, Princes, and States, That yf any person or persons which shall hereafter be of the said Company or plantation, or any other, by lycense or appointment of the said Governor and Company for the tyme being, shall at any tyme or tymes hereafter, robb or spoyle by sea or by land, or doe any hurt, violence, or unlawfull hostility to any of the subjectes of us, our heires or successors, or any of the subjectes of any Prince or State being then in league and amytie with us, our heires and successors, and that upon such injury don, and upon just complaint of such Prince or State, or their subjectes, WEE, our heires or successors, shall make open proclamation within any of the partes within our realme of England commodious for that purpose, That the person or persons haveing committed any such roberie or spoyle, shall within the terme lymytted by such a proclamation make full restitution or satisfaction of all such injuries don, soe as the said Princes or others soe complayning maie hould themselves fullie satisfied and contented. And that yf the said person or persons having committed such robbery or spoile shall not make or cause to be made satisfaction accordinglie within such time soe to be lymytted, That then it shalbe lawfull for us, our heires and successors, to putt the said person or persons out of our allegiance and protection: And that it shalbe lawfull and free for all Princes to prosecute with hostilitie the said offendors and every of them, their and every of their procurers, ayders, abettors, and comforters in that behalf. PROVIDED also, and our expresse will and pleasure is, And wee doe by theis presentes, for us, our heires and successors, ordeyne and appoint, That theis presentes shall not in any manner enure, or be taken to abridge, barr, or hinder any of our loving subjectes whatsoever to use and exercise the trade of fishing upon that coast of New England in America by theis presentes mentioned to be graunted: But that they and every or any of them shall have full and free power and liberty to continue and use their said trade of fishing upon the said coast in any the seas thereunto adjoyning, or any armes of the seas or saltwater rivers where they have byn wont to fishe, and to build and sett up upon the landes by theis presentes graunted such wharfes, stages, and workehouses as shalbe necessarie for the salting, drying, keeping, and packing up of their fish, to be taken or gotten upon that coast: And to cutt downe and take such trees and other materialls there groweing, or being, or shalbe needefull for that purpose, and for all other necessarie easementes, helpes, and advantage concerning their said trade of fishing there, in such manner and forme as they have byn heretofore at any tyme accustomed to doe, without making any wilfull waste or spoyle, Any thing in theis presentes conteyned to the contrarie notwithstanding. AND WEE DOE further, for us, our heires and successors, ordeyne and graunte to the said Governor and Company, and their successors, by theis presentes, That theis our letters patentes shalbe firme, good, effectuall, and availeable in all thinges, and to all intentes and constructions of lawe, according to our true meaning herein before declared, and shalbe construed, reputed, and adjudged in all cases most favourablie on the behalf and for the benefitt and behoofe of the saide Governor and Company and their successors. ALTHOUGH expresse mention of the true yearely value or certenty of the premisses, or of any of them, or of any other guiftes or grauntes by us or any of our progenitors or predecessors to the foresaid Governor or Company before this time made, in theis presentes is not made, Or any statute, acte, ordinance, provision, proclamation, or restrainte to the contrarie thereof heretofore had, made, published, ordeyned, or provided, or any other matter, cause, or thinge whatsoever to the contrarie thereof in any wise notwithstanding. IN

WITNES whereof, wee have caused theis our letters to be made patentes. WITNES ourself at Westminster, the fourth day of March, in the fourth yeare of our raigne.

Per Breve de Privato Sigillo.

WOLSELEY.

PRAEDICT' Matthaeus Cradocke Juratus est de Fide et Obedientiâ Regi et Successoribus suis, et de Debitâ Exequutione Officij Gubernatoris iuxta Tenorem Presentium, 18° Martij, 1628. Coram me, Carolo Caesare, Milite, in Cancellariâ Mro.

CHAR. CAESAR.[1]

The Records of the Governor and Company of The Massachusetts Bay in New England.[1]

x   x   x   x   x   cast in the ballast of the shipps, and 2 lode of chalke, 10 thousand of bricks;   and 5 chauldron of sea coales.

Naieles;	Iron, 1 tun;	Fr: Johnson.
Lead.	Steele, 2 ffagotts;	Raphe White, at corner
Iron.	Lead, 1 ffodder;	of Philpot Lane, for
Steele.	Read lead, 1 barrill;	aquavite.
x d lead.		
x ayles.		
Salt.		
Sayle cloth.		
Hopps.		

---

[1] Affixed to the above letters patent, by party-colored strings of braided silk, is the broad seal of Charles I., and inscribed on the back of one of the four sheets of parchment on which the instrument is beautifully engrossed (the initial letter containing a well-executed representation of the king) is the following: "A perpetuity graunted to Sir Henry Rosewell and others, of parte of Newe England in America. [Signed] WOLSELEY."

[1] The first page, supposed to be in the handwriting of John Washborne, and before his appointment to the office of Secretary of the Company of the Massachusetts Bay in New England, evidently relates to the early outfitting of vessels destined for New England, and bears no date of the year in which it was written. The ten succeeding pages of the manuscript are apparently in the same handwriting, with the exception, perhaps, of part of the record of the 17th of March, the whole of those of the 19th and 23rd of March, 1628-9, and of the 11th of May, 1629, and also portions of the record of the 13th of May following, which are in an unrecognized hand.

Apparell ffor 100 men:—

400 peare of shewes;

300 peare of stockings, whereof 200 peare Irish, about [*11d*] 13d
 a peare, Mr. Deputy, 100 peare of knit stockings, about 2s 4d
 a peare, Mr. Treasurer;

 10 dussen peare of Norwich garters, about 5s a dussen peare;

400 shirts;

100 sutes doublett and hose, of leather, lyned with oild skyn
 leather, the hose and dublet with hookes and eyes;

100 sutes of Norden dussens, or Hampsheere kerseis, lyned, the
 hose with skins, the dublets with lynen;

 of Gilford or Gedlyman kersyes, 2s 10d to 3s a yard, 4½ to 5
  yards a sute;

400 bands, 300 playne falling bands, at the George in South-
 warke; 100 *x* band *x* ;

100 wastcoates of greene cotton, bound about with red tape;

100 lether girdles;

100 Munmouth capps, about 2s a peece;

100 black hatts, lyned in the browe with lether;

100 redd knitt capps, milled, about 5d a peece;

200 dussen hookes and eyes, and small hookes and eyes for man-
 dillions;

 16 dussen of gloves, whereof 12 dussen of calfs lether, and 2
 dussen tanned sheepes lether, and 2 dussen kyd;

 ells sleice lynnen ffor handkerchers;

 ½ a deker of lether, of the best bend lether;

 50 matts to lye under 50 bedds aboard shippe; 50 ruggs;

 50 peare of blanketts of Welsh cotton; 100 peare of sheetes;

 50 bedtykes and bolsters, with wool, to put them in Skotsh tick-
 ing;

 lynnen ffor towells and tableclothes and napkins;

 sea chests;

 3 C. poppering hopps, and 1 C. particuler.

Mr. Vassall. { 16 March. Agreed the apparell to bee, 100 man-
 dillions lyned with white cotton, 12d a yard,
 breeches and wastcote; and 100 lether sutes,
 dubletts and breeches of oyled lether. 100 peare
 breeches of lether, to serve to weare with boeth
 there other sutes.

> *x*   at Sherbrooke by tomorro in the afternoon.
> *x*   ticon to hinder the
> *x*   ting guns and gunpower.
> *x*   member if cattell.
> *x*   blud   *x*   to helpe them
> *x*   sea.

To provide to send for Newe England:—

Ministers;

Pattent under seale;

A seale;

Men skylful in making of pitch, of salt.

Vyne Planters.

Wheate, rye, barly, oates, a hogshed of each in the eare; benes, pease;

Stones of all sorts of fruites, as peaches, plums, filberts, cherries;

Peare, aple, quince kernells, pomegranats;

Woad seed;

Saffron heads;

Liquorice seed, rootes sent and madder rootes;

Potatoes;

Hoprootes;

Hempseede;

Flaxe seede, agenst wynter;

Connys;

Currant plants;

Tame turkeys;

Shewes;

Lynnen cloth;

Woollen cloth;

Pewter botles, of pyntes and quarts;

Brass ladells and spoones;

Copper kettells, of the F[ren]ch making, without barrs of iron about them;

Oyled skynnes of lether;

Madder seede.

23 February, 1628.

THIS day delivered a warrant to Mr. George Harwood, Threasurer, to pay Mr. Barnard Michell one hundred pounds, in parte

of the ffreight of the   , Heneri Gawden Mr., from Waimouth
to Nahumkeke, the goods shipt per bill of lading dated 20 June
last, beeing per bill of ladinge 46½ tuns of goods, besyds the
chardge of Capten John Endecott, his wiffe and   persons
  x his company, theire passage and dyett.

26th. William Sherman hath liberty for 14 daies to fech his
keynes in Northampton, neare *x* ferry.

26 February, 1628.

*Necessaries conseaved meete for our intended voiadge for
Newe England to bee prepared forthwith.*

FOR our 5 peeces of ordnance, longe sence bowght and payd
ffor, John Humphry is intreated and doeth promiss foorthwith
to cause *x* to bee delyvered to Samuell Sharpe, who is to
take care *x* having fytt cariadges made for them.

Armes ffor 100 men:—

 3 drums, to ech 2 pere of hedds;
 2 ensignes;
 2 partizans, for capten and lieftenant;
 3 halberts, for 3 sarjants;
80 bastard musketts, with snaphances, 4 ffoote in the barrill,
  without rests;
06 longe ffowlinge peeces with muskett boare, 6 foote longe, ½;
 4 longe ffowlinge peeces, with bastard muskett boare, 5½ foote
  longe;
10 ffull musketts, 4 foote barrill, with matchcocks and rests;
90 bandeleers, for the musketts, ech with a bullett bag;
10 horne fflaskes, for the longe fowling peeces, to hould a pound
  a peece; and
100 swoordes *x* and belts;
60 cosletts, and 60 pikes; 20 halffe pikes;
12 barrills powder, 8 barrills for the forte,
  4 ffor small shott;
  shott, 1 pound to a bandeleere;
 8 peecs of land ordnance for the forte, whereof 5 alreddy provided; namely, 2 demie culverings, 30 C. weight a peece,
     3 sackers, ech weigne 25 C. weight;
  to provide $\begin{cases} \text{1 whole culveringe, as long as may bee,} \\ \text{2 small peecs, iron drakes;} \end{cases}$

For great shott, a ffitt preportion to the ordnance;
A sayne, beeing a nett to ffish with.

For the Talbut, if 100 passingers, and 35 maryners, 3 monthes,
the maryners accounted doble:—

45 tun beere, whereof 6 tun 4s ⎱ beere; Mallega and Canari caske
           39 tun 6s ⎰ 16s a tun;

6 tuns of water;
12 m of bread, after ¾ C. to a man;
22 hogsheds of bieffe;
40 bushells peas, a peck a man the voyadg;
20 bushells oatmeale;
14 C. haberdyne, 62 cople ech C., ech cople makes p. 1, per ½
    a p.a man per day;
8 dussen pounds of candeles;
2 terces of beere vyneger;
1½ bushells mustard seede;
20 gallons oyle, Gallipoly or Mayorke, a quart a man;
2 fferkins of soape;
2 runlett Spanish wyne, 10 galls a person;
4 thowsand of billets;
10 firkins of butter;
10 C. of cheese;
20 gallons aquavite.

26 February, 1628.

AGREED with Jno. Hewson to make 8 pere of welt neates leather
sheues, c[losed] on the out sydes with a seame, to bee substanciall,
good over leather, of the best, and 2 soles, the inner soale of
good neates leather, and the owter sole of tallowed backs, to bee
2 pair of 10 inches, 2 pair 11 inches, 2 pair of 12 inches, and 2
pair of 13 inches size.

The preportions wee intend is,
        1 of 10 inches, ⎤
        3 of 11 inches, ⎟
        3 of 12 inches, ⎬ 2 7d.
        1 of 13 inches, ⎦

2 of 8 inches, ⎫ 2 4d, and hee to refer it to
2 of 9 inches, ⎬ the Company whether to alow
            ⎭ 1d per pair more.

2 Marche, 1628.

PRESENT, Mr. Governor   Mr. Adams,
          Mr. Deputy,   Mr. Nowel,
          Mr. Wright,   Mr. Whetcombe
          Mr. Vassall,   Mr. Perry,
          Mr. Harwood,   Mr. Huson.
          Mr. Coulson,

THIS day James Edmonds, a saylor, ffisher, and a couper, was prepounded to serve the Company; as also Sydrach Miller, a couper and a clever; who demanding £45 for him and his man the first yeere, £50 a yeere the second and third yeere, and Edmonds demands being £10 the first yeere, £15 the second, and £20 the third yeere, boeth held to deere for the Company to be at chargs withall.

Also, for Mr. Malbon, it was propounded, he having skyll in iron works, and willing to put in £25 in stocke, it should bee accepted as £50, and his chargs to bee bore out and home for Newe England; and uppon his returne, and report what may bee done about iron works, consyderation to be had of proceeding therein accordingly, and ffurder recompence, if there be cause to intertayne him.

Towching making of salt, it was conseaved ffytt that commoddetty should bee reserved for the generall stocks benefitt; yeet with this proviso, that aney planter or brother of the Company should have as much as he might aney way have occasyon to make usse of, at as cheape rate as themselves cowld make it; provided, if the Company bee not sufficiently provided for themselffs, then particuler men may have liberty to make for there owne expence and usse aney way, but not to transporte nor sell.

Towching Jno. Oldam, the Governor was ordered to conferr with him uppon aney indifferent course that might not bee prejudiciall to the Company.

Also, it beeing prepounded by Mr. Coney, in the behalfe of the Boston men, (whereof dyvers had promised, though not in our booke underwritten, to adventure £400 for the joint stock,) that now there desire was that 10 persons of them might underwrite £25 a man in the joint stock, they withall promisinge with theise shippes to adventure in there particuler above £250 more, and to provide abell men to send over for manadging the bussines; which though it bee prejudiciall to the generall stock, by the abatement of so much money thereout, yeet appearing realley to conduce more to the good of the plantation, which is most desired, it was condiscended unto.

3 Marche, 1628.

PRESENT, Mr. Governor,   Mr. Nowel,
Mr. Deputy,   Mr. Sharpe.
Mr. Wright,

IT was at present debated howe some good course might bee setteled for the devision of the lands, and that all men intendinge to goe in person or to send over, might underwrite and seale some instrument to bee made, whereby every man to bee tyed to such orders as shalbee agreed uppon here; and that a coppey of this agreement bee sent to Dorchester, ffor all men to underwrite and seale, that intend to take theire passage in the Lyons Whelpe, or ells order to bee taken that the shippe proceede without [them.]

Mr. Samuell Sharpe, with whome there hath beene an agreeyment made in behalffe of the Company to geeve him ten pounds per   *x*   for three yeeres, to have the oversight of the ordnance to bee planted in the ffort to bee built uppon the plantation, and what ells may concerne artillery bisines to geeve his advize in. But ffor all other implyments was left to bee intertayned by aney particular brethren of the Companie, who for other occasions had intertayned   *x*   alreddy, and held not fytt to bee at furder chardge in that kynd;   *x*   *x*   the sayd Sharpe is also intertayned to oversey the   *x*   and implyments of certen particuler men of the Company. But for the generall presented a bill ffor three drums and other particulers, amountinge to fyve pounds, xix shillings; which the Treasurer hath order to paye.

The 5 Marche, 1628.

PRESENT, The Governor,   Mr. Wright,
Mr. Deputy,   Mr. Nowel,

Mr. Threasurer,   Mr. White,
Sir Rich: Saltonstal,   Mr. Whetcombe,
Capt. Ven,   Mr. Whitchcombe.

A NEWE proposition beeinge made in the behalfe of Mr. Oldum to bee intertayned   x   this Company, it was deferred to furder consideration.

Also, Jno. Washborne beeinge propounded for Secretary to the Company, it was conseaved fytt to intertayne him, but deferred till another   x

A proposition beeing made by Sir William Bruerten to the Governor, of a p   x   graunted him of lands in the Massachusets Bay by Mr. Jno. G[orges], and that if this Company would make him a promisse, so as he con   x   to underwrite with this Company, it might not bee prejudi   x   to his pattent; it was resolved this answere should [bee] geeven him, nameley: That if he pleased to underwrite with us without aney condition whatsoever, but to come in [as] all other adventurers doe, he should bee welcome uppon the same conditions that wee have.

A proposition beeinge made to intertayne a surgeon for   x   plantation, Mr.   Pratt was propounded as an abell man uppon theis conditions, nameley: That £40 should bee allowed him, viz., for his chist, £25, the rest [for] his owne sallery for the first yeere; provided, if he con   x   3 yeeres, the Company to bee at charge of transporting his wiffe and a yo   x   ,   x   have £20 a yeere for the other 2 yeeres, and to build him a house [at] the Company chardge, and to allott him 100 acres of ground; but if he stay but one yeere, then the Company to be at chardge of his bringing back for England, and he to leave his serv[ant], and the chist for the Company service.

Agreed with Robert Morley, servant to Mr. Andrewe Mathewes, late barber surgeon, to serve the Company in Newe England for three yeeres; the first yeere to have 20 nobles, the second yeere   x   x   ,   x   x   yeere 20 markes, to serve as a barber and a surgeon,   x   x   occasyons belonging to his calling, to aney of this   x   that are planters, or there servants; and for his [chist,] and all in it, whereof he hath geeven an inventory,   x   x   x   sight of it, it bee approoved, ffyve pounds is   *x*   *x*   *x*   and payed to him ffor it, and the same to bee fo[rthwith payd].

The buissines concerning the devission of the lands, propounded the 3d of this monthe, was agayne taken into consideration, and it was resolved that Capten Waller, Captain Ven, Mr. Eaton and Mr. Addams, Mr. Whetcombe, Mr. Wright, Mr. Vassall, Mr. Threasurer, with the Governor and Deputy, shall consyder seriously of the buissines, calling to there assistance Mr. Graves, Mr. Sharpe, or aney other, and to sett downe in writinge what course they conseave fytt to bee held herein, whereby an equallety may bee held, to avoyd all contention twixt the adventurers; and Tuesday morning appoynted for thiese Committees to meete about this buissines.

This Court also, Mr. Thomas Graves was propounded to goe over with the shippes nowe bound for Newe England, to have his chargs borne out and home; and beeinge a man experienced in iron workes, in salt workes, in measuring and surveyinge of lands, and in fortiffications, in lead, copper, and allam mynes, etc., havinge a chardge of wiffe, 5 children, a man and mayd servant; after some conference with him, he tendring his implyment to goe and returne with one of our shyps, to the company discression ffor his sallery in that tyme, it was thought fytt that he should consyder twixt this and tomorrow what to demand in case he did returne presently with the shippe he should take his passage in; and what his demands would bee if the Company should contyneue him there, and bee at chardges of the transportation of his wiffe and ffameley thether in theire next shippes, if he take lyking to contyneue in Newe England.

Mr. Jno. Malbon beeing also desyred to bee heere, after conference had with him touching the proposition made in his behalffe the 2 of this monthe, he was wished to consyder what further proposition he would make, that the Company might take it into consyderation.

The 6 Marche, 1628.

AGREED with Mr. Thomas Steevens, armorer in Buttolph Lane, for 20 armes, viz., coslett, brest, back, culet, gorgett, tases, and hed peece to ech, varnished all black, with lethers and buckles, at

17s ech armour, excepting 4, which are to bee with close head peeces, and theis 4 armours at 24, a peece, to bee delivered all by the 20th of this monthe; whereof one left nowe for a sample.

Agreed with Jno. Wise, shoemaker in Marke Lane, ffor

1	dussen	pere sheues	of tens,	
3	dussen	" "	of 11,	at 2s 7d a pere;
3	dussen	" "	of 12,	
1	dussen pere	"	of 13,	
1	dussen pere	"	of 8,	at 2s 5d a pere;
1	dussen pere	"	of 9,	

10 dussen pere to bee delivered by the 20th of this monthe.

The 9 Marche, 1628.

THIS day John Washborne is intertayned for Secretary for one whole yeere, to enter the Courts, to keepe the Companys accounts, to make warrants for all moneys to bee browght in or payd out, and to geeve nottice at every meeting of such as are backward in payment of there subscriptions, as also for all provission to bee made reddy, to call uppon such as have the chardge thereof, whereby the shippes nowe bound ffor Newe England may bee dispatched by the 25 of this month at ffurdest; his sallery ffor this yeere is te   x   x   , he in the premisses, and the office of a Secretary, to perf[orme] ffaithfull, dilligent, and tr[eue i]n-devours wherunto he doeth fulley   x   and agree.

JNO. WASHBORNE

Agreed with John Gace, of London, turner, ffor 40 bande-leers,   x   x   x   neates lether, broad girdles, ech with 12 charges, whereof one a priming b   x   ,   x   of wood, covered with black lether, at 2s a peece, to bee delivered next [weeke]; the boxes to bee for bastard muskett sise, excepting 10 for full mus[ketts,] and these to be marked M., the other for bastard musketts B.

More, agreed with him for ten dozen of shovels and spades, at eyghten shillings the dozen, of three severall sises, wherof the smalest proportion to be of the smallest sises; and three spads and thre shovels left heer for sa[mples].

This day theise things were ordered to bee provided by theise men; 120 men's provissions.

| Mr. Thomas Hewson, | { 120 fflitches bacon, |
| | { 120 gallons sweete oyle; |

	{ 150 quarters of meale,
	{ 30 quarters of pease, at 26s,
Mr. Deputy,	{ 15 quarters of greats, at 4s, full dryed,
	{ 20 fferkins of butter, 17s,
	{ 60 quarters of malt, 17s 6d,
	{ 30 C. of cheese.

THIS 10th March, 1628, I, Thomas Graves, of Gravesend, in the County of Kent, gentleman, and by my proffession skillfull and experienced in the discovery and finding out of iron mynes, as also of lead, copper, minerall salt and [allam], in ffortiffications of all sorts, according to the nature of the plase, in surveying of buildings and of lands, and in measuringe of land, in describing a country by mappe, in leading of water   x   to prepare usses for milles or other usses, in fynding out [all] sorts of lymestones and materials for buildings, in manufacturing, etc., have this present day agreed to serve the Newe England Company, and in there ymplyment to take my passage for Newe England in such shippe as thei shall appoynt mee; and during my stay there, according to the conditions heereafter expressed, to doe my true and uttermost indevour, in all or aney the particulers abovementioned, for the most good and benefitt of the said Companie; and I do heereby faithfulley promisse to do my uttermost indeavour for the discovery of owght that may be beneficiall to the Companie, and not to conceale owght ffrom them whome I shalbee injoyned to reveal the same unto, that may tend or conduce to the good and proffit of the sayd Company: Neither that I shall or   x   disclose owght that they shall injoyne me to keepe secrett, to any man whomesoever; but in all things to bend my uttermost skyll and abillity to do the Companey the best, treue, and ffaithffull service I may or cane perfforme. In consyderacion whereof, the said Companey are to beare all my chardgs by sea into Newe England, together with my charges duringe my staie in there implyments in Newe England, and my charges at sea in my returne home, apparrell only excepted, which is to bee allwaies at my owne chargs; and it is [agreed] moreover, that from the tyme of my

ffirst landing in Newe England, to the tyme of the returne from thence for London of such shippe as shalbee sent from London next after Michelmas next, and in which I shall take my passage for London, that there shalbee allowed [unto] me ffyve pounds for ech month that I shall contyneue in Newe [England] as afore said, for my sallery or wages, but nothinge to bee allowed [for] my charges during the tyme of my beeing at sea, outward and   *x*   , with this furder proviso, that in case the said Company, [after I] shall have contynewed 6 or 8 months in the countrey   *x*   , shall desyre my contynuance in   *x*
x   three yeeres from the tyme of my f   *x*   , I will and [doe hereby]   *x*   *x*   *x*   *x*   *x*   *x*   there intent to retayne me in there service to the end of three yeeres, doe heereby promise to bee at the chardge of the transportation into Newe England of my wiffe, ffyve children, a boy, and a mayd servant, and withall to build mee a convenient house for my selffe and my sayd ffameley, at there chargs, and therto to assyne me one hundred acres of land, and to have parte thereof planted at the Companies chardge against the coming of my ffameley, whereby they may subsiste till I shall be possessed of my ffameley to perfforme the same, or otherwise to alloue me some competency of necessary victualls for the subsistance of me and my ffameley till the next season of plantinge and reapinge after there arryvall: And it is furder agreed, that yf I contyneue in the Companies implyments ffor three yeeres, the payment of ffyve pounds per month ffor my sallery is to bee utterly voyde, and my yeereley allowance in money, ffrom the tyme of my ffirst arrivall in Newe England to the end of three yeeres, to bee after the rate of ffyftey pounds by the yeere, provided alwayes that my sayd ffameley, goinge over as aforesaid, there shalbee such a preportion of land alloued me for them heereafter as if they had nowe taken there passage with me in the shippes nowe bound for Newe England; and ffor furder recompence for my treue and faithfull indeavours in the sayd Companies implyments, which I doe promisse with Gods assistance to perfforme trulye and sincereley to the best of my abillity and understandinge, I doe and shall refferre my selffe wholey to the Companies discression, as my treue indevours and the suckcesse thereof, through Gods mercy, shall incorradge them to doe. In wyttness of all the premisses I have heereunto sett my hand and

seale this present xth daye of Marche, Anno. 1628, in London.
    Wittness heereunto: THO: GRAVES.[2]
        George Harwood,
        John Venn.

The 10th Marche, 1628.

PRESENT, The Governor,   Mr. Eaton,
         Mr. Deputy,   Mr. Adams,
         Capt. Ven,   Mr. Whetcomb,
         Mr. Threasurer,   Mr. Hutchins.
         Mr. Vassall,

A PROPOSITION was made this day by Samuell Sharpe, who was formerley intertayned to doe his indevour in the Companies implyments concerning artillery bissines, as appereth the 3d of this monthe, that all or the better part of his sallery might be paid him nowe, to provide him apparell withall; and if he should happen to dye before he had deserved it, his said apparell should satisfye it; uppon debate whereof, it was thought ffitt that twenty pounds should bee paid him; and this to bee the Treasurers warrant for payment thereof, uppon his sallery of £10 a yeere, ffor three yeeres; I say twenty pounds to be paid him presently.

This day beeing apoynted to take into consyderation towching the devission of the lands in Newe England, where our first plantation shalbee, it was, after much debate, thowght ffytt to referre this buissines to the Governor, and a committee to bee chosen to that purpose to assist him; and whatsoever thei shall doe heerein, that to stand ffor good.

This day order was geeven to the Threasurer for payment of twenty pounds more to Mr. Jno. Humphry towrds chardges of our pattent; and this to bee his warrant ffor the payment thereof.

Capten Ven, Mr. Eaton, Mr. Samuell Vassall, and Mr. Nowel, and Mr. Whetcombe, [or any] three [of] them, are intreated once more to conferr with Mr. Jno. Ouldam   x   x   x
commodation may bee made twixt the Company and him, that
    x   x   x   commodated.

---

[2] The above agreement of Mr. Thomas Graves was undoubtedly intended to be an original instrument, as well as a record of the transaction; all the signatures to it are autographs, and that of Graves is accompanied with an impression of a seal in wax.

[*12 Marche, 1628.*]
PRESENT, Mr. Wri[ght,]   Mr. Threasurer,
          Sir Rich: Saltonstal,   Mr. Nowel.

JOHN BROWNE, gentleman, and Mr. Samuell Browne, of Rox-
well, in Essex,   *x*   *x*   take there passage in the Company
shipps ffor Newe England, at   *x*   chardge, and intending to
plant there, it is agreed by theise   *x*   , that for there passage
and dyett they shall pay ffyve pounds [each]; and that for there
incowragement land shalbee allotted to them [there], as if they
had subscribed fyty pounds in the generall stock, [with such]
pryveledge as others that are in the pattent doe.
                                           JOHN BROWNE,
                                           SAMUELL BROWNE.

RICHARD CLAYTON, aged 34 yeeres, or thereabouts, carpenter,
who beeing desirous to transport himselffe. his wiffe, one daughter
[of]   *x*   yeeres ould, his sister of 14 yeeres ould, his brother
Barnaby C[laydon,] aged 23 yeeres, and his brother in lawe
Thomas Hanscombe, ag *x*   *x*   *x*   , for Newe England in the Company shippes, it is promised [this] daye, that he
beeing abel to ffurnish £40 towrds the chardge of him and his,
what shalbee wantinge the Company will [supply] uppon this
condition, that uppon theire arryvall [in Newe] England, what
he shalbee indebted to the Companie shalbee [paid] by the labor
of himselffe and his 2 servants, or brothers aforesaid, allouing
them all three 3s the day for so long tyme [until] they have paid
this debtt, and in that tyme fynding [these] 3 persons dyett at
the Companie chardge, and whilest   *x*   *x*   earning out
this dett to instruckt aney of the Company   *x*   in the trade
of a ploue wright; and there is land to bee [allotted] to him and
his, as is ussuall, by the Company orders, to th *x*   that
transporte themselves; written this 12 March, 1628.
   Cannotte goe this viodge.   RICHARD CLAYDON.

The 16 March, 1628.

BESPOKEN by Mr. Durbridge, at 2s 7d a pair, 6 dussen pere of
shewes, to bee delivered this weeke, viz., 1 dussen pere of tens,
                                   2 dussen pair of 11,

2   of   12,
1 dussen pair of 13;
4 pair delivered.

The 16th of March, 1628.

BESPOKE of Mr. Maio, at 10½d per yard, ffor beds and boul-
sters, 20 bed tikes, Scotch tikeing, ¾ broad, 2¹⁄₁₆ long, and 1½
yards broad; 11 yards each bed and boulster.

Bespoke the day abovesaid, 8 dussen pair neats leather shewes,
of Robert Harret,

1 dussen 10,
3 dussen 11,   At 2s 7d per pair, to bee good liquored
3 dussen 12,   neats leather, according to the pat-
1 dussen 13,   terne.

*Estimat of 100 men, chardge of them and theire provissions,
with others noted:—*

100 men, there chardge, £15 a man, ...		1500
Freight of the shippe Talbut, 5 monthes,		
£80 per month, ...	400	750
Victualls and wages 32 men, £70 a monthe, ...	350	
The Lyons Whelpe sett to sea, ...		500
20 cowes and bulls, £4 a peece, ...	80	
10 mares and horses, £6 a peece, ...	60	610
Charges of theis, ...	470	
		3360

[17 March, 1628.]

AGREED with [Joseph] Churchell ffor 100 swoords with   x
blades, at 4s 6d a peece, to have all chapes, and 10 short
swoords, at 2s a peece; and Polonia hilts, at 3s 4d, as maney as
wee like, to   delivered within 8 dayes.

Bowght of Felix Boreman, dwelling in Fleete Lane:

14 swoords, at 4s 6d a peece,
7   ditto, at 3s a peece,   £4 12 00
4   ditto, at 2s a peece,
___
25 swoords.

Agreed with Mr. Raphe White, in Philpot Lane, for 12 gallons aquavite, 2s 6d a gallon.

12 sydes of bacon delivered by Jno. Gladwing, at Mr. Goffs, of 74 stone ½, ech st. £8, at 2s 5d a stone.

17 Marche, 1628.

A WARRANT was made ffor payment of £120 to Mr. Nathaniell Wright, for so much paid by him to Mr. Jarvis Kerke, Mr. William Barkley, and Mr. Robert Charlton, ffor the shippe.

Also, to pay ffor iron and steele.

Also, to pay ffor burrs to make milstones, 110, 2s a pair, bowght of

Edward Casson, of London, merchantayler, ...	11	0	0
14 C. of plaster of Parris, 18d per C.	1	1	0
	12	1	0
and portridge, weig the plaster and casting out of the burrs, 12d and 23d, ...		3	0
	12	4	0

The 19th of March, 1628.

A WARRANT was made ffor payment of twelve pounds and twelve shillings unto Mr. Gawen Helme and Thomas Brickhed ffor two coppers for the Lyons Whelpe. I saye for,   £12 and 12s 00d

The 19th of March, 1628.

A WARRANT was made for payment of eyghtene pounds unto Mr.   Browne, and is for one bayle of French cloth, ffor the Lyons Whelpe. I saye,   £18

The 19th of March, 1628.

A WARRANT was made for payment of twenty-ffive pounds, ffyfftene shillings, unto Mr. Jno. Whitt, of Reddinge, for thirtye quarters of maulte, to goe in the shipps. I say £25 15s 00d, £26 05s[3]

---

[3] The £26 5s. is an alteration of the record.

[23] March, 1628.

PRESENT, The Governor,   Mr. Humffry,
             Deputy,   Mr. William Vassall,
             Sir Rich: Saltonstall, Mr. Whetcomb,
             Mr. Davinport,   Mr. Nowell.
             Capt. Venn,

AT this meeting intimation was given by Mr. Nowell, by letters ffrom Mr. Izake Johnson, that one Mr. Higgeson, of Lester, an able minister, proffers to goe to our plantation; who being approved for a reverend, grave minister, fitt for our present occasions, it was thought by thes present to entreat Mr. Jno. Humfry to ride presently to Lester, and, if Mr. Higgeson may conveniently be had to goe this present vioage, that he should deale with him; ffirst, if his remooue from thence may be without scandall to that people, and approved by the consent of some of the best affected amonge them, with the approbation of Mr. Heldersham, of Asheby, dallisouch; secondly, that in regard of the shortnes of the time, the Companye conseave it woulde be best, if hee so thought good, to leave his wiffe and ffamily till towards Bartholomew, for ther better accommodation; yet if this should be held inconvenient, [it] may be referred to himselfe to take [his wife and tw]o children with him; thirdly, that for his entertaynment the Company [will give him such accommodation as any they have yet intertayned or are in parly with, or rather better, and doubt not but such as will be to his content.][4]

The 23 March, 1628.

THIS day, according to the tenour of the charter, these persons following were sworne for the performance of their severall places and offices according to the tenour of their severall oathes.

Mr. Thomas Goffe tooke the oath of Deputy to this Company, by the name of the Governor and Company of the Massachusetts Bay in New England.

---

[4] Here is an hiatus in the original manuscript. The record of the 23d of March, 1628–29, is incomplete, and the first portion of that of the 30th of April, 1629, is wanting. The lost portion was supplied from an early copy, which was in the possession of Thomas Aspinwall, Esq., at the time when the Massachusetts Records were first published.

Sir Richard Saltonstall, Captaine Venn, Mr. John Humfrey, Mr. Symon Whetcombe, Mr. Thomas Adams, Mr. Samuel Vassall, Mr. George Foxcrofte, Mr. William Vassall, Mr. Increase Nowell, Mr. Richard Perry, and Mr. Thomas Hutchins tooke the oath of Assistants to the said Companye.

Mr. George Harwood tooke the oath of Treasuror.

Humfrey Scale tooke the oath of Beadle.

A motion was made by the Governor that 6 of the Company would take the paynes as daylie to see when the Companyes servants are imployd, and how they demeasne themselves, to the end if there be cause such as shall be found idle or debosht may be dismissed; whereupon these following have promised to see the same performed, viz.:

Mr. Thomas Adams,	Mr. Increase Nowell,
Mr. Thomas Hughson,	Mr. George Foxcroft,
Mr. Daniel Winche,	Mr. Owen Rowe,
Mr. Thomas Hutchins,	Mr. Symon Whetcombe.

Thomas Beard, of St. Martins, shoomaker, single man, aged 30 yeares, desirous to goe over at his owne charge, there is 50 acres of land to be assigned to him by order of this Company, and £5 payd by him for his passage to the Treasuror.

Wee William Riall and Thomas Braid, coopers: the Company hath agreed that they shall goe halfe, at the charge of Mr. Governor the one halfe, and at the charge of the Company the other halfe, and so the Governor is to appoint them men, the Governor one halfe and the Company the other halfe.

It is agreed that every person that shall goe over at his owne charge shall have fifty acres of land.

Further, it is agreed, that if any of the Company send over any servants or others, they shall have fifty acres of land to be at their masters disposinge at their pleasure.

Delivered a bill to Mr. Brereton, for £12 15s 0, for a cable and 86 yards of sayle cloath, delivered to the Lyons Whelpe.

Delivered a bill to John Gibes for £15, for disbursements for the Lyons Whelpe, and he to give account for it.

Delivered a bill to John Wighte, for 30 qrs. of malte, at 17s 6d per qr., £26 5s 0.

Delivered a bill to Robert Harrett, for 8 dussen of shooes at 2s 7d per pair, £12 8s od.

30 March, 1629.

DELIVERED Mr. John Wise, shoomaker, a warrant for £18 4s, being for 12 dussen payre of shooes.

8 dussen pair, at 2s 7d a pair,
$$\left\{\begin{array}{l} \text{1 dussen of 13,} \\ \text{3 dussen of 12,} \\ \text{3 dussen of 11,} \\ \text{1 dussen of 10.} \end{array}\right.$$

And 4 dussen of 8ts. and 9nes., at 2s 5d a pair.

Delivered John French a warrant for 3 dussen of Irish spades, at 3s 8d a peece, steele spades shodd cleane over.

John Slanie, plaisterer, doth desire you to pay unto his mother, Mary Slanye, the summe of twenty shillings within 10 dayes after the Company is a board, in parte of his wages, I say.................................... } 20s

JOHN SLAYNYES   mark.

Witness, John Washbourne.

A warrant to Mr. Molton, for
To Mr. Robert Molton, a warrant for } .... £10.

A warrant to Mr. John Goose, for.................... £13.

Delivered a warrant to Mr. John Hughson,
    shoomaker, for .... £22 14s 6d.

Delivered a warrant to Mr. Tayler, for worke upon the
    Lyons Whelpe, for............................. £30.

Delivered a warrant to Mr. Clarke, in part of caske delivered, £30.

Delivered a warrant to Mr. Tanner, in part of caske delivered, £30.

Warrants delivered the 30th of March, for moneys to be payd to the Treasuror, as followeth:—

Mr. William Backhouse,	£25	Mr. John Pococke,	£25
Mr. Owen Rowe,	25	Mr. George Foxcrofte,	25
Mr. John Bowles,	25	Mr. Daniel Hudson,	25
Mr. Robert Crane,	25	Mrs. A. C.,	25

Mr. Daniel Winche, ... 25   Mr. William Crowther, . . . 25
Mr. Joseph Caron, ... 25   Mr. John Venn, ... 50
Mr. Richard Tuffnayle, . . . 50   Mr. Richard Yonge, ... 50
Mr. John Davenporte, ... 25   Mr. Thomas Hutchins, . . . 25
Mr. Samuel Aldersey, ... 75   Mr. Nathaniel Manesly, . . 25
Mr. Richard Poorye, ... 25   Mr. Theophilus Eaton, . . . 25
Mr. Nathaniel Wright, . . . 25   Mr. Christofer Coulson, . . 25
Mr. Richard Davys, ... 25   Mr. Charles Witchcote, . . 50
Mr. Increase Nowell, ... 25   Mr. Edward Forde, ... 25
Mr. Edmond White, ... 25   Mr. Samuel Vassall, ... 50
Mr. John Humfrey, ... 25   Mr. Simon Whitcombe, . . 85
Mr. Hugh Peter, ... 25   Mr. Edward Ironside, ... 25
Mr. Joas Glover, ... 25

1629. A Note of the Tooles provided and viewed by William Ryall.

2 barge axes, 2s a peece, ... 0   4s 0
2 howells, 1: 18d and 1: 12d, ... 0   2   6
2 two hollow tap bores and stockes to them, 18d a peece, 0   3   0
2 bung bores, 2s a peece; too deare, 6d a peece, ... 0   4   0
2 pesters stockt, 8d a peece;
1 adds of 2s; 1 other adds, 20d, is naught;
2 felling axes, 2s the one, the other 18d, ... 0   3   6
1 round shave, ... 0   1   4
1 joynter iron, 1s; 2 smale irons for planes, 5d and 3d, 0   1   8
1 spoke shave, 8d; a knyfe, 8d.
1 steele sawe, 3s 4d; 1 heading knife, 2s 6d,
    6d too deare, ... 0   5   10
1 marking iron; 1 hammer;
2 wimbles; 1 gowge; 1 skraper, 16d;
1 croze iron, 8d;
1 holdfast, 8d; a drawing knife, 10d, naught;
2 dussen of perser bitts;
1 broad axe, 2s 8d, 2d too deare;
1 bill, 15d; a cressen iron;
1 great cleaving iron.

Brought in by William Ryall.

1 croze with an iron to it; a paire of compasses; 1 adds; 1 howell; 2 tap bores, 1 hollowe, 1 round; 1 barge axe; 1 shave.

Ordinance received of Mr. Edward Turvile, as followeth:—

16	2	0	16	2	0
16	2	0	12	2	0
16	2	0	12	01	0
16	3	0	41	1	0
16	3	0	83	0	0
83	0	0	124	1	0 at 13s per C. is £80 15s 3d.

A warrant, delivered to Mr. Trasuror, to pay the said money the 2d of Aprill, 1629, to Mr. Turvile, for the ordinance above-mentioned delivered aboard the Lyons Whelpe.

A warrant delivered unto Mr. Anthony Webster, the 2 of Aprill, 1629, for the summe of two pounds fifteene shillings, ...£2 15s.

The 2 of Aprill, 1629.

THIS day these persons following were present: Mr. Mathewe Cradocke, Governor, Mr. Tho: Goffe, Deputy, Mr. George Harwood, Treasuror, and the rest following: Mr. William Vassall, Mr. John Browne, Mr. Francis Webb, Mr. Richard Perry, Mr. Increase Nowell, Mr. Thomas Adams, Mr. Sam: Vassall.

It is ordered, that Mr. Moulton, carpenter, and two or three men are to goe to New England, and Mr. Governor is to beare a third of the charge of these men.

The 6th of Aprill, 1629.

THIS day these persons in the margin mett and consulted.

Mr. Math: Cradocke, Governor,
Mr. Tho: Goffe, Deputy,
Sir Rich: Saltonstall,
Mr. Rich: Davys,
Mr. Sam: Vassall,
Mr. Sim: Whetcombe,
Mr.   Yonge,
Mr. Tho: Adams,
Mr. Jo: Pococke,
Mr. Increase Nowell,
Mr.   Coulson,
Mr. Rich: Perry,
Mr.   Crane,
Mr. Treasurer,
Mr.   Hughson,
Mr. William Vassall,

Mr. Daniel Winche,	Mr. Webbe,
Mr. Owen Rowe,	Captaine Waller,
Mr. George Foxcrofte,	Captaine Venn.

It is agreed, that all the cattell that Mr. Governor shall shippe shall be halfe for the Company and the other halfe for the Governors use. Also, for sending the Lyons Whelpe to the Isle of Wight, and if she may have sufficient company to send her speedily, to appoint some to see the hay put a board.

These were appointed to be committees for making orders and power for meet government of New England, to write letters to Captaine Endicott, to order divisions of land and whatsoever may concerne the Companyes affayres, and to appoint a committee to joyne with the Governor any five of these with Governor or Deputy, to divide your company in familyes by the said committee:—

Mr. Davenporte,	Mr. Adams,
Mr. Higgeson,	Mr. Eaton,
Mr. Waller,	Mr. Vassall,
Mr. Venn,	Mr. Coulson,
Sir Rich: Saltonstall,	Mr. Treasuror.
Mr. Wright,	

The Company is content to give unto Mr. Bright £5 towards his losse of his wages in the country, and his charge being in London.

Mr. Wright and Mr. John Browne tooke the oath of Assistants this day.

Appointed Mr. Deputy to gett the lord treasurors letter to the customs.

Appointed to Mr. Whetcombe to gett the Exemplification of the Letters Patents.

To have such cattell changed as are unfitt to carry.

The 8th Aprill, 1629.

PRESENT,	Sir Rich: Saltonstall,	Mr. Skelton,
at Mr. Treasurers,	Mr. Davenporte,	Mr. Bright,
	Mr. Higginson,	Mr. Coulson,
	Mr. Glover,	Mr. Humfrey,
	Capt: Waller,	Mr. Whetcombe,

Capt: Venn,   Mr. William Vassall,
Mr. Adams,   Mr. John Pococke.

MR. FRANCIS HIGGESON and Mr. Samuel Skelton intended ministers for this plantation, and it being thought meete to consider of their intertaynement, who expressing their willingnesse together, also with Mr. Francis Bright, being now present to doe their true endevour in their places of the ministery as well in preaching, catechizing, as also in teaching, or causing to be taught, the Companyes servants and their children, as also the salvages and their children, whereby to their uttermost to further the maine end of this plantation, being, by the assistance of Allmighty God, the conversion of the salvages, the propositions concluded on with Mr. Francis Bright, the 2 of February last, were reciprocally accepted of by Mr. Francis Higgison and Mr. Samuel Skelton, who are in every respect to have the like conditions as Mr. Bright hath, onely whereas Mr. Higgeson hath 8 children it is intended that £10 more yearely shall be allowed him towards their charge. And it is agreed that the increase of the improvement of all their grounds during the first 3 yeares shall be at the Companies disposing, who are to fynde them dyett during that time, and tenne pounds more to Mr. Higgeson towards his present fitting him and his for the voyage.

FRANCIS HIGGINSON,
SAMUEL SKELTON.

8 Aprill, 1629.

TOUCHING Mr. Ralfe Smith, order was given to the Governor to conferr with him, and if he will give it under his hand not to exercise the ministery within the lymitts of our plantation, neither publique nor private, without the consent and approbation of the goverment there established by us, that then he shall be accommodated in his passage, and so as during his being within the lymitts of our plantation he promise not to disturbe our proceedings, but to submitt to such orders as shall be there established.

13 Aprill, 1629.

PRESENT, The Governor,   Mr. Sam: Vassall,
Mr. Deputy,   Mr. Tho: Addams,
Mr. Treasurer,   Mr. William Backhouse.

THIS day notice was given that Mr. William Backhouse had freely bestowed upon this Company to send for New England these bookes following, for which thankes was given by the Governor and those present to the said Mr. Backhouse in the Companies behalfe.

The Englishe Bible in folio, of the last print;

The Booke of Common Prayer;

Aynsworths Works, in folio;

Bishop Babingtons Works;

Calvins Institutions;

Fotherby against Atheists;

Malderott upon St. Johns Gospell;

A booke called The French Country Farme.

    To provide to send for New England.

12 barrills powder, whereof 3 fine;

3 C. weight of shott for bastard musketts;

6 C. weight of shott for fowlinge;

1 fodder of lead;

Shott for the great ordinance, rammers, spunges, ladles, and wadhooke.

The 16th of Aprill, 1629.

PRESENT, Mr. Governor, Mr. Browne,
this day, Mr. Deputy, Mr. Bright.
    Mr. Adams,

Mr. Skeltons Note of Bookes.

1 Gerards Meditations,	o	1	2
1 Helpes to Faith,	o	o	9
1 Rogers Workes,	o	7	o
1 Donhams Guide,	o	10	o
1 Aynsworth,	o	13	o
1 Downhams Warfare,	o	13	o
1 Maire on the Epistles,	o	3	o
1 Dod on the Commandments,	o	2	2
1 Robinsons Essayes,	o	2	8
1 Dr. Berd of Antichrist,	o	2	o
1 Practise of Piety,	o	1	6
1 Dyke on the Heart,	o	2	o

1 Of Conscience, ...	0	1	0
1 Downham on the Commandments, ...	0	1	6
1 Communion per Saints, ...	0	1	6
1 Arrow against Idolatry, ...	0	0	6
1 Scudder on the Lords Prayer, ...	0	1	2
1 Helpe to Happinesse, ...	0	1	0
1 Scudders Directions, ...	0	1	6
1 Dr. Tayler, ...	0	1	0
	3	6	3

Chemnitii Harmon;   in Prophetas Minores;
Pareus de Imaginibus;   in Proverbia et Cantica;
Piscator in Genesin;   in Jobam;
      in Exod;   in Isaiam;
      Deuteronomin;   Buxtorfii Synagoga Judaica;
      in Chronicles;   Bellarminus Enervatus, 2 vol;
      Samuel;   1 Ametii Medulla, 12;
      in Regum;   . Molerus.
      in Psalmos;

Amount unto £3 15s.

A Note of the rest of the Bookes, 16th of Aprill, 1629.

1 Scapula, ...	0	13	0
1 A Concordance, ...	0	15	0
1 Pareus in Rom., ...	0	7	0
1 Dr. Wilcox Works, ...	0	6	0
1 Paget against Aynsworth, ...	0	2	6
1 Wemes his Image, ...	0	2	0
1 Bernard against Brownists, ...	0	1	8
1 A Bible, ...	0	6	0
1 Raising Brownisme, ...	0	0	8
1 Moses Unvayled, ...	0 ⎱	1	4
1 Popish Glorying, ...	0 ⎰		
1 Clenards Grammer, ...	0	1	6
1 Camdens Grammer, ...	0	1	2
1 Esp. Greeke and Latin, ...	0	1	2
2 Ainsworths Psalmes, ...	0	1	4
2 dussen and ten Catechismes, ...	0	3	0
1 Rider London, ...	0	7	0
	3	10	4

16 Aprill, 1629.

80 women and mayds;
26 children;
300 men with victualls, armes, and tooles, and necessary apparell for them;
12 faggotts of steele;
5 tunnes of iron;
340 hogsheads of meale;
120 hogsheads of malte;
64 quarters of pease;
60 waie of cheese;
80 waie of salt;
60 firkins of butter;
140 head of cattell, with hay and provender for them;
40 goats;
40 hogsheads of beife and pork;
8 pieces of ordinance;
40 barrills of powder;
200 musketts;
60 pykes;
3 fother of lead.

In merchandize of severall kyndes, as kettles, bugles, spoones, knives, scissers, combes, linnen, and woollen cloath and other things, in all the value of £350.

After my hearty commendations, whereas his majesty, in and by his letters patents, under the great seale of England, bearing

The 27th of Aprill, 1629.

PRESENT, Mr. Governor,
this day, Mr. Treasurer,
  Mr. Adams,
  Mr. Nowell,
  Mr. Humfrey,
  Mr. Crane,
  Mr. Burnet,
  Mr. Warren,
  Mr. Backhouse,
  Mr. Webb,

Mr. Deputy,
Sir Rich: S[altonstall,]
Mr. William [Vassall,]
Mr. H[ughson,]
Mr. Whe[tcombe,]
Mr. Pincheon,
Mr. Winche,
Mr. Colbron,
Mr. Ballard.

A WARRANT delivered this day to Mary Slaynie, for 20s.

Mr. Pincheon was sworne unto the Company Assistant.

The letters that are written unto Captaine Endicott are approved of, and copies of them to be taken notice of.

The 30th of Aprill, 1629.

PRESENT, Mr. Governor,
this day, Mr. Deputy,
  Mr. Treasurer,

Mr. Humfreys,
Mr. Hutchinson,
Mr. Sam: Vassall,

Mr. Adams,	Mr. Sam: Aldersey,
Mr. Foxcroft,	Mr. William Vassall,
Mr. Nowell,	Mr. Rich: Perry,
Mr. Huson,	Mr. Tho: Walgrave,
Mr. Pincheon,	Mr. Herbert Pelham.

DELIVERED a warrant unto Richard Trott for 2 seales in silver, the summe of £5.

To Mr. John Clarke for........................ £5 4s.

Unto Richard Bowry for two parts of his agreement, .. £12.

To Mr. Thomas Prince, ... £6 4s.

It is agreed for the three shippes that are to goe forth now for New England, the one halfe of the charge to be the Governors, and the other to be at the Companies charge.

The letters read, which were sent in the George and Talbut, and confirmed.

Mr. Samuel Aldersey tooke his oathe of Assistant.

Mr. John Endecott and Mr. Samuell Sharpe being both put to election for Governor of the Plantation in the Mattachusetts Bay, Captaine John Endecott was chosen by a full and free election for the yeare following to be Governor, and the yeare to begin from the time he shall take his oath.

Mr. Francis Higgenson, Mr. Samuel Skelton, Mr. Francis Bright, Mr. John Browne, Mr. Samuel Browne Sharpe, or any one of them, but in the case of all their absence, Abraham Palmer or Elias Styleman are to administer the oath sent herewith, to the said Governor, Mr. Endecott, for the execution of his place.

Mr. Francis Higginson, Mr. Samuel Skelton, Mr. Francis Bright, Mr. John Browne, Mr. Samuel Browne, Mr. Thomas Graves, Mr. Samuel Sharpe, these by free election of hands were chosen to be of the counsell of the Mattachusetts Bay for the yeare ensuing, after they have taken their oaths, to assist the Governor, Captaine John Endecott, or his deputy, being such as shall be thereto chosen.

By erection of hands the old planters there that will live under our government are hereby authorized to choose 2 of the discreetest men among themselves to be of the Counsell; but in case they refuse, then the Governor, or Deputy, and the 7 of the Counsell abovementioned, or the major parte of them, are to choose 2 in lieu of them to be of the Counsell.

By erection of hands the Governor, or Deputy, and the 7 of the Counsell abovenamed, or the major parte of them, are to choose 3 more, to be of the Counsell, such as they shall esteeme fittest thereto.

It is ordered that the Governor and the Counsell, or the major parte of them, shall choose a Deputy Governor for the yeare ensuing, to assist the Governor and the Counsell in his absence, and that the Governor shall give the Deputy and the Counsell their oathes appertayning to their places, a coppy whereof is sent herewith.

It is ffurder ordered by theise present, that the Governor, Deputy, and Counsell afforesayd, or the major parte of them, shall make choice of a Secretary, and such other officers as shall in there discressions seeme requesyte and neydffull, ffor   x   peasable and quyett goverment of the plantation; and   x   frame such oethes, and to administer the same to every of them, for the execution of his plase and office for the yeere insuing next after they shall have taken their oethes, as they in there discressions, or the greter number   x   them, shall thinke good.

And it is ordered, that the said Governor, Deputie, Councell, and other officers aforenamed, shalbe established and continue in their said severall places for one whole yeare, or untill this Court shall thinke fitt to chuse others in the place or places of them, or any of them; and in case of death, etc.

It is ffurder ordered, that the said Governor, Mr. Endecott, or his   x   and the said Counsell, beeing chosen as afforesayd, and having taken   x   oethes respectyvely to there places, or the greater number, whereof the Governor or Deputy to bee always one, at aney there meetings, (which the sayd Governor, at his discretion, or in his absence the Deputy, is hereby authorized to apoynt, as oft as there shalbee occasyon,) shall have ffull power and authoritey,   x   x   are heereby awthorized by power deryved from his   x   letters pattents, to make, ordeyne, and establish, all manner of wholsome and resonable orders, laues, statuts, ordinances, direc[tions] and instrucktyons, not contrary to the laws of the realme of England, ffor the present goverment of our plantation, and the inhabitants residinge within the lymitts of our plantation; a coppy of all which orders is from tyme to tyme to bee sent the Company in London.

It is ordered by theise presents, that a coppye of the acts and orders made this present day for settelling the goverment in the plantation of the Massatchusetts Bay aforesayd, shalbee fayreley ingrossed, and sent under the Companies seale, subscribed by the Governor and Deputy, by the speedyest conveyance for Newe England that   x   bee had.

All this conffirmed by erection of hands.

Mr. Walgrave, Mr. Pelham, and Mr. Humphry, and Mr. Nowel, are intreated [to] fframe the forme of the oeth for the Governor, Mr. Endecott, also for his Deputy, and for the Counsell, which   x   x   x   sent over and bee administred them in Newe England.

A Generall Court, holden at London, the 30th Day of Aprill, 1629, by the Governor and Company of the Mattachusetts Bay in New England.[5]

WHERAS the Kings most excellent Majesty hath bin gratiously pleased to erect and establish us, by his letters pattents, under the great seale of England, to bee a body corporate, entytuled the Governor and Company of the Mattachusetts Bay in New England, and therby hath endowed us with many large and ample pruiledges and immunities, with power to make good and wholsome lawes, orders, and ordinances, for the better maintenance and support of the said pruiledges, and for the better and more orderly and regular government, to bee observed in the prosecution and propagation of our intended voyages and the plantation there, authorising us to nominate, and appoint, and select fitt persons amoungst ourselves for the managing, ordering, and governing of our affaires, both in England and in the places speyed and graunted unto us by vertue of his majesty's said charter, wee have, in the prosecution of the said power and authoritie given us, and in conformitie thereunto, and to the purpose and intent thereof, and not otherwise, thought fitt to settle and establish an absolute government at our plantation in the said Mattachusetts Bay in New England, which, by the vote and consent of a full and ample Court

---

[5] This entry, carrying out the order just agreed upon, is in the handwriting of Secretary William Burgis and was originally bound into the records in the midst of the entry for May 13, 1629.

now assembled, is thought fitt, and ordered as followeth, viz.:—

That thirteene of such as shalbe reputed the most wyse, honest, expert, and discreete persons resident upon the said plantation, shall, from tyme to tyme, and at all tyme hereafter, have the sole managing and ordering of the government and our affaires there, who, to the best of their judgments, are to endeavour soe to settle the same as may make most to the glory of God, the furtherance and advancement of this hopeful plantation, the comfort, encouragement, and future benefitt of us and others, the beginners and prosecutors of this soe laudable a worke. The said 13 persons soe appointed to bee entytled by the name of the Governor and Councell of Londons Plantation in the Mattachusetts Bay in New England.

And having taken into due consideration the meritt, worth, and good desert of Capt. John Endecott, and others lately gone over from hence with purpose to resyde and continue there, wee have, with full consent and authoritie of this Court, and by erection of hands, chosen and elected the said Capt. John Endecott to the place of present Governor in our said plantation.

Also, by the same power, and with the like full and free consent, wee have chosen and elected Mr. Fra: Higgeson, Mr. Sam: Skelton, Mr. Fr: Bright, Mr. John Browne, Mr. Sam: Browne, Mr. Tho: Graves, and Mr. Samuell Sharpe, these seaven, to bee of the said councell, and doe hereby give power and authoritie to the said Governor and those seaven to make choice of 3 others, such as they, or the greater nomber of them, in their discretions, shall esteeme and conceive most fitt thereunto, to bee also of the said councell.

And to the end that the former planters there may have noe just occasion of exception, as being excluded out of the pruiledges of the Company, this Court are content, and doe order, by erection of hands, that such of the said former planters as are willing to live within the lymitts of our plantation shalbe enabled, and are hereby authorized, to make choice of 2 such as they shall thinke fitt, to supply and make upp the nomber of 12 of the said councell, one of which 12 is, by the Governor and councell, or the major part of them, to bee chosen Deputie to the Governor for the tyme being.

And further, the Court doth authorize and give power to the said Governor and councell, or the major part of them, (wherof the Governor or Deputie to bee alwayes one,) to make choice of a Secretary, and such other subordinate officers, to attend them at their courts, meetings, or otherwise, etc., as in their discretions shall seeme meete and needfull.

And to the end that every one of the forenamed officers, aswell Governor, Deputie, and councell as others who they shall thinke fitt to nominate and chuse, may bee the more carefull in perform-ance of the charge committed unto them, it is by this Court thought fitt and ordered, that each of them shall take an oath proper to that place hee shalbe elected and chosen to, which is to bee admin-istred unto him or them at the tyme of his or their election or admittance into the said severall place or places.

And we doe hereby authorize
to administer unto the Governor the oath to his place appertain-inge, and that the Governor, having taken his oath as aforesaid, shall administer the oath to the Deputie appertaining to his place. And wee doe further hereby authorize the Governor or Deputie, or ether of them, to administer the oath to the rest of the councell, and unto all others the severall officers respectively, which said oathes are to bee administred in a publique court, and not elswhere.

It is further concluded on and ordered by this Court, that the said Governor. Deputie, and councell, before named, soe chosen and established in their severall places, shall continue and bee confirmed therin for the space of one whole yeare from and after taking the oath, or untill such time as this Court shall thinke fitt to make choice of any others to succeed in the place or places of them or any of them.

And if it shall please God that any of them, or any others to bee hereafter chosen to any office there, shall depart this lyfe before th'xpiration of the tyme they were soe chosen, or for any misdemeanor or unfittnes shalbe held unmeete for the place hee was formerly chosen unto, that then the Governor or Deputie and councell, or the greater nomber of them, at an ample Court assemb[led], shall have power, and hereby are authorized, not only to remove and displace such unfitt person or persons, but also to nominate and choose a fitt person or persons to succeed him or them soe deceased, removed, or displaced, as aforesaid, into the said place or places, for the residue of the tyme unexpired.

And it is further agreed on and ordered, that the Governor for the tyme beeing shall have power, and is heereby authorized, to call courts and meetings in places and at tymes convenyent, as to his discretion shall seeme meete, which power is heereby also conferred upon the Deputie in the absence of the said Governor; and the said Governor or Deputie, togeather with the said councell, being chosen and assembled as aforesaid, and having taken their oaths respectively to their severall places, they, or the greater nomber of them, wherof the Governor or Deputie to bee alwayes one, are authorized by this act, grounded on the power derived from his majesty's charter, to make, ordaine, and establish all manner of wholsome and reasonable lawes, orders, ordinances, and constitutions, (soe as the same bee noe way repugnant or contrary to the lawes of the realme of England,) for the administring of justice upon malefactors, and inflicting condigne punishment upon all other offendors, and for the furtherance and propagating of the said plantation, and the more decent and orderly government of the inhabitants resydent there.

Thursday, the 7 May, 1629.

PRESENT, The Governor,   Mr. Cowlson,
    Mr. Deputy,   Mr. Nowell,
    Mr. Aldersey,   Mr. Humphry,
    Mr. Addams,   Mr. Tho: Pulyston.
    Mr. Hutchins,

THE last Court was read and confirmed by these present.

A fforme of an oeth for the Governor beyond the seas, [and] of an oeth for the Counsell there, was drawen and delivered to Mr. Humphry to sheue to Counsell.

Letters are to bee written about lands to bee allotted to ech adventurer; also about Mr. Fra: Webbs buiseynes for a mill, etc.

To have those punnished beyond seas that sell guns.

To have some mens lands layd together.

The 11th of Maye, 1629.

PRESENT,   Mr. Deputy,   Mr. Humfryes,
this day,   Mr. Tresurer,   Mr. William Vassell,
    Sir Rich: Saltinstall,   Mr. Peeters,
    Mr. Addams,   Mr. Pinchen,
    Mr. Nowell,   Mr. [Fox]crafte.
    Mr. Hutchens,

THIS daye Mr. Oldum propounded unto Mr. White, that he would have his patten examined; and its agred by the Courte not to have any treatye with him about it, by resone its thought he doth it not out of love, but out of some synister respect.

A warrant delivered unto Mr. Seale for   x   dozen and two hats, at ii shillings per dozen, for the somme of   20s iiii d

The 13th of Maye, 1629.

PRESENT,	The Governor,	Mr. Pinchen,
this day,	Mr. Deputy,	Mr. Hutchens,
	Mr. Tresurer,	Mr. Hewson,
	Mr. Glover,	Mr. Backhouse,
	Sir Rich: Saltingstall,	Mr. Ballard,
	Mr. Addams,	Mr. Crowther,
	Mr. Offeild,	Mr. Whichcote,
	Mr. Whetcombe,	Mr. White,
	Mr. Foxcraft,	Mr. Peeters,
	Mr. William Vassall,	Mr. Crane,
	Mr. Perry,	Mr. Humphry,
	Mr. Nowell,	Mr. [Sam: Vass]all.

DELIVERED a warrant unto Richard Bowry for twelve pounds, £xii, as ⅔ parts of £18, the other ⅓ beeing to bee paid per the Governor, and is for his apprentice, Robert Seale, his tyme.

Mr. Mathew Cradocke is this daye chosen by the consent of the generallity of the Company to be Governor to the New England Companye for the yeare followinge; Mr. Thomas Goffe, Deputy; also, Mr. George Harwood, Tresurer to the said Company.

The Assistants beeing this day to bee chosen, 2 of the former Assistants, mentioned in the pattent, viz., Mr. Jno. Endecott and Mr. John Browne beeinge out of the land, the other 16 were confyrmed, viz., Sir Rich: Saltonstall, Mr. Izaack Jonson, Mr. Samuell Aldersey, Mr. John Ven, Mr. Jno. Humphry, Mr. Symon Whetcombe, Increase Nowel, Rich: Perry, Nathaniell Wright, Sam: Vassall, Theophilus Eaton, Thomas Addams, Tho: Hutchins, George Foxcroft, William Vassall, and William Pinchion; and to make up the nomber of 18, Mr. John Pocock and Mr. Chr: Cowlson were chosen Assistants; and of theise all, exceptinge Mr. Iz: Jonson, Sam: Aldersey, Jno. Ven, Nathaniel Wright, Sam:

Vassal, Theophilus Eaton, and Chr: Cowlson, tooke there oathes apertayning.

William Burges, Humphrey Lewes, Jno. Washborne, and Lawrence Roe, beeing all putt in election for the plase of Secretary, by a free election, Mr. William Burges was chosen Secretary for the yeere ensuinge.

Humphry Seale chosen and sworen Beadle.

It is this day ordered, that whensoever any Court of Assistants shalbee summoned, whosoever of the Assistants comes not, twixt 25 March and 29 of September, before eight of the clock in the morning, and from 29 September to 25 March, before 9 of the clock in the morning, shall forfett twelve pence for every such offence; and if he come not within towe howers after either of the said howres respectyveley, then towe shillings for every defalt; ech man to fforffett and pay, and for want of payment within daies after demand made by the officer [of] the Company, the ffyne doble, to bee sett uppon his accomte; allwayes   x uppon   x   of the Governor   x   no ffull ex   x approbation   x   x   x   x   x   x   x   x x   x   x   x   x

It is also agreed, that for aney that shall have pryvat conference, after the Court is summoned, by the Governor, or his Deputy, knocking of the hammer thrice on the table to sitt downe and attend the Court, that six pence by every person for every such offence shalbee payd.

It is agreed, that three pounds shalbee paid Jno. Washebourne for his paynes as Secretary to the Companie for the tyme past.[6]

The Names of the Governor, Deputie, Tresorer, and Assistants, for the Yeare 1629, and other Officers.
Mr. Matthew Cradocke, Governor;
Mr. Tho: Goffe, Deputy;
Mr. George Harwood, Tresorer;
Assistants.

Sir Richard Saltonstall,   Mr. Samuel Vassall,
Mr. Isack Johnson,   Mr. Theophilus Eaton,

[6] Here the Records cease to be in the handwriting of Secretary John Washborne; and the subsequent pages of the manuscript, as far as Feb. 10, 1629–30, were written by Secretary William Burgis.

Mr. Sam: Aldersey,	Mr. Thomas Adams,
Mr. John Venn,	Mr. Thomas Hutchins,
Mr. John Humfrey,	Mr. Georg Foxcroft,
Mr. Symon Whetcombe,	Mr. William Vassall,
Mr. Increase Nowell,	Mr. William Pinchion,
Mr. Richard Perry,	Mr. John Pocock,
Mr. Nathaniell Wright,	Mr. Chistopher Cowlson;

William Burgis, Secretarie;
Humphrey Seale, Beadle.

At a court of Assistants, on Munday, the 18th of May, 1629.

PRESENT, Mr. Governor, Mr. Tho: Adams,
Mr. Deputie, Mr. Sym: Whetcombe,
Sir R: Soltonstall, Mr. Ri: Perry,
Mr. Geo: Harwood, Mr. Jo: Pocock,
Treasurer, Mr. Geo: Foxcroft.
Mr. Jno: Humphrey

WILLIAM BURGIS, chosen by the last Generall Court to bee Secretarie for the yeare ensuinge, was now admitted and sworne accordingly; upon the salarie of xx Marks from the day hee was chosen, for the said yeare.

The Acts made at a Court the 30th of April last, for chusing and establishing a Governor, Deputie, Councell, and other officers in New England, was now read; and this Court thought fitt to add thereunto, that they shalbe established in their said severall places for one whole yeare, or till such tyme as the Company heere shall thinke fitt to chuse others in the places of them, or any of them; and that in case any of them shall depart this lyfe before th'xpiration of the tyme they were soe chosen for, that the Governor, or Deputie, and Councell, at an ample Court assembled, shall have power to nominate and chuse fitt person or persons to succed him or them soe deceased in the said place or places for the residue of the tyme unexpired.

Mr. Humphreys and Mr. Addams are desired to meete and consider what provisions are fitt to bee now sent over to Capt: Jo: Indicott and his ffamylie, and to provyde the same accordingly.

The names of all the adventurers to bee now sent over, with the severall sommes by them underwritten; and it bee ordered that

the Governor and Councell there shall have power to allott unto
every particuler adventurer that shall desire the same by himselfe
or his assignees, 200 acres of land upon the somme of £50 adventure in the generall stock in this first devident, and proportionably
for more or less according to their severall adventurers.

And Mr. Governor, Deputie, Mr. Whyte, and Mr. Addams,
and Mr. Whetcombe are to meete at Mr. Governors house to
morrow morning at six of the clock, to advise and conclude of
this business.

The 19th of May, 1629.

[PRESENT,] Mr. Governor,   Mr. Whetcombe,
     Mr. Whyte, Mr. Adams.

CONCERNING the allottment of land to those persons as are
adventurers in the common stock, it is thought fitt that letters be
writt to the Governor to sett out and allott unto them after the
proportion of 200 acres of land ffor £50 adventer, and after that
rate for more or less, to the intent to build their houses and to
improove there labors theron; and if within 10 dayes after their
arrivall, and demand made by aney particuler adventerrer in the
common stock, or his servant ffor him, the same be not soe allotted,
then each man, being an adventurer, is heereby permitted ffree
liberty to build in aney plase where himselfe shall thinke most
convenient, with reservation not to build or manure that alreddy
built on or manured; provided, that if the plott of ground whereon
the towne is intended to bee built bee sett out, that it bee pub-
liqueley knowne to bee intended for that purpose, that then noe
man shall presume to build his howse aney where else, (unless it
bee in the Massachusetts Bay, and there according to such directions as shalbee thowght meete for that plase;) but in case his
allotment be not sett out within the towne where he shall build,
and having [in] his owne name, or in the behalfe of his master,
made request to the Governor to have the same assigned to him,
if it bee not done within 10 daies after his arryvall, it shalbee
ffreey ffor aney in such case, beeing an adventrer in the common
stock, to build his howse within the foresaid plott of ground sett
out for the towne to bee built on, and to impale to his owne usse
preportionable to halffe an acre of ground for £50 adventer in
the common stock, unless a greter or lesser preportion be formerley

determyned of by the Governor and Counsell; in which case, that proportion is to bee made use of and appropriated to ech man within the liberties of the plott sett out ffor the towne to bee built; and it is ordered, that conveyance bee made in the Companies name, with the common seale of the Companie to it, to aney that shall desire it, for ech mans peasable injoying of the land he holds, at the chardge of the Company.

It is further thought fitt, and ordered, That all such persons as goe over at their owne charge, and are adventurers in the common stock, shall have lands allotted to them for themselves and their families forthwith, 50 acres of land for each person; but being noe adventurers in the common stock, shall have 50 acres of land for the Master of the familie, and such a proportion of land more, if there bee cause, as, according to their charge and qualitie, the Governor and Councell of New England shall thinke necessary for them, whereby their charge may bee fully and amply supported; unless it bee to any with whom the Company in London shall make any other particuler agreement; to which relation is to bee had, in such case.

And for such as transport servants, land shalbe allotted for each servant, 50 acres to the master; which land the master is to dispose of at his discression, in regard the servants transportation, wages, etc., is at the masters charge.

A Court of Assistants, on Thursday, the 21th of May, 1629.

PRESENT, Mr. Governor.

Mr. Goff, Deputie,	Mr. Eaton,
Mr. Harwood,	Mr. Bilson,
Treasurer,	Mr. Th: Huson,
Mr. Addams,	Mr. Inc: Nouell
Mr. Whichcoyte,	Mr. Humphrey,
Mr. Foxcroft,	Capt: Waller,
	Mr. Hutchins.

MR. EATEN tooke the oath of Assistant. And hee is desired to accompany Mr. Humphrey to Mr. Whyte, the Councellor, to bee satisfied concerning the administering othes to the Governor and Councell in New England. Mr. Whetcombe is also desired to bee with them.

The Court of the 18th of May was now read, as also the order conceived by Mr. Governor, and others, concerning the allottment of lands, and a part of the letter formerly written in this particuler was confirmed; whereunto this Court thought fitt to add, if, within 10 dayes after arrivall of these shipps, and demand made by any person, adventurer in the common stock, or his or their servant, of their allottment of land, the same not being done, that in a convenyent place not formerly built nor manured, then each person be permitted to seate himselfe, and build his house, and incose the same to his or their use, not exceeding the one halfe of that proportion which by the former order of this Court is allowed; and when the devydent is made, to bee free to make his choice within the said allottment, if hee dislike that hee had formerly chosen.

It is thought fitt that the Secretary draw out at large the orders concerninge the establishment of the Governor and Councell in New England, as also the order made concerning the allotment of lands; and Mr. Governor, Mr. Deputie, Mr. Tresurer, Mr. Addams, Mr. Eaten, Mr. Hutchins, Mr. Nowell, Mr. Whetcombe, Mr. William Vassal, or any 4 of them, wherof the Governor or Deputie to bee alwayes one, are desired and appointed to meete and resolve of these orders, and to affix the Companyes seale therunto, as also for preparing letters to bee now written, and to resolve and determine of all other business requisite for dispatch of these shipps.

At a Court of Assistants, on Thursday, the 21th of May, 1629.[7]

THIS Court, taking into due and mature consideration how necessary it wilbe that a devydent bee forthwith made of some competent quantitie of land in the London plantation in New England, both for the present accommodation of the people lately gone thither, aswell to build them houses as to inclose and manure, and to feede their cattle on, have thought fitt and ordered, that the Governor, Deputie, and councell there shall make a devydent accordingly, and allott the same unto the severall adventurers and others, as followeth, viz.:—

That 200 acres of land bee by them allotted to each adventurer for £50 adventure in the common stock, and soe after that rate, and according to that proportion, for more or less, as the adventure

---

[7] This entry, carrying out the order just given, was originally bound into the records in the midst of the entry for May 13, 1629.

is, to th'intent they may build their houses and improve their labours thereon.

That every adventurer in the common stock, or his servant for him or on his behalfe, shall make request or demand to the Governor or Deputie and councell to have a proportion of land allotted unto him accordingly; and if, within ten dayes after such request or demand made, the same bee not sett out and allotted unto him, then such person or persons are, by vertue of this act, permitted and authorized to seate him or themselves, and build his or their house or houses, and inclose and manure ground, in any convenyent place or places not formerly built upon or manured; provyded, that the land soe made choice of by any such person or persons doe not exceede in quantytie the one halfe of the land which is to bee allotted unto him or them by devydent, according to this order above written; with liberty also, when the first devydent shalbe made, to take his or their allottment of land as others doe, in leiu of this, if in the meane tyme the first choice shalbe disliked by them or any of them.

And for further explanation of this act, it is thought fitt that if the platt of ground wheron the towne is to bee built bee sett out, and that it bee publiquely knowne to bee intended for that purpose, that then noe man shall presume to build his house in any other place, (unless it bee in the Mattachusetts Bay, and there according to such direction as shalbe thought meete for that place;) and in case his allottment for building his house within the platt of ground sett out for building of the towne bee not appointed unto him within 10 dayes after demand or request to the Governor or the Deputie and councell for the same, it shalbe free for any, being an adventurer in the common stock, or his servant for him, or on his behalfe, to build his house in any place within the said platt sett out for the towne, and to impale to the quantitie of halfe an acre of ground for each £50 adventure in the common stock, unless a greater or lesser proportion bee formerly determined by the Governor and councell, by which each builder is to bee guided and directed.

It is farther thought fitt and ordered, that all such as goe over in person, or send over others at their owne charge, and are adventurers in the common stock, shall have lands allotted unto them for each person they transport to inhabite the plantation, aswell servants as all others; which 50 acres of land, soe allotted to servants or others, is heereby ordered to bee to and for the use of his master or setter forth, being an adventurer in the common stock, to dispose of at his discretion, in regard the master, etc., is at the charge of the said servant and others, their transportation, wages, and otherwise; but for such as, being noe adventurers in the common stock, shall transport themselves and their famylies, it is ordered, that 50 acres of land shall   allotted and sett out for the master of the ffamilie, and such a proportion of land more, if there bee cause, as, according to their charge and qualitie, the Governor and councell of the plantation there shall thinke necessary for them, wherby their charge may bee fully and amply supported, unless it bee to any with whom the Company in London have or shall make any other particuler agreement, to which relation is to bee had in such case.

And to the end every adventurer may the more safely and peaceably enjoy their said lands allotted unto them or chosen by them, and the houses they build therupon as abovesaid, it is thought fitt and ordered by this Court, that conveyances shalbe made therof unto each particuler man for the land hee possesseth, in the Companyes name, and the common seale of the Company to bee therunto affixed by the Governor and councell there, at the charge of the Company; which common seale is by this Court thought fitt and ordered to bee committed to the charge and keeping of the Governor for the tyme beinge, and in his absence to his Deputie there.

All which premisses before mentioned the Company doe by generall consent ratyfie, establish, and confirme; and doe also order, that coppyes of these acts shalbe sent over to the Governor and councell there resydent, subscribed by the Governor, Deputie, and six of the Assistants heere, and sealed with the common seale of the Companie.

A Meeting at the Governors House, on Friday, the
22th of May, 1629.
PRESENT, Mr. Governor,   Mr. Adams,
                Deputie,   Mr. Humphrey.
THE orders drawne for th'stablishment of the Governor, Deputie, and Councell, and other officers in the plantation at the

Mattuchusetts Bay in New England, as also the orders for the devyding and allottment of land there to the adventurers and others, were now read, advised on, corrected, and concluded on, etc., togeather with the generall letter from the Company heere to the Governor and Councell there. All which are appointed to bee fairely engrossed, and the said orders to bee sealed with the common seale of the Companie, and sent over upon the shipps now ready to depart for New England.

A Generall Court, the 11th of June, 1629.

PRESENT, Mr. Governor,   Mr. William Vassall,
Mr. Deputie,   Mr. Webb,
Mr. Harwood,   Mr. Humfrey,
Treasurer,   Mr. Crane,
Mr. Adams,   Mr. Pulliston,
Mr. Jo: Venn,   Mr. Foxcroft.
Mr. Backhouse,

THIS Court was appointed to take consideration of raising of monyes for payment of divers debts and bills; and therupon an estimate was made of what was owing, per severalls bills, and which are of necessitie to bee presently paid.

That another day bee appointed, and the whole Company to bee summoned by ticketts, which is thought fitt to bee on Wensday next.

Mr. Godden, master of the shipp   , made demand of ffraight pretended to bee due unto him for his last voyage; but hee not expressing a certaine somme, this assembly thinke fitt to deferr him till the next Court; and in the meane tyme hee is desired to bring in a note of what is due, as also to give securitie to the Company to free them from any further demands, etc., and therupon a fynall conclusion therof to bee made.

A Generall Court, at the Deputyes House, on Wensday, the 17th of June, 1629.

PRESENT, Mr. Governor,   Mr. Cooke,
Mr. Deputie,   Mr. Clarke,
Sir R: Saltonstall,   Mr. Ballard,
Mr. Geo: Foxcroft,   Mr. Pulison,

Mr. Ri: Perry,	Mr. Walgrave,
Mr. Adams,	Mr. Backhouse,
Mr. Whitcombe,	Mr. Davis,
Mr. Pococke,	Mr. Edm: Whyte,
Mr. Johnson,	Capt. Waller,
Mr. Noell,	Capt. Venn,
Mr. Harwood,	Mr. Davis,
Treasurer,	Mr. Tho: Andrewes,
Mr. Whyte,	Mr. Aldersey,
Mr. Pelham,	

MR.   Johnson was sworne an Assistant of this Company,
being chosen therunto at a Court, the 13th of May, 1629.

Mr. Governor moved that a course might bee setled for bringing
in of moneyes; and Mr. Treasurer returned a note concerning the
Lecestershire men. It was propounded,—

To encrease their former subscriptions;

To invyte others to underwryte;

To borrow mony for a tyme, to supply th'occasions;

To take upp mony at interest.

That those heere present doe furnish 200 or 100 a peece, to
have allowance for it.

   Names of those in Court that underwritt to lend:—

Sir R: Saltonstall,	......£100	Sym: Whetcomb,	...... £25
Mr. Governor,	 150	Tho: Hutchins,	 25
Mr. Deputie,	 050	Edw: Cooke,	 50
Perrie,	 025	Dan: Ballard,	 25
Addams,	 050	Edm: Whyte,	 20
Increase Noell,	 25	Joseph Caron,	 25
George Harwood,	 50	Aldersey,	 50
Rich: Whyte,	 25	Tho: Andrewes,	 25
Mr. Clark,	 25		

The Court taking into consideration the necessitie of a present
supply of the somme of ffifteene hundred pounds, for discharging
of debts and bills, and that the monyes underwritten by the adventurers, and not yett brought in, nor not likely to bee brought in,
in convenyent tyme for satisfaction of those debts and bills which
are of necessitie to bee presently paid; upon several propositions
made, it [is] desired and concluded on, that those of the Company

heere present would each of them voluntarilie lend such a somme of mony as hee shall thinke fitt, for advancing the somme wanting, and to have the common seale of the Companie for the repayment therof, according to the tyme for which hee or they soe lend the same; and also that the Secretarie bee appointed, to goe to such others of the Companie not present as Mr. Governor shall name, to intimate the same unto them, and to desire them to underwryte what sommes they will lend for this occasion, according as many of the Company heere present have done.

And it is ordered, that the common seale of the Company bee given to them, and all others that will lend, for repayment therof at such tyme as they shall desire the same.

Auditors appointed for auditing the accompts, viz., Mr. Symon Whetcombe, Mr. Nathaniell Wright, Mr. Noell, Mr. Perry, Mr. Crane, Mr. Clarke, Mr. Eaton, and Mr. Andrewes; these 8, or any 4 or more of them, to meete at a convenyent tyme and place to audite the accompts.

A committee for reducing of all former orders into a methode, viz., the Governor, Mr. Whyte, Mr. Davenport, Mr. Johnson, Capt. Waller, Capt. Venn, Mr. Aldersey, Mr. Adams, Mr. Wright, and Mr. Darby, they or any 4 of   , and to present the same to the next Generall Court, to bee ratyfied and confirmed, in part or in whole, as shalbe then thought fitt; which are then by the Secretary to bee entered into a faire booke to bee kept for that purpose, according to the usage and custome of other Companyes.

A Generall Court, holden for the Company of the Mattachusetts Bay, in New England, at Mr. Deputyes House, on Tewsday, the 28 of July, 1629.

PRESENT, Mr. Matt: Cradock, Governor,
Mr. Thomas Goff, Deputie,
Mr. George Harwood, Treasurer,
Mr. Thomas Adams,
Mr. Nathaniell Wright,
Mr. Theophilus Eaton,
Mr. Richard Perry,
Mr. Increase Noell,
Mr. Symon Whetcombe,
Mr. John Pococke,
Mr. Colson,
Mr. Hutchins,
Mr. William Pinchon,
Mr. Sam: Vassall, Assistants,

Mr. Jos: Bradshawe,   Mr. Tho: Hewson,
Mr. Burnell,   Mr. Woodgate,
Mr. Rivet,   Mr. Webb,
Mr. Dan: Ballard,   Mr. Crane, Generalitie.
Mr. Spurstowe,

THE business treated on at the last meeting was now read; and therupon the accompts of Mr. Governor, Mr. Deputie, and Mr. Treasurer, being now presented to this Court, the Auditors, formerly appointed for auditing the Company accompts, were now desired to meete and peruse and audite these accompts; which they have agreed to doe to morrow in th'afternoone.

It was moved by Mr. Governor, that a shipp of 400 tonn and of good force being now to bee sold, should bee bought for the Companyes use, upon their generall stock; or that some particuler members of the Company would undertake to buy the said shipp, in regard the Company are not now in cash; and that the Company will not only imploy that shipp, but take other shipps of them of less defence, for transport of their cattle and all other commodities, from tyme to tyme, soe long as they shalbe willing to furnish such shippinge; wherupon Mr. Governor declared that hee was willing to take ⅛ part of the said shipp, or under.

and did wryte . . . . . . ⅛ part.	Mr. Revell, ... 1⁄16 part.
Mr. Deputie, ... 1⁄16	Mr. Aldersey, ... 1⁄16
Mr. Adams, ... ⅛	Mr. Milburne, ... ⅛
Mr. Wright, ... ⅛	Mr. Huson, ... 1⁄16
Mr. Eaton, ... 1⁄16	The Company, ... ⅛
Mr. Whetcombe, . . . 1⁄16	etc.

A letter of the 27th of May from Mr. Jo: Endecott was now read, wherin, amongst other things, hee complaines of the prophane and dissolute living of divers of our nation, former traders to those parts, and of their irregular trading with the Indians, contrary to his late Majesties proclamation, desiring that the Company would take the same into their serious consideration, and to use some speedy means heere for reformation thereof. Wherupon the proclamation made in Anno 1622 was read; and it is thought fitt that suite bee made to his Majesty or the lords for renewing therof, with addition of such benefitiall clauses as shalbe needfull for reforming so great and unsufferable abuses; and Mr. Governor, Mr. Aldersey, Mr. Wright, and Mr. Eaton are desired to repaire to the Lord Keeper and Mr. Secretary Coke to acquaint their honours herewith, and afterwards a petition to bee presented to the Councell Board accordingly.

A note of divers propositions offred to the consideration of this Company by one John Betts was read, pretending that hee is able to discover divers things for the good and advancement of the plantation, and the benefitt of this Company; wherupon some of those heere present were desired to enquire further of him, not only of his abilitie, but of his deportment in his lyfe and conversation, and then the Company to treat with him as they shall thinke fitt.

Also, Mr. Webb moved concerning a French man, being a phisitian, and otherwise well qualifyed, who is desirous to goe over to live upon the Companys plantation, and gave good commendations both of his suffyciency and of his godly lyfe and conversation; and of one Mr. Gardner, an able and expert man in divers faccultyes; who are to bee further enquired of and treated with, against the next meeting of the Companie.

It is also thought fitt and ordered, that letters bee written to those in the country to pay in what they are behinde upon their subscriptions; and that some tradesmen heere in London that have occasion to travell into any of those parts, bee desired to receive the mony on the Companys behalfe.

And lastly, Mr. Governor read certaine propositions conceived by himselfe, viz., that for the advancement of the plantation, the inducing and encouraging persons of worth and qualitie transplant themselves and famylyes thether, and for other weighty reasons therein contained, to transferr the government of the plantation to those that shall inhabite there, and not to continue the same in subordination to the Company heer, as now it is. This business occasioned some debate; but by reason of the many great and considerable consequences therupon depending, it was not now resolved upon; but those present are desired privately and seriously to consider hereof, and to sett downe their particuler reasons in wryting pro and contra, and to produce the same at the next Generall Court; where they being reduced to heads, and maturely considered of, the Company may then proceede to a fynall resolution ther[on]; and in the meane tyme they are desired to carry this business secretly, that the same bee not divulged.

A Generall Court, holden at Mr. Deputyes House,
the 28 of August, 1629.

PRESENT, Mr. Goff, Deputie,   Mr. Adams,
Mr. Harwood, Treasurer,   Capt. Venn,
Sir Richard Saltonstall,   Mr. Pocock,
Mr. Johnson,   Mr. Perry,
Mr. Davenport,   Mr. Colston,
Mr. Humfreys,   Mr. Pinchion,
Mr. William Vassall,   Mr. Whetcombe,
Mr. Nowell,   Mr. Smith,
Mr. Foxcroft,   Mr. Revell,
Mr. Whyte,   Mr. Davis,
Mr. Cooke,   Mr. Eaton,
Mr. Ballard,   Mr. Colbrand.
Mr. Wright,

MR. Deputie acquainted this Court, that the espetiall cause of their meeting was to give answere to divers gentlemen, intending to goe into New England, whether or noe the chiefe government of the plantation, togeather with the pattent, should bee settled in New England, or heere.

Wherupon it was ordered, that this afternoone Mr. Wright, Mr. Eaton, Mr. Adams, Mr. Spurstowe, and such others as they should thinke fitt to call unto them, whether they were of the Company or not, to consider of arguments against the setling of the chiefe government in New England.

And, on the other syde, Sir Richard Saltonstall, Mr. Johnson, Capt. Venn, and such others as they should call unto them, to prepare arguments for the setling of the said government in New England; and that to morrow morning, being the 29th of August at 7 of the clock, both sydes should meete and conferr and weigh each others arguments, and afterwards, at 9 of the clock, (which is the tyme appointed of meeting for a Generall Court,) to make report therof to the whole Company, who then will determine this business.

*A Generall Court, at Mr. Deputyes House, the 29th
of August, 1629.*

PRESENT, Mr. Deputie,   Mr. Harwood, Treasurer,
      Sir Ri: Saltonstall,   Mr. Perry,
      Mr. Johnson,   Mr. Foxcroft,
      Mr. Davenport,   Mr. Davys,
      Mr. Aldersey,   Mr. Ironsyde,
      Mr. Humfrey,   Mr. Pinchon,
      Capt. Waller,   Mr. William Vassall,
      Capt. Venn,   Mr. Rowe,
      Mr. Adams,   Mr. Ballard,
      Mr. Eaton,   Mr. Nowell,
      Mr. Sam: Vassal,   Mr. Webb,
      Mr. Wright,   Mr. Whetcombe,
      Mr. Colston,   Mr. Colbrand.
      Mr. Pocock,

THIS day the committees which were appointed to meete yesterday in the afternoone to consider of arguments pro and contra
touching the setling of the government of the Companyes plantation in New England, being according to the order of the last
Court mett togeather, debated their arguments and reasons on
both sydes; where were present many of the Assistants and generalitie; and after a long debate, Mr. Deputie put it to the question,
as followeth:

As many of you as desire to have the pattent and the government
of the plantation to bee transferred to New England, soe as it
may bee done legally, hold up your hands: Soe many as will not,
hold upp your hands.

Where, by erection of hands, it appeared by the generall consent
of the Company, that the government and pattent should bee setled
in New England, and accordingly an order to bee drawne upp.

*A Generall Court holden at Mr. Deputyes House,
the 19th of Sept., 1629.*

PRESENT, Mr. Matt: Cradock, Governor,   Mr. Colson,
      Mr. Tho: Goff, Deputy,   Mr. Pinchon,
      Mr. Geo: Harwood, Treasurer,   Mr. Hutchins,
      Mr. Spurstowe,   Mr. Perry,

Mr. Pocock,   Mr. Whetcombe,
Mr. Wrighte,   and others.

AT this Court letters were read from Capt. Endicott and others from New E.; and wheras a difference hath falne out betwixt the Governor there and Mr. John and Samuell Browne, it was agreed by the Court, that for the determination of those differences, Mr. John and Samuell Browne might choose any 3 or 4 of the Company on their behalfe, to heare the said differences, the Company choosing as many: Wherupon the said Mr. John and Samuell Browne made choice of Mr. Sam: Vassell, and Mr. William Vassell, Mr. Symon Whetcombe, and Mr. William Pinchion; and for the Companie there were chosen Mr. John Whyte, Mr. John Davenport, Mr. Isack Johnson, and Mr. John Wynthropp; who, with the Governor or Deputie, are to determine and end the business the first Tewsday in the next tearme; and if any of the aforenamed partyes bee absent, others to bee chosen by ether partyes in their steade.

For the unlading of the shipps now come, viz., the Lyons Whelpe and the Talbott, it was desired that the Governor and Deputie would take such order therin as they should thinke fitt.

And lastly, for the 5 boyes returned from New England upon the Talbutt, it is to bee advised on what course to bee taken for their punishment, ether by procuring Mr. Recorder his warrant, by complaning to the Judge of the Admiraltie or otherwise.

A Generall Court holden at Mr. Deputyes House, on Tewsday, the 29th of Sept., 1629.

PRESENT, Mr. Matthew Cradock, Governor, Mr. Andrewes,
Mr. Thomas Goff, Deputy,   Mr. Roe,
Capt. Waller,   Mr. Revell,
Capt. Venn,   Mr. Huson,
Mr. Nath: Wright,   Mr. Webb,
Mr. Tho: Adams,   Mr. Woodgate,
Mr. Geo: Foxcroft,   Mr. Puliston,
Mr. Richard Perry,   Mr. Bateman,
Mr. Nowell,   Mr. Wynche.
Mr. Sym: Whetcombe,

AT this Court were read the orders made the 28th and 29th of August last, concerning the transferring of the pattent and government of the plantation into New England: but that business, being of great and weighty consiquences, is thought fitt to bee deferred for determina[tion] untill Sir R. Saltonstall, Mr. Johnson, and other gentlemen bee come upp to London, and may bee heere present; and in the meane tyme it was propounded that a committee should bee appointed to prepare the business;

To take advice of learned councell whether the same may be legally done or noe;

By what way or meanes the same may be done, to corispond with, and not to prejudice the government heere;

To consider of the tyme when it willbe fitt to doe it;

To resolve on whom to conferr the government; and divers other circumstances materiall to bee resolved on, etc.

The next thinge taken into consideration was the letters from Mr. Jo: and Samuell Browne to divers of their private freinds heere in England, whether the same should bee delivered or detained, and whether they should bee opened and read, or not; and for that it was to bee doubted by probable circumstances, that they had defamed the country of New England, and the Governor and government there, it was thought fitt that some of the said letters should bee opened and publiquely read, which was done accordingly; and the rest to remaine at Mr. Deputyes house, and the partyes to whom they are directed to have notice, and Mr. Governor, Mr. Deputie, Mr. Treasurer, and Mr. Wright, or any two of them, are intreated to bee at the opening and reading thereof, to the end the Company may have notice, if ought bee incerted therein which may bee prejudiciall to their government, or plantation in New England.

And it is also thought fitt that none of the letters from Mr. Sam: Browne shalbe delivered, but kept to bee made use of against him as occasion shalbe offred.

The business of cleering the 2 shippes lately come home, paying and discharging the men, and housing the goods, is recommended to the care of Mr. Deputie, who hath undertaken the same.

It is also thought fitt and ordered, that the Secretary shall wryte out a coppy of the former grant to the Erle of Warwick and others, which was by them resigned to this Company, to bee presented to his Lordship, as hee having desired the same.

Mr. Governor moved to knowe the resolution of the Company concerning buying the shipp Eagle; and it was concluded on, as formerly, that the said shipp should bee bought by those hereafter named, viz.,

The Governor,	⅛	Mr. Revell,	1/16
The Deputie,	1/16	Mr. Aldersey,	1/16
Mr. Adams,	⅛	Mr. Milburne,	⅛
Mr. Wright,	⅛	Mr. Huson,	1/16
Mr. Eaton,	1/16	The Companie,	⅛
Mr. Whetcombe,	1/16		

And Mr. Governor is desired to goe on and conclude the bargaine upon such tearmes as hee can: And it was further thought fitt and resolved on, that this shipp, being of good force, and bought for the safety and honor and benefitt of the plantation, shall alwayes bee preferred in that voyage before any other shipp, and to have some consideration in her fraight above other shipps accordingly.

It is also thought fitt, for the present raysing of mony, that sale bee made of the beavor skins; and, to that purpose, a rate was now sett upon them of 20s per pound; and Mr. Nathaniell Wright, being heere present, is to have tyme till to morrow to accept of them at that rate, or to returne his answer; and in the meane tyme the skins not to bee sold under that rate, the sale of them being referred to Mr. Governor and Mr. Deputie.

Also some speech was had concerning the delivery of the petition to the Lords of the Councell; but this is deferred till their Lordships coming to London.

Mr. Treasurer and Mr. Adams are desired to make an abstract of those who are behinde with their subscriptions, to the end some course may bee taken to call in for those monyes.

For the 12 cowes, and 3 calfes, and 2 mares, and 2 foles, it is thought fitt that they bee forthwith sold, rather then kept at charges all this winter; which is recommended to the care of Mr. Bateman and Mr. Huson.

Also, concerning the 5 boyes returned in the Talbott, Mr. Whetcome and Mr. Noell are desired to acquaint Sir Hen: Martyn with their misdemeanour, and to advise what punishment may bee inflicted upon them, and how the Company may bee legally discharged of them.

Upon the desire of Mr. John and Samuell Browne, it is thought fitt and ordered, that they should have a coppy of the accusation sent from New England against them, to the end that they may bee the better prepared to make answere therunto.

Mr. Wright is desired to take care of the sale of the clapboard and other wood.

Also, letters from Robert Moulton, the shipwright, and from the cowpers and cleavers of wood, consisting of divers perticulers, were now read; which are to bee abrevyated, and fitting answers to bee made unto them by the returne of the next shipps to New England.

A Generall Court at the Deputyes House, on Thursday,
the 15 of Octo., 1629.

PRESENT, Mr. Matt: Cradock, Governor,
         Mr. Geo: Harwood, Treasurer,
         Sir Richard Saltonstall,
         Mr. John Davenport,
         Mr. Isack Johnson,
         Mr. Samuell Aldersey,
         Mr. John Humfry,
         Mr. Nath: Wright,
         Mr. John Venn,
         Mr. Tho: Adams,
         Mr. William Vassall,
         Mr. Symon Whetcombe,
         Mr. William Pynchion,
         Mr. Geo: Foxcroft,

Mr. Increase Noell,
Mr. Ballard,
Mr. Revell,
Mr. Dudley,
Mr. Winthrop,
Mr. Webb,
Mr. Huson,
Mr. Young,
Mr. Whichcoyte,
Mr. Crane,
Mr. Owen Roe,
Mr. Forde, with
    divers others of
    the generalitie.

THE espetiall and only occasion of this meeting beinge to consider and resolve of the setling the trade in New England, (now upon transferring the government thither,) for th' incouragment aswell of the adventurers in the joynt stock heere, as of those who already are, and of others who intend to goe over in person to bee planters there, and for their mutuall corispondence and behoofe, and the advancement of the plantation to the end which was at first intended: The Court tooke the same into due and mature consideration; and after a long debate, and sundry opinions given, and reasons why the joynt stock (which had borne the brunt of the charge hetherto, and was likely to beare much more) should have certaine commodityes appropriate therunto, for reembursment and defrayment thereof, and divers objections being made to those reasons, all which was largly discused and well weighed, the Court, in conclusion, for accomodation of both parts, fell upon a moderation, as followeth, viz.:

That the Companye's joint stock shall have the trade of beavor and all other ffurrs in those parts soly, for the tearme of 7 yeares from this day, for and in consideration of the charge that the joynt stock hath undergone already, and is yett annually to beare, for th' advancement of the plantation.

That for the charge of ffortyfications, the Companyes joint stock to beare the one halfe, and the planters to defray the other, viz., for ordnance, munition, powder, etc.: But for laborers in building of fforts, etc., all men to bee employed in an equall proportion, according to the nomber of men upon the plantation, and soe to continue untill such fitt and necessarie works bee finished.

That the charge of the ministers now there, or that shall hereafter goe to resyde there, as also the charge of building convenyent churches, and all other publique works upon the plantation, bee in like manner indifferently borne, the one halfe by the Companyes joynt stock for the said tearme of 7 yeares, and the other halfe by the planters.

That the ordnance already provyded for fortyfication bee rated as they cost, as also all powder and munition whatsoever concerning armes, soe as the same bee delivered there for publique use; and this to bee accompted as part of the joynt stock of the Company.

All which beeing severall tymes read, was by Mr. Governor put to the question, and by generall consent, by erection of hands, was agreed and concluded on, and ordered accordingly.

And forasmuch as by former order the pattent and government i[s] to bee transferred to New England, a committee is appointed, part of the adventurers heere, and part of those that intend to goe over, viz.:

Mr. Davenport,	Mr. Adams,
Mr. Wright,	Mr. Whetcombe,
Mr. Perry,	Mr. Young,
Capt. Waller,	Mr. Spurstowe,
Capt. Venn, and	Mr. Revell;
Sir R: Saltonstall,	Mr. Dudley,
Mr. Johnson,	Mr. Va[ssall],
Mr. Winthrope,	Mr. [Pinchon,]
Mr. Humfry, and	Mr. [Downing;]

who are desired to meete tomorrow morning, to conferr of and drawe fitt and convenyent clauses to bee incerted in articles of agreement, which may bee commodious for ether part, and to prepare the same for a Court of Assistants, appointed that afternoone to determine therof.

A Court of Assistants at the Deputies House, on Fryday, the 16 of Octo., 1629.

PRESENT, Mr. Matth: Cradock, Governor,	Mr. Geo: Harwood, Treasurer,
	Mr. Winthrop,
Sir R: Saltonstall,	Mr. Huson,
Mr. Is: Johnson,	Mr. Whetcombe
Mr. Dudley,	Mr. Perry,
Mr. Jo: Humfry,	Mr. Pocock,
Mr. William Vassall,	Mr. Spurstowe,
Mr. Revell,	Mr. Pinchon,
Mr. Geo: Foxcroft,	Capt. Venn,
Mr. Adams,	Mr. Sam: Vassall.

THIS Court was appointed to treat and resolve, that upon the transferring of the government to N. England, what government shalbe held at London, wherby the future charge of the joynt stock may bee cherished and preserved, and the body politique of the Company remaine and increase.

What persons shall have the charge of the managing of the joynt stock, both at London and in N. England; wherin it is conceeved fitt that Capt. Endecott continue the government there, unless just cause to the contrarie.

These and other things were largely discussed; and it was thought fitt and naturall that the government of persons bee held the   the government of trade and marchandizes to be heere;

That the joynt stock being mutuall, both heere and there, that some fitt persons bee appointed for managing therof in both places;

But for that there is a great debt owing by the joynt stock, it was moved that some course might bee taken for cleering therof, before the government bee transferred; and to this purpose it was first thought fitt that the accompts should bee audited, to see what the debt is; but the business not admitting any such delay, it was desired that Mr. Governor and Mr. Treasurer would meete to morrow, and make an estimate of the debts, and prepare the same against a meeting to bee on Monday next, to determine this question.

The Shipp Eagle is to bee fraighted from Bristoll.

Lastly, letters were read and signed to Mr. Endecott, Mr. Skelton, and Mr. Higgison, as appears by the entryes of them in the booke of coppyes of letters.

A Meeting at Mr. Deputies House, on Monday,
the 19th of Octo., 1629.

PRESENT, Mr. Matth. Cradock,   Mr. Adams,
              Governor,   Mr. Foxcroft,
        Mr. Geo: Harwood,   Sir R. Saltonstall,
              Treasurer,   Mr. Isack Johnson,
        Mr. Na: Wright,   Mr. Davenport,
        Capt. Venn,   Mr. Whyte, the Preacher,
        Mr. Pinchon,   Mr. Whyte, the Councellour,
        Mr. William Vassall,   Mr. Wynthropp,
        Mr. Huson,   Mr. Dudley.
        Mr. Noell,

TH'OCCASION of this meeting being to resolve of the alteration of the government, and therin to consider how the debts upon the joynt stock shalbe first discharged, and how the same shalbe hereafter managed; and herein what was formerly treated on, was againe related, and for that divers questions will arise to bee determined in this business, which will take upp much tyme, and cannot bee soe convenyently done at a Court, it was thought fitt that certaine committees bee appointed on ether part to meete and make propositions each to other, and sett the same downe in wryting; and if they can, to agree and conclude of a fitt end to bee made for the good of the plantation; and if any difference happen which they cannot agree on, that then the same bee referred to the umperage and determination of some of the preachers to bee chosen to that purpose; who are desired to sett downe in wryting what they shall thinke in conscience is fitt to bee done, indifferently for the good of the worke and the encouragement both of planters and adventurers: And to this purpose, articles betweene the planters and adventurers for performance of what shalbe determined, was now drawne by Mr. Whyte, the councellour, read and approved, and are to bee presented to morrow at a Generall Court, to bee ratyfyed, and then sealed; and at that Court the Governor and Assistants to bee chosen for the Government in N. England.

A Generall Court holden at Mr. Goff the Deputyes House, on Tewsday, the 20th of Octo., 1629.

PRESENT, Mr. Matthew Cradock, Governor,
Sir Richard Saltonstall,
Mr. Isack Johnson,
Capt. Jo: Venn,
Mr. Aldersey,
Mr. Nath: Wright,
Mr. Geo: Harwood, Treasurer,
Mr. Jo: Humfry,
Mr. William Vassall,
Mr. William Pinchon,
Mr. Geo: Foxcroft,
Mr. Increase Noell,
Mr. Chr: Colson,
Mr. Rich: Perry,
Mr. Tho: Adams,
Mr. Jo: Pocock,
Mr. Tho: Hutchins, Assistants;

Mr. Davenport, } Clerks:
Mr. Whyte,
Mr. Wenthrop,
Mr. Dudley,
Mr. Puliston,
Mr. Ballard,
Mr. Job Bradshaw,
Mr. Cooke,
Mr. Revell,
Capt. Waller,
Mr. Ballard,
Mr. Woodgate,
Mr. Stephens,
Mr. Fr: Flyer,
Mr. Spurstowe,
Mr. Huson,
Mr. Roe,
Mr. Webb; with some others of the generalitie.

MR. Governor caused to bee read the order formerly made concerning the buying of the shipp Eagle, and desired to knowe the pleasure of the Court for confirmation thereof: wherupon some debate being had, the order was well approved of; but for that it is wished that the gentlemen that are to goe over should have the ⅛ part of the said shipp which was formerly allotted to the Companie, (the Companie being out of cash, and for other reasons,) they not having notice thereof till now, desired tyme till the after noone to consider thereof, and to give their answere; which was condiscended unto, and the same is then to bee determined accordingly.

After which Mr. Governor acquainted those present, that the espetiall occasion of summoninge this Court was for the election of a new Governor, Deputie, and Assistants, the government being to bee transferred into New England, according to the former order and resolution of the Company. But before the Court proceeded to the said election, certaine articles of agreement, conceived at a meeting yesterday betweene the adventurers heere at home and the planters that are to goe over, aswell for the mannaging and setling of the joynt stock as for reconcilinge of any differences that may happen upon this change of government, was now read and recommended to the Court for their approbation, and for the nomination and appointment of a compitent nomber of committees to meete and treat and resolve of these businesses. The articles themselves were approved of, and 5 committees on ether part were therupon chosen, viz., Sir Richard Saltonstall, Mr. Winthrop, Mr. Dudley, Mr. Johnson, and Mr. Humfrey for the planters; and for the adventurers was chosen, Mr. Governor, Mr. Aldersey, Mr. Wright, Mr. Hutchins, and Capt. Venn. And in case the said committee, or the greater nomber of them, should differ in any one or more particulers, and not agree theron, there was chosen for umpiers, Mr. Whyte, the councellour, Mr. Whyte, of Dorchester, and Mr. Davenport, to whom the desition and determination of all such differences is referred, according to the tenure of the said articles of agreement. And it being further taken into consideration, that, in regard of the shortness of the tyme limitted to the committees, many things of waight and consiquence in this soe great a business may ether not bee at all thought on, or otherwise left unresolved by them and the said umpiers, it is therefore thought fitt by this Court thatt the said committee and umpiers shall continue till the end of this tearme; and whatsoever materiall things for the good of the plantation shall in that tyme bee treated on and resolved by them, the same to bee as valide and effectuall as if it had bin done before the expiration of the tyme limitted by the articles. And it was further thought fitt that all such others of the Company as will may, from tyme to tyme, have access to the said committee, to propound such things as they conceive benefitiall for the business, or to present their opinions in wryting, but not to debate with them for interrupting their proceedings.

All which, being put to the question, was approved of, and, by erection of hands, ordered accordingly.

And now the Court, proceeding to the election of a new Governor, Deputie, and Assistants, which, upon serious deliberation, hath bin and is conceived to bee for the espetiall good and advancement of their affaires, and having received extraordinary great commendations of Mr. John Wynthrop, both for his integritie and sufficiencie, as being one every well fitted and accomplished for the place of Governor, did putt in nomination for that place the said Mr. John Winthrop, Sir R: Saltonstall, Mr. Is: Johnson, and Mr. John Humfry; and the said Mr. Winthrop was, with a generall vote and full consent of this Court, by erection of hands, chosen to bee Governor for the ensuing yeare, to begin on this present day; who was pleased to accept therof, and therupon tooke the oath to that place appertaine . In like manner, and with like free and full consent, Mr. John Humfry was chosen Deputie Governor,

and Sir R: Saltonstall,	Mr. Thomas Sharpe,
Mr. Is: Johnson,	Mr. John Revell,
Mr. Tho: Dudley,	Mr. Matt: Cradock,
Mr. Jo: Endecott,	Mr. Thomas Goff,
Mr. Noell,	Mr. Aldersey,
Mr. William Vassall,	Mr. John Venn,
Mr. William Pinchon,	Mr. Nath: Wright,
Mr. Sam: Sharpe,	Mr. Theoph: Eaton, and
Mr. Edw: Rossiter,	Mr. Tho: Addams,

were chosen to bee Assistants; which said Deputie, and the greatest part of the said Assistants, being present, tooke the oaths to their said places appertaining respectively.

*A Court of Assistants, at Mr. Goffs House, on Fryday, the
20th of Novemb., 1629.*

PRESENT, Mr. John Wynthrope,   Mr. Hutchins,
        Governor,   Mr. Tho: Goff,
    Mr. John Humfry,   Mr. William Pinchion,
      Deputy Governor,   Mr. Colson,
    Sir Richard Saltonstall,   Mr. Matt: Cradock,
    Mr. Thomas Dudley   Mr. George Harwood,
    Mr. Thomas Adams,   Mr. John Revell,
    Mr. Nathaniell Wright, Mr. Increase Noell.

THE espetiall occasion of this meetinge was to advise of a course
for bringing in of monyes, for payment of marryners wages, fraight
of shipps, and other debts; and therupon Mr. Cradock acquainted
those present what sommes hee had disbursed for accompt of the
Company, and what more was owing for marryners wages upon the
shipps Talbot, Mayflower, and Fower Sisters, and for the fraight
of those shipps, amounting to £1200 and upwards; which the
Court thinke fitt, and order, to bee first paid before any other
debts. And Mr. Governor desiring to have power from the Court
to graunt warrants for payment of monyes, as was formerly accustomed, the same was condiscended unto; and a warrant was
now made and signed by the Governor and Deputie, directed to
Mr. Harwood, the Treasorer, for payment of [£]800 to Mr.
Cradock, soe soone as mony shall come to his hands.

Some debate was had concerning Mr. John and Sam: Browne
complayning that their goods, praised in New England, are under-
valued, and divers things omitted to bee praised; wher[ein] they
desire to have releife and justice done. It is therupon thought fitt,
that if they can produce proofe therof, then they are to bee re-
leived heere; otherwise, the same is to bee suspended, and all the
objections they can make to bee taken notice of and recommended
to Mr. Governor, to bee considered of and determined after his
arrivall in New England, when hee may heere the praisers answers
to those objections; and, in the meane tyme, Mr. Cradock to pay
the mony charged upon him for the same.

Mr. Beecher, Master of the shipp Talbot, desired to have in a
bond, which hee entered into, to Mr. Pratt, for wages or allowance
to a chirurgion for the Lyons Whelpe, who was to have 2s 6d for

every person in the shipp, according to an agreement made with
them, the nomber of the persons being about 125, of which Mr.
Beecher had formerly delivered a particuler note to Mr. Goff. The
Court conceiving the said allowance to bee exorbitant, and more
then is usuall in like cases, doe desire that the chirurgion bee
appointed to bee heere the next Generall Court, and then such
conclusion is to bee made with him as shalbe fitt.

Lastly, Mr. Smith, the accomptant, attended them with their
accompts; and, after perusal therof, it appearing that divers were
behynde with their whole subscriptions, or part therof, it was
thought fitt, that, for the present supply of monys, ticketts should
bee sent unto them to desire them to send in the sommes by them
underwritten; to which purpose a list of their names and sommes
was now drawne out; and ticketts are forthwith to bee made
accordingly.

A Generall Court, on Wensday, the 25 of Novem., 1629.

PRESENT, Mr. Jo: Winthrope,
            Governor,
      Mr. Jo: Humfry, Deputy,
      Sir R: Saltonstall,
      Mr. Isack Johnson,
      Mr. Thomas Adams,
      Mr. Nathaniell Wright,
      Mr. Theoph: Eaton,
      Mr. William Pinchion,
      Capt. Venn,
      Mr. Encrease Noel,

Mr. Matthew Cradock,
Capt. Waller,
Mr. Whyte,
Mr. Davenport,
Mr. Huson,
Mr. Backhouse,
Mr. Foxcroft,
Mr. Woodgate,
Mr. Bradshawe,
      and others.

A LETTER of the fift of September, from Mr. Endecot, the Governor, and others in New England, was now read; as also Mr.
Governor acquainted those present with certaine testymony sent
over against one William Rovell, master of a shipp of   , concerning some insolent and misbeseeming speeches uttered by him
in contempt of the Companyes pruiledges and government; which
is to bee taken into further consideration, and bee proceeded
against, when other certyficates are come, which are expected, concerning that business.

This day being one of the 4 quarter dayes appointed by the

charter for keeping a Generall Court, the generall business of the
plantation should have bin treated on; but by reason of the small
appearance, and shortness of tyme, nothing was done therin: only
the Governor made relation of the proceedings of the joynt committee concerning the setling of the joynt stock: That notwithstanding there had bin all good concordencie and faire proceeding betweene them, yett, by reason of the greatness of the business, and
the smalness of the supplyes, they could not bring the same to a
wished effect, but only had reduced it to certaine proposions to
bee represented to the consideration of the Company, to receive
their resolution therin.

The accomptant having made an estimate of the accounts, the
joynt stock appeares to bee in arreare £3000 and upwards. Towards which £3000 there is 1900 in subscriptions not yet brought
in, and about 8 or 900 pounds upon fraight of shipps.

There wilbe a necessitie for supply of necessaryes for the ⎱
    Companyes servants, ... ⎰ 2000
    for marchandizes for trade, ... 0500
    for munition and artillery for ffortification, ... 0500

Soe as there being an inevitable necessitie of supply of money,
ether to revyve the old stock, or to raise a new, the propositions
were now expressed, viz.,

    1.   That all the former adventurers should double their former
subscriptions;

    2.   That the servants, cattle, and all marchandizes or provisions
belonging to the joynt stock, should bee sold, and the underwryters
bee paid their proportions of what shall accrew or arise thereof;

    3.   Or lastly, that the old stock bee putt over to certaine under-
takers, upon such conditions as can bee agreed on, and they to goe
on with the worke, and mannage the business, to beare all charges,
and to stand to profitt and loss, and to pay the underwryters their
principall by them brought, at the end of 7 yeares; and this to bee
understood not to exclude any who have affection to this business,
but that they may come in under those undertakers for such sommes
as they shall thinke fitt to adventure; but that for the better furtherance and facilitating the business, the same to bee managed by
few hands. And for th'incouragment of such undertakers, the committee have thought of certaine inducements: viz.,

That they shall have the one halfe of the beavor;

The sole makeing of salt;

The sole transpor[tation] of passengers; servants and goods to bee transported at reasonable rate;

To bee allowed a reasonable profitt upon all such provisions as they shall keepe in magazine there for the use and releife of th'inhabitants.

All which premises the Governor recommended to the consideration of those present; but by reason of the small appearance, nothing could bee determined, and therefore a spetiall Court is appointed for this purpose on Munday next, and the whole Company to bee summoned by ticketts to bee present.

Lastly, upon the motion of Mr. Whyte, to the end that this business might bee proceeded in with the first intention, which was cheifly the glory of God, and to that purpose that their meetings might be sanctyfied by the prayers of some faithfull ministers resident heere in London, whose advice would bee likewise requisite upon many occasion, the Court thought fitt to admitt into the freedome of this Company Mr. Jo: Archer and Mr. Phillip Nye, ministers heere in London, who being heere present, kindly accepted thereof: Also Mr. Whyte did recommend unto them Mr. Nathaniell Ward, of Standon.

A Generall Court at Mr. Goffs House, on Monday, the last of November, 1629.

PRESENT, Mr. John Winthrop, Governor;

Mr. John Humfry, Deputy;   Mr. Geo: Harwood, Treasurer;

Assistants,

Sir Richard Saltonstall,	Mr. Thomas Adams,
Mr. Isack Johnson,	Mr. Theophilus Eaton,
Mr. Thomas Goff,	Mr. Encrease Noell,
Mr. Tho: Dudley,	Mr. John Revell,
Mr. Nath: Wright,	Mr. William Pinchon;
Mr. Matt: Cradock,	

with many of the generalitie.   25.

IT was propounded to the Court that whereas the joynt stock was engaged to the value of £2500, present debt, and there was necessarilie required £1500 present disbursment for maintenance of the servants now in the plantation, and for commodities for truck and munition, that the adventurers would bee pleased to double their former subscriptions; which being not assented unto by the Court, it was propounded and agreed by generall consent that ten persons should bee chosen, 5 of the adventurers, and five of the planters, which should take the joynt stock at the true value, and take upon them the engagements and other charges; for which there should bee appropriated to the joynt stock, for 7 yeares, these pruiledges which follow, viz.:

1. Halfe the trade of the beavors, and all other furrs;
2. The sole making of salt;
3. The ffurnishing of a magazine at sett rates;
4. The sole transportation of passengers and goods at certaine rates.

For which end there was a committee appointed to value the joynt stock, viz.:

Mr. White, of Dorchester,   Mr. Webb,
Mr. Thomas Goff,   Mr. Increase Noell;

who, taking upon them the charge of the said business, did the next day (the Court then sitting upon adjornment) make certificate of their proceedings to this effect, viz.:

The first, the 10th month, 1629.[8]

That wheras divers sommes had bin disbursed in publique charges, as transporting of ministers and their ffamilies, amunition, etc., which were not now to bee valued to the undertakers, as beinge to remaine alwayes to the plantation; and wheras many of the servants, which were transported at extraordinary charge, doe not prove soe usefull as was expected, and soe will not yeild the undertakers any such benefitt as may answere their charge, divers of the cattle and provisions likewise miscarryinge, through want of experience in the begininge of such a worke, they could not fynde the said stock to remaine cleere and good, (the debts discharged,) above one third part of the whole somme which hath bin adventured from the first to this present day; which value, upon due examination and long debate, was allowed by all the Court.

Wherupon it was propounded and agreed by the whole Court, that the old adventurers (in leiu of this abatement of ⅔ of their adventurs) should have an addition of a double proportion of land, according to the first proportion of 200 acres for £50, and that

---

[8] This date is not in the handwriting of the Secretary but is an ancient interpolation, apparently very nearly contemporaneous with the record.

they should have libertie to putt in what sommes they pleased, to bee added to their former adventures, soe as they subscribed the same before the first day of January now next followinge; and such as live in the country, remote from the cittie of London, to enter their subscriptions before the second of February next: And that any of the said adventurers may take out their adventures after the aforesaid rate: And further, that it should bee lawfull for all other persons (with consent of any 3 of the undertakers) to put in what sommes of mony they please, to bee traded in the joynt stock, (upon such allowance to the common stock for publique uses, in regard that they shall beare noe part in the former losses,) as the said adventurers, or 3 of them, shall agree with them for, from tyme to tyme, and that all adventurers shall pay in their adventures in such tyme and manner as shalbe agreed betweene them and the said undertakers, or any three of them.

It was also agreed by the Court, that in regard the undertakers should beare the greatest charge and burthen, and all other adventurers should have equall part of the gaine, if any did proceede, that therfore they should have £5 in the hundred cleere gaines of the said joynt stock, both in and out, all charges beinge deducted.

And that the joynt stock being thus managed, at the end of 7 yeares, (to bee accompted from this day,) aswell the said stock, as the proceede and profitt therof, to bee devyded to every man proportionably, according to his adventure; and all the said previledges then to cease, and all persons to bee at libertie to dispose of their parts in the joynt stock at their owne pleasures.

Hereupon the Court thought fitt to desire the gentlemen hereunder named to undertake the joynt stock upon the tearmes before propounded, viz.:

Mr. John Winthrop, the Governor,	Mr. Matt: Cradock,
Sir Richard Saltonstall, Knight,	Mr. Nathaniell Wright,
Isack Johnson, Esquire,	Mr. Theophilus Eaton,
Mr. Thomas Dudley,	Mr. Thomas Goff,
Mr. John Revell,	Mr. James Younge;

which gentlemen (upon much entreaty of the Court) did accept of the said charge, and accordingly were chosen to bee undertakers, to have the sole managinge of the joynt stock, with all things incydent therunto, for the space of 7 yeares, as is aforesaid.

And it was agreed to desire and nominate Mr. Aldersey to bee treasorer for the said Companie; and that all monyes which shall come in to the joynt stock, or that shalbe given to the common stock, shalbe paid unto him, and to bee issued out upon warrant under the hands of the said undertakers, or any three of them, as occasion shall require.

It was also ordered by the Court, that the undertakers should provyde a sufficient nomber of shipps, of good force, for transporting of passingers, at the rate of £5 a person, and £4 a tonn for goods, which shalbe ready to sett saile from London, by the first day of March; and that if any passingers bee to take shipp at the Isle of Wight, the shipps shall stopp there 24 howers; and that all such as intend to pass over shall give in their names, with 40s towards their fraight to one of the said undertakers abyding in London, in the Michaelmas tearme before, and shall deliver their goods on shipp board before the 20th of February following, and shall give security for the rest of their fraight as they can agree with the said undertakers, ether for mony to bee paid heere, or for commoditie to bee delivered in the plantation.

Further it was agreed, that for the transportation of children this rate shalbe kept, viz.: Sucking children not to bee reckoned; such as under 4 yeares of age, 3 for one; under 8, 2 for one; under 12, 3 for 2. And that a shipp of 200 tonn shall not carry above 120 passengers compleate; and soe of other shipps after the same proportion. And for goods homewards, the fraight shalbe for beavors £3 per tonn, and for other commodities 40s per tonn; and such as will have their good assured shall pay £5 per C.

Concerning the magazine,   is likewise agreed, that the undertakers should furnish the plantation with all such commodities as they shall send for; and the planters to take them off and retaile them at their pleasure, allowing the undertakers £25 in the hundred above all charges; and the planters to have liberty to dispose of their part of the beavors at their owne will; and every man may fetch or send for any commoditie for his owne use, where or how hee please, soe as hee trade not with interlopers, soe long as hee may bee furnished suffitiently by th'adventurers at the rates aforesaid.

Lastly, it is ordered, that in regard this Court could not sett downe particuler direction for every thinge which may bee fitt to be considered and provyded for, in all or any of the matters aforesaid, therfore the said undertakers should have power to meete and consult about the premises; and what orders and directions they or the greater nomber of them shall sett down, shalbe accompted legall, and to bee duly observed untill it shalbe thought fitt by this Court to alter or determyne the same.

Provyded alwayes, that if those that intend to inhabite upon the plantation shall, before the first of January next, take upon them all the said engagments and other charges of the joynt stock, then the power and pruiledges of the undertakers to determine, and all trade, etc., to bee free.

A Generall Court, holden at Mr. Goffs House, on the
15th of Decemb., 1629.

PRESENT, Mr. Jo: Humfry, Deputy;

Assistants,

Sir Richard Saltonstall,	Mr. John Revell,
Mr. Matth: Cradock,	Mr. Geo: Harwood,
Mr. Nathaniell Wright,	Mr. William Pinchion,
Mr. Increase Noell,	Mr. Thomas Adams;
Capt. Venn,	

with divers of the generalitie.   17.

MR. DEPUTIE caused to bee read the acts and orders made at the last Generall Court of the 30th of November; which being of great consiquence, as namely for setling the joynt stock, and managing of the whole busines, it was desired the same should receive confirmation by this Court. Upon debate wherof, some exceptions was taken by those who had double[d] their adventures, conceiving themselves to bee wronged in having both their sommes drawne downe to soe lowe a rate as $\frac{1}{3}$ part; alleadinge that the second somme was paid in upon a proposition of trade, which went not forward, and not as unto the joynt stock for the plantation.

This business received a large discussion, and Capt. Waller and Mr. Vassall were content to give the first £50 to the plantation, soe as their other £50 might goe on wholy in this new stock; but forasmuch as this concern'd divers others who were in the same case, and that it could not bee done without alteration of the act made the 30 of November, which was done by a Generall Court, upon mature and deliberate consideration, and that the undertakers would not continue their said undertaking but upon the same conditions which were then propounded and concluded on.

This Court, in conclusion, put it to the question, and by erection of hands every particuler of the former Court was ratyfied and confirmed. And the matter in difference with them who had doubled their adventures being noe more to each of them then betweene £50 and £33 6s 8d, was by mutuall consent referred to the 3 ministers heere present, Mr. Davenport, Mr. Nye, and Mr. Archer, who are to reconcile the same betweene the new undertakers and them.

*A Generall Court, holden at Mr. Goffs House, on Wensday, the
10th of Febr: 1629–30.*

PRESENT, Mr. John Winthrope,   Mr. Thomas Adams,
Governor,   Mr. George Harwood,
Mr. John Humfry,   Mr. Increase Noell,
Deputy,   Mr. Nathaniell Wright,
Mr. Isack Johnson,   Mr. John Revell,
Mr. Matthew Cradock,   Mr. William Pinchon;
Mr. Theophilus Eaton,
with many others of the generalitie.

FORASMUCH as the furtherance of the plantation will necessarylie require a great and continuall charge, which cannot with convenyence bee defrayed out of the joynt stock of the Company, which is ordained for the maintenance of the trade, without endangering the same to bee wasted and exhausted, it was therfore propounded that a common stock should bee raysed from such as beare good affection to the plantation, and the propagation therof, and the same to bee employed only in defrayment of publique charges, as maintenance of ministers, transportation of poore famylyes, building of churches and ffortyfycations, and all other publique and necessary occasions of the plantation; and the Court doe thinke fitt, and order, that 200 acres of land shalbe allotted for every £50, and soe proportionable for what sommes shalbe brought in by any to this purpose. And Mr. George Harwood is chosen Treasurer for this accompt of the common stock, which hee accepted of: who is to receive all such mony as shalbe by any sent in, and to issue out the same upon warrant under the hands of any 2 or more of the undertakers. And it is further agreed on and ordered, That an order bee drawne upp and published under the seale of the Company, to signifie and declare to what uses all such monyes as are given to the common stock shalbe employed, and what land shalbe allotted to each man that gives therunto, aswell for their sattisfaction as th'incouragment of others to soe laudable and charitable a worke; and it was further taken into consideration, and ordered that this allottment or devision of land shall not prejudice the right of any th'adventurers who are to have land, and have not yett the same allotted out unto them, nor unto those whose land is already sett out according to the former order and direction of this Court; yett nevertheless, it is further agreed that if for good and weighty reasons, and for the benefitt of the plantation in generall, there shalbe occasion to alter any particuler mans allottment, the said party is to have such due recompence for the same as, in the wisdome of the Governor and Company there resident, shalbe thought reasonable and expedient.

Motion was made on the behalfe of Sir William Brewerton, who, by vertue of a late pattent, pretends right and tytle to some part of the land within the Companys pruiledges and plantation in New England; yett nevertheless hee intends not to contest with the Company, but desires that a proportionable quantitie of land might be allotted unto him for the accommodation of his people and servants now to bee sent over. Which request the Court taking into due consideration, doe not thinke fitt to enter into any particuler cappitulation with him therin, nor to sett out any allottment of land for him more then the 600 acres hee is to have by vertue of his adventure in the joynt stock, nor to acknowledg any thinge due unto him as of right by vertue of his said pattent, nor to give any consideration in case hee should relinquish his pretended right; but they are well content hee should joyne with them in the prosecution of this business, according to their charter, and doe promise, in the meane tyme, that such servants as hee shall send over to inhabite upon the plantation shall receive all courteous respect, and bee accommodated with land, and what els shalbe necessary, as other the servants of the Company. Which answere was delivered unto those that were sent from him; and the Court desired also that Capt. Waller and Mr. Eaton would signifie the Companyes affection and due respect unto him, hee having written to them about this business.

A wryting of grevances of Mr. Samuell and John Browne was presented to this Court, wherin they desire recompence for loss and damage sustained by them in New England; which this Assembly taking into consideration, doe thinke fitt that upon their submitting to stand to the Companys fynall order for ending of all differences between them, which they are to signifie under their hands, Mr. Wright and Mr. Eaton are to heare their complaint, and to sett downe what they in their judgments shall thinke requisite to bee allowed them for their pretended damage sustained, and soe to make a fynall end with them accordingly.

Mr. Roger Ludlowe was now chosen and sworne an Assistant in the roome of Mr. Samuell Sharpe, who by reason of his absence had not taken the oath.

And lastly, upon the petition of Humphry Seale, the beadle of this Company, the Court were content, and agreed to give him 20 nobles, for his yeares salary ending at Christmas last; which is to bee paid by Mr. Aldersey, the Treasorer, out of the joynt stock.[9]

Att a Meeteing of Assistants att Southampton, March 18th, 1629–30.

PRESENT, Mr. Governor,   Mr. Humfrey,
           Sir Richard Saltonstall,   Mr. Nowell,
           Mr. Johnson,   Mr. Pinchion,
           Mr. Dudley,   Mr. Goffe.

IT was ordered and concluded, by erection of hands, that Sir Brian Janson, knight, Mr. William Coddington, and Mr. Simon Bradstreete, gentleman, shalbe chosen in the roomes and places of Assistants of Mr. Nathaniell Wright, merchant, Mr. Theophilus Eaton, and Mr. Thomas Goffe, of London, merchants.

Sir Brian Janson was sworne an Assistant before the Governor and Mr. Dudley, the same day.

March 23th, 1629.

MR. WILLIAM CODDINGTON, Mr. Simon Bradstreete, and Mr. Thomas Sharpe, being formerly chosen Assistants, did nowe take the oath of Assistants before the Governor, Mr. Dudley, and other Assistants.

---

[9] Here the records cease to be in the handwriting of Secretary Burgis. The remaining records were written by Simon Bradstreete.

Att a Court of Assistants aboard the Arbella, March 23th, 1629.
PRESENT, Mr. John Winthrop,   Mr. William Coddington,
    Governor,   Mr. Tho: Sharpe,
   Sir Rich: Saltonstall,   Mr. William Vassall,
   Mr. Isaack Johnson,   Mr. Simon Bradstreete.
   Mr. Thomas Dudley,

MR. JOHN HUMFREY (in regard hee was to stay behinde in England) was discharged of his Deputy-shipp, and Mr. Thomas Dudley chosen Deputy in his place.

The first Court of Assistants, holden att Charlton,
August 23th, Anno Domini 1630.
PRESENT, Mr. Jo: Winthrop,   Mr. Roberte
    Governor   [Roger] Ludlowe,
   Mr. Tho: Dudley,   Mr. Edward Rossiter,
    Deputy Governor,   Mr. Tho: Sharpe,
   Sir Rich: Saltonstall,   Mr. Will: Pinchion,
    knight,   Mr. Sim: Bradstreete.

IMPR., it was propounded howe the ministers should be mayntayned, Mr. Wilson and Mr. Phillips onely propounded.

It was ordered, that houses should be built for them with convenient speede, att the publique charge. Sir Rich: Saltonstall undertooke to see it done att his plantation for Mr. Phillips, and Mr. Governor, att the other plantation, for Mr. Wilson.

It was propounded what should be their present maynetenance.

Ordered, that Mr. Phillips should have allowed him 3 hogsheads of meale, 1 hogshead of malte, 4 bushells of Indean corne, 1 bushell of oatemeale, halfe an hundred of salte fishe; for apparell, and other provisions, xx pounds, or els to have xl pounds given him in money per annum, to make his owne provisions if hee chuse it the rather, the yeare to begin the first of September nexte.

Item, that Mr. Wilson should have after xx pounds per annum till his wife come over; his yeare to begin the 10th of July last. All this to be att the common charge, those of Mattapan and Salem onely exempted.

It was propounded what should be Mr. Gagers maintenance.

Ordered, that hee should have a house builded him against the nexte springe; is to have a cowe given him, and xx pounds in money for this yeare, to begin the 20th of June, 1630, and after xxx pounds per annum. All this to be att the common charge.

It was ordered, that James Penn should have 20 nobles per annum, and a dayes worke of a man att springe, from every able famyly, to helpe build his house, his yeare to begin the 1th of September nexte. His imployement to be as a beadle to attend upon the Governor, and alwaies to be ready to execute his commands in publique businesses.

It was ordered, that there should be a Court of Assistants helde att the Governors howse on the 7th day of September nexte, being Tuesday, to begin att 8 of the clocke.

It was propounded, whither there should not be a Court helde every first Tuesday in every moneth, and a Generall Court the last Wednesday in every tearme.

It was ordered, that, in all civill actions, the first processe or summons by the beadle or his deputy shalbe directed by the Governor, or Deputy Governor, or some other of the Assistants, being a justice of the peace; the next processe to be a capias or distringas, att the discretion of the Court.

It was ordered, that Morton, of Mount Woolison, should presently be sent for by processe.

It was ordered, that carpenters, joyners, brickelayers, sawers, and thatchers shall not take above 2s aday, nor any man shall give more, under paine of x shillings to taker and giver; and that sawers shall not take above 4s 6d the hundred for boards, att 6 scoore to the hundred, if they have their wood felled and squared for them, and not above 5s 6d if they fell and square their wood themselves.

It was ordered, that the Governor and Deputy Governor, for the tyme being, shall alwaies be justices of the peace; and that Sir Rich: Saltonstall, Mr. Johnson, Mr. Endicott, and Mr. Ludlowe shalbe justices of the peace for the present tyme, in all things to have like power that justices of peace hath in England for reformation of abuses and punishing of offenders; and that any justice of the peace may imprison an offender, but not inflict any corporall punishment without the presence and consent of some one of the Assistants.

It was ordered, that noe person shall use or take away any boate or cannoe without leave from the owner thereof, in paine of ffyne and imprisonment, att the discretion of the Court.

Memorand.—To estimate, the nexte Court day, the charges that Mr. Governor hath beene att in entertaineing severall publique persons since his landing in Newe England.

A Court of Assistants, holden att Charlton the 7th of September, 1630.

PRESENT, The Governor,   Mr. Nowell.
           Deputy Governor,   Mr. Coddington,
           Sir Rich: Saltonstall, knight, Mr. Ludlowe,
           Mr. Johnson,   Mr. Rossiter,
           Mr. Endicott,   Mr. Pinchon,
           Mr. Sharpe,   Mr. Bradstreete.

CAPT. ENDICOTT, beinge formerly chosen an Assistant, did nowe take the oath of an Assistant in the presence of the Court.

It was ordered, that every third Tuesday there should be a Court of Assistants helde att the Governors howse, (for the tyme being,) to begin att 8 of the clocke in the morneing, every Assistant not being present att that tyme to be fyned att the discretion of the Court.

James Penn did now take the oath of beadle.

Mr. Ludlowe, Mr. Rossiter, and Mr. Pinchon, by the generall consent of the Court, is fyned a noble a peece for their absence from the Court after the tyme appoyncted.

It is ordered by this present Court, that Thomas Morton, of Mount Wolliston, shall presently be sett into the bilbowes, and after sent prisoner into England, by the shipp called the Gifte, nowe returneing thith[er]; that all his goods shalbe seazed upon to defray the charge of his transportation, payement of his debts, and to give satisfaction to the Indians for a cannoe hee unjustly tooke away from them; and that his howse, after the goods are taken out, shalbe burnt downe to the ground in the sight of the Indians, for their satisfaction, for many wrongs hee hath done them from tyme to tyme.

It is ordered, that Mr. Clearke shall pay unto John Baker the somme of xxxviii shillings, in recompence for the damage hee receaved by a bargaine of cloath, wherein Mr. Clearke dealte fraudylently with the said John Baker, as hath beene proved upon oath.

It is ordered, that Mr. Patricke and Mr. Underhill shall have allowed them, for halfe a yeares provision, 2 hogsheads of meale, 4 bushells of malte, 10 pounds of powder, and leade to make shott; also howseroome provided for them, and £15 12s in money, to make other provisions. All this to be done att the publique charge, their yeare to begin from the tyme they begin to keepe howse.

It is ordered, that Trimountaine shalbe called Boston; Mattapan, Dorchester; and the towne upon Charles Ryver, Waterton.

It is ordered, that noe person shall plant in any place within the lymitts of this pattent, without leave from the Governor and Assistants, or the major parte of them.

Also, that a warrant shall presently be sent to Aggawam, to command those that are planted there forthwith to come away.

A Court of Assistants, holden att Charlton, 28th of September, 1630.

PRESENT, The Governor,   Mr. Coddington,
Deputy Governor,   Mr. Bradstreete,
Capt. Endicott,   Mr. Rossiter,
Mr. Ludlowe,   Mr. Pinchon.
Mr. Nowell,

IT is ordered, that those of Dorchester whoe bought certayne cattell of the merchants of Dorchester shall pay unto Nich: Stower 9 bushells of meale or of Indian corne, or 9 pounds of beavor, for the keepeing of the said cattell, according to an agreement made with him.

It is ordered, that noe person whatsoever shall, either directly or indirectly, imploy, or cause to be imployed, or to their power permitt, any Indian to use any peece upon any occasion or pretence whatsoever, under payne of x pounds ffyne for the first offence, and for the 2 offence to be ffyned and imprisoned att the discretion of the Court.

It is further ordered, that noe servant, either man or maide, shall either give, sell, or trucke any commodytie whatsoever, without lycence from their maister, dureing the tyme of their service, under paine of ffyne and corporall punishment, att the discretion of the Court.

John Woodbury is chosen constable of Salem, and Thomas Stoughton constable of Dorchester, to contynue in that office for a yeare and after, till newe be chosen.

John Woodbury did nowe take the oath of a constable.

It is ordered, that all Rich: Cloughes stronge water shall presently be seazed upon, for his selling greate quantytie thereof to severall mens servants, which was the occasion of much disorder, drunckenes, and misdemeanor.

It is ordered, that noe maister carpenter, mason, joyner, or brickelayer shall take above 16d a day for their worke, if they have meate and drinke, and the second sort not above 12d aday, under payne of x shillings both to giver and receaver.

It is ordered, that Mr. Patricke and Mr. Underhill shall have allowed them £6 8s in money, to buy them howseholde stuffe, and for helpe to washe, brewe, and bake, xx shillings.

Thomas Gray is injoyned, under the penalty of x pounds, to attend on the Court in person this day 3 weekes, to answer to dyvers things objected against him, and to remove himselfe out of the lymetts of this pattent before the end of March nexte.

Sir Rich: Saltonstall is ffyned 4 bushells of malte, for his absence from the Court.

It is ordered, that noe person, inhabitting within the lymitts of this pattent, shall, either directly or indirectly, give, sell, trucke, or send away any Indian corn to any Englishe without the lymitts of this pattent, or to any Indian whatsoever, without licence from the Governor and Assistants.

It is ordered, that John Goulworth shalbe whipped, and afterwards sett in the stocks, for fellony committed by him, whereof hee is convicted by his owne confession; also, that Henry Lynn shalbe whipped for the like offence, and John Boggust and John Pickryn to sitt in the stocks 4 howers togeather, att Salem, for being accessary thereunto.

It is ordered, that there shalbe collected and levied by distresse out of the severall plantations, for the maintenance of Mr. Patricke and Mr. Underhill, the somme of £50, viz.: out of Charlton, £7; Boston, £11; Dorchester, £7; Rocsbury, £5; Waterton, £11; Meadford, £3; Salem, £3; Wessaguscus, £2; Natascett, £1.

It is ordered, that labourers shall not take above 12d a day for their worke, and not above 6d and meate and drinke, under paine of x shillings.

September 28th, 1630.

A Jury impanneld to inquire concerning the Death of Austen Bratcher:—

Rich: Browne,	John Johnson,
William Aspynwall,	Edward Converse,
Abraham Palmer,	Ralfe Sprage,
Nich: Stower,	Giles Sexton,
Peter Palfry,	Abraham Pratt,
Roger Williams,	Francis Smyth,
William Bunell,	George Dyar.
Nich: Upsall,	

Austen Bratcher, dyeing lately att Mr. Cradocks plantation, was vewed before his buryall by dyvers persons, viz:

Tho: Graves,	Thomas Reade,
James Crugott,	Rich: Lynton,
Thomas Ward,	John Jarvis, } Absent.
Thomas Paynter,	Arthur Ellis,
William Barsham,	

The Juryes Verdict:—

Wee finde that the strookes given by Walter Palmer were occationally the meanes of the death of Austen Bratcher, and soe to be manslaughter.

Walter Palmer hath bound himselfe in £40, and Ralfe Sprage and John Sticklett hath bound themselves in £20 a peece, for Walter Palmers personall appearance att the nexte Courte, to be holden att Boston the 19th of October nexte, to answer for the death of Austen Bratcher.

September 18th, 1630.

Upon vew of the dead body of William Bateman.

An Inquisition taken att Charlton, the 18th day of September, Anno Domini 1630, before John Winthrop, Esquire and Governor, and Isaack Johnson, Esquire, one of the Assistants, and Justice of Peace.

Upon the oathes of

Walter Norton, Esquire	Roberte Hardinge,
Nich: Stowre,	Richard Garrett,
Ralfe Sprage,	Thomas Williams,
Will: Cheesebrough,	Daniel
John Stickland,	John Baker,
Rich: Norman,	William Bateman;
Richard Browne,	

whoe say, upon their oathes, that the aforesaid William Bateman was sett on shore upon the necke of land neere Pullen Poynte, in the bay of Mattachusetts, by a shallop of one Mr. Wright, (which brought him from Plimouthe,) upon Wednesday last, being very sicke and weake, and beinge lefte there with one Mr. Ralfe Glover and others, whoe hadd a shallop in that place; but being forced to leave her there, because the wind was contrarie, they, returneing home, lefte him such provisions as they hadd, and a fire; but when they returned to their boate, upon Friday last, they found the said William Bateman dead, about the highwater marke, neere their boate, aboute a stones cast from the place where they lefte him. Soe the jury presents that he dyed by Gods visitation.

Evidences, Mr. Ralfe Glover, Elias Maveracke, Giles Sexton, and James Browne, etc.

A Generall Court, holden att Boston the 19th of October, 1630.

PRESENT, The Governor,	Capt. Endicott,
Deputy Governor,	Mr. Nowell,
Sir Rich: Saltonstall,	Mr. Pinchon,
Mr. Ludlowe,	Mr. Bradstreete.

FOR the establishinge of the government. It was propounded if it were not the best course that the ffreemen should have the power of chuseing Assistants when there are to be chosen, and the Assistants from amongst themselves to chuse a Governor and Deputy Governor, whoe with the Assistants should have the power of makeing lawes and chuseing officers to execute the same. This was fully assented unto by the generall vote of the people, and erection of hands.

Ralfe Sprage is chosen constable of Charlton, John Johnson of Rocksbury, and John Page for Waterton, for the space of one whole yeare, and after till newe be chosen.

It is ordered that sawers shall not take above 12d a scoore for saweing oake boards, and 10d a scoore for pyne boards, if they have their wood felled and squared for them.

Walter Palmer made his personall appearance this day, and stands bound, hee and his suerties, till the nexte Court.

The Names of such as desire to be made Freemen.

Mr. Samuell Maveracke,
Mr. Edw: Johnson,
Mr. Edw: Gibbins,
Mr. Will: Jeffries,
Mr. John Burslin,
Mr. Samuell Sharpe,
Mr. Tho: Graves,
Mr. Roger Conant,
John Woodbury,
Peter Palfry,
Mr. Nath: Turner,
Mr. Samuell Freeman,
Eprahim Childe,
Mr. William Clerke,
Mr. Abraham Palmer,
John Page,
Nich: Upsall,
Stephen Terree,
Henry Smyth,
Roger Williams,
John Woolridge,
Tho: Lumberd,
Bigatt Egglestone,
John Grinoway,
Christopher Gibson,
John Benham,
Thomas Williams,
　alias Harris,
Rich: Garrett,
John Howman,
John Crabb,
Capt. Walter Norton,
Mr. Alex: Wignall,
Mr. Roberte Feake,
Mr. William Pelham,
Mr. Ben: Brand,
Mr. Will: Blackstone,
Mr. Edmond Lockwood,
Mr. Rich: Browne,
John Strickland,
Ralfe Sprage,
Mr. George Ludlowe,
James Penn,
Henry Woolcott,
Thomas Stoughton,
William Phelpes,
George Dyar,
John Hoskins,
Thomas Ford,
Mr. John Warham,
Mr. Samuel Skelton,
Mr. Will: Colbron,
Mr. Will: Aspinwall,
Edw: Converse,
Mr. Rich: Palgrave,
John Taylour,
Rich: Church,
Rich: Silvester,
Will: Balstone,
Roberte Abell,
Mr. Giles Sexton,
Roberte Seely,
John Mills,
John Cranwell,
Mr. Ralfe Glover,
William Hulbird,

Mr. William Jennison,
Mr. Thomas Southcoate,
Mr. Rich: Southcoate,
James Pemberton,
Mr. John Dillingham,
John Johnson,
George Alcocke,
Mr. Robert Coles,
Jehu Burr,
Thomas Rawlins,
Rich: Bugby,
Rich: Hutchins,
Ralfe Mushell,
Thomas Lambe,
Will: Throdingham,
William Chase,
                Foxewell,
Mr. Charles Gott,
Henry Harwood,
Mr. George Phillips,
Mr. John Wilson,
Mr. John Maveracke,

Edmond James,
John Pillips,
Nath: Bowman,
John Doggett,
Laurence Leach,
Daniell Abbott,
Charles Chadwicke,
Will: Drakenbury,
John Drake,
John Balshe,
Mr. Samuell Coole,
Mr. Will: Traske,
Will: Gallard,
Will: Rockewell,
Henry Herricke,
Samuel Hosier,
Rich: Myllett,
Mr. Abraham Pratt,
William James,
William Allen,
Samuell Archer.

A Court of Assistants, holden att Boston, November 9th, 1630.

PRESENT, The Governor,
          Deputy Governor,
          Sir Rich: Saltonstall,
          Mr. Ludlowe,

Capt. Endicott,
Mr. Coddington,
Mr. Pinchon,
Mr. Bradstreete.

IT is ordered, that whereas the usuall rate of beavor hath beene after 6s the pound, it shalbe hereafter lefte free for every man to make the best proffit and improvement of it that hee can.

It is ordered, that every Englishe man that killeth a wolfe in any parte within the lymitts of this pattent shall have allowed him 1d for every beast and horse, and ob. for every weaned swyne and goate in every plantation, to be levied by the constables of the said plantations.

It is further ordered, that whoesoever shall first give in his name to Mr. Governor that hee will undertake to sett upp a fferry betwixte Boston and Charlton, and shall begin the same att such tyme as Mr. Governor shall appoynt, shall have 1d for every person, and 1d for every 100 waight of goods hee shall soe transport.

Mr. Clearke is prohibited cohabitation and frequent keepeing company with Mrs. Freeman, under paine of such punishment as the Court shall thinke meete to inflict.

Mr. Clearke and Mr. Freeman hath bound themselves in xx pounds apeece that Mr. Clearke shall make his personall appearance att the nexte Court, to be holden in March nexte, and in the meane tyme to carry himselfe in good behavior towards all people, and espetially towards Mrs. Freeman, concerneing whome there is stronge suspicion of incontinency.

It is ordered, that Rich: Diffy, servant to Sir Richard Saltonstall, shalbe whipped for his misdemeanor towards his maister.

A Jury impannell for the Tryall of Walter Palmer, concerneing the Death of Austin Bratcher.

Mr. Edmond Lockwood,	Rich: Morris,
William Rockewell,	William Balston,
Christopher Conant,	William Cheesbrough,
William Phelpes,	John Page,
William Gallard,	John Balshe,
John Hoskins,	Laurence Leach.

The jury findes Walter Palmer not guilty of manslaughter, whereof hee stoode indicted, and soe the Court acquitts him.

A Court of Assistants, holden att Boston, November 30th, 1630.

PRESENT, The Governor,	Mr. Nowell,
The Deputy Governor,	Mr. Pinchon,
Sir Rich: Saltonstall,	Mr. Coddington,
Mr. Ludlowe,	Mr. Bradstreete.

SIR RICH: SALTONSTALL is fyned v pounds for whipping 2 severall persons without the presence of another Assistant, contrary to an act of Court formerly made.

It is ordered, that whosoever imployeth William Knopp or his sonne in any worke shall pay the one halfe of their wages to Sir Rich: Siltonstall, and whoever buyeth boards of them shall pay one halfe of the price to Sir Richard, till the money hee hath disbursed for them be satisfyed.

Bartholmewe Hill is adjudged to be whipt for stealeing a loafe of breade from John Hoskins, which himselfe confesseth.

It is ordered, that there shalbe £60 collected out of the severall plantations followeing, for the mainetenance of Mr. Wilson and Mr. Phillips, viz.: out of Boston, £20; Waterton, £20; Charlton, £10; Rockesbury, £6; Meadford, £3; Winnett-semett, £1.

It is ordered, that John Baker shalbe whipped for shooteing att fowle on the Sabboth day, etc.

It is further ordered, that Thomas Moulton shall pay unto Mr. Ralfe Glover xl shillings before the 8th day of December nexte, or els to be whipped for the wronge hee did Mr. Glover in comeing from Plymoth, being maister of his boate, and leaveing him without a pylott.

A Court of Assistants, holden att Boston, 1th of March, 1630–31.

PRESENT, The Governor,   Mr. Pinchon,
Deputie Governor,   Mr. Nowell,
Sir Rich: Saltonstall,   Mr. Sharpe,
Mr. Ludlowe,   Mr. Coddington,
Capt. Endicott,   Mr. Bradstreete.

IT is ordered, that Mr. Aleworth, Mr. Weaver, Mr. Plastowe, Mr. Shuter, Cobbett, and Wormewood shalbe sent into England by the shipp Lyon, or soe many of them as the ship can carry, the rest to be sent thither by the 1th of May nexte, if there be opportunitie of shipping, if not, by the nexte shipp that returnes for England, as persons unmeete to inhabit here; and that Sir Christopher Gardner and Mr. Wright shalbe sent as prisoners into England by the shipp Lyon, nowe returneing thither.

Further, it is ordered, that the busines concerneing Mr. George Ludlowe, expressed in a certaine petition sent out of England, to the Governor, etc., shalbe referred to t[he] Governor and Deputy Governor; and the rest of the Assistants, resident att Boston, or some 3 of them, the Governor and Deputie being 2 thereof, to receave his answer, and determyne the busines.

Mr. Tho: Stoughton, constable of Dorchester, is ffyned v pounds for takeing upon him to marry Clement Briggs and Joane Allen, and to be imprisoned till hee hath paid his ffyne.

It is ordered, that if any person within the lymitts of this pattent doe trade, trucke, or sell any money, either silver or golde, to any Indian, or any man that knowes of any that shall soe doe, and conceale the same, shall forfeit twenty for one.

Further, it is ordered, that whatever person hath receaved any Indian into their ffamylie as a servant shall discharge themselves of them by the 1th of May nexte; and that noe person shall hereafter intertaine any Indian for a servant without licence from the Court.

Nich: Knopp is fyned v pounds for takeing upon him to cure the scurvey by a water of noe worth nor value, which he solde att a very deare rate, to be imprisoned till hee pay his ffine, or give securitye for it, or els to be whipped, and shalbe lyable to any mans action of whome hee hath receaved money for the said water.

Jost Weillust is chosen surveyer of the ordinanc and cannouneere, for which hee is to have allowed him £10 per annum.

John Ellford hath bound himselfe in C marks, and Roger Connant and John Woodbury hath bound themselves in £40 a peece, for John Ellfords personall appearance att the first Court to be holden in November nexte, to answere for the death of Thomas Puckett.

Mr. William Pelham and Mr. Edmond Lockewood hath promised to pay to the Court the somme of v pounds, for Nich: Knopp, before the last Court of May nexte.

Att a Court att Waterton, March 8th,
1630–31.

PRESENT, The Governor,   Mr. Nowell,
    Deputie Governor,   Mr. Pinchon,
    Sir Rich: Saltonstall,   Mr. Coddington,
    Mr. Ludlowe,   Mr. Bradstreete.

UPON a complaynte made by Saggamore John and Peter for haveing 2 wigwams burnt, which, upon examination, appeared to be occasioned by James Woodward, servant to Sir Rich: Saltonstall, it was therefore ordered, that Sir Richard should satisfie the Indians for the wronge done to them, (which accordingly hee did by giveing them 7 yards of cloath,) and that his said servant should pay unto him for it, att the end of his tyme, the somme of 1s.

It was ordered, that Tho: Foxe, servant to Mr. Cradocke, shalbe whipped for uttering mallitious and scandilous speeches, whereby hee sought to traduce the Court, as if they hadd taken some bribe in the busines concerneing Walter Palmer.

Further, (in regard the number of Assistants are but fewe, and some of them goeing for England,) it was therefore ordered, that whensoever the number of Assistants resident within the lymitts of this jurisdiction shalbe fewer than 9, it shalbe lawfull for the major parte of them to keepe a Court; and whatsoever orders or acts they make shalbe as legall and authenticall as if there were the full number of 7 or more.

Att a Court of Assistants, holden att Boston, March 22th, 1630–31.
PRESENT, The Governor,   Mr. Nowell,
         The Deputie   Sir Rich: Soltonstall,
           Governor,   Mr. Pinchon,
         Mr. Ludlowe,   Mr. Sharpe,
         Mr. Coddington,   Mr. Bradstreete.

IT is ordered, (that whereas the wages of carpenters, joyners, and other artificers and workemen, were by order of Court restrayned to particular sommes) shall nowe be lefte free and att libertie as men shall reasonably agree.

Further, it is ordered, that every towne within this pattent shall, before the 5th of Aprill nexte, take espetiall care that every person within their towne, (except magistrates and ministers,) as well servants as others, furnished with good and sufficient armes allowable by the capt. or other officers, those that want and are of abilitie to buy them themselves, others that are unable to have them provided by the towne, for the present, and after to receive satisfaction for that they disburse when they shalbe able.

It is likewise ordered that all persons whatsoever that have cards, dice, or tables in their howses, shall make away with them before the nexte Court, under paine of punishment.

Rich: Johnson confesseth to owe unto Sr: Richard Saltonstall (all accompts cleared) the somme of £13, which hee promiseth to pay after 2s per weeke; therefore it is ordered, that those that setts Johnson on worke shall pay unto Sir Richard out of his wages the said 2s per week.

It is ordered, that Benjamyn Cribb, John Cable, and Morris Trowent shalbe whipped for stealeing 3 piggs of Mr. Ralfe Glovers.

Rich: Louge confesseth to owe unto Mr. Ludlowe the somme of £3, 8s, 4d, which hee promisseth to pay him after 2s per weeke till it be all satisfied.

It appeares by Sir Rich: Saltonstalls note of disbursements that William Knopp owes him the some of £19 v shillings, as was evidenced to the Court by Richard Browne and Ephraim Childe, being men indifferently chosen betwixte them to judge thereof.

A Court of Assistants, holden at Boston, April 12th, 1631.
PRESENT, The Governor,   Mr. Nowell,
                Deputie Governor,   Mr. Pinchon,
                Mr. Ludlowe,   Mr. Bradstreete.

IT is ordered, that there shalbe a watch of 4 kept every night att Dorchester, and another of 4 att Waterton, the watches to begin att sunsett.

Further, it is ordered, that if any person shall shoote of any peece after the watch is sett, hee shall forfeict 40s, or if the Court shall judge him unable, then to be whipped; the second fault to be punished by the Court as an offence of an higher nature.

It is likewise ordered, that every man that findes a muskett shall, before the 18th day of this moneth, (and soe alwaies after,) have ready 1 pound of powder, 20 bulletts, and 2 fathome of match, under penaltie of x shillings for every fault.—Moderated 470.

It is ordered, that every captaine shall traine his companie on Saterday in everie weeke.

Further, it is ordered, that noe person shall travell single betwixte theis plantations and Plymouthe, nor without some armes, though 2 or 3 togeather.

A Court of Assistants, holden att Boston, May 3, 1631.
PRESENT, The Governor,   Mr. Nowell,
                Deputie Governor,   Mr. Pinchon,
                Mr. Ludlowe,   Mr. Bradstreete.
                Capt. Endicott,

IT is ordered, that Thomas Chubb shall be freed from the service of Mr. Samuell Maveracke, and shall become servant to William Gayllerd, of Dorchester.

It is ordered, that John Legge, servant to Mr. Humfry, shalbe severely whipped this day att Boston, and afterwards soe soone as conveniently may be, att Salem, for strikeing Richard Wright, when hee came to give him correction for idleness in his maisters worke.

Tho: Walford, of Charlton, is ffyned xl shillings, and is injoyned, hee and his wife, to departe out of the lymits of this pattent before the 20th day of October nexte, under paine of confiscation of his goods, for his contempt of authoritie and confrontinge officers, etc.

It is ordered, that for this yeare if the cowes, horses, or goates, of any mans, in any plantation, (Salem excepted,) shall trespasse and doe hurte in the corne of another, that the owner of the cattell shall make full satisfaction for the damage done by them, and that all swine that are found in any mans corne shalbe forfeit to the publique, out of which the partie damnyfied shalbe satisfied, if the swine soe forfeicted be of that value; if not, the owner is to make full recompence in other goods.

It is ordered, that Thomas Bartlett, servant to Mr. Pelham, shalbe whipped for his unjust selling of his maisters tooles, and that Samuell Hosier and John Page shall returne either the tooles they bought of him, or the prices thereof, to Mr. Pelham.

John Norman, senior, is ffyned x shillings for his not appearing att the Court, being summoned.

A Jury impanneld to inquire concerneing an action of battry, complayned of by Thomas Dextor against Capt. Endicott.

Rich: Browne,	Henry Wolcott,
William Clearke,	Samuell Hosier,
Alex: Wignall,	John Strickland,
John Dillingham,	Isaac Sternes,
John Gosse,	Daniell Fince,
John Johnson,	Edw: Converse.

The jury findes for the plantiffe, and cesses for damages xl shillings.

A Generall Court, holden att Boston, the 18th day of May, 1631.
PRESENT, Mr. Winthrop,   Capt. Endicott,
         Governor,   Mr. Nowell,
      Mr. Dudley,   Mr. Pinchon,
         Deputy Governor,   Mr. Bradstreete,
      Mr. Ludlowe,   Assistants.

JOHN WINTHROP, Esquire, was chosen Governor for a whole yeare nexte ensueinge by the generall consent of the Court, according to the meaneing of the pattent, and did accordingly take an oathe to the place of Governor belonginge.

Tho: Dudley, Esquire, is also chosen Deputy Governor for this yeare nexte ensuing, and did in presence of the Court take an oath to his place belonginge.

For explanation of an order made the last Generall Court, holden the 19th of October last, it was ordered nowe, with full consent of all the commons then present, that once in every yeare, att least, a Generall Court shalbe holden, att which Court it shalbe lawfull for the commons to propounde any person or persons whome they shall desire to be chosen Assistants, and if it be doubt-full whither it be the greater parte of the commons or not, it shalbe putt to the poll. The like course to be holden when they, the said commons, shall see cause for any defect or misbehavior to remove any one or more of the Assistants; and to the end the body of the commons may be preserved of honest and good men, it was likewise ordered and agreed that for time to come noe man shalbe admitted to the freedome of this body polliticke, but such as are members of some of the churches within the lymitts of the same.

Tho: Williams hath undertaken to sett upp a fferry betwixte Winnettsemett and Charlton, for which hee is to have after 3d a person, and from Winnettsemett to Boston 4d a person.

It is ordered, that every plantation within the lymitts of this pattent shall before the last day of June nexte provide common measures and waights, which shalbe made by some that the Governor hath already sealed, and by which also all others that will have waights and measures of their owne are to be made.

It is ordered, that noe person shall kill any wilde swine without a generall agreement att some Court.

Rich: Norman is fyned ii shillings vi pence for his negligence in watching.

Daniell Abbott is fined v shillings for refuseing to watch, and for other ill behavior, shewed towards Capt. Pattricke.

Chickataubott and Saggamore John promised unto the Court to make satisfaction for whatsoever wronge that any of their men shall doe to any of the Englishe, to their cattell or any other waies.

Mr. Roger Connant promiseth to deliver to Mr. Thomas Dudley, Deputy Governor, 4 bushells of Indian corne before the last day of October nexte.

A Court, holden att Boston, June 14th, 1631.
PRESENT, The Governor,   Mr. Nowell,
    Deputy Governor,   Mr. Pinchon,
    Mr. Ludlowe,   Simon Bradstreete.
    Capt. Endicott,

IT is ordered, that noe man within the limitts of this jurisdiction shall hire any person for a servant for lesse time than a yeare, unles hee be a setled housekeeper; also that noe person whatsoever shall travell out of this pattent, either by sea or land, without leave from the Governor, Deputy Governor, or some other Assistant, under such penalty as the Court shall thinke meete to inflict.

It is ordered, that the constables of the severall plantations shall give notice to the creditors of Capt. Levett, John Boggust, and Henry Lauson, to be att the nexte Court, to make proofe of their debts, that they may receive satisfaction for the same, soe farr as their goods will afford.

Upon the reading of certaine artickles concerneing a generall trade of beaver agreed upon by Capt. Endicott and dyvers others, it was ordered, that the persons interest therein shall give a meeteing before the nexte Court, att such tyme and place as Capt. Endicott shall appoynct, to discide such differences as are betwixte them, and for such as they cannot end to bring them to the nexte Court, there to be determined.

Mr. John Maisters hath undertaken to make a passage from Charles Ryver to the newe towne, 12 foote broad and 7 foote deepe, for which the Court promiseth him satisfaction according as the charges thereof shall amount unto.

It is ordered, that Phillip Swaddon shalbe whipped for running away from his maister, Robert Seely, intending to goe to Virginia.

It is ordered, that Phillip Ratliffe shalbe whipped, have his eares cutt of, fyned £40, and banished out of the lymitts of this jurisdiction, for uttering mallitious and scandulous speeches against the government and the church of Salem, etc., as appeareth by a particular thereof, proved upon oath.

It is ordered, that noe person whatsoever shall buy corne or any other provision or merchantable commodity of any shipp or barke that comes into this bay, without leave from the Governor or some other of the Assistants.

Chickataubott is fyned a skyn of beaver for shooteinge a swine of Sir Richard Saltonstalls.

William Almy is ffyned ii shillings vi pence for takeing away Mr. Glovers cannoe without leave.

Edw: Converse hath undertaken to sett upp a fferry betwixte Charlton and Boston, for which hee is to have ii pence for every single person, and id a peece if there be 2 or more.

It is ordered, that Mr. Pelham shall pay unto Tho: Goilthayt the somme of v pounds (whereof 5 nobles is already paid) which the Court hath awarded him to pay, to make good a covenant betwixte them.

A Court of Assistants, holden att Boston, July 5th, 1631.
PRESENT, The Governor,   Mr. Nowell,
           Deputy Governor, Mr. Pinchon,
           Mr. Ludlowe,   S: Bradstreete.

IT is ordered, there shalbe levyed out of the severall plantations the somme of thirty pounds for the makeing of the creeke att the new towne, viz.: Winettsemett, 15s; Wessaguscus, 40s; Saugus, 20s; Natascett, 10s; Waterton, v pounds; Boston, v pounds; Dorchester, £4 10s; Rocksbury, £3; Salem, £3 5s; Charlton, £4 10s.

Further, it is ordered, that all the ilelands within the lymitts of this pattent, viz., Conants Ileland, Noddles Ileland, Tompsons Ileland, togeather with all other ilelands within the lymitts of our pattent, shalbe appropriated to publique benefits and uses, and to remaine in the power of the Governor and Assistants (for the time being,) to be lett and disposed of by them to helpe towards publique charges, and that noe person whatsoever shall make any use or benefitt of any of the said ilelands, by putting on cattell, felling wood, raiseing slate, etc., without leave from the Governor and Assistants for the time being. This order to take place immediately after the first of October nexte.

It is further ordered, that every Assistant shall have power to graunt warrants, summons, and attatchments, as occasion shall require, and that the acts of the Court shalbe authenticall if they passe onely under the Secretaryes hand, (for the time being.)

The Saggamore of Aggawam is banished from comeing into any Englishe mans howse for the space of a yeare, under the penalty of 10 skins of beaver.

Att a Court, holden att Boston, July 26th, 1631.
PRESENT, The Governor   Mr. Nowell,
             Deputy Governor,   Mr. Pinchon,
             Mr. Ludlowe,   S: Bradstreete.
             Capt. Endicott,

FOR the preservation of howses, hay, boards, timber, etc., it was ordered, that noe person whatsoever within the lymitts of our pattent shall burne any ground any yeare till the first of March, under such penalty as the Court shall thinke meete to inflict; and if any person be desirous to burne any of his owne ground for corne before that time, hee shall make full satisfaction for the damage it doeth, in case any be occasioned thereby.

Lucy Smyth is bound as an apprentice with Mr. Roger Ludlowe for 7 yeares, dureing which tyme hee is to finde her meate, drinke, and cloathes, and att the end of her yeares to give her the somme of v pounds.

It is ordered, that there shalbe a watch of sixe and an officer kept every night att Boston, 2 whereof are to be of Boston, 2 of Charlton, and 2 of Rocksbury.

It is further ordered, that every first Thursday in every moneth there shalbe a generall traineing of Capt. Underhills company att Boston and Rocksbury, and every first Friday in every moneth there shalbe a generall traineing of the remainder of them who inhabitt att Charlton, Misticke, and the newe towne, att a convenient place aboute the Indian wigwams, the traineing to begin att one of the clocke in the afternoone.

It is ordered, that Frauncis Perry shalbe whipped, for his ill speeches and misbehavior towards his maister.

Mr. Frauncis Aleworth is chosen Leifetenant unto Capt. South-coate, and Capt. Southcoate hath liberty graunted him to goe for England, promiseing to returne againe with all convenient speede.

A Court of Assistants, holden att Boston, August 16th, 1631.
PRESENT, The Governor,   Mr. Nowell,
                Deputy Governor,   Mr. Pinchon,
                Mr. Ludlowe,   S: Bradstreete.

IT is ordered, that any bill assigned to another shalbe good debt to the party to whome it is assigned; also that such debts due upon bill shalbe paid before any other, and that the party that giveth such bills shall renewe them upon demaund and delivery in of the olde bill.

It is ordered, that Mr. Shepheard and Roberte Coles shalbe ffyned 5 marks a peece, and Edward Gibbons xx shillings, for abuseing themselves disorderly with drinkeing to much stronge drinke aboard the Frendshipp, and att Mr. Maveracke his howse at Winettsemett.

Mr. Alex: Wignall is ffined 5 marks for the like offence att the same time.

It is further ordered, that the executors of Rich: Garrett shall pay unto Henry Harwood the somme of 20 nobles, according to the proportion that the goods of the said Rich: Garrett shall amount unto.

It is ordered, that Phillip Swaddon shalbe sett free from his maister Roberte Seely, upon the payement of x shillings to his maister.

Mr. William Gennison is chosent anchient to Capt. Pattricke.

A Court of Assistants, holden att Boston, September 6th, 1631.
PRESENT, The Governor,   Mr. Nowell,
                Deputy Governor,   Mr. Pinchon,
                Mr. Ludlowe,   S: Bradstreete.

IT is ordered, that Henry Lynn shalbe whipped and banished the plantation before the 6th day of October nexte for writeing into

England falsely and mallitiously against the government and execution of justice here.

There is graunted to Mr. Governor 600 acres of land, to be sett forth by marks and bounds neere his howse att Misticke, to enjoy to him and his heires for ever.

It is ordered, John Dawe shalbe severely whipped for intiseing an Indian woman to lye with him. Upon this occasion it is propounded wither adultery, either with English or Indian, shall not be punished with death. Referred to the nexte Court to be considered of.

Mr. Alex: Wignall is ffined 40s, bound to his good behavior, and enjoyned to remove his dwelling to some setled plantation before the last of May nexte, for drunkenes and much misdemeanor by him committed att the plantation where nowe hee dwelleth.

A Court of Assistants, holden at Boston, September 27th, 1631.
PRESENT, The Governor,   Mr. Nowell,
Deputy Governor,   Mr. Pinchon,
Mr. Ludlowe,   S: Bradstreete.

IT is ordered, that sawers shall not take over 12d a scoore for boards, if they have their wood felled and squared for them, and not above 7s the hundred, after 5 scoore to the hundred, if they fell and square their wood themselves.

William Phelpes is chosen constable of Dorchester.

It is ordered, that Josias Plastowe shall (for stealeing 4 basketts of corne from the Indians) returne them 8 basketts againe, be ffined v pounds, and hereafter to be called by the name of Josias, and not Mr., as formerly hee used to be, and that William Buckland and Tho: Andrewe shalbe whipped for being accessary to the same offence.

A Court of Assistants, holden att Boston, October 18th, 1631.
PRESENT, The Governor,   Mr. Nowell,
Deputy Governor,   Mr. Pinchon,
Mr. Ludlowe,   S: Bradstreete.
Capt. Endicott,

IT is ordered, that if any man shall have carnall copulation with another mans wife, they both shalbe punished by death.

The constable of Rocksbury returnes the receipt of Mr. Shepheards ffine of 5 marks, and soe it remaines in his hands to be accomptable for it. Mr. Governor is to have 40s of it, which hee paid for ferryeing the watch from Charlton to Boston.

It is ordered, that Thomas Grayes howse att Marble Harbor shalbe puld downe, and that noe Englishe man shall hereafter give howseroome to him or intertaine him, under such penalty as the Court shall thinke meete to inflicte.

It is ordered, that there shalbe taken out of the estate of Mr. Crispe and his company the somme of xii pounds i shillings v pence, and delivered to John Kirman, as his proper goods, and after the whole estate to be inventoryed, whereof the said John Kirman is to have an 8th parte; this to be done with all convenient speede by theis 5 commissioners, or any 3 of them, viz.: Mr. John Masters, Mr. Roberte Feakes, Mr. Edward Gibbons, Epharim Childe, Daniell Fynch, etc.

It is further ordered, that corne shall passe for payement of all debts at the usuall rate it is solde for, except money or beaver be expressely named.

Att a Meeteing of Assistants att Boston, February the 3, 1631.
PRESENT, The Governor,   Mr. Nowell,
         Deputy Governor,   Mr. Pinchon,
         Mr. Ludlowe,   S: Bradstreete.
         Capt. Endicott,

IT was ordered, there should be three scoore pounds levyed out of the severall plantations within the lymitts of this pattent towards the makeing of a pallysadoe aboute the newe towne, viz.: Waterton viii pounds, the new towne, iii pounds, Charlton vii pounds, Meadford iii pounds, Saugus and Marble Harbor vi pounds, Salem iiii pounds x shillings, Boston viii pounds, Rocksbury, vii pounds, Dorchester vii pounds, Wessaguscus v pounds, Winettsemett xxx shillings.

Thomas Knower hath bound himselfe in x pounds to make his personall appearance att the nexte Court, to be holden att Boston the first Tuesday in March nexte, to answer to such things as shalbe objected against him.

A Court of Assistants, holden att Boston, March 6th, 1632.

PRESENT, The Governor,   Mr. Nowell,
           Deputy Governor, Mr. Pinchon,
           Mr. Ludlowe,   S: Bradstreete.
           Capt. Endicott,

IT is ordered, that noe planter within the lymitts of this jurisdiction, returneing for England, shall carry either money or beaver with him without leave from the Governor, (for the time being,) under paine of forfecting the money or beaver soe intended to be transported.

As an addition to an order made the 22th of March, 1630, it is ordered that if any single person be not provided of sufficient armes allowable by the captain or leifetenants, before the 10th of Aprill nexte, shalbe compelled to serve by the yeare with any maister that will retaine him for such wages as the Court shall thinke meete to appoynte.

It is ordered, that Courts hereafter shalbe helde every first Tuesday in every moneth.

It is further ordered, that Roberte Coles, of Rocksbury, shalbe fined xx shillings for being drunke at Charlton in October last, and is injoyned to confesse his fault to the Court, (nowe committed in extenuateing his offence,) the nexte Court, and after att the Generall Court.

Tho: Knower hath bound himselfe in x pounds to make his personal appearance att the nexte Court, to answer to such things as shall be objected against him.

A Court of Assistants, holden att Boston, April 3, 1632.

PRESENT, The Governor,   Mr. Nowell,
           Deputy Governor, Mr. Pinchon,
           Mr. Ludlowe,   S: Bradstreete.
           Capt. Endicott,

THO: KNOWER was sett in the bilbowes for threateing the Court that, if hee should be punist, hee would have it tryed in England whither hee was lawfully punished or not.

It was ordered, that noe person whatsoever shall shoote att fowle upon Pullen Poynte or Noddles Ileland, but that the said places shalbe reserved for John Perkins to take fowle with netts.

Upon Roberte Coles confession of his faulte committed the last Court, in extenuateing of his offence of drunkenes, the Court remitted his ffyne, and further confession enjoyned him the last Court.

Sarah Morley is putt as an apprentice to Mr. Nathanaell Turner, of Saugus, for the space of nyne yeares from this Court, for which tearme hee is to finde her meate, drinke, and cloathing.

The Ileland called Conant's Ileland, with all the liberties and previlidges of fishing and fowleing, was demised to John Winthrop, Esquire, the present Governor, for the tearme of his life, for the ffine of fforty shillings, and att the yearely rent of xii pence, to be paid to the Treasurer upon the 25th day of March; and it was further agreed, and the said John Winthrop did covenant and promise to plant a vineyard and an orchyard in the same, in consideration whereof the Court did graunt that, att the end of the said tearme, the lease hereof should be renewed to the heires or assignes of the said John Winthrop for one and twenty yeares, payeinge yearely to the Governor, for the time being, the fifth parte of all such fruicts and proffitts as shalbe yearely raysed out of the same, and soe the same lease to be renewed from time to time unto the heires and assignes of the said John Winthrop, with the said reservation of the said fifth parte to the Governor for the time being, and the name of the said ileland was changed, and is to be called the Governors Garden; provided, that if the heires or assignes of the said John Winthrop shall att any time suffer the said ileland to lye wast, and not improve the same, then this present demise to be voide.

March 6th 1632.

IT is agreed upon by the partyes whose names are here underwritten, by vertue of an order of Court ffor the appoincted and setting out the bounds of Charles-Towne and Newe Towne.

First, it is agreed that all the land impaled by Newe Towne men, with the necke thereunto adjoyneing, whereon Mr. Graves dwelleth, shall belonge to the said Newe Towne, and that the bounds of Charles Towne shall end att a tree marked by the said pale, and to passe alonge from that tree, by a straight lyne unto the mydway betweene the westermost parte of the great lott of land of John Winthrop, Esquire, nowe Governor of the Englishe colony in the Massachusetts, and the neerest parte thereto of the bounds of Waterton. In witnes whereof, wee have hereunto sett our hands, the day and yeare aforesaid.

THO: MAYHEWE,
NATH: TURNER,
GEORGE ALCOCKE.

A Generall Court, holden att Boston, May 9th, 1632.

PRESENT, The Governor,   Mr. Nowell,
Deputy Governor,   Mr. Pinchon,
Mr. Ludlowe,   S: Bradstreete.

IT was generally agreed upon, by erection of hands, that the Governor, Deputy Governor, and Assistants should be chosen by the whole Court of Governor, Deputy Governor, Assistants, and freemen, and that the Governor shall alwaies be chosen out of the Assistants.

John Winthrop, Esquire, was chosen to the place of Governor (by the generall consent of the whole Court, manefested by erection of hands) for this yeare nexte ensueing, and till a newe be chosen, and did, in presence of the Court, take an oath to his said place belonging.

Thomas Dudley, Esquire, was in like manner chosen to the place of Deputy Governor for this yeare nexte ensueing, and till a newe be chosen, and did, accordingly, take an oath to his place belonging.

Mr. Roger Ludlowe, Mr. Increase Nowell, Mr. William Pinchon, S: Bradstreete, Capt. John Endicott, John Humfrey, Esquire, Mr. William Coddington, and Mr. John Winthrop, Junior, was chosen into the place of Assistants for this yeare nexte ensueing, and till newe be chosen.

It was ordered, that there should be two of every plantation appointed to conferre with the Court about raiseing of a publique stocke:—

Mr. Oldeham and Mr. Masters, for Waterton;
Roberte Coles and John Johnson, for Rocksbury;
Mr. Will: Colbran and Will: Cheesebrough, for Boston;
Rich: Wright   for Saugus;

Mr. Lockwood and Mr. Spencer for Newe Towne;
Mr. Gibbons and Mr. Palmer, for Charlton;
Mr. Conant and Peter Palfry, for Salem;
William Felpes and John Gallard, for Dorchester.

It was ordered, that the towne of Waterton, shall have that priviledge and interest in the wayre they have built upp Charles Ryver, according as the Court hereafter shall thinke meete to confirme unto them.

Mr. Edmond Lockwood was chosen constable of New Towne for this yeare nexte ensueing, and till a newe be chosen.   Jur.

Mr. Clerke was chosen constable of Waterton for this yeare nexte ensueing, and till a newe be chosen.   Jur.

A Court of Assistants, holden att Boston, June 5th, 1632.
PRESENT, The Governor,   Mr. Ludlowe,
            Deputy Governor,   Mr. Winthrop, Junior,
            Mr. Nowell,   S: Bradstreete.
            Mr. Pinchon,

THE Court, takeing into consideration the greate mercy of God, vouchsafed to the churches of God in Germany and the Pallattinate, etc., hath appoyncted the 13th day of this present moneth to be kept as a day of publique thanksgiving throughout the severall plantations.

It is ordered, that the goods of the company of husbandmen shalbe inventoryed by the beadle, and preserved here, for the use and benefitt of the said company.

It was further ordered, that there shalbe 200 acres of land sett out by marks and bounds, on the west side of Charles Ryver, over against the newe towne, to enjoy to Thomas Dudley, Esquire, Deputy Governor, to him and his heires for ever.

It was likewise ordered, that every planter inhabiting within this pattent shall pay to the Court, towards the defrayeing of publique charges, xii pence for every pound of beaver that hee shall trade for with any Indian within this pattent, or that hee brings into the pattent, haveing traded the same with any forraine Indean.

Also, it is agreed that there shalbe a trucking howse appoyncted in every plantation, whither the Indians may resorte to trade, to avoide there comeing to severall howses.

There is a commission graunted to Mr. Pinchon and Mr. Mavericke, Senior, to make inquiry, and to take depositions of the creditors of Josias Plastowe and there witnesses, that it may appeare what debts are oweing by him, and soe his estate to be preserved here till the nexte Court.

A Court, holden att Boston, July 3, 1632.

PRESENT, The Governor,   Mr. Pinchon,
Deputy Governor,   Mr. Winthrop,
Mr. Ludlowe,   S: Bradstreete,
Capt. Endicott,   Mr. Nowell.

CAPT. ENDICOTT, being chosen an Assistant att the Generall Court, did nowe take an oath to his place belonging, in the presence of the Court.

It is ordered, that Joist Weillust shall have allowed him v pounds towards his transportation into his owne country, whither, according to his desire, hee hath free leave to goe.

It is ordered, that Thomas Dextor shalbe bound to his good behavior till the nexte Generall Court, and ffined v pounds for his misdemeanor and insolent carriage and speeches to S: Bradstreete, att his owne howse; also, att the Generall Court is bound to confesse his fault.

There is a necke of land lyeing aboute 3 myles from Salem, containing aboute 300 acres of land, graunted to Capt. Jo: Endicott, to enjoy to him and his heires for ever, called in the Indean tonge Wahquainesehcok, in English Birchwood, bounded on the south side with a ryver called in the Indean tounge Soewamapenessett, commonly called the Cowe Howse Ryver; bounded on the north side with a ryver called in the Indean tongue Conamabsquenooncant, commonly called the Ducke Ryver; bounded on the east with a ryver leadeing upp to the 2 former ryvers, which is called in the Indean tongue Orkhussunt, otherwise knowen by the name of Wooleston Ryver; bounded on the west with the maine land.

There is another necke of land, lyeing aboute 3 myles from Salem, containing aboute 200 acres, graunted to Mr. Samuell Skelton, to enjoy to him and his heires for ever, called by the Indeans Wahquack, bounded on the south upon a little ryver called by the Indeans Conamabsquenooncant; upon the north abutting on another ryver, called by the Indeans Pouomeneuhcant; and on the east, on the same ryver, also there is graunted to Mr. Skelton one acre of land, on which his howse standeth, and 10 acres more in a necke of land abutting on the south ryver, upon the harbor ryver on the north, upon William Allens ground on the east, and upon Mrs. Higgensons ground on the west.

Likewise there is graunted to Mr. Skelton 2 acres more of ground, lyeing in Salem, abutting on the south ryver on the east, upon the maine upon the west, on Capt. Endicotts ground on the south, and on John Sweetes ground on the north.

William Parks doeth promise, if Serjeant Bateman comes noe more, to satisfie Mr. Pinchon what shalbe thought meete by 2 indifferent men for 3 leaden waights by him lost, and 12 paire of stockins which the said Bateman solde to Mr. Pinchon for good ones, but proved badd and moath-eaten.

John Smithe is bound as an apprentice with Mr. John Wilson for fyve yeares from this Court, dureing which tearme Mr. Wilson is to finde the said John Smyth meate, drinke, and apparell, and att the end of the said time is to give unto him the somme of fforty shillings.

It is likewise ordered, that those goods which were sent over with the said John Smythe shall remaine in the hands of Mr. Wilson, for which hee is to be accountable to those that sent them over.

Bryan Bincks and Peter Johnson hath bound themselves joynctly and severally in x pounds a peece, that they shall not depart out of the pattent without leave from the Governor, and shalbe ready to attend upon the Court, when they shalbe called to give an account of their company goods.

John Smyth hath likewise bound himselfe in x pounds to be accomptable for his companyes goods nowe inventoryed, and remaineing in his hands.

Mr. James Parker is ffined xl shillings, and bound to his good behavior till the nexte Court, for his misdemeanor and drunkenes, committed aboard the Virginia shipp.

Mr. Samuell Dudley is ffined xl shillings for the like offence att the same time.

It is ordered, that the captain and officers shall take especiall care to search all peeces that are brought into the ffeild for being charged, and that noe person whatsoever shall att any time charge any peece of service with bulletts or shott, other then for defence of their howses, or att commaund from the captain, upon such penallty as the Court shall thinke meete to inflict.

A Court, holden att Boston, August 7th, 1632.

PRESENT, The Governor,   Mr. Pinchon,
            Deputy Governor,   Mr. Winthrop,
            Mr. Ludlowe,   S: Bradstreete.
            Mr. Nowell,

UPON further consideration of justice to be done upon the murder of Walter Bagnall, and upon readeing a letter from those of Plymouthe, being written in answer to a letter sent to them aboute it, it is ordered that a boate shall be sent forth, sufficiently manned, with commission to deale with the plantation to the eastward, and to joyne with such of them as shalbe willing thereto, for examination of the murder of the said Walter Bagnall, and for apprehending of such as shalbe found guilty thereof, and to bring the prisoners into the Bay; it is referred to the Governor to take order herein.

It is ordered, that the remainder of Mr. Allens stronge water, being estimated aboute 2 gallands, shalbe delivered into the hands of the deacons of Dorchester, for the benefitt of the poore there, for his selling of it dyvers tymes to such as were drunke with it, hee knowing thereof.

It is ordered, that James Woodward shalbe sett in the billbowes for being drunke att the newe towne.

There is iii pounds of Knops fine of v pounds remitted.

It is ordered, that the captains shalbe maintained by their severall companies.

Mr. William Pinchon is chosen Treasurer for this yeare nexte ensueing, and till a newe be chosen.

A Court, holden att Boston, Sept. 4th, 1632.

PRESENT, The Governor,   Mr. Tresurer,
            Deputy Governor,   Mr. Nowell,
            Mr. Ludlowe,   Mr. Jo: Winthrop,
            Capt. Endicott,   S: Bradstreete.

IT is ordered, that Roberte Shawe shalbe severely whipt, for wicked curseing, sweareing, justifyeing the same, and gloryeing in it, as hath been proved by oath.

John Stickland is ffined iii pounds, for his refuseing to watch, att the captain's commaunds.

Saggamore John, etc., promised against the nexte yeare, and soe ever after, to fence their corne against all kinde of cattell.

Josuah Barnes is bound as an apprentice to Mr. Paine for 5 yeares from his landing, for £4 per annum wages, and v pounds att the end of his tearme, to be paid to him by his said maister.

It is ordered, William Hamon shalbe sett in the bilbowes, for being drunke.

Mr. Turner is chosen constable of Saugus for this yeare, and till a newe be chosen, and did nowe take an oath to his place belonging.

There is order given to Mr. Treasurer to pay 40s to Richard Waterman, for killing a woulfe aboute 2 monthes since, in Salem plantation.

There is likewise order graunted to Mr. Treasurer to pay Capt. Underhill and Capt. Pattricke a quarters exhibition.

Mr. Roberte Feakes is chosen into the place of leifetenant to Capt. Pattricke.

It is ordered, that Richard Hopkins shalbe severely whipt, and branded with a hott iron on one of his cheekes, for selling peeces and powder and shott to the Indeans. Hereupon it was propounded if this offence should not be punished hereafter by death. Referred to the nexte Court, to be determined.

A Court, holden att Boston, October 3, 1632.

PRESENT, The Governor,   Mr. Tresurer,
            Deputy Governor,   Mr. Nowell,
            Mr. Ludlowe,   Mr. Winthrop,
            Capt. Endicott,   S: Bradstreete.

Mr. Tresurer hath promised to give xxv pounds for this yeare, for his beaver trade, for which his 12d in the pound is remitted.

It is ordered, that there shalbe a howse of correction and a house for the beadle built att Boston, with what speede conveniently may be.

Mr. Batcheler is required to forbeare exerciseing his guifts as a pastor or teacher publiquely, in our pattent, unlesse it be to those hee brought with him, for his contempt of authority, and till some scandles be removed.

It is agreed, that the beadle shall have viii pounds exhibition for this yeare.

It is ordered, that James Woodward shalbe whipt, for runing from his maister, Mr. Gibbons, and absenting himselfe from his service; in recompence whereof hee shall doe him 6 weekes worke when his time comes out.

Edward Burton is ffined v pounds for his contempt of authority, in refuseing to come to the Court, being summoned by the Governor, and 40s for drunkenes.

It is ordered, that Saugus plantation shall have liberty to build a ware upon Saugus Ryver; also, they have promised to make and continually to keepe a good foote-bridge upon the most convenient place there.

It is ordered, that Alex: Miller and John Wipple shall give iii shillings iiii pence a peece to their maister, Israell Stoughton, for their wastfull expence of powder and shott.

Leifetenant Aleworth hath liberty graunted him to returne to England by the shipp Lyon.

There is 60 acres of meadowe ground graunted to Simon Bradstreete, in the marshe ground against the oyster banke, where hee shall chuse, to injoy to him and his heires for ever.

It is ordered, that Nicholas Frost, for thefte by him committed att Damerills Cove upon the Indeans, for drunkenes and fornication, of all which hee is convicted, shalbe fined v pounds to the Court, and xl pounds to Henry Way and John Holman shalbe severely whipt, and branded in the hand with a hott iron, and after banished out of this pattent, with penalty that if ever hee be found within the lymitts of the said pattent, hee shalbe putt to death; also it is agreed that hee shalbe kept in boults by Henry Way and John Holman, till his ffines be paid, dureing which time hee is to beare his owne charges.

It is thought, by generall consent, that Boston is the fittest place for publique meeteings of any place in the Bay.

It is ordered, that from the 1th of March nexte, every person shall satisfie for the damages his swine shall doe in the corne of another.

It is further ordered, that noe person shall take any tobacco publiquely, under paine of punishment; also that every one shall pay i pence for every time hee is convicted for takeing tobacco in any place, and that any Assistant shall have power to receave evidence and give order for the levyeing of it, as also to give order for the levyeing of the officers charge; this order to begin the 10th of November nexte.

George Dyar is chosen constable of Dorchester for this yeare nexte ensueing, and till a newe be chosen, and did nowe take an oath to his place belonging.

A Court, holden att Boston, November 7th, 1632.

PRESENT, The Governor, Mr. Nowell,
    Deputy Governor, Mr. Winthrop,
    Mr. Ludlowe, S: Bradstreete.
    Mr. Tresurer,

FOR preservation of good timber for more necessary uses, it is ordered, that noe man shall fell any wood for paleing but such as shalbe vewed and allowed by the nexte Assistant, or some whome they shall depute to doe the same; this order not to extend to ground that is or shall be assigned to particular persons.

It is ordered, that the difference betwixte Charles-Towne and Newe-Towne, for ground, shalbe referred to Mr. Mavericke, Junior, Mr. Alcocke, Mr. Turner, and John Johnson, to vewe the ground, wood, and meadowe, and soe to sett downe the bounds betwixte them.

It is ordered, that the necke of land betwixte Powder Horne Hill and Pullen Poynte shall belonge to Boston, to be enjoyed by the inhabitants thereof for ever.

It is likewise ordered, that the inhabitants of Boston shall have liberty to fetch wood from Dorchester necke of land for 20 yeares, the propriety of the land to remaine to Dorchester.

Capt. Traske, Mr. Conant, William Cheesebrough, and John Perkins are appoincted by the Court to sett downe the bounds betwixte Dorchester and Rocksbury. Ralfe Sprage is chosen umpire.

There is 100 acres of land graunted to Mr. Roger Ludlowe, to injoy to him and his heires for ever, lyeing betwixte Musquantum Chappell and the mouthe of Naponsett.

John Finch is ffined x shillings for wanting armes for his man, and for being absent himselfe from traineing.

Henry Lynn is ffined x shillings for absenting himselfe from traineing.

Mr. Mathewe Cradocke is ffined iiii pounds for his men being absent from traineing dyvers times.

It is ordered, that the captains shall traine their companyes but once a monethe.

It is ffurther agreed, that Sir Richard Saltonstall shall give Saggamore John a hogshead of corne for the hurt his cattell did him in his corne.

It is ordered, that neither Englishe nor Indeans shall have any more rewards given them for killing woolfes.

There is aboute 50 acres of mead ground graunted to John Winthrop, Esquire, present Governor, lyeing betwixte Cobbetts howse and Wanottymies Ryver.

It is referred to Mr. Turner, Peter Palfry, and Roger Conant to sett out a proportion of land in Saugus for John Humfry, Esquire.

Mr. Phillips hath 30 acres of land graunted him upp Charles Ryver, on the south side, begininge att a creeke a lyttle higher then the first pynes, and soe upwards towards the ware.

It is ordered, that Robert Huitt and Mary Ridge shalbe whipt for committing fornication togeather, of which they are convicted.

There is iiii pounds of Tho: Dexters ffine of v pounds forgiven him.

6th March, 1632.

IT was agreed by the parties appointed by the Court, etc., that all the ground impaled by Newe towne men, with the neck whereon Mr. Graves his house standeth, shall belong to Newe towne, and that the bounds of Charles-towne shall end at a tree marked by the pale, and to passe along from thence by a straight line unto the midway betwixt the westermost part of the Governors greate lot and the nearest part thereto of the bounds of Watertowne.

A Court, holden att Boston, March 4th, 1632.

PRESENT, The Governor,   Mr. Tresurer,
Deputy Governor,   Mr. Nowell,
Mr. Ludlowe,   Mr. Winthrop, Junior,
Capt. Endicott,   S: Bradstreete.

THERE is administration graunted to Roger Ludlowe, Esquire, of the goods and chattells of John Knight, whoe disceased in November last.

The Court hath reversed the last act against Mr. Batcheler, which restrained him from further gathering a church within this pattent.

It is ordered, that Thomas Dexter shalbe sett in the bilbowes, disfranchized and ffined xl pounds for speakeing reproachfull and seditious words against the government here established, and findeing fault to dyvers with the acts of the Court, sayeing this captious government will bring all to naught, adding that the best of them was but an atturney, etc.

It is agreed, that the bounds formerly sett out betwixte Boston and Rocksbury shall continue, onely Rocksbury to enjoy the conveniency of the creeke neere thereunto.

Boston is cessed v pounds, Charlton iiii pounds, Rocksbury vi pounds, Waterton vi pounds, Newe-Towne vi pounds, Meadford iii pounds, for the maintenance of Capt. Underhill and Capt. Pattricke for halfe a yeare.

Serjeant Morris is chosen ancient to Capt. Underhill.

Thomas Wincall is ffined xx shillings for drunkennes.

A Court, holden att Boston, April 1th, 1633.
PRESENT, The Governor,   Mr. Tresurer,
                Deputy Governor,   Mr. Nowell,
                Mr. Ludlowe,   S: Bradstreete.
                Capt. Endicott,

THERE is xi shillings v pence allowed to Edward Converse for ferryeing officers over the water.

It is ordered, that noe person whatsoever shall goe to plant or inhabitt att Aggawam, without leave from the Court, except those that are already gone, viz.: Mr. John Winthrop, Junior, Mr. Clerke, Roberte Coles, Thomas Howlett, John Biggs, John Gage, Thomas Hardy, William Perkins, Mr. Thornedicke, William Serjeant.

The price of corne, formerly restrained to 6s the bushell, is nowe sett at liberty to be solde as men can agree.

Noddles Ileland is graunted to Mr. Samuell Maveracke, to enjoy to him and his heires for ever, yeilding and payeing yearely att the Generall Court, to the Governor for the time being, either a fatt weather, a fatt hogg, or xl shillings in money, and shall give leave to Boston and Charles-Towne to fetch wood contynually, as their neede requires, from the southerne parte of the said ileland.

It is agreed, that Mr. William Blackestone shall have 50 acres of ground sett out for him neere to his howse in Boston, to injoy for ever.

Ezekiell Richardson is chosen constable of Charlton, for this yeare nexte ensueing, and till a newe be chosen.

It is ordered, that if any swine shall, in fishing time, come within a quarter of a myle of the stage att Marble Harbour, that they shalbe forfected to the owners of the said stadge, and soe for all other stadges within theis lymitts.

It is ordered, that Joyce Bradwicke shall give unto Alex: Becke the somme of xx shillings, for promiseing him marriage without her ffrends consent, and nowe refuseing to performe the same.

John Sayles being convicted of fellonyously takeing away corne and fishe from dyvers persons the last yeare and this, as also clap-boards, etc., is censured by the Court after this manner: That all his estate shalbe forfected, out of which double restitution shalbe made to those whome hee hath wronged, shalbe whipt, and bound as a servant with any that will retaine him for 3 yeares, and after to be disposed of by the Court as they shall thinke meete.

John Sayle is bound with Mr. Coxeshall for 3 yeares, for which hee is to give him £4 per annum; his daughter is also bound with him for 14 yeares. Mr. Coxeshall is to have a sowe with her, and att the end of her time hee is to give unto her a cowe calfe.

A Generall Courte, holden att Boston, May 29th, 1633.

PRESENT, The Governor,   Mr. Coddington,
           Deputy Governor,   Mr. Winthrop, Junior,
           Mr. Tresurer,   S: Bradstreete.
           Mr. Nowell,

JOHN WINTHROP, Senior, Esquire, was chosen to the place of Governor for this yeare nexte ensueing, manefested by generall erection of hands, and did in presence of the Courte take an oath to his place belonging.

In like manner, Tho: Dudley, Esquire, was chosen to the place of Deputy Governor for this yeare nexte ensueing, and did in presence of the Court take an oath to his place belonging.

Mr. Roger Ludlowe, Mr. William Pinchon, Mr. Will: Codding-ton, Mr. Increase Nowell, Mr. Simon Bradstreete, and Mr. John

Winthrop, Junior, was chosen to the place of Assistants for this yeare nexte ensueing, and till newe be chosen, and did in Courte take the oath to their place belonginge.

Mr. John Endicott, Sir Richard Saltonstall, John Humfry, Esquire, was chosen to the place of Assistants for this yeare nexte ensueing.

It was ordered, that the ffort att Boston shalbe finished with what convenient speede may be, att the publique charg.

Mr. John Benjamyn chosen constable of Newe-Towne for this yeare nexte ensueing, and till a newe be chosen.

The nexte Court is to be holden the 2 Tuesday in June.

A Court, holden att Boston, June 11th, 1633.

PRESENT, The Governor, Mr. Nowell,
    Deputy Governor, Mr. Coddington,
    Mr. Ludlowe, Mr. Winthrop,
    Mr. Tresurer, S: Bradstreete.

IT is ordered, that William Dixon shalbe sett in the bilbowes for disordering himselfe with drinke.

It is likewise ordered, that John Pemerton shalbe whipt, bound to his good behavior, and enjoyned to make his appearance att the nexte Court, for committing fornication with Eliz: Marson.

John Webb is sett at liberty from his maister, William Parks.

There is leave graunted to Tho: Sellen to plant att Aggawam.

The 19th day of this moneth is appoyncted to be kept as a day of publique thanksgiveing throughout the severall plantations, etc.

A Court, holden att Boston, July 2, 1633.

PRESENT, The Governor, Mr. Nowell,
    Deputy Governor, Mr. Coddington,
    Mr. Ludlowe, Mr. Winthrop,
    Mr. Endicott, S: Bradstreete.
    Mr. Tresurer,

Mr. Endicott, being chosen an Assistant att the Generall Court, did nowe take an oath to his place belonging.

Mr. Ludlowe, Mr. Tresurer, and Mr. Nowell are chosen as committees to take an accompt of the debts due to the Governor, and to certifie the same att the nexte Court, that they may be discharged.

It is ordered, that there shalbe cl pounds [£150] given to the Governor for this present yeare, towards his publique charges and extraordinary expences.

Roberte Allen is ffined v shillings for absenting himselfe from Court, being summoned to be there as a witnes, etc.

James White is ffined xxx shillings for drunkenes by him committed att Marblehead, on the Sabboth day.

John Bennett is ffined x shillings for being drunke att Marblehead.

It is ordered, that noe person shall sell either wine or stronge water without leave from the Governor, or Deputy Governor. This order to take place a fortnight hence, and after the constable of the same plantation hath published the same, and that noe man shall sell, or (being in a course of tradeing,) give any stronge water to any Indean.

It is ordered, that if any corne fence shalbe by the inhabitants of the towne judged insufficient, and the owner thereof forbeare mending of it more then 2 dayes after warneing given, the inhabitants shall mend the said fence, and the corne of the owner of the said fence shalbe liable to pay the charges of the mending thereof.

Mr. Woolridge and Mr. Gibbons are appoyncted to joyne with Mr. Graves and Mr. Geneson to inventory the goods and chattells of Alex: Wignall.

It is ordered, that the ground lyeing betwixte the North Ryver and the creeke on the north side of Mr. Maveracks, and soe upp into the country, shall belonge to the inhabitants of Charlton.

Order is given to the Tresurer to deliver to Leifetenant Mason x pounds for his voyage to the eastward, when hee went about the takeing of Bull.

There is demised to Tho: Lambe, of slate in Slate Ileand, 10 poole towards the water side, and 5 poole into the land, for 3 yeares, payeing the yearely rent of ii shillings vi pence.

Administration is graunted to Mr. Mayhewe of the goods and chattells of Mr. Ralfe Glover, disceased, etc.

It is ordered, that it shalbe lawfull for any man to kill any swine that comes into his corne: the party that ow[n]es the swine is to have them, being kild, and allowe recompence for the damage they doe, etc.

A Court, holden att Boston, August 6th, 1633.
PRESENT, The Governor,   Mr. Nowell,
    Deputy Governor,   Mr. Coddington,
    Mr. Ludlowe,   Mr. Winthrop,
    Mr. Tresurer,   S: Bradstreete.

MR. JOHN WOOLRIDGE is ffined 1 shilling for distempering him-selfe with drinke, aboard Mr. Graves his shipp.

It is agreed, that there shalbe a sufficient cartbridge made in some convenient place over Muddy River, and another over Stony Ryver, to be done att the charge of Boston and Rocksbury. Mr. Coddington, Mr. Colbran, and Mr. Samford are chosen to see it done for Boston, and Mr. Tresurer, Jehu Burr, and John Johnson for Rocksbury.

It is further ordered, that if any ram goate be found amongst ewe goates betwixte the first of July and 10th of November, it shalbe lawfull for any man to sease on him before witnesses, and to convey him to some safe place till the said 10th of November, and then halfe of him is to goe to the publique, and the other halfe to the party that seases on him. This order to take place on Thursday nexte.

A Court, holden att Boston, Sept. 3, 1633.
PRESENT, The Governor,   Mr. Nowell,
    Deputy Governor,   Mr. Coddington,
    Mr. Ludlowe,   Mr. Winthrop,
    Mr. Tresurer,   S: Bradstreete.

JOHN SHOTSWELL is ffined xl shillings for distempering him-selfe with drinke att Aggawam.

Roberte Coles is ffined x pounds, and enjoyned to stand with a white sheete of paper on his back, wherein a drunkard shalbe written in great letters, and to stand therewith soe longe as the Court thinks meete, for abuseing himselfe shamefully with drinke, intiseing John Shotswell wife to incontinency, and other mis-demeanor.

It is ordered, that the goods of Thomas Walford shalbe seques-tred, and remaine in the hands of Anchient Gennison, to satisfie the debts hee owes in the Bay to severall persons.

There is administration graunted to William Gallard and William Rockwell, of the goods and chattels of John Russell, of Dorchester, whoe disceased August 26th, 1633.

Administration graunted to Mr. John Moody of the goods and chattells of Thomas Desbre disceased, and soe to remaine in his hands, to be accomptable for them.

By consent of John Billingham, Richard Wright, and Thomas Dexter, the differences betwixte them are referd to Mr. Endicott and Mr. Nowell, and power is graunted them by the Court to depose witnesses, heare, and determine the said differences.

Capt. John Stone for his outrage committed in confronting aucthority, abuseing Mr. Ludlowe both in words and behavour, assalting him and calling him a just as, etc., is ffined c pounds, and prohibited comeing within this pattent without leave from the Government, under the penalty of death.

It is ordered, (according to a former order att the Generall Court,) that every hand (except magistrates and ministers) shall aford there helpe to the finishing of the ffort att Boston, till it be ended.

Mr. Palmer is ffined x shillings for absenting himselfe, being warnd to serve of a jury.

Alex: Wignall is ffined x pounds for drunkenes, quarrelling, breach of an order of Court, and contempt of aucthority.

Administration graunted to William Stitson of the goods and chattells of Richard Arnoll, of Wenetsemett, disceased.

There is liberty graunted to Mr. John Winthrop, Junior, and to his assignes, to sett upp a trucking howse upp Merrymak Ryver.

Mr. John Barcrofte doeth acknowledge to owe unto our Soveraigne, the King, the somme of xl pounds and Mr. Samuell Maveracke the somme of xx pounds, etc. The condition of this recognizance is, that Jane Barcrofte, wife of the said John, shall be of good behavior towards all persons.

> *A Court, holden att Boston, October 1th, 1633.*
> PRESENT, The Governor,   Mr. Nowell,
>   Deputy Governor,   Mr. Coddington,
>   Mr. Ludlowe,   S: Bradstreete.
>   Mr. Tresurer,

IT is ordered, that Serjeant Perkins shall carry 40 turfes to the ffort, as a punishment for drunkenes by him committed.

Also, it is ordered, that Thomas Dexter shalbe ffined xx shillings for the like offence.

It is ordered, that if any trained solder shalbe absent from traineing, upon their traineing dayes, haveing lawfull warneing, shall forfect v shillings, and that it shalbe lawfull for one of the serjeants appoyncted by the captain of the company to levye; unles within 2 dayes after it be demaunded, the party offending bring a certificate from the nexte Assistant that hee had a necessary occasion to be absent.

It is ordered, that maister carpenters, sawers, masons, clapboard-ryvers, brickelayers, tylars, joyners, wheelewrights, mowers, etc., shall not take above 2s a day, findeing themselves dyett, and not above 14d a day if they have dyett found them, under the penalty of v shillings, both to giver and receaver, for every day that there is more given and receaved. Also, that all other inferior worke-men of the said occupations shall have such wages as the constable of the said place, and 2 other inhabitants, that hee shall chuse, shall appoynct.

Also, it is agreed, that the best sorte of labourers shall not take above 18d a day if they dyett themselves, and not above 8d a day if they have dyett found them, under the aforesaid penalty, both to giver and receaver.

Likewise, that the wages of inferior labourers shalbe referd to the constable and 2 other, as aforesaid.

Master taylours shall not take above 12d a day, and the inferior sorte not above 8d, if they be dyeted, under the aforesaid penalty; and for all other worke they doe att home proportionably, and soe for other worke that shalbe done by the greate by any other artificer.

Further, it is ordered, that all workemen shall worke the whole day, alloweing convenient tyme for foode and rest. This order to take place the 12th of this present moneth.

It is further ordered, that noe person, howse houlder or other, shall spend his time idlely or unproffitably, under paine of such punishment as the Court shall thinke meete to inflicte; and for this end it is ordered, that the constable of every place shall use spetiall care and deligence to take knowledge of offenders in this kinde, espetially of common coasters, unprofittable fowlers, and tobacco takers, and to present the same to the 2 nexte Assistants, whoe shall have power to heare and determine the cause, or, if the matter be of importance, to transferr it to the Court.

In regard of the many and extraordinary mercyes which the Lord hath beene pleased to vouchsafe of late to this plantation, viz., a plentifull harvest, ships safely arrived with persons of spetiall use and quallity, etc., it is ordered, that Wednesday, the 16th day of this present moneth, shalbe kept as a day of publique thanksgiveing through the severall plantations. And whereas it is found by common experience that the keepeing of lectures att the ordinary howres nowe observed in the fore-noone to be dyvers wayes prejudiciall to the common good, both in the losse of a whole day and bringing other charges and troubles to the place where the lecture is kept, it is therefore ordered, that hereafter noe lecture shall begin before one a clocke in the afternoone.

It is ordered, that there shalbe £400 collected out of the severall plantations, to defray publique charges, viz:—

Boston,	£48 00s 00d	Saugus,	£36 00s 00d
Rocksbury,	48 00 00	Salem,	28 00 00
Newe-Towne,	48 00 00	Wenetsemett,	08 00 00
Waterton,	48 00 00	Meadford,	12 00 00
Charlton,	48 00 00	Aggawam,	08 00 00
Dorchester,	80 00 00		

Summe tot: £412 00 00.

A Court, holden att Boston, November 5th, 1633.
PRESENT, The Governor,   Mr. Tresurer,
       Mr. Ludlowe,   Mr. Coddington,
       Mr. Nowell,   S: Bradstreete.

IT is ordered, that when all the plantations in the Bay hath done 2 dayes worke a peece att the ffort, there shall order goe forth to Salem, Aggawam, and Saugus, to send in their money for 3 dayes worke towards it, for every man, except magistrates and minister.

It is ordered, that proces shall be directed by the Secretary to the beadle, for the warning of 24 jurors, 14 dayes before the Court, to be named by the Secritary.

It is likewise ordered, that corne of the country shall passe att 6s the bushell till the nexte Court.

Further, it is agreed, that noe man shall give his swine any corne but such as, being vewed by 2 or 3 neighbors, shalbe judged unfitt for mans meate.

Also, that every plantation shall agree howe many swine every person may keepe, winter and summer, aboute the plantation; this order to take place 10 dayes hence.

Mr. Rich: Browne is allowed by the Court to keepe a fferry over Charles Ryver, against his howse, and is to have 2d for every single person hee soe transports, and 1 pence a peece if there be 2 or more.

Ensigne Morris is discharged of his place of ensigne, and Mr. Thomas Mooteham chosen in his roome.

Serjeant Stoughton is chosen ensigne to Capt. Mason.

It is ordered, that James Penn, the beadle, shall have allowed him by the Tresurer the somme of £30, to builde a howse, which is to be for his use while hee remaines in the place of beadle, and after to be disposed of as the Court shall thinke meete.

November 8th, 1633.

WHEREAS, by order of Court, holden in October last, the wages of workemen were reduced to a certainety, in regard of the great extortion used by dyvers persons of little conscience, and the greate disorder which grewe hereupon, by vaine and idle wast of much precious tyme, and expence of those immoderate gaynes in wyne, stronge water, and other superfluities, nowe, least the honest and conscionable workemen should be wronged or discouraged by excessive prizes of those commodityes which are necessary for their life and comfort, wee have thought it very just and equall to sett order also therein. Wee doe therefore hereby order, that after publique notice hereof, noe persons shall sell to any of the inhabitants within this jurisdiction any provision, cloathinge, tooles, or other commodities, above the rate of ffoure pence in a shilling more then the same cost or might be bought for ready money in England, upon paine of forfecting the valewe of the thinge solde, (except cheese, which, in regard of the much hazard in bringing, and wyne, oyle, vinegar, and stronge waters, which, in regard of leakeing, may be solde att such rates (provided the same be moderate) as the buyer and seller can agree.)

And for lynnen and other commodities, which, in regard of their close stowage and small hazard, may be afforded att a cheap rate, wee doe advise all men to be a rule to themselves, in keepeing a good conscience, assureing them that, if any man shall exceede the bounds of moderation, wee shall punish them severely.

A Court, holden att Boston, March 4th, 1633.

PRESENT, The Governor,   Mr. Tresurer,
         Deputy Governor,   Mr. Nowell,
         Mr. Ludlowe,   Mr. Coddington,
         Capt. Endicott,   S: Bradstreete.

IT is ordered, that all the swamps conteyneing above 100 acres, either belonging to any towne or not, shall lye in common for any free inhabitant to fetch wood att seasonable tymes, without prejudice to the inhabitants where the same is, (that swampe onely excepted lyeing within the Newe-Towne pale, towards the bay.)

It is ordered, that Mr. Dumer shalbe rated viii pounds to the publique stocke, viz.: v pounds x shillings for his estate in Rocksbury, and 1 shilling in Saugus; the tresury is to lose the rest that hee was rated in Saugus.

The Court hath ordered, that Mr. Dillingham shalbe rated for the cattell hee is possessed of, of Mr. Downeings.

It is ordered, that there shalbe a markett kept att Boston upon every Thursday, the fifth day of the weeke.

Mr. Nath: Turner is chosen captain of the millitary company att Saugus.

It is ordered, that John Sayles shalbe severely whipt for running from his maister, Mr. Coxeall.

It is ordered, that v pounds of the judgement against Joseph Twitchwell shalbe abated, it appeareing to the Court that Joseph Mannering hadd not paid the same, as was formerly conceaved.

Mr. Rich: Morris is chosen leifetenant to Capt. Underhill.

It is ordered, that noe person whatsoever shall buy any land of any Indean without leave from the Court.

Christopher Tarling is to be whipt for stealeing victualls from his master, and for running away.

Mr. William Dennison is chosen constable of Rocksbury.

John Chapman is ffined xx shillings for selling boards att 8 shillings per 10 x, contrary to an order of Court, and is remitted, upon promise of 300 of 4 inch planke towards the sea ffort.

Rich: Williams is ffined 40s for drunkenes committed att Bowmans howse.

William Cooley is ffined 40s for the like offence.

Tymothy Hawkins and John Vauhan ffined xx shillings a peece

for mispending their tyme in company keepeing, drinkeing stronge water, and selling other, contrary to an order of Court.

Allowed to the witnes bound over to the Court, to give evidence against them, v shillings.

Edward Howe is ffined xx shillings for selling stronge water, contrary to an order of Court.

It is ordered, that Roberte Coles, for drunkenes by him committed att Rocksbury, shalbe disfranchized, weare aboute his necke, and soe to hange upon his outward garment, a D, made of redd cloath, and sett upon white; to contynue this for a yeare, and not to leave it of att any tyme when hee comes amongst company, under the penalty of xl shillings for the first offence, and v pounds the second, and after to be punished by the Court as they thinke meete; also, hee is to weare the D outwards, and is enjoyned to appeare att the nexte Generall Court, and to contynue there till the Court be ended.

Josuah Harris is bound as an apprentice with Frauncis Weston, for 5 yeares from this day, his said maister findeing him meate, drinke, and cloathes.

Ensigne Stoughton, Tho: Ford, and William Felpes, and William Galard are appoyncted to sett out the bounds betwixte Boston and Rocksbury, which is nowe in difference betwixte them.

The ware att Misticke is graunted to John Winthrop, Esquire, present Governor, and to Mr. Mathewe Cradocke, of London, merchant, to enjoy to them and their heires for ever.

Upon consideration of the usefullness of a moveing ffort to be builte, 40 ffoote longe and 21 ffoote wide, for defence of this colony, and upon the ffree offer of some gentlemen lately come over to us of some large sommes of money, to be imployed that way, it is thought fitt that this matter shalbe moved to such men of ability as have not borne their parte in the great charges of the ffoundation of this colony; and for this end it is desired that every Assistant shall undertake the busines for treateing with such as are within the towne where they dwell, and if they see fitt, they may desire some other of the Assistants to joyne with them.

There is x pounds promised Mr. Stevens, for his care and expedition in this worke, to be paid when the worke is finished.

Gyven and promised towards the Sea Fort:—
Mr. Haynes, ... 1 pound

Capt. Turner, ... x pounds
Mr. Coxeall, ... v pounds
Rich: Wright, 4 inch plancke, ... 400
John Chapman, 4 inch planke, ... 300
Mr. Aspinwall, ... l shillings
John Johnson, ... xx shillings
Mr. Nowell, ... iii pounds
Frauncis Johnson, ... xl shillings
Josuah Hewes, ... xx shillings
James Penn, ... xx shillings
Mr. William Dennison, ... xl shillings
Mr. Harding, ... iii pounds
Mr. George Alcocke, ... xl shillings
Mr. Israell Stoughton, to be paid
   within 9 or 10 monthes ...... xx pounds
Mr. John Coggin, ... v pounds
Tho: Reade, ... xx shillings
Mr. Parker, of Rocksbury, ... l shillings
Mr. Dumer, ... xxx pounds
Phillip Tabor, 4 inch plancke, ... 200
Garrett Church, 4 inch plancke, .. 200
Mr. John Wilson, ... iii pounds

      £144 and
        1100 4 inch plank.

A Court, holden att Boston, Aprill 1th, 1634.
PRESENT, The Governor,   Mr. Nowell,
        Deputy Governor,   Mr. Coddington,
        Mr. Ludlowe,   Mr. Winthrop,
        Mr. Endicott,   S: Bradstreete.
        Mr. Tresurer,

THERE is a thousand acres of land, and greate p   x
graunted to John Haynes, Esquire, ffyve hundred acres graunted
to Thomas Dudley, Esquire, Deputy Governor, x hundred to Mr.
Samuell Dudley, and two hundred acres   x   Daniell Dennison, all lyeing and being above the ffalls,   x   easterly side
of Charles Ryver, to enjoy to them and   x   heires for ever.
    There is two hundred acres of land graunted to Mr. I. Nowell,
lyeing and being on the west side of the North Ryv, otherwise
called the Three Myle Brooke.

There is ffyve hundred acres of land graunted to Mr. Jo: Oldham, lyeing neare Mount Feakes, on the north-west of Charles Ryver.

It is ordered, that if any man that hath any great quan x of land graunted him, and doeth not builde upon it or improve x within three yeares, it shalbe ffree for the Court to disp x of it to whome they please.

There is two hundred acres of land graunted to Mr. Jo: Wilson, pastor of the church of Boston, lyeing nexte the land graunted to Mr. Nowell on the south, and nexte Meadford on the north.

It is ordered, that John Lee shalbe whipt and ffined for calling Mr. Ludlowe false-hearted knave, and hard-heart knave, heavy ffriend, etc.

Thomas Foxe is ffined x shillings for want of appearance, being summoned to give evidence against John Lee.

Robert Moulton is chosen constable of Charlton, and sworne.

Mr. Israell Stoughton hath liberty graunted him to builde a myll, a ware, and a bridge over Naponsett Ryver, and is to sell the alewyves hee takes there att 5s the thousand.

It is ordered, that if any boy (that hath bene whipt for running from his maister) be taken in any other plantation, not haveing a note from his maister to testifie his business there, it sh[albe] lawfull for the constable of the said plantation to whip him a[nd] send him home.

There is power graunted to Mr. Ludlowe and Mr. Coggin to inventory, and take into safe keeping the goods and chattells of Mr. John Tilley, to satisfie such debts as hee ownes in the Bay.

The price of corne is lefte at liberty to be solde as men can agree.

Mr. Chester hath bound himselfe in x pounds to appeare at the next Court, to be holden in June, to answer to such things as shalbe objected against him.

Garrett Church and Phillip Tabor hath bound themselves [in] xl shillings a peece, to appeare then to give testimony agst Mr. Ch x for selling commodities contrary to order.

Long Iland, Deere Iland, and Hogg Iland graunted to Boston for e x, for the yearely rent of ii pounds, to be paid x x Treasurer x first day of the second moneth yearely.

It was further ordered, that every man of or above the age of twenty yeares, whoe hath bene or shall hereafter be resident within this jurisdiction by the space of sixe monethes, as an householder or sojorner, and not infranchised, shall take the oath hereunder written, before the Governor, or Deputy Governor, or some two of the nexte Assistants, whoe shall have power to convent him for that purpose, and upon his refuseall, to binde him over to the nexte Court of Assistants; and upon his refuseall the second tyme, hee shalbe banished, except the Court shall see cause to give him further respite.

THE OATH.

I DOE heare sweare, and call God to witnes, that, being nowe an inhabitant within the lymitts of this jurisdiction of the Massachusetts, I doe acknowledge myselfe lawfully subject to the aucthoritie and goverment there established, and doe accordingly submitt my person, family, and estate, to be protected, ordered, and governed by the lawes and constitutions thereof, and doe faithfully promise to be from time to time obedient and conformeable thereunto, and to the aucthoritie of the Governor, and all other the magistrates there, and their successors, and to all such lawes, orders, sentences, and decrees, as nowe are or hereafter shalbe lawfully made, decreed, and published by them or their successors. And I will alwayes indeavor (as in duty I am bound) to advance the peace and wellfaire of this body pollitique, and I will (to my best power and meanes) seeke to devert and prevent whatsoever may tende to the ruine or damage thereof, or of the Governor, Deputy Governor, or Assistants, or any of them or their successors, and will give speedy notice to them, or some of them, of any sedition, violence, treacherie, or other hurte or evill which I shall knowe, heare, or vehemently suspect to be plotted or intended against them or any of them, or against the said Common-wealth or government established. Soe helpe mee God.

It was further ordered, that the constable and foure o[r] more of the cheife inhabitants of every towne, (to be chosen by all the ffree men there, att some meeteing there,) with the advise of some one or more of the nexte Assistants, shall make a surveyinge of the howses backeside, corne feildes, moweing ground, and other lands, improved, or inclosed, or graunted by speciall order of the Court, of every ffree inhabitant there, and shall enter the same in a booke, (fairely written in words att lenght, and not in ffigures,) with the severall bounds and quantities, by the neerest estimation, and shall deliver a transcript thereof into the Court, within sixe monethes nowe nexte ensueing, and the same soe entered and recorded shalbe a sufficient assurance to every such ffree inhabitant, his and theire heires and assignes, of such estate of inheritance, or as they shall have in any such howses, lands, or ffranke-tenements.

The like course shalbe taken for assurance of all howses and towne-lotts of all such as shalbe hereafter enfranchised, and every sale or graunt of such howses or lotts as shalbe from time to time entered into the said booke by the said constable and foure inhabitants or their successors, (whoe shalbe still supplyed upon death or removeall,) for which entry the purchaser shall pay sixe pence, and the like summe for a coppy thereof, under the hands of the said surveyors, or three of them.

Att a Generall Courte, holden att Boston, May 14th, 1634.

PRESENT, The Governor,   Mr. Tresurer,
         Deputy Governor,   Mr. Nowell,
         Mr. Ludlowe,   Mr. Coddington,
         Mr. Endicott,   Mr. Bradstreete;

         Mr. Goodwin,   Mr. Coxeall,
         Mr. Spencer,   Edmond Quinsey,
         Mr. Talcott,   Capt. John Underhill,
         Mr. Feakes,   John Johnson,
         Mr. Browne,   William Heath,
         Mr. Oldham,   Mr. Alcocke,
         Mr. Beecher,   Mr. Israell Stoughton,
         Mr. Palmer,   William Felpes,
         Roberte Moulton,   George Hull,
         Capt. Turner,   Mr. Conant,
         Mr. Willis,   Frauncis Weston,
         Mr. Edw: Tomlins,   etc.
         Mr. Holgrave,

IT was agreed and ordered, that the former oath of ffreemen shalbe revoked, soe farr as it is dissonant from the oath of ffreemen here under written, and that those that receaved the former oath shall stand bound noe further thereby, to any intent or purpose, then this newe oath tyes those that nowe takes the same.

THE OATH OF A FREEMAN.

I, A. B., being, by Gods providence, an inhabitant and ffreeman within the jurisdiction of this commonweale, doe freely acknowledge my selfe to be subject to the goverment thereof, and therefore doe heere sweare, by the greate and dreadfull name of the everlyveing God, that I wilbe true and faithfull to the same, and will accordingly yeilde assistance and support thereunto, with my person and estate, as in equity I am bound, and will also truely indeavor to mainetaine and preserve all the libertyes and previlidges thereof, submitting my selfe to the wholesome lawes and orders made and established by the same; and further, that I will not plott nor practise any evill against it, nor consent to any that shall soe doe, but will timely discover and reveale the same to lawfull aucthority nowe here established, for the speedy preventing thereof. Moreover, I doe solemnely bynde myselfe, in the sight of God, that when I shalbe called to give my voice touching any such matter of this state, wherein ffreemen are to deale, I will give my vote and suffrage, as I shall judge in myne owne conscience may best conduce and tend to the publique weale of the body, without respect of persons, or favor of any man. Soe helpe mee God, in the Lord Jesus Christ.

Further, it is agreed, that none but the Generall Court hath power to chuse and admitt ffreemen.

That none but the Generall Court hath power to make and establishe lawes, nor to elect and appoynct officers, as Governor, Deputy Governor, Assistants, Tresurer, Secretary, Captains, Leiuetenants, Ensignes, or any of like moment, or to remove such upon misdemeanor, as also to sett out the dutyes and powers of the said officers.

That none but the Generall Court hath power to rayse moneyes and taxes, and to dispose of lands, viz., to give and confirme proprietyes.

Thomas Dudley, Esquire, was chosen Governor for this yeare next ensueing, and till a newe be chosen, and did, in presence of the Court, take an oath to his said place belonginge.

In like manner, Roger Ludlowe, Esquire, was chosen [to] the

place of Deputy Governor, for this yeare nexte ensueing, and till a newe be chosen, and did take an oathe, in presence of the Court, to his said place belonginge.

John Winthrop, Senior, John Humfrey, John Haynes, John Endicott, Esquires, Mr. William Pinchon, Mr. Increase Nowell, Mr. William Coddington, Mr. John Winthrop, Junior, Mr. Simon Bradstreete, were chosen to the place of Assistants for this yeare nexte ensueing, and till newe be chosen, and did, in presence of the Court, take an oath to the said place belongeing, Mr. Humfry and Mr. Winthrop, Junior, onely excepted, whoe were absent.

Mr. William Coddington was also chosen Tresurer for this yeare nexte ensueinge, and till a newe be chosen.

In like manner, Mr. Simon Bradstreete was chosen Secretary for this yeare nexte ensueinge, and till a newe be chosen.

The sentence of Court inflicted upon Roberte Coles, March 4th, 1633, for drunkenes, etc., by him committed, is nowe reversed, upon his submission, and testimoney being given of his good behavior.

It is agreed, that there shalbe x pounds ffine sett upon the Court of Assistants, and Mr. Mayhewe, for breach of an order of Court against imployeing Indeans to shoote with peeces, the one halfe to be payde by Mr. Pinchon and Mr. Mayhewe, offending therein, the other halfe by the Court of Assistants then in being, whoe gave leave thereunto.

It was further ordered, that the constable of every plantation shall, upon proces receaved from the Secretary, give tymely notice to the ffreemen of the plantation where hee dwells to send soe many of their said members as the proces shall direct, to attend upon publique service; and it is agreed, that noe tryall shall passe upon any, for life or banishment, but by a jury soe summoned, [*or by the Generall Courte.*][10]

It is likewise ordered, that there shalbe foure Generall Courts held yearely, to be summoned by the Governor, for the tyme being, and not to be dissolved without the consent of the major parte of the Court.

It was further ordered, that it shalbe lawfull for the ffreemen of every plantation to chuse two or three of each towne before

---

[10] The last five words are in the handwriting of Increase Nowell.

every Generall Court, to conferre of and prepare such publique busines as by them shalbe thought fitt to consider of att the nexte Generall Court, and that such persons as shalbe hereafter soe deputed by the ffreemen of [the] severall plantations, to deale in their behalfe, in the publique affayres of the commonwealth, shall have the full power and voyces of all the said ffreemen, deryved to them for the makeing and establishing of lawes, graunting of lands, etc., and to deale in all other affaires of the commonwealth wherein the ffreemen have to doe, the matter of election of magistrates and other officers onely excepted, wherein every freeman is to gyve his owne voyce.

All former orders concerneing swine are repealed. And it is agreed that every towne shall have liberty to make such orders aboute swine as they shall judge best for themselves, and that if the swine of one towne shall come within the lymitts of another, the owners thereof shalbe lyeable to the orders of that towne where their swine soe trespasseth.

Upon a complaynte made to John Winthrop, Esquire, then Governor, by a kinsman of John Hocking, lately slaine att Kenebecke, by one of the Plymouthe plantation, desireing that justice might be done upon the offender, the Court, takeing into consideration the same, hath ordered that Mr. John Alden (being there present when the said Hocking was slaine) shalbe detained here, till answer be received from those of Plymouthe, whither they will trye the matter there or noe, or that sufficient security shalbe taken that hee, the said John Alden, shall not departe out of the lymitts of this pattent, without leave from the Court or Governor.

Mr. John Alden doeth acknowledge to owe unto our Soveraigne Lord the King the somme of two hundred pounds; and Mr. Tymothy Hetherly and Leiuetenant Rich: Morris, in an hundred pound a peece, to be levyed of their goods and chattells, etc.

The condition of this recognizance is, that John Alden shall not departe out of the lymitts of this pattent without leave from the Court or Governor.

There is leave graunted to the inhabitants of Newe Towne to seeke out some convenient place for them, with promise that it shalbe confirmed unto them, to which they may remove their habitations, or have as an addition to that which already they have, provided they doe not take it in any place to prejudice a plantation already setled.

It was further ordered that Roberte Way shall remaine with the Deputy Governor till Mr. Way come out of England, for which hee is to allowe the said Roberte Way such recompenc as the Court shall thinke meete.

Furthermore, the Court hath ordered, that Boston shall have convenient inlargement att Mount Wooliston, to be sett out by foure indifferent men, whoe shall drawe a plott thereof, and present it to the nexte Generall Court, when it shalbe confirmed. Mr. Oldham, Mr. Aspinwall, Mr. Coxeall, Serjeant Stoughton, and William Felpes are chosen to vewe the place, and to certifie the nexte Generall Court thereof.

It was ffurther ordered, that Winetsemet, and the howses there builte and to be builte, shall joyne themselves either to Charlton or Boston, as members of that towne, before the nexte Generall Court, to be holden the first Wednesday in September nexte, or els to be layde then to one of those two townes by the Court.

Mr. Beecher, Mr. Peirce, and Roberte Moulton are desired to treate and bargaine with Mr. Stevens and Mr. Mayhewe, or with either of them, for the building of the seaffort by the greate, and the Court promiseth to performe what bargaine they shall soe make, for manner and time of payement.

Mr. Edward Tomlyns and Mr. John Samford are intreated by the Court to take notice of the ordinances, powder and shott, and to make reporte to the nexte Court in what condition they are in.

It is ordered, that Dorchester shall have three peeces of ordinances, to ffortifie themselves withall, one drake and two other peeces, to be hadd from Charlton.

It was ffurther ordered, that if any Assistant, or any man deputed by the ffreemen to deale in publique occasions of the commonwealthe, doe absent himselfe without leave in tyme of publique busines, hee shalbe ffined att the discretion of the Court.

It was ordered, that there shalbe a ward of two kept every day att the ffort att Boston, dureing the tyme of any shipps rydeing there, to be borne by the publique, and to be ordered by Capt. Underhill; and it is agreed that those plantations that (by reason of their remotenes) are unwilling to send men, shall pay ii shillings a day for a man, to such as Capt. Underhill shall hire, when it comes to their turne.

It is further ordered, that in all rates and publique charges, the townes shall have respect to levy every man according to his estate, and with consideration of all other his abilityes, whatsoever, and not according to the number of his persons.

Mr. Roberte Harding, William Baulston, and Ralfe Sprage are chosen serjeants to Captaine Underhill, and John Ollyver chosen corporall to the said captaine.

Richard Damford was chosen ensygne to Capt. Traske.

It was further ordered, that there shalbe a watch of two a night kept in every plantation till the nexte Generall Court.

The Deputy Governor, Mr. Israell Stoughton, and Mr. Coxeall are desired by the Court to take an accompt of John Winthrop, Esquire, for such commodityes as hee hath received of the common stocke.

There is 500 acres of land graunted to Mr. Simon Bradstreete, lyeing nore west from the lands of John Haynes, Esquire, and above the falls of Charles Ryver, neere the weire; provided, there be not just reason shewed against it att the nexte Court, why it may not be graunted him.

There is liberty also graunted to Mr. Israell Stoughton and Mr. Wulcott to looke out ffermes for themselves, with promise to accommidate them.

Freemen of the Colony of the Massachusetts Bay in New England.
18 May 1631—14 May 1634

The Names of such as tooke the Oath of Freemen. [18 May, 1631.]

Mr. John Maveracke,	Jehu Burr,
Mr. Jo: Warham,	Simon Hoytt,
Mr. William Blackestone,	Charles Chadwicke,
Mr. George Phillips,	William Parks,
Mr. Rich: Browne,	Ralfe Mushell,
Capt. Daniell Pattricke,	William Hudson,
Capt. Jo: Underhill,	Walter Palmer,
Capt. Southcoate,	Henry Smyth,
Mr. Tho: Graves,	Tho: Ford,
Capt. Walter Norton,	Jonas Weede,
Mr. George Throckmorton,	Mr. Edw: Tomlyns,
Mr. William Colbran,	Mr. Rich: Saltonstall,
Serjeant Morris,	Edw: Gibbons,
Serjeant Stickland,	Mr. Alex: Wignall,

Mr. Roger Conant,
Mr. Charles Gott,
Ralfe Sprage,
Laurence Leach,
John Horne,
Mr. Samuell Coole,
John Woodbury,
Mr. John Oldeham,
Edmond Lockewood,
John Page,
Mr. Rich: Palgrave,
John Doggett,
Rich: Sprage,
Francis Johnson,
Tho: Stoughton,
Abraham Palmer,
John Johnson,
Eprahim Childe,
Bray Rossiter,
Roberte Seely,
Biggott Egglestone,
Mr. Will: Clearke,
William Noddle,
Mr. Roberte Feakes,
William Agar,
Nich: Stower,
John Benham,
William Balstone,
Stephen Terre,
Samuell Hosier,
Roberte Hardinge,
William Woods,
Mr. George Alcocke,
Roberte Moulton,
Peter Palfry,
Mr. Edw: Belchar,
John Edmonds,
George Phillips,
Roger Williams,

Mr. William Gennison,
Daniell Abbott,
Tho: Rawlins,
Rich: Bugby,
John Warren,
Mr. William Jeffry,
Davy Johnson,
Nich: Upsall,
William Bateman,
Daniell Finch,
Mr. Jo: Burslyn,
Mr. John Maisters,
John Peirce,
Griffin Crofte,
George Dyar,
William Rockewell,
Tho: Moore,
John Taylour,
Ezekiell Richardson,
Edw: Converse,
Roberte Abell,
Mr. John Dillingham,
Isaacke Sterne,
Roger Mawry,
Tho: Lambe,
Tho: Williams,
John Ferman,
John Gosse,
John Grinnoway,
Gyles Sexton,
Tho: Lumberd,
Mr. Edw: Jones,
William Gallerd,
William Allen,
Rich: Bulgar,
Rich: Foxewell,
William Felpes,
John Perkins,
Mr. Samuell Skelton,

John Balche,	Mr. Edw: Johnson,
John Moore,	William Cheesebrough,
Henry Herricke,	Anthony Dixe,
John Hoskins,	Frauncis Smyth,
Math: Grant,	Frauncis Aleworth.

March 6th, 1631.

Mr. John Ellyott,	Gregory Baxter,
Jacob Ellyott,	William Frothingham,
Abraham Browne,	Samuell Moore,
James Pennyman,	John Blacke,
Isaack Perry,	John Mylls.

Aprill 3, 1632.

Mr. John Winthrop, Junior,	John Sampeford,
Mr. William Aspinwall,	William Hulbert.

July 3, 1632.

Mr. Nath: Turner,	Mr. John Wilson,
John Ruggles,	Mr. Samuell Sharpe,
Elias Stileman,	John Moore.
Mr. William Dennison,	

August 7th.

John Phillips,	John Hull,
Valentine Prentice,	Samuell Wakeman.

October 2, 1632.

Mr. Samuell Mavericke.

Nov. 6th, 1632.

Mr. Tho: Weld,	William Goodwin,
Mr. Tho: James,	John Benjamin,
Mr. Jo: Willust,	John Talcott,
Mr. Jo: Coggeshall,	James Olmstead,
Mr. Rich: Dummer,	John Clerke,
Mr. Tho: Ollyver,	William Leawis,
Mr. John Branker,	Nath: Richards,
Mr. Tho: Beecher,	William Wadsworth,
Tho: French,	Rich: Webb.

March 4th, 1632.

William Curtis,	John Neweton,
Thomas Uffott,	John White,
John Perry,	William Spencer,
Isaack Morrall,	John Kirman,

William Heath,   Tymothy Tomlyns,
George Hull,   Henry Harwood,
Eltweed Pummery,   Richard Collocott,
Nich: Denselowe,   William Brakenbury,
Gyles Gibbs,   John Smyth.

April 1th, 1633.

Serjeant Greene,   William Dady.
Rise Coles,

June 11th, 1633.

William Stilson,   Tho: Smyth,
Rich: Millett,   David Wilton,
Rich: Lyman,   John Witchfeild,
Jesper Rawling,   Elias Maveracke.

Nov. 5th, 1633.

Mr. Israell Stoughton,   John Porter,
Mr. John Coggin,   Frauncis Weston,
Mr. William Hill,   John Watson,
Mr. John Moody,   John Holgrave.

March 4th, 1633.

Thomas Grubb,   James Browne,
Edmond Hubbert,   Mr. John Woolridge,
Edw: Hutchingson,   Josuah Hewes,
Mr. Tho: Leveritt,   Roberte Turner,
Mr. Gyles Ferman,   John Biggs,
Edmond Quinsey,   Tho: Matson,
William Collishawe,   Walter Merry,
Thomas Minor,   Rich: Tappin,
Tho: Howlett,   Mr. Atterton Hough,
John Gage,   William Andrewes,
Samuell Wilboare,   Rich: Walker,
John Levens,   George Ruggles,
John Cranwell,   Mr. Nich: Parker.
Edw: Mellowes,

April 1th, 1634.

Mr. Daniell Dennison,   Bernard Lumbert,
George Minott,   Henry Wulcott,
Rich: Gridley,   Rich: Hull,
Thomas Reade,   John Gallop,
George Hutchingson,   Richard Silvester,

Roberte Roise,   William Horseford.
John Pemerton,

May 14th, 1634.

John Haynes, Esquire, Samuell Finch,
Phillip Sherman,   George Williams,
Daniell Brewer,   Edw: Gyles,
Tho: Gaildthaite,   William Dixy,
Roberte Gamlyn, Senior, George Norton,
Thomas Hale,   Thomas Eborne,
Edward Riggs,   Daniell Wray,
John Walker,   Abraham Mellowes,
Thomas Wilson,   John Ollyver,
Samuell Basse,   Roberte Hale,
Tho: Pigg,   Tho: Cakebread.
William Hill,

Freemen made att the Generall Court, May 14th, 1634.

Tho: Squire,   Tho: Faireweather,
Roberte Houlton, William Hedges,
Richard Fairebancks, John Hoskins,
Phillip Tabor,   Peter Woolfe,
Gregory Taylour, William Chase,
John Chapman,   William Talmidge,
William Learned, Mr. John Cotton,
Mr. Tho: Hooker, Nath: Gillett,
Mr. Samuell Stone, Daniell Howe,
Edw: Howe,   Myles Reddin,
Bartholomewe Greene, John Eales,
Rich: Wright,   Mr. William Peirce,
John Steele,   Mr. Tho: Mahewe,
Edm: Stebbins,   Josuah Carter,
Andrewe Warner, Thomas Talmage,
George Steele,   Roberte Walker,
Rich: Butlar,   Phillipp Randill,
Thomas Spencer, Tho: Holcombe,
Edw: Muste,   Tho: Dewey,
Rich: Goodman, Tho: Jeffry,
John Pratt,   James Parker,
John Haward,   Walter Filer,

Andrewe Ward,
Joseph Twitchwell,
Tho: Hatch,
George Whitehand,
Jerad Hadden,
John Odlyn,
Roger Clapp,
Joseph Reddings,
Anthony Colby,
John Bosworth,
Frauncis Plummer,
Humfry Pynny,
Bray Wilkins,
James Rawlyns,
Jacob Barny,
Tho: Lowthrop,
Steven Hart,
Jeffery Massy,
Rich: Brakenbury,
John Haydon,
Edmond Harte,
William Hathorne,
Steven French,
Christopher Hussey,
Edw: Bendall,
John Button,
Rich: Raymond,
Jonathan Wade,
Tho: Coldham,
James Tompson,
Tho: Hubbard,
John Hall,
John Baker,
Mr. William Brenton,
John Capen,
Frauncis Dent,
Henry Feakes.

Letters from the Governor and Company of the Massachusetts Bay in New England.

Letter from Matthew Cradock, Governor of the Company.[11]

WORTHY Sir, and my lovinge Freynd: All dew commendations premised to your self and second self, with harty well wishes from my self and many others, well willers and adventurers in this our plantation, to your self and the rest of your good company, of whose safe arryvall beinge now throughlie informed by your letters bearinge date the 13 September last, which came to my hands the 13 this instant February, we doe not a little rejoyce; and to heare [that] my good cozen, your wyfe, were perfectly recovered of her healthe would be [ac]ceptable newes to us all; which God graunt in his good tyme that wee may. Mea[nwh]ile, I am, in the behalf of our whole company, (which are much inlarged sence your departure out of England,) to give you harty thankes ffor your lardge advize [contained in thi]s your letter, which I have fully imparted unto them, and, farther, to [give proof tha]t thei intende not to bee wantinge by all good meanes to furd[er the] plantation; to which purpose (God willinge) you shall heare more at [another time], and that speedily; there beeinge one shipp bought for the co[mpany of] xxo tunnes, and 2 others hyred of about 200 tunns each of them, 1 of 19 [and 1 of] xo peeces of   rdnance, besides not unlike but one other vessell shall [come in] companie with theise; in all which shipps, for the generall stocke and property [of the ad]ventures, there is likelye to be sent thether twixt 2 and 300 persons, wee ho[pe to res]ide there, and about 100 head of cattell; wherefore, as I wrote you in [full, and sen]t by Mr. Allerton of New Plimouth in November last, soe the desire of them [is, that] you would endevour to gett convenient howsinge, fitt to lodge as manye as you can, against they doe come; and withall what bever, or other commodities, or ffishe, if t[he mean]es to preserve it, can be gotten readie, to returne in the foresaid shipps; [and like]wise

---

[11] The following letter, in a very worn condition, is preserved loose in the first volume of the Colony Records; and although it bears no superscription, was evidently intended for Mr. John Endicott, who, at the date thereof, was in New England. The lost portions were restored chiefly from Prince's Annals, and the printed collections of the Massachusetts Historical Society.

wood, if noe better ladinge be to be had; that you would endevor
to get in [a rea]dines what you can, whereby our shipps, whereof
twoe are to returne backe [direc]tlye heather, maye not come
wholye emptye. There hath not bine a better tyme [for sa]le of
tymber theise twoe seaven yeres then at present; and therefore
pittye [these] shipps should come backe emptye, if it might be
made readie that they neede [not stope 1 daye] for it; otherwise
mens wages and victualls, together with the shipps, will quicklie
rise too high, if to be reladen with wood, and that the same be
not readie to [put] aboord as soone as the shipps are discharged of
theire outward ladinge. [I] wishe alsoe that there be some sassaf-
fras and sarsaparilla sent us, as a[lsoe good st]ore of shoomacke, if
there to be had, as wee are informed there is. The l[ike do]e I
wishe for a tun waight at least of silke grasse, and of ought elce
that maye be usefull for dyinge or in phisicke; to have some of ech
sent, and advise given withall what store of each to be had there,
if vent maye be found here for it. Alsoe, I hope you will have
some good sturgion in a readines to send us; and if it be well
cured, 2 or 300 ffirkins thereof would helpe well towards our
charge. Wee are very confident of your best endevors for the
generall good; and wee doubt not but God will in mercye give a
blessinge upon our laboures; and wee trust you will not be unmind-
full of the mayne end of our plantation, by indevoringe to bringe
the Indians to the knowledge of the gospell; which, that it maye be
speedier and better effected, the earnest desire of our whole company is, that you have dilligent and watchfull eye over our owne
people, that they live unblameable and without reproofe, and demeane themselves justlye and curteous towards [the Indians],
thereby to drawe them to affect our persons, and consequentlye
our religion; as alsoe to endevour to gett some of theire children to
trayne up to readinge, and consequentlye to religion, whilest they
are yonge; herein to yonge or olde to omitt noe good opportu-
ni[tye] that maye tend to bringe them out of that woefull state and
condition they now are in; in which case our predecessors in this
our land sometymes were, and but for the mercye and goodnes of
our good God might have continued to this daye; but God, whoe
out of [the] boundles ocean of his mercye hath shewed pittie and
compassion to our land, he is alsuffitient, and can bringe this to
passe which wee now desire in that countrye likewise. Onlie let

us not be wantinge on our partes, n[ow]e wee are c[alled] to [this] worke of the Lords; neither, having put our handes to the [plowe, let us look back, but goe on cheerfullye, and depend upon God for a blessing upon our labours]; whoe by weake instruments is able (if he see it good) to bringe glori[ous thinges to passe].

Be of good courage, goe on, and doe woorthilye, and the Lord prosper your [endeavor].

It is fullie resolved, by Gods assistance, to send over twoe ministers, [at the least, with the] shippes now intended to be sent thether; but for Mr. Peters, he is now [in Holland, from] whence his returne hether I hold to be uncertaine. Those wee send sh[all be by the appro]bation of Mr. White, of Dorchester, and Mr. Davenport. For whatsoev[er else you have given] advise, care shall be taken, God willinge, to performe the needefull, as [neere as wee can], and the tymes will permitt; whereof alsoe you maye expect more amp[le advertisement, in] theire generall letter, when God shall send our shipps thether. The c[ourse you have taken], in givinge our countrymen theire content in the point of pl[antinge tobacco] there for the present, (theire necessitie considered,) is not disallowed; [but, wee trust in] God, other meanes will be found to imploye theire tyme more comfor[table, and profitable] alsoe in the end; and wee cannot but generallie approve and commend th[eir good resolution] to desist from the plantinge thereof, when as they shall discerne howe [to imploye their] laboures otherwise, which wee hope they will be speedilye induced unto [by such precepts] and examples as wee shall give them. And now, mindinge to conclude [this, I maye not] omitt to put you in mynde, how ever you seeme to feare noe enimies the[re, yet that you have] a watchfull eye for your owne saftye, and the saftye of all those of [our nation with you], and not to bee too confident of the ffidellitie of the salvages. It [is an old proverb, yet] as true, The burnt childe dreades the fyre. Our countrymen [have suffered by] theire too much confidence in Virginea. Let us by theire harmes [learne to beware]; and as wee are commanded to be innocent as doves, soe withall wee [are enjoined to be] wise as serpents. The God of heaven and earth preserve and keepe [you from all forayne] and inland enimies, and blesse and prosper this plantation, to the enl[argement of the kingdom] of Jesus Christ, to whose mercifull protection I recommend you [and all your assotiates] there, knowne or unknowne. And soe, tyll my next, which shall [be, God willinge, by our] shipps, whoe I make account will be readie to set sayle fro[m hence about the 20th of] this next moneth of Marche, I end, and rest

       Your [assured loving friende] and cussen,

               MATHEWE CRADOCK.

[From] my howse in Swithens Lane, neere London Stone, this 16th Februarye, 1628,
  stilo A[ngl]iae.

First General Letter of the Governor and Deputy of the New England Company for a Plantation in Massachusetts Bay, to the Governor and Council for London's Plantation in the Massachusetts Bay in New England.[12]

               [LAUS DEO!

         In Gravesend, the 17th of April, 1629.]

LOVING Freinds: Wee hartylie salute yow. Wee have r[eceived your] letter of the 13th of September, by which wee take notice [of your safe] arriveall, blessing God for it. Wee have formerly [requested] Mr. Cradock, our Governor, to wryte yow of the receipt ther[eof, and to] give advice how wee purposed to proceed in seting forward our plantation, whose letters, if they bee come to your hande, (as wee hope they are,) will putt lyfe into your affaires, and encourage yow to provyde for the entertainment of such as are now cominge.

Since your departure, wee have, for the further strengthening of our graunt from the councell at Plymoth, obtayned a confirmation of it from his majesty by his letters pattents, under the broad seale of England; by which said letters pattents wee are incorpo-, rated into a body pollitique, with ample power to governe and rule all his majesty's subjects that reside within the limitts of our plantation, as by the duplicate thereof under the broad seale, which wee have delivered to Mr. Sharpe to bee delivered to yow, doth fully appeare.

[12] This and the following letters, in the handwriting of Secretary Burgis, are evidently intended to be a portion of the records of the Governor and Company, and are preserved in the oldest volume of records in the Suffolk Registry of Deeds. The volume in which they are found is undoubtedly the "book of copies of letters" alluded to on October 16, 1629, and was converted to its present purpose soon after the removal of the Company to America.

And for that the propagating of the gosple is the thing [wee] doe profess above all to bee our ayme in setling this plantation, wee have bin carefull to make plentyfull provision of godly ministers, by whose faithfull preachinge, godly conversation, and exemplary lyfe, wee trust, not only those of our owne nation wilbe built up in the knowledge of God, but also the Indians may in Gods appointed tyme bee reduced to the obedyence of the gosple of Christ. One of them is well knowne to yourselfe, viz., Mr. Skelton, whom wee have the rather desired to beare a part in this worke, for that wee are informed yourselfe have formerly received much good by his ministry; hee cometh in the George Bonaventure, Mr. Thomas Cox. Another is Mr. Higgeson, a grave man, and of worthy commendations; he cometh in the Talbott. The third is Mr. Bright, sometymes trained upp under Mr. Davenport, who cometh in the Lyons Whelp. Wee pray yow, accommodate them all with necessaryes as well as yow may, and in convenyent tyme lett there bee houses built them according to the agreement wee have made with them, coppyes wherof, as of all others wee have entertained, shalbe sent yow by the next shipps, tyme not permitting it now. Wee doubt not but these gentlemen, your ministers, will agree lovingly togeather; and for cherishinge of love betwixt them, wee pray yow, carry yourselfe impartiallie to all. For the mannor of the exercising their ministrie, and teaching both our owne people and the Indians, wee leave that to themselves, hoping they will make Gods word the rule of [their actions], and mutually agree in the discharge of their duties; and because their doctrine will hardly bee well esteemed whose persons are not reverenced, wee desire that, both by your owne example and by commanding all others to doe the like, our ministers may receive due honour.

Wee have, in prosecution of that good opinion wee have alway had of yow, confirmed yow Governor of our plantation, and joyned in commission with yow the three ministers, namely, Mr. Francis Higgonson, Mr. Samuell Skelton, and Mr. Francis Bright, also Mr. John and Mr. Samuell Browne, Mr. Thomas Graves, and Mr. Samuell Sharpe; and for that wee have ordered that the body of the government there shall consist of 13 persons, wee are content the old planters that are now there within our plantation and lymitts therof shall chuse 2 of the discreetest and juditiall men from amongst themselves to bee of the government, that they may see wee are not wanting to give them fitting respect, in that wee would have their consent (if it may bee) in making wholsome constitutions for government; alwayes provyded, that none shalbe chosen, or meddle in their choice, but such as will live amongst us, and conforme themselves to our government. But if they shall refuse to performe this our direction, then wee hereby authorise yow, and those nominated to bee of the councell aforesaid, to nominate and elect two such men as in your opinions yow shall hold meete for that place and office; and for the other three which wilbe wanting to make upp the full number of 13, (which wee have styled the Councell of the Mattachusetts Bay,) wee hereby authorize [you], with the aforenamed seaven persons, to chuse and nominate them out of the whole body of the Companie, aswell of those that are there as of those that are to come now, not doubting but, all partialitie sett apart, yow will make choice of such men as may bee most usefull and carefull to advance the generall good of our plantation.

And that it may appeare, aswell to all the world as to the old planters themselves, that wee seeke not to make them slaves, (as it seemes by your letter some of them thinke themselves to bee become by meanes of our pattent,) wee are content they shalbe partakers of such priviledges as wee, from his majesty's espetiall grace, with great cost, favour of personages of note, and much labour, have obtained, and that they shalbe incorporated into this socyetie, and enjoy, not only those lands which formerly they have manured, but such a further proportion as, by th'advice and judgment of yourselfe and the rest of the councell, shalbe thought fitt for them or any of them. And besides, it is still our purpose that they should have some benefitt by the common stock, as was by your first commission directed and appointed, with this addition, that if it bee held too much to take 30 per cent and the fraight of the goods for and in consideration of our adventure and disbursment of our monyes, to bee paid in bevor at 6s per lb., that yow moderate the said rate as yow, with the rest of the [councell,] shall thinke to bee agreeable to equitie and good conscience. And our further orders is, that none bee partakers of any the aforesaid pruiledges and profitts but such as bee peaceable men, and of honest lyfe and conversation, and desirous to live amongst us, and conforme themselves to good order and government.

And as touching the old planters their earnest desire for [the] present to continue the planting of tobacco, (a trade by the Companie generally disavowed and utterly disclaymed by some [of the] greatest adventurers amongst us, who absolutely declared themselves unwilling to have any hand in this plantation if wee intend to cherish or permitt the planting therof, or any other kinde than for a mans private use for meere necessitie,) wee are of opinion the old planters will have small encouragment to that employment, for wee fynde heere, by late experience, that it doth hardly produce the fraight and custome; nether is there hope [of] amendment, there being such great quantities made in other parts that ere long it is like to bee little worth. Nevertheless, if the old planters (for wee exclude all others) conceive that they cannot otherwise provyde for their livelyhood, wee leave it to the discretion of yourselfe and the councell there to give way for the present to their planting of it in such manner, and with such restrictions, [as] yow and the said councell shall thinke fittinge, having an espetiall care, with as much convenyence as may bee, utterly [to] suppress the planting of it, except for meere necessitie; but, however, wee absolutely forbidd the sale of it, or the use of [it], by any of our owne or particuler mens servants, unless upon urgent occasion for the benefitt of health, and taken privately.

Mr. John Oldham came from New England not long before your arrivall there, by whom wee have had noe small disturbance in our business, having bin cast behinde, at the least, two months tyme in our voyage, through the varyetie of his vast conceipts of extraordinary gaine of 3 for one, propounded to bee made and raised in 3 yeares, if hee might have the managinge of our stock, preferring to bee contented for his owne employment, soe hee might have the overplus of the gaines; with whom, after long time spent in sundry treaties, fynding him a man altogeather unfitt for us to deale with, wee have at last left him to his owne way; and, as wee are informed, hee, with some others, are provyding a vessell, and is mynded, as soone as hee can despatch, to come for New England, pretending to settle himselfe in Mattachusetts Bay, clayming a tytle and right by a grant from Sir Ferdinando Gorges son, which wee are well satisfyed by good councell is voyde in lawe. Hee will admitt of noe tearmes of agreement, unlesse wee leave him at libertie to trade for beavor with the [Indians], which wee deny to the best of our owne planters; nether is hee satisfyed to trade himselfe with his owne stock and meanes, which wee conceeve is so small that it would not much hinder us, but hee doth interest other men, who, for ought we knowe, are never likely to bee benefitiall to the planting of the country, their owne particuler profitts (though to the overthrowe of the generall plantation) being their chiefe ayme and intent. Now, as wee shall unwillingly doe any act in debarringe such as were inhabitants before us of that trade, as in conscience they ought to enjoy, soe shall wee as unwillingly permitt any to appropriate that to their owne private lucar which wee, in our religious intentions, have dedicated to the common charge of building houses for Gods worshipp and fforts to defend such as shall come thither to inhabite. Wee feare that as hee hath bin obstinate and vyolent in his opinions heere, soe hee will persist and bee ready to drawe a partie to himselfe there, to the great hinderance of the common quiett. Wee have therfore thought fitt to give yow notice of his disposition, to the end yow may beware how yow meddle with him, as also that yow may use the best meanes yow can to settle an agreement with the old planters, soe as they may not harken to Mr. Oldhams dangerous though vaine propositions. Wee fynde him a man soe affected to his owne opinion as not to bee removed from it, nether by reason nor any perswasion; and unlesse hee may beare sway, and have all things carryed to his good likinge, wee have little hope of quiett or comfortable subsistance where he shall make his aboad.

And therefore, if yow shall see just cause, wee hereby require yow and the councell there to exercise that power wee have, and our previledges will beare us out in it, to suppresse a mischiefe before it take too great a head. Not that wee would wrong him or any man that will live peaceably within the limitts of our plantation; but as the preservation of our pruiledges will cheifly depend (under God) upon the first foundation of our government, soe, if wee suffer soe great an affront as wee fynde is intended towards us by the proceedings of Mr. Oldham and his adherents in our first beginnings, wee may bee sure they will take hart, and bee emboldned to doe us a farr greater injurie hereafter. And therefore wee pray yow and the councell there to advise seriously togeather for the maintenance of our pruiledges and peaceable government, which, if it may be done by a temperate course, wee much desire it, though with some inconvenyence, soe as our government and pruiledges bee not brought in contempt, wishing rather there might bee such an union as might drawe the heathen by our good example to the embracing of Christ and his gosple, then that offence should bee given to the heathen, and a scandall to our religion, through our disagreement amongst ourselves. But if necessitie require a more severe course, when faire meanes will not prevaile, wee pray yow to deale as in your discretions yow shall thinke fittest for the generall good and safety of the plantation and preservation of our pruiledges. And because wee would not omitt to doe any thinge which might strengthen our right, wee would have yow (as soone as these [shipps, or any] of them, arrive [with yow, whe]reby [yow may have men to do it]) send 40 or 50 [persons] to Mattachusetts [Bay to inhabite there, which we] pray yow not to protract, but to doe it with [all] speede; and if [any] of our Company in particuler shall desire to setle themselves there, or to send servants thither, wee desire all accommodation and encouragment may bee given them therunto, whereby the better to strengthen our possession there against all or any that shall intrude upon us, which wee would not have yow by any meanes give way unto, with this caution, notwithstanding, that for such of our countrymen as yow finde there planted, soe as they bee willing to live under government, yow endeavor to give them all fitting and due accommodation as to any of ourselves; yea, if yow see cause for it, though it bee with more then ordinarie pruiledges in point of trade.

Mr. Raph Smith, a minister, hath desired passage in our [shipps], which was graunted him before wee understood of his difference of judgment in some things from our ministers. But his provisions [for] his voyage being shipt before notice was taken therof, through many occasions wherwith those intrusted with this business have bin employed, and forasmuch as from hence it is feared there may growe some distraction amonst yow if there should bee any syding, though wee have a very good opinion of his honesty, wee shall not, hope, offend in charitie to feare the worst that may grow from their different judgments. Wee have therfore thought fitt to give yow this order, that unless hee wilbe conformable to our government, yow suffer him not to remaine within the limitts of [our] graunt.

Wee take notice that yow desire to have Frenchmen sent yow

that might bee experienced in making of salt and plantinge of vynes. Wee have enquired diligently for such, but ca[nnot] meete with any of that nation. Nevertheless, God hath not left us altogeather unprovyded of a man able to undertake that worke, for that wee have entertained Mr. Thomas Groves, a man commended to us as well for his honestie as skill in many things very usefull. First, hee professeth great skill in the making of salt, both in ponds and panns, as also to fynde out salt springs and mynes; secondly, hee is well seene in mynes and mineralls, espetially about iron ore and iron workes; thirdly, hee is able to make any sort of fortyfications; fourthly, hee is well able to surveigh and sett forth lands. Hee hath bin a travillor [in] divers forraigne parts to gaine his experience. Therfore wee pray yow take his advice touching the premises, and where yow intend to sett downe in to fortyfie and build a towne, that it may bee qualified for good ayre and water, according to your first instructions, and may have as much naturall helpe as may bee, wherby it may with the less labor and cost bee made fitt to resist an enemie. Soe soone as yow have made tryall of his sufficiencie, wryte us your opinion how long yow [conceive] it [will be fitt for us] to continue him in our service; [for] that he is tyed to [serve] us one whole yeare absolutely, and two yeares more if wee should give him order to stay soe long. Soe wee hope to receve your advice tyme enough [to] give him order to stay out full 3 yeares, or to come home at [the end] of one yeare. His salarie costs this Companie a great somme of mony, besides which (if hee remain with us) the transporting of his wyfe, and building him a house, wilbe very chargable, which wee pray yow take into your consideration, that soe wee may continue or surcease this charge as occasion shall require.

In our next wee intend to send yow a particuler of such as are to have land allotted and sett out unto them, that soe yow may appoint unto each man an equall proportion by lott, according to what is to bee allowed in the first devident, touching which wee shall then give yow more large instructions. Meane while, for such as have sent over servants and cattle in these shipps, and for such as have more to come in two other shipps, which wee hope wilbe ready to sett saile within ten dayes, our desire is, they should ether bee accommodated at Nahumkeeke or in Mattachusetts Bay, or in both places if they desire it, with all the convenyence that may bee; and for such grounds as shalbe allotted unto them, that the same bee conveyed unto them, if they desire it, at any tyme within one yeare after their entring upon it, and to bee accompted as part of their first devident. But if they shall dislike it at any tyme before a generall distribution bee made by lott to all the adventurers, then they may have libertie to doe it, and take in lieu therof as by lott shall fall out amongst other private adventurers.

Wee recommend unto yow Sir Richard Saltonstall and Mr. Isack Johnson, who send over servants and cattle in these shipps, desiring yow will take care for their present accommodation as aforesaid; and as for them, soe wee may not omitt to pray yow likewise to give all good accommodation to our present Governor, Mr. Matthew Cradock, who, with some particuler brethren of our Company, have deepely engaged themselves in their private adventures in these shipps and those to come; and as wee hold these men that thus deepely adventure in their private to bee (under God) spetiall instruments for the advancing and strengthning of our plantation, which is done by them without any charge to the Companyes generall stock, wherin, notwithstanding, they are as deepe or deeper engaged then any other, soe being contented to bee debarred from all private trading in furrs for 3 yeares, wee doe hold it very requisite in all other their desires to give them all accommodation and furtherance that reasonably may be propounded by them, or any for them; their good beginnings in the infancie of our plantation worthylie deserving of us all favor and furtherance.

Wee have caused a common seale to bee made, which wee send by Mr. Sharpe.

If yow want any swyne, wee have agreed with those of New Plymouth that they deliver yow six sowes with pigg, for which they are to bee allowed £9 in accompt of what they owe unto Mr. Goffe, Deputie; and for goats, wee have bought 42 for the generall and particuler mens accompts, which shalbe sent yow by these and the next shipps, or at least wise soe many of them as they can convenyently carrie.

Wee have followed your advice, and sent most of our guns snaphance, bastard muskett bore; and wee have also sent store of powder and shott, grayne for seede, both wheat, barley, and rye, in the chaff, etc. As for fruit stones and kernells, the tyme of the yeare fitts not to send them now; soe wee purpose to do it per our next. Tame turkyes shalbe now sent yow (if may bee); if not, per other shipps. Wee are disappointed of the provisions ordered to have bin sent yow for yourselfe and Mrs. Endecote; but, God willing, they shall come by the next.

Wee have made our servants apparell of cloth and lether, which lether is not of oyle skins, for wee found them over deere; yett if this prove not profittable, upon your second advice wee will send yow oyle skinns.

For such of our nation as sell munition, gunns, or other furniture, to arme the Indians against us, or teach them the use of armes, wee would have yow to apprehend them and send them prisoners for England, where they will not escape severe punishment, being expressly against the proclamation.

Yow have had former caution given yow to take heede of beeing too secure in trusting the Indians, which wee againe commend to your care; and that yow may bee the better able to resist both forraigne enemies and the natives, if ether should assaile yow, wee pray yow lett all such as live under our government, both our servants and other planters and their servants, bee exercised in the use of armes, and certaine tymes appointed to muster them, in which business Mr. Sharpe and Mr. Graves wilbe assistant to yow. Mr. Sharpe is by us entertained to bee master gunner of our ordnance, in which service hee is to employ soe much of his tyme as the charge of that office doth require, and in the rest hee is to follow other imployments of our governors and others, for whose employment hee is particularly sent over.

Inclosed yow shall receive a factory of such provision of victuall and other necessaryes as wee have sent for the generall accompt, to which wee referr yow, nothing doubting but yow wilbe a provident steward to husband our provisions to the best advantage. Wee also send yow the particuler names of such as are entertained for the Companyes service, amongst which wee hope yow will fynde many religious, discreete, and well ordered persons, which yow must sett over the rest devyding them into famylies, placing some with the ministers, and others under such as, beeing honest men, (and of their owne calling as neere as may bee,) may have care to see them well educated in their generall callings as Christians, and particuler according to their severall trades or fitness in disposition to learne a trade. And wheras amongst such a nomber (notwithstanding our care to purge them) there may still remaine some liberties, wee desire yow to bee carefull that such (if any bee) may bee forced, by inflicting such punishment as their offences shall deserve, which is to bee (as neere as may bee) according to the lawes of this kingdome, to conforme themselves to good order; with whom, after admonition given, if they amend not, wee pray yow proceede without partiallitie to punish them as the nature of their fault shall deserve; and the like course yow are to hold both with planters and their servants, for all must live under government and a like lawe. And to the end yow may not doe any thing contrarie to lawe nor the power graunted us by his majesty's letters patents, wee have, as aforesaid, sent yow the duplicate of the letters patents, under the great seale of England, ordering and requiring yow and the rest of the councell there not to doe any thinge, ether in inflicting punishment on malefactors or otherwise, contrarie to or in derogation of the said letters pattents; but if occasion require, wee authorise yow and them to proceede according to the power yow have. Nevertheless, wee desire (if it may bee) that errors may bee reformed with lenitie or mylde correction; and if any prove incorrigable, and will not bee reclaimed by gentle correction, ship such persons home by the Lyons Whelpe, rather than keep them there to infect or to bee an occasion of scandall unto others; wee being fully perswaded that if one or two bee soe reshipped back, and certificate sent home of their misdemeanor, it wilbe a terror to the rest, and a meanes to reduce them to good conformitie. And, above all, wee pray yow bee carefull that there bee none in our precincts permitted to doe any injurie (in the least kinde) to the heathen people; and if any offend in that way, lett them receive due correction. And wee hold it fitting yow publish a proclamation to that effect by leaving it fixed under the Companyes seale in some eminent place, for all to take notice, at such tyme as both the heathen themselves, as well as our people, may take notice of it. And for the avoyding of the hurt that may follow through our much familiaritie with the Indians, wee conceive it fitt that they bee not permitted to come to your plantation but at certaine tymes and places to bee appointed them. If any of the salvages pretend right of inheritance to all or any part of the lands graunted in our pattent, wee pray yow endeavor to purchase their tytle, that wee may avoyde the least scruple of intrusion.

Wee have, in the former part of our letter, certyfyed yow of the good hope wee have of the love and unanimus agreement of our ministers, they having declared themselves to us to bee of one judgment, and to bee fully agreed on the manner how to exercise their ministry, which wee hope wilbe by them accordingly performed. Yett, because it is often found that some busie persons (led more by their will then any good warrant out of Gods word) take opportunitie [of] moving needless questions to stirr up strife, and by that [meanes] to begett a question, and bring men to declare some different judgment, (most commonly in things indifferent,) from which small beginnings great mischeifs have followed, wee pray yow and the rest of the councell, that if any such disputes shall happen among yow, that yow suppress them, and bee carefull to maintaine peace and unitie.

Wee desire yow to take notice of one Lawrence Leech, whom we have found a carefull and painfull man, and wee doubt not but hee will continue his dilligence; lett him have deserving respect. The like wee say of Richard Waterman, whose cheife employment wilbe to get yow good venison.

Wee have sent six shipwrights, of whom Robert Molton is cheif. These mens entertainment is very chargable to us; and by agreement it is to bee borne two thirds at the charge of the generall Companie, and the other third is to bee borne by Mr. Cradock, our Governor, and his assotiatts interested in a private stock. Wee hope yow wilbe carefull to see them soe employed as may countervaile the charge, desiring yow to agree with Mr. Sharpe that their labour may bee employed ⅔ for the generall Companie, and ⅓ for Mr. Cradock and his assotiats; praying yow to accommodate the said Mr. Cradocks people in all fitting manner, as hee doth well deserve.

Such cattle, both horss, mares, cowes, bulls, and goates, as are shipped by Mr. Cradock, are to bee devyded in equall halfes twixt him and the Companie, which was omitted to bee done heere for avoyding partiallitie; soe yow must doe it equally there.

Wee pray yow to bee carefull to make us what returnes yow possibly may, the better to enable us to send out a fresh supply. Wee hope yow have converted the commodities yow carryed with yow for truck into beavor, otter, or other ffurrs, which wee pray yow send us by the Talbot, as also any other commodities yow have provyded in readyness against the shipps coming thither; but pray doe not detaine her any longer tyme to cutt tymber or any other gross ladinge, for shee is at £150 a month charges, which will soone eat out more then the goods shee should stay for is worth. Wherfore, pray make what expedition yow can to unlade her goods, and to put such things aboard her as yow have ready, and send her hetherward againe as soone as yow may.

Wee have sent five weigh of salt in the Whelpe, and ten weigh in the Talbot. If there bee any shallopps to bee had to fish withall, and the season of the yeare fitt, pray lett the ffishermen, (of which wee send 6 from Dortchester,) togeather with some of the shipps company, endeavour to take ffish, and lett it bee well saved with the said salt, and packed upp in hogsheads or otherwise, as shalbe thought fitt, and send it home by the Talbott or Lyons Whelpe. Now, forasmuch as the Lyons Whelpe belongeth to the Companie, yow may (if there bee hope to doe good by it) keepe her there some tyme after the Talbott; but unless it bee to very good purpose, doe not detaine her, but lett her come home in companie of the Talbott. The Georg Bonaventure is to land her passingers and other things belonging to the generall Companie or to particuler men, and soe sett sayle for New Found Land; and wee pray yow lett it be your care to dispatch her as soone as may bee.

William Ryall and Thomas Brude, coopers and cleavors of tymber, are entertained by us in halfes with Mr. Cradock, our Governor. Pray joyne others that can assist them unto them, and lett them provide us some staves and other tymber of all sorts, to bee sent us by the Talbott, Whelpe, or the other 2 shipps that come after. But wee pray yow consider the charge of these shipps, and detaine them not for small matters. Rather use all dilligence to send them away.

If, at the arivall of this shipp, Mr. Endecott should bee departed this lyfe, (which God forbidd,) or should happen to dye before the other shipps arrive, wee authorise yow, Mr. Skelton and Mr. Samuell Sharpe, to take care of our affaires, and to governe the people according to order, untill further order. And to the end the Saboth may bee celebrated in a religious manner, we appoint, that all that inhabite the plantation, both for the generall and particuler imployments, may surcease their labour every Satterday throughout the yeare at 3 of the clock in the afternoone, and that they spend the rest of that day in catichising and preparation for the Saboth, as the ministers shall direct.

If it shall please God to take away by death any of the 13 that shalbe chosen and appointed for the councell, (of which yourselfe or your successor is to bee one,) in such case the then being Governor and the survyving councell shall from tyme to tyme make choice of one or more to supply the place of such as shalbe wanting; and that there may noe difference arise about the appointing of one to bee minister with those yow send to inhabite at Mattachusetts Bay, wee will have yow (in case the ministers cannot agree amongst themselves who shall undertake that place) to make choice of one of the three by lott; and on whom the lott shall fall hee to goe with his famylie to performe that worke.

Wee have advised yow of the sending of William Ryall and Thomas Brude, cleavers of tymber; but, indeed, the said Thomas his name is Brand, and not Norton. But there is one Norton, a carpenter, whom wee pray yow respect as hee shall deserve.

There is one Richard Ewstead, a wheelewright, who was commended to us by Mr. Davenport for a very able man, though not without his imperfections. Wee pray yow take notice of him, and regard him as hee shall well deserve. The benefitt of his labour is to bee [⅔] for the generall Companie, and ⅓ for Mr. Cradock, our Governor, being his charges is to bee borne according to that proportion; and withall wee pray yow take care that their charges who are for partable employment, whether in halfes or thirds, may bee equally defrayed by such as are to have benefitt of their labours, according to each partyes proportion. Their severall agreements, or the coppyes therof, shalbe (if God permitt) sent yow by the next shipps.

Wee have entertained Lambert Wilson, chirurgion, to remaine [with] yow in the service of the plantation; with whom wee are agreed, that hee shall serve this Companie and the other planters that live in the plantation for 3 yeares, and in that time apply himselfe to cure not only of such as came from hence for the generall and particuler accompts, but also for the Indians as from tyme to tyme hee shalbe directed by yourselfe or your successor and the rest of the councell. And, moreover, hee is to educate and instruct in his art one or more youths, such as yow and the said councell shall appoint, that may bee helpfull to him, and, if occasion serve, succeed him in the plantation; which youth or youths fitt to learne that profession lett bee placed with him; of which Mr. Hugessons sonne, if his father approve therof, may bee one, the rather because hee hath bin trayned up in litterature; but if not hee, then such other as yow shall judg most fittest, etc.

The 21 of April, in Gravesend.

The aforewritten is, for the most part, the coppie of our generall letter sent you togeather with our pattent, under the broad seale and the Companyes seale in silver, by Mr. Samuell Sharpe, passinger in the George, who wee thinke is yett ryding in the Hope; but, by meanes of stormy weather, the Talbot and Lyons Whelpe are yett att Black Wall. By these shipps that are to follow wee intend, God willing, to supply both in our advice and in our provisions what is wanting now. In the mean whyle wee pray yow accommodate business with your true endeavours for the generall good in the best and discreetest manner that yow may. For the better accommodation of businesses, wee have devyded the servants belonging to the Company into severall famylies, as wee desire and intend they should live togeather; a coppy wherof wee send yow heere inclosed, that yow may accordingly appoint each man his charge and dutie. Yett it is not our intent to tye yow soe strictly to this direction but that in your discretion, as yow shall see cause from tyme to tyme, yow may alter or displace any as yow shall thinke fitt.

Our earnest desire is, that yow take spetiall care, in setlinge these ffamilies, that the cheife in the familie (at least some of them) bee grounded in religion; wherby morning and evening famylie dutyes may bee duely performed, and a watchfull eye held over all in each familie by one or more in each famylie to bee appointed thereto, that soe disorders may bee prevented, and ill weeds nipt before they take too great a head. It wilbe a business worthy your best endeavours to looke unto this in the beginninge, and, if neede bee, to make some exemplary to all the rest; otherwise your government wilbe esteemed as a scar crowe. Our desire is to use lenitie all that may bee, but, in case of necessitie, not to neglect the other, knowing that correction is ordained for the ffooles back; and as wee intend not to bee wanting on our parts to provyde all things neefull for the maintenance and sustenance of our servants, soe may wee justly, by the lawes of God and man, require obedyence and honest carriage from them, with fitting labour in their severall employments; wherin if they shalbe wanting, and much more if refractory, care must bee taken to punish the obstinate and disobedyent, being as necessary as food and rayment. And wee hartely pray yow, that all bee kept to labour, as the only meanes to reduce them to civill, yea, a godly lyfe, and to keepe youth from falling into many enormities which by nature wee are all too much enclyned unto. God, who alone is able and powerfull, enable yow to this great worke, and graunt that our cheifest ayme may bee his honour and glory. And thus, wishing yow all happy and prosperous success, wee end, and rest

   Your assured loving friends,
  The Governor and Deputie of the New England Company
   for a Plantation in Mattachusetts Bay.

Through many businesses wee had almost forgotten to recommend unto yow 2 brethren of our Company, Mr. John and Mr. Sam: Browne, who, though they bee noe adventurers in the generall stock, yett are they men wee doe much respect, being fully perswaded of their sincere affections to the good of our plantation. The one, Mr. John Browne, is sworne an Assistant heere, and by us chosen one of the councell there—a man experienced in the lawes of our kingdome, and such an one as wee are perswaded will worthylie deserve your favour and furtherance, which wee desire hee may have, and that in the first devision of lands there may bee allotted to ether of them 200 acres.

I finde Mr. Oldhams graunt from Mr. Gorge is to him and John Dorrell for all the lands within Mattachusetts Bay between Charles River and Abousett River, cont. in lengt, by a streigth lyne, 5 myles up the said Charles River, into the maine land north west from the border of the said bay, including all creekes and points by the way, and 3 myles in length from the mouth of the foresaid river of Abousett up into the maine land, upon a streight lyne s. w., including all creeks and points, and all the land in bredth and length betweene the foresaid rivers, withall prerogatives, ryall mynes excepted. The rent reserved is 12d on every

100 acres of land that shalbe used; William Blaxton, clerk, and William Jeffryes, gentleman, authorised to putt John Oldham in possession. Having a sight of his graunt, this I found, though I hold it voyde in lawe, yett, his clayme being to this, yow may in your discretion prevent him by causing some to take possession of the cheife part therof.

Second General Letter of the Governor and Deputy of the New England Company for a Plantation in Massachusetts Bay, to the Governor and Council for London's Plantation in the Massachusetts Bay in New England.

London, 28 May, 1629.

AFTER our harty commendations: Our last unto yow was of the 17th and 21th Aprill, sent by the last shipps, viz., the Geo. Bonaventure, Thomas Cox master, who sett saile from th'Isle of Wight the 4th of this month, and seconded by the Talbott, Thomas Beecher master, and the Lyons Whelpe, John Gibbs master, who sett saile also from th'Isle of Wight about the 11th of this month; which letter, being large and consisting of many particulers, hath bin confirmed heere; and herewith yow shall receive a coppy therof, desiring yow to take espetiall care of the performance and putting in execution of all things materiall therein mentioned, and particulerly, amongst others, that point concerninge publication to bee made that noe wrong or injurie bee offered by any of our people to the natives there. To which purpose wee desire yow, the Governor, to advise with the councell in penning of an effectuall edict, upon penalty to bee inflicted upon such as shall transgress the same; which being done, our desire is the same may bee published, to the end that all men may take notice therof, as also that yow send a coppy therof unto us by the next returne of the shipps.

Wee have, sithence our last, and according as wee then advised, at a full and ample Court assembled, ellected and established yow, Captaine John Endicott, to the place of present Governor in our plantation there, as also some others to bee of the councell with yow, as more particulerly yow will perceive by an act of Court herewith sent, confirmed by us at a Generall Court, and sealed with our common seale; to which act wee referr yow, desiring yow all punctually to observe the same, and that the oathes wee herewith send yow, (which have bin heere penned by learned councell,) to bee administred to each of yow in your severall places, may bee administred in such manner and forme as in and by our said order is particulerly expressed, and that yourselves do frame such other oathes as in your wisdomes yow shall thinke fitt to bee administred to your Secretary or other officers, according to their severall places respectively.

Wee have further taken into our consideration the fittness and convenyencie, or rather a necessitie, of making a devident of land, and allotting a proportion to each adventurer, and otherwise, and to this purpose have made and confirmed an act, and sealed the same with our common seale, to the particulers wherof wee referr yow, desiring yow with all convenyent expedition to put the same in execution; and for your better direction in the allottment, wee have herewith sent yow (as by our last wee promised) a list of all the severall adventurers, and of the somme by each of them adventured, desiring that upon the devydent each adventurer may have his allotment of land, as also such others as are noe adventurers, coming in person at their owne charge, and the servants of adventurers sent over to reside upon the plantation, may have such a proportion of land allotted unto and for them as by our said order is appointed.

And wheras divers of the Companie are desirous to have the lands lye together, wee, holding it fitt herein to give them all accommodation, as tending to the furtherance of the plantation, doe pray yow to give way therunto for such as shall desire the same, whether it bee before a devident bee made according to our direction or at the tyme of the allotment to observe the same course.

Yow shall also receive herewith the coppys of all the severall agreements made with the servants and others sent over in the 3 last shipps for accompt of the Companie, togeather with their severall names, for your better direction in employing them in their severall places according to those agreements, as also the names of the servants of such particuler members of the Company as went over in the said shipps; desiring you that a due register bee taken and kept from tyme to tyme of all the persons formerly sent over, or that shall hereafter come to the plantation, both of the names, and qualitie, and age, of each particuler person, and for or by whom they are sent over.

Wee send yow also herewith a particuler of all the goods and cattle sent in those forenamed shipps, as also of what goods, cattle, or other provisions, wee now send upon these 3 shipps, viz., the Mayflower, of Yarmouth, William Peirse master, the Fower Sisters, of London, Roger Harman master, the Pilgrim, of London, William Woolrige master, amongst which wee have remembred yow, the Governor there, with certaine necessaries promised by our last; and if in ought wee have bin now wantinge, wee shall, upon notice from yow, see the same supplyed by our next.

Wheras in our last wee advised yow to make composition with such of the salvages as did pretend any tytle or lay clayme to any of the land within the teretoryes graunted to us by his majesty's charter, wee pray yow now bee carefull to discover and finde out all such pretendors, and by advice of the councell there to make such reasonable composition with them as may free us and your-selves from any scruple of intrusion, and to this purpose, if it might bee convenyently done, to compound and conclude with them all, or as many as yow can at one tyme, not doubting but, by your discreet ordering of this business, the natives wilbe willing to treat and compound with yow upon very easie conditions.

Wee pray yow, as soone as these shipps are discharged, to cause a particuler to bee taken, and sent us at their returne for England, of the names of all such persons as come upon them to remaine in the country, as also a note of the cattle and all manner of goods of what kinde soever landed out of them, with the severall marks and names of the owners therof; the like wherof wee desire to receive from yow of the former 3 shipps, viz., the George, Talbott, and Lyons Whelpe, to the end wee may compare the same with the invoyces heere, and receive fraight, if any bee omitted.

The charge wee are at in sending over servants for the Com-pany is very great, the recompense wherof (under God) depends upon their labour and endeavours; and therefore our desire is, that yow appoint a carefull and dilligent overseer to each familie, who is to see each person employed in the business hee or they are appointed for. And to the end both yourselves there and wee heere may from tyme to tyme have notice how they employ their tyme, wee have sent yow divers paper bookes, which wee pray yow to distribute to the said overseers, who are to keepe a perfect register of the dayly worke done by each person in each familie, a coppy wherof wee pray yow send unto us once every halfe yeare, or as often as convenyently yow may. But if yow conceive that the said register may bee too much to wryte particulerly every day, wee desire that a summary may bee taken therof at the least evry weeke, registred in the booke kept for that familie, and at each weeks end the same to bee examined and subscribed by two, three, or fower such discreet persons as yow shall thinke fitt to appoint for that purpose.

And for the better governing and ordering of our people, espetiallie such as shalbe negligent and remiss in performance of their dutyes, or otherwise exorbitant, our desire is, that a house of correction bee erected and set upp, both for the punishment of such offendors, and to deterr others by their example from such irregular courses.

Richard Claydon, a wheelwright, recommended unto us by Dr. Wells to bee both a good and painfull workman, and of an orderly lyfe and conversation, our desire is, that upon all occasions hee may have your furtherance and good accommodation, as yow shall finde him by his endeavours to deserve; to whom, as to all others of fitness and judgment, lett some of our servants bee committed, to bee instructed by him or them in their severall arts, etc.

There is also one Richard Haward and Richard Inkersall, both Bedfordshire men, hyred for the Company, with their famylies, who wee pray yow may bee well accommodated, not doubting but they will well and orderly demeane themselves.

Our Governor, Mr. Cradock, hath entertained 2 gardnors, one of which hee is content the Company shall have use of if neede bee; and wee desire that Barnabie Claydon, a wheelwright, may serve Mr. Sharpe for our said Governor heere, or some other person in lieu of him, that may give him content.

Some things wee are desired by Mr. Whyte, the minister, to recommend unto your care, viz.: that yow would shew all lawfull favour and respect unto the planters that came over in the Lyons Whelpe out of the countyes of Dorset and Somersett; that yow would appoint unto William Dodg, a skilfull and painfull husbandman, the charge of a teame of horses; to appoint Hugh Tillie and William Eedes for servants to Sir Richard Saltonstall; to give approbation and furtherance to Francis Webb in setting upp his saw mill; and to take notice that all other persons sent over by

Mr. Whyte are servants to the Company, whatsoever hee hath written to the contrary, this being now his owne desire.

The charge of these 3 shipps now sent, though every man that hath any private adventure in them is to pay for his particuler, yett the hazard of profitt and loss by the fraighting of them all, and mens wages and victuall, with victuall for the passengers, is to bee borne ½ by the Companyes generall stock, and ½ by the Governor and his partners their private stock; soe is also the ffishing to bee returned by them, as the salt sent in them is. Wherfore wee pray yow, when your shipps are discharged, if any surplus shalbe in victualls that they can spare, as also of other provisions that was provided for the passingers accommodation, lett the same bee equally devyded, ½ to the Governor there for the Company, th' other halfe to Mr. Samuell Sharpe for the use of Mr. Cradock, our Governor, and his partners. All provisions for the fishing at sea is heere equallie borne in halfes; soe are all the provisions for shipping of all the cattle in these 3 shipps; and accordingly wee desire the deales and cask may be devyded there.

The provisions for building of shipps, as pitch, tarr, rozen, okum, old ropes for okum, cordage, and saylcloth, in all these shipps, with 9 fferkins and 5 halfe barrells of nayles in the 4 Sisters, are ⅔ for the Company in generall, and ⅓ for the Governor, Mr. Cradock, and his partners, as is also the charge of one Georg Farr, now sent over to the six shipwrights formerly sent. Our desire is, a storehouse may bee made apt for the provisions of the ship-wrights and their tooles, wherof Robert Moulton to have the cheife charge, and an inventory to bee sent us of all the tooles, the new by themselves and the old by themselves, that are sent over for the use of the said shipwrights, or any of them, in these and the former shipps, in like manner of all provisions any way concerning shipping, to the end wee may heere examine and fynde that the Company may bee duly charged with their ⅔ parts of the charge, and noe more, and the Governor likewise and his partners with ⅓ part, and noe more; and our desire is, that these men bee kept at worke togeather, adding to their helpe such of the Com-panyes servants as yow shall fynde needfull, and proportionably ½ as many of Mr. Cradocks, which course wee hold most equall, and that accordingly as any vessells bee built, first that both partyes may bee accommodated for the present occasion, but soe soone as 3 shallops shalbe finished, two of them to bee sett out for the Companie by lott, or as yow shall agree there to make an equall devision, and one for our Governor, and his partners, with whose agent, Mr. Sharpe, if yow shall thinke fitt to agree upon equall tearmes, ether in thirds or halfes, to fish togeather when yow shall have vessells fitting, or for setting any other designe forward that may conduce to the good of all partyes, the charge to bee borne indifferently by each partye proportionably, wee leave to your care and good discretions, desiring and hartely praying that love and unitie may bee continued without any hartburninge. And as our Governor hath engaged himselfe beyond all expectation in this business, not only in his particuler, but by great sommes disbursed for the generall, to supply the wants therof, soe our desire is, that yow endeavour to give all furtherance and freindly accommodation to his agents and servants there, not doubting butt yow shall fynde them likewise ready to accommodate the Company in what they may, the Company standing in neede of their helpe.

The cattle now and formerly sent have bin all provyded by the Governor, excepting 3 mares that came out of Lecestershire; but aswell those as all the rest are agreed upon to bee shipt, the one halfe at the charge and upon the adventure of the generall Company, the other ½ for the Governor and his partners. And because all occasions shalbe avoyded of just exceptions in their devision, it is agreed, the devision shalbe made after the arrivall there, that soe whatsoever it shall please God to send thither in safety, a devision may bee then made therof by lott, or in such equall manner as yow, the Governor there, and Mr. Sharpe, shall hold to bee indifferent; and in case Mr. Samuell Sharpe should bee sick or absent, the Governors desire is, that Henry Haughton supply his place herein, and in other his occasions there.

And as in our former, soe now againe wee espetially desire yow to take care that noe tobacco bee planted by any of the new planters under your government, unless it bee some small quantitie for meere necessitie, and for phisick, for preservation of their healths, and that the same bee taken privately by auntient men and none other, and to make a generall restraint therof, as much as in yow is, by perswading the old planters to employ themselves in other business, according to our example, and not to permitt that any tobacco bee laden there upon our shipps.

Since th'above written, wee have, upon further consideration, resolved, that the charge of the six fishermen sent over in the Lyons Whelpe, and 3 more now sent by our Governor, should bee borne, ⅔ by the generall Company, and ⅓ by Mr. Cradock and partners; the like for salt and other necessaryes for ffishing. In consideration wherof, and for that they will have a like interest in the shallops, our desire is, that the benefitt of their labours, both in ffishinge and otherwise, (the trade of beavor excepted, in which, if yow use any of these fishermen as seamen, yow must recompence their labours by other men to supply their place,) bee equally devyded, ⅔ for th'use of the generall Company, and ⅓ for our Governor, Mr. Cradock, and partners, proportionably; and for such others as are to bee assisting to these men in the ffishing, yow are to appoint ⅔ of them to bee of the generall Companyes servants, and ⅓ of the servants of Mr. Cradock and his partners, accordingly.

The charge of the fraight of these 3 shipps, their men, victualls, etc., will stand us in about £2400, and their fraight outward will nothing neere countervaile that charge. Wherfore wee pray yow to ease it what yow may by sending us returnes in ffish or other lading; and wee desire you to give them all expedition, for otherwise their monthly pay, being about £400 per month for these 3 shipps, will soone swallow up the gaines wee shall make of any thinge they may bring home from thence.

Wee have now sent by these 3 shipps 29 waigh of salt, viz., 11 weigh in the May Flower, 15 in the Fower Sisters, and 3 waigh in the Pilgrim, togeather with lynes, hookes, knives, bootes, and baruells, necessary for ffishinge; desiring our men may bee employed, ether in harbor or upon the banke, to make use therof for lading our shipps; wherin wee desire yow to conferr and advise with Mr. Peirce, who hath formerly fished there. And if yow send the shipps to fish at the banck, and expect them not to returne againe to the plantation, that then yow send our barke, that is already built in the country, to bring back our ffishermen and such provisions as they had for fishing, viz., of salt, if any remainder bee, as also of hookes, lynes, knives, bootes, and baruells, which to them wilbe of noe use, their fishing being ended, but may bee of use to yow upon all occasions.

And as wee have hereby desired that a storehouse bee built for the shipwrights and their provisions, and an inventory kept therof, soe wee desire likewise that the same course bee observed for the ffishermen, and an inventory bee duly kept of all the provisions and implements for fishinge, and a coppy therof to bee sent unto us, and that such a carefull person bee appointed to take care and charge therof, to preserve the same from loss and spoyle, as yow in your discretions shall thinke fitt, which wee pray yow take into your espetiall care and consideration, and soe to order this and other business, by distributing the care thereof to severall persons, that the burthen bee not too heavy to any particuler, and soe the business itselfe suffer. And this care wee desire may bee taken, for that wee know not how soone wee may resolve of some other devision.

Thomas Beard, a shoomaker, and Isack Rickman, being both recommended to us by Mr. Symon Whetcombe to receive their dyett and houseroome at the charge of the Companie, wee have agreed they shalbe with yow, the Governor, or placed elsewhere, as yow shall thinke good, and receive from yow, or by your appointment, their dyett and lodging, for which they are to pay, each of them, after the rate of £10 per annum. And wee desire to receive a certificate, under the hand of whomsoever they shalbe soe dyetted and lodged with, how long tyme they have remained with them, in case they shall otherwise dispose of themselves before the yeare bee expired, or at least wise at the end of each yeare, to the end wee may heere receive payment according to the said agreement. The said Tho: Beard hath in the shipp the May Flower divers hydes, both for soles and upper leathers, which hee intends to make upp in bootes and shoes there in the country. Wee pray yow let Mr. Peirce, the master of the said shipp, viewe the said leather, and estimate what tonnage the same may import, that soe the said Beard may ether pay unto yow there after the rate of £4 per tonn for fraight of the same, the like for his dyett if there bee occasion to use any of his commodities, or otherwise, upon your advice, wee may receive it of Mr. Whetcombe, who hath promised to see the same discharged. Wee desire also the said Tho: Beard may have 50 acres of land allotted to him as one that transports himselfe at his owne charge. But as well for him as all others that shall have land allotted to them in that kinde, and are noe adventurers in the common stock, which is to support the charge of ffortyfications, as also for the ministrie and divers other affaires, wee holde it fitt that these kinde of men, as also such as shall come to inheritt lands by their service, should, by way of acknowledgment to such from whom they receive these lands, become lyable to the performance of some service certaine dayes in the yeare, and by that service they and their posteritie after them to hold and inherite these lands, which wilbe a good meanes to enjoy their lands from being held in capite, and to support the plantation in generall and particuler.

Wee may not omitt, out of our zeale for the generall good, once more [to] putt yow in mynde to bee very circumspect, in the infancie of the plantation, to settle some good orders wherby all persons resident upon our plantation may apply themselves to one calling or other, and noe idle drone bee permitted to live amongst us, which, if yow take care now at the first to establish, wilbe an undoubted meanes, through Gods assistance, to prevent a world of disorders and many grevious sinns and sin[ners].

The course we have prescribed for keeping a dayly register in each familie of what is done by all and every person in the famylie wilbe a great helpe and remembrance to yow, and to future posteritie, for the upholding and continuance of this good act, if once well begun and setled, which wee hartely wish and desire as aforesaid.

And as wee desire all should live in some honest calling and profession, soe wee pray yow to bee unpartiall in the administration of justice, and endeavour that noe man whatsoever, freeman, or servant to any, may have just cause of complaint herein. And for that it cannot be avoyded but offences wilbe given, wee hartely pray yow to admitt of all complaints that shalbe made to yow, or any of yow that are of the councell, bee the complaints never soe meane, and pass it not sleightly over, but seriously examine the truth of the business, and if yow fynde there was just cause for the complaint, endeavour to right the oppressed in the best manner yow can. But, howsoever, take some strict course to prevent the like; and such as are by us put in authoritie as subordinate governors of ffamylies, if they shall abuse any under their government, and after a gentle admonition doe not reforme it, faile not speedylie to remove them, as men more fitt to bee governed then to governe others, and place more fitt and sufficient men in their steed. But if yow fynde any complaint to bee made without just cause given, lett not such a fault escape without severe punishment, and that forthwith, and in publique, wherby to teryfie all others from daring to complaine against any that shalbe sett over them without a just cause. Wee pray yow take this earnestly to hart, and neglect not the due execution therof upon plaintiff or defendant, according to the nature of the offence. It wilbe a meanes, through Gods mercy, of preventing many inconvenyencies and disorders that otherwise will undoubtedly befall yow and the whole government there.

And amongst other sinns, wee pray yow make some good lawes for the punishing of swearers, wherunto it is to bee feared too many are adicted that are servants sent over formerly and now. These and other abuses wee pray yow who are in authoritie to endeavor seriously to reforme, if ever you expect comfort or a blessing from God upon our plantation.

We have discharged divers servants heere that wee had entertained, and bin at great charges with some of them, yett, fearing their ill lyfe might bee prejudiciall to the plantation, wee rather thought fitt to dismiss them, and loose our charges, then to burthen the plantation with them. Amongst others in like manner dismissed by the Governor, 2 of the 3 ffishermen of his, formerly mentioned, are gone. Wee doubt not but God will in due tyme provyde us sufficiently with honest and able servants; and wee hope these sent wilbe conformable to good government, which if they doe willingly and cheerefully wilbe the greater comfort to yow and us; if otherwise, we doubt not but yow, in your good discretions, will know how to proceede with such. Wherin, and in all things els yow goe about, wee beseech the Almighty soe to direct yow as that God alone may have the glory, and yow and wee comfort heere temporally and hereafter perpetually.

Wee pray yow to take notice that in these and the former shipps ther is shipped in cattle and other provisions according to particuler invoyces heere inclosed; but whether all things bee incerted in the same invoyces wee make doubt, and therfore pray yow to bee carefull a due register bee kept of all putt ashore.

Wee pray yow endeavour, though there bee much strong waters sent for sale, yett soe to order it as that the salvages may not for our lucre sake bee induced to the excessive use, or rather abuse of it, and at any hand take care our people give noe ill example; and if any shall exceede in that inordinate kinde of drinking as to become drunck, wee hope yow will take care his punishment bee made exemplary for all others. Lett the lawes bee first published to forbidd these disorders, and all others yow feare may growe up, wherby they may not pretend ignorance of the one nor pruiledg to offend, and then feare not to putt good lawes, made upon good ground and warrant, in due execution. And soe, recommending yow and all your affaires to the protection of the Almighty, wee conclude and rest

Your, etc.

Gravesend, 3 June, 1629.

To the Worshipfull our very loving friends, Capt. Jo: Endecott, Esquire, Governor, Fr: Higgenson, Samuell Skelton, Fr: Bright, Jo: and Sam: Browne, Sam: Sharpe, Tho: Graves, and the rest of the Councell for Londons Plantation in the Mattachusetts Bay, in New England.

Letter from the Governor and Company to the Ministers.

REVEREND Freinds: There are lately arrived heere (being sent from the Governor, Mr. Endecott, as men ffactious and e[vil] conditioned) John and Samuell Browne, being brethren, who, since their arrivall, have raised rumours (as wee heare) of divers scandalous and intemperate speeches passed from one or both of yow in your publique sermons or prayers in New England, as also of some innovations attempted by yow. Wee have reason to hope that their reports are but slanders, partly for that your godly and quiett conditions are well knowne to some of us, and also for that these men, your accusers, seeme to bee imbittered against yow and Capt. Endecott for injuries which they conceive they have received from some of yow there. Yett, for that wee all knowe that the best advysed may overshoote themselves, wee have thought good to informe yow of what wee heare, that if yow bee innocent yow may cleare yourselves, or, if otherwise, yow may heereby bee entreated to looke back upon your miscarriage with repentance, or at least to take notice that wee utterly disallowe any such passages, and must and will take order for the redress therof, as shall become us. But hoping, as wee said, of your unblameableness heerein, wee desire only that this may testyfy to yow and others that wee are tender of the least aspersion which, either directly or obliquely, may bee cast upon the state heere, to whom wee owe soe much duty, and from whom wee have received soe much favour in this plantation where yow now reside. Soe, with our love and due respect to your callings, wee rest

Your loving freinds,

London, 16 Octo. 1629.

R: SALTONSTALL,   MATT: CRADOCK, Governor,
ISA: JOHNSON,   THO: GOFFE, Deputy,
                     GEO: HARWOOD, Treasurer,
                     JOHN WINTHROP,
                     THO: ADAMS,
                     SYM: WHETCOMBE,
                     WILLIAM VASSALL,
                     WILLIAM PINCHON,
                     JOHN REVELL,
                     FRANCIS WEBB.

Mr. Skelton and Mr. Higgison.

Letter from the Governor and Company to Governor Endecott.

SIR: As wee have written at this tyme to Mr. Skelton and Mr. Higgison touching the rumours of Jo: and Sam: Browne, spread by them upon their arrivall heere, concerning some unadvysed and scandalous speeches uttered by them in their publique sermons or prayers, soe have wee thought meete to advertise yow of what they have reported against yow and them concerninge some rash innovations begun and practized in the civill and ecclesiasticall government. Wee doe well consider that the Brownes are likely to make the worst of any thing they have observed in New England by reason of your sending them back against their wills for their offencive behaviour, expressed in a generall letter from the Company there. Yett, for that wee likewise doe consider that yow are in a government newly founded, and want that assistance which the waight of such a business doth require, wee may have leave to think that it is possible some undigested councells have too so-dainely bin put in execution, which may have ill construction with the state heere, and make us obnoxious to any adversary. Lett it, therfore, seeme good unto yow to bee very sparing in introduceing any lawes or commands which may render yourselfe or us distastefull to the state heere, to which (as wee ought) wee must and will have an obsequious eye. And as wee make it our mayn care to have the plantation soe ordered as may bee most for the honour of God and of our gratious soveraigne, who hath bestowed many large pruiledges and royall favours upon this Companie, soe wee desire that all such as shall, by word or deede, doe any thinge to detract from Gods glory or his majesty's honour, may bee duly corrected, for their amendment and the terror of others. And to that end, if yow knowe any thinge which hath bin spoken or done, either by the ministers (whom the Brownes doe seeme tacetly to blame for some things uttered in their sermons or prayers) or any others, wee require yow, if any such thinge bee, that yow forme due process against the offendors, and send it to us by the first, that wee may, as our duty bindes us, use meanes to have them duly punished. Soe, not doubting but wee have said enough, wee shall repose ourselves upon your wisdome, and doe rest

Your loving freinds.

Dated and signed as the former letter to Mr. Skelton and Mr. Higgison. To the Governor, Capt. Endecott.